ENGLISH PLACE-NAME SOCIETY. VOLUME LXXXII
FOR 2004

GENERAL EDITOR

RICHARD COATES

THE PLACE-NAMES OF SHROPSHIRE

PART V

THE SURVEY OF ENGLISH PLACE-NAMES
UNDERTAKEN WITH THE APPROVAL AND SUPPORT OF
THE ARTS AND HUMANITIES RESEARCH COUNCIL
AND
THE BRITISH ACADEMY

THE PLACE-NAMES OF

SHROPSHIRE

BY

MARGARET GELLING
in collaboration with
the late H. D. G. FOXALL

PART FIVE

THE HUNDREDS OF PIMHILL AND BRADFORD NORTH

NOTTINGHAM
ENGLISH PLACE-NAME SOCIETY
2006

Published by the English Place-Name Society,
School of English Studies, University of Nottingham,
Nottingham NG7 2RD.

Registered Charity No. 257891

© English Place-Name Society 2006

All rights reserved.
No part of this publication may be reproduced,
stored in a retrieval system or transmitted
in any form or by any means,
without prior permission of the English Place-Name Society.

ISBN-10: 0 904889 76 9
ISBN-13: 978 0 904889 76 5

Typeset by Paul Cavill & Printed in Great Britain
by Woolnough Bookbinding, Irthlingborough, Northants.

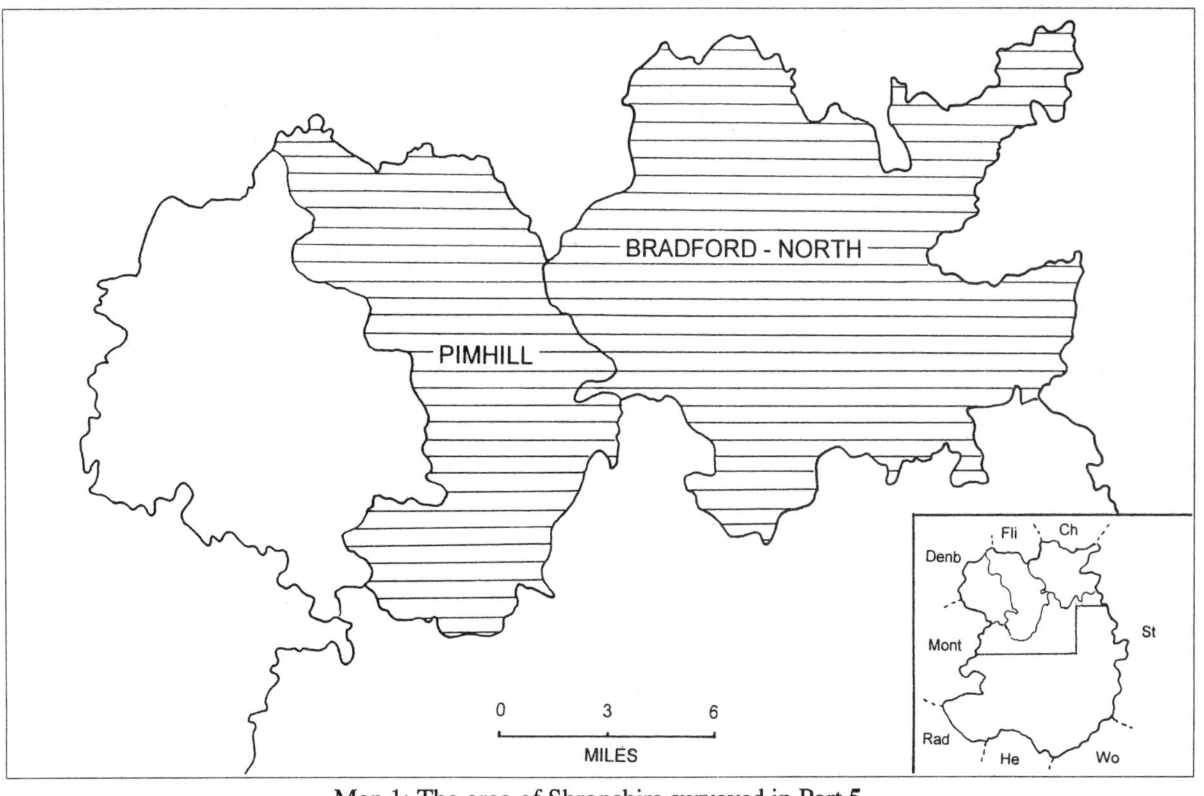

Map 1: The area of Shropshire surveyed in Part **5**.

CONTENTS

MAPS

ACKNOWLEDGEMENTS

A great debt is owed to Dr Paul Cavill, the Principal Research Fellow of the English Place-Name Society, who turns my old-fashioned typescripts into print and provides help and encouragement at every stage of the laborious process of producing these volumes. I could not continue to publish the Shropshire place-name material without his assistance.

I am deeply grateful to Dr Richard Morgan for his invaluable help with Welsh minor names and field-names in Pimhill Hundred. I hope it will be possible eventually to obtain his collaboration in work on the hundreds of Oswestry, Chirbury and Clun.

I am (as ever) grateful to Ann Cole, who turns my scribbled sketches into excellent maps.

My debt to the late George Foxall is apparent throughout, and it is appropriate to note that much of the material from early sources, both printed and manuscript, was extracted by members of a Birmingham University extra-mural class which ran from 1961 to 1988.

September 2006 Margaret Gelling

INTRODUCTION

This volume presents the place-name material for two of the three northernmost Shropshire hundreds, Pimhill and Bradford North. In the south west the area adjoins those of the Liberties of Shrewsbury, covered in Part **4**, and Ford Hundred, covered in Part **2**. It has Oswestry Hundred, not yet covered, on the west, and its eastern limit is the Shropshire/Staffordshire boundary.

This is the first part of the county to be dealt with without any assistance from the regional volumes of the Victoria County History. Parts **2** and **3** relied heavily on VCH volumes VIII, X and XI, and for Part **4** I was able to benefit from Bill Champion's material, collected for the projected Shrewsbury volume. Now the place-name survey is on its own, and there is consequently less detail, particularly about manorial descents, history of buildings and identification of open fields. The availability of the place-name material may, however, be useful to future compilers of VCH volumes, and it is fair that the benefit should flow in the other direction.

PLACE-NAMES IN RELATION TO THE GEOGRAPHICAL SETTING

North Shropshire is a low-lying land of glacial lakes, marshes and heaths. There is some woodland, particularly in the north east, and this is marked, as usual, by the term **lēah**; but there are -ley names also in marshy areas, and in these the term seems more likely to have been used in its late Old English senses, 'pasture, meadow': examples include Audley, Bagley, Bletchley, Cloverley, Hordley, Kempley, Noneley. Possibly the only area in these two hundreds where a group of settlements were in clearings in ancient woodland is that between the Rivers Roden and Tern, where Lee Brockhurst, Marchamley, Booley, Hopley and Weobley are. North of that, on the north/south watershed between the Tern and the R. Duckow, there is a cluster of -ley names in which **lēah** seems more likely to refer to pasture or meadow. These include Cloverley and (across the Cheshire border) Butterley Heys. This late usage also seems likely to the west, by the R. Perry especially in the marshy land between Ellesmere and Baschurch. For some names, e.g.

Wolverley and Tilley in Wem, it is difficult to say whether woodland or pasture is more likely to be indicated. Some -ley names in Hinstock, Soudley, Lockley and Pixley, are on the western fringe of a belt of **lēah** names running along the west boundary of Staffordshire, and these probably reflect the presence of ancient woodland.

In most of northern Shropshire woodland was probably a limited and treasured resource. There is a Grafton, in the southern part of Pimhill Hundred, which probably refers to a coppiced wood, and Haywood in Cheswardine was near an enclosed wood. The two northernmost townships of Ellesmere parish, Hampton Wood and Northwood, may have provided timber for the whole of this great estate, as the other two Northwoods may have done for the large parishes of Prees and Wem. The terms **stoccing** and ***ryding** are frequent in field-names throughout the two hundreds, but these probably refer to the clearing of brushwood rather than to inroads into forest. Prees is a Brittonic name meaning 'brushwood'. Names in **hyrst** and **sceaga** indicate woods of limited size. Threapwood, 'disputed wood', occurs as a field-name in Ightfield.

The glacial lakes of north-west Shropshire gave rise to a cluster of settlement-names in **mere** (Colemere, Ellesmere, Fenemere, Merehouse, and two Martons) which is the densest in the country (*v.* map on p. 24 of LPN). The marsh terms, **mersc**, **mōr**, **mos** occur occasionally in settlement-names, as in the two Moretons, Moston and Bilmarsh, but they are more frequently used to denote unsettled areas of wet land, such as Baggy Moor, Muckmoor, Radmoor and Smithy Moor. **mōr** is the commonest of the three terms. Wet ground is also noted in the names Lacon and Wem.

In the drier areas of Bradford North Hundred there is a considerable amount of heathland. Here are two Hattons (High and Hungry) and a large area called Hine Heath. Parishes here have their own heaths, known by the parish-name: Whitchurch Heath and Prees Higher Heath are among the larger instances. It was suggested in Part **4**, xvii–xviii, that the frequent occurrence of **bryce** 'newly-broken-in land' in the area north of Shrewsbury pointed to reclamation of heathland, and this term is frequent in field-names in Pimhill and Bradford North Hundreds, particular in the latter. Stands of birch trees have given rise to three settlement-names, Birch in Baschurch and Ellesmere and The Birtles in Woore, and there are frequent references to this heathland tree in minor names and field-names (though in the latter it cannot always be distinguished from **bryce**).

HABITATIVE NAMES

The commonest habitative term, **tūn**, is the generic in 52 names in these two hundreds. **tūn** usually has a complementary distribution to that of **lēah**, and this distinction is largely present in north Shropshire, though there is some complication due to the probable occurrence of **lēah** in its late sense 'meadow, pasture'. The distribution of **tūn** names in Pimhill and Bradford North Hundreds shows a notable relationship to rivers; they line the banks of the Perry, Roden, Meese and Tern. In addition to these riverine **tūn** names there are clusters round the Ellesmere lakes and round the marshes on the upper course of the R. Perry. These 52 names are not spread randomly across the area.

The other habitative terms evidenced are **cot**, **wīc** and **worðign**. **cot** is the commonest, but none are very frequent. The five names — Carradine, Cheswardine, Ridgwardine, Shrawardine, Stanwardine — constitute something like a concentration, since this element is nowhere common, but they are widely scattered over the area of the two hundreds. Three of them are Domesday manors.

PLACE-NAMES IN RELATION TO POST-ROMAN HISTORY

The problem presented by the general paucity of pre-English names in Shropshire, which was discussed in the Introduction to Part **1**, is less acute in the northern part of the county than elsewhere. Hodnet and Prees together with the river-name *Giht* in Ightfield form an impressive cluster, and to these can be added the river-names Roden and Tern. The river-name Perry (a doublet of Peover Eye PN Ch **1** 33) is Welsh *Pefr* 'bright one' with Old English **ēa** 'river'. These names provide firm evidence for co-existence of Welsh- and English-speaking people during the absorption of the region into the Kingdom of Mercia.

Welsh minor names and field-names occur occasionally in Bradford North Hundred and much more frequently in the west of Pimhill, but these are 'modern' Welsh (modified by English pronunciation and orthography) and cannot be considered evidence for language survival from earlier times.

PLACE-NAMES IN RELATION TO ARCHAEOLOGY

The element **hlāw** occurs in seven names in these two hundreds: Blakeley Hill, Blakelow, Catlow, Drakeley, Longslow, Lowe and Peplow; and there are other instances in field-names. It is probable that these names refer to burial mounds, either prehistoric or dating from the earlier decades of Mercian domination. Longslow ('Wlanc's tumulus') has the best claim to refer to an Anglian burial: names of this sort in

Cheshire, Shropshire and Herefordshire are listed and discussed in M. Gelling, *The West Midlands in the Early Middle Ages*, 48–52. Unfortunately no remaining traces of tumuli have been noted at any of the Shropshire places with **hlāw** names.

The other main class of ancient monument which is frequently noted in place-names consists of hill-forts and analogous defensive structures of the Bronze Age and the Iron Age. These have a better survival rate than tumuli. The element **burh**, which is regularly used to refer to such earthworks, can also refer to a defended Anglo-Saxon manor house, but in practice it is not difficult to distinguish between the two usages. Two noteworthy instances of the 'archaeological' usage in north Shropshire are The Berth in Baschurch (from the nominative **burh**) and Chirbury in Hodnet (containing the dative *byrig*). Shawbury is the only name in these two hundreds in which **byrig** is likely to mean 'manor house'.

FIELD-NAMES

The large quantity of field-name material presented in this and in earlier volumes is taken mainly from the late George Foxall's wonderful 6" maps which reproduce the delineation of the numbered fields as shown on the 19th-century tithe award maps, printing in each field the names as set out in the accompanying schedule. For the purposes of the place-name survey these names have been put into alphabetical order, which is an essential prerequisite if they are to become readily available for linguistic study. Alphabetisation obscures the connection between the names and the fields as shown on the tithe award maps; but in order to compensate for this I have looked at the drawing of every field while inserting its name into the alphabetical list. In this way it has been possible to comment on the appropriateness or otherwise of shape-names and acreage-names, and to note significant factors in the situation of the field.

It is unlikely (in fact inconceivable) that names in this quantity should have been taken from the Foxall maps and alphabetised by one person working on this scale without some errors of transcription and some unintentional omissions; but the lists will serve as a general indication of the nature of the county's place-name stock, and as a guide for local historians embarking on more detailed parish studies. The Foxall maps can be seen at the Shrewsbury Records and Research Centre, and copies will be supplied on request. Checking with the maps is advised for any in-depth study. An excellent overview of field-names for the whole county is available in Mr Foxall's book *Shropshire Field-Names*, published by the Shropshire Archaeological Society.

The field-name material presented in this volume has not been systematically analysed, and many points of lexicographical interest will not be fully appreciated until such an analysis is undertaken. The type of contribution which a comprehensive collection of field-names can make to lexicography is well illustrated by the Clemley names discussed on pp. 198–200. These had been noted occasionally in other counties (*v*. PN Ch **3** 47) and had been accorded variant etymologies. North Shropshire has a denser concentration of these names than any area so far studied, and observation of their situation on the tithe award maps and of the nature of adjacent field-names makes it abundantly clear that they are 'infertility' names based on the verb *clem* 'to starve'. In townships in these two hundreds there are seven fields called *Cleml(e)y*, two called *The Clemley*, eight called *Cleml(e)y Park* (with three variants *Chumley Park*, *Clem Park*, *Clemsons Park*). There is also a *Clemley Meadow*, a *Clemson*, a *Clemstead* and (most significantly) a *Clem Guts*. With the contexts noted on p. 199 there can be little doubt about the significance, although the reasons for -ley in *Clemley* and the significance of *Park* remain open to discussion. As noted on p. 200 there is a reference from 1615 which, for the first time, takes these names back beyond the 18th and 19th centuries.

The field-names of Pimhill and North Bradford Hundreds contain numerous examples of 'derogatory' names and some of the less frequent 'complimentary' ones, the range of these being similar to those found in field-names everywhere except for the concentration of *Clemley*. There are many comments on soil quality and consistency, and many references to coarse grass by the terms *feg*, *feggy* and *hassocks*, to heather, often using the Welsh-derived word *grig*, and to gorse, using the dialect forms *gorst(y)*.

Names referring to the distinctive shape of fields are frequent, and comment on these has obviously been facilitated by the availability of the Foxall maps. Particularly interesting in this respect are the *Harp* names (occasionally *Welsh Harp*). By consulting the maps it can be seen that this is not simply another term for a triangular field, like *Brandart*, *Triangle*, *Three Cornered Piece* and the common *Shoulder of Mutton*. Most of these fields actually bear a resemblance to the shape of the musical instrument. It would be interesting to check whether this applies to *Telyn* in Welsh field-names. Other shape-names refer to clothing, like *Cocked Hat*, *Sleeve*, *The Shirt*, *Stomacher*, or to human or animal body parts, like *Leg and Foot*, *Cowtail*, *The Horn*. Cuts of meat feature: in addition to the common *Shoulder of Mutton* there is *Leg of Mutton*, and *Slensh* in Dudleston (p. 40), *Haunch* in Marchamley (p. 155). *Round* is regularly used of fields which have slightly curved sides, sometimes only one or two.

Some common field-name terms have not yet been precisely interpreted. *Shut* occurs frequently in these two hundreds, but nothing has been noted which clearly identifies it with any feature of topography or of open-field farming arrangements. *Criftin* has been assigned to an OE ***cryfting** 'small croft', but the fields so called in north Shropshire are of average or above-average size. There are a few names (*Leans* in Loppington, *Leen(s)* in Prees, possibly Lionlane in Ellesmere) which may derive from ME **leyne**, noted in EPN as a recognised place-name element but of obscure significance.

Place-name scholars have naturally concentrated on the linguistic interest of field-names, but it is important to remember that these are, in John Field's classic definition, "names of all pieces of land forming part of the agrarian economy of a town or village". Many names which do not stand out from the mass record the agrarian history of their township and the resources and installations which were of primary concern to farmers.

The northern plain of Shropshire is a "dairying area" (VCH IV, map on p. 4), and field-names referring to cows and calves are ubiquitous. *Cow Pasture* and *Calves Close* are often adjacent, and there are numerous *Milking Banks*. Ubiquitous also are *Barn Fields*, which presumably refer to cattle shelters. The numerous *Cote Fields* where no buildings are shown on the maps presumably refer to structures connected with stock management, and *Outlet*, *Foredraught* to stock movement. Horses are quite frequently mentioned and *Horse Wash Croft* in Moreton Say may be a clue to the meaning of *Wash Pit* in other parishes.

North Shropshire was a land of windmills. These appear frequently in field-names, occasionally in minor names (Windmill in Weston-under-Redcastle, Mill House in Wem) and once in a township-name, Millenheath in Prees. Most townships had a *Brickkiln*, many had quarries referred to as *Gravel Hole* or *Sand Hole*. Rabbit warrens are frequently indicated by the variant spellings of *coneygree*. VCH IV, p. 147, notes that hemp and flax were the most widely grown industrial crops in the northern dairy region, and the common name *Gig Hole* refers to arrangements for drying the stalks of these plants. In large parishes field-names referring to such facilities are often found in each township, suggesting a township-based economy.

FURTHER RESEARCH

There is as much material in this volume as can conveniently be handled within the scope of one of the English Place-Name Society's volumes. It should, however, be noted that only a small portion of the material in the Shropshire Records and Research Centre has been used, and there are doubtless sources known to local historians which have not been drawn upon. Interpretations based on map study should ideally be checked by field-work. Because of the lack of a regional VCH volume references to events and people which are known to local historians will have been overlooked. This volume should be seen as a starting point for further study rather than as a definitive account of the place-names of Pimhill and Bradford North Hundreds.

ABBREVIATIONS AND BIBLIOGRAPHY

Abbreviations printed in roman type refer to printed sources and those in italic to manuscript sources.

a. — *ante.*

Abbr — *Placitorum Abbreviatio* (RC), 1811.

acc. — accusative.

AD — *Catalogue of Ancient Deeds* (PRO), 1890 and in progress.

AddCh — Additional Charters in the British Library.

adj. — adjective.

APW — *Calendar of Ancient Petitions relating to Wales*, ed. W. Rees, Cardiff 1975.

ASC — *The Anglo-Saxon Chronicle.*

Ass — Assize Rolls (PRO).

ASWills — *Anglo-Saxon Wills*, ed. D. Whitelock, Cambridge 1930.

Ave. — Avenue.

Baugh — Robert Baugh's Map of Shropshire 1808, Shropshire Archaeological Society 1983.

BBCS — *The Bulletin of the Board of Celtic Studies.*

Bd — Bedfordshire.

Berks — Berkshire.

Bk — Buckinghamshire.

BL — Documents in British Library.

Blome — Richard Blome, *A General Mapp of Shropshire with its Hundreds* (c.1675).

BM — *Index to the Charters and Rolls in the Department of Manuscripts, British Museum*, ed. H. J. Ellis and F. B. Bickley, 2 vols., 1900–12.

Bodl — *Calendar of Charters and Rolls in the Bodleian Library*, ed. W. H. Turner and H. O. Coxe, Oxford 1878.

Bowcock — E. W. Bowcock, *Shropshire Place-Names*, Shrewsbury 1923.

Burton — *Charters of Burton Abbey*, ed. P. H. Sawyer, *Anglo-Saxon Charters* II, British Academy 1979.

c. — *circa*: about.

Ca — Cambridgeshire.

Cant — *The Register of Thomas de Cantilupe*, Canterbury and York Society II, 1907.

CartAntiq — *The Cartae Antiquae Rolls* 1–10, PRS NS 17, 1939; 11–20, PRS NS 33, 1960.

CDEPN	V. Watts, *The Cambridge Dictionary of English Place-Names*, 2004.
cent.	century.
Ch	Cheshire.
Ch	*Calendar of Charter Rolls* (PRO), 1903–27.
Ch 1, Ch 2	regnal dates, t. Charles I or II.
Champion	W. Champion, contributions to VCH Sa VI, forthcoming.
ChanR	*Calendar of various Chancery Rolls*, A.D.1277–1326 (PRO), 1912.
Charles	B. G. Charles, 'The Welsh, their Language and Place-Names in Archenfield and Oswestry', in *Angles and Britons: O'Donnell Lectures*, University of Wales Press 1963, pp. 85–110.
ChR	*Rotuli Chartarum*, ed. T. D. Hardy (RC), 1837.
Cl	*Calendar of Close Rolls* (PRO), in progress.
ClR	*Rotuli Litterarum Clausarum*, ed. T. D. Hardy (RC).
Co	Cornwall.
Coin(s)	spellings taken from coin-legends.
CorbetMaps	Survey and valuation of Sundorn and Haughmond Abbey Demesnes near Shrewsbury and other estates in the Hundreds of Bradford South and Pimhill, and Liberties of Shrewsbury in the County of Salop belonging to John Corbet, 1777, *SRO 3182/1* (photocopy).
CorbetMaps 2	Corbet Estate Maps in SRO for Besford, Charlton Grange, Child's Ercall, Preston Brockhurst.
CornEl	O. J. Padel, *Cornish Place-Name Elements*, EPNS 56/57.
Corn.R.O.	Buller MSS in Cornwall Record Office, Truro.
CourtR	Moreton Corbet Roll Book, *SRO 322/1/1* (names supplied by R. Collingwood).
Cox	B. Cox, *English Inn and Tavern Names*, Nottingham 1994.
Craven	Surveys of the Craven Estates in Shrewsbury Record Office (Class M.S.Accession 2480–3).
Ct	Court.
Cu	Cumberland.
Cur	*Curia Regis Rolls* (PRO), in progress.
CurR	*Rotuli Curia Regis* (RC), 1835.
CV	R. Coates and A. Breeze, *Celtic Voices, English Places*, Stamford 2000.
D	Devon.
dat.	dative.
Db	Derbyshire.
DB	Domesday Book.
Denb	Denbighshire.
DEPN	E. Ekwall, *The Concise Oxford Dictionary of English Place-Names*, 4th ed., 1960.
Do	Dorset.
Du	County Durham.
Dugdale	W. Dugdale, *Monasticon Anglicanum*, 6 vols. in 8, 1817–30.

Duignan	W. H. Duignan, *Notes on Staffordshire Place-Names*, London 1902.
e.	early.
E.	East.
ECWM	H. P. R. Finberg, *The Early Charters of the West Midlands*, Leicester 1972.
Ed 1, Ed 2 etc.	regnal dates, t. Edward I, t. Edward II, etc.
EDD	J. Wright, *The English Dialect Dictionary*, 6 vols., 1898–1905.
Ekwall Street-Names	E. Ekwall, *Street-Names of the City of London*, Oxford 1954.
el.	place-name element.
Eliz	regnal date, t. Elizabeth I.
EPN	A. H. Smith, *English Place-Name Elements*, Parts 1 and 2 (EPNS 25, 26), Cambridge 1956.
EPNS	publications of the English Place-Name Society.
ERN	E. Ekwall, *English River-Names*, Oxford 1928.
ERY	East Riding of Yorkshire.
Ess	Essex.
et freq	*et frequenter*: and frequently (thereafter).
et seq	*et sequenter*: and subsequently.
Eyton	*SRO 665/37–8*, an uncatalogued collection of 16th, 17th and e.18th cent. indentures from the Condover estate which came to SRO from the Eyton family.
Eyton	R. W. Eyton, *Antiquities of Shropshire*, London 1854–60.
f, fs	folio(s).
FA	*Feudal Aids* (PRO), 1899–1920.
FCI	H. D. G. Foxall, card index of Shrewsbury place-names in Shropshire Records and Research Centre.
Fees	*The Book of Fees* (PRO), 1920–31.
Feilitzen	O. von Feilitzen, *The Pre-Conquest Personal Names of Domesday Book*, Uppsala 1937.
fem.	feminine.
ff.	and the pages following.
FF	*Feet of Fines* (PRSoc 17, 20, 23, 24), 1894, 1896, 1898, 1900. Some FF forms have been taken from SAS vols.; these are referenced (e.g.) SAS 2/X(FF).
FFW	*Fouke Fitz Warin, Roman du XIV*^{e} *Siècle* ed. Louis Brandon, Paris 1930.
Fine	*Calendar of Fine Rolls* (PRO), in progress.
Fli	Flintshire.
Fm	Farm.
f.n., f.ns.	field-name(s).
FN	H. D. G. Foxall, *Shropshire Field-Names*, Shrewsbury 1980.
For	*Select Pleas of the Forest*, ed. J. G. Turner, Selden Soc. 13, 1901.
ForProc	Forest Proceedings in PRO.
Fr	French.
freq	*frequenter*: frequently.
G	German.

Garbet	S. Garbet, *History of Wem*, 1818, reprinted Shrewsbury 1982.
Gazetteer	H. D. G. Foxall, *A Gazetteer of Streets, Roads and Place Names in Shropshire,* 2nd ed., Shrewsbury 1967.
gen.	genitive.
GeolSurv	T. H. Whitehead and R. W. Pocock, *Dudley and Bridgnorth*, Memoirs of the Geological Survey of England and Wales, HMSO 1947.
Gir	*Giraldi Cambrensis Opera* (RS), 1861–91.
Gl	Gloucestershire.
Gough	R. Gough, *The Antiquities and Memoirs of Myddle*, 1700, published from MS 1875, reproduction of 1875 edition published by the Records Committee of Salop County Council.
GR	national grid reference.
GT	*The Glebe Terriers of Shropshire Part 1 (Abdon to Llanfair Waterdine), Part 2 (Llanyblodwel to Wroxeter)*, ed. S. Watts, Shropshire Record Series Volume 5, Keele 2001.
Ha	Hampshire.
HAC	*The Cartulary of Haughmond Abbey,* ed. Una Rees, Cardiff 1985.
Harl 433	*British Library Harleian Manuscript 433*, ed. Rosemary Horrox and P. W. Hammond, 4 vols., Richard III Soc. 1979–83.
He	Herefordshire.
HePN	B. Coplestone-Crow, *Herefordshire Place-Names*, *British Archaeological Reports* 214, 1989.
Hey	D. Hey, *An English Rural Community: Myddle under the Tudors and Stuarts*, Leicester 1974.
Ho	House.
Hobbs	J. L. Hobbs, *Shrewsbury Street-Names,* Shrewsbury 1954.
Howard	C. Howard, *The Roads of England and Wales*, 1883.
Hrt	Hertfordshire.
HTR	*The Shropshire Hearth-Tax Roll of 1672*, ed. W. Watkins-Pitchford, Shrewsbury 1949.
Hu	Huntingdonshire.
Hunt	*Henrici Huntendunensis Historia Anglorum* (RS), 1879.
Hy 1, Hy 2 etc.	regnal dates, t. Henry I, t. Henry II etc.
ib, *ib*	*ibidem* (referring respectively to published and unpublished sources).
InqMisc	*Calendar of Inquisitions Miscellaneous* (PRO), in progress.
Ipm	*Calendar of Inquisitions Post Mortem* (PRO), in progress.
IS	L. C. Lloyd, *The Inns of Shrewsbury: Their Signs and Their Stories*, Shrewsbury 1942, reprinted by Shrewsbury County Library 1976.
Jas 1, Jas 2	regnal dates, t. James I, t. James II.
JEPN	*Journal of the English Place-Name Society.*
John	regnal date, t. John.
K	Kent.
Kelly	*Kelly's Directory of Shropshire*, 1934.

Kynnersley Brown Letter from W. J. Kynnersley Brown, The Hall, Leighton, date 31st Jan. 1933, filed in E. W. Bowcock's material.

l. late.

L Lincolnshire.

La Lancashire.

LCA *Index to Llyfr Coch Asaph, Archaeologia Cambrensis* 3rd series, Vol. 14, 1868.

LDR Glebe terriers in Lichfield Diocesan Registry.

Lees R. B. Lees, *A History of Hinstock Church and the Chapels*, Hinstock Village History Series, 1990.

Lei Leicestershire.

Leland *Leland's Itinerary in England and Wales*, ed. L. Toulmin Smith, 5 vols., London 1964.

LHEB K. Jackson, *Language and History in Early Britain*, Edinburgh 1953.

Lib *Calendar of Liberate Rolls* (PRO), in progress.

Lil *The Cartulary of Lilleshall Abbey*, ed. Una Rees, Shropshire Archaeological and Historical Society 1997. This replaces *Lil* in Bibliographies to Parts **1** and **2**.

Lilco Records of the Lilleshall Company.

LP *Letters and Papers Foreign and Domestic, Henry VIII*, PRO 1864–1933.

LPN M. Gelling and Ann Cole, *The Landscape of Place-Names*, Stamford 2000.

LVD *Liber Vitae Dunelmensis*, Surtees Society Publications 13, 1841.

m. mid.

Margary I. D. Margary, *Roman Roads in Britain,* 2 vols., London 1955–7.

masc. masculine.

ME Middle English.

MemR *The Memoranda Roll of the King's Remembrancer for 1230–31* (PRS NS 11), 1933; ~ *for the Michaelmas Term of the First Year of the Reign of King John* (PRS NS 21), 1943.

MGS C. H. Drinkwater, *The Merchants' Gild of Shrewsbury*: a series of articles in SAS. Most of these are bound in a volume in the Local Studies Library, Shrewsbury (D 36.1 Acc No 1695).

MHG Middle High German.

Mills A. D. Mills, *Dorset Place-Names: Their Origins and Meanings*, Wimborne 1986.

MinAcc Ministers' Accounts (PRO).

MM *Mappa Mundi* in *The Historical Works of Gervase of Canterbury*, ed. W. Stubbs, Vol. II (RS), 1880.

ModE Modern English.

Mont Montgomeryshire.

Morden *The County Maps from William Camden's Britannia 1695* by Robert Morden. A Facsimile (1972).

Morgan R. Morgan, *Welsh Place-Names in Shropshire*, Cardiff 1997. This replaces *MorganTS* in Bibliographies to Parts **1** and **2**.

MS, MSS Manuscript(s).

Mx Middlesex.

n., ns.	name(s)
N.	North.
Nankivell	J. W. Nankivell, *Chapters from the History of Ellesmere*, 1992.
Nb	Northumberland.
NCPNW	B. G. Charles, *Non-Celtic Place-Names in Wales*, London 1938.
n.d.	undated.
NED	*A New English Dictionary*, ed. J. A. H. Murray and others, Oxford 1888–1933. This is now *The Oxford English Dictionary*.
Nf	Norfolk.
NLW	MSS in the National Library of Wales.
NLWCat	Online catalogue of *NLW* (forms supplied by R. Morgan).
nom.	nominative.
Norwich	*The Valuation of Norwich*, ed. W. E. Lunt, Oxford 1926.
NRY	North Riding of Yorkshire.
NS	New Series in a run of publications.
Nt	Nottinghamshire.
Nth	Northamptonshire.
O	Oxfordshire.
OB	H. Owen and J. B. Blakeway, *History of Shrewsbury*, 1825.
obl.	oblique case.
OE	Old English.
Ogilby	J. Ogilby, *Itinerarium Angliae*, London 1675.
OHG	Old High German.
OLG	Old Low German.
ON	Old Norse.
OrdVit	*The Ecclesiastical History of Ordericus Vitalis*, ed. M. Chibnall, 6 vols., Oxford 1968–80.
OS	Ordnance Survey.
p.	page.
p.	*post*: after.
(p)	place-name used in a person's surname.
P	Pipe Rolls (PRS), in progress.
part.	participle.
Pat	*Calendar of Patent Rolls* (PRO), in progress.
Peake	Rev. J. Peake, *Ellesmere*, 1889, and H. J. Peake, *Historical Guide to Ellesmere*, 1897. There are copies of these in SRO.
pers.n.	personal name.
P.H.	Public House.
Pk	Park.
pl.	plural.
Pltn	Plantation.
Plymley	J. Plymley, *General Survey of the Agriculture of Shropshire*, London 1803.
p.n., p.ns.	place-name(s).
PN	EPNS survey of the county indicated by the abbreviation which follows.

PN Du	V. Watts, *A Dictionary of County Durham Place-Names*, EPNS 2002.
PN EF	H. Wyn Owen, *The Place-Names of East Flintshire*, Cardiff 1994.
PN Ha	R. Coates, *The Place-Names of Hampshire*, London 1989.
PN La	E. Ekwall, *The Place-Names of Lancashire*, Manchester 1922.
PR	*Shropshire Parish Registers*, Shropshire Parish Register Society. (H) Hereford Diocese; (L) Lichfield Diocese; (StA) St Asaph Diocese.
PRAlveley etc.	MS transcripts of parish registers in Shrewsbury Record Office.
PrGerm	Primitive Germanic.
PRO	Public Record Office.
PRS	Pipe Roll Society.
PrW	Primitive Welsh.
PW	*The Parliamentary Writs and Writs of Military Summons . . .* (RC), 1827–30.
QW	*Placita de Quo Warranto* (RC), 1818.
R.	River.
R 1, R 2 etc.	regnal dates, t. Richard I, t. Richard II etc.
Rad	Radnorshire.
RB	Romano-British.
RBE	*The Red Book of the Exchequer*, ed. H. Hall (RS), 3 vols., 1896.
RC	Record Commission.
Rd	Road.
Redin	M. Redin, *Studies on Uncompounded Personal Names in Old English*, Uppsala 1919.
RentSurv	Rentals and Surveys in PRO.
RH	*Rotuli Hundredorum* (RC), 1812–18.
Rocque	J. Rocque, Map of Shrewsbury, 1746.
RS	Rolls Series.
RTH	*The Registers of Thomas Higgins of Wem, in Shropshire*: in *Shropshire Historical Documents: A Miscellany*, Shropshire Record Series 4, Keele 2000 (Higgins was a man-midwife).
Ru	Rutland.
S	P. H. Sawyer, *Anglo-Saxon Charters, an annotated list and bibliography*, Royal Historical Society, 1968.
S.	South.
s.a.	*sub anno.*
Sa	Shropshire.
SAC	*The Cartulary of Shrewsbury Abbey,* ed. Una Rees, 2 vols., National Library of Wales, 1975.
Saints	*Die Heiligen Englands,* ed. F. Liebermann, Hanover 1889.
SaltNS	*Collections for a History of Staffordshire*, The William Salt Archaeological Society, New Series.
SAS	*Transactions of the Shropshire Archaeological Society.* The series is numbered in arabic figures, the volume in roman, e.g. 1/IX, 4/III. If no series is given the ref. is to the current series, and the volume no. is in arabic.

Saxton — Saxton's *Map of Shropshire*, 1577.
SBL — A collection of Shropshire documents formerly in the Local Studies Department of Shropshire Libraries, Shrewsbury. These documents are now in SRO. The numbering is the same as previously, but prefixed by 6000.
Searle — W. G. Searle, *Onomasticon Anglo-Saxonicum*, Cambridge 1897.
Sf — Suffolk.
SHC — *Collections for a History of Staffordshire*, William Salt Society.
ShelveMap — Map of 1650 displayed in Shelve church.
sing. — singular.
Slack — *The Lordship of Oswestry 1393–1602*, ed. W. J. Slack, Shrewsbury 1951.
s.n. — *sub nomine.*
SNQ — *Shropshire Notes and Queries* Vols. I and II, Shrewsbury 1886 (items collected from *The Shrewsbury Chronicle* 1884–86).
So — Somerset.
Sr — Surrey.
SR — *The Shropshire Lay Subsidy Roll of 1 Edward III, 1327*, ed. W. G. D. Fletcher, reprinted from SAS, Oswestry 1907. *The Lay Subsidy Roll of 1334*, ed. R. E. Glasscock, British Academy 1975.
SRO — Documents in Shropshire Records and Research Centre, formerly Shropshire Record Office.
St — Staffordshire.
Strain — M. J. Strain, *A Short History of Lockley Wood*, Hinstock Village History Series 1994.
Strange — *Le Strange Records*, ed. Hamon le Strange, London 1916.
StRO — Documents in Staffordshire Record Office.
s.v. — *sub voce*: under the word.
SWB — G. F. Jackson, *Shropshire Word Book*, London 1879.
Swin — *Registrum Ricardi de Swinfield, Episcopi Herefordensis*, ed. W. W. Capes, Canterbury and York Society VI, 1909.
Sx — Sussex.
t. — *tempore.*
TA — Tithe Award.
Talbot — *Accounts of the Stewards of the Talbot Household at Blakemere 1392–1425*, ed. B. Ross, Shropshire Record Series 7, Keele 2003.
TAMap — Map accompanying *TA.*
Templars — *Records of the Templars in England in the Twelfth Century*, ed. B. A. Lees, British Academy 1935.
Tengstrand — E. Tengstrand, *A Contribution to the Study of Genitival Composition in Old English Place-Names*, Uppsala 1940.
TN — *Taxatio Ecclesiastica Angliae et Walliae, auctoritate Papae Nicholai IV c. 1291*, ed. S. Ayscough and J. Caley, London 1802.
Tong — G. Griffiths, *A History of Tong, Shropshire*, Newport 1894.

Townson — R. Townson, 'A Sketch of the Mineralogy of Shropshire' in *Tracts and Observations in Natural History and Physiology*, London 1799.

TRE — *tempore Regis Edwardi*, the DB term for 'on the day that King Edward the Confessor was alive and dead'.

VCH — *The Victoria History of the County of Shropshire*, in progress.

VCH — Victoria County History notes, held at Shropshire Record Office. Sometimes followed by note of ultimate source, e.g. *VCH(Longleat)*, *VCH(Hereford)*.

VE — *Valor Ecclesiasticus*, ed. J. Hunter (RC), 1810–34.

VEPN — *The Vocabulary of English Place-Names (Á–Box)*, ed. D. Parsons and T. Styles with C. Hough, *(Brace–Cæster)*, ed. D Parsons and T. Styles, Centre for English Name-Studies, Nottingham 1997, 2000, *(Ceafor–Cock-pit)*, ed. D. N. Parsons, English Place-Name Society, Nottingham 2004.

v.r. — variant reading.

W — Wiltshire.

W. — West.

WATU — M. Richards, *Welsh Administrative and Territorial Units*, Cardiff 1973.

Wd — Wood.

We — Westmorland.

WMidl — west-midland.

Wo — Worcestershire.

Wom — Wombridge Cartulary, *BL EgMS 3712*.

WRY — West Riding of Yorkshire.

WSax — West-Saxon.

Wt — Isle of Wight.

Y — Yorkshire.

* — a postulated form.

Words printed in bold type, e.g. **āc**, **tūn**, are recognised place-name elements. Most of these are discussed in EPNS 25–26; some are to be found in the Elements sections of later volumes.

Dates such as '1271–2 *Ass*' indicate that the spelling cannot be precisely dated within those limits. Dates such as '1347, 54 Ipm' indicate that the same spelling occurs in 1347 and 1354.

Long and short vowels are indicated thus: **ā**, ă.

ABBREVIATIONS USED IN FIELD-NAME SECTIONS

Fd	Field	Mdw	Meadow
Flg	Furlong	Pce	Piece
Lsw	Leasow	Yd	Yard

Field-names are arranged in lists headed (a) and (b), the former containing those names known to have been in use in the 19th century or later.

Capitalisation in field-names has been rationalised; the use in sources of small or capital initials has not been reproduced.

ADDENDA AND CORRIGENDA TO THE PLACE-NAMES OF SHROPSHIRE PARTS **1–4**

PART **1**

pp. 299–300 s.n. WATTLESBOROUGH. Professor J. Beverley Smith has established that the Welsh name for Wattlesborough is Trefrudd 'red settlement' (*ex inf.* R. Morgan).

PART **2**

p. 96 s.n. Boars Den. The field is described in FN 44 as "a spectacular hollow which has only been filled in in recent years".

pp. 108–9 s.n. *Gamelesbrugg'*. Cf. the discussion of *gannow* in Part **5** 60–1.

p. 171 s.n. Spy Bank. The discussion is superseded by that in Part **5** 32. This is one of three instances in the county, and probably contains *spy* referring to a look-out place.

p. 184 s.n UNDERHILL HALL. Cf. Richard *de Underhull'* 1327 SR, listed under Cardington: *v.* **under**, **hyll**.

PART **3**

p. 67 s.n. OLD HALL. Earlier references are *The Old Hall* 1736 PR(L) 18, 1808 PR(L) 20.

p. 240 BALAAM'S HEATH. Another instance of *Balaam* names has been noted in Wo. A group in Sheriff and Church Lench comprises *Balaam Slade* in an Enclosure Award and *Balaams Way*, *North Balaam* in a Tithe Award (*ex inf.* P. Knight).

PART **4**

p. 7 s.n. WAXCHERE. The word *shere* 'shed' occurs in GT2 under Llanyblodwell, 1685: "the house has 2 rooms per floor and a small 'sheere' called a buttery".

pp. 49, 88 s.n. *Coleham*. Delete *Carnecolne*. All the forms noted for this name have *-cole*, not *-colne*. Dr D. Horovitz has noted a doublet of this name in St. *Rough Carncoe* is shown on 1833 OS, ½ mile S. of Willoughbridge Lodge (SJ 730388) near the Sa border, E. of Norton in Hales, and early forms are *Carnecole* 1585, *Garnecoale* 1617. In view of this and of the deletion of the erroneous *-colne* form for the Sa name it now seems likely that the Shrewsbury name is not connected with Coleham, as suggested in Part **4**, the proximity being coincidental. *Carnecole* should be noted as a recurrent minor name, for which no etymology is at present available.

p. 63, s.n. *Bagbridge*. An earlier form for the Coleham name is *Bagbrigge* "super aquam vocat' Meole Watyr" 1450 *SRO 322/260.*

p. 98 s.n. ACTONLEA. *The Lea* 1588 *SRO 322/1/1* probably belongs here.

p. 99 s.n. Chelmley Park. This is *Clemley*, *Clemley Parke* 1615 *SRO 322 box 2*. This reference is considerably earlier than *Clemly* 1756, noted on p. 91. *v.* discussion of Clemley names *infra* 198–200.

pp. 98–9, Acton Reynald field-names, s.ns. Flaxmoors, Hamstocks, Outland Pits add *Flax More*, *Hampstock*, *Owtelands Gate*, *Owtelande Lane* 1615 *SRO 322 box 2*. Add (b) *Badgers Dore*; *Brodwater*; *The Double Harrowes*; *Geryes Dole*; *Ladye Furlong*; *Stanmylle Damme* (all 1615 *SRO 322 box 2*).

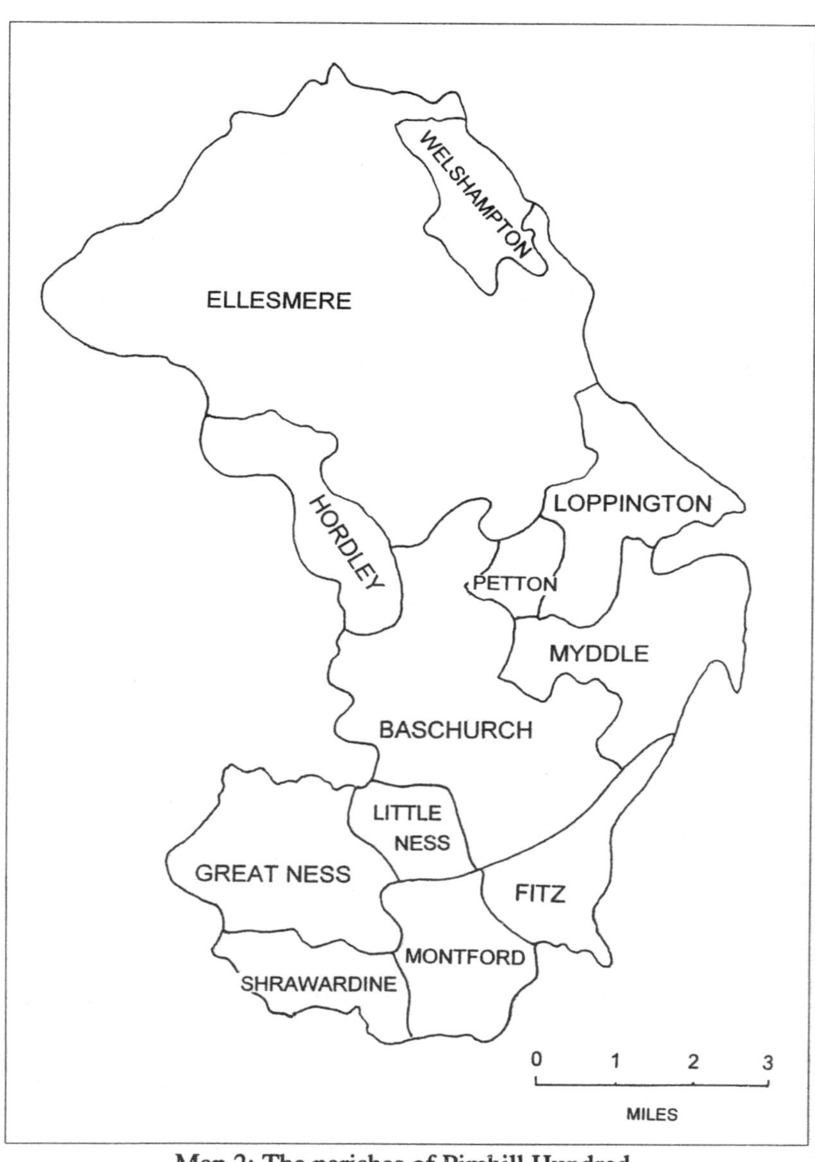

Map 2: The parishes of Pimhill Hundred.

PIMHILL HUNDRED

The area treated here is mainly that of the hundred as shown on a map by H. D. G. Foxall entitled *County of Salop: The Hundreds in 1831*. The exception is the inclusion of Dudleston, which Foxall places in Oswestry Hundred. The material is arranged under parishes and townships as shown on the Tithe Award maps. The large civil parish of Pimhill, created in 1934, has been ignored.

The hill from which the Hundred is named is in Preston Gubbals, on the boundary between that parish and Myddle. Preston Gubbals became part of the Liberties of Shrewsbury, and the name was therefore discussed in Part **4**, 156–8. The first element, **pymba*, is unexplained.

The hill is a typical meeting-place, in open country, on the boundary of two parishes and near a road-junction. It is likely that this was always the meeting-place, though the DB name for the Hundred was Baschurch. Most of the places in this section were in Baschurch Hundred at the time of the Domesday Survey. The renamed Hundred of Pimhill appears in records from the early 13th century. A number of the manors in its southern half were taken into the Liberties of Shrewsbury, and these were treated in Part **4**.

Lost DB manors entered as in Baschurch Hundred are:

Cheneltone, a one-hide estate, which was waste TRE and in 1086;

Estone, a one-hide estate, waste TRE but functioning in 1086;

Slacheberie, a one-hide estate, waste in 1086: this place is entered in 1255 RH as *Slachbur'*, held by William *de Hochton'*, i.e. Haughton in Ellesmere township;

Sudtelch, a half-hide estate which follows Sleap in the Survey: a note in the Phillimore DB expresses doubt about the hundredal ascription;

Udeford, a one-and-a-half-hide estate, perhaps a member of Ruyton-XI-Towns with which the DB entry links it: if so, it was in the post-Conquest Lordship of Oswestry, so in Oswestry Hundred.

It is seldom advisable to offer firm etymologies for names recorded only in DB, but *Estone* may fairly be considered an 'east settlement', and *Udeford is* probably 'wood ford'. *Slacheberie*, in view of the *-bur'* of 1255, probably has **burh** as second element; the first may be a late OE antecedent of ME *slack* 'valley, hollow', ultimately from ON **slakki**.

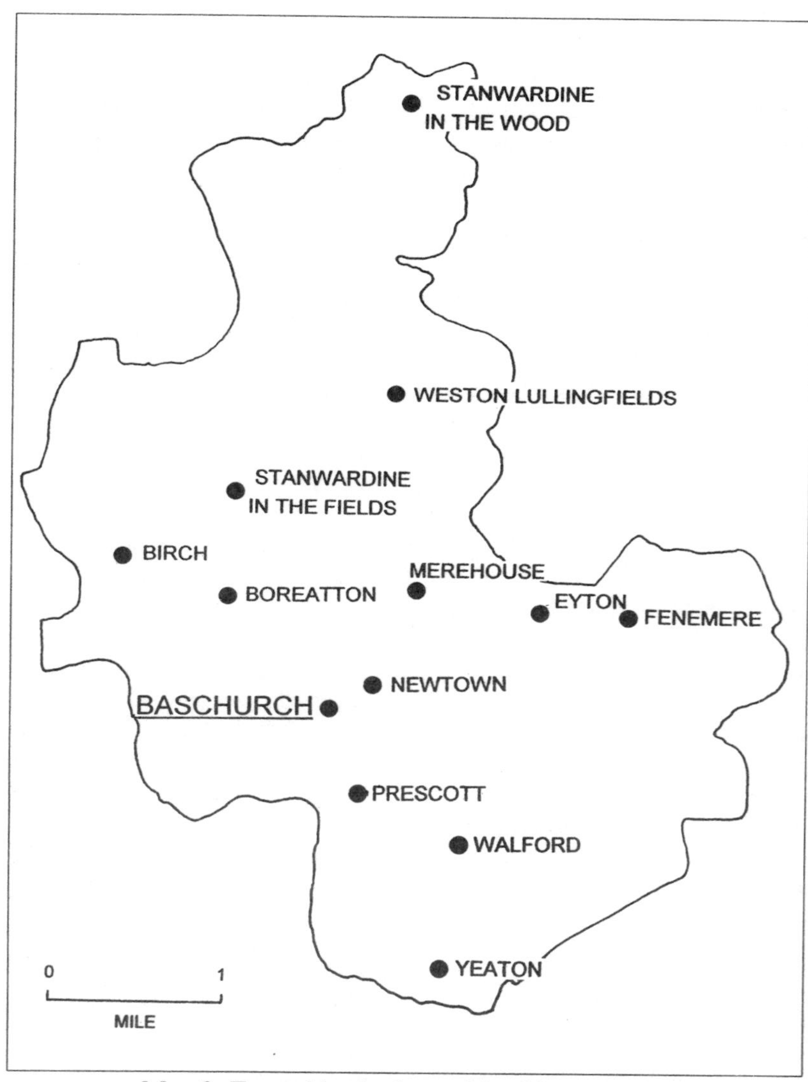

Map 3: Townships in the parish of Baschurch.

Baschurch

The parish contained 13 townships: Baschurch, Birch, Boreatton, Eyton, Fenemere, Merehouse, Newtown, Prescott, Stanwardine in the Fields, Stanwardine in the Wood, Walford, Weston Lullingfields, Yeaton. George Foxall drew a composite Tithe Award map, which he dated 1841–4. He marked the township boundaries on this, and the place-name material is presented here in accordance with those divisions.

The 13 townships are small areas, some with minimal settlement, but field-names suggest that they operated as discrete agricultural units. Six are in DB: Baschurch, rated at three-and-a-half hides, Fenemere at half a hide, Eyton at one, Stanwardine in the Fields, Walford and Yeaton at two. Yagdon, in Yeaton township, is also in DB, with an assessment of half a hide.

1. BASCHURCH (SJ 220425)
The name, which means 'Bassa's church' is discussed in Part **1**.

NOBOLD (lost). The *TA* field-names *Nobold Meadow* and *Nobold Moor*, on the southern edge of Baschurch village and straddling the boundary with Prescott township, may preserve the name of a lost hamlet. Gazetteer lists "Nobold Baschurch" as an extant name, but it does not appear on maps later than *TA*. If this is an ancient name it is a third 'new building' to add to Nobold in Meole Brace and a lost *Newbold* in Cound (Part **4** 149, Part **2** 135).

A possible early reference occurs in a deed of 1377, *SBL 3603*. This disposes of a holding "in villa et campis de Neubald" and a curtilage in the suburbs of Shrewsbury. The witnesses include John of *Shotton'*, William of *Weston* and Hugh of *Atton*. These places — Boreatton and Weston in Baschurch and Shotton in Hadnall — are close enough to support the placing of *Neubald* in Baschurch, but Nobold in Meole Brace, on the outskirts of Shrewsbury, is perhaps likelier.

ASH COPPICE.

MOOR FM, 1841–4 *TA*, *La More* 1327 SAS 3/V (p), *The Moors*, *Great*, *Little*, and *Nearmost Moors* 1794 *SBL 17441*; *v.* **mōr**. On *TAMap*

Great Moor, *Moor Head*, *Perry Moor*, *Milford Moor*, *Parks Moor*, and *Moor Meadow* lie between the farm and the R. Perry.

NEW BUILDINGS 1833 OS. *TAMap* shows *Hill Fm* here.

WHITMORE COTTAGES and LANE. The lane and the three cottages at the end of it are shown, but not named, on *TAMap*. One of the fields abutting the lane is *Whit Mill Leasow* on the Foxall map, and *Whitmill Lane* occurs 1792 *SBL 17439*.

Mrs H. G. Letts has informed us that the cottages were demolished in 1960, but the lane continued to be maintained by householders living near the village end of it. Locally the name Whitmore Lane is rejected, and the true name is considered to be World's End Lane, which Shrewsbury Post Office recognises as an official address. World's End is appropriate to the cottage-site at which the lane ends, but no early references have been found for it. Whitmore is probably a conflation of *Whitmill* with the Moor names for which *v.* Moor Fm *supra*. *Whitmill* may have referred to a windmill.

In 1792 *SBL 17439* there is a piece of land called *Phillips's Whitmill*. Gazetteer lists PHILLIPS ST in Baschurch village, which may contain the same surname.

Field-Names

Forms in (a) for which no date is given are 1841–4 *TA*. Those dated 1805 are *SBL 16898*.

Sources for names in (b) are: 1539–40 and Hy 8, *RentSur*; 1545 (1773), 1609, 1719, 1792, 1794 *SBL 17285*, *17410*, *17532*, *17439*, *17441*; 1612 and 1682, GT.

Some names in (b) may be in other townships. In addition to all early-recorded names for which there is positive evidence of location in Baschurch township the list includes names for which there is no evidence of exact location in the parish.

(a) Blaze Bank (perhaps referring to a bare spot, *v.* FN 28); Bowling Alley (perhaps referring to a level surface rather than to the game, cf. *Bowling Green* 1719); Calves Yd; Church Mdw; Croft, Great, Far, Near, Garden, House, Hincksmans (round the outskirts of Baschurch village); Field, Long, Upper; Great Lsw; Hempyard (in the village); (The) Hill Top, Near Hill Top, Lower Hill, Croft below the Hill (The Hill 1805); Holly Croft; Juglars Grave (also 1805); Kings Flg, Far, Near (also 1805, in a sharp projection of the N. boundary of the township); Lambs Lsw, Higher, Lower 1805 (*The Lambs Leasowe* 1609); Lime Lsw 1805 (1719); Lanacres, First, Second, Fourth (Third, Fourth ~ 1794); Long Lsw 1800 *SBL 16976*; Long Shade; Meadow, Far, Near, Long (The Meadow 1805); Middle Fd, Lower 1805; Milford Moor (Milford is in Little Ness *infra*); Millington's Yd 1805;

Moor Head (1792, 4 *SBL 17439*, *17441*); Motley Hill (also 1805); New Inclosure and Pce (*The New Inclosure* 1792); New Pce, Far (New Pce 1805); Nobold Moor (1794), Nobold Mdw, Far and Near Nobold Mdw (*v. Nobold supra*); Old Leys (Old Lays 1805); Parks Moor, Lower, Upper (*Parks's First*, *Second*, *Third Moor* 1792, 4); Perry Moor, Big, Further, Middle ~ ~ (by R. Perry); Pissant Graves, Great, Little (also 1805, dialect *pissant* 'ant', Graves perhaps referring to nests under the ground); Pool Mdw, Baschurch Pools and Pltn; The Pool Moor 1805; Sandy Lsw; Sandy Pce; Shop Yd 1805; Stanwardine Cross, Big ~ ~ (Big, Little ~ ~ 1805, by crossroads on road to Stanwardine in the Fields); Stoney Yd 1805; Tanhouse Fd, Far, Near, ~ Mdw (on boundary with Prescott township, *TAMap* shows buildings by R. Perry); Townsend (1805, *Farthermost*, *Nearmost* ~ 1792, at W. edge of village); Vicarage Croft, Mdw; Way Lsw; Whit Mill Lsw (*v.* Whitmore *supra*); Yard, Home, Millingtons, Stony (on N. edge of village).

(b) *Adcote Way Furlong* 1612 (Adcote is in L. Ness *infra*); *Le Dame Yardes* Hy 8, *Lez* ~ ~ 1545 (1773); *Blacke Pole* Hy 8 ('black pool'); *Le Bryer Yard'* Hy 8; *Calde Wall' Feld* Hy 8, *Caldwall Feilde* 1545 (1773) ('cold spring'); *Chapel Croft or Winters Croft* 1682; *Claypit Furlong* 1612 ("in Peyrie Field", "5 butts" also mentioned); *Le Colders* Hy 8, *Coldars* 1545 (1773) (a derogatory name, 'cold arse', there is an earlier instance PN Ch **4** 248); *Collys Headland* 1682; *Conygree* 1609 ('rabbit warren'); *Cow Leasowe* 1609, *Little Cow Leasow* 1719; *Croft* 1612; *Croft Meadow* 1682; *Edove Pool* Hy 8; *Eldertree Furlong* 1612 (in *Heath Field*); *Flowers Meadow* 1612; *Le Foxmore* Hy 8, *Foxmore* 1545 (1773) ('fox marsh'); *Le Gold Smythes* Hy 8; *Gorsty Hurst* Hy 8, *Grostie-hurst* 1545 (1773) (*v.* ***gorstig**, **hyrst**); *Gryffiths Leasowe* 1609; *Grymley Yate Furlong* 1612; *Heath Field* 1612; *Hopyard Leasow* 1719; *The Horse Pasture* 1609; *Howelles Leasowe and Yard* 1609; *John' Jonys Hey* Hy 8, *John Johns Hey* 1545 (1773); *Le Kylne* Hy 8, *Le Kilne* 1545 (1773); *Leafields* 1609; *Leppydge Furlong* 1612; *Little Field* 1609; *Long Acre Pole* Hy 8 ('~ ~ pool'); *Long Furlong* 1682; *Middle Paddock* 1719; *The Mill Meadow* 1609; *New Leasowe* 1609; *The Oxhouse Yard* 1792; *Ox Leasow* 1719; *Peyrie Field* 1612; *Roowood Co'men* Hy 8, *Rough Wood* 1545 (1773) (*v.* **rūh**); *Roughe Leasow* 1609; *Segge Pole* Hy 8 ('sedge pool'); *Shawe*, *High*, *Le Lowe* Hy 8, *Highshawe*, *Lowshawe* 1545 (1773) (*v.* **sceaga**); *Thorneforde* 1539–40; *Tong Hill* 1682; *Townepole* Hy 8 ('township pool'); *Tythe Barn* 1792; *The Wall Hill* 1609; *Waltons Piece* 1682; *Wildingsley* 1609; *Woodfield* 1612.

2. BIRCH (PARK) (SJ 404234)

Bircha 1194–5 SAC, *Birch* c.1270 SAC, 1672 HTR, *Byrche* Hy 8 *RentSur*, *Leybyrch* 1545 (1773) *SBL 17285*, *Birche Growndes* 1609 *SBL 17410*, *Birch Park* 1833 OS.

v. **birce** 'birch tree'. The forms give no indication of a plural, such as is found in those for Much and Little Birch He (HePN 33) and Birch Hall Db (PN Db 115), so this name may derive from a collective use of the singular. Another instance of such usage may be Birch Fm in Frilsham, Berks (PN Berks 246), which is *Birche*, *Burch'* 1202. The 1545 form has the French definite article prefixed.

Kelly's Directory for 1934 describes Birch Park as a hamlet, but maps from *TA* onwards show only a single large house. The earliest reference is to the enlargement of John Lestrange's park here. The second is from a grant by Ivo *de Birch* to Shrewsbury Abbey of all his father's land in the *villa de Birch*.

ALDERSLEY, *Aldersley Meadow* 1833 OS, ~ ~ *and Thicket* 1841–4 *TA*.

BOREATTON PARK, 1833 OS, 1841–4 *TA*. This is a mile N.W. of Boreatton Hall. The large house shown on 1900 6" map is not shown on *TAMap*.

THE DRUMBLE, *Drumble Meadow*, *The Drumble Wood* 1841–4 *TA*. The R. Perry flows in a gorge here. Gazetteer lists this and six other instances of Drumble(s) in the county. There is a larger number in Cheshire. The discussion in PN Ch **5.1** 162 treats it as a S. and E. Cheshire ModE dialect variant of the more widespread Dumble, and gives the meaning 'a wooded dell, a ravine'. EDD says 'a dingle, a ravine' and ascribes the word to Cheshire, Staffordshire and Shropshire. Cf. Dumble Hole in Lyneal, *infra*.

DUNNING WD, 1833 OS, *Donyngwoode* Hy 8 *RentSur*, *Doningswood* 1609 *SBL 17410*, (*Broomy*) *Donings Wood* 1719 *SBL 17532*, *Dunnings Wood* 1841–4 *TA*.

MILLDALE, 1841–4 *TA*, *Mill Dale* 1719, 1800 *SBL 17532*, *16976*, by Platt Mill in Boreatton.

Field-Names

Forms in (a) are 1841–4 *TA*.

(a) Clear Sand in Boreatton Park (this is the n. given to most of the Park area); Foxholes Lsw, Far, Near, Foxholes Mdw, East, West, Foxholes Pltn (*Foxholes*, ~ *Meadow* 1719 *SBL 17532*); Home Mdw (by Birch Park); Milking Bank, Little (adjoins Birch Park); Mill Fd, Millway (not by the river, probably a windmill); Pail Mdw (on the edge of Boreatton Park); Park Pltn, Further, Near, Upper, Lower Park Mdw (on W. edge of Boreatton Park); Twenty Shillings Pce and Nine Days Math; Wellwood Paddock, Far, Middle and Near, Little Paddock (*v*. Stanwardine in the Fields f.ns. for Wellwood).

3. BOREATTON (HALL) (SJ 413230)

Acton' 1291–2 *Ass*, Hy 8 *RentSur*, *Acton* 1545 (1773) *SBL 17285*
Boreatton 1577 Saxton *et seq*, *Borow Attoon* 1600 OB, *Bore Atton* 1600 OB, 1609 *SBL 6146*
Boare Acton 1649 SAS 4/VII, *Boracton* 1672 HTR

This is one of eight Sa examples of the name meaning 'oak settlement', the significance of which is discussed in Part **1** under Acton.

The prefix *Bore-* was probably added for distinction from the Acton in neighbouring Ruyton-XI-Towns which became Shotatton. The *Shot-* forms for the Ruyton name are recorded earlier, but the *Bore-* form of the Baschurch name may go back further than its first appearance in records. *Bor-* is perhaps most likely to be the animal name 'boar'.

Like Birch, Boreatton is the name of a single large house.

THE LAPWING, *The Lappwing* 1609 *SBL 17410*, *Lapperwing Wood* 1719 *SBL 17532*, *Lapwingwood* 1800 *SBL 16976*, 1841–4 *TA*. This is a small wood near the larger one called The Forest.

Lapwing names are not confined to the north-west Midlands, but they are concentrated in Shropshire and Cheshire. Two f.n. instances were noted in PN Sa **2** (164, 219), and one in Part **3** (219), Gazetteer notes Lapwing in Stottesdon, and there is a *Lapwings Leasow* in the *TA* for Trench in Ellesmere. PN Ch **5.1** 227 lists five instances. The 1609 reference to the present instance is probably the earliest noted, though PN Db 643 has a field-name *Lapwingeflight* 1673.

These names have generally been regarded as straightforward references to the bird, but in CornEl 62, Dr Oliver Padel makes an alternative suggestion. Discussing the place-name use of the Modern Cornish name for the bird (*kodna huilan*) he points out that, in Cornwall, English dialect *horniwink* is used both for the lapwing and for a tumbledown place, and that a Welsh name for the bird, *cornicyll*, is used for a shieling. A transferred use of this sort would be especially suitable for simplex examples of Lapwing.

EDD gives *hornywink* as Dev. Corn., and defines the adjective *hornywinky* as 'desolate, outlandish, like a moor where horniwinks resort'. Also, from Cornwall, "an old tumble-down house has been revilingly described as an old shabrag horny-wink place".

MUCKMOOR: *Knokynmore* Hy 8 *RentSur*, *Knockymore* 1609 *SBL 17410*, *The Nuckimore Meadow*, *Knuckimore Wood* and *Plain* 1719 *SBL 17532*, *Nuckemoor Meadow*, *Wood*, *Coppice Piece* 1841–4 *TA*. The substitution of M- for N- may be due to popular etymology. 'Knockin marsh', *v.* **mōr**. Knockin is five miles west, so this was presumably outlying marshland.

PLATT BRIDGE, 1771 *Craven*, is *Le Plattebrugge* 1343 *SBL 8387*, *The Platt Bridge* 1700 Gough, *Plat Bridge* 1719 *SBL 17532*, 1784

PR(Baschurch). PLATTMILL is *molendinum de Plattebrug'* 1194–5 *SAC*, *molendinum de Platte* c.1272 *SAC*, *Platte Mylle* Hy 8 *RentSur*, *The Platt Milles* 1609 *SBL 17410*, *Platt Mills* 1771 *SBL 6549*. This is a well-recorded example of ME **plat**[1] 'footbridge', found in La (PN La 31, 102) and fairly frequently in Ch (PN Ch **5.1** 308). The footbridge perhaps led to the island in R. Perry called *Bylet* on *TAMap*.

BOREATTON MOSS, 1833 OS, *The Moss* 1841–4 *TA*.

THE FOREST, 1833 OS, *The Forrest* 1609, 1719 *SBL 17410*, *17532*. This is a small wood, so an unusual use of *forest*. The 1609 reference is to pasture.

NEW PLTN, *Boreatton Ash Plantation* 1841–4 *TA*.

Field-Names

Forms in (a) are 1841–4 *TA* except where otherwise stated.

(a) Bime, Great 1805 *SBL 16898*, Byme Pltn, Higher and Way Byme (*Upper Byme* 1719 *SBL 17532*); Calves Croft (1609, 1719, 77 *SBL 17410*, *17532*, *16874*); Cunnery ('rabbit warren', by Boreatton Hall); Cow Lsw, Far, Near; Dove House Fd; East Moss Pltn (by Boreatton Moss); Great Yd; The Green; Hays Mdw, Big, Little, Lower; Hop Mdw and Yd; Lambs Lsw, Little, Great, Lower, Higher; Lane Lsw; Long Lsw, Lower, Upper; Middle Fd, Lower, Upper; Milking Bank Croft, Great Milking Bank (by Boreatton Hall); Moss Top Pltn (by Boreatton Moss); Ox Lsw; Sandy Lsw; Skreen Pltn (2, on outskirts of Boreatton Hall grounds).

(b) *Acherley Medowe* Hy 8 *RentSur*, 1545 (1773) *SBL 17285*; *Le Kydhey Yard* Hy 8 *RentSur*, *Le Kydhey* 1545 *SBL 17285* ('kid enclosure').

4. EYTON (SJ 441229)

This is one of four Sa Eytons and the name is discussed in Part **1**. It means 'island farm', referring to the situation on raised ground in an area of pools and marshes.

BIRCHGROVE, 1833 OS, BIRCHGROVE POOL, *Birch Groves Pool* 1841–4 *TA*: cf. *Byrche Greves* Hy 8 *RentSur*. The WMidl variant **grǣfe** has interchanged with **grāfa** 'coppice'.

EYTON CROSSING, a cluster of houses at the Baschurch-road crossing of the railway.

Field-Names

Forms in (a) are 1841–4 *TA*.

(a) Bakehouse Mdw; Banky Lsw; Barn Lsw; Big Mdw (2); (The) Black Ditches, Far, Near, Big, Little, Long, Lower, Upper and Middle ~ ~, Black Ditches Mdw (a group of small fields W. of Eyton straddling the boundary with Newton township); Brazen Nook, Far, Near; Brook Croft; Broomy Lsw; Calves Croft (2); Calves Yd; Cottons Fd, Little Cottons Hill; Grove Lsw; Heath, Lower, Higher, Big, Little and Long, Heath Bank; Hempbutt; Horse Mdw; Kitchen Fd (adjoins Birch Grove); Little Mdw; Little Yd; Lower Lsw, Far; Marlpit Lsw; Merchants Mdw; Moss (several); New Lsw (5 fields); Sniggle Bogs (SWB notes *sniggle-grass* as 'a kind of coarse grass growing in boggy places'); Squires Mdw; Townsend, Big (S. of the hamlet); Wallbrook Lsw and Mdw (*v.* War Brook *infra*); Waltons Croft; Ware Mdw ('weir'); Yards End.

5. FENEMERE (SJ 445230)
The GR is that of the lake. The name, which means 'mouldy lake', is discussed in Part **1**. The township is surprisingly well recorded considering the minimal nature of settlement. In DB it is recorded as ½ hide and waste.

The 1833 1" map shows two farms called Upper and Lower Fenemere. *TAMap* shows small buildings at both these sites without naming them. The 1900 6" map marks the one nearest the lake as Fenemere and the other as Lower Fenemere, and gives the name Upper Fenemere to a farm on the north boundary of the township which is shown but not named on *TAMap*, and not shown on the 1833 1" map. The 1999 2½" map also calls this northern-boundary farm Upper Fenemere, and gives the name Fenemere Manor to the southernmost of the three. It is not likely that there was ever a hamlet.

A slip in E. W. Bowcock's writing notes *Fennymere alias Linches* 1652 *SBL 10*, with the comment "know nothing of this alias 'Linches' locally": this name is documented *infra*, under Myddle.

Field-Names

Forms in (a) are 1841–4 *TA*.

(a) Aldery Croft; Aliens Croft; Bake House Yd; Barn Fd; Big Mdw (2); Brick Kiln; Bridge Croft; Broad Mdw; Broad Moors; Broomy Lsw; Burnt Tree Lsw; Butchers Mdw; Copper Lands; Cot Bank; Cot Lsw (with a small building in corner); Dairy Mdw; Dones Croft; Dry Bank; Duck Pits; Dukes Fd; Fat Lsw; Foxes Fd; Hall Banks; Heath Ground; Higher Ends; Holly Moor; Hook Lsw (one pointed corner); Horse Croft; Lee Fd and Mdw; Little Lsw; Little Mdw (2); Little Moor; Lloyds Lsw; Long Lsw (2); Marl Lsw; Marlpit Fd; Marlpit Lsw (not near preceding); Moor(s), Moor Bank; New Garden; New Lsw; Old House Yd (no building); Ox Lsw; Pool Lsw; Pool Mdw, Big, Little (by Marton Pool); Rough Lsw; Round Hill; Rushley, Cross, Long, ~ Mdw, ~ Pool; Rushy Moor; Rye Croft; Slade (Sa dialect for a wet patch in a field); Stable Mdw; Stair Mdw; Syllings Yd; Thistly Fd; Warehouse Croft; Warehouse Mdw (not near preceding); Warehouse Moor (not by other Warehouse fields); Watsons Patch; Well Lsw; Well Mdw; White Lsw; Wood Lsw.

6. MEREHOUSE (SJ 430230)

Mara 1199 SAS 2/X, *La Mere* m.13th, c.1270 (p) SAC, 1292, 1311 HAC, *Maire* 1523 SAS 2/XI, *Le Mere* Hy 8 *RentSur*, *Meyer* 1545 (1773) *SBL 17285*, *Meere* 1655 SAS 1/XLVII, *The Mere* 1833 OS, *Merehouse Farm* 1841–4 *TA*

v. **mere**, which is here used for the feature called The Berth Pool, which lies within the northern boundary of the township. *v. infra* for the name Berth. The Index to Tithe Award map gives the farm-name as *The Mere* and prints *Merehouse* in capitals, presumably to indicate that the latter is the name of the township.

Field-Names

Forms in (a) are 1841–4 *TA*. Those in (b) are SAS 2/XI.

(a) Barn Yd; Byrth Pool Pltn (*v.* The Berth *infra*); Holly Fd, Far, Near; Home Croft; Hoven Yd (probably 'oven'); Leasow, Near, Further; Little Croft; Little Pltn; Moor Mdw; Pool Lsw; Pool Mdw; Stanks, Far, Near (adjoining Long and Short Stanks in Eyton township and by an area called The Moss: the reference is probably to a construction for controlling water, but the exact sense is unclear); Tanhouse Bank, Croft, Mdw (by a brook on E. parish boundary); Taylors Lsw, Big, Little; Way Lsw.

(b) *The Mores Ledyate* 1296–1328 ('swing gate of the marsh', *v.* **mōr**, **hlidgeat**); *Le Mulenor Long* (*sic*), *Le Mulnestr* c.1290, *Mulnefeld* (an open field) 1296–1317 ('mill field', the final els. in the c.1290 forms are uncertain); *Ronlowesfeld* 1296–1317 (probably *recte Rou-*, 'rough tumulus', *v.* **rūh**, **hlāw**, the n. may be preserved in Rewley Hill in Newtown township, on the boundary with Merehouse: this was an open field).

SAC p. 112 has a deed of c.1250 recording a gift of nine acres "in campo qui vocatur la Mere", five of which are in "la dale atte bruches". This is 'the hollow at the broken-in land', *v.* **bryce**. ME *dale* appears to be used of hollows in Sa, cf. Part **4** 65.

7. NEWTOWN (SJ 425222)

Newetowne 1516 *SBL 3651*, *New Towne* Hy 8 *RentSur*, *Newtowne* 1545 (1773) *SBL 17285*, 1554 SAS 2/XI, *Newton* 1777 *SBL 16874*. This is an early ModE version of the common name Newton. NED notes the spelling *town* from the 15th cent. The settlement is on the edge of Baschurch village.

BASCHURCH STATION.

BOREATTON ARMS HOTEL.

DUNCAN ARMS P.H., *Duncan's Head Inn* 1841–4 *TA*.

THE YESTERS. On the 1900 6" map this name is given to a boggy wood on the S.E. boundary of the township. *TAMap* has *Yesters Bog*, *Yesters Plantation* here, and also a group of fields to the west called *Big*, *Lower*, *Top* and *Gorsty Yesters*. Possibly **eowestre** 'sheep-fold'.

Field-Names

Forms in (a) are 1841–4 *TA*. Those in (b) are Hy 8 *RentSur*.

(a) Brick Kiln Lsw; Eytons Cross, Far, Lower, Top, Near (by a T-junction on Eyton boundary); Ferny Croft; Green (a tiny tenement in the village); Leasow, Big, Little, Long, School (adjacent fields N.E. of village, the school is shown on *TAMap*); Longshoots, Far, Near and Lower Longshoots, Longshoots Croft (the fields are furlong-shaped); Lower Croft; Motley Hill (near, but not adjacent to, the same n. in Baschurch township); Newtown End (on township boundary); Old Fd, Far, Near; Rewley Hill (possibly *Roulow* 'rough tumulus' in the Merehouse f.n. *Roulowesfeld*: the field is now crossed by a railway); Warwithy (the hoar withy or whitebeam tree); Yard, Dove House, Far, Great, Little (on the outskirts of the village).

(b) *Estall* (probably 'east nook', *v.* **halh**); *Le Meyres Mosse* (probably 'Mere(house) bog'); *Le Peretre Yorde* ('peartree yard').

8. PRESCOTT (SJ 425210)

Prestecote 1190, 1 P (p) *et freq* with variant spellings *-cot*, *-kote* to 1327 SR (p)

Prescot 1508 AD *et freq* with variant spellings *-cott*, *-cote*

'Priests' cottage(s)'. There is a second Sa instance in Stottesdon. The name occurs also in Co, Gl, La, O, but it is much less common than Preston.

ADCOT MILL, *molendinum de Addecota* c.1240–52 HAC, *Adcote Mylne* 1516 (1773) *SBL 17285*, *Atcott Mylle* Hy 8 *RentSur*, *Attcot Mill* 1793 PR(L) 4, *Addcot Mills* 1771 *SBL 6549*, ~ *Mill* 1841–4 *TA*. Adcot is in Little Ness *infra*.

FRANKBROOK COTTAGE. *TAMap* shows *Frank Bridge Croft* with the cottage in a corner, and *Frank Brook Field*, *Lower Frank Brook* adjoining in Yeaton township. The stream is the lower course of War Brook, for which *v.* Walford *infra*.

NEW POOLS PLTN, cf. "drye pytte called newe poole" Hy 8 *RentSur*.

Field-Names

Forms in (a) are 1841–4 *TA*. Earlier forms for these, and names in (b), are 1771 *Craven*.

(a) Alder Crofts; Backside, Lower, New (on outskirts of hamlet); Barn Lsw and Garden; Bent Mill Lsw, Benby Lsw (*Bent Mill* was in Little Ness *infra*); Big Mdw; Brickkiln Lsw; Colemoor Wall (*Cummex Wall Leasow*, by *Wall Brook*, modern War Brook *infra*); Copmoor, Big and Little ~ (*The Cop Moor*: an earlier instance is *Le Copmor* l.13th PN Ch **2** 208, perhaps 'embanked marsh': *Coppedemor* 1240 PN Nth 267 may be related); Crofts (*v.* Four Butts); Cross Lsw, Dry, Way (either side of a road junction); Fennimere and Newtown End (large field on boundary with Newtown, but Fenemere is some distance E.); Footway Lsw; Fords (by R. Perry); Four Butts (The ~ ~: adjoining the hamlet on the east are three fields called Crofts, with Four Butts along one end of them, this looks like a minuscule open field); Furlong (a group of fields S. of Prescott contains Big, Had, Long, Sty and Yea Furlong, which were probably components of a small open field); The Green (a roughly triangular field at S. end of Baschurch village); Guy's Croft, ~ Cross (the Cross is by the same road-crossing as Posts and Gates *infra*); Hare Fd, Big, Little; Higher Fd (1771); Hole; Little Fd (*Nigher*, *Further* ~ ~); Lloyds Croft (2, *Loyd's* ~); Lower Ground, Big, Middle and Upper ~ ~, Lower Ground Croft and Banks (*Lower Ground*, the fields are spread out in an area by R. Perry); Lower Mdw; Moor, ~ Mdw (*The Moor*, near Moor Fm in Baschurch); New Lsw; Nobold Mdw and floor (*v. supra*); Old Man's Fd; Patch (tiny enclosure in angle between road and township boundary); Perry Mdw (1771, by R. Perry); Posts and Gates, Big, Middle and Near ~ ~ ~ (5 fields by an off-set crossroads); Sexton's Lsw and Mdw; Shaw Hill, Big, Little (*Great*, *Little*, *Lower* ~ ~); Slang, Lower, Upper (not slang-shaped); Slead, Little Field Slead (*Slade Meadow*, 'wet patch'); Smith Yd; Tythers Mdw; Yard (the hamlet is surrounded by Yards, including Barn, Higher, Lower, Upper, Smith and Poolyards); Yea Furlong (one of the Furlong ns. listed *supra*, this one is by R. Perry, so 'river furlong', *v.* **ēa**).

(b) *Bridge Furlong*; *Hewitt's Croft*; *Newtown Lsw*; *The Seven Butts* (cf. Four Butts *supra*).

The 1221 Feet of Fines published in SAS 3/VI include one for *Prestecote*, which the author of the article identifies as Prescott in Baschurch. The land in question is a half virgate consisting of seven acres in *Arildewell*, five in *Chesterfordfeld* and four in *Hinesmere*. These have not been listed above as the identification requires confirmation. *Chesterfordfeld* seems inappropriate here.

9. STANWARDINE IN THE FIELDS (SJ 414240)

The name, which means 'enclosed settlement on stony ground', is discussed in Part **1**, and forms for the affix are set out there. The earliest appearance noted of the affix is 1271–2 *Ass* (*Alchamp* and *in Le Felde*). Another Baschurch township, separated from this one by Weston Lullingfields, is Stanwardine in the Wood *infra*.

CLARENCE VILLA.

FISHPOOL COTTAGE.

LIMPIT HILL, 1784 *PR(Baschurch)*, 1833 OS, 1841–4 *TA*. Probably 'lime pit', referring to a place where lime was burnt, but the vowel of *lime* is not usually shortened in place-names.

THE ROUGH, *Rough* 1841–4 *TA*.

STANWARDINE PARK (a large house), *The Park* 1833 OS.

Field-Names

Forms in (a) are 1841–4 *TA*.

(a) Adderhill; Alder Rough Lsw (by The Rough); Bagley Moor (part of an extensive area on either side of R. Perry the correct n. of which is Baggy Moor, *v. infra*); Barley Flg; Blaze Bank (the same n. occurs in Baschurch township *supra*); Church Hill (3 fields in a road fork at approx. GR 416237, this may be a corruption of *crūc-hyll*, referring to an abrupt hill); Coppice Lsw; Cow Lsw, Little ~ ~; Croft(s) (*freq*, round village, on S. edge of Limpit Hill, etc.); Cross Gates, Further and Higher ~ ~ (surrounding a crossroads); Field, First, Second, Fifth, Sixth (4 small enclosures); Fish Croft, Fishpool Croft (pool shown); Gosty Fd ('gorsy'); Green Lsw; Hatton Corner; Hopyard Mdw; Kirkhams Croft; Long Slang (slang-shaped); Moor Mdw; New Croft, Higher ~ ~; New Lsw (7 fields on E. boundary of township); Oaktree Fd; Old Fd (very small, adjoins Barley Flg); Painters Yd; Patch (some tiny enclosures among Croft(s)); Pool Lsw, Big and Higher ~ ~; Rose Orchard; Sions Mdw; Stackyard; Stanwardine Croft (on township boundary); Stone Marl; Tedsmore Lsw, Far, Near; Tench (adjoining Fish ~ ns. so presumably named from the presence of tench in the fishpool); Walnut Tree Yd; Weir Mdw; Weston Gate (on Weston Lullingfields boundary); Wightwick Mdw (*Whittock Style* 1705 *SBL 273*); Willwood (4 fields), ~ Croft (adjoining Wellwood Paddock in Birch, *Willow Wood* 1771 *Craven*); Wingdale (an adjacent field is Winsdale); Wood Croft; Wood Ground, Mdw, Woodground Lsw; Yewtree Lsw.

(b) *Earl's Wood* 1771 *Craven*; *Stanworthinnesfeld* c.1250 SAC ('Stanwardine field'); *The Territt* 1705 *SBL 273* (Gazetteer lists "Territs, Stanwardine in the Fields", but the n. is not on maps); *The Town Ditch* 1635 (copy) *SBL 10293*.

10. STANWARDINE IN THE WOOD (SJ 428278)

Stanewrd' Ric I Cur, *Stanewardyn in Bosco* 1291–2 *Ass* (p)

Stanwardin 1193 P (p), *Stanwurthin* 1221–2 *Ass* (p)

Stanword' in Bosco 1231 SAC (p) *et freq* with variant spellings *Stanwordyn(e)* ~ ~ to 1615 (copy) *SBL 15755*

Stanworhin in Le Wude 1291–2 *Ass*, *Stanwarthynythewode* 1317 Ch, *Stanwarthyn-in-the-Wode* 1326 Ipm, *Stanwardine in the Woode* 1452 *SBL 4525*, *Stanwardyn in Le Wode* 1508 AD

Stannerton 1577 Saxton

This settlement is 2½ miles N.E. of Stanwardine in the Fields, and the areas of the two townships do not adjoin. Stanwardine in the Wood may have been a detached area of woodland belonging to the other settlement which evolved into a separate settlement, as detached woodland pastures often did.

WYCHERLEY HALL (1833 OS, 1841–4 *TA*), *Wycchersley* 1271–2 *Ass* (p), *Wycherley* 1396 *SBL 3599*, *Wychurley* 1397–8 MGS, *Wycherley*, *Wicherley* 1615 (copy) *SBL 15755*, *Witcherley* 1731 PR(L) 7, *v.* **lēah**. For the first element, a derivative of **wice** 'wych-elm' might be suspected, but the evidence for *-er* formations from tree-names is rather thin.

EPN **1** 156 says "A few tree-names appear to have secondary forms with a suffix *-er* (as *hæseler* from *hasel*, *mispeler* from *mispel*, ME *medler* from *medle*)"; and in PN NRY and PN ERY Smith derived Heslerton and (Kirby) Misperton from ***hæsler** and ***mispeler**. These etymologies were rejected in DEPN, but are accepted by Watts in CDEPN. For the present name **wicer* 'wych-elm' may be tentatively proposed, but more evidence for such formations would be welcome.

Wyteleye 1291–2 *Ass*, mentioned with *Stanworhin in le Wude* and *Bagleye*, is probably a garbled form for Wycherley.

LEA GORSE.

NILLGREEN, ~ COTTAGES, *Knill Green* 1661 *SBL 5950*, *Nil-Green* 1804 PR(L) 7, *Nill Green* 1833 OS, *v.* ***cnyll** 'hillock'.

ROWSEL WD, *Roushill Coppice* 1833 OS, *Roushill* 1841–4 *TA*.

STANWARDINE HALL, 1841–4 *TA*.

STONEHILL, *Stone Hill* 1833 OS, 1841–4 *TA*.

Field-Names

Forms in (a) are 1841–4 *TA*.

(a) Bagley Moor (a large area which extends into Stanwardine in the Fields; Bagley is in Hordley *infra*); Bath Mdw (beside the moat at Stanwardine Hall); Big Mdw; Bostons Bank; Boult Mdw (NED gives *bolt* sb[1] 13 'an obsolete or local name for some plants'); Calves Pce; Clover Lsw; Cow Lsw; Croft(s) (*freq*, at Stonehill and round Nillgreen); Dones Big Lsw, ~ Yd; Dones Mdw (not near preceding); Green Croft; Higley; Holdings Ground; Horse Pce; Kitchen Fd; Lawn, Far, Near, Middle (adjoining Park); Lea Fd; Limekilns; Lower Way Lsw; Masseys Pce, Big, Little; Middle Lsw; Moat Mdw (by Wycherley Hall); Newfound Land (on parish boundary); Orchard Mdw; Park, Big, Little, Middle (these and the 3 Lawn Fds may occupy the area of a park belonging to Stanwardine Hall; there is also a Park Fd N. of the Hall);

The Park (S.E. of Wycherley Hall); Pembridge Mdw; Reeves's Mdw; Riddings Bank ('clearing'); Road (a long, narrow strip on the edge of Bagley Moor); Rough Lsw; Round Bank (three-quarters curved); Ryegrass Fd, Flat, Long; Sandfords Pce; Walk Pce; Wharf Mdw (by canal); White Lsw and Mdw; Williams Croft; Wycherley Fd, Lsw, Mdw (*v. supra*); Yard, Lower and Upper Yd (by Wharf Mdw on the canal); The Yeld ('slight slope', *v.* **helde**).

11. WALFORD (SJ 435206)

Forms for the name are set out in Part **1**. It means 'spring ford', with most of the spellings indicating derivation from **wælle**, the WMidl form of **well**. This is one of four examples of the name, the others being Walford He (near Leintwardine) and Welford Gl, Nth. Ekwall (DEPN) takes **waelle**, **well** in these names to mean 'stream', though he allows 'spring(s)' as an alternative in the Gl example. The usual meaning of **well** in place-names is, however, 'spring', and, although it is not obvious why a spring should be the defining characteristic of a ford, this etymology is the likeliest. The road through Walford crosses War Brook at the southern end of Walford Pool, which is a large wide place in the brook, so there is little likelihood of the water from a spring being of exceptional value as a resource for travellers or residents.

ASH COPPICE.

THE HAYES, *Hayes Meddowe* 1609 *SBL 17410*, ~ *Meadow* 1719 *SBL 17532*.

WALFORD COTTAGES, HALL, MANOR, POOL.

WAR BROOK, 1833 OS, *Wall Brook* 1771 *Craven*. *TAMap* shows *Wallbrook Leasow* and *Meadow* on the N. side of the brook in Eyton township. It is possible that the name was **Walford Brook*, with the middle element dropped and *Wal-* corrupted to *War-*.

Field-Names

The Baschurch Tithe Award names only Calcott Hill and Ox Leasow in this township. Mr E. Wadlow supplied a list of field-names which were in use 1903–21 on Walford House Fm, and names in (a) are from this. Mr Wadlow also supplied names from a survey of Bank Fm and Hall Fm made for Thomas Presland in 1773. Names in (b) are taken from this.

(a) Back Orchard; Brickill or Brickhill (*Brick Kiln Leasow* 1773); Calcot Hill (1773, Calcott ~ 1841–4 *TA*); Cowpasture; Craft (dialect form of Croft); Diah or Dia Lane; End Mdw; Jays Cross; Kents Mdw; The Leasowes; Middle Mdw; Newtons Mdw (1773); Prescott Mdw; Sandy Pit Fd.

(b) *Backside Pce*; *Barn Yard*; *Beamdales*; *Broomy Yard*; *Calves Croft*; *Cow Leasow*; *Duvehouse Field*; *Duckpit Leasow*; *Frame Yard*; *Frank Bridge* (*v.* Frank Brook *supra*); *Green Leasow*; *The Gunnery*, *Gunnery Meadow* (for *Cunnery*, one of the many forms developed from **coninger** 'rabbit warren'); *Heath Leasow* (Walford Heath is in Yeaton); *Hollands*, *Big*, *Little*; *Hollings* (possibly 'holly', *v.* **holegn**); *Hoop Pool Mdw*; *Lambpit Leasow*, *Lower*, *Upper* ('loam pit'); *Malthouse Meadow*; *Mill Croft* and *Field*; *New Leasow*; *Oak Meadow*; *Ox Leasow* (this is one of the only two fields named in *TA*); *The Quabs* ('marsh', *v.* ***cwabba**); *The Slang*; *Tanners Leasow*; *Weavers Meadow*; *Weir Croft*; *White Croft.*

ME names are *Bradele* 1307 HAC, *Bradeley*, *Simondesleye* 1335 *HAC* ('broad clearing' and 'Sigemund's clearing', both pieces of land were in Walford wood).

12. WESTON LULLINGFIELDS (SJ 428248)

Weston 1255 RH, 1271–2 *Ass*, 1276 Cl, 1309 Ipm, 1510, 42 *SBL 4459*, *3652*

Weston' sup' Lullingfeld' 1291–2 *Ass*, *Weston super Lollingefelde* 1324 HAC, *Weston Bullyngesfelde* 1399 Cl, *Weston' sup' Lollyngeffeld* 1399, 1400 *SBL 4523*, *4*, *Westone in Lollyngfeld'* 1516 *SBL 3651*, *Weston Lullingfields* 1554 *SBL 3606*, *Lullingefeld* 1655 SAS 1/XLVII, ~ *Lullingfeild* 1672 HTR

Lullyngfeld 1497 Ipm

This Weston, one of ten examples in the county, is probably named from its position in the area called Lullingfield. The settlement is north, not west, of Baschurch.

The affix is a separate place-name referring to a district. DEPN says "Lullingfield would seem to mean 'FELD of *Lull*(*a*)'s people'", and the two 14th-cent. forms with *-inge-* support this. The garbled *Bullyngesfelde* should probably be disregarded. **feld**, 'open space', is frequently compounded with the genitive of group-names in **-ingas**, but most examples are in south-east and eastern England. Names containing **-inga-** are very rare in the Welsh Marches, but this appears to be one such. Lullingfield should probably be accepted as an indication of early Mercian settlement.

As used in place-names **feld** implies a contrast with land which is wooded, hilly, or marshy. Here the contrast is likely to be with the belt of marshy land between Weston and Baschurch.

THE BERTH, BERTH POOL, *The Burgh Poole* 1700 Gough, *Berth Hill*, *Pool* 1833 OS, *Byrth*, *The Byrth Pool* 1841–4 *TA*.

The name is that of the large Iron-Age fortification which adjoins the pool. It derives from **burh** 'fort', with substitution of *-th* for the *-f* which, though not documented, must have developed from OE *-h*, ME *-gh*, pronounced [χ]. Development of **burh** to Burf can be seen in Abdon and Clee Burf in this county. Interchange of *f* with *th* is well evidenced in modern dialects. Gough's form appears to show the more usual development to Burgh or Borough, but the pronunciation could have been *Burf.*

In Part **1**, s.n. Wattlesborough, it was suggested that in Sa the nominative **burh** was more likely to be used than the dative **byrig** when the reference was to an ancient earthwork, as opposed to the term being used for a manor house.

The Berth has long been of special interest to historians of the Welsh Marches. The Welsh poem cycle known as *Canu Heledd* names *Eglwysseu Bassa*, i.e. Baschurch, as the burial place of Cynddylan, ruler of Powys. In this poetry the central place of Cynddylan's kingdom is called *Pengwern*. *Pengwern* has been considered to be an earlier name of Shrewsbury, but the meaning, '(place at) the end of the alder swamp', is more appropriate to The Berth, which stands near the junction of an area of small lakes and meandering streams with the higher ground on which Stanwardine in the Fields and Weston Lullingfields are situated. The small amount of excavation which has so far taken place at The Berth produced Iron Age pottery, with a single Neolithic sherd, but a cauldron which has been considered to be of Dark-Age date was earlier found in nearby marshland. It is possible that the fort was re-used in the post-Roman period and became a centre of power after the abandonment of Wroxeter; but if the Dark Age occupants were Celtic Christians it may be difficult to recover archaeological proof of their presence.

In Staffordshire, about 30 miles N.E. of Baschurch, there is a replica of the situation at The Berth. The village called Maer (DB *Mere*) is beside a small lake which adjoins an earthwork called Berth Hill. Maer has the same name as Merehouse *supra*, and to complete the symmetry there is a DB settlement called Weston adjacent to Maer. It is unlikely that this is due to anything other than coincidence.

BOGGYMOOR, *The Boggymoor* 1777 *SBL 16874.*

CHELSEA COTTAGE.

CLAYPIT HALL, *Clay Pit Hall* 1833 OS. Cf. *The Clay Pitts* 1792 *SBL 17439*, *Clay Pits* 1794 *SBL 17441*, *Claypit Leasow* 1841–4 *TA*. 'Hall' is ironic.

PENNYRUSH, 1833 OS.

WESTONCOMMON, *Weston Common* 1833 OS.

WESTON VILLA, shown but not named on *TAMap.*

WESTONWHARF, *Weston Wharf* 1833 OS, on the Shropshire Union Canal. *TAMap* shows *Boat Inn* in Westonwharf.

Field-Names

Forms in (a) are 1841–4 *TA*.

(a) Bagley Moor (part of a large area, *v.* Bagley in Hordley, *infra*); Bambarts; Big Fd (very small); Big Wheat End; Birch Croft; Brantail Croft (a bird n., *brandtail* is a dialect term for the redstart); Broad Doors, Big, Little (the meaning is not clear: PN Ch **5.1** 163–4 lists a number of f.ns. in which *door* refers to a farmhouse entrance, but that does not suit here); Broad Lsw, Higher, Lower; Broomy Fd; Burlton Style; Byrth Fd, ~ Mdw (*v.* The Berth *supra*); Carthouse Fd; Claypit Lsw (*v.* Claypit Hall *supra*); Clover Lsw (2); Common Lsw; Coppice Fd; Corax, ~ Fd, Lsw, Mdw, Bank; Cordale; Court Mdw (not near a building); Cow Lsw, Big and Little ~ ~; Croft(s) (*freq*, on either side of N. boundary, round Westonwharf and in a large cluster on Westoncommon); Crooked Croft (2, both irregularly shaped); Crows Nest, Big (4 fields on parish boundary, E. of village, the n. may refer to elevation); Damesdale (adjoins Cordale); Field, Field Lsw; Gorsty Fd (*v.* **gorstig**); Great Nell, Big, Little; Hall Lsw, ~ Yard Mdw (by Claypit Hall); Hatch, Far, Near, Marton (Westonhatch Pltn in Myddle adjoins); Hay Shults; Inclosure, Great and Near ~ (on E. edge of Bagley Moor); Little Green Hill; Little Fd; Long Lsw; Marl Croft; Marton Fd, Big and Little ~ ~ (on boundary with Marton in Myddle); Meadow, Higher, Little, Rough, Big, Dukes (adjoining fields between the village and Bagley Moor); Middle Mdw (adjoins Court Mdw); Milking Bank (a large field not immediately adjacent to a farm); New Croft; New Lsw, Far, Near; Old Hens; Oxen Hill; Pail Pce (probably referring to a paled fence); The Park (minute enclosure); Petton Fd (a group of fields adjoining Petton boundary); Pool Mdw; Roberts Mdw; Rye Hill, ~ Fd; Salt Hill, ~ ~ Mdw; Smiths Mdw; Thieves Pce; Top Fd; Weavers Mdw (2, on either side of village); Well Mdw; Weston Fd (small field on S. township boundary); Weston Mdw (small field on E. boundary); White Lsw, ~ Moor (adjoining); Withy Croft; Wood Fd; Yard, Broomy, Far, Near, Dories, Little, Winterbrook, The Yard (enclosures round the village).

13. YEATON (SJ 433194)

The township-name, which means 'river settlement', is discussed in Part **1**.

The township contains a second DB manor, Yagdon, whose name survives in Yagdons Lane, GR 457193. There is a moated site at GR 448191, which is surrounded on *TAMap* by fields called Yagdens. This name, which means 'cuckoos' hill', is also discussed in Part **1**.

HOME FM is by Yeaton Pevery park. Two lodges are also shown on 1900 6".

LOWER MILL, *Mill* 1841–4 *TA*.

MANOR FM.

PARRY'S PLTN, *Plantation* 1841–4 *TA*.

UPPER MILL, *Mill* 1833 OS, 1841–4 *TA*.

WALFORD HEATH, 1747 PR(L) 4, adjoining Walford *supra*.

YAGDONS LANE, *v. supra*.

YEATON LO, *Yeaton Villa* 1841–4 *TA*.

YEATON PEVERY. This house is described in Kelly 1934 as "an extensive mansion of red stone . . . standing in park-like land of 250 acres". The mansion and park are shown on the 1900 6" map, but the area is farmland on *TAMap*. Pevery is the old form of Perry, the name of the adjoining river.

Field-Names

Forms in (a) are 1841–4 *TA*.

(a) Banky Fd; Barn Yd, Big ~ ~ (in hamlet); Beach; Beech's Lane Fd, ~ South Fd (not near preceding); Broad Lsw; Broomy Lsw, Far, Middle; Calves Yd; Common Pce (7 fields by Walford Heath); Cow Pasture, Ploughed ~ ~ (Calves Yd adjoins); Cow Pasture (not near preceding, adjoins Horse Pasture); Croft(s) (by Walford Heath); Dale Fd and Mdw; Drain Lsw; Dry Lsw; The Esps ('aspens'); Far Heath Croft (by Walford Heath); Ferringtons Fd, ~ Yd (near but not adjacent); Footway Lsw (2); Fox and Does (an unremarkable field in N.E. corner of township); Heath Croft, Near ~ ~ (outskirts of Walford Heath); Horse Pasture; Key Fd (might be considered key-shaped); Lawn (outskirts of Walford Park); Lily Pool Fd; Little Fd (2); Little Lsw (adjoins Big New Lsw); Lunns; Mare Fd, Mere Fd (3 fields on parish boundary, *v.* **(ge)mǣre**); Marl Lsw; Meadow, Far, Near; Mere Fd, Little ~ ~ (small pond shown, *v.* **mere**); Mill Fd (by Upper Mill); New Lsw, Big ~ ~ (6 fields); Old Gates; Old Wood Fd, Lsw, Pce; Patch (by Walford Heath); Peas Fd; Perry Mdw; Plantation (several); Pool Lsw; Reans, Big, Little (drainage channels); Shop Lsw (by two small houses on Shrewsbury road); Slang Mdw (slang-shaped); Townsend (E. end of hamlet); Upper Mdw; Walford Corner; Yelds ('gentle slope', *v.* **helde**).

Cockshutt

The ecclesiastical parish of Cockshutt was formed in 1872, from Ellesmere, and it became a civil parish in 1896. The name, which is discussed in Part **1**, is a term for a woodland glade where nets were stretched to catch woodcock.

The area contains five townships: Cockshutt and Crosemere; Frankton; Kenwick Park; Kenwick, Stockett and Whettall; Kenwick's Wood. Each of these has its own *TA* survey as a township of Ellesmere. The place-name material has been arranged within these divisions according to George Foxall's *TAMaps*.

1. COCKSHUTT AND CROSEMERE

CROSEMERE (SJ 437294)

Craulesmare 1255–6 *Ass* (p)

Croulesmere 1279–80 *RentSur*, 1309 Eyton, 1319 Pat, 1337 HAC (p), 1421 *SBL 3650*, *Crowlesmeere* 1685–6 *SBL 6223*, 1690–1 *SBL 5230*

Crolesmere 1427 *SBL 4028*, 1563 *SBL 3646*, *Crollesmere* 1496 *SBL 3644 et freq* to 1588 *SBL 3648*

Crosemere 1557 SAS 4/X *et seq*, *Crosemeare* 1615 (copy) *SBL 15755*, *Croesmere* 1716 *SBL 1066*, 1799 *PR(Cockshutt)*

Crolsemere 1588 *SBL 3647*

Crowsmeere 1672 HTR

Crosmere 1784 PR(StA) 2

v. **mere**: the lake is on the N. boundary of the township, about ¾ mile from the settlement, which adjoins Cockshutt.

An OE ***creowel** 'fork' is considered to be the first element of Croughton PN Nth 51 and Cryfield PN Wa 181–2, and the genitive of this word may be the qualifier in Crosemere. The Nth and Wa names have early forms with *Cruil-*, *Cr(e)ul-* (Cryfield) and *Criwel-*, *Creul-*, *Crewel-*, *Cruel-* (Croughton), so the parallel is not exact. Croughton, however, has *Crou(e)l-*, *Crowel-* forms also, and the editors of PN Nth comment that "OE *creowel* would give ME *crewel* and *crowel*". There is no obvious topographical fork near the lake.

CROSEMERE HALL.

CROWN INN.

EAST LO, by Petton Park.

LLOYD'S MOSS and WD, *Moss*, *Plantation* 1839 *TA*.

RED LION INN. *TA* has *Far*, *Middle* and *Near Red Lion Piece* N.W. of the village.

STANWARDINE GRANGE.

WACKLEY LO, 1833 OS: *v*. Wackley in Petton *infra*.

Field-Names

Forms in (a) are 1839 *TA*.

(a) Ashmoor, Big; Banky Mdw; Barn Fd; Barn Yd (several); Big Fd (very large); Birch Flg; Birchin Croft ('birchen', i.e. growing with birches); Blue Strine Mdw (dialect *strine* 'water channel'); Braddock Moss; Brickkiln Fd (several); Broad Lsw; Brook Croft, Big and Little ~ ~; Broom Hill (*Bromehull'* 1392–3 *SRO Bridgewater 212/box 72*); Broomy Lsw; Brush Croft; Bumpers Mdw; Coat Mdw (no building); Cobbler's Croft, Little; Cockshutt Fd, Mdw; Coppy Fd, Little; Cordwell, Near ~; Cottage Mdw; Cow Pasture; Crabtree Fd; Crabtree Lsw (not near preceding); Croft, Big, Little, Far, Hop and Cherry Tree ~ (adjoining, N.W. of village); Croft(s) (many small enclosures round Cockshutt and Crosemere, some with pers.ns., e.g. Betty Huntley's, Drury's, Malley's, Nancy Dicks: also Far, Near, Cherry, Footway, Gorse, Marlpit ~); Dale Croft; Dingle Fd; Dintail (not near Dipthill, earlier Diptail, in Frankton); Dry Pits; Dudmoor Brook, Big, Little (Deadman's Brook adjoins, Dudmoor Mdw is near); Edward Fd; Evans Dale; Far Fd (2); Field before the House; Field next Lane; Five Day Math ('five days' mowing'); Footway Fd, Mdw; Four Cornered Croft (irregularly shaped); Furlong Croft; Gander Pool; Gate Lsw (2); Gorsy Bank (2); Gravel Pit Fd; Green Fd (2); Haybridge, ~ Mdw (in drained marshland); Hesp, Far, Near, Hesp Mdw (possibly 'aspen'); Hollybush Pasture; Kenwick Lsw (on boundary with Kenwick township); Keay Bottoms, Keays Fd and Mdw, Dry Kayse (adjoining fields between village and drained marshland); Lake's Lsw; Lawns, Big, Little; Lea Fd (near Lea Fm *infra*); Lodge Fd (by Wackley Lo); Long Fd (2); Long Mdw; Low Mdw; Maltman's Fd; Maltman's Mdw (not near preceding); Marlpit Croft; Mat's Rough; Meadow (~ Mdw ns. in the marshland on E. boundary of township include Gotheleys, Harper's, Maltmans and Reynard's Mdw, Far, Near and Footway Mdw, (The) Chapel Mdw, and Round Mdw, with one very slightly curved side); Mere Croft, Mere Fd, Big ~ ~ (by Crosemere Mere); Mere Lsw, Little ~ ~ (on S. boundary of township, *v*. **(ge)mǣre**); Milestone Croft (by Shrewsbury road); Moliner's Wd, Far, Near; Moor (~ Moor ns. on E. boundary include Butler's and Morris's ~, and Fluggy, Huggy, Rushy and Smithy ~: this area may be *The Moore* 1588 *SBL 3647*); Mountain Fd; Nash Croft; Near Fd; New Hay Ground; Next up to Faulks Wood Rough; Old Hill, ~ ~ Mdw; Old Mdw; Park Hill (near Kenwick's Park boundary); Patch Croft; Pit Fd; Porter Lsw; Primrose Mdw; Ragman's Fd; Ratcliffe; Reeke Pool; Rough Lsw; Sandhole Fd; Shagger Dobbin; Shed Fd; Shippa; Span, Big, Little (*v*. Frankton f.ns. *infra*); Stockett Croft, Fd, Lsw (on boundary with Stockett *infra*); Stony Croft; Thatch Croft (adjoins Patch ~); Three Cornered Fd; Townsend, Far, Near (at S. end of Cockshutt village); Waggon Shed Fd; The Walmsleys; Ware Mdw ('weir', by Crosemere Mere); Wet Mdw; Whattall Dale (on boundary with Whattall); Wilson's Fd; Wood, Big, Little (adjoining Kenwick's Wood); Woodcote Mdw; Wood's Yd; Yard, Big, Low, New, Dovehouse (by Cockshutt).

(b) *Cokshotegrene* 1496 *SBL 3644* ("Crollesmere et ~": one of the Green Fd ns. in (a) adjoins Crosemere settlement); *Kocschetemere* 1421 *SBL 3650* (perhaps an alternative n. for Crosemere Mere); *Le Monmedewe ib* ('common meadow', *v.* **(ge)mǣne**); *Wythimere* 1278–9 *RentSur* ('willow pool').

2. (ENGLISH) FRANKTON (SJ 453297)

The township-name, which means 'Franca's estate', is discussed in Part **1**. The relationship of this settlement to Welsh Frankton, 5 miles W.N.W., is also discussed there.

SPAN (SJ 446301). OS maps do not name this tiny settlement, but buildings by the road to Cockshutt are shown from 1833 to the 1999 Explorer, and Gazetteer lists Span Cottage. The *TAMap* for Frankton has fields called *Span* on either side of the road, and the Cockshutt and Crosemere *TAMap* has fields called *Big* and *Little Span* a short distance W. on the N. side of the road. An earlier reference is *Spon Croft* and *Meadow* 1713 *SBL 6254*.

OE **spann** 'hand's breadth' has been noted in a number of minor place-names, but its toponymical meaning has not been ascertained. Well-evidenced examples include Span Fm, near Wroxall Wt, which is *Spanne* c.1280, and Spon End in Coventry Wa, which is *Spanna* c.1144. The street leading to Spon End is *Spannestrete* 1332. EPN cites other examples under **spann**[1], noting that the element is commonest in the West Midlands. In the West Midlands [a] followed by a nasal consonant usually becomes [o], and in Spon End development to *Sponne* is recorded in 1250. West Midland simplex names recorded from the 13th century which have only *Sponne* forms can safely be attributed to **spann**[1]. PN Ch **5.1** 345 lists some examples, and there are several in St. The Sa name Spunhill or Spoonhill in Ellesmere, however, which Smith lists under **spann**[1] is more likely to contain **spōn** 'wood shaving', *v. infra*.

The place-name senses suggested in EPN for **spann**[1] are 'strip of land', 'foot-bridge' and 'strip of woodland', but no firm topographical evidence has been adduced for any of these. Dodgson, PN Ch **1** 200, notes that in several of the Ch instances the reference could be to a moorland tract separating areas of cultivated land. In the present instance the settlement and the field-names are shown by *TAMaps* to be on a narrow belt of ground separating two areas of drained marshland. The field which adjoins *Big* and *Little Span* is called *Haybridge*, but this may be a corruption of *-britch* from **bryce.**

CORK HALL, 1798 RTH, 1833 OS, 1839 *TA*.

DIPTHILL PLTN, *The Two Dipdales* 1713 *SBL 6254*, *Diptail* 1839 *TA*.

FRANKTON GRANGE, *Frankton Grove* 1839 *TA*.

GARDEN PLTN.

LUKE'S COTTAGE, *Luke's Place* 1839 *TA*.

QUAIKIN, ~ PLTN, *Quakin* 1833 OS, *The Quiykin* 1839 *TA*: 'mountain ash', ME **quiken**.

SLANGS PLTN, narrow strip.

WOOD FM. The building is shown but not named on *TAMap*, and there are fields called *The Wood*, *Big Wood* and *The Wood Meadow* to the W. of it. On 1833 OS *The Wood* is printed across this area.

Field-Names

Forms in (a) are 1839 *TA*. Earlier forms and those in (b) are 1713 *SBL 6254*.

(a) Aldery Mdw; Barn Yd (several); Big Fd (2); Big Lsw and Crabtree Croft; Big Mdw (smaller than nearby Little Mdw); Big Yd (large field on outskirts of Frankton); Black Mdw; Blacksmith's Mdw; Brickkiln Fd; Broad Lsw; Brook Croft; Broomy Lsw; Calves Croft; Clemly Park (a recurrent f.n. referring to poor soil, *v*. Prees f.ns. *infra*); Clerk's Lsw; Coalpit Fd (referring to charcoal burning); Colts Fd; Cordwood Lsw; Cork Mdw (a short distance from Cork Hall); Corner Croft, Three Cornered Croft (adjoining, in road junction angles); Cow Lsw; Crabtree Fd; Croft (very small fields by Brownheath are Corner, Footroad, Footway, Hollybush, Pit, Road and Sandhill Croft); Croft (small enclosures round Frankton include Back, Far, Jenks, Little, Long, Middle, Near, Potato and Small Croft); Croft (enclosures clustered by an unnamed building a short distance S. of Frankton are Croft, Far, Low, High and Blacksmith's Croft: a large field adjoining is Wheat Croft); Croft, High and Lower ~ (by Wood Fm); Croft on the Banks; Cross Pce and False Flg; The Cross Pce (by a road junction); Double Mdw; Drypit; Dunne Bridge (*Duna Britches*, *v*. **bryce**); Earth Fd; Far Ground, Near ~ ~ (on township boundary); Field, Little, Middle; Field before the House; First Fd (by Quaikin); The Five Lands (adjoins Big Fd on outskirts of Frankton); Flax Pit, ~ ~ Mdw (*Flax Pitt*); Footway Fd, ~ Lsw; The Four Acres; Frankton Fd (on S. boundary of township, this is the n. of two large fields separated by Farther and Near Fd); Frankton Mount, Higher, Lower; Gale Mdw (1713), The Gale (*gale* is bog myrtle); Garden Fd; Gillans Wall; Goosey Pce; Green Croft; Guiners Fd; Higher Lsw; Hill Fd; Horse Pasture; Horses' Fd; The Intack; Lawn (by Frankton Grange); Lawn Fd (adjoins Cork Hall); Leasow, Higher, Lower; Leg and Foot (a shape n.); Little Mdw (2); Long Fd; Marle Fd; Meadow (very small fields on the outskirts of Brownheath are Brown, Corner, First, Second, Heath, Little, Middle,

Moss and Wet Mdw); Middle Fd; Moor Flg; Moss Fd, Mdw (by Brownheath Moss in Loppington); Moss Pool, Lower, Upper, Mossy Pools (*Mossey Pool*); New Lsw (1713); Orchard Fd; Pea Bank; Pickering's Yd (in Frankton); Ploughing, North, South, West (very small fields on outskirts of Brownheath); Pools, Broad, Low, Near and Humphreys Pools (5 adjoining fields); Portsand Flg; Quigkin Mdw (2, *v.* Quaiken *supra*); Rough Fd, First, Second, Third; Rough Wd, East, West; Round Bank (small rectangular field by Brownheath); Rye Hill (1713); Shutt Corner (*Shut* ~ 1713, possibly short for Cockshutt ~); Slang (not near Slangs Pltn); Slang Mdw, Big (not near other Slang ns.); Smithy Wd; Spring Moor; Stack Yd (2, both in Frankton); Thatchers Croft; Three Butts (near Big Fd and The Five Lands: there may have been a very small open field E. of Frankton); Tinkers Patch; Tinsdale Lsw; Top Croft; Top Fd; Townsend (at S. end of hamlet); Ware Croft; Way Bridge, Lower, Upper (on the approach to a small stream); The Way Lsw, Lower ~ ~, Highway Lsw; Well Mdw (2); Whattall Croft, The Whattall Mdw, Lower Whattall (adjoining Whattall *infra*, cf. *Whettalls Crofte*).

(b) *Greenwood Croft* (possibly Green Croft in (a)); *Windmill Fd.*

3. KENWICK, STOCKETT AND WHATTALL

KENWICK (SJ 421304): *Kenewic* 1203–4 *Ass et freq* with variant spellings *-wike*, *-wiche*, *-wyk* to 1344 HAC, *Kenwike* 1339 HAC, *Kenwick* 1577 Saxton. 'Cēna's farm', *v.* **wīc**. *TAMap* shows Upper and Lower Kenwick.

STOCKETT (SJ 426307) (lost)

Stocgate 1186–94 HAC

Stokeita 1197–8 HAC, *Stockiet'* 1203–4 *Ass*, *Stokeieta* 1205–c.1210 HAC, *Stokeyete* 1253 HAC, *Stokeyate* 1326 HAC (p), 1539–40 *RentSur*

Stocheta 1235–c.1260 HAC, *Stokeyte* 1246–53 HAC, *Stockeyth* 1280 Strange, *Stokytt* 1516 (1773) *SBL 17285*, *Stockett* 1615 (copy) *SBL 15755*, 1672 HTR *et seq* to 1839 *TA*

Stockyate 1289 *SBL 5844* (p), *Stokyate* 1336 Pat, 1336, 7, 44 HAC, *Stokȝate* 1337 HAC

Probably 'tree-stump gate', *v.* **stocc**, **geat**, but **stoc** 'dependent farm' is a possible first element.

No buildings are shown here on the 1900 6" or on later OS maps, and Kelly's Directory for 1934 describes Stockett as "non-existent for many years". The 1833 1" map shows the name beside the Shrewsbury road, where *TAMap* has *Stockett Cottages*, and shows it again for a building to the east which *TAMap* calls *Mere House*. It seems clear that whatever existed by way of a settlement lay along the north edge of Crose Mere.

WHATTALL (SJ 438310), 1833 OS, 1839 *TA*: *Whetall* 1535 VE, *Whottall* 1655 SAS l/XVII, 1672 HTR, *Whettals Crofts* 1681 *SBL 6254*. The references are late, but this is probably 'wheat nook', *v.* **hwǣte, halh**, identical with Wheathall Part **2** 124. On the *TAMap* there are three fields called *Whattall Moss* and three called *Whattall* and *Big, Little Whattall* spread over the eastern projection of the township area, so **halh** may have its administrative sense.

GESENOK (lost): *Gesnok'* 1279–80 *RentSur* (p), *Gesenok, -oc* 1323 HAC (p), (fields of) *Gesenok* 1337 HAC, *Gesenok iuxta Ken(e)wike* 1339, 40 HAC. This is an unusual name. As regards the second element, the choice appears to lie between **āc** 'oak' and ME **nok** 'nook', which is sometimes used as a measure of land. If the name were a compound with **āc** the *-n-* would belong to the first element, and the problem would be that *Gesen-* seems to be inexplicable. ME **nok** seems a more hopeful candidate, especially as in HAC *noke* is regularly used for pieces of land granted to the abbey. Instances are listed in Dr Rees's index. *Ges(e)nok* could be a ME name meaning 'geese noke'.

There was a habitation here. HAC has charters by which Roger son of Thomas of Gesenok grants land here to Haughmond. One of these charters locates a "little meadow" as lying between an assart called *le Litulheybruch* and a "stadium" called *le Berewyn*. The "stadium" is probably a furlong, so it appears possible that *Gesenok* had a minute field system as well as a house where the de Gesenok family lived. Another charter locates an acre of meadow in the fields of *Gesenok* as lying between *le Heybruche* and *Smethemore*. Smithy Moor is shown on the *TAMap* as occupying most of the N.W. corner of the township, so *Gesenok* was probably N.W. of Kenwick. *Oldegosenoke* 1483–4 *SRO Bridgewater 212/box 72* may indicate that the settlement was then deserted.

SMITHY MOOR, 1839 *TA*, is *Smethemore* 1337 HAC. 'Smooth marsh', *v.* **smēðe, mōr**.

THE BIRCHES, *Birch Copy Moss* 1839 *TA*.

THE SPRINGS, SPRINGS BROOK. Two adjacent houses are *Springs* and *Lower Springs* 1839 *TA*. Perhaps *spring* in the sense 'plantation, coppice'.

SWEAT MERE, *Swetemore* 1483–4 *SRO Bridgewater 212/box 72*, *Swet Mere* 1839 *TA*: this may be *Swotlemere* 1309 Eyton, which follows Crosemere in a list of lakes. 'Sweet lake', *v.* **swēte**.

WHATTALL MOSS, 1839 *TA*.

Field-Names

Forms in (a) are 1839 *TA*. Those in (b) are all HAC. HAC has a charter of c.1344 (no. 659) which lists land in Kenwick lying in three fields called *Collefelde*, *Longeheystowesfeld* and *Winmullefeelde*. Within these there are furlongs, butts, headlands and pieces called *bruche*. One of the furlongs, with ten butts, is called *le Bruche*. Some butts are "in diversis locis" in the fields.

(a) Ashton Pltns; The Backside (by Upper Kenwick); Bank Pce; Bank, Lower, Higher; Barn Fd; Big Fd (several); Big Mdw (2); Big Wd; Bran Pce; Brock Hill; Calves Croft, Little ~ ~ (by Upper Kenwick); Calves Croft (by Springs); Carter's Mdw; Crabtree Fd, Lsw; Croft, Higher, Lower and Top ~ (by Stockett Cottages); The Croft (by Whattall); Foxgloves, ~ Corner; Foxhole, Big, Little ~ Mdw; Furlong Mdw (near the likely site of *Gesenok*, *v. supra*); Garden Croft, Fd (by Kenwick); Garden Fd (adjoins Whattall); Haystack Yd (in Lower Kenwick); Hollins, Big, Little (*v.* **holegn**); Holly Bank Croft, Moor, Moss; Hooton, Big, Little, ~ Mdw; Horse Moor (3); Hunts Bank; Lawn, Big, Little (3 large fields S.W. of Kenwick); Little Fd (adjoins Big Fd and is of comparable size); Long Mdw; Long Wd; Lower Fd; Malthouse (in Upper Kenwick); (The) Meadow (several); Meadow, Brook, Long, Middle; Mere Croft (by Crosemere Mere); Moss, ~ Mdw; Moss, Far, Higher, Middle; New Lsw, Big ~ ~; New Pce; Old Wd (the charter of c.1344, referred to *supra*, mentions "uno Grosebosci vocato Oldehille": Old Wd may be short for *Oldhill Wd); Oliver's Yd; Patch, Lower, Higher; Pinfold Fd; Plantation Mdw, Far ~ ~; Quab, Lower and Higher ~ (*v.* ***cwabbe**); Rabbit Banks; Ryegrass Fd; Springs Mdw (not adjacent to Springs); Stackyard Croft (by Springs); Stockett, ~ Bank (fields on W. side of Shrewsbury road); Stony Croft; Three Days' Math (i.e. mowing); Turfcote Lsw ('hut made of turf', PN Ch **5.1** 373 lists 5 instances); Wall Fd; War Bank; Well Fd; Well Mdw; Whattall Pit (small circular enclosure); Winnets Bank, Lsw; Wood Lsw.

(b) *Le Berewyn* 1339 (a "stadium", probably 'furlong', the n. is obscure); *Brokkelondes* c.1344; *Le Bruche* c.1344 (a furlong in *Collefelde*, *v.* **bryce**); *Bukbyesyorde* c.1344 (an "ortus", which perhaps has the sense 'yard' here); *Collefelde* c.1344 (a "campus", first el. uncertain); *Crofte unde reyordes* c.1344 (a furlong in *Collefelde*, perhaps 'croft under the yards': **croft** is an unusual term for a furlong); *Le Lytelheibruche*, *Muchilhebruche*, *Le Muchileibruche* 1335, *Le Heybruche* 1337, *Le Litulheybruche* 1339 (*v.* **hēg**, **bryce**, **mycel**, **litel**); *Le Heimore* 1335 (a meadow, *v.* **hēg**, **mōr**); *Longeheystowesfelde* c.1344 (a "campus": **hege-stōw** occurs in charter-bounds and field-names: Dodgson, PN Ch **5.1** 220, accepts Toller's translation 'place with a hedge', but there are other possible interpretations); *Oldehille* c.1344 (a wood by *Winmullefeelde*, 'old hill'); *Stevonsmedowe* c.1344 (in *Collefelde*); *Totewike* 1323, 33, *Oldetotewike*, *Le Newtotewike* 1335, *Oldetotewike*, *Le Newtotewike*, *Totewike*, *Totewikesmedowe* c.1344 (perhaps 'Tota's farm': the 1323 reference locates this land between the court of Roger Gesenoc and a dry marlpit: the contexts do not suggest that *Totewike* was an extant settlement in the 14th cent., but the element **wīc** probably indicates that there was a farm when the name arose: this small township appears to have contained a surprising number of discrete habitation sites); *Wallemedowe* c.1344 (by *Winmullefeelde*, 'spring meadow'); *Willebruche* c.1344 (a "bruche" in *Winmullefeelde*, 'Willa's broken-in land'); *Winmullefeelde* c.1344 (a "campus", 'windmill field').

4. KENWICK PARK (SJ 414297), 1833 OS, *Kenwyke Parke* 1585 *SBL 1571*, *Kenwicke* ~ 1634 PR(L) 20, *Kenwicks Parke* 1602 Peake, 1672 HTR, ~ *Park* 1686 PR(L) 7 *et freq* to 1839 *TA*.

KENWICK LO, LOWER HO and TOP HO are shown but not named on *TAMap*. TOP HO is called *Kenwick Park* on 1833 OS.

Field-Names

Forms in (a) are 1839 *TA*.

(a) Back House Croft (by Lower Ho); Backside (by a house); Bakehouse (by Lower Ho); Banky Fd; Barn Yd (several); Beats Lsw; Big Fd; Big Hill; Big Lsw (2); Big Mdw (several); Birches Lsw, Far ~ ~; Brickkiln Fd (not near Kiln Fd); Briery Croft (2); The Butts; Butches Bank; Calf Gate Lsw; Calves Croft (several, by houses); Care Makes, Low, High; Cattys Croft; Clover Fd; Coalpit Croft (probably referring to charcoal burning); Cockshutt Croft, Fd, Mdw (adjoining Cockshutt township); Copy Bank; Copy Banks, Flat, High, Little; Copy Fd, Big, Little; Cow Lsw; Cow Pasture, High, Low, Near; Cranks; Croft (several, small enclosures by buildings); The Dingle; Foxholes; Garden Fd; Giggle Fd (probably *gig-hole*, variant of *gig-pit*, FN 31, a hole in the ground where rotted flax was dried by fire); Glass Fd; Gorsy Fd (2); Gravel Hole Mdw; Green Fd (several); High Park Fd (not near Kenwick Park); The Hill (2); Hook up the Wood, Lower, Top; Hungry Croft; Kiln Fd (*TAMap* shows buildings by the road from Kenwick Park to Ellesmere, Explorer map has Brickhill Fm here); Ladies Pce, Big, Little; Lawns, Big, Little, First, Second (6 fields near E. boundary of township); Leasow, Cross, Far, Haycock, Middle (adjoining fields); Little Fd; Long Fd, Far, Near; Long Lsw (2); Lows Fd, Mdw; Marlpit Fd (several); The Meadow (several); Meadow, Big, Little; Middle Fd (several); Muck Fd; Nook Fd; Park Fd, Big, Little (adjoining Stanwardine Hall); Park Mdw (not near Kenwick Pk); Pickering's Fd, Low, Top; Pinfold, Higher, Lower; Pen Fd, Higher, Lower; Pit Mdw; Road Pce; Robert Lsw; Rough Fd, Mdw; Rough Mdw; Round Fd (one curved side); Rye Lsw, Big, Little; Sandy Hole, Big, Little; Sawpit Fd (2); Says Fd; Square Fd; Stack Yd (by Kenwick Lo); Stubble Fd; Thorny Bank; Three Cornered Pce; Top Fd; Top Marl Pit; Traps Pce; Tudor's Lsw; Way Lsw; Well Mdw (several, some with Well Croft or Fd adjoining).

5. KENWICK WOOD (SJ 415296), 1753 *SBL 1998*, *Kenewykeswode* 1309 Eyton, *Kynwyges Woode* 1369 *SBL 3599*, *Kenwicks Wood* 1557 SAS 4/X *et freq* to 1839 *TA*, *Kenwicks Wood als Under Kenwicks Wood* 1615 (copy) *SBL 15755*.

The *TA* for this township shows it as three distinct units. One of these consists of fields surrounding some buildings which, although not named on *TAMap* or on 1833 OS, may be the main habitation site for the township. The 1999 Explorer map marks Kenwick Park and Kenwick Wood as adjacent buildings; and Kenwick Wood, which is the eastern unit, roughly corresponds to the unnamed buildings on *TAMap*. The GR given above is for this. There is a strip of Cockshutt township between these buildings and another building with four fields. These two small areas are treated as (i) for the purpose of presenting field-names.

The small area treated as (ii) is about two miles S.E. of (i). It contains Lea Fm, GR 435274.

The largest portion of the township consists of a curving strip on the W. boundary of Cockshutt parish, bordering Hordley. This contains the settlements called Ferney Hough, Shade Oak, Lower Hordley and Outcast. Field-names in this strip are presented under (iii).

FERNEY HOUGH (SJ 417279), *Fernenhalgh*, *Vernihalh* 1279–80 *RentSur* (p), *Fernihaughe*, *Fearnyhaugh* 1607 Peake, 'ferny hollow', *v.* **fearnig, halh**, the earliest forms show alternation with ***fearnen** 'growing with ferns'.

LEA FM (SJ 437273), *The Lea* 1637 *SBL 6434*, 1833 OS, 1839 *TA*, *v.* **lēah.** This is a detached portion of Kenwick Wood township.

OUTCAST (SJ 403315). This building is *Oldcast* on 1833 OS, but this must be erroneous. Ground called *The Outcaste* is mentioned 1602 Peake and *TAMap* shows fields called *Outcast*, *Big* and *Little Outcast*, *Outcast Meadow* south of the building. EDD gives the meaning 'a quarrel, contention, disagreement' for *outcast*, noting that this is recorded in Scotland, Yorkshire, Lincolnshire and Shropshire, and this seems appropriate for land in the boundary strip which contains the largest part of this scattered township. The name can be classed with those from **calenge** and **þrēap**, which refer to disputed ownership. A single instance in Cheshire, *Outcast Moss* in the *TA* for Haslington, was ascribed by Dodgson, PN Ch **5.1** 297, to the standard sense 'rejected', and considered to refer to worthless land, but the dialect sense noted in EDD seems more satisfactory.

SHADE OAK (SJ 411276), 1747 *SBL 1862*, 1833 OS, *Schurdook* 1369 *SBL 3599*, *Shade Oake* 1706 PR(StA) 5, *Shad Oak* 1737 *SBL 1861*: *v.* **āc**, first element possibly **sceard** adj. 'notched, mutilated'.

HAYCOCK (lost?). This farm is not named on later OS maps but it is *Haycock* on 1833 OS, and a field called *The Haycocks* adjoins it on *TAMap*. Kelly's Directory for 1934 lists Haycock as a residence in Kenwick Wood. It is one of the group of buildings noted *supra* in the (i) section of the township.

LOWER HORDLEY, 1833 OS, is on the boundary with Hordley *infra*.

PARK HO is shown but not named on *TAMap*. Nearby fields are *Park Field* and *Big*, *Little*, *Near Park Field*.

SHADE OAK COPPICE.

WHINNETT HILL: the area *is Kenwick Wood Field* 1839 *TA*.

Field-Names

Forms in all three sections are 1839 *TA*.

(i) Back House Lsw; Back of the Yard; Barn Fd; Big Mdw; Black Pits; Croft; Garden Fd; Gate Lsw; Gorsy Lsw; Hacksey; Heasel Husk, Little ~ ~; (The) Meadow (3); Thistly Fd; Well Fd; Wood Fd; Wood, Far, Nearest.

(ii) Banky Fd; Barn Yd; Birchers Croft; Brickkiln; Croft; Drain Fd; Iron Gate Fd; Lloyd's Lsw; Rookery Fd; Savage's Mdw; Stockyard; Well Mdw, Near ~ ~.

(iii) The Acre; Backside (by Outcast); Bagley Mdw (adjoins Bagley in Hordley); Big Fd (several); Big Mdw (2); Blackhurst, Big, Little; Brickiln Fd; Briery Croft; Burroughs Stubble; Cabbage Croft; Canal Croft; Carthouse Fd (by Park Ho); Copy Fd (Wood, Wood Mdw and Leasow adjoin and trees are shown on map); Copy Fd (2, not near preceding); Corner Croft (large field); Croft, Middle, Top (fairly big fields); Croft, Big, Little (in Lower Hordley); Croft, Barn, Bellis, Cockshutt, Milk (by Ferney Hough); Crow Rook; Cut Fd (by Ellesmere and Chester canal); Desorts; Foxholes; Gorsy Fd (2); Green Yd; Ground Fd, Low, Near; Hall Mdw; Hare Pit; Home Bridge; Horse Pasture; Hungust; Lesters Ground Far, Near; Limekiln Fd (Limekiln and Wharf shown in corner); Little Mdw; Long Croft (2); Long Mdw; Lord's Mdw; Marlepit, Lower; Marlepit Fd (not near preceding); The Meadow; Morris Ground; Plain Lsw; Shop Fd, Lower, Top (by Lower Hordley); Stackyard Fd (by Park Ho); Stockings, Far, Near (*v.* ***stoccing**); Three Cornered Pce; Wakeley, Far, Near (some distance from Wackley in Petton); Wheat Bridge (by canal); Wilkets Stockett (*v.* ***stoccet**, synonymous with ***stoccing**: these names may indicate the clearing of the wood which gave name to the township); Windmill Fd; Wood Fd; Wood Mdw; Wycherley Fd (adjoins Wycherley *supra*).

(b) *Brodepull'*, *Le Brodepol* 1392–3 *SRO Bridgewater 212/box 72* ('broad pool'); *Risebrugge ib* (**hrisbrycg* 'brushwood causeway', a widespread minor p.n.).

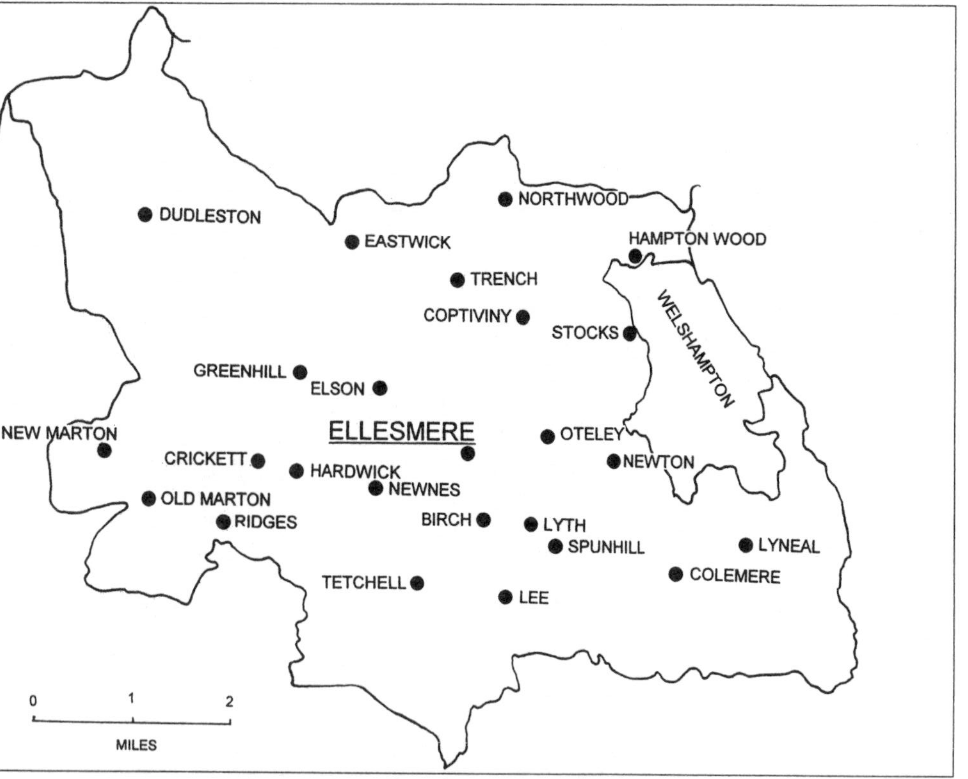

Map 4: Townships in the parish of Ellesmere.

Ellesmere

The parish-name, which means 'Elli's lake', is discussed in Part **1**. The same personal name occurs in the township-name Elson.

The *TA* for Ellesmere recognises 19 townships: Birch and Lyth; Colemere; Crickett; Dudleston; Eastwick; Ellesmere; Elson and Greenhill; Hampton Wood; Hardwick; Lee; Lyneal; New Marton; Newnes; Northwood; Oteley, Newton and Spunhill; Ridges, Stocks and Coptiviney; Tetchill; Trench. Old Marton, though here included with New Marton, was a township of the neighbouring parish of Whittington for the purposes of the Tithe Survey.

These townships vary greatly in size. The largest, Dudleston, is as big as many parishes, but at the other extreme Crickett, Eastwick, Newnes, and Stocks and Coptiviney are tiny. The varying sizes are reflected in the length of the field-name lists.

There were three DB manors in the area: Colemere, Ellesmere and Broom in Tetchill; and Lee is recorded c.1090. Some of the later-recorded settlements may be of similar antiquity, but the large number of township centres first noted in records of the 12th–14th centuries may indicate an expansion of settlement in the post-Conquest period.

1. BIRCH AND LYTH

BIRCH HALL (SJ 403336), 1839 *TA*: *Berch'* (p), *Byrch'* 1255–6 *Ass*, *Birche* 1280 Strange, *Berche* 1309 Eyton, 1403 *SBL 15668*, *Byrch* 1549 Pat. 'Birch tree', *v.* **birce**, probably used collectively. 1833 OS shows *Birch* for Birch Hall, and a few houses called *The Birch* further north on the boundary with Ellesmere township. *TAMaps* for both townships have *Birch* ~ f.ns. at this last site.

THE LYTH (SJ 411336), 1839 *TA*: *Lithe*, *Lythe* 1279–80 *RentSur* (p), *Lythe* 1309 Eyton, *La Lithe* 1335 HAC (p), *Lithe* 1403 *SBL 15668* (p), *Lith* 1655 SAS 1/XLVII, *Lyth* 1672 HTR, *Lyth Hall* 1833 OS, *v.* **hlið**.

In the southern half of Shropshire and in north Herefordshire **hlið** is consistently used for a hill with a hollow in the side, *v.* the discussions of Pontesford Hill (earlier *Ponteslithe*) in Part **1** 51, and Ragleth, Part **2**

226. In northern England, however, the ON equivalent **hlíð** is used in the naming of settlements at the foot of a long slope, and it is possible that the OE word has this sense in the northern part of Shropshire and in its occasional occurrences in Cheshire.

The topography at Lyth near Ellesmere is indeterminate as between the two senses. There is a long slope on the east side of the A45 in which there are some slight hollows.

SPY BANK (?lost, Gazetteer gives the n. as extant), 1833 OS, 1839 *TA*, across the road from Birch Hall. There was another Spy Bank in Castle Pulverbatch (Part **2** 171), and Gazetteer notes a third instance in Worfield. In Part **2** the Pulverbatch name was tentatively ascribed to ***spǣg** 'brushwood', but it now seems more likely that the source is the word *spy*, either referring to a look-out place or perhaps in the obsolete sense (NED 3) 'ambush'. The word has been noted occasionally in other counties. PN Ch **3** 215 notes Spy Hill, and another occurrence is indexed in PN WRY **8**, but with an incorrect page reference. Spying How, PN We **2** 227, may be compared. The only instance noted with early references is Spye Park PN W 252, for which *Spyestret* 1409, *Le Spye* 1426, *Spyegate* 1430 are given. As noted in PN W this place has a commanding situation, so perhaps the 'viewpoint' interpretation is the correct one.

STAPELEY WD, *Stapeley* 1392–3 *SRO Bridgewater 212/box 72*. 'Post wood', *v.* **stapol, lēah**. This is a recurrent p.n. compound. *TAMap* shows a field called *Stapeley* with another called *Wood and Plantation* adjoining, and the latter corresponds to Stapeley Wd on 6".

BEECH HO: *TAMap* shows *Canal Office*, *Workshops and Wharf* here.

FOSTER'S HAYS: 1833 OS marks *Birch Lythe* here, *TAMap* shows a house.

ST OSWALD'S COLLEGE: Kelly's Directory for 1934 says the school was opened in 1884.

Field-Names

Forms in (a) are 1839 *TA*.

(a) Adwick; Bank Mdw; Banky Mdw; Big Fd; Bill's Mdw; Birch Fd, Far and Near ~ ~, Birch Croft, Far, Near, Long and Square ~ ~ (a group of small fields a short distance N.W. of Birch Hall); Birch Fd (2 fields a short distance S.W. of Birch Hall); The Bottom; Brickkiln Fd, Upper ~ ~, ~ Croft; Brickkiln Fd (not near preceding); Briery Yd; Butchers Fd; Canal Mdw; Croft (an average-sized field), Meadow near

Croft; Cross Fds (between a road and the canal); Cut Fd, Little ~ ~ (adjoining the canal); Garatree Fd (possibly a corruption of *Gallitree* 'gallows'); Garden Fd (by The Lyth, adjoining small fields are Barn, Far, Near and Middle Field and another Garden Fd); Gravel Hole Fd; Green Fd, Big; Hall Fd, Far, Near, Side (a short distance W. of Birch Hall); Hall Mdw (by Birch Hall); Hazle hill; Home Heath; Horse Pasture; Hown Heath (adjoins Home Heath); Lawn(s), North, South (on either side of The Lyth); Marlpit Fd; The Meadow, Big and Little ~, Chidley's, Grindleys and Langfords ~ (a group of fields on N.W. boundary); Mere Fd (by White Mere); Moss Fd; Mystical Bank, Far ~ ~; New Mdw; Nursery Mdw; Park Fd, Far, Near (by The Lyth); Peartree Fd; Pedlar's Mdw; Plantation and Fishing Cottage (by White Mere); Pleasure Ground (by The Lyth); Rough Mdw; Salisbury, Big, Little (adjoining Mystical Bank, both ns. are of obscure significance); Sandy Hole; Stanks, Big, Little, Canal, Far and Lane ~, Stanks Fd, Near and Little ~~, Stanks Mdw (the fields are on either side of the canal, covering a wide area: NED *stank*[2] 'a dam to hold back water, a weir or floodgate' may be more relevant than the commoner sense 'pond'); Tetchill Fd, Big, Little (a short distance from the boundary with Tetchill); Well Mdw; Whelps Croft (*v*. Ellesmere f.ns., this field is on the boundary); Windmill Fd; Yewtree Mdw.

(b) *Wollonheth et Stapeley* 1392–3 *SRO Bridgewater 212/box 72* (*Stapeley* is Stapeley Wd *supra*).

2. COLEMERE (SJ 433327)

The township-name, which means 'Cūla's lake', is discussed in Part **1**.

WHITE MERE, 1833 OS, 1839 *TA*, *Witemere* 1205–c.1210 HAC, *Le Witemere* 1326 ib, *Whitemere* 1344 ib, *v*. **hwīt**, **mere**. The early references do not indicate that there was a settlement. The lake was granted to Haughmond as an appendage to an estate at Newton.

BAYSIL WD, 1833 OS, *Basehill* 1839 *TA*.

COLEMERE BOATHOUSE WD.

COLEMERE WOODS, ~ *Wood* 1833 OS; the house is shown but not named on *TAMap*.

LITTLE MILL, 1833 OS.

PIKESEND FM and MOSS, *Pikes End* 1799 *PR(Cockshutt)*, *Pikes-end* 1833 OS, *Pikesend Moss* 1839 *TA*. The S.E. projection of the township may have been considered a 'point', *v*. **pīc**.

POLE WD: *Pole Field*, 1839 *TA*, is a small field with a Plantation adjoining at this point on the S. edge of White Mere.

WOOD LANE, 1833 OS.

YARNEST WD, *Heron Nest*, ~ ~ *Pltn* 1839 *TA*, a short distance from White Mere.

Field-Names

All forms are 1839 *TA*.

(a) Bankers Hill (*sic*, probably for Bunkers Hill: J. Field, A *History of English Field-Names* p. 158, notes that Bunkers Hill, "a Pyrrhic victory during the War of American Independence appears to have made an indelible impression on English minds, and occurs so frequently among minor names and field-names . . . as to seem like a remedial incantation"); Ben's Mdw; Big Fd; Birchy Lsw, ~ Ross; Bran Tree; Brickkiln Fd; Broom Fd, Little ~ ~; Broomy Corner; Calves Pce; Chumley Park Mdw (probably a corruption of Clemley Park, *v.* Clem Guts in Northwood township *infra*); Clayhead Lands (adjoins Brickkiln Fd); Copy Shutt (not near Shutt Croft or Pole Shutt); Corner Fd (in road-fork); Corner Pit (also in road fork); Cow Lsw, Little ~ ~, Uncle's Big and Little ~ ~, Stokes ~ ~, William Wenlock's ~ ~, Our Own ~ ~; Croft (*freq*, clustered round Colemere village); Cross Bank, ~ Hill; Dale Fd; Dark Lane Fd; Dovey Pool; Drumble Pits (variant of *dumble* 'hollow', *v.* Dumble Hole in Lyneal *infra*); Ellesmere Croft (3 average-sized fields); Elley Pit; Far Moor; Fords Bank, Mdw (Ford's Coppice in Lyneal adjoins); Garden Fd; Godfrey; Gorse Bank; Grass Hill; Gravel Hill Fd; Green (3 fields, in Colemere village); Hawk Moss, Big ~ ~; Hays, Big and Little ~, Gravel Pit ~, Hays Mdw, Hay Pit (a group of fields by Wood Lane: Hay probably derives from a conflation of OE (**ge**)**hæg** 'enclosure' and Norman French *haia* 'part of a forest fenced off for hunting'); Heath Moss; Hell Hole (not L-shaped, so probably derogatory); Hill(s) (Far Hill, ~ ~ Mdw, Middle Hills, Nearest Hill adjoin); Hill Mdw (Mill Hurst and Big Rill adjoin, so the correct form is uncertain); Hill Top, Big, Little, Rough and Young's ~ ~; Horse Moor; Hungry Bank; Hursty Canel; Kebley (5 fields on S.E. boundary); Lady Oak (other instances occur in Minsterley and Cressage, Part **2** 27, 140); Lee Fd, ~ Mdw (on boundary with Lee township); The Leg and Foot (a shape name); Ley Fd; Light Wd, Lightwood Fd; Limekiln Lsw; Lineal Hatch, Mdw (on boundary with Lyneal township); Little Fd; Little Wood Fd; Long Croft; Longum Lannet (a narrow, curved field); Marl Croft; Meadow (several); Mere Fd, ~ Mdw (by Cole Mere); Mere Fd, Near, Middle, Mereside Croft (by White Mere); Milking Bank (by the house called Colemere Woods on 6"); Moss, Far, Near; Mill Hurst (adjoins Hill Mdw, possibly M- for H-); Moorside, Big, Little, ~ Mdw; Nantigodale; Ox Close, Big, Little and Far ~ ~; Pinfold Croft; Pole Shutt (a short distance from Shutt Croft); Richmond Hill (probably a transference of the London n.); Rough Lsw; Rough Mdw(s) (several); Rough Mossill; Sand Hill, Big and Little ~ ~; Sandy Bank; Sayers Ditch; Shutt Croft (the meaning of Shutt in Sa f.ns. is uncertain, *v.* the discussion in Part **4** 113); Smithfield, ~ Mdw; Snoggs (3 small fields by Colemere crossroads, FN 11 observes that Snog(g)s is mainly confined to Ellesmere, Ruyton-XI-Towns and West Felton, though *The Seven Snogges* is recorded in Berrington, S. of Shrewsbury, in 1593: the Berrington n. was discussed in Part **2** 100 with the tentative suggestion that it might be a corruption of *nokes*, *noke* being a measure of land: this is doubtful, but established NED and EDD senses of *snog* are not likely to be relevant to the f.n. term); Stock Pce; Ten Shilling Croft (perhaps the purchase price, it is an average-sized field); Thistly; Thorns; Tinkers Path, Low ~ ~ (tiny enclosures by Pikesend); Titch Croft (very small); Turner's Wd; Turnpike Fd (by the Ellesmere road); Weigh Bridge (by Pikesend, the road from Loppington crosses a small stream); White Moss

(White Fd adjoins); Whitlands Croft; Woodgate Fd (by the turnpike road); Woodwell Lsw; Yard, Back, Barn, Far, Higher, Stock (in Colemere village).

3. CRICKETT (SJ 364346)

Crickcote 1194–7 HAC, *Criccote* 1197–1203 ib, *Crikott* 1309 Eyton, *Krikot* 1638–41 Morgan

Crycatt 1332 Morgan, *Crickett* 1672 HTR, *Cricket* 1695 Morden

Krikod 1645–1728 Morgan

Probably 'cottage by an abrupt hill', with **cot** added to the hill-term, PrW **crūg**, which was taken into the OE place-name-forming vocabulary in the forms **crūc**, **crȳc**. In Crickett we may have the Welsh word, anglicised to *cric*.

Modern maps show Crickett and New Crickett. These tiny settlements are *Old* and *New Crickett* 1837 OS, 1839 *TA*.

BRICK KILN WD. The *TAMap* shows a few trees here.

Field-Names

All forms are 1839 *TA*.

(a) Backhouse Mdw (by Old Crickett); Barn Fd; Boosey Pasture (pasture used by an outgoing tenant, *v*. FN 34); Bryn Gyb(s) (W **bryn**, 'hill', probably with a pers.n.); Copley Mdw; Croft(s) (small enclosures round Perthy Fd); Foxglove Fd, ~ ~ Moss; Gapleys; Heath Mdw, ~ ~ Bank; Higher Gwernn (Welsh *gwern* 'alder swamp'); Maes Issa (Welsh, 'lower field'); Meadow, Rough Mdw, Mdw Bank; New Fd; Ox Pasture, Big, Little; Payns Mdw; Pontellin, Big, Little (Welsh *pont* 'bridge', probably with a pers.n., the road to Ellesmere crosses a stream here); Perthy Fd (on the boundary with Perthy *infra*); Pool Mdw; Windmill Fd; Wood, Big, Far, Little, Wood Pond.

4. DUDLESTON (SJ 346385)

Dodeleston(e) 1267, 72 Ipm, 1271–2 *Ass*, 1330 Ch

Dudleston' 1272 Cl, *-ton* 1598–9 PR(StA) 4 *et seq*, *Duddleston* 1745 PR(L) 7

Dodleston 1330 Ch, 1609 PR(StA) 4

Dudeleston 1427, 37 *SBL 4028*, *3600*

Duddiston 1535 VE

Dudlyston 1549 Pat, *Dudliston* 1669 *SBL 4153*, 1672 HTR, 1736 PR(L) 7

Dydleston 1577 Saxton, 1593 PR(StA) 4, 1600 Slack, *Didleston* 1607 Slack

Didelston 1602 Slack
Dydliston 1612–13 PR(StA) 4
Dydlaston 1716 PR(StA) 2
Deedliston 1804 PR(StA) 2

'Dudel's estate', *v.* **tūn**. Later forms may show some indication of a pronunciation with Welsh stress on the middle syllable. Welsh forms of the name are discussed in Morgan, p. 26. One of these Welsh forms, *Didlystun*, from a poem, *Gwaith Cynddelw Brydydd Mawr*, dates to the second half of the 12th century, so is the earliest evidence.

Dodleston Ch, PN Ch **4** 156–7, has a predominant *-o-* in ME spellings, so is more likely to contain a pers.n. **Dod*(*d*)*el* than to be a doublet of the Sa name.

BALCARRES HO, shown but not named on *TAMap*.

BARTIE, *The Barkty* 1716 *SBL 4129*, *The Bartie* 1839 *TA*: possibly 'bark house' Welsh *tŷ* and *barc* (a loan-word from English). This may be the equivalent of Tanhouse.

BLACK WD.

BRYN DANIEL, 1839 *TA*, BRYNDANIEL BROOK, *Bryn Danyell* 1583 *NLWCat*.

BRYN-GOLEU, 1837 OS, *Bryn Golly* 1839 *TA*, perhaps 'fair hillside', with Welsh *golau*.

BRYNORE, 1705 *NLWCat*, 1837 OS, BRYNORE HALL, *Brynoer* 1837 OS, Welsh 'cold hillside'.

BRYN-Y-COCHIN. A cluster of houses and crofts is shown, but not named on *TAMap*.

CAIA FM (1961 1"), CAE-HIR (1899 6"), *Caeau* 1837 OS, *The Kyah* 1839 *TA*. Welsh *caeau*, pl. of *cae* 'field'. Cae-Hir on the 6" map shows interpretation as 'long field'.

THE CASTLE, 1738 *NLWCat*, 1837 OS, 1839 *TA*, CASTLE DINGLE.

CHAPEL HO is *Chapel Farm* 1839 *TA*.

CRIFTINS, *y Kryfftons* 1509 *NLWCat*, *Maes y Crifton* 1530 *ib*, *Cryftin* 1837 OS, *High* and *Low Criftons* 1839 *TA*, *v.* ***cryfting**. This rather rare field and minor name term is formally a diminutive of **croft**, but modern fields so called are not always small, and its use as a farm-name implies a holding of some size.

THE CRIMPS. *TAMap* shows *Pentrecoed Cottage* here. Cf. Crimps Fm *infra*.

CROSS LANES, 1837 OS, 1839 *TA*, LITTLE CROSSLANES, CROSSLANE FM. The house on 19th-cent. maps corresponds to Little Crosslanes on the 1899 6" map. The house called Cross Lanes on 6" is a short distance S., by the T-junction which is the 'cross'.

DEEFIELDS, *Dee Fields* 1839 *TA*: the R. Dee is 3 miles away. 1837 OS has *Tan House* here.

DEE SIDE, 1839 *TA*, adjoining R. Dee.

DUDLESTON GROVE, ~ *Groves* 1839 *TA*.

DUDLESTON HALL, 1837 OS, 1839 *TA*.

DUDLESTON HEATH, 1837 OS, *Didleston Heath*, *Ros Didleston* 1602 Slack. The large, scattered settlement here is shown on *TAMap*. Peake 1897 quotes a rhyme

Dilluston yeth
Wher the devil ketched is djeth

Peake also says that a hostelry called *The Pigeons* once stood there: this is *Pigeons Inn* 1839 *TA*.

DUDLESTON PARK.

ERWAY, 1839 *TA*, Welsh *erwau*, pl. of *erw* 'acre, field'.

THE FIRS.

FLANNOG, 1837 OS, *The Flaneg* 1602 Slack, *The Flannag* 1839 *TA*.

FLANNOG DINGLE, 1837 OS, ~ WD.

GADLAS, 1837 OS, *Gadlass* 1839 *TA*, GADLAS FM and HALL, Welsh *cadlas* 'enclosure, yard'.

GRAVEL HOLE, 1339 *TA*.

GREENHILL BANK, *v*. Greenhill *infra*.

GREYHOUND P.H.

GRIFFIN FM.

THE HOLLIES.

KILHENDRE FM, HALL, *Kelhendre* 1580 *NLWCat*, *Kylhendre* 1600 *ib*, *Keelhendrey* 1664 *ib*, *Cilhendre*, *Little* ~ 1837 OS, *Kilhendre* 1839 *TA*. Welsh *hendref* with *cil* 'nook'. One of the meanings of *hendref* is 'old or ancestral home'. Kelly's Directory for 1934 says that the house incorporates a small portion which dates from the reign of Henry III.

LONG WD.

LOWER WD.

NEW HALL, 1839 *TA*, *Place Eignyon Vaughan alias Newe Hall* 1586 *NLWCat*.

THE PANT, 1839 *TA*, *Pant Mill* 1738 *NLWCat*, 1837 OS, Welsh *pant* 'hollow'.

PENTRE-COED, *Pentre Koed* 1454 *NLWCat*, *Pentre'r Coed* 1536 *ib*, *Pentrecoyd* 1549 Pat, *Pentrecoed* 1839 *TA*. *TAMap* shows *Pentrecoed Pottery*. 'Farm by a wood', Welsh *pentref* and *coed*. In this area *pentre(f)* has lost its earlier, more dignified, sense of 'chief settlement' and appears to mean 'large farm'.

PENTREHEYLIN, *Pentre Haylin* 1839 *TA*; PENTRE MADOC, 1837 OS, 1839 *TA*, *Pentremaddock* 1680 *SBL 5727*; PENTRE MORGAN, 1837 OS, 1839 *TA*, *Pentremorgan* 1656–7 PR(StA) 4. The affixes to these three names are Welsh personal names.

PEN-Y-BRYN, Welsh 'end of the hill'.

PLAS IOLYN (*sic*, on 1899 6", YOLYN on later maps), *Plasiolyn* 1745 *NLWCat*, *Plas Iolyn* 1837 OS, 1899 6", *Plas Yollen* 1839 *TA*; PLAS THOMAS; PLAS WARREN, 1839 *TA*. Welsh *plas* 'residence' with owners' names.

PLAS-YN-COED 1839 *TA*, *Plas yn coed* 1837 OS, 'house in the wood'.

ROCK, 1839 *TA*, ROCK DINGLE.

ROUND WD.

SHELL BROOK, SHELLBROOK HILL, *Schalbrok* 1454 *NLWCat*, *Shellbrook Hill* 1837 OS, *Shelbrook* 1839 *TA*. 'Shallow brook', *v.* **sceald**.

SODYLT BANK, *The Bank* 1837 OS, FORD, HALL, LO. *TAMap* shows two houses, *Sodylt* and *Sodylt Hall*, and another two called *Higher Sodylt* and *The Bank*. The n. is *Sodill* 1562 *NLWCat*, *Sodhill* 1584 *ib*, *Sodylth* 1672 *ib*. Morgan p. 50 suggests that *Sothull* in the designation of Johannes de Pryers *de Sothull*, a juror in Bradford Hundred in 1346 FA, may be this place. If this identification be correct, the name is identical with Soothill PN WRY **2** 193, 'soot hill'. Sodylt Ford is *Smith Ford* 1837 OS.

STREET DINAS, *Street y Dynas* 1664 *NLWCat*, *Street-y-dinas* 1837 OS, *The Lane*, 1839 *TA*. This is a scatter of houses by the road from Oswestry. The *dinas* could perhaps be Old Oswestry hill-fort: *dinas* is sometimes used in Wales for hill-forts.

VRON, *The Fron* 1839 *TA*, Welsh *bron* 'breast (of a hill)'.

YEWTREE HO.

Field-Names

Dudleston, although administratively a chapelry of Ellesmere, is the size of a parish, and the Tithe Award lists 1585 fields. The (a) list presented here is not a complete tally of the names of these fields. Categories omitted are: Welsh names in which Cae is qualified by personal names or surnames (e.g. Cae Davee, ~ Beddow, ~ Dicken); English names in which Field is similarly qualified (e.g. Harpers ~, Parry's ~); and names like Field below Barlows, ~ by Jenny Jones, ~ facing the Tailor's.

Richard Morgan has supplied the *NLWCat* forms and has given much-needed help with Welsh names in this township. He points out that a number of 'English' terms, such as *cockshut*, *coppy*, *slough*, were borrowed into Welsh from English and occur elsewhere in Wales without the anglicised restorations found in Dudleston field-names.

All forms in (a) are 1839 *TA*. Earlier forms dated 1602 are Slack, those dated 1597, 1669, 1702, 16, 17 are *SBL 3601*, *4153*, *5367*, *4129*, *6194*.

(a) The Acre; Alder Croft; Anagram (unexplained, the field is small and diamond-shaped); Aved; The Bank; Banky Fd (several); Banky Mdw; Barn Fd (*freq*); Bartre Fd (near The Bartie); Big Fd (*freq*); Big Gate Fd (by a road junction); Big Mdw (several); Bin Fd; Black Acre; Blackwood Fd; Blind Woman's Mdw, Far, Near; Bottom Fd; Boundry Pce (*sic*, on S.W. boundary); Bowling Fd, ~ Green (among the cluster of buildings by St Mary's Church); Bready Croft; Brickkiln Fd (several, one with Brick Yd adjoining); Bridge Fd; Briery Banks; Broad Fd (several); Brook Fd (several); Broomy Fd; Bryn Tangles (possibly Welsh *tanglai* 'fire clay'); Bryn y backers (perhaps 'slope with a bakehouse'); Brynn yn Dollas (possibly *Bryn y Ddol Las ('slope of the verdant meadow'); Bryn y Fires (perhaps Welsh/English 'slope with fir trees'); Bryn y Slough Mdw; Burnt Fd; Bushy Mdw; Cae Cannal ('middle field'), Cae cle Mandee ('dovecot field', Welsh *colomendy*, by Gadlas); Cae Coppice; Cae Gwin ('white field'); Cae Ket, Caeket Croft (*Kae Keede* 1600 *NLWCat*); Cae Mach, High, Low; Cae Marle ('marl field'); Cae Mawr (2, 'big field'); Cae Rhos ('heath field'); Cae Withings (perhaps Welsh/English 'willows field'); Calves Croft; Carthouse Fd (several); Chapel Fd (near St Mary's church); Chapel Fd (by a chapel at Gravel Hole in Dudleston Heath); Chapel Mdw (not near a church or chapel, but near Plas Yolyn, where *NLWCat* has *The Chaple Ffyld* 1600: cf. *Capella ste Elene vocata Le Bettus* 1437 *SBL 3600*, *v.* **bettws**); Cherrytree Fd (2); Claypit Fd; Clover Fd (several); Coalpit Fd (by The Flannog); Coed Bowkir (probably 'Bowker's wood'); Colley Benyon, Big, Little ('Benyon's hazels', Welsh **cyllau* from *coil*, *v.* PN EF 237–8); Corner Fd; Corner Pce (triangular); Cote Fd (no building); Cottage Fd (several); Cowhouse Fd; Cow Pasture (several); Crabmill Mdw; Crashen (probably Welsh *crachen* 'poor piece of land'); Crickel Gammon (possibly Welsh *crigyll* 'hillocky place': the field is very irregularly shaped); Crimpy Fd (not near The Crimps but probably containing a related term, *v.* Crimps Fm *infra*); Croft(s) (*freq* near settlements, the Dudleston Heath settlement consists mainly of Crofts); Crooked Fd (2, irregularly shaped); Cuckoo Fd (2); Dale Fd; Double Styles; Dove House Fd; Eakes Mdw; Esquire's Mdw (2); Far Fd (several); Far Mdw; Fenn y Turner; The Fig Mdw (by Plas Yollen); Fingerpost Fd; Five Oaks; Five Pits Fd; Footroad Fd (4: PN Ch **5.1** lists 2 instances and says it is modern dialect for *footway*); Foxhole Fd; Garden Fd; Gighole, Big ~, ~ Fd (by Pentrecoed); Gighole Fd (by The Kyah) (pit in which a fire was lit for drying flax, noted in PN Ch **5.1** 193, but more frequent in Sa); Gorsy Bank; Gorsy Fd (several); The Grass Fd; Grassy Bank; Gravel Hole Fd (not near Gravel Hole *supra*); Green Fd; Grogriery; Grosvener; Gutter Fd (3); Hale Fd (in a road curve, possibly ME reflex of **halh** 'nook'); Hay Mdw; Head Girn (the field has two points, Girn from Welsh *cyrn* 'horns'); Hell Fd (L-shaped); Higgins Barn, Mdw, Lane; High Fd (2); Hill Fd; Hopyard (Fd) (several); Horse Fd; Horse Pasture (several); Horse Pit; House Fd; House Mdw (by Plas-yn-coed); Hurders (*Heeredir* 1622 *NLWCat*, Welsh *hirdir* 'long land'); The Kellin (Welsh *celyn* 'holly'); Kenric, Little; Kilkings, Kilking Mdw; Kiln Fd, Copy, Croft; Kiln Mdw (2); Lane Fd; Leekes Fd (2); Link Fd; Little Fd (several); Long Fd (*freq*); Long Lane Fd; Long Mdw (several); Low Cae Dee, Far, Near (by R. Dee, so possibly using the English form of the r.n., but Welsh *du* 'black' is perhaps more likely); Low Fd; Lowermost Fd; Maes y Criftin (*v.* Criftins *supra*); Maes Hewen (possibly Welsh *ywen* 'yew'); Maes Y Glothia (possibly Welsh *cloddiau* 'ditches'); Maes y Rhos ('heath field'); Magpie Fd (adjoins Cuckoo Fd); Marlpit Fd; The Meadow (*freq*); The Meadow, Far, Near, Wood and Hopyard Mdw (a group of fields on N.E. boundary); Middle Field (*freq*); Milking Bank Fd (by The Kyah); Milking Bank (by Pentrecoed, *v.* FN 39); Moat Fd (W. of Plas Warren); Moat Mdw, Long ~ ~ (by The Pant); Moss (*freq* in Dudleston Heath); The Mount; Mowing Fd; Muck Fd; New Lsw; Old House Fd (2); The Old Mdw; Outlet (4, FN defines this as pasture adjoining winter cattle sheds); Owl's Nest; Ox Lsw; Paddock; Ox Pasture, High, Low; (The) Park (fields with these ns. are by Dee Side and Plas Yolyn, and there is a third which is not by a house); The Patch (average-sized); Peartree Croft; Peas Fd; Pigeon Fd (several); Pigeon House Fd; Pinfold Fd (*The Pinfould Close* 1672 *NLWCat*); Pit Fd (several); Plantation Fd; Pleasant Ma-celley; Pleasure Ground (by Plas Yolyn); The Plough Mdw; Pool Fd; Pottery Fd (2 mile from Pentrecoed Pottery); Present Bind Mdw; Quiners Mdw; Rabbit Banks; Ragman's Fd; Red Mdw; Road Fd (several); Rosy Mdw (adjoins Red Mdw); Round Fd (two curved sides, perhaps identical with *Kae Crwn* in (b)); Sandy Fd; Sandyhole/Sandhole Fd (*freq*); Sawpit Croft; Sawpit Fd (several); Scullery; Seeky Fd (land with drainage channels, ultimately from **sīc**); Seven Acres; Shanny Lease; Sheep Cote; Sheep Fd; Shivelee Fd; Shoulder of Mutton (2); Shutt Fd (5 examples and one Shutt Mdw: the meaning of *shut*(*t*) in Sa f.ns. is uncertain, *v.* the discussion in Part **4** 113); Slensh, Far, Middle, Near (probably a shape n., EDD *slench*[2], recorded from Sa, is 'a hind leg of beef from the first joint, including the upper round and part of the flank': the three fields together seem appropriate to this); Smith's Shop Fd; Smithy Fd; Sour Fd; Spanks, Far, Near (cf. *Kay yr Spanck* 1586 *NLWCat*); Square Fd (2); Stable Fd (2); Stackyard Fd (several); Stackyard Mdw; Stony Croft; Stony Fd; Summer House Fd; Sycamore Fd (2); Tan House Fd, Mdw (by Dee Fields, Tanner's Croft adjoins); Tathole; Thistly Fd (2); The Thole (*The Ddole* 1705 *NLWCat*, the shape resembles that of a rowing-boat thole: the field is not near a stream, so Welsh *dol* 'water-meadow' is unlikely); Three Cornered Croft (2); Three Cornered Fd; Top Fd (*freq*); Turnip Fd; Turnpike Fd (by Ellesmere road); Tyn y Cellyn (a large field by Plas Jolyn with no buildings, but apparently 'smallholding in the holly', with Welsh *tyn*, from *tyddyn*); Weaver's Mdw; Well Fd (*freq*); The Wet Mdw; Wheelwright's Fd; Wintley Fd; Wood Fd (*freq*); Wood(s) (*freq*, for fields and for strips of woodland); Yellow Fd; Yewtree Fd.

(b) With the possible exception of *Horsoll* the (b) ns. are Welsh, probably recorded at a time when the Welsh language was imperfectly understood. There are many Welsh field-names, not included here, in *NLWCat*.

Cae Ty Bithel Ucha 1716, *Cae Ty Bithel* 1717 ('field of Bithel's house'); *Ero Dyth Alt* 1602; *Erowe Goonynge* 1557 *NLWCat*, *Maes y Cynnyn* 1602 ('rabbit acre and field', Welsh *cwning*); *Erw Gwnog* 1702, *Erw Gownog* 1716 'reedy ploughland' from *erw* and *cawnog*); *Y Gardd Ruffith* 1669, *Gardd Riffith* 1716 ('Gruffudd's enclosure'); *Gilros* 1602 (perhaps 'heath nook' from *cil* and *rhos*); *Horscoll* 1583 *NLWCat*, *Horsoll* 1597; *Kae Cokshut* 1702, *Cae Cockshutt* 1717 ('field with a cockshoot'); *Kae Crwn* 1702, *Cae Crwnucha*, *Cae Crwnissa* 1717 ('round field' with 'higher' and 'lower'); *Kay Dykyn alias Kay Atha Weeth* 1586 *NLWCat*, *Awydd Fydd* 1717 (*Atha Weeth* may be 'left-handed Adam'); *Kay Evan alias Yorwerth ap Ithell* 1669; *Kay Garth y Bythel Issa* 1669, *Kay Garth y Bethel* 1702 (if *y* is intrusive 'field of Bithel's enclosure'); *Kay Gronow* 1669 ('Goronwy's field'); *Kay Krion Kanol*, ~ ~ *Issa* 1669 (perhaps 'field with pigsties', Welsh *creuon*, with 'middle' and 'lower'); *Kay Mayr* 1597 (possibly Welsh *maer* 'steward'); *Lli yr Hen Velyn* 1602, *Ker Hen Vellin otherwise the Brooke* 1738 *NLWCat* (*Hen Velyn* is 'old mill', *Lli* may be a poor spelling for *Lle* 'place'); *Ros David Velyn* 1602 ('heath of David of the mill'); *Ty-in-y-Lluyny* 1602 ('house in the groves', Welsh *llwyni*); *Y Werglodd* 1717 ('hayfield'); *Y Wyddfud* 1669, *Clwyddfyd* 1716 (probably *gwyddfid* 'thorn enclosure').

5. EASTWICK (SJ 380380)

Astwick' (p), *Astwik'* 1279–80 *RentSur*, *Astwik* 1280 Strange
Estwic c.1561–85 Morgan
Eastwick 1602 Slack, *-wicke* 1672 HTR, *-wich* 1730 *SBL 1355*

'East dairy farm', *v.* **ēast**, **wīc**. The significance of the name is not obvious. Eastwick is E. of Dudleston, but it is not the most easterly township in the parish, and it is N.W. of Ellesmere.

GROVES MOSS, 1839 *TA*, PLTN, 1839 *TA*, WD: by Plas-yn-Grove.
PLAS-YN-GROVE, *Pleasant Grove* 1837 OS, ~ *Groves* 1839 *TA*. Assuming that the modern form is the correct one, this is a hybrid Welsh/English name, 'house in the grove'.
TAN HO, 1837 OS, 1839 *TA*.

Field-Names

Forms in (a) are 1839 *TA*.

(a) Acre Fd; Barn Fd; Bedling, Little, Near, Bedlings Mdw; Big Mdw; Brickkiln Fd (2); Brook Mdw; Brynn y Goch; Cae Dee, Big, Little (not near R. Dee); Cae Ears, Far, Near; Cae Hollins, Big, Little, Middle ('holly field'); Calves Croft (3); Cote Fd (a large field with Eastwick farm in a corner); Cowslip Mdw; Croft (some small enclosures by what looks like an extension of Dudleston Heath); Double Pit Fd; Eastwick Mdw, Big ~ ~; First Fd; French Wheat Fd; Garden Fd; Goblin Dale (*v.* Goblindale in Trench *infra*); Gravel Hole Fd, Lower, Upper, ~ ~ Bank (Sandhole Fd adjoins); Hendear Fd, Mdw (Welsh *hendir* 'old or unploughed land'); Hengoer (adjoins Hendear, perhaps a corrupt version of that n.); Hevin, Big (Near Trevin adjoins, correct form uncertain); Higher Wd; Intack ('newly cultivated land', adjoins Maes y Rhos); Little Mdw; Long Mdw; Maes y Rhos ('heath field', Intack adjoins); Marle Fd; Marsh Mallows (perhaps a reference to soil consistency: the plant from which the sweetmeat was made grows in salt marshes); The Meadow, Far, First and Second Mdw; Meadow, Far, Long; Mill Fd (by Shell Brook); Moss, ~ Mdw (by

Groves Moss); Plantation; Road Fd; Rushy Mdw; Sandhole Fd; Slang, Higher, Lower (strips by road); Tan House Fd (3 fields by Tan Ho); Top Fd; Turnip Patch; Well Fd; Wet Mdw.

6. ELLESMERE (SJ 398349)

HAUGHTON (SJ 404359)

Houton' 1255–6 *Ass* (p)
Hochton m.13th HAC (p), *-ton'* 1255 RH (p)
Horton 1284 ChanR
Hoghton 1309 Eyton, *Hougton* 1549 Pat
Haughton alias Houghton 1607 Peake, *Haughton* 1703 PR(L) 7 *et seq*

The ChanR form is probably erroneous. The other spellings indicate **hōh-tūn**, with **hōh** referring here to a low spur of ground. In Part **1** 160, s.n. Horton, the 1284 form was erroneously cited as evidence for a lost *Horton* ('dirt farm') in Ellesmere.

A reference to *Oldehoghton'* 1392–3 *SRO Bridgewater 212/box 72* suggests that there were two settlements.

THE AVENUE.

CASTLE, *Castle Parke* 1664 *SBL 5250.*

CREMORNE GARDENS. Nankivell 45 says that this landscaped garden was laid out on land where tanneries had stood, and was named "after the notorious London Cremorne Gardens".

CRIMPS COTTAGES, *v.* Crimps Fm *infra.*

THE GRANGE, 1839 *TA*, *Grange* 1833 OS.

THE HOLLIES.

MENTONE HO.

THE MERE. Elias *del Mere* is mentioned 1278–9 *RentSur.*

Street-Names

As was done for Shrewsbury in Part **4**, this section takes account of the streets shown on the 1900 6" map. Few of these are named on the OS map, however, and names for those which are there shown blank have been taken from the *County Red Book: Shropshire*, Estate Publications 2001. These have been collated with G. Foxall's drawing of the plan of Ellesmere town which is included in *TA*.

H. J. Peake, *Historical Guide to Ellesmere*, 23–4, gives Love Lane, St John's Hill and Sandy Lane as the route of Colonel Mytton's escape from Prince Rupert in 1643.

BIRCH RD (*sic* on 2001 map, BIRCH ROW in Peake 1897), *Birch Lane* 1839 *TA*.

BROWNLOW RD, after Lord Brownlow who inherited the Bridgewater properties in Ellesmere. The road is not shown on *TAMap*, but it is shown and named on the 1900 6".

CHAPEL ST, 1839 *TA*. *TAMap* shows *Chapel* and *Chapel School.*

CHARLOTTE ROW, 1839 *TA*.

CHURCH HILL, 1839 *TA*.

CHURCH ST, 1839 *TA*.

CROSS ST, 1839 *TA*.

GRANGE RD.

HIGH ST, 1839 *TA*.

LOVE LANE, 1839 *TA*. Peake 1897 suggests that this was a postern entrance to the castle.

MARKET ST, *Swine Market* 1839 *TA*.

PINFOLD ST, *Pynfold* 1483–4 *SRO Bridgewater 212/box 72*; *Pinfold Lane* 1839 *TA*. Cf. *Pinfolde Yardes* 1602 Peake.

ST JOHNS HILL, 1839 *TA*. The Knights Hospitallers of St John were given land here in the 13th century.

SANDY LANE, 1839 *TA*.

SCOTLAND ST, 1839 *TA*, *Scotland Streete* 1521–2 *SRO Bridgewater 212/box 92*; *strete callid Scotland* 1585 *SBL 15671*. *Scotland Croft* adjoins the road on *TAMap*. Cf. John Field, *A History of English Field-Names* p. 152, "the ambiguity of *Scotland* names has long been recognised". The choice is between a reference to the payment of some tax and a reference to remoteness.

SWAN HILL, 1839 *TA*, by the Mere.

TALBOT ST. The stretch of road between Spar Bridge and the N. end of Watergate St has this name on the 2001 map, and Talbot Lane is on the N. side of the road. *TAMap* shows *Talbot Inn.*

TRIMPLEY ST, *Trympley Lane* 1585 *SBL 15671*, *Trimpley* 1839 *TA*. The street is called Trimpley, without St or Lane, in Kelly's Directory for 1934.

WATERGATE ST, 1839 *TA*. The second element is 'gate', not the Norse-derived word for 'street'. The name occurs in Chester and London, and there are a number of instances which are not in towns. There was presumably a gate at the junction with Church or Talbot St which gave access to the lakeside.

WHARF RD, leading to the canal installations.

WILLOW ST, 1839 *TA*.

The *TAMap* of Ellesmere town shows *Rope Walk* alongside Charlotte Row, and marks *The Mount* on the W. side of Pinfold Lane.

Buildings shown on *TAMap* are: *Black Lion Hotel, Bull and Dog, Dead House* (by the church), *Dolphin Inn, Eagles, Hearse House, Kiln* (2), *Limehouse, Madras School, Manor Place, Market Hall, Mixing Holes* (2, by Kiln and by Limehouse), *Old Kiln and Gig House, Post Office, Prison, Red Lion, Stone Yard, Swan, Timber Yard, Unicorn Inn, Vicarage House, Warehouse, White Hart Inn, Wood Yard.*

The area by the wharf has *Canal Tavern, Candle House, Gas House, Woodhouse, Wood Yard.*

Field-Names

Forms in (a) are 1839 *TA* except where otherwise stated. Earlier forms dated 1343, 1602 are Peake 1897, 1889, those dated 1392–3, 1483–4, 1521–2, 1595–6 are *SRO Bridgewater 212/box 72, 92, 382*, 1664 are *SBL 5250.*

(a) Arragon Croft; Fd; The Bank; Banky Fd (several); Barn Fd (several); Big Fd (several); Big Lsw; Big Mdw; Birchin Pool; Birch Mdw; Blackbird Fd; Blackwaters Mdw (*Blackwater* 1664: Nankivell 29 notes that this stream runs out of the S.E. end of the Mere, Gazetteer notes that Blackwater occurs on 1st ed. 6" map); Brick Kiln; Brickkiln Fd (several); Bridge Fd, Higher, Lower; Brook Fd, Mdw; Burgage, Big ~ (4 small fields on N. outskirts of town); Chopping Pce; Clem Park (2, *v.* Clemley in Prees *infra*); Corner Fd; Cote Fd (2, no buildings); Croft (a few round Haughton, and elsewhere used for many small enclosures and some normal-sized fields); Croft of the Hill; Cross Fd, Far and Near ~ ~ (by Cross in Trench township); Dab Badgers Fd; Daisy Fd; Diglake Mdw, Little ~ ~ (*v.* **dīc**, **lacu**, the n. occurs twice in Ch, PN Ch **2** 291, **3** 82); Dole Yd; Elson Fd (5 fields adjoining Elson and Greenhill township); Fakeaway; Footroad Fd (2, *v.* Dudleston f.ns. *supra*); Foxholes, Big, Little; Further Fd; Gambick Mdw; Garden Fd; George's Fd; The Go(w)ers; Grange Croft, Big, Little (by The Grange); Greenfield; Hanmer's Mdw; Haughton Fd, Near and Middle ~ ~ (N.W. of Haughton); Honey Dale, Big, Little, Long and Far ~ ~, ~ ~ Mdw (*Horry Dale Feildes* 1602); Hop Yd; Horse Pasture; Hown Fd (*TAMap* shows a few houses here which are shown on 1899 6" without a n.); Industry Pce (by House of Industry); Jenny's Clays Fd; Judy's Pasture; The Lawn (near The Grange); Lawyer's Mdw; Leasow, Big, Long; Leasow, Little, New; Leg of Mutton Fd (an excellent description); Ley Mdw; Lime Mdw; Little Haughton, ~ ~ Mdw, ~ ~ Seven, Nine and Ten Acres (a group of fields on N.E. boundary, ½ mile from Haughton); Long Fd (several); Long Mdw, North, South; Martin's Orchard (*Le Martyn Orchard* 1483–4, *Merton Orchard* 1521–2, associated with *Martonfeld* 1521–2, *Martins Feild* 1664); Meadow (*freq*); Mere Fd; Mere Mdw; Middle Fd; Mill Fd (2, one adjoining Windmill Fd); Moor; More Mdw; Moss Croft and Mdw; New Fd; Newnes Bridge Fd, Mdw, The Newnes Fd (by Newnes township); Old House Fd; Old House Mdw; Pit Fd, Big and Little ~ ~; Pitch Croft, Big and Little Pitchmoor, Pitchmoor Fd

(*Pittlesmore* 1343, *Pitelesmor* 1392–3, *Pettesmore* 1483–4, *Pyttesmore*, *Pychmore* 1521–2, 'hawk's marsh', *v.* **pyttel, mōr**); Plantation Fd; Pontons Fd; Pool Fd; Road Fd; Roberts Backside; Rough Mdw (2); Ryegrass Fd, Little ~ ~; Sandy Hill Fd; Scotland Croft (by Scotland St); Shutt Fd (*v.* Part **4** 113); Sickhouse Mdw (adjoins House of Industry); The Squirrel (FN 44 notes another occurrence in Bitterley); Stackyard Fd; Tan Yd; Toby's Mdw; Trimpley Croft, Fd, Mdw (by the road called Trimpley, *v. supra*); Trunk Lsw; Vetch Fd; Well Bank, Far, Near; Whelpscroft 1897 Peake (1343, *Whelpescroft* 1595–6, *v.* **hwelp** 'young animal', here perhaps a pers.n. or nickname); Windmill Fd (2, cf. *Wynmylnefeld* 1483–4, *Windemill Feilde* 1602); Wood, Far, Near.

TA names two artificial islands in the Mere: Cohill and Eleanour Islands. Nankivell 42 gives an account of the construction of Cohill Island in 1812–13: it was first called *Moscow*, then *Charlotte Island*, "and eventually became Cowhill".

(b) *Billings Croft* 1664; *Brome Croft* 1664; *Collyes Feilde* 1602; *The Coneygree* 1664; *Gatebruggemore* 1392–3 (probably 'goat bridge marsh'); *Hawries Cross* 1343; *Ye Mearhead* 1343; *Ye Mile Dam* 1343 (probably 'mill dam'); *Miskill More* 1602; *Rounhull* 1392–3 (probably 'rough hill', *v.* **rūh**); *Walton* 1343 (this is the penultimate n. in a sparse boundary of Ellesmere: Peake 1897, p. 26 says "Walton lay near Haughton", but no other reference has been found).

7. ELSON AND GREENHILL

ELSON (SJ 384358)

Ellesdon' 1279–80 *RentSur*, *-dene* 1309 Eyton
Elston Greville 1602 Slack, *Elston* 1672 HTR
Elliston 1711 PR(StA) 5
Elson 1837 OS

'Elli's hill', *v.* **dūn**. The pers.n. occurs also in Ellesmere.

GREENHILL (SJ 374356)

(*vill' de*) *Grenhull'* 1279–80 *RentSur*, *Grenhulle* 1309 Eyton
Greenhill 1672 HTR, *Green Hill* 1837 OS

'Green hill', *v.* **grēne, hyll**.

THE HOLLIES.

LOOP FM, near the loop line connecting Cambrian with Wrexham and Ellesmere railway.

OSBORNE HO.

WALLFORD HO.

Field-Names

Forms in (a) are 1839 *TA*.

(a) Barn Fd; Barn Yd; Big Fd; Big Mdw; Biggest Fd; Brick Yard; Bridge Fd; Broad Fd (Broad Lsw adjoins); Brook Fd; Brook Lsw (2); Broomy Croft; Broomy Fd; Charles Pit; Cleml(e)y (2, *v.* Clemley in Prees *infra*: Clemley ns. are frequent in this part of Sa, but it is surprising to have two in this small township); Cocking Mdw; Cote Lsw (no building); Cow Pasture; Crook Fd, Little (irregularly shaped); Croft (a few near settlements); Dolly's Fd (Peggy's Fd and Nanny's Fd are in the same area); Far Pit Mdw; Footroad Fd (2, *v.* Dudleston f.ns. *supra*); Green Fd (one of the fields surrounding Greenhill, others are Greenhill Fd and Lsw); Half Mile Fd (by the Ellesmere road, ½ mile from Elson); Hawthorn Tree Fd; Higher Fd; Hook, ~ Mdw (a shape n.); Hopyard Mdw; Horse Mdw; Kahen, Great, Little; Lanscroft; The Lilly Mdw; Long Croft; Long Fd; Long Mdw; Maes y Gwalley (on N. boundary, there is nothing appropriate to derivation from Welsh *gwaliau* 'walls': Wallford Ho, on 6" map, adjoins, but this is probably not an old n.); Marl Croft (2); Marl Fd; The Meadow; Meadows; Narrow Pce; New Lsw; Nick Fd; Oak Fd; Ox Lsw; Pease Brush; Pentelling (a field called Pontelling is nearby, perhaps Welsh *pont* 'bridge', the fields are near a stream-crossing on W. boundary); Pit Fd (2); Polymaster(s) Mdw, Big and Little ~ ~; Pritchard's Mdw; Roundabout Fd (irregularly shaped); Sandy Hole; The Slang (very narrow strip); Stallions Fd; Thistly Fd (2); Vronn (Welsh, 'breast of a hill'); Wet Mdw; White Moors, Farther, Near; The Wood.

(b) *Wodemulne* 1392–3 *SRO Bridgewater 212/box 72* ('wood mill').

8. HAMPTON WOOD (SJ 428377)

Hamptonwode 1349, 1436 AD, *Hampton Wode* 1377 *SBL 3597*, 1403 Pat, ~ *Wod* 1451 AD, ~ *Woode* 1615 (copy) *SBL 15755*

Hamtonneswode 1392 AD, *Hamptons Wood* 1672 HTR, 1833 OS

'Wood belonging to Welshampton'. Morgan 30 gives a 1526 form *Hamtonswode otherwise Coyde hempton,* and this partly Welsh version appears on Morden's map of 1695 as *Coidhampton.*

The township adjoins Welshampton *infra*, and was presumably an area of woodland belonging to that parish before becoming a settlement and a township of Ellesmere. The *TAMap* for Hampton Wood shows an area of Welshampton in the middle of the main part, and small detached areas of Hampton Wood in the south of Welshampton. For the purpose of the place-name survey the main part of Hampton Wood has been treated as a unit, with field-names for the space in the middle taken from Welshampton *TA*, and names in the scattered areas of detached land have been incorporated into the Welshampton list.

BISHOP'S HO, 1839 *TA*.

BISHOP'S WD, *Baylins Wood* 1833 OS, *Wood* 1839 *TA*.

BROOK MILL, 1833 OS, 1839 *TA*.

CAMBRIAN WD: on 1839 *TAMap* an adjacent field is called *Camaran.*

CRYNOS FM. On 1839 *TAMap* two fields a short distance east are called *Higher* and *Lower Crynos*.

HAMPTON WD FM, *Hamptons Wood* 1833 OS, 1839 *TA*.

HILL TOP, *The Hill* 1839 *TA*.

KNOLLS WD, *Wood* 1839 *TA*. Adjacent fields are *Big* and *Little Knowld* 1839 *TA*. Knolls Fm in Bettisfield Fli is nearby.

LEWIS'S WD.

MILL WD, *Wood Mill Cover* 1833 OS, *Wood* 1839 *TA*.

NEW COPPICE.

WOOD MILL, 1833 OS. This is the mill from which Mill Wd is named.

WOODSIDE, *Wood Side* 1839 *TA*.

Field-Names

Forms in (a) are 1839 *TA*. The list includes some names from Welshampton *TA*, *v. supra*.

(a) Banky Pce; Barn Yd (several); Big Fd (2); Big Mdw (3); Birch Fd; Brickkiln Fd (2); Cae Buchan (Welsh, 'little field'); Calves Croft; Carters Fd; Clover Fd (2); Coffins Fd; Comonacks, High, Low; Croft (a few, small enclosures); Cross Lane Fd (by a crossroads); Dingle, Big, Little; Far Fd (2); Gough's Wd, Big, Little; Green Fd (2); Horse Pasture; House Fd; Lane Croft, Far, Near; Little Fd; Long Fd; Lower Fd; (The) Meadow (several); Mere Fd (not by a lake or a boundary); Milking Bank Fd (by Hampton Wd Fm); Orchard Fd; The Outlet (not near a building); The Patch (in a stream junction, larger than most Patch fields); Pit Fd; Post Lsw; Reddings (*v.* ***ryding**); Rough Lsw (2); Round Bank (small enclosure with two curved sides); Sandyhole Fd (2); Sheep Fd; Shell Fd; Shutt, Croft (Corner Croft and Square Croft are in the same group of small enclosures); Slade Fd (a field with a wet patch, *v.* FN 18); Slang (narrow strip); Thistly Fd; Top Fd (2); Well Fd; Widdows Fd; Wood Fd (several); Yard, Pit, Lower (by Hill Top).

9. HARDWICK (SJ 369345)

Herdewick' 1279–80 *RentSur*, *-wyk* 1284 Pat, Ch, *-wike* 1309 Eyton
Hardwick 1577 Saxton, ~ *Hall* 1837 OS, 1839 *TA*

'Herd farm', *v.* **heord-wīc**. Other Sa examples are in Hadnall, Norbury and Stottesdon.

The precise sense of this common place-name has not been ascertained. It has been translated 'sheep farm' (DEPN), and it has been considered to denote "that part of a manor devoted to livestock as distinct from the **bere-wīc** which was that part devoted to arable farming" (EPN, followed by CDEPN). NED, s.n. *herdwick*, notes that the earliest occurrence is in DB for Gloucestershire, and the Phillimore translation renders this 'dairy farm'. This last meaning was given for Hardwick in Hadnall in Part **4**, 130–1, but it should be noted that none of these meanings can be proved to be correct.

BEECH WD.

FRIESLAND, this is woodland in the grounds of Hardwick Hall.

HARDWICK COTTAGE: the building is in the corner of *Cottage Field* on *TAMap*.

HARDWICK LO, 1839 *TA*, *Lodge* 1837 OS.

HARDWICK POOL, *New Pool* 1839 *TA*.

OLD HARDWICK, 1837 OS, 1839 *TA*. This little settlement, ½ mile W. of the Hall, is not named on the 1961 1" map.

PERTHY, 1837 OS: Welsh *perthi* 'hedges'. This is a row of buildings in the S.W. corner of the township, with numerous *Crofts* on *TAMap*, which are shown as small rectangular enclosures on the 1900 6".

POOL COVERT, by Hardwick Pool.

ROCKERY WD.

Field-Names

Forms in (a) are 1839 *TA*.

(a) Ashtree Fd; Back Fd (by Hardwick Lo); Barn Fd; Basin Fd; Beechtree Fd; Big Fd; Brickkiln Croft; Brynn David ('David's hill'); Bush Fd; Clover Fd (2); Coachman's Fd (by Hardwick Hall); Croft (a few by Old Hardwick and on S. edge of Hardwick Park, a very large group at Perthy); Fingerpost Fd (by a road junction); Four Acres; George's Croft; Horse Moor; Horse Pasture; John Davies's Pltn; Ka Cockshutt, Big, Little ('field with a cockshoot', Ka from Welsh *cae*); Ka Fenny (Welsh/English, 'marshy field'); Ka Glase (Welsh, 'green field'); Kagroes ('cross field', by a road junction); Ka Kiln ('kiln field', not near Brickkiln Croft); Lawn (2, by Hardwick Lo and by the Hall); Long Mdw; Maes Gwynn (Welsh 'white field'); Meadow, Big, Little, Moss; Mowing Mdw, Big; Orchard Fd; Ox Pasture; The Park (a large field, not part of Hardwick Park); Perthy Fd (a short distance from Perthy); Pool Croft, Fd, Mdw (by Hardwick Pool); Round Bank (with three slightly curved sides).

10. LEE (SJ 404325)

Lega c.1090, 1138, c.1150, c.1235, l.14th SAC

Leye 1280 Strange, *Legh'* 1291–2 *Ass*

Lee c.1300 *SBL 3586*, 1577 Saxton *et seq*
Leigh 1654 PR(StA) 4

'Clearing', *v.* **lēah**. In SAC the form *Legha in lima* in a charter of 1167–82 (p. 299) is indexed as Lee in Ellesmere, but this is High Legh near Lymm in Cheshire.

LEE BRIDGES, 1833 OS, 1839 *TA*.
LEE NEW FM, *New Farm* 1833 OS, 1839 *TA*.
LEE WD, *Coppice* 1839 *TA*.
MERE WD, *Moss* 1839 *TA*.
OLD HALL, *Lee Hall* 1839 *TA*.
THE ROOKERY.

Field-Names

Forms in (a) are 1839 *TA*.

(a) Ashton Plants; The Banks; Barn Fd (2); Big Corner; Big Mdw; Birchen Hill, New Birchin Hill; Birch Gate, Big ~ ~, ~ ~ Mdw (by the Ellesmere road, on boundary with Birch and Lyth township); Brook Inclosure, Lsw, Mdw; Burrow Hill, Mdw; Charlton's Bank; Clover Lsw; Coalpit Fd (S. of hamlet, Pit Fd adjoins, both are large); Corner Mdw; Cote Lsw (no building); Cow Pasture; Croft(s) (several round hamlet, a cluster near S. boundary where 6" map marks Meth. Chapel, a few by the Hadwick fields on W. boundary); Cross Greys; Daisy Fd; Dale Fd; Drainhurst; Far Croft (2); Farthest Fd; Five Pound Lsw; Foster's Hayes, Big, Little; Four Day Math; The Foxholes; Gighole Fd (a reference to flax drying, *v.* Dudleston f.ns. *supra*); Godfrey, ~ Mdw (the n. Godfrey applies to two fairly large fields); Gorsy Bank; Gravelhole Fd; Gravel Pit Fd; Hadwick, Far, Middle, Gorsy, The Hadwick Mdw (these ns. apply to a line of small rectilinear enclosures which adjoin the village of Tetchill in the neighbouring township: this is the only record of the n. Hadwick); Hempyard; Hollin Banks (*v.* **holegn**); Horse Pce, Big, Little; The Husk, Near Husk (possibly **hassuc** 'coarse grass', which has become Haske in D, PN D 419); Lawn (in hamlet); Long Fd; Long Lsw; Low Enclosure; Martin's Mdw; Meadow, Big, Croft, Far, Horse, Hugh's, Little, Long, Middle, Nonsuch, Peels (a series of narrow fields along a brook on S.E. boundary); Meadow below Orchard; Mere Fd, Banky, Big and Little ~ ~, Mere Croft (by White Mere); Middle Bank; Middle Croft; Moody's Mdw; Moor Side, Far ~ ~; New Lsw; Nursery Croft; Oaktree Fd; Pigeon Mdw; The Radnor; Round Bank (no curved side); Round Moss (two slightly curving sides); Rye Lsw; Sheep Lsw; Shop Fd (in hamlet); The Slade (Sa dialect for a field with a wet patch); Southard, Big; Sparks Mdw; Sturdys Yd; Three Acre Mdw (Two ~ ~ adjoins); Titchell Fd (by Tetchill); Ways Fd (Way Lsw adjoins, not by a path or road); Well Fd (2); White Mdw; Windmill Fd; Winsbury Hill; The Wood, Big Wood, Woods by Titchell Moor, Woods Mdw (group of fields along S.W. boundary); Wych Croft.

(b) (moor of) *Leyemor* 1309 Eyton.

11. LYNEAL (SJ 446332)

Lunehal' 1221 SAS 3/VI
Lunyhal' 1221–2 *Ass*
Lunyal 1279–80 *RentSur* (p)
Luneyale 1309 Eyton
Linial 1326 HAC, *Linyal* 1328 HAC, *Lynniall* 1622 PR(L) 9, 1632–3 *SBL 4199*, *Liniall* 1655 SAS 1/XLVII
Leonayles 1396 Cl
Lenyall 1577 Saxton

Second element **halh**, probably in the sense 'slight hollow'. The forms indicate a first element **lunig* or **hlunig*, probably an adjective, which appears to be unique to this place-name. No etymology is available for this. Ekwall's suggestion (DEPN, under Lineal) of OE **hlin** 'maple' does not suit, nor does **hlyn** 'torrent'. The vowel of the first syllable is *-u-*, with development to *-i-* as seen in Dinnington Nb, So, WRY, Dinton Bk, W and Dinworthy D, from the personal name *Dunna*.

BLACK COPPICE.

BRIDGE VILLA.

CLAPPING GATE, 1833 OS, variant of *clap-gate* 'kissing gate'.

DUMBLE HOLE (not on map, in Gazetteer, *v.* f.ns.). *Dumble* is a variant of *Drumble*, for which *v.* The Drumble in Birch township *supra*. EDD, *s.v. drumble*, has a quotation referring to this place which illustrates the interchange between the two forms:

> "I got to goo to Lineal toneet, an I dunna know 'ow to pass
> the drumby-'ole near the Cut bridge fur they sen theer's
> frittenin theer."

DUNBUCK MOOR: *TA* has fields called *Dunsbridge Moor* and *Meadow*, *Dunsbridge*, *Dunbricks Field* on either side of the canal here. This may be the Cut bridge in the quotation *supra*.

FORD'S COPPICE, *Fords Plantation* 1839 *TA*. *TA* also has four fields called *Fords* and two called *Big* and *Little Fords*. The 1999 Explorer map has The Fords. The road from Lyneal Hall crosses marshy ground here.

HAMPTON BANK, 1833 OS, by the road to Welshampton.

HATCH, 1839 *TA*.

LYNEAL GORSE.

LYNEAL HALL, *Lineal Hall* 1839 *TA*.

LYNEAL MILL, cf. *Mill Croft*, *Mill Tail* 1839 *TA*.

LYNEAL MOSS, ~ ~ COTTAGE, *Lineal Moss* 1839 *TA*.

LYNEAL WD, 1833 OS.

ROWE, *Rotten Row* 1833 OS, *The Roe* 1839 *TA*, 'rat row', a name usually found in towns, cf. Part **4** 7.

VILLAGE FM.

YELL BRIDGE, WD, *Yells* 1839 *TA*, *v*. **helde** 'gentle slope'.

YETCHLEYS COPPICE, *Yetchleys*, 1833 OS. *TA* has fields called *Eachleys*, *Big* and *Far* ~, and *Eachley Bar* is shown on *TAMap* by *Turnpike Gate* on the road from Ellesmere.

Field-Names

Forms in (a) are 1839 *TA*.

(a) Aldershutt Mdw, Big and Little Alder Shutt (the meaning of Shutt is uncertain, *v*. Part **4** 113); Balmer Fd (Balmer is in Welshampton); Barn Fd; The Bank; Big Fd (several); Big Lsw; Big Mdw; Big Stubble; Big Yd; Blake Castle, Bank (in S.E. corner of township); Bottom; Bradley, Big and Little ~, ~ Fd, Mdw (9 fields E. of Lyneal Mill); Breech (several, **bryce** 'newly-broken-in land'); Brickkiln Lsw; Brook Fd, ~ ~ Mdw; Brynada (first el. probably Welsh *bryn* 'slope'); Cart Door; Chapel Fd (chapel shown on *TAMap*); Clare Pits (by Clarepool in Welshampton); Close, Far, Richards, Middle, Big, Low, Higher, New (adjacent fields on W. boundary); Cordwell; Corny Fd; Cote Croft (no building); Cote Fd (with a small building); Croft(s) (*freq*: there is a cluster in the northern tip of the township, one by Northwood in Wem and one round Lyneal village); Crooked Style; Cut Patch (a tiny enclosure by the canal); Ditch Croft Mdw; Downs Ground; Dumbleditch, Far and Near ~ (*v*. Dumble Hole *supra*: this f.n. locates the feature on the W. boundary, a short distance N. of Cole Mere); Far Lsw; Field below the Wood; Far Mdw; Fox Cover; Gaphills; Gravel Hole Fd; Gighole (*v*. Dudleston f.ns.); Green (a tiny triangle between Eachleys and Lyneal Moss); Greenway, ~ Slade; Hackney Lake, Near (Lake from **lacu** 'drainage channel'); Hale Pit; Hampton Fd (by Welshampton); High Rough Hill, Far, Near; Holdings Lsw; Honey Spot Mdw; Horse Pasture; Jones Bank; Kebley, Big, Rough and Little ~ (4 fields on S.W. boundary); Long Croft (2 fields S. of Lyneal Moss, these with Tithebarn Croft and one of the Snailhouse fields are 4 adjacent strip-shaped enclosures); Long Fd; Long Flg, Near, Middle and Old ~ ~ (4 fields E. of village); Long Lsw; Lord's Fd; Mannering (3 fields near W. boundary); March Mdw (on S. boundary); Meadow (*freq*); Meadow, Far, Little, Potato, House, Middle, Big (small enclosures in a cluster of small fields on E. boundary of township); Mere Fd (on W. boundary); Mere Lsw (not near a boundary or a pond); Moor, Grazing, Mowing, Rushy; Moors (a large area with a grid field-pattern on N.E. boundary); Moss (*freq*); Mossell Mdw, Far, Near; Mowing Slade; Near Lsw (2); New Lsw (2); Oak Lsw; Old House Fd; Oliver's Heath; Orms Butt; Ox Lsw; Peat Moss; Pissing Graves, Far ~ ~ (3 fields between the canal and the Welshampton road, *v*. Pissant Graves in Baschurch *supra*); Pit Fd (2); Plant Yd; Polletts Mdw; Profeat Yd (this and Plant Yd are on the edge of Moor and Moss fields near The Rowe); Quiykin, Big, Far, Little (near Quaiken in Cockshut, *q.v.*); Rogers Pce; Round Mdw (curvilinear sides); Rushy Flatt; Shase (3 fields on E. boundary, probably the plural of *shay*, variant of *shaw*, 'copse'); Sheveleng; Snail House (4 fields on the edge of Lyneal Moss); Sourdock Fd (*sourdock* is a n. for sorrel); Square Fd; Stony Riln; Sydney; Three Cornered Pce; Three Part Mdw; Tithebarn Fd (a small enclosure called Tithe Barn adjoins); Vann, Big, Little (in S.E. corner of township, not a marshy area, so probably not **fenn**); Ware Fd, Moor (7 fields E. of Cole Mere in a network of streams, 'weir'); Weirbank; Well Fd; Well Lsw; Westlynns, Far Weslynns; Whattall, Big ~; Wheat Croft; Windmill Fd; Wolverley Fd (Wolverley is in Wem); Wood, Big, Little, Menlove's; Woodal Croft (a normal-sized field); Woody Faugh (possibly *fall* 'place where trees have been felled', the form is better suited to **falh** 'land broken up for cultivation', but other words are used for that in Sa); Wykey Fd; Yellow Lawn (in the village).

12. MARTON, NEW (SJ 340347) AND OLD (SJ 351343)

New Marton and Old Marton are shown as distinct townships on the Index to Tithe Survey map, and G. Foxall's set of drawings from *TAMaps* puts Old Marton with the townships of the neighbouring parish of Whittington. It is convenient to treat the two units together here, but with separate field-name lists.

MARTON is *Marton* 1284 Pat *et seq.*

OLD MARTON is *Oldemarten* 1544 *SBL 6176*, *Old Merton 1657* PR(StA) 4, *Ould Marton* 1667 PR(L) 9, 1672 HTR.

NEW MARTON is *New Marton* 1577 Saxton *et seq*, *Newe Morton* 1609 PR(StA) 4, *New Martin* 1695 Morden.

Marton is probably 'mere settlement' like the other Sa Martons, which are in Chirbury and Myddle. There is no lake here now, but (*ex inf.* Ann Cole) there is a belt of alluvium running alongside the Shropshire Union canal, and this could be a silted-up lake. The other possibility is 'boundary settlement', from **(ge)mǣre**, which could be a reference to the boundary with Oswestry Hundred.

Some references in PR(StA) 2 mention another name: *Old Merton als yr Heol* 1625, *Old Merton y Rheal* 1626, "Marye of Oulde Marton dwellinge in a place called the Neol there" 1648. This is Welsh *heol*, *hewl* 'street, road, way, path; enclosure, close' (PN EF 382), which has given Rhewl near Gobowen, 2 miles west.

Field-Names

Names in (a) are 1839 *TA*: (a:i) and (a:ii) are for New and Old Marton.

(a:i) Banks; Banky Fd (adjoins Banks); Barn Fd; Barn Yd; Brickkiln Fd; Broomy Croft, Fd; Broomy Fd (not near preceding); Brown's Mdw; Brynns; Calves Croft; Claly Vath; Clunhill; Croft(s) (a few in the hamlet and a few on N. boundary); Cuff by Allard; Godrell; Kabricks (Ka- is probably Welsh *cae* 'field', perhaps 'brick field'); Karderwaun (perhaps Cae'r Dderwen 'oak-tree field'); Ka ban y du; Kachaun; Kaclany; Kacoed ('wood field'); Kamore (perhaps 'big field'); Little Fd; Long Fd; Long Mdw; Marshmoles (4 large fields on N.E. boundary); Mathers Fd; (The) Meadow (several); Moat Fd (the moat is shown, in the grounds of New Marton Hall); Moss; Narrow Lane Fd; New Marton Fd (on boundary with Old Marton); Outlet (by New Marton Hall); Pistol Lsw (Welsh *pistyll* 'spout', by a small stream on N. boundary); Rabber Acre; Redgate; Rough Bowens; Rough Mdw; Rough Yellick, Lower ~ ~ (adjoining Rough Bowens); Runybank; Sandy Bank; Shop Bank (in hamlet); Shop Mdw (by a line of small buildings along a road N.W. of hamlet); Stacks, Highermost, Lowermost; Sycamore Fd; Three Cornered Croft; Voils; Weigrinns; Well Fd; Wickey Fd, Big Wickey; Woods, Big, Far and Near ~.

(a:ii) Aber Oer (Welsh, 'cold stream', PN EF gives 'stream' as one meaning of *aber*); Barn Croft; Barn Fd, Further; Barn Yd; Big Mdw; Brickkiln Lsw; Bryn y Fallan ('hill of the apple-tree', Welsh *afallen*); Bryn y Fanne; Bryn Mawr ('big hill'); Cae Cam ('crooked field'); Cae Wean (perhaps Welsh *gwaun*, with roughly the same meanings as OE **mōr**: PN EF 376 cites forms *Waen* and *Wain* from this); Calves Croft; Castle Fd (small building shown); Clover Fd; Clover Lease; Coppice; Criftins, Middle ~ (*v*. Criftins in Dudleston *supra*: Gazetteer lists the Old Marton n. as extant); Croft, Croft by Jones's (adjacent); Cyfions (Welsh *cyffion* 'stocks', with English pl. added); Gorsty Fd (2); Grass Fd; Green Fds; Hall Mdw; Little Mdw; Marl Fd; Marlpit Fd; Middle Fd; New Inn (no building); New Mdw; Orchards; Perthy Fd (2, by Perthy in Hardwick *supra*); Rough Mdw; Round Mdw (irregularly shaped with short, straight lengths of boundary and one small curve); Rushes; Thistly Fd; Town Fd, Big, Little (2 fields W. of the single building which constitutes the Old Marton settlement); Walk Fd; Walk Mdw (probably referring to fulling, *v*. FN 41); Well Fd; Well Mdw; Worldy Ladder, Worldymost Hawthorn (these 2 fields are ½ mile apart on E. and W. boundaries of the northern tip of the township).

13. NEWNES

NEWNES (SJ 383343)

Newenes 1309 Eyton
Newmans 1549 Pat
Neawnes 1672 HTR, 1695 Morden
Newns 1687 PR(StA) 5
ye Niewns 1687 PR(StA) 5

This name is unsolved. Formally it could be a compound of **nes** 'promontory' with **nīwe** 'new', but this does not give satisfactory sense, nor does it suit the topography. This is an area of low relief. The settlement is on rising ground, but there is no prominent feature of the type usually denoted by **nes**.

Field-Names

Names in (a) are 1839 *TA*.

(a) Big Fd; Blackwell Mdw; Boosey Mdw (land on which an outgoing tenant had pasture rights, FN 34); Brook Mdw; Brook Lsw; Broomy Fd; Bryn y Garrick (possibly 'slope of the stone', Welsh *bryn*, *carreg*); Bryn y gossell; Cackenell (Cackett adjoins); Cote Mdw (2, no buildings); Far Mdw; Footroad Fd (*v*. Dudleston f.ns.); Greenhill Lsw (probably connected with Greenhill *supra*, but not adjacent); Hatch (by a brook, so probably a sluice gate); Higher Lsw; Hill, Big, Little; Horse Mdw; Kancewaths; Karalls; Long Croft; Long Mdw; Long Pool; Marlpit Fd; New Lsw; Nursery, ~ Mdw; Pitchmoor; Pola Pusent, Big, Little; Quiykin Moss (cf. Quaiken in Cockshut); Senyards; Tetchill Fd (on boundary with Tetchill township); Town Mdw; Vaughan's Yd; Well Fd.

(b) *Schadewallemor* 1392 *SRO Bridgewater 212/box 72*, *Shadwalmore* 1483–4 *ib* ('boundary-spring marsh', *v*. **scēad**, **wælle**, **mōr**: Shadwell is a recurrent p.n.).

14. NORTHWOOD

NORTHWOOD HO (SJ 404387)
Nordwode 1197–1203 HAC
Northwude 1309 Eyton, *Northwodd* 1549 Pat
Nordewode c.1324 APW

'North wood', this is one of the northernmost Ellesmere townships. The HAC document confirms a gift of Crickett, 3½ miles S.W., with pannage for 100 pigs in *Nordwode*, and the 1309 reference is to a *bosc*. A good deal of the area is woodland on 19th-cent. and modern maps.

Morgan, p. 42, identifies Northwood with *Coetsowyth* 1283, *Coyde soith* 1425, *Koid swydd* 1543, *Coytsoyd* 1548, giving *SRO Bridge* as the reference for these forms. This Welsh name is identical with Coed-swydd in Radnorshire, and is a compound of *coed* 'wood' and *swydd* 'office, manor'. It may be the equivalent of the English name Woodhouse, eight Sa examples of which are listed in Part **1** 322, with the suggestion that this denoted a building with a special function in relation to woodland.

CROSSFIELD WD: *Cross Field* 1839 *TA* is at the S. end of the strip of woodland.

DESK COPPICE: *TAMap* has an adjoining field called *The Desk*, which could be considered desk-shaped.

EVAN'S WD, *Wood* 1839 *TA*.

GAMEBUCK ROUGH: *TA* has seven fields called *Gamebuck*, *Top* and *Lowermost ~*, *Gamebuck Field*, *~ Meadow*, *Gamebrick Meadow*. There are two Gamebuck Fields, at the N. and S. ends of the group. FN 44 lists Gamebuck among hunting names, but the substantive use in some of these field-names tells against a reference to an animal of the chase.

GREEN BANKS, "a little house called the Greenbanks" 1897 Peake.

LIONLANE WD, *Lions Lane*, ~ ~ *Wood* 1833 OS, *Lion Lane Field* 1839 *TA*. The lane is a straight road with the wood on one side and small buildings on the other. *Lion* in minor names and field-names has been considered as an occasional development of ME **leyne**, a word discussed somewhat inconclusively in several EPNS surveys. EPN gives "**leyne**, **lain** ME, 'a layer, a tract of arable land'", and NED has "lain sb^2. A layer, a stratum" from 1577, and "Laine, local. A name given to certain tracts of arable land at the foot of the Sussex Downs" from 1754. This last instance is discussed in PN Sx 310. The Northwood instance, if it be indeed this word, does not obviously support an association with tracts of arable land. For other possible instances of development of **leyne** to Lion *v*. PN O 456, PN W 439.

LOMAX WD, *Lomacks Coppice* 1833 OS, *Wood* 1839 *TA*.

NANTCLIMBERS WD, 1833 OS. Nantclimbers is over the county boundary, in a detached portion of Flintshire.

NORTHWOOD FM, shown but not named on *TAMap*, HALL, HO.

OLD COPPICE, *Wood* 1839 *TA*.

PARK HALL, 1833 OS, 1839 *TA*.

SANDHOLE PLTN: the 6" map shows Old Sand Pit in the wood, and *Sandhole Field* 1839 *TA* adjoins.

SPOUT, probably a spring. *TAMap* shows a curvilinear enclosure with a building called The Spout a short distance N. of the building shown on 6" map. SPOUT WD is *Spout Coppice* 1833 OS, *Wood* 1839 *TA*.

WELL COPPICE: *Well Field* occupies the area on *TAMap*.

WOOD MILL, 1839 *TA*.

Field-Names

Names in (a) are 1839 *TA*. Early forms dated 1392–3, 1521–2, 1523–4 are *SRO Bridgewater 212/box 72, 192*, those dated 1548 are *SRO 3322/1*.

(a) Acorn; Back House; Backhouse Croft; Backhouse Fd (probably 'bakehouse' in all 3 instances); Banky Fd (several); Banky Mdw; Barclay's Fd, Mdw; Barn Fd (2); Barnhill Mdw; Barn Mdw (2); Barn Yd; Birch Fd, Big, Little; Birchin Hill, Low, Higher (***bircen** 'growing with birch trees' is fairly common in p.ns.); Bitchey Gwynn (Gwynn is Welsh *gwyn* 'white', Bitchey is obscure); Boosey Lsw (*v*. Newnes f.ns. *supra*); Bottom Fd (2); Braynes Lsw, Big, Little; Brennulth, Lower ~ (a compound of *bryn* and *allt*, both hill terms); Brickkiln Fd (2); Broad Fd (2); Cae Jem;

Cae Mawr ('big field'); Cae Panwell (perhaps 'hollow field' with Welsh *pannwl*); Calves Croft; Catwood Fd; Clarks Mdw; Clem Guts (a derogatory name: this use of Clem suggests that the Clemley ns. refer to hunger, *v.* Clemley in Prees *infra*); Clempark (a variant of Clemley Park, which is unusually common in this area of Sa); Clover Fd (several); Coal House Mdw; Coptiveny Croft, Mdw (on boundary with Coptiviney); Copy Fd, Mdw ('coppice', at S. end of Spout Wd); Cottage Fd; Croft (*freq*, small enclosures); Dale Fd; Davies Fd; Delva (a field called Little Delva is some distance away); Edge's Mdw; Far Fd (several); Far Moor; Field, Big, Little, Long (2), Near, Middle, Five Acre, Ash, Ellesmere, Stable (an adjoining group in S.W. of township); Foot Full Fd; Gilase (perhaps 'green nook', Welsh *cil* and *glas*); Goblin Mdw (cf. Goblindale in Trench *infra*); Gorsy Fd (2); Graves Pce; Green Fd; Haybank; Higher Lsw; Horse Pasture (2); The House Mdw; Lane Fd (2); Lawns, Bottom, Top (by Park Hall); Leasow, Far, Long; Little Park (not near a house); Little Patch (tiny enclosure); Long Croft; Long Fd (several); Lower Fd; Meadow (*freq*, with qualifiers such as Little, Long); Middle Fd (2); Moor (several); Moor Bank; Moors (a long strip on N.E. boundary); Morris Fd; Old Fd; Old House Fd; Old Orchard (2); Oxen Lsw, Pasture; Penfold Fd; Pit Fd (several); Polly Taylor's Fd; Powell Lsw, Bottom, Top; Rabbit Croft; Races Croft; Rhon y dee, Big, Little, Ripery; Roberts Wd; Round Croft (one slightly curved side); Round Fd (three curved sides); Sand Fd; Sandhole Fd; Sawpit Fd; Shade Fd; Shutt Fd (*v.* Part **4** 113 for a discussion of Shut(t) ns.); Slang, Far, Near; Square Fd (2); Tallow Bottoms; Thistly Fd (2); Three Acre Fd, Big, Little; Three Pound Fd; Well Fd (several); Well Mdw; Wood, Higher, Lower; Wood Fd (several); Yewtree Fd.

(b) *Gilursstockyng* 1392–3 (*v.* ***stoccing**); *Griggy Lesows* 1548 (cf. Grig Lsw in Balderton *infra*, Welsh *grug* 'heather'); *Holynhurst* 1521–2 (*v.* **holegn**, **hyrst**); *Kae Gwinn* 1548 ('white field'); *Kae Rheig* 1548 ('rye field'); *Le Vaghaime* 1521–2, *Le Baghenne* 1523–4 (probably the same name, but the form is uncertain).

15. OTELEY, NEWTON AND SPUNHILL

NEWTON (SJ 421344)

Newentonia 1165–70 HAC

Newtona c.1190–95 HAC *et freq* with variant spellings *-ton*(*ia*), *Neuton iuxta Elesmere* 1327 HAC, ~ *juxta Elsemere* 1535 VE, *Neuton* 1336 Pat

'New settlement'. This is one of the commonest English place-names, and there are more than a dozen examples in Sa.

OTELEY (SJ 413348)

Otleg' 1279–80 *RentSur* (p), *Otleye* 1322 Pat (p), c.1300 *SBL 3586*, 1379 *SBL 4413* (p), *Otley* 1577 Saxton

Otale 1279–80 *RentSur*, *Othale* 1309 Eyton, 1328 HAC, *Otehall'* 1483–4 *SRO Bridgewater 212/box 72*

Ottleye 1371 *SBL 4412* (p), *Ottley* 1695 *SBL 5889*

Oteley 1380 Fine (p), 1427 *SBL 3608*
Oateley 1672 HTR, *Oatley* 1695 Morden

The second element is probably **lēah** in spite of the spellings which suggest a compound with **halh**. The name appears to have been interpreted as 'oat clearing', and this is probably correct. However, **āte** is not a common place-name element, and some forms suggest the personal name **Otta*.

SPUNHILL (SJ 413334)
Spenhull' 1255–6 *Ass*
Sponhul m.13th HAC (p)
Spone Hill 1602 Peake
Spoonell 1672 HTR
Spunhill 1833 OS
Spoonhill 1839 *TA*

Spunhill is a compound of **spōn** 'wood shaving' and **hyll**. ON **spánn**, which is cognate with **spōn**, means 'wooden shingle-tile', and this has been suggested for the OE word when used as a place-name element. Spoonley, Part **1** 275–6, is a compound with **lēah**, and this can be interpreted as a woodland name referring to a product, but this is not so clearly appropriate to a compound with **hyll**. A comparable formation with **dūn** is, however, found in Spondon PN Db 605.

Spondon Db was *Spoondon* in 17th- and 18th-cent. references, so the shortening of the vowel was late, as appears to be the case in Spunhill.

BIRCHES. *TAMap* shows a small enclosure here marked *Wood and Plantations*, one of several in this township.

BLAKE MERE, *Blakemere* 1309 Eyton, *Blackmere* 1602 Peake, *Black Mere* 1833 OS. 'Dark lake', contrasting with nearby White Mere in Colemere township. There is another Blake Mere in Whitchurch.

BURNS WD, 1833 OS, 1839 *TA*.

CATHAY'S MOSS.

CRIMPS FM, *The Crimps* 1755 PR(L) 19, 1833 OS, 1839 *TA*. In addition to the farm, *TAMap* shows large fields called *Little*, *Long* and *Far Crimps*. For *crimp* EDD gives the meaning 'a little bit, a crumb'. This word is likely to be one of a group which are related to OE *cruma*, ModE *crumb*. In PN Ch **2** 171 Dodgson gives a list of ns. in Ch which he derives from an OE **cryme* 'small piece of land'. A number of the Ch ns. have forms with *-b-*, such as *Crymbe*. None has *-p-*, but the evidence of the dialect word *crimp* supports such a variant. The assumption that Crimps derives from one of the 'crumb' words raises a problem analogous to that discussed under Criftins in Dudleston *supra*, of why such a term should be appropriate to a farm.

DEER PK, *Oatley Parke* 1700 Gough, 1839 *TA*, *Oteley Park* 1833 OS.

DOVE POOL, *Doves Pool* 1839 *TA*.

GEORGE'S WD, *George Wood* 1833 OS.

HAMPTON MOSS, *Moss* 1839 *TA,* by Welshampton.

ELLESMERE LO, *Lodge* 1839 *TA*, on the Park boundary, by the Ellesmere road.

KETTLE MERE, 1833 OS, 1839 *TA*, *Chetelmere* 1309 Eyton, *Chettle Mere* 1602 Peake. OE **cetel** 'kettle' is sometimes a valley-term in place-names, but when used in water-names, as here and in Kettlewell WRY, it probably refers to bubbling or swirling water. The lake is a small one, near Blake Mere.

LEA WD, *Old Wood* 1839 *TA*, cf. *Le Leefelde* in f.ns. *infra*.

MYSYCH, *Little Mae Such* 1839 *TA*: the *TA* field is by a small stream, and *Such* is probably from **sīc**.

NEWTON LO, on the Park boundary, by Newton.

NEWTON MERE, 1833 OS, 1839 *TA*.

PADDOCK WD, 1839 *TA*.

THE RAN, a strip of wood by Blake Mere, possibly **rand** 'shore'.

Field-Names

Forms in (a) are 1839 *TA*. Earlier forms are HAC except where otherwise stated.

(a) Bean Bank; Barclam's Ground; Big Fd, Near, Further; Big Mdw; Boathouse Fd (by Newton Mere); Brick Fd, Far, Middle, Near, Brickkiln Fd, Further ~ ~; Brickkiln Fd (2, not near preceding); Brimswood Fd, Mdw; Broomfield, Big and Long ~; Callumdick; Cally's Yd; Cherry Croft; Clover Fd, Little, Long; Copy Bank; Crabtree Fd (2); Crooked Croft (irregularly shaped); Cuckoo Croft; Cureton's Fd; Far Fd; Field below the Keeper's; Foxglove Fd; Gighole Fd (*v*. Dudleston f.ns. *supra*); Gravelhole Wd; Greens Bridge; Hampton's Wd, Wood Mdw (adjoining Welshampton); Higher Side of the Road; Hill, Far, Middle, Near; Horse Pasture Wd; Lawns, Far, Near (near Oteley Park); Lead Hill; Leek's Mdw; Lee Moss (*Le Leemos*, *Le Parva Lemos*, one of the open fields of Newton was *Le Leefelde*, *infra*); Limekiln Fd, Limekilns, Offices belonging to Limekilns (adjoining, by Cole Mere); Lowermost Mdw; Low Hill (possibly **hlāw** 'tumulus', the field has a spot height at approx. GR 417358); Mere Fd, Mdw (by Ellesmere Mere); Mere Fd, New ~ ~ (by Newton Mere); Moat Mdw (on N. boundary); Moss Fd; Mur Fd; Newfoundland (on E. township boundary); New Lsw (2); Orchard Mdw; Paddock Mdw, Wd; Park Fd (by Oteley Park); Patch(es) (enclosures in Newton); The Pearl (*v*. Part **3** 130, where evidence is presented for the meaning 'spring' in Sa and St); Pickin; Pole Croft; The Rough; Sheep Pasture; Shutt Lsw (2, meaning uncertain, *v.* Part **4** 113); Spoonhill Lsw; Square Fd; Stackyard Mdw (2); Stocks Wd (adjoining Stocks in adjacent township); Townsend (3, on outskirts of Newton); Two Butts (a small strip near Newton hamlet, perhaps a remnant of Newton's Middle Field, *infra*); White Mdw; Windmill Fd (3); Yard(s), Clover and Higher Yd (in Newton); Yewtree Fd, Far, Near.

(b) All the HAC names are in Newton. In the 1326 and 1328 documents the names are listed under *Le Leefelde*, *Le Middelfelde* and "field towards Lineal". These must have been small open fields. The lists have been amalgamated for presentation here. The translation 'strip' is used for *land* because the names refer to component parts of open fields. A property called *Wyn Kenescroft* is said to abut on Oteley field, which shows that the field-system in HAC pertained only to Newton, not to the whole township.

Berganesgrene 1326 (*v.* **grēne**[2] 'grassy space'); *Le Brodeforlonge* 1328 ('broad furlong'); *Le Brodelonde* 1328 ('broad open-field strip'); *Le Calewe*, *Le Calwewey* 1328 (*v.* **calu** 'bare hill', **weg**); *Cariare Crofte* 1539–40 *RentSur*; *Cathulleslonde* 1326, *Le Cathull* 1328 ('cat hill'); *Le Coumbes* 1326, *Le Combes* 1328 (the plural of **cumb** 'short valley'); *Le Croslonde* 1326, 8 ('open-field strip lying athwart'); *Le Dalelonde* 1328 (*dale* perhaps in the sense 'hollow' noted in Coton, Part **4** 65); *Dylemos* 1328 (*v.* **mos**, first el. the plant-name **dile**); *Le Ellenelonde* 1328 ('elder-tree strip', *v.* **elle(r)n**); *Elotonhull* 1326; *Le Guldenelonde* 1326 ('golden strip'); *Hamptonestroys* 1328 (Welshampton adjoins, the second el. might be 'trees'); *Hamptoneswey* 1326; *Heslonde* 1326, *Le Hesellonde Magna* 1328 ('hazel-tree strip'); *Le Holtepoll'* 1328; *Le Leefelde* 1326, 8 (Lea Wd *supra* may preserve part of this open-field name, as may Lee Moss in (a): Lee may have one of the later senses of **lēah**, such as 'pasture, meadow'); *Le Longeforlonge* 1326; *Le Longelonde* 1326; *Le Longelonde* 1328 (in a different field from preceding); (*Le*) *Longemore* 1326, 8; *Le Middelfelde* 1326, 8; *Moderleslond* 1326; *Modlas* 1328; *Le Oldehelde* 1328 ('old slope', *v.* **helde**); *Ovenaldestre* (second el. probably 'tree', first el. obscure); *Le Raytrowe* 1328 (second el. 'tree'); *Rowelonde* 1328, *Le Rowlonde* c.1330 ('rough strip'); *Schornhull* 1328 (*v.* **hyll**, first el. **scoren**, 'cut off' or 'precipitous'); *Slangbury* c.1330; (*Le*) *Wetemos* 1326, 8 ('wet bog'); *Le Withinepoll'* 1328, c.1330 ('willow pool', *v.* **wīðign**, **pōl**); *Wudelonde* 1328 ('wood strip'); *Wothull* 1326; *Wyn Kenescroft* 1316 (said to be "a piece of land in Newton village"); *Wyteforlonge* 1326, *Whiteforlonge* 1328.

16. RIDGES

HIGHER RIDGE (SJ 359336), LOWER RIDGE (SJ 341330)

Rugge 1279–8 *RentSur*, c.1300 *SBL 3586* (p), *Rugg* 1309 Eyton, *Rudge* 1770 PR(StA) 2

Lower Ridge 1603 PR(StA) 2, *Ridge* 1604 ib, *Higher Ridge* 1627 ib, *Ridge & Ridge* 1672 HTR, *Lower Ridge*, *High Ridge* 1839 *TA*

'Ridge', *v.* **hrycg**. Higher Ridge is on a spur of raised ground. The modern plural refers to the two settlements.

GANNOW HILL (SJ 357330), *Geannok* 1255–6 *Ass* (p). It seems clear from the context that Ric. *de Geannok* came from this place. The case concerns pasture rights in Hordley on land bordering the manor of Ellesmere, and another person involved is from Tetchill.

The occurrence of an early form *Geannok* corresponding to modern Gannow is relevant to discussion of two unexplained terms which are well evidenced and widely distributed in minor place-names.

ME **gannok** is found in Ca (3), Hrt (3), L (2), Mx, Nf and YWR. ME **gannow** has been noted in Db, Gl, He, La, Wa, Wo (2). These distributions could be regarded as complementary between eastern and western counties.

As regards dates of recording, there is a 1287 reference for Gannock in Sandon Hrt, and some other Gannocks have 14th- and 15th-century forms. The Sa 1255–6 reference appears to be the earliest so far noted. For **gannow** the earliest form available is *Gannon* (?*recte Gannou*), c.1225, from a surname which can be linked with Gannah Fm He, HePN 104. Gannow in Bromsgrove Wo has a form from 1330.

The most revealing context for a **gannok** name comes from the 14th-century records of Norwich Cathedral Priory, where there are several references to a pig-keeper at *Le Gannok* in King's Lynn, and the editor comments that this was "evidently a farm" (H. W. Saunders, *An Introduction to the Obedientiary and Manor Rolls ofNorwich Cathedral Priory*, Norwich 1930, p. 100, n. 1). Other instances of both terms are sometimes field-names, but a significant number refer to dwelling-sites. The *gannok* instances discussed in PN Ca 326 are field-names, as is the single instance noted PN WRY **7** 191; but two of the three instances in Hrt (PN Hrt 164) are dwelling-sites, as, probably, is Ganwick Corner PN Mx 77. The status of the Db instance of **gannow** cannot be ascertained from the discussion in PN Db **2** 274, nor can that of Gannow in Whalley La from PNLa 33. *Gannow*(*e*) PN Gl **1** 227 is stated in 1628 to be a *sheepcote*. Gannaway Gate PN Wa 206–7, in Claverdon, refers to some houses at a crossroads. The two instances of Gannow in Wo are both farm-names (PN Wo 327, 341).

There has been much discussion of the meaning of **gannok** and of its relationship, or lack of it, to **gannow**. The Sa instance appears to be the only one noted in which the two terms are associated. Since it is not likely that **gannok** would develop into **gannow**, this relationship may indicate that the terms could interchange. However, with only a 13th-cent. and a modern form, the history of the Sa name cannot be firmly established.

The most recent discussion of **gannow** is by David Horovitz and Richard Coates, 'Gnosall and the Middle English Word *genow*' in *Celtic Voices, English Places*, R. Coates and A. Breeze, 2000, pp. 184–92. These authors discount the possibility of identity between **gannow** and **gannok**, and eliminate the Sa Gannow Hill from their analysis, implying that the 1255–6 form shows it more likely to be from **gannok**. They present a case for **gannow** being an English borrowing of the Welsh word *genou*, 'mouth', and have assembled topographical evidence for a meaning 'mouth of a valley', which they consider suitable for the first element of Gnosall St and for the La, Wo, He, Wa and Db names derived from **gannow**.

The meaning of **gannok** is not addressed in the Coates and Horovitz article. The three main suggestions which have been put forward are:

1. a compound of **gamen** 'sport' with **āc** 'oak', denoting a tree which was a marker for sporting activities (PN Hrt 164);
2. a transfer from Wales of *Gannoc*, which is a Latinisation of the name of the fortress of Deganwy (*Review of English Studies* 16, 1942);
3. a word meaning 'shelter', conjectured on the basis of the recorded ME *ganneker* 'alehouse keeper' (EPN).

The third suggestion is perhaps the one best suited to both terms as used in place-names. There is no consistent association with any type of topographical feature, or with fortified sites.

For the moment, both terms can be considered to lack definitive explanation. The Coates and Horovitz suggestion of an English derivative of Welsh *genou* 'mouth' is plausible for Gnosall St, but the assumption that it also lies behind the **gannow** names ignores the probability that the two ME terms are connected. It seems unlikely that these two similar minor names have distinct origins, and *genou* will not do for **gannok**.

Gannow Hill is situated in a sharply pointed projection of the E. boundary of Ellesmere parish. The group of buildings to which the name is given on the 1900 6" and 1961 1" maps is not there on 1833 OS or *TAMap*, so the name would seem to have been that of a piece of ground. The name does not appear in the *TA* for Ridges or for the adjacent area of Whittington parish.

A field-name in Condover, Part **2** 108–9, may be another instance of **gannow**, but the forms are not conclusive.

THE BRYN, *Brynns* 1839 *TA*: Welsh *bryn* 'hill, rise'.

RIDGE COTTAGE.

The 1900 6" map shows canal bridges called Paddock Bridge no. 1, no. 2, Broom's Bridge and Pollett's Bridge.

Field-Names

Forms in (a) are 1839 *TA*. Early forms dated 1696, 1697 are *SBL 6158, 6145(6)*.

(a) Arr y coed, Far ~ ~ ~ (perhaps Welsh *argoed* 'edge of woodland'); Balvers Fd; Banky Fd; Big Fd; Brickkiln Fd; Broomy Fd; Brynn Gwynn ('white slope'); Brynnyrace Fd; Bryn y yarnan (perhaps *Bryn a Wernon* 1697); Butchers Mdw; Cae Boody; Cae Dowells, Big, Little, Middle; Cae Marle ('marl field'); Cae Mawith; Cae Porth (in High Ridge hamlet, probably *porth* 'door'); Cae Sennye; Cae Vin y maes; Calves Croft; Cannall Fd, Nearmost, Middlemost, Farmost (not adjacent to the canal, Welsh *canol* 'middle', *v.* Six Butts *infra*); Cannalls (not adjoining Cannal Fd or near the canal); Croft (there is a line of Crofts on the boundary with Hardwick township); Farthings (*Maes y Forthing* 1697, **feorðing** 'quarter'); Field before the House (2); Field behind the House; Floating Mdw; Garden Fd; Golphins; Henliss; Holly Green, Big, Little; Horse Pasture; Indy; Limekiln Mdw; Long Fd; Lower Ridge Fd (not near either Lower or High Ridge); Meadow (*freq*, qualifiers include Big, Little, Square, Cottage, Barn, Canal); Morris Mdw; Newin; Old House Fd; Ox Pasture, Far ~ ~; Pea Fd; Perthy Fd (by Perthy in Hardwick township); Pistol (Welsh *pistyll* 'spring'); Price's Mdw; Romans Croft; Rye Fd; Sandhole Fd; Six Butts (adjoining the 3 Cannall Fds, there may have been a small open field here); Square Fd; Stang; Tailor's Croft; Tommy Hall, Little ~ ~; Turnpike Fd (by Oswestry/Ellesmere road); Well Fd; Well Mdw; Wived, Big, Little, Long; Yewtree Fd.

(b) *The Backside* 1696, *Cae Gwenith* 1696 ('Gwynedd's field'); *Ca Newidd* 1697 ('new field'); *Gwern y groes* 1697 ('marsh of the cross', perhaps referring to a crossroads); *Gwier glodd heilin* 1697 ('Heilyn's hayfield'); *The Hempyard* 1696.

17. STOCKS AND COPTIVINEY

COPTIVINEY (SJ 408369). The only early forms available are *Coptivena* 1521–2, 23–4 *SRO Bridgewater/box 92*, *Captiveny* 1672 HTR. The modern spelling occurs 1833 OS, 1839 *TA*. The name is entirely mysterious. R. Morgan comments "probably not Welsh".

STOCKS, LOWER (SJ 419370), HIGHER (SJ 427366)
Stockes 1279–80 *RentSur* (p), *Stokes* 1309 Eyton, *Le Stocks* 1370 ib, *Stox* 1672 HTR

'Tree-stumps', *v.* **stocc**. Higher Stocks is The Stocks on 1961 1" map.

THE JONALLS: this is a wood which is shown but not named on *TAMap*.

Field-Names

Forms in (a) are 1839 *TA*.

(a) Barn Fd; Big Mdw (very big, Little Mdw adjoins); Birchin Croft; Birchin Fd (not near preceding: ***bircen** 'growing with birch trees'); Black House Croft; Boggy Croft; Brickkiln Fd; Broomy Fd; Broomy Lsw (not near preceding); Bryn Ruston (Little Ruston adjoins); Cae Cooper; Cae Werley; Calves Croft; Claypit Mdw; The Copy, Copy Mdw ('coppice'); Crabtree Fd, ~ Croft; Croft(s) (a few small enclosures); Cross Flg (not near a crossroads); Dockyard Fd; Ellesmere Fd, Big, Little (on boundary with E. township); Far Flg (narrow field adjoining Stocks); Felly; Fishpond Mdw; Foxhole Fd; Glade Fd; Greenyard; Heath Fd, Far, Near; High Ashes; Lower Mdw; Maes Crigh (possibly Welsh *crych* 'crumpled'); Milking Bank (adjoining buildings at Coptiviney); Mill Fd (adjoins Mill Wd in Hampton Wood); Moor (3 fields along stream on E. boundary); Old House Fd; Old Oat Stubble; Pantowna, Hollow, Round (first el. Welsh *pant* 'hollow', there is an indentation in the 300' contour here); Park Fd, Higher, Lower (adjoining Old House Fd); Parsley Bank; Pinfold Fd; Rogers Mdw; Sandyhole Fd; Slang (between a road and a stream); Swine Croft; Washpit Fd; Well Mdw (2).

18. TETCHILL (SJ 390327)

Tetneshull, *Tetleshull* 1255–6 *Ass* (p), *Tetneshul* 1278–9 *RentSur*, *-hulle* 1309 Eyton, *Tetnushall* 1392–3 *SRO Bridgewater 212/box 72*, *Tetteneshull'* 1483–4 *ib*

Teteshull' 1255–6 *Ass*

Tetushull' 1427 *SBL 4028*

Tetshull 1549 Pat

Tateshull 1549 Pat

Tech Hill 1577 Saxton, *Tettishill alias Techil* 1607 Peake, *Techell* 1672 HTR, *Tetchel* 1700 PR(L) 29, *Tetchil* 1772 PR(StA) 2, *Tetch Hill* 1791 ib

Tetsill in Neen Sollers, a DB manor for which forms are set out in Part **1**, has a similar run of spellings to Tetchill. In Part **1** the etymology '*Tǣtel's hill' was offered for Tetsill, the *Tetnes* forms being explained as due to Norman French confusion of *-l-* and *-n-*. The same etymology is formally applicable to Tetchill. **Tǣtel*, which would be a variant of the recorded *Tātel*, is considered to occur in a number of other place-names, including Tetsworth PN O 143–4 and Tatton PN Wo 173–4. CDEPN, however, prefers a personal name **Tetīn* for the two Sa names.

There is some awkwardness in the assumption that an individual named **Tǣtel* (or **Tetīn*) was twice associated with a feature called **hyll** in the county of Shropshire. Comparable problems are presented by the two names Estell in Minsterley and Tedstill in Chetton, which both appear to mean 'Tydi's stile', and Edgebold in Meole Brace and Edgebolton in Shawbury, which both appear to mean 'Ecgbald's village'. Estell and Tetsill are discussed in Part **2** 24, and Edgebold and Edgebolton in Part **1** 118, Part **4** 148.

The evidence for these sets of names can only be presented: no explanation of the phenomenon is available.

Tetchill is surrounded by low hills. One of the references in CDEPN — Studies 1936. 12 — is erroneous.

BROOM. This is a DB manor for which forms are set out in Part **1**. It is one of three Sa settlements with this name.

THE BROW, 1837 OS, also *Brow Bank.*

BROW WD, *Windmill Plantation* 1839 *TA.*

BRYN-ALLT. On *TAMap* the farm is called *Tab yn gwynt.* The *TA* f.n. *Brinnulth* may lie behind the modern name. There is a field called *Brinnulth* adjoining the farm, and there are other fields called (*The*) *Brinnulth* scattered over an area extending ½ mile to the east. Brennulth in Northwood f.ns. *supra* appears to be the same compound of *bryn* and *allt*, both Welsh hill-terms.

BUILDING FM, *New Farm* 1837 OS, *The Buildings* 1839 *TA.*

CAENUMBAS.

COACHMAN'S BRIDGE, 1897 Peake.

COPPICE HO, adjoining Wood Fm: *TAMap* shows *Copy Leasow* and *Meadow.*

ONSTON, 1839 *TA*, cf. Winston *infra.*

SALTER'S ROUGH, *Plantation* 1839 *TA.*

SHERWOOD'S ROUGH, *Sherwood Piece* and *Rough* 1839 *TA.*

SPRINGS BROOK.

TETCHILL MOOR, *Techill More* 1602 Peake, (*Techel &*) *ye Moore* 1672 HTR, *Techill Moor* 1721 PR(L) 7, *Tetch hill Moor* 1833 OS. This is a large area of drained and enclosed wetland.

WINSTON, 1839 *TA.* Winston and Onston do not appear on 1833 OS, and no early forms have been found for them.

WOOD FM, 1839 *TA*, *The Wood* 1837 OS.

Field-Names

Forms in (a) are 1839 *TA* except where otherwise stated. Earlier forms are *SRO Bridgewater 212/box 72, 92.*

(a) Abb y Salt; Acre (in T. Moor); Barrow's Pce (in T. Moor); Basin Mdw (by canal); Big Fd; Big Frith ('scrubland', *v.* **fyrhð**); Big Mdw (several); Big Roots (in T. Moor); Birches Fd; Bradley, ~ Mdw, Little and Richards Bradley (a group of fields in S.W. corner of township); Bridge Fd (by canal bridge); Brincoe, Far, Big, Little and Near ~ (a group of fields on W. boundary of township); Broad Mdw; Brown Moss (in T. Moor); Brynn Bedoe ('birch-tree hill', Welsh *bedw*); Burnt Patches (in T. Moor); Cae Bouts; Cae Hughes; Cae miah; Caenynies; Caet y nel Wd (*sic*, by Building Fm); Canal Fd (by canal); Carey Tulth (perhaps *recte* Cae'r Twll, 'hole field'); Claypit, ~ Lsw, Big and Little Claypit (this is the n. of a house and croft, as well as fields: 1837 OS names a small building here *Clipet*); Common Moors (on S.W. boundary, along canal); Cote Lsw (no building); Cow Pasture (in T. Moor); Criftons, ~ Mdw (*v.* Criftins in Dudleston *supra*); Croft (fields surrounding Broom are Broomy, Hares, Long and Limekiln Croft, enclosures by Brynn-allt are Garden and Top Croft, Tetchill village consists mainly of very small Crofts with larger fields called Jones and Townfield Croft on the western outskirts); Dodnell, Far, Near; Dodness; The Field (small enclosure); Fold House, Far, Near, ~ ~ Mdw; Four Day Math (in T. Moor); Gamms (Gamm is a Welsh surname, but this f.n. could be the adj. *cam* 'crooked': one edge is jagged); Grass Ford; Gwynnmiebre; Hamstill (adjoins Homestead); Harding's Yd; Hempyard (in Tetchill); Hill Lsw; Holliers, Far, Near (adjoining Holliness); Holliness, Higher, Lower; Homestead, Far and Near ~ (no building); Hordley Bridge, ~ ~ Fd, Mdw, Hordley Fd (Hordley parish adjoins); Kandwadding, Lower ~; Kitchpump; Kurst; Lawns (by Building Fm); Little Fd; Little Mdw; Llan y Werm (perhaps Glan y wern 'edge of the alder marsh'); Long Mdw; Lower Lsw; Lower Mdw; Manbridge, Middle ~ (4 fields by Claypit); The Meadow; Meadow under the Wood; Mersey Mdw, Big, Little, Far; Milliners Fd; New Lsw (2); New Mdw; Nursery Croft; Pearl Fd (S.W. of Winston), Pearl Mdw, Far, Middle, Near, ~ Lsw (5 fields N.W. of Onston: Pearl, from ME *pirle*, means 'spring' in Sa and St, *v.* Part **2** 130); Pringle (FN 11 lists this as a variant of *pingle* 'small plot'); Quakin Moor ('mountain ash', ME **quiken**); Quaking Broom (a short distance from Broom); Road Pce; Robber Hill; Rowley, ~ Mdw; Sandy Hole; Seven Acres (in T. Moor); Sidnall, Big, Little, ~ Bank, Mdw (4 fields on N. boundary); Slade (Sa dialect, field with a wet patch, in Tetchill Moor); Slang; Snelsall, ~ Fd and Mdw; Square Mdw; Stackyard Fd; Sweetmuck; Top Fd; Town Fd (2, either side of Tetchill village); Tynn y brynn ('hill house'); Rosy Vall, Rossy Vall Mdw and Bottoms (*v.* Vall *infra*, Ros(s)y may be from Welsh *rhos*, here 'marsh'); The Vall, Big ~, ~ Lsw, Vall Hill, Near and Side Vall Hill Fd (a group of fields N.W. of Winston, 1837 OS has Val Hill here: Vall is probably 'place where trees were felled', *v.* PN Ch **5.1** 173 *s.v.* *(**ge**)**fall**); Well Lsw; Wet Mdw Croft; White Mill, Near ~ ~ (large fields on N.E. boundary); The White Moor (*Whytemore* 1521–2); Widow's Fd.

Tetchill Moor is divided into small, rectangular fields on *TAMap*. Some of the f.ns. are listed *supra*. Those with ~ Bank, ~ Croft, ~ Meadow, ~ Moor, ~ Piece are summarised here.

Bank ns. in Tetchill Moor: Daisy, Far, Jack's, Near, Wall.

Croft ns. in Tetchill Moor: Barn, Hungry, Orchard, Potato.

Meadow ns. in Tetchill Moor: Alder, Bakehouse, Big, Broad, Brook, Cook's, Ellis, Far, Folly, Jack's, Lady, Little, Long, Moss, Near, Nook, Orchard, Peel's, Plat, Plate (not near preceding, both may refer to footbridges), Rushy, Sedgey, Sherwood, Small Man's, Spencer's, Spring, Tetchill Moor, Withy Tree.

Moor ns. in Tetchill Moor: Clark's, Davies, Edwards, Far, Middle, Near, Rushy.
Piece ns. in Tetchill Moor: Barrows (6 fields), Susan's.
(b) *Baylesmede* 1521–2; *Grenemedewe* 1392–3.

19. TRENCH

THE TRENCH (SJ 398376). Trench appears on 1833 OS and 1839 *TAMap*, but no earlier references have been found. In spite of this, the name must be Middle English. OFr, ME **trenche** had the specialised sense of a woodland road with linear clearings on either side to provide greater security for travellers. There is another settlement called Trench in Oakengates, which is discussed in Part **3** 40. A reference is given there for the use of this term in Sa t.John.

The Trench and Trench Fm are beside the road which leads to Penley in the detached portion of Flintshire which adjoins Shropshire here. There is another farm called Trench, 1¼ miles N.W., in Flintshire, which lies on a road running parallel to the Ellesmere/Penley one. The area is well wooded on modern maps.

CAEGOODY. This name does not appear on the 1899 6" map, but the 2000 Explorer map (240) has Caegoody at SJ 387364 and Caegoody Lane. The lane, which runs from Elson to near Cross, is listed in Gazetteer. On *TAMap* the name is applied to a number of fields near the junction of the three townships of Ellesmere, Trench, and Elson and Greenhill. Elson has *Cae Goody Toll Bar*, where the lane joins the Chirk/Ellesmere road, and a field by the junction is *Long Cae Goody*. Trench has fields called *Big* and *Little Cae Goody*, W. of the buildings to which the name is applied on the Explorer map. Ellesmere has *Cae Goody Field*, a short distance E. of the other names.

This appears to be a Welsh field-name of the common type in which *cae* 'field' is qualified by a personal name or nickname. It is not clear why it should have multiple occurrences in this area where three townships meet. *Goody* is presumably the English term for an elderly woman.

BIRCH HILL, *Birchin Hill* 1839 *TA*, *v.* ***bircen**.

CROSS, CROSS FM, *The Cross* 1833 OS, 1839 *TA*, at the road fork on the S. boundary of the township. Cross frequently refers to road junctions in this county. Peake 1897 identifies this with *Ithiel's Cross* in 1343 bounds of Ellesmere.

GOBLINDALE FM, PLTN, *Goblin Dale* (a field) 1839 *TA*.

SANDYHILL, ~ COTTAGE, *Sandy Hill* 1839 *TA*.

TRENCH WD.
VALVE HO.

Field-Names

Forms in (a) are 1839 *TA*. Those in (b) are 1586 *SRO 3322/1*.

(a) Bank; Banky Fd; Barclay's Croft; Barn Fd; Barn Yd; Big Fd (2); Big Hollins Fd; Bog Mdw; Brickkiln Croft; Brickkiln Fd; Bridge Fd; Cabin Fd, Mdw; Cae Grig ('heather'); Cae Jenkins, Far ~ ~; Cae merd well; Cae Mine; Cae Rally, Far, Near; Cae Roughin; Calf Gate Fd; Carthouse Fd (2); Carthouse Mdw; Cote Mdw; Cottage Fd; Croft (a few small enclosures); Crooked Croft (an irregularly shaped field); Dunsyall; Eastwick Mdw (adjoins Eastwick township); Elson Fd, Big, Little (adjoining Elson township); Far Fd (3); Far Mdw; Field by the House; Flashy Mdw; Five Cornered Fd (irregularly shaped); Footroad Fd (2, both beside roads); Four Acre Fd; Goat Lsw; Goer; Graves Pce; Green Fd; Half Corket; Hill Fd, Mdw, Far and Near Hill; Horse Pasture; Horses Fd; Humphreys Fd; Joys Mdw; Lady Mdw; Lane Fd; Lapwings Lsw (*v*. The Lapwing in Boreatton *supra*); Little Fd; Little Mdw; Long Fd (several); Long Mdw (several); Long Slang; Low Mdw; Luke's Mdw; Maes Trench, ~ ~ Mdw; Meadow, Big, Little; Old Man's Pce; Outlet (3, by The Cross, Trench Fm and The Trench, pasture adjoining winter cattle sheds); Payne's Fd; Pear Yd, Far, Near; Pit Fd; Pritchard Mdw; Road Fd; Rough, Big, Little; Rough Mdw; Round Fd (one curved side); Sandy Sadler's Mdw; Sandpits; Sandy Fd, Big, Sandyhole Fd (by Sandy Hill); Sawpit Fd; Sawyer's Fd; Shone's Mdw; Shutt Fd (2, *v*. Part **4** 113); Slades Croft; Square Pce; Stockings (*v*. ***stoccing**); Tithebarn Fd; Trotting Man Fd (adjoins Trotting Mare P.H. in Overton Fli); Well Mdw; Wood Fd; Woodfield.

On *TAMap* there are small buildings with crofts running parallel to the road along the road from Ellesmere to Overton Fli. These are flanked on one side by fields called Back of Fleet's, Jones, Higleys and Lloyds, and one field called Face of Haynes.

(b) *Caye Hibbard*; *Coed Madoc* ('Madog's wood'); *Maes Ellisdoun* ('Elson's field); *Pille Duon* ('black pools', Welsh *pyllau* and *duon*).

The Bridgewater documents in SRO contain a number of Ellesmere names which cannot be assigned to specific townships. These include: *Backockesfeld* 1483–4; *Battesmore* 1483–4; *Bettersych'* 1483–4 (*v*. **sīc**); *Le Blakheth'* 1483–4 ('black heath'); *Chamberleynbrugge alias Genetbrygge* 1483–4; *Dorysfeld* 1521–2; *Glynbyrche* 1483–4; *Hokebyesȝate* 1392–3 (*v*. **geat**); *Holbach'* 1392–3, *Holbych'broke* 1483–4 (*v*. **hol**[2], **bæce, brōc**); *Hollemor* 1392–3; *Honeydale* 1521–2, *Honydale* 1523–4 ('honey hollow', *v*. **hunig**, **dæl**); *Keyglasse* 1521–2 (Welsh 'green field'); *Kylthmere* 1483–4; *Mondcroftes* 1521–2, *Monecroftes* 1523–4; *Newmere* 1521–2; *Okenmore* 1483–4 ('marsh with oak trees'); *Soliesfeld* 1392–3; *Strifwod* (a mill) 1392–3 ('disputed wood'); *Watton'heye* 1392–3; *Wentyshey* 1483–4; *Wetteley'* 1392–3 (associated with 'old Haughton'); *Wildhurst* 1392–3 (*v*. **wilde**, **hyrst**); *Wrygh'brugge* 1483–4.

Fitz

The parish-name, which means 'Fitt's spur of land', is discussed in Part **1**.

GRAFTON (SJ 433190)

Grafton 1221–2 *Ass et freq*
Grafton' 1306–7 *Ass*
Graffeton' 1539–40 *RentSur*

The meaning is probably 'settlement with an area of coppiced woodland'. Arguments in favour of this interpretation of OE **grāfa**, (ModE *grove*) and the variant **grǣfe** are presented in LPN pp. 226 ff.

Grafton is a widespread recurrent **-tūn** name.

MYTTON (SJ 453170)

Mytton is a DB manor and accordingly discussed in Part **1**. The name means 'river-junction settlement', referring to the confluence of R. Perry with R. Severn.

ALBION HAYES, 1833 OS, *Alburnehey* 1616 PR(L) 4, *The Albon Heys* 1646 ib, *The Alborne Heyes* 1684 ib, *The Albarnhey Farm* 1722 ib, *The Albion Hayes* 1733 *et seq* ib, *Alburn Hayes* 1784, 9 ib. Final el. ME *hay* 'enclosure'. The origin of *Alburne-*, *Alborne-*, which has been rationalised to Albion, is obscure. A name in **burna** 'clear stream' is improbable as that word is rare in Sa and no stream is shown here on maps.

BANK HO, 1833 OS, *Banky Field* adjoins on *TAMap*, as do other Bank ~ ns. in Montford *infra*.

BARN PIECE COVERT, a small wood in a large field which was called *Barn Field* 1838 *TA*.

BLACK COPPICE.

BRICKKILN PLTN, *Plantation Pool* 1838 *TA*.

BYLET, an island in the Severn.

COPPY BANK FM, *Coppice Bank* 1838 *TA*, 1833 OS has *Bank Fm* and *Fern Bank* here.

FITZ COPPICE, 1833 OS.

FITZ MANOR, MANOR FM, *The Mannor House* 1722 PR(L) 4.

FITZ MILL, 1833 OS, *Mill* 1838 *TA*.

THE GORSE.

GRAFTON HO, LODGE, both shown but not named on *TAMap*. *The Lodge* appears on 1833 OS.

MEADOW PLTN.

MEDLEY FM, shown but not named on *TAMap*.

MERRINGTON PLTN, *Plantation* 1838 *TA*.

MOCK HALL, 1833 OS, *Mock Hall Field* and *Meadow* 1838 *TA*. Probably an abbreviation of Mockbeggar Hall.

THE MOSS, *The Moss Plantation* 1833 OS.

MYTTON HALL, HO, MILL. The mill is shown on *TAMap* with *Mill Leasow*, *Meadow* and *Patch*; it is *Mitton Mill* 1785, 8 PR(L) 4.

NEW MEADOW PLTN, *New Meadow* 1838 *TA*.

PUNCH'S DRIVE, a wood.

THE ROOKERY.

THE ROUGH.

ROUND COPPICE, *Cutbury Coppice* 1838 *TA*.

WEIR MEADOW PLTN, *Weir Meadow Coppice* 1838 *TA*.

Field-Names

Forms in (a) are 1838 *TA*, except where otherwise stated. Early forms for which no source is given are GT.

(a) Adcott Fd (Adcot in Little Ness adjoins); Backhouse Croft (not near Bakehouse, but both are near Mytton); Backside (by Coppy Bank Fm); Bakehouse Croft; Banky Fd; Banky Lsw; Barley Croft; Barn Croft; Barn Yd (several); Boat Lands (by Severn); Brade Mdw; Brickkiln, Lower, Nether; Brickkiln Lsw; Brickkiln Pce; Broad Lsw (2); Broom Fd (a short distance E. of Broomfields in Montford); Bylet (island in Severn); Bylets (islands in Perry); Cabin Lsw (no building); Calves Croft (3, one adjoins Cow Pasture); Calves Yd; Cart House Fd; Chapel Fd (adjoins church); Claypits, Claypit Fd; Cockshutt Hill, East, West; Common Fd (small field in N.E. extension of parish, 2 fields called Field adjoin); Common Pce, Near, Middle, Farther, Common Fd, Further ~ ~, Common Lsw (10 fields in centre of parish); The Common Pce, Common Pces, Common Fd (on outskirts of Broomfields in Montford); Coppice (several); Coppice Lsw; Cote Fd (no building); Cow Pasture (2); Creek Flg, Little ~ ~ (3 furlong-shaped fields E. of Mytton); Criftin Mdw, Big Criftin; Criftin (not near preceding, *v.* Criftins in Dudleston *supra*: these are not small fields); Crinkham, Little (the adjoining field is Heath Close or Crankham: these are small, irregularly-shaped fields with sharp corners, and Crinkham, Crankham are probably related to the words discussed in NED *s.v. crank* sb.[1], sb.[2] and *crink* sb., with the meanings 'bend, twist': EDD records *crinkum-crankum* 'engineering or mechanical device', but that is probably not relevant here); Croft(s) (several); Ddol

Bank (apparently Welsh *dol* 'meadow', but this would be an isolated Welsh term in an area of English f.ns.); Drain Fd; Elm Fd; Far Yd; Ferny Flat; Field by the House; Fitz Fd, Near, Far, Fitz Pce, Great, Little (by Mytton); Fitz Fd (not near preceding); Five Days Math (Twelve Days' Math, which adjoins, is only slightly larger); Flash Fd (a *flash* is a shallow floodwater pool, FN 19); Flat Fd; Flood Mdw (by Severn); Footway Pce (footpath shown); Foxhole Doors; Garden Pce; Garden Yd; Gayley Bank; Gorsy Patch, Little; Gravelly Croft, Ham or Gravelly Flg; Green Lsw (2); The Grudy (an obscure n., the field is a strip along R. Severn); Hams, Big, Little, Higher, Lower (an area enclosed by R. Severn, this ancient sense of **hamm** survived in Sa dialect); Hargroves, Further and Upper ~ (*v.* Hengreave *infra*); Hedge Croft; Hemp Yd; Hengreave, ~ Mdw, Upper Hengraves (6 fields on N. boundary, *Hengreave* 1612, 82, 94: first el. probably **henn**, perhaps referring to water-hens as the fields are by R. Severn, second el. **grǣfe** 'coppice': an adjoining field is Hargroves); Higher Lsw; Hill Fd; Hovel Fd (no building); The Lawn (in Mytton park); Little Dicks; Little Moss (tiny enclosure on outskirts of Broomfields); Llyddiate Lsw (*v.* **hlid-geat** 'swing gate': the field adjoins Ddol Bank and the Ll- spelling may be another indication of Welsh influence); Long Croft (2); Long Lsw (3); Long Mdw (2); Long Slang (narrow strip); Lower Mdw; Maidenhead Lane (by R. Severn, perhaps transferred from Berks); Mannings Croft; Mare Fd, Further, Lower, Middle, Near (6 fields on N. boundary, *v.* **(ge)mǣre**); The Meadow (2); Middle Lsw; Mitton Fd and Mdw; Middle Pce; Moses Pce; New Lsw (2); New Pce; Nicholls Britch (**bryce** 'newly-broken-in land'); The Nook (tiny enclosure in the outskirts of Broomfields); Old House Yd (in Grafton); Old Orchard; Olive Bush Lsw (FN 49 cites 2 other Olive ns. in Sa, the reference is obscure); Onion's Lsw; Osiers; Paddock; Park Bank (a strip along R. Severn by Fitz Manor); Patch (several, small enclosures); Peartree Lsw; Perry Fd; Perry Mdw; Perry Mouth (where R. Perry joins Severn); Robin Hill's Fd; Rough Ground; Rough Mdw; Roundabouts (R. Severn on three sides); The Sands, Lower Sands; Sed or Sead Gear; Seven Lands (probably open-field strips); Shop Mdw (on outskirts of Grafton); Sitch Croft and Mdw (*v.* **sīc**); Springs, Near, Far (probably ME **spring** 'young plantation': earlier *Spring* ns. are *Spring Croft* 1682, ~ *Close* 1694, ~ *Coppy* 1712); Square Lsw; Square Mdw, Little; Stable Yd (2); Swan's Nest; Thistly Fd; Townsend (on outskirts of Grafton); Tyne Mdw (a derivative of ME **tining** 'enclosure'); Wall Lsw; Well Croft 1841 GT (1682, 94, 1712, *Wall Croft* 1612); Well Lsw (2); Well Mdw (2); Wheat Fd, Great, Little; Wheelwright's Shop (in Grafton); Wilmore, ~ Bank and Mdw; Withy Stiles (Upper ~ ~ is several fields away); Wood Fd, Little, Great, Middle, Near, Upper (adjoining Spring and Coppice ns. on N. boundary); Yard (a number of enclosures in the part of Broomfields which is in the S.W. corner of the parish: cf. *Yards* 1712, 1828, *The Yards* 1722 PR(L) 4); Yeld Fd, Farther, Near ('gentle slope', *v.* **helde**).

(b) *Grafton Croft* 1694; *Grafton Leasow* 1612; *The Heath Croft* 1722 PR(L) 4; *The Hengrians, croft called*, ib; *Parsons Croft* 1682, 94; *Pine Meadow* 1722 PR(L) 4; *Wood Leasow* 1612.

Hordley

The parish contains the two townships of Bagley and Hordley.

1. BAGLEY (SJ 405273)

Bageleia c.1090 SAC, *Bagel'* 1236 SAS 4/IV(FF), *Bageleye* l.14th SAC

Baggeleia 1209 P *et freq* with variant spellings *-ley*(*a*), *-leg'* to 1396 *SBL 3599*

Baggylecth 1271–2 *Ass* (p)

Bagleye 1291–2 *Ass*, c.1306 APW, *Bagligh* 1397 Pat, *Baglay* c.1550 SAS 1/VI, *Bagley* 1577 Saxton

The recurrent p.n. Bagley (Baguley in Ch) is usually translated 'badger wood', but it is not certain that this is the appropriate meaning for the Sa example. OE ***bagga** 'bag', which occurs frequently with non-habitative generics in place-names and charter boundaries, is taken to be a transferred use of 'bag' to denote a bag-shaped animal, and this is generally convincing. In the case of the Sa Bagley, however, **lēah** probably has its late OE sense of 'meadow, pasture', and badgers may not be appropriate to the marshy environment.

Discussions of the various senses of **lēah** (e.g. EPN, DEPN, CDEPN) agree that in the later Anglo-Saxon period the term lost its association with woodland and developed the meaning 'meadow, pasture', and this late sense seems appropriate to a number of -ley ns. in north Shropshire, particularly near Wem and in the marshy ground along the R. Perry where Bagley and Hordley are situated.

Bagley is on the eastern edge of Baggy Moor, through which the R. Perry flows for 2½ miles; and Baggy Moor, *infra*, may be an independent name with the same first element. It is possible that in these names ***bagga** is used as a descriptive term for the marsh. The oval-shaped wetland is divided into small portions by the drainage channels, and most of these have ~ Meadow ns. in *TA*. VEPN cites comparable instances where 'badger' is not appropriate. These include *Bag Lane* for a cul-de-sac, and a f.n. (*pastur' voc*) *le Bagge* in Gl.

BAGGY MOOR, *Baggemor'* 1343 *SBL 8387*, *Baggamore* 1612 *SBL 8480*, 1717 *SBL 9005*, *Bagamoor* 17th *SBL 6151*, *Bagamore* 1672 *SBL 8545*, *Baggymoore* 1683 *SBL 6146*, *Baggimore* 1685 *SBL 10258*, *Baggley Moor* PR(L) 7, *Bagamoor* 1777 *SBL 16874*, *Bagemore* 1780 PR(L) 7, *Baggymoor Meadow* 1788 *SBL 9864*. Possibly 'bag-shaped marsh', *v.* ***bagga**, **mōr** and the discussion of Bagley *supra*. The moor is partly in West Felton parish. *Baggy Moor* occurs as a *TA* f.n. in Lacon *infra*.

BAGLEY HALL.

BAGLEY MARSH, 1701, 6 PR(L) 7. This is a scattered settlement N. of Baggy Moor.

BROMLEY, 1689 PR(L) 7, 1833 OS. If an ancient name this will be another instance of **lēah** used for a settlement on the edge of marsh.

BROMLEY GREEN, 1736 PR(L) 7, *Bromley-green* 1727–8 ib.

FOX P.H.

HORDLEY GROVE.

THE OAKS, 1800 PR(L) 7, *Big and Little Oaks* 1849 *TA*.

THE RAKES, 1782, 7 PR(L) 7, *The Rakes Field* 1849 *TA*. ME **rake** 'narrow path'.

Field-Names

Forms in (a) are 1849 *TA*. Many of the ~ Meadow ns. and some of the Bank ns. belong to rectangular strips in the drained land of Baggy Moor.

(a) Abbots Fd, Mdw; Bagley Moor (small patch in Baggy Moor); Banky Fd, Sandy ~ ~; Barn Croft; Big Hinds; Big Mdw (2); Black Ground; Brickkiln Fd; Brick Mdw; Butchers Croft, Big and Little ~ ~; Chapel Fd (by Chapel in Bagley); Clough Banks (adjoins fields called Hough); Common, Bayleys, Far, Near, Middle (a group of small fields in Bagley Marsh); Cow Mdw at Bromley; Cow Mdw at Home; The Crabbs; Croft (there is a cluster of Croft fields in Bagley Marsh); David's Mdw; Duckley Fd (adjoins ~ Mdw in Hordley township); Far Fd, Mdw; Far Mdw; Ferny Bank; Field, Far, Near, Lower, Upper, Marsh, Moat, Big (these adjoin in the area between Bagley and Bagley Marsh); Furlongs Yd (adjoins Bagley); Garden Fd; Gorshy Bank; Gravel Hole Fd, Far, Near, ~ ~ Mdw; Griffiths Fd; Hazlehurst, Hazle Mdw, Far, Near; Hill Fd, Lower, Higher and Upper ~ ~ (adjoining Field ns. *supra*); Hollybush Mdw; Honey Croft, Near (a short distance from Honey Spot); Honey Spot (probably referring to sticky soil); Horse Croft, Far, Near, Little, Lower, Higher, Horse Croft Fd, Mdws (a group of fields by The Rakes); Hough, Big, Little, Haugh Mdw (*sic*); Intake; Kettles, ~ Mdw (*kettle* occurs in some plant-names); Lea Flg (near Bagley Marsh); Leatons Lsw; Left Hand Mdw (one of the small rectangular fields in Baggy Moor); Little Mdw; Little Mdw near Paddocks; Long Lsw (2); Long Lsws; Long Mdw; Marl Croft, Lower ~ ~; Marsh Fd (2, in Bagley Marsh); Meadow, Far and Near Mdw; Meadow, Big, Little; Middle Mdw (several); Moss Fd; Mowing

Mdw (2); New Mdw; Park Mdw (by Hordley Grove); Patch (tiny enclosure in Bagley Marsh); Peat Moor; Pedlars Mdw; Perry Mdw (several by R. Perry); Pit Mdw; Plantation Mdw; Pole Lsw, Mdw; Rushy Mdw; Slang (narrow strip); The Slang Mdw (narrowest of the Meadow strips along R. Perry); Small Patch; The Snabbs (in a projection of township boundary, but ***snæp** 'boggy land' is perhaps more likely than ***snabbe** 'projection'); Timothy Mdw, Little Timothy; Town Fd (a large field adjoining Bagley) Trevor Croft, Big, Little; Warrens Bank, Near, Further; Weavers Mdw; Whitcherley Mdw; Williams Croft, Mdw; Withy Mdw; The Yard, Big and Little Yd, Hemp Yd (in Bagley Marsh); (The) Yard, Towns Yd (in Bagley); Yewtree Fd.

2. HORDLEY (SJ 382308)

The name was discussed in Part **1**. It is a compound of **hord** 'hoard' and **lēah**, the first element perhaps referring to finds of Roman coins such as have occurred here in modern times. The second element was rendered as 'wood or clearing' in Part **1**, but it is more likely that here, as in Bagley, **lēah** has its late OE sense of 'meadow, pasture'.

CHURCH HO.

DANDYFORD, 1837 OS. This is the name of a house which is shown but not named on *TAMap*. There is no river-crossing.

THE GRANGE: the house is shown but not named on *TAMap*.

HAWK'S WD, *The Hawkes Wood* 1698, 9 *SBL 5777/8*, 1849 *TA*, *Hawkwood* 1752 *SBL 6253*. This is a small rectangular stand of trees.

HORDLEY BRIDGE, 1837 OS, a canal bridge.

HORDLEY COTTAGES.

HORDLEY HALL, 1707 PR(L) 7.

LOCKGATE BRIDGE, 1837 OS, a canal bridge.

LOCKMOOR COTTAGE, *Big and Little Lockmoor* 1847 *TA*, by Lockgate Bridge.

SPRINGS BROOK.

SYCAMORE HO, shown but not named on *TAMap*.

SYCAMORE TREE, 1837 OS.

WILDERNESS.

Field-Names

Forms in (a) are 1849 *TA* except where otherwise stated. Early forms dated c.1550 are SAS 1/VI, 1698, 9 are *SBL 5777/8*.

(a) Back House Croft; Bakehouse Croft; The Banks; Banks Mdw; Barn Field, Lower, Upper; Barnyard Fd (2); Bartley Hill (*Barkley Hill* 1698, *Berkley Hill* 1699, first el. possibly **berc** 'birch'); Berghill Mdw (2 non-adjacent fields on N.W.

boundary, cf. *Lower Berghill Moore* 1698); Big Fd (2); Big Garden; Big Mdw (2); Botany Bay (near N.W. boundary); Brickkiln Bank; Calfs Croft (*The Calfe Croft* 1698); Carthouse Croft and Fd (by Horse Mdw, *The Cart House Field* 1698); Clarks Mdw; Common Moor, Near, Middle, Further; Corner Mdw (triangular); Cote Lsw (no building); (The) Cote Mdw (2, no buildings); Culvert Mdw; Dodds Mdw; Duckley Mdw; Far Fd; Feggy Mdw (*feg* is coarse grass); Field in Front of House; Flooded Mdw; Four Acre Mdw (smaller than adjoining Six ~ ~); French Wheat Bank (*The French-wheat Banke* 1698, French wheat is buckwheat, *v*. PN Ch **5.1** 186); Garden Fd; Gorshy Bank, Big, Little (not near Gorshy Bank in Bagley); Gravel Hole Fd (cf. *The Gravel Pitt Field* 1598); Gunnery Fd ('rabbit-warren', *v*. **coninger**); Hawthorn Tree Fd; Heath Mdw; Hopyard Croft and Fd; Horse Croft, Mdw, Patch (*The Horse Meadow* 1698); Lees Pltn; Little Fd; Little Mdw (*The Little Meadow* 17th PR(L) 7); Long Croft; Long Lsw; Louseley Mdw; Maddocks Leys; Matthews Ley; The Meadow; Middle Meadow (2); Mill Fd, Hayes and Mdw (by Rednal Mill in West Felton, cf. *The Mill Heys* 1698); Moor, Further, Near (*Moor Piece*, *Little Moor* 1698, *The Moor Piece* 17th PR(L) 7); Moss Fd, Mdw, Near and Far Moss Fd (*The Moss* 1698); New Buildings Fd (*TAMap* shows a small building called Smithy Shop Hole); New Lsw; Old House Fd (no building); Ox Pasture, Higher, Upper, Middle 1845 GT (*The Oxe Pasture* 1698); The Paddock, Meadow in Paddock (*the little meadow by the paddocks* 1698); Parsons Mdw; Perry Mdw, Far, Near, Middle and Bottom ~ ~; Pike Mdw 1845 GT (*Pike Meadow*, *Pike Moore Meadow* 1612 GT, *The Pick Moors* 17th PR(L) 7, *Pick Moor* 1698 GT); Pikes Bank; Pole Mdw, Further ~ ~ (perhaps a pool in R. Perry); Rough Mdw (3 non-adjacent fields on N.W. boundary); Rough Mdw (not near preceding); Round Mdw (rectangular, but has Round Pltn, a small circle, on one side); Ryegrass Fd; St Mary's Fd (from church dedication); Sandhole Fd; Sheep Lsw; Shop Fd (no building); Six Acre Mdw; The Slang (long, narrow strip); Spring Coppice; Stable Croft; Ten Acre Fd; Ware Mdw (by R. Perry, *The Weir Meadow* 1698); Wet Ends, ~ ~ Mdw (*The Wet Ends and Woods* 1698); Wash Mdw; Will Croft; Winters Bank; Woodcock Fd; Woodcote Mdw 1845 GT; The Wood Lsw; Yew Tree Croft 1845 GT; Yewtree Fd.

(b) *Edy Pole* (*field called*) c.1550; *Frankton's Wood* 1687 PR(L) 7, *Franctonswood* 1704 ib, *Francton Common* 1706 ib (Welsh Frankton is in the adjoining parish of Whittington); *The Great Leasow*, *The Great Meadow* ib; *Griffiths Moore* ib; *The Great Hough*, *The two Houghs next the land*, *The Further Hough* 1698 (perhaps **halh** in one of its 'watery' senses: in a list of fields belonging to Hordley Hall, so not connected with Hough in Bagley, *supra*); *Jallincallin* 1698; *Knokyhurst*, *Knokemore*, *Hey by Knokyhurst* c.1550; *The Long Moore* 1698; *Warrener's Meadow* ib; *The Weaver's Meadow* ib.

Loppington

The parish-name was discussed in Part **1** and an etymology 'estate associated with Loppa' was proposed. Further discussion is offered under Loppington township *infra*.

There are three townships, Burlton, Loppington and Noneley.

1. BURLTON (SJ 458260)

Burcheltun 1194–7 HAC (p), *Burghelton'* 1221–2 *Ass*, *-ton* 1240 SAS 4/VI (FF), *Burghulton* 1284–5 FA, *Borughulton'* 1291–2 *Ass*

Bor(e)welton' 1255–6 *Ass et freq* with variant spellings *Burwelton*, *Borwolton'*, *Burwalton'* to 1327 SR (p)

Burleton 1255 RH, *-ton'* 1255–6 *Ass*, *Borelton'* 1291–2 *Ass*

Burleton' 1271–2 *Ass et freq* with variant spelling *-ton* to 1588 *SBL 3988*, *Borleton* 1334 SR, *-ton* 1397 InqMisc *Bourlton* 1785 PR(StA) 3

OE *burh-hyll-tūn*, 'settlement by a hill with a fort'. An air photograph has shown a multivallate enclosure at SJ 453263, W. of Burlton village (*ex inf.* E. Jenks), and this may be the **burh**.

ALLESLEY HO.

BROOK HO, 1833 OS, 1838 *TA*.

BURLTON GRANGE, 1833 OS and *TAMap* show *Burlton Mill* here.

BURLTON GROVE, 1838 *TA*.

BURLTON HALL, shown but not named on *TAMap*.

THE COPPY, 1833 OS: *Coppice Field* and *Meadow* adjoin the house on *TAMap*.

CROSS KEYS P.H.

THE FOREST.

MOOR HO. Cf. *Burlton Moor* 1682 GT2 and f.ns. *infra*.

OLD WD, *Burlton Wood* 1838 *TA*, cf. *boys de Burleton* 1344 *SBL 3621*.

PICKHILL, 1838 *TA*, *Pickell* 1833 OS.

LITTLE WACKLEY, WACKLEY BROOK, Wackley is in Petton *infra*.

YEW TREE HO: 1833 OS shows *Golden Heart*, probably a P.H., here. The house is shown but not named on *TAMap*.

Field-Names

Forms in (a) are 1838 *TA*. Early forms dated Hy 8 are *RentSur*.

(a) Archers Moor, Far, Middle and Near ~ ~; Artilla Fd, Mdw; Barn Yd, Higher, Lower; Beasts Bridge; Bells Fd, Lower, Upper; Big Fd (2); Big Lsw; Big Mdw (2); Big Rough; Big Yd; Black Croft, Far and Near ~ ~; Boggy Croft; Brickkiln Fd; Brickkiln Yd; Broad Lsw (2); Broomy Croft and Fd; Burlton Lsw; Calves Croft; Carthouse Fd; Carthouse Lsw; Cobets Croft; (The) Coppice, Near ~; Coppice Fd, Mdw (by house called The Coppy); Corporation (a large field by the road to English Frankton, the reference may be to allotments, cf. Corporation Lane Part **4** 61); Cote Lsw (no building); (The) Cow Lsw; Croft (Owen's, Near, Upper, Middle ~ adjoin near S.E. boundary); The Croft (a fairly large field on N. boundary); Cronkhill, Big, Little, ~ Moor (probably 'crane hill', *v.* **cranoc**); Dairy Lsw, New ~ ~; Denston, Far and Little ~, Near, Further and Chidloes Dunstan (6 fields in S.E. corner, possibly a form of Dunstall, from ***tūn-stall** 'farm site'); Dole Mdw; Edge Lane; Forge Fd; Furlong, Big, New, Little, Brook House, Moor Lane (5 fields N. of Burlton hamlet); George Mdw; Gorsy Croft; Gravel Fd; Grove Fd (by Burlton Grove); Harvest Pce (2, *v.* The Moor); Herbage; Higher Wheat Fd (on N. boundary, not near other Wheat ns.); Hillock Lee; Himbo; Hopyard; Horse Moor, Far, Near; House Fd; House Pce; Intake, Big, Little (tiny enclosures either side of a road); Jockey Pce; Lawn Croft; Lea Steel; The Leg and Foot (so shaped); Little George Mdw; Long Croft; Long Lsw; Long Mdw; Loppington Lsw (on boundary with L. township); The Lyde, Long ~, Lyde Lane, Lsw, Mdw (Lyde is usually from **Hlȳde**, a n. for a noisy stream, but OS maps show no stream here: another possibility is **hlið**, discussed under Lyth in Ellesmere *supra*: the fields are by Yew Tree Ho); Marl Lsw; Marlpit Slade; Marton Fd; Meadow, Big, Little, Old, Rough (adjoining); Mill Fd, Far, Near, Middle, Mill Hills, Lsw, Mdw (by Burlton Grange *supra*); The Moor (strips on E. boundary are Common Moor (9), Cuckhold Moor (4), Griggy Moor (3, dialect *grig* 'heather'): The Moor is a single strip in the middle of the series, and Moor and Big Moor adjoin to the W.: these are separated by Mill Mdw ns. from another series of strips called Belle Moor, Cronkhill Moor, Galey Moor (*Galy Moore* 1698 *SBL 5777*, bog-myrtle), Griggy Moor, Harris Moor, The Long Moor: both series have strips called Harvest Pce); Moor Lane, Lsw; The Moors (adjoining Archers Moor on N.W. boundary); New Fm (4 fields on E. boundary with the Moor ns., no buildings); (The) New Lsw (2); Old Croft; Orchard Fd, Old Orchard; Park Fd (adjoins Petton Pk); Peters Fd; Petton Fd (on Petton boundary); The Pits, Pit Fd; Pit Croft (not near preceding); Pool Banks, Croft, Mdw; Pool Banks with Pits and Rough (not near preceding); Rabbit Burrows; The Randle; Ryegrass Fd; Scotch Croft; Severn Side (by Wackley Brook); Sheepcote Lsw; The Slade (2, Sa dialect for a field with a wet patch); Spencer's Wd; Step Mdw; Stocket Mdw (***stoccett** 'place with tree-stumps', a rare p.n. term); The Swathes, Far and Near Swathes (**swæð** 'strip of mowing grass' is rarely used as a simplex n. but another instance is noted PN Nth 270); The Turfs, Dry Turfs, Turf Mdw; Wackley, Big, Little, Burlton, Cross, Wackley Croft (Wackley is in Petton *infra*); Way Lsw; Well Fd; Well Lsw; Wheat Croft, Little ~ ~, Lower and Upper Wheat Lsw (a group of fields in S.W. corner); Wood Lsw, Big, Little; Yard Croft.

(b) *Bernardesmedowe* 1344 *SBL 3621*; *Blacke Pole* Hy 8; *Le Brodemedowe* 1344 *SBL 3622*; *Byrcheley* Hy 8 (perhaps 'birch wood'); *Goughes Wood* 1650 *SBL 1018*;

Long Acre Pole Hy 8 (the Pole ns. in this document are in a list of pools); *Newe Pool* Hy 8 (a "drye pytt"); *Segge Pole* Hy 8 ('sedge pool'); *Towne Pole* Hy 8; *Le Vernehale* 1291–2 *Ass* ("Rog. in ~ ~ de Browelton"', 'ferny nook', *v.* **fearnig**, **halh**); *Wymberley* Hy 8.

2. LOPPINGTON (SJ 471293)

Forms for this name are set out in Part **1**, with the suggested derivation from **-ingtūn** and a personal name **Loppa*, which would be derived from OE *loppa* 'spider'.

Two other etymologies have been put forward. One is by Dr G. Fellows-Jensen, who mentioned the name in a paper (*Sydsvenska Ortnamnssallskapets Årsskrift* 1974) which questioned the assumption that most names of this type have a personal-name base rather than a significant term or an earlier place-name to which the suffix **-ing** has been added. She suggested that Loppington could contain a noun **lopping*, 'spider place'. This possibility is repeated in CDEPN, with an additional suggestion by V. Watts of an **-ing** formation based on a hill-term **lop*. In defence of this last Watts says that both Loppington and Lopham in Norfolk occupy hill sites. Both places could, however, more precisely be said to stand on raised ground overlooking marsh. These are not conspicuous hill sites, and they do not add significantly to the slender evidence for an OE **lop* 'hill'.

An **-ingtūn** formation with a personal name **Loppa* seems to the present writer to be the most convincing explanation of this name.

THE AVENUE.

BROWNHEATH, *Browneheth* 1483–4 *SRO Bridgewater 212/box 72*, *Brown Heathe* 1602 Peake, *Brown Heath* 1833 OS. BROWNHEATH MOSS, *Brown Moss* 1838 *TA*.

THE FIELDS: ~ Field ns. surround the house on *TAMap*.

THE HOLLIES.

HOLYWELL LO, HOLYWELLMOOR, ~ COPPICE, *Holywell Moor Meadow* 1682 GT, *Holywell Moor* 1833 OS, *Holywell Moor Farm* 1863 PR(L) 18. *TAMap* shows *Hollywell Moor* and *Meadow* along R. Roden, E. of the house called Holywellmoor. Probably 'holy well'.

JUBILEE PLTN.

LOPPINGTON HALL.

LOPPINGTON HO, shown but not named on *TAMap*.

LOPPINGTON WINDMILL, the mill is marked on *TAMap*.

LYNEAL LO, Lyneal in Ellesmere adjoins.

MILL COTTAGE, HO, near Loppington Windmill.

NEW FM.

THE NOOK.

OLD HO 1833 OS, *Old House Field* and *Meadow* 1838 *TA*.

THE ROUGH, ROUGH HAYS, *Rough Hayes Plantation* 1838 *TA*.

SALTERS LANE: *TAMap* has *Salters Plantation* and 4 fields called *Salters Croft*(*s*) alongside the lane.

THE SHAWS, 1838 *TA*, *v*. Shays Cottage in Noneley, *infra*.

SLANGS PLTN, *The Slangs* 1838 *TA*.

SPENFORD BRIDGE, cf. *Big Spendford*, *Great Spendford Meadow* 1838 *TA*. The name is given as *Penceford Bridge* 1818 in Garbet's *History of Wem*, and this accords with *Pensford Leasow* 1653 *SBL 2503*. The original form is uncertain.

WILLOW BED, *Holywell Moor Willow Bed* 1838 *TA*.

WOODGATE, 1833 OS, *Big* and *Little Wood Gate Field* 1838 *TA*.

Field-Names

Forms in (a) are 1838 *TA* except where otherwise stated. Early forms for which no source is given are GT.

(a) Allanseeds, Anniseed (adjacent, FN 31 lists references to the crop aniseed in Sa f.ns.); The Anderley, Far and Near ~; Banky Pce; Barkley's Crofts; Barn Fd; Barn Flg; Big Fd, Far, Near; Big Mdw (2); Black Lakes, Big, Little, Long and Round Black Lake ('black drainage channels', *Lake* is here a reflex of **lacu**: Round ~ ~ has one slightly curved side); Brand Hawthorn, Far ~ ~ (probably 'burnt'); Breakfast Croft (one of a cluster of Croft ns., *v. infra*); Brickkiln Lsw (cf. *Brick Leasow* 1785); Bridges (adjoins Black Lake ns., perhaps a reference to causeways); Britch (a group of fields N.W. of Loppington village contains Brown's and Sheet ~, Britch Lane Cover, Birch Lanes, Mdw, Pools Bridges, cf. *Britchlane Croft* 1612, 21, *Brichlane* ~ 1682: 'newly-broken-in land', *v*. **bryce**); Broomy Lsw (2); Burlton Moors (the northern extremity of the marshes along the E. boundary of Burlton township); Burtmoss Croft; Calves Croft; Chemley Park, Big and Little ~ ~ (on the edge of Brownheath Moss, *v*. Clemley in Prees *infra*); Cherrytree Fd; Clover Fd; Cottage Croft; Cow Pasture, Big, Little; Crabtree Lsw; Croft (a large group of ~ Croft ns. in the N. of the township includes Bottom, Bostocks, Corner, Long, Rough, Thorny, Vetch, First, Second ~: another group N. of Woodgate includes First, Second, Far, Near, Middle, Big, Little, Barn, Cottage ~: Breakfast Croft is in the latter group); Crossing Croft, Cross Lanes (by road junction); Cross Lanes Croft (in a road junction); Dangmoor Hayes, Far and Near; Edmunds Pce; Espes, Far, Near, Long and Round Espes ('aspens', ultimately from **æspe**); Far Pool; Fawkes Pit; Field up to Road; Fox Moor; Frog Pool; Frog Pool Mdw (not near preceding); Furlong, The Furlong (2 fields S.W. of. Loppinton Ho, cf. *parcel called Furlong* 1621); Further Lsw; Garden Fd (by Loppington Ho); Gorse Cover; Gravel Hole Pltn; Half Acre; Hall Yd (by Loppington Hall); Hand Lane, ~ ~ Croft (cf. *Handhay Croft* 1682, 1785: possibly referring to a signpost, the *TA* ns. are by the Ellesmere/Loppington road); Hard Ryegrass; The Haycocks; Heath Ground, Gravelly, Little, Rough and Mosspit

~ ~, Heath Ground Banks (cf. *Heath Field* e.17th, *Heath Leasow* 1682, 1785); Heath Mdw; Hollins Bank ('holly', *v.* **holegn**); Horse Pce; House Fd; Ladies Pce; Lampeth Oak (1785, *Lampreach Oak Meadow* 1682); Lawn (by Woodgate); Lawn, Front, Round (in the grounds of Loppington Ho); Leans, Croft, Big Leans (*v.* **leyne**, a f.n. term of uncertain meaning, and cf. Lionlane in Ellesmere *supra*); Leasow, Far, Middle, Gorsty; Little Mdw (several, one 1785); Little Yd; Long Pce; Loppington Mdw (a large field in N. tip of township); Marlpit Lsw; Marsh, Big, Little; Meadow (several); Meadow below the House; Middle Fd; Middle Hayes Mdw; Mill Fd (2, by Loppington Windmill); Mill Fd, Near, Far and Second Mill Lsw (S. of Loppington village, not near Windmill ns.); New Lsw (1612, 21, 82); Noneley Croft (near Noneley boundary); Oak Fd; Old Lane; Outlet (land adjoining winter cattle sheds); Owl Lsw; Pool Croft (Loppington Ho); The Possels (EDD records, from Sa, *possel* 'a state of soft, swampy saturation'); Quaiken Ground (adjoins Quaiken in Ellesmere *supra*); Red Mdw, Big and Little ~ ~; Rough Mdw; Round Mdw (one curved side); Ryegrass Fd; Sandhole Fd (adjoins Gravel Hole Pltn); Sawpit Mdw 1841 GT; Sheep Yd; Slade (a tiny enclosure in Loppington); Slang, First, Second, Third, Fourth (strips on W. boundary); Snal Oak, Snab Oak Mdw (*sic*, adjoining); Stony Furlong, ~ ~ Croft, Far Furlong Croft (3 small fields W. of Loppington village); Tanpit Mdw; Thistly Fd; Timber Yd; Townsend (on outskirts of Loppington); The Two Acres; War Corner, Weir Corn (*sic*, these fields are near but not adjacent); The Wheat Hurst; Wickytree, Lower, Higher ('mountain ash', *v.* FN 48); Wintill (*Wintle Croft* 1682, *Wyntle* ~ 1785); Wood Lsw; Yard, Barn, Far, Haycocks, Higher, Lower, Smith's (adjacent, S. of Loppington); Yewpit Lsw; Yewtree Fd (2).

(b) *Barnyard Close* 1621; *Boultons Croft* 1682, 1785; *Bryar Meadow* 1682, 1785; *Croft between the Meadows* 1682; *Flaxbutts* 1682, *Flax Butts Croft* 1789; *Rough Croft* 1682, 1785; *Wallcroft* 1612, *Wall Leasow Croft* e.17th, *Well Croft* 1621, *Wellcroft* 1682 ('spring'); *Wood Field* e.17th.

3. NONELEY (SJ 481280)

Noneleia c.1090 SAC, *Noneley* 1535 VE, *Nonely* Hy 8 *RentSur*, *Nonneley* 1623 PR(L) 9, *Noneley* 1811 PR(L) 10

Noniley c.1220–30 HAC (p), *-lege* 1271–2 *Ass*, *Nonylegh'* 1291–2 *Ass*, *-lie* 1292–5 *Ass*, 1327 SR (p), *-ley* Hy 8 *RentSur*, c.1550 SAS 1/VI

Numleg' 1221 SAC, *Nunnleg'* c.1235 SAC

Nunnileg' m.13th SAC, *Nunily* 1656 PR(L) 20

Nuneley Hy 8 *RentSur*, 1649 SAS 4/V11, *Nunneley* 1577 Saxton, 1658 *et seq* PR(L) 9

First element the personal name *Nunna*, second element **lēah**, here probably in its late OE sense 'meadow, pasture' which was postulated for Bagley and Hordley *supra*. This marshy area is not likely to have had the ancient forest environment implied by the earlier senses of **lēah**.

The spellings suggest that there was a form with connective **-ing-** as well as one with the personal name in the genitive.

BENTLEY, 1833 OS. The house is shown on *TAMap* with *Bentley Meadow* nearby.

COMMONWOOD, *Common Wood* 1833 OS. This is the n. of a scatter of houses over an area which is called *Common Right* on *TAMap*, with large fields called *Common Meadow* and *Wood Leasow* adjoining.

FORESTERS ARMS P.H.

NONELEY HALL.

RUEWOOD, *Roowood Commen'* Hy 8 *RentSur*, *The Rowewood* 1596 PR(L) 9, *Rooewood* 1656, 8 ib, *Roowewood* 1681 *et seq* ib, *Rue Wood* 1726 *SBL 1619*, 1833 OS. 'Rough wood', *v.* **rūh**. The same name occurs in Ch with the modern form Roewoods, PN Ch **1** 120.

THE SHAYS, SHAYS COTTAGE. This name must be considered together with The Shaws in Loppington. On *TAMap* this and The Shaws are at the E. and W. ends of a belt of fields called Big, Little, Middle, Far, Near, Long Shaws, Shaws Pltn (in Loppington) and Big, Near, Further, Noneley Shaws, Shaws Meadow (in Noneley). The two map-names are just under ½ mile apart. There must at one time have been a small wood here, but on 19th-cent. and modern maps there is only the tiny stand of trees called The Shaws at the western end.

OE **sceaga** is used in place-names for strips of woodland which are peripheral to more heavily wooded areas. The distribution is discussed in LPN pp. 245–6. The interchange between the modern forms Shaw and Shay is discussed in *Nomina* 12, pp. 103–4, and 13, pp. 109–14.

Field-Names

Forms in (a) are 1838 *TA*. Early forms dated Hy 8 are *RentSur*.

(a) Appletree Fd; Ash Flg; Banky Fd; Barn Croft; Barn Fd; Barn Lsw; Boat Mdw (by Sleap Brook); Brickkiln Fd, Big, Little; Brickkiln Yd; Broad Mdw with Slade (*Brademedewe* m.13th SAC, *v.* Slade *infra*); Bromley, Near, Middle, Far, Long; Bush Moor Mdw, Far Bush Moor, Near Bush Moor with Slade, Bush Moor Croft (7 fields in N. tip of township, *Byschmore* Hy 8, 'marsh with thickets', *v.* **bysce**, **mōr**); Canal Fd (perhaps referring to a drainage channel); Catchlow, Middle and Hedges ~; Cote Fd (no building); Cote Lsw (no building); Cowdust, Near, Further; Cow Pasture; Croft (several round Noneley hamlet); Dry Marlpit Fd; Dunstall Pool (S. of Noneley, perhaps ***tūn-stall** 'farm site'); Far Lsw; Field (14 adjoining, small fields in S.E. corner are Big, Pit, Orchard, Gravel Hole, Pool, Clover, Barn, Lane, Middle, Turnip, Left Hand, Right Hand Field); Field before House; Fox Moor; Furlong, Near, Far (2 furlong-shaped fields E. of hamlet); Garden Lsw, Little Garden Pce; Green Lane; Handys Mdw; Haycock Yd, Far ~ ~; Hedleys (7 fields near Sleap Brook, Hedleys Mdw and Hedley Side adjoin the group); Hemp Croft; Hemp Yd; The Henshaw; Hoarstone (not on a boundary); Holly Husk (perhaps *hussocks* 'clumps of coarse grass'); Homestead (by The Shays); Leasow, New, Part; Lidgate with Slade, The Lidgate ('swing-gate', the fields are either side of a road); Long Croft; Longley Bank, Mdw; Lop Mdw; Maiden's Hurst (in S.W. corner of township: 1900 6" map shows two small stands of trees here and the ground is slightly raised, so a **hyrst** is possible); Mannerings Mdw; Marl Lsw; Martins Croft; Meadow (adjacent small fields in S.E. corner are Far, Near, Barn, Little Meadow; another group on W. boundary contains Yard, Barn, Further, Butt Field, Further Field Meadow); Meadow Bank; Moor Side with Slade, Moor Side (near, not adjacent); Moors, Rushy, Second, Near and Far Moor; Moss Pit Fd; New Gates; New Lsw; Noneley Croft; Noneley Mdw; Nuttree Fd; One Acre (tiny enclosure in Noneley); Outlet (by Bentley); Patch (tiny enclosure by Commonwood); Pillow Brook (Pillow in f.ns. is considered to be a derivative of **pil-āte** 'pill oats', *v.* FN 32, PN Ch **5.1** 305); Pool Mdw, Big and Great ~ ~ (5 fields along R. Roden, Pool Croft and Fd adjoin); Ryegrass Fd; Sandhole Fd (sandpit marked on 1900 6"); Six Days Math (Two Days, Four Days and Twelve Day Math are nearby, the ns. refer to mowing); Slade (several fields are named "x with Slade", and there is one called Slade in Meadow: these were probably fields with patches too wet to plough, *v.* FN 18); Slape Brook Mdw (by Sleap Brook); The Snab (probably ME ***snabbe** in the sense 'projection into marsh'); The Stanmoors; The Stew ('fish pond', on edge of Noneley hamlet); Stackyard Fd; Three Corner Pce; Townsend (3 fields along E. side of hamlet); The Two Oaks; Wheat Croft; Wintell, Big, Little (adjoining Wintill in Loppington township); Wood Lsw; Yewtree Fd.

(b) *Caldewall' Feld* Hy 8 ('cold spring'); *Le Colpytt* Hy 8 (a reference to charcoal burning); *Wellecroft* c.1235 SAC ('spring croft'); *Le Westmore Feld Hy* 8 ('west marsh').

Montford

The parish-name is discussed in Part **1**, with a suggested etymology 'ford where meetings took place'.

In a glebe terrier of 1612 (GT) it is stated that "there are 3 small townships in the parish Montford, Forton and Ensdon". The *TA*, however, treats the parish as a single unit.

ENSDON (SJ 409169)

Edenesdon' 1271–2 *Ass et passim* with variant spelling *-don* to 1327 Pat
Edeneston 1272 Cl, *-tone* ib, 1320 *SBL 8396*
Hedenesdon 1284–5 FA
Ednesdon' 1291–2 *Ass*, 1302 Ipm, 1320 *SBL 8396*, 1404–5 MGS
Eneston 1418–20 *SBL 6041*
Endsdon 1637, 56 PR(L) 7, 1654 PR(L) 4
Ensdon 1644 PR(L) 7 *et seq*
Enson 1656, 92 PR(StA) 3, 1695 Morden

'Ēden's hill', *v.* **dūn**. The personal name, which is considered to be a hypocoristic form of names in *Ēad-*, is found also in Edensor PN Db 91, Edstone PN NRY **5** 8 and Edge Knoll PN Du 38.

FORTON (SJ 430161)
This is a DB manor, so the name, which means 'settlement near a ford', is discussed in Part **1**.

MONTFORD BRIDGE, *pons de Muneford* 1255–6 *Ass*, *Moneford' Brughe* 1361 *SBL 3610*, *Moneford Brugge* 1369 *SBL 3636*, *Monfordbrigg* 1374–7, 81 Pat, *Mundeford Brugge* 1386 Cl.

There are 17th- and 18th-cent. references in PR(L) 4 and 7 to people who lived in the settlement by the bridge, the south part of which is in Preston Montford parish. The settlement north of the bridge is called Allen's Hill on 19th- and 20th-cent. maps, except for the 1999 Explorer, which gives Montford Bridge for both settlements.

Leland, c.1540, notes *Mountford/Monford Bridge* "a fayre Stone Bridge . . . of late renewed". The present bridge was built by Telford in 1792.

NIB HEATH, 1833 OS, *Knibheath* 1677 PR(L) 20, *Nib-Heath* 1680 PR(L) 7, *Nibheath* 1682, 3, 92 ib, *Nibb Heath* 1692 ib. OE ***hnybba** 'nib' is used in place-names for a projecting piece of land. Early forms for North Nibley, PN Gl **2** 240, and a Gl charter-boundary mark take this word back to OE, but it is not certain that the Montford name is of such antiquity, rather than being a ME or ModE use of *nib*. The name refers on maps to a small cluster of houses on the N. boundary of the parish, adjacent to a sharp projection of the boundary. This last may be the 'nib', but the entry of 1677 in PR(L) 20 says that John Bamford "unfortunately broke his neck on Knibheath", and this might indicate broken ground with a projecting feature which could have been referred to in a name of earlier origin.

ALLEN'S HILL, 1833 OS, 1844 *TA*.

BEAM HO, 1833 OS, 1844 *TA*. Fields called *Beamhurst* in Great Ness *TA* are a short distance N., and Beam Ho may have been *Beamhurst Ho. Beamhurst was perhaps a stand of trees from which timber was obtained.

BLAKELEYS CLUMP, *Blakeleys* 1844 *TA*.

BROMLEY'S FORGE. This is a group of houses which is shown but not named on *TAMap*. They are at the junction of R. Perry with R. Severn, and *TAMap* marks 'Site of Forge'. Cf. "the Fordge, p. of Monford" 1674, 92, 99 PR(L) 4.

BROOMFIELDS, 1844 *TA*, *Broom Field* 1833 OS.

THE COTTAGE, COTTAGE PLTN, 1844 *TA*, COTTAGE POND, ~ POOL, 1833 OS, 1844 *TA*: *TA* also has *Cottage Bank* and *Meadow*.

CRIT PLTN, *Crit*, *Crit Houses* 1844 *TA*. This is a scatter of houses with small Crofts and Closes, like that at Bromley's Forge a short distance E. *crit* is a Sa word for a cabin or small hut (EDD).

DEN PLTN, LITTLE DEN. 1833 OS has *Foxhole Rough or Plantation* here, 1844 *TA* has *Far* and *Near Devil's Den* and *Devil's Den Pltn*. These look on maps like ordinary fields and woods.

ENSDON BANK PLTN, *Ensdon Pltn* 1833 OS.

ENSDON HO, 1833 OS, 1844 *TA*, *Endsdon House* 1701 *SBL 6559*.

FORTON BANK, COTTAGE, VILLA.

FORTON HEATH, 1833 OS.

HORSE MOORS, 1833 OS.

HUNGER HILL, *High* and *Low* ~ ~ 1844 *TA*.

THE KNOWLES, *Far* and *Near Knowles* 1844 *TA*.

LITTLE ENSDON. The hamlet is shown but not named on *TAMap*.

MILLERS CLUMP.

NEW POOL.

RODEFERN, *The Two Radifearnes* 1703 *SBL 4134*, *Raddifrans Meadow* 1789 *SBL 6200*, *Roderfern* 1833 OS, *Rhuddy Fern Leasow* 1844 *TA*.

ROYAL HILL, 1844 *TA*.

SCHOOL, *School House* 1833 OS, *School and Schoolhouse* 1844 *TA*.

WEIR FM, *Weir House* 1844 *TA*.

YELL BANK, 1844 *TA*, also ~ ~ *Pltn* and *Meadow*, 'gentle slope', *v.* **helde**.

TAMap shows the following buildings: *Montford Barley Fm*, *Montford Lodge*, *Montford School House* (in village), *Powis Arms Inn*, *Turnpike Ho* (in Montford Bridge).

Field-Names

Forms in (a) are 1844 *TA*, except where otherwise stated. Early forms dated 1320, 1418 are *SBL 8396*, *6041*, those dated 1612, 35, 85, 1701, 5 are GT, 1736 are PR(L) 7.

(a) Adcote Lane Pce (Adcote is in Little Ness); Alloe Brook ('alders', *v.* FN 47); Armour Mdw; Bank near Charles's; Bank Head Fd, Bank Lsw (by Bank Ho in Fitz); Banky Lsw (several); Banky Pce, Big, Little; Barn Fd and Patch (in Montford village); Barn Mdw; Barn Pce (2); Bay Moss, Rushy ~ ~, Moss; Beggar Hill; Bell Mdw (cf. *The Bell Yard* 1736: an innkeeper "at the Bel at Ensdon" is mentioned 1656 SAS 2/VII); Big Bank; Big Lsw (several); Black Marsh, Little; Black Parks (a large field on S.W. boundary with a building called Lodge in one corner, The Park adjoins on Shrawardine *TAMap*: cf. *Park Stile*, ~ *Pale* 1612, *Park Stile Leasow* 1635, 85, 1705); Bowling Green Lsw; Brade Mdw, ~ ~ Corner; Bridge Lsw, Big, Little, Lower (by Montford Bridge); Broad Lsw (2); Brook Lsw; Broomfield, Near, Farther, Middle, Paddocks (S. of Broomfields hamlet); Brooms; Broomy Lsw; Burnt House Lsw; Bylet (tiny enclosure in Bromley's Forge, island in Severn nearby); Cabbage Lsw; Calves Close (several); Caethrog; Close(s) (clusters occur round hamlets, one group of larger Close fields is near Montford Vicarage); Coach Road Fd (by road to Oswestry); Coltsfoot Lsw; Common Field, Second, Third, Fourth, Fifth (by Forton Heath, Near, Far, Middle ~ ~ are on the other side of the road to Leaton: the adjacent small enclosures round Bromley's Forge include Common Bank and Lsw and Higher Common); Coppice, Piece by Coppice (no trees on *TAMap*, or on 1901 6"); Cow Pasture (several); Crimes, Jeffreys ~ (probably the same term as in Crimps Fm in Ellesmere, *q.v.*); Cross Gates, Bowkers, Little (by road junction on W. boundary); Depsile, Lower, Upper; Far Gates; Far Ground; Far Lsw (several); Fernhill Bank 1845 GT; Field adjoining Pltn; Field Pce, Big, Little; Footway Pce; Footing Mdw; Four Acres; Foxhole Lsw; Franks Bank; Furlong, Big ~ (5 small fields S. of Ensdon);

Furlong, Far, Long, Middle (adjoining strips N.E. of Ensdon); Furlong (3 strips S. and S.W. of Forton); Furlongs (large field by Forton); Furnival's Fd; Further Cow Pasture; Further Lsw; Garbells Corner, Big, Little; Garden Fd (2); Garson's Heath; Glebe Corner; Goutern Lsw (*v.* FN 27 for various meanings of *gout* in f.ns.); Grafton Stile; Gravel Hole Close; Gravel Hole Fd (not near preceding); Halfpenny Oak; Heath Lsw; High Oaks; High Stone Gates; Hill Fd (2); Hollytree Lsw; Horse Moss; Horsemoss Pltn (not near preceding); Horse Pasture; Hovel Lsw (2, no buildings); Isle, Big, Little (E. of the village, not by the river); Jeffreys Pce; John's Lsw; Jones's Lsw; Lawn (by Ensdon Ho); Lawn and Cottage (by Forton); Little Lsw; Little Mdw (several); Lodge Mdw (adjoins Lodge in Black Park); Long Croft (a large field); Long Lsw (several); Long Pce (2); Lower Fd; Meadow (several); Meadow, Big, Long, Grassy (tiny enclosures in Forton); Middle Lsw (2); Middle Pce; Miles's Pce; Millers Gate; Mitton Pce, Far, Near, Middle (by road to Mytton); Moss and Slang, Far Moss, Moss (in Broomfields); Mossy Lsw; Near Park (close to Park Side on Shrawardine *TAMap*); New Lsw; New Pce (several); Oat Lsw; Old House (in Forton); Orchard Mdw (2); Osier Bed, Rough ~ ~ (the first is an island in Severn, the other a riverside field); Park Fd, Lower, Upper (by R. Severn, upstream from Montford Bridge); Patch(es) (several, small enclosures in hamlets); Piery's Lsw; Pig Bank (2, on either side of Montford village); Pinfold Croft; The Pitacres and Quoitings (FN 68 lists Quoitings as a "Sports and Pastimes" n.); Pit Lsw (several); The Plain (a big rectangular field); Pool Patch (by Ensdon Ho); Preston Fd, Mdw (Preston Montford is across R. Severn); Pump Lsw; Purslow's Yd; Raven Mdw; Raventree Lsw; Rise, Lower, Upper; Rough Mdw; Roundabout (a bend in the road gives the field one curved side); Roundabout (a rectangular strip with a slight curve in one side); Round Mdw (one side formed by a curve in Severn); Sandhole Pce; Sandy Lsw; Severn Mdw, Near, Middle, Upper; Sheep Wood; Shop Lsw; Shoulder of Mutton (triangular); The Six Acres; Slang (several, all but one slang-shaped); Stanbridge, Higher, Far and Lower Stanbridge (by the Montford/Ensdon road, possibly a causeway, there is a gap between Stanbridge and the other fields); Stonehouse Lsw (no building); Teinter Yd (cloth-stretching frame); Thornwell; Three Corner Fd; Three Corner Pce; Townsend (by Montford); Townsend, Far, Near (by Forton); Upper Mdw; Vicarage Bank 1845 GT; Vicarage Fd, Big, Little (cf. *The Vicarage Croft* 1736); Wall Hill; Wardrocks, Lower, Top; Wards Fd; Watthill; Weir Lsw, Far, Near (by weir in Severn); Well Mdw (3); Well Yd; Wheelwright's Shop (in Forton); White Fd; Wigmores; Wintlin, Big; Withy Doors; Yard, Far, Lower, Long, Middle, Near, Well (small enclosures N. and S. of Broomfields); Yard, Calves, Long, Little, Timber (in Ensdon); Yard, Little, Paynes (*Payne's Yard* 1736), Well (in Montford); Yewtree Lsw.

(b) *Alrenenemor* 1320, *Aldermore* 1418, *Alderley Moore* 1655 SAS 1/XLVII ('alder marsh', *Alrenene* is a garbled form from **ælren**); *Astwode* 1320, 1418 ('east wood'); *Bridgefield* 1612; *Cross Field* 1612, 85; *Edpool* 1736 (in Forton); *Faleswyk'* 1418; *The Field Ground* 1736; *The Gill Yard* 1736; *The Green* 1701, 36; *Gylvor* 1612, *Gilver* 1635, 85, *Gilver Leasow* 1701, *Gilford* 1705, *The Gilver* 1736; *The Hemp-Butt* 1736; *Knell Booth* 1635; *Marsh* 1612, 35, 85, 1705; *Middle Field* 1612, 85; *Montford Green* 1635; *Mosspit* 1701, *The Mosspit Leasow* 1736; *New Piece* 1701; *Le Peyreue* 1418; *Rowney* 1418 (probably 'rough island', *v.* **rūh**, **ēg**); *The Sheepcott* 1736; *The Short Butt* 1736; *The Tith Yard* 1736; *Water's Yard* 1736; *The Well Leasow* 1736.

Myddle

The arrangement under townships of the place-name material for this parish presents formidable problems, and the solutions adopted here are to some extent arbitrary.

There is no available guide to the exact boundaries of Myddle townships. George Foxall's drawing of the Tithe Map does not show internal boundaries. There is a sketch map showing townships in D. Hey's 1974 book *An English Rural Community: Myddle under the Tudors and Stuarts* (which is an analysis of Gough), but this is not sufficiently detailed for transference to larger-scale maps. The townships on Hey's map are Alderton, Balderton, Houlston, Marton, Myddle and Newton. He shows Sleap (the area defined *infra* under Sleap Hall) and Webscott as detached areas of Balderton. Alderton has a small detached area and Newton has two. This is the administrative pattern of the 17th century.

The 19th-cent. Index to Tithe Survey map shows Alderton, Balderton, Marton and Newton as discrete townships. Here, as on Hey's map, Sleap and Webscott are shown as detached areas of Balderton. Newton is accorded two detached portions, one with a boundary, the other without. Alderton, however, is not accorded the small detached portion shown on Hey's map, and Houlston is not given township status. Hey, p. 11, notes that "Houlston was absorbed into Myddle township when its five tenements were amalgamated into a single farm". Alderton is shown on the Tithe Map for Hadnall, but it is treated here as a Myddle township, and is accorded the few detached fields which constitute its outlying area on Hey's map.

For the purposes of the place-name survey, boundaries shown on the Index to Tithe Survey map have been transferred as precisely as possible to the 1900 6" map and to George Foxall's drawing of the Tithe Award map, which is also on the 6" scale; but assignment of borderline fields to one township or its neighbour can only be approximately correct.

The parish-name is discussed in Part **1**, with a suggested derivation from an OE ***gemȳðel**, diminutive of **gemȳðe** 'river-junction'. There can never have been a river-junction here, but there might have been a place where several small streams joined. The forms set out in Part **1** tell strongly against Ekwall's etymology (DEPN under the spelling Middle) of **gemȳðe** and **lēah**.

1. ALDERTON (SJ 496240)
Elureton c.1180 SAS
Alverton 1195–6 Eyton, *Alverton super Bylemars* 1280–90 ib
Allerton 1279 Eyton, 1495 Ipm
Alderton 1624 *SBL 3407*

The misleading modern form may be due to influence from the neighbouring Balderton. The c.1180 and 1195–6 spellings suggest a compound of **tūn** with a personal name in *Ælf-*, probably Ælfhere, which would be uninflected: *v.* the discussion of Balderton *infra*.

In Part **4**, p. 130, this name was mistakenly said to be 'alder settlement', owing to failure to note the two earliest forms.

As noted *supra*, the administrative situation of Alderton is complicated. It could have been considered as part of Hadnall and included in the Liberties of Shrewsbury in Part **4**, but it has seemed most convenient to treat it as a township of Myddle.

BULLSHOP, 1833 OS, 1839 *TA*. *TAMap* shows *Big* and *Little Bull Field* here.

Field-Names

Forms in (a) are 1839 *TA*. These are divided into (i), which is the main part of the township, and (ii), a detached portion which is a strip of land a mile N.E. of Alderton hamlet.

(a) (i) Astenfield, Further, Nearer, Astern Fd, Big, Little, Aster Fd, Near, Far, Middle (this group of fields adjoins Well Fd in Balderton: Gough, 1700, notes a well called *Ast-well* or *Astawell* or *Easterwell* in this area: the first el. of these ns. is **ēasterra** 'more eastern'); Billimarsh Fd, Little ~ ~, ~ Mdw (*v.* Bilmarsh *infra*); The Billings, ~ ~ Mdw (the fields are on the edge of Bilmarsh); Black Pit, Far, Near; Cross Flg (a rectangular field N. of Alderton); Field below B2 (this refers to the numbering in the Award schedule); Field near Shones; Field up to Hollow; Long Fd; Newtons Croft (on boundary with Newton township); Oat Croft; Old Mdw; Pump Mdw; Windmill Fd; Withyford Croft (across a road from Black Pit, perhaps a causeway).

(ii) Banky Fd; Far Fd; Floated Mdw; Footroad Fd (*v.* Dudleston f.ns. *supra*); Lyons Wd Fd (Lyon's Wd in Broughton (Part **4** 120) is fairly close: the n. may contain the term discussed under Lionlane in Northwood *supra*); Rough Fd; Slang (narrow, curved strip).

2. BALDERTON, with the detached areas of SLEAP and WEBSCOTT

BALDERTON (SJ 481240)

Balderton c.1175–8 HAC *et freq* with variant spellings *-ton'*, *-tona*
Baldreton 1221–2 *Ass* (p) *et freq* with variant spellings *-tun(a)* to 1330 Ch
Ballederton 1486 Ipm

There are three instances of this name, the others being in Nottinghamshire (PN Nt 209–10) and Cheshire (PN Ch **4** 157). It appears to be a compound of **tūn** with *Baldhere*, with the personal name uninflected. As PN Nt notes, this type of name is common in that county. The omission of genitival *s* in such compounds is not common in Shropshire, though there are some examples, neighbouring Alderton being probably one of them.

BROOMHURST FM (in Gazetteer, not on maps: Hey 85 says it adjoins Balderton Hall): *Bromehurste* 1334 HAC, *Farme called Bromehurst* 1602 Hey, *Broomehurst Farme* 1700 Gough, *v.* **brōm**, **hyrst**.

WITTERAGE GREEN, *Le Whiterusche* 1334 HAC, *Whitrish House*, *Lane* 1700 Gough. 'White rush-bed', *v.* **hwīt**, **risc**.

The name is applied to different places on 1833 OS and 1900 6" maps. On 1833 OS it is shown at the road junction where the 6" map marks a Methodist chapel. On 1900 6" and on *TAMap* the name is shown ½ mile east of this, where there is a single house. The latter site is accorded the name on the 1961 1" map and on the 1999 Explorer. On the Explorer map the road-junction houses have acquired the curious name Grumpy.

BALDERTON HALL, 1833 OS, is the site for which the GR is given *supra*.

SLEAP (SJ 486267), 1622 PR(L) 19, 1833 OS, 1839 *TA*, *Aula Slepe* 1603 PR(L) 19, *Slip Hall* 1606 ib, *Aula Sleep* 1608 ib. The main settlement of Sleap is in Wem in N. Bradford Hundred, *infra*; but an area S. of the Wem/Myddle boundary (and the hundredal boundary), which includes Sleap Hall, was a detached part of Balderton township. This is probably *Parua Slepe super Bilemers* 1291–2 *Ass*.

SLEAP GORSE, 1563 Hey, *Slepegorstes* 1334 HAC, *Sleeps Gorse* 1602 Peake, *Heaps Gorse* (*sic*) 1839 *TA*. *v.* **gorst**.

WEBSCOTT (SJ 465228)

Weblescowe 1172 (e.14th) HAC, *Weblescho* 1243–8 HAC, *Webblescove* a.1233, 1383 Lil, *Weblescove*, *Webleshoue* c.1250 Lil, *Webluscowe* 1383 Lil (p)
Wellestowe c.1175–8 HAC
Weblestowe 1178–80 HAC, *Web(b)lestowe* 1333 HAC
Weblescote 1271–2 *Ass* (p), 1297 Strange, *Webblescote* 1291–2 *Ass* (p)
Weblestone 1325–46 HAC
Webscowe 1392–9, 97 InqMisc, *Webbescowe* 1487 Ipm, *Webscoe* 1545 PR(L) 19 *et freq* with variant spellings -*sco*(*o*) to 1602 Peake
Webscott 1617 PR(L) 19, 1624 *SBL 3407*, *Webscoe or Webscott* 1663–4 *SBL 1402*

Early spellings show that the final element of Webscott is ME *scogh*, ultimately from ON **skógr**, cognate with OE **sceaga** 'small wood'. It is unlikely that there is any direct contact with Norse speech; but the term makes an occasional appearance in the adjoining county of Cheshire (PN Ch **5.1** 339), and this instance may be considered an outlier from the generally northern distribution.

The first element appears to be unique to this name. The only suggestion available is a personal name, which could be an -*el* derivative of the recorded *U*(*a*)*ebba,* which Redin (p. 80) suggests may be from OE *webba* 'weaver'. A late OE origin for Webscott would provide a possible context for a combination of an OE personal name with a word of ultimate ON origin.

There is probably mistranscription in some of the printed spellings, and there has been some substitution of commoner generics, the latter resulting in the modern -*cott.*

Hey 116–17 says that in the 16th/17th century there were two houses, Higher Webscott on the original site and Lower Webscott nearer Harmer.

Field-Names

The field-names of this township are presented in three sections: (i) contains names in the main portion of the township, (ii) and (iii) contain those in the detached areas of Sleap and Webscott. The (a) forms in all sections are 1839 *TA*. In (b, i) early forms dated c.1240–60, 1334 are HAC, 1662 are Hey: in (b, ii) 1661 and 1787 are *SBL 1784*, *1789*.

(a, i, Balderton) Adderfield; Appletree Lsw, Mdw; Birch Hill; Broomy Lsw; Cow Lsw, Big, Little, Near; Crifton (*v.* ***cryfting** and cf. Criftins in Dudleston *supra*: the field is of similar size to its neighbours); Drayton Hill, Big, Little; Grig Lsw (FN 50 suggests that *grig* is Welsh *grug* 'heather'); Marl Pce; Pink Yd; Rough Croft; Witherage Green Fd (*v*. Witterage *supra*); Within Hill, Far ~ ~, ~ ~ Mdw (*The Within Hills* 1700 Gough, *v*. **wīðign**).

(b, i) *Baldertonslow* 1334 (possibly **hlāw** 'tumulus'); *Bilmerspol* 1334 ('Bilmarsh pool'); *The Bromehurst Feild* 1662 (*v*. Broomhurst *supra*); *Colledge Leasow, First, Second* 1662; *The Farthings* 1662 (*v*. **feorðung**); *Gorsthurst* 1334 (*v*. **gorst**, **hyrst**); *The Gorsty Field* 1662 (*v*. ***gorstig**); *Le Haghfelde* 1334 (*v*. **haga**[1] 'enclosure'); *Holstedemore* c.1240–60, *Holstedestowe* 1334 (apparently a p.n.) *Holstede* 'hollow place') with **mōr** 'marsh' and **stōw** 'assembly place': **stede** and **stōw**, like **haga** *supra*, are unusual in Sa); *Great Poole Pasture, Lower* and *Upper Little Poole Meadow, Rush Pool Meadow* 1662; *Taylors Feild* 1662.

(a, ii, Sleap) Big Bushes; Bilmarsh Mdw (*v*. Bilmarsh *infra*); Cow Lsw, Further, Middle, Near (*Cow Leasowe* 1661); Cow Pasture, Far; Honey Croft; The Lessage, Far and Big, The Near Lessage (*The Lessuages* 1700 Gough); Lower Hayes; Marl Pce, Higher, Lower; Park Fd, Mdw (a short distance from Sleap Hall); The Patch; The Water Mdws; Way Fd, ~ ~ Croft, Little ~ ~; Wikey, Big, Little (perhaps 'mountain ash', *v*. FN 48).

(b, ii) *Byshops Yard* 1787; *Cornells Meadows* 1661; *The Further Moore* 1661; *The Heaths* 1787; *Hollinsfield* 1787; *The Marled Leasowe* 1661; *Matthews Yorde* 1661; *Ye Moores* 1787; *Newcrofts* 1787; *New Lane* 1787.

(a, iii, Webscott) Banky Mdw; Big Mdw; Brandy Lsw (FN 29 suggests that Brandy in f.ns. refers to clearing by burning); Coppice Lsw; Crifton, Big, Little (*v*. *supra*, Big Crifton is a large field); Croft(s); Fox Holes, Near and Further Fox Hole; Gutter Fd; Harmer Close, Long ~ ~ (by Harmer in Newton township); Horse Pasture; Ox Lsw; Rosy Mdw (FN 27 cites several examples and suggests a connection with Welsh *rhos* 'moor, heath'); Well Lsw.

(b, iii) *Le Hethilyghe* 1333 HAC (*v*. **hǣðiht**, **lēah**); *Webbestowlone* ib ('Webscott lane').

3. MARTON (SJ 443239)

Marton' iuxta Mudle 1292–5 *Ass*, *Marton'* 1327 SR (p)
Merton 1452 *SBL 4525*
Martin in Middle parish 1684 PR(StA) 5

'Lake settlement', *v*. **mere**, **tūn**, identical with Marton in Chirbury, Part **1** 199–200. Instances in other counties have variant modern forms Marten, Martin, Merton. The whole corpus, numbering about 30, is discussed by Ann Cole in *Journal* 24, pp. 30–41.

The village is at a road-junction, ¼ mile from the small lake called Marton Pool.

Marton Pool was earlier (*aqua de*) *Bassemare* 1271–2 *Ass*, *Bassemere* 1324 HAC. This may be short for **Bassechirchmere*. The lake is bisected by the boundary between Baschurch and Myddle parishes.

THE BUTTS, 1833 OS, *Gravelly Butts* 1839 *TA*. This is **butte** in the sense 'headland in an open field'. The house occupies a strip of land in what appears from *TAMap* to have been a small open field N.W. of the village.

FIRTREE COTTAGE.

MARTON COPPICE.

MARTON FM.

MARTON GRANGE.

MARTON HALL, 1833 OS, 1839 *TA*.

MARTONTAN HO (TAN HO in Gazetteer): Gough 10 says "it is likely that a mill stood here formerly, but now there is onely a tan house, which was first erected by Richard Acherley, great grandfather of Andrew Acherley, now living". Hey 100 notes that Thomas Atcherley was named as a tanner in a Chancery case of 1623.

MARTON VILLA.

WESTONHATCH PLTN, *Westons Hatch* 1839 *TA*.

Field-Names

Forms in (a) are 1839 *TA*. Early forms dated 1756 are *SBL 8609*.

(a) Appletree Fd; Aldrey Croft (probably 'alder'); Ashing Hill; Banky Fd; Banky Lsw, Near; Bar, Lower, Higher (by road to Loppington); Barnyard (2, both large); The Basnetts, Upper ~; Bowen's Lsw; Bradley Gate (*Bradely Gate* 1756); Broomy Crofts, Big Broomy Leasow; Circuits, Lower, Middle, Big (in the angle made by junction of Marton/Myddle road and road to Loppington); Clemley Park (*Clemly* 1756, *v*. Clemley in Prees *infra*); Cloddy Green, ~ ~ Mdw (at E. edge of village); Cote Lsw, Big (no building); Croft (several, small enclosures on edge of village and by Myddlewood); Crows Nest, Lower (fields called The Middle and The Higher Nest adjoin: there is nothing on 6" map to account for the n.); Dairy Pce; Eytons Bridge (a road crosses a brook here, on boundary with Eyton in Baschurch); Far Fd (3); Far House Mdw; Field (an area adjoining the hamlet of Myddlewood has small fields called Big and Little Field, Field by Mr Griffiths, Mr Scotts, Mr Morris's, Field before Door, Far Pit Field: an adjacent area is divided into small fields called Common Field, Big, Far and Near Field, this area is divided between Marton and Myddle); Field back of House, Field behind House; Four Acre and Two Acre Fd; Four Acres, Five Acres (adjoining, with Six Acres nearby: there is another Four Acres a short distance away); Freehold Lsw; Fridays, Lower and Higher ~ (*The Two Fridays* 1756, *v*. FN 25 for a discussion of *Friday* in Sa f.ns.); Gib Socket (?socket for a gibbet); Gorsty Mdw; Grassy Pool; Gravelly Butts (*v*. The Butts *supra*); Leasow, Clover, Glassy, Higher; Little Boat Mdw (by Marton Pool); Little Mdw (several); Long Acre; Long Bine (possibly referring to bindweed); Long Lsw (2); Marlpit Fd; Marsh, Big, Little; Martons Moors (*Marton More* 1602 Peake); Meadow by Paynes, ~ by Shintons; New Lsw; New Pce; Nine Shilling Lsw (perhaps *Nines Leasows* 1756); Nine Shilling Mdw (not near preceding); The Nook, The Near

Nooks, The Big Nooks or Hooks, Far Hooks; Oak Lsw; Old Mill Lsw (1756, cf. *The Old Mill Brook* 1700 Gough); Orchards; Owens Croft (*The Two Ownes Crofts* 1756); Park Fd, Lsw (either side of Clemley Park); Pencils Lsw; Pool Mdw (by Marton Pool); Poors Mdw; Quol Lsw; Rushy Fd; The Slane; Slang (narrow strip); Stackyard Mdw; Stanways Fd; Tailors Croft; Thorns Mdw; The Three Cornered Fd; Town Mdw, Little (*Town Meadow* 1756); Upper Fd, Lsw; Well Lsw; Westons Hatch, ~ ~ Mdw (on boundary with Weston Lullingfield); Wooderley Fd; Woodhouse Fd; Wood Lsw.

(b, except for *The Rowlands* all forms in this section are 1756) *Crumnis Croft*; *Field Pce*; *Grass Yards*, *The Two*; *Little Fields*, *The Two*; *Rough Leasow*; *The Rowlands* 1700 Gough (probably 'rough land'); *Three Way Leasow*; *Trevors Croft*, *Meadow*; *The Yard by the House.*

4. MYDDLE, including HOULSTON

BILMARSH (SJ 494252)

Bilemersch 1250–5 Eyton *et freq* with variant spellings *Byle-* and *-mars*, *-mers*, *-mersche* to 1529–30 *SBL 6305*
Bilmarshe 1579 PR(L) 19

v. **mersc**. The first element is **bile** 'bill, beak', used in place-names for "a pointed projection, either with reference to topography . . . or to the shape of a boundary" (VEPN). The boundary-shape sense is probably found here. *TAMap* shows a field called *Bilmarsh Meadow*, ¾ mile N. of the settlement, which suggests that the marsh extended into the sharply pointed projection on the N.E. boundary of Myddle parish (*v.* Map 2).

Gough p. 33 refers to a "small common" called *Billmarsh Green*, and Hey p. 14 refers to *Little Bilmarsh*, purchased in the mid-17th cent. Gough, p. 38, also mentions a spring called *Bill-well*, the stream from which runs through *Billa Meadows*. The latter may be the *TA Bilmarsh Meadow*.

BRANDWOOD (SJ 469262): *Le Barndewode* m.13th *SBL 6305*, *Brand Wood* 1545 PR(L) 19, *Brandwhoode* 1558 *et seq* to 1590 ib, *Brandwhod* 1559 *et seq* to 1591 ib, *Brandwood* 1601 ib, *Braindwood* 1692, 1701 ib. 'Burnt wood', *v.* **brend**, **wudu**.

HOULSTON (SJ 479248)

Le Hulston 1447–8 *SBL 2482*, *Hulston* 1470–1, 77, 78, 82 *SBL 115*, *182*, *97*, *116*, 1575 *et seq* to 1624 PR(L) 19
Houlston 1547 PR(L) 19, *Hoolston* 1729 ib
Houlson 1603 PR(L) 19
Houston 1629 PR(L) 19, *Howston* 1635 ib

Housan 1632 PR(L) 19
Hooson 1672 HTR

If the final element is **tūn** no suggestion can be offered for the qualifier. If it is **stān** this could be a compound with ***hugol** 'small hill, mound', found in Howle, Part **1** 161. There are no hills, but a mound would be conspicuous in this low-lying area.

Houleston on 1833 OS corresponds to Houlston Manor on modern maps, and the above GR is for this site. The 1999 Explorer map gives the name Houlston to a farm ½ mile N. which is Lower Houlston Farm on 1961 1". The 1900 6" map has Houlston for this site and Houlston Farm for the Manor.

LINCHES or LINCH LANE (Gazetteer): *Lynches subtus Mudlewode* 1291 *Ass*, *Fennymere alias Linches* 1652 *SBL 10*, *Linches Hall*, *The Linch Lane* 1700 Gough. Gough says that Linch Lane marked the W. side of Myddle Park and was named from Linches Hall "which stood on a small bank in Fenymeare ground, neare the side of this lane". This identifies the lane with the narrow road which runs past Myddle Park Wd to Merrington, and is now part of the Marches Way. **hlinc** is regularly used in place-names for a terraced road, *v.* LPN 180.

MYDDLEWOOD (SJ 452239): *Muddelwode* m.13th *SBL 6305*, *Bosc of Mudle* 1250–5 Eyton, *Mudleswode* 1291–2 *Ass*, *Muddleswode* 1297 Strange, *Mydle Wood* 1604, 7 PR(L) 19, *Middlewood* 1811 PR(L) 10. 'Wood belonging to Myddle'. Gough 33 gives an account of Myddle Wood Common and the tenements and cottages which were there in 1700. The settlement was probably made by squatters.

ALFORD FM. It is probable that this is a modern name. Kelly's Directory for 1934 notes repairs to the Castle in 1849 by Viscount Alford. The buildings are not named on 1833 OS or on 1839 *TAMap.* The occurrence of Alford as a surname in 1291 *Ass* (Thom' *de Alford*, mentioned in connection with property at Myddlewood) is probably a coincidence.

BRANDWOOD COTTAGE (~ HO on modern maps).

BURLTONLANE FM, *Burlton Lane* 1795 RTH, by the road to Burlton in Loppington.

CASTLE FM, *The Castle Farme* 1700 Gough. Hey, note to Plate 6, says that the Lord of Myddle was given licence to build the castle in 1308, and the building was allowed to go to ruin in the early 16th cent. Eyton,

X 67, says the remains of the castellated mansion are still to be seen.

EAGLE FM (Gazetteer). Hey 87 n. says "it acquired the name of Eagle Farm after the Gittins family had moved to Castle Farm and let the property to Thomas Jux, who put up the sign of the Eagle and Child (the coat of arms of the Lords Strange . . .) and sold ale there". Richard Gittins was at this farm in 1528.

THE GROVE.

HOLLINS, 1608 PR(L) 19, 1833 OS, 1849 *TA*, *Hollens* 1541 PR(L) 19 *et seq* to 1592 ib, *Hollans* 1573 ib, *The Hollins* 1691 ib, *Halling* 1695 Morden: *v.* **holegn** 'holly'.

MYDDLE HILL, *Middle Hill* 1689, 98 PR(L) 19, 1839 *TA*. Roger *de la Hull* is listed 1327 SR in Myddle.

MYDDLE PARK WD, *Park Wood* 1839 *TA*, cf. *Le Park du Mudle* 1333 HAC. Gough 29 (1700) speaks of the park in the past tense.

Field-Names

Forms in (a) are 1839 *TA*. Early forms for which no date or source is given are 1700 Gough.

(a) Allens Lsw, Lower, Higher; Bank; Banky Mdw; Barn Croft; Barn Fd (several); Barn Yd (2); Bean Fd; Big Fd (2); Big Mdw; Billings Croft, Higher, Lower; Breach Croft, Far, Little, Near, ~ ~ Mdw (*v.* **brēc**); Brickkiln Croft, ~ Fd (near but not adjoining); Brickkiln Lsw; Brick Yd; Bringwins or Bringwyas; Brook Mdw; Broomy Lsw; Calves Croft; Cherry Lsw; The Clemley (*v.* Clemley in Prees *infra*); Clover Croft; Clover Fd; Club Mdw, Little Club Lsw (perhaps a reference to a friendly society, cf. Club Fm, Part **3** 182); Cockpit (by Houlston Manor); College, Far ~, College Stiles; Colts Croft; Coppy Fd (2); Cow Lsw; Cow Pasture; Cows Pasture; Croft, Long, Middle, Top, Croft below Garden (small enclosures S. of Brandwood, 1900 6" shows a cluster of houses here); Croft(s) (numerous small enclosures N.W. of Myddle village, others by Myddle Hill); Croft adjoining Flash; Cross Fd (near a road junction); Dogkennel Lsw; Dry Pit Fd; The Eight Acres (Six Acres, slightly smaller, adjoins); The Farthing, Near ~ (a quarter of some unit, *v.* **feorðung**); Fiddlers Bridge Mdw; Field adjoining Mr Shingler's Coppy; Field adjoining Wright's; Field adjoining Fox's, Menlove's, Stanways (3 adjoining enclosures); Field before the House (2); Field near Eyton's; Floyds Yd, Higher, Lower; Footway Fd, Lower, Upper; Four Moors; Fox Hole; The Furlong (a small field N.W. of Myddle village); Gorsy Lsw (2); Gravel Hole Fd; Green Fd; Guest Croft; Halls Fd; Headed Lion, Big, Little; Heady Croft, Big; Higher Ground; Hill Fd, Lsw (by Myddle Hill); Husk, Big, Little, Near (perhaps *hassock* 'clump of coarse grass'); Inch Lane Mdw (perhaps *innage* 'newly-enclosed land'); John Wynn's Breakfast (cf. Breakfast Croft in Loppington); Kiln Croft; Little Croft; Little Mdw (several); Little Square Fd; Long Croft, Near ~ ~; Long Fd (2); Long Flg; (The) Long Lsw (2); Lower Fd; Lyons Bank (possibly **leyne**, *v.* Part **2** 108); Maddox's Lsw, Near, Little; Mail Lsw; Mail Pce (not near preceding); Mall Lsw; Mansells Fd;

Manure Lsw; Marl Bank; Marl Pce (*The Marle Peices*); Marsh, ~ Mouth; Marsh adjoining Shone's, Far ~ ~ ~; Meadow, Big, Little, Hanmers, Nunnerley, Rogers (these are adjoining fields, Rogers Croft and Fd adjoin the last item); Meadow Pce; Moor, Alder Tree, Big, Little, Far, Near, Middle ~ (adjacent fields on N.E. boundary); Moss Pit Lsw; Mowing Mdw; Mowing Pce; New Fd (several); New Lsw (several); New Mdw; Old House Croft; Old House Fd (not near preceding); Old Mdw; Ox Pasture; Park, Higher, Park Mdw, Wide Park, Little Park Fd, Field below Park (*v.* Myddle Park Wd *supra*); Parsons Croft; Partridge Mdw (1700 Gough); Near Partridge Fd; Peartree Lsw (2); Peas Lsw; Penbooke Croft (*sic*, Gough 12 gives the n. Penbrooke to the stream here, which is the stream crossed by *Bristle Bridge*); Pigs Croft, The Pig Fd; Pit Fd (several, one with Pit Mdw adjoining); Pool Croft, Near, Upper; The Pools, Pools adjoining Road; Principals; Priscilla's Croft; Rail Pce and Far Wood Lsw; Road Croft; Rooks, Far, White; The Rough; Rough Moor; Rushy Lsw; Rushy Mdw; Ryegrass Pce; Sandy Bank; Seeky Croft; Seven Acres (2); Sharrats Croft; Sheet Groves, Further, Third ~ ~; The Six Acre Fd; Six Acres (adjoins Five Acres); Six Acres (adjoins Seven Acres); Sleap Croft, Fd (on boundary with Sleap); Sleap Fd (not near Sleap Hall or Sleap in Loppington); The Sling (an unremarkable shape); The Slugs; Square Fd; Stubble Fd; Sturdy, Big, Little; Tailors Fd; Ten Acres; Three Acres; Top Fd; Warwick Fd (*Werwick Feilde* 1592–3 *SBL 2483*); Way Fd; Well Lsw; Well Mdw; Wheat Fd; Wheat Hill; White Fd; Within Hill, Far and Near ~ ~ (*v.* **wīðign**); Woodfine Bank; Wood Ground; Wood Lsw (3); Wynbury Fd; Yewtree Fd.

(b) *Le Barn de Wodesford juxta le Barndewode* l.13th Gough; *Bristle Bridge* (Gough 11–12 recounts a local belief that a monstrous boar was killed here: from Gough's description the bridge would be at approx. GR 469244, on the Ellesmere/Shrewsbury road); *Dearie Leasowe* 1592–3 *SBL 2483*; *Diblin Woode* 1602 Peake, *Dublin's Wood* 1642 PR(L) 19, *Divlin Wood* (Gough 37 mentions *Divlin Lane alias Taylor's Lane* as well as the wood, and says that the n. is "not now used": it appears to be a transferred use of Dublin); *Draken Hill* ('dragon hill'); *The Goblin Hole* (Gough 11–12 says this is a cave by *Bristle Bridge*, inhabited t.Eliz.); *The Harhouse Banke* (Gough 29 says that the Harhouse "now pulled down" was S. of the Castle); *Hell Hole or Heild Hole* (the spring called *Bill-well* rises here); *The High Hursts*; *The Hill Leasows*; *Holloway Hills* (Gazetteer gives this n. as extant: Gough 30 says it referred to a wood which was cut down in his lifetime); *The Hooke of the Wood*; *The Intake*; *The Lane* (on E. side of Castle Park); *Myddle Pools*; *The Setts* (Gough 37 says this was "a sort of crosse way", so called because corpses were put down on the way to burial and prayers said "in the time of popery"); *Shoton Banke* (earlier *Broadway Bank*); *The Sling Lane*; *The Wood feild Lane* (Gough 37 says this was the road running to the top of Myddle Hill).

5. NEWTON ON THE HILL (SJ 486235)

Neutone 1194–5 SAC, *-ton'* 1255–6 *Ass*, *Newton* 1499 Ipm, 1577 Saxton, *Neuton sup' Le Hull* 1436 *SRO 322/245*, *Newton one the Hill* 1601 PR(L) 19, ~ *Supra Montem* 1615 ib, ~ *of ye Hill* 1639 ib, ~ *on ye Hill* 1672 HTR

Neventon c.1217 SAC

Neweton 1350 *SBL 3656*

'New settlement', OE *nīwantūne*. This is probably the commonest of all English settlement-names, *v*. CDEPN 436–9. There are about a dozen instances in Sa.

The map in Hey (p. 19) shows two very small detached portions of the township, and these are arrowed to Newton on the 19th-cent. Index to Tithe Survey map. For the purposes of the place-name survey these have been included in the township of Myddle.

HARMERHILL (SJ 490212)

Haremor' 1325–46 HAC, *-mor(e)* 1383 Lil, *-more* 1636 PR(L) 19
Haremere 1602 Peake, *-meare* 1655 SAS 1/XLVII, 1697, 1709 PR(L) 19
Harmer or Armour Hill 1833 OS, *Harmer Hill* 1839 *TA*

'Hare marsh', *v*. **hara**, **mōr**. Cf. *Haremor*, Part **4** 140, which, however, is more likely to have **mere** as second element.

The 14th-cent. references are to land, and Harmerhill is probably not an ancient settlement. HARMER MOSS FM, which is called *Harmer* on 1833 OS, may be an earlier settlement-site. HARMER MOSS PLTN is *Harmer Moss* on this map, *The Moss* 1839 *TA*. Gough 30 says that *Haremeare Mosse* was an island in the mere, and that the mere was drained and converted to meadow and pasture. This probably does not constitute evidence that **mere** 'lake' was the original generic, as the area drained is more likely to have been marsh than a glacial lake.

There was also a heath (*Harmer Heath vel Newton Heath* 1611 PR(L) 19, *Haremeare Heath* 1700 Gough) and a warren (*the Haremeare Warren* 1700 Gough).

BRIDGEWATER ARMS P.H.

CLIFFS COTTAGE.

HIGHER AND LOWER RD. These names are given on the 1999 Explorer map to the two branches of the Shrewsbury road S. of Webscott. This may be an antiquarian revival, echoing Gough's *Higher* and *Lower Way* for these two roads.

STONEYCROFT.

Gough 11–12 mentions *The Meare House* in Harmer.

Field-Names

Forms in (a) are 1839 *TA*. Early forms are Gough and those for which no date is given are 1700.

(a) Banky Lsw; Banky Mdw; Barn Yd (2); Bells Lsw; Big Fd; Birds Pce; Bull Mdw; Calves Croft; Clemley Park, Park Sides (*v.* Prees f.ns. *infra*); Common Fd, Near; Cow Lsw, Far, Near; Croft(s) (*freq*, along roads and in Harmerhill); Crooked Pce (T-shaped); Dee Bank; Docky Lsw; Field, First, Second, Third, Fourth, Far (5 rectangular enclosures S.W. of Harmerhill); The Flash (shallow floodwater pool); Footway Croft; Garden Pce; Gorsy Croft; Grassy Lsw; Heath Pce (2); Hill Fd, Far, Second, Third, Fourth (4 fields straggling the township boundary N. of Harmerhill, with fields called Hill Lsw at N. and S. ends of the series, also Hill Croft); Higleys Pce; The Last Skin, ~ ~ ~ Croft; Little Mdw; Long Croft; Long Harmer (a short distance from Harmerhill); Lower Mdw; Marl Pce; Middle Pce; The Moss; Pimhill Mdw (Pim Hill is in Hadnall Part **4** 156–8); Pit Fd, Far, Near; Pit Lsw (not near preceding); Pryces Lsw; Road Croft, Field adjoining Road; Rushy Mdw; Rushy Mdw, Moor (not near preceding); Salt Pce; (The) Slang (3, all narrow strips); Smith's Pce, Upper ~ ~; Square Fd; Stone Rock; Tailors Pce, Big, Little; Three Cornered Lsw; Triangle Croft; Walmsleys Croft; White Horse Fd, Long, Upper, Lower; Wink Hill Bank; Wycherley's Croft; Yards End.

(b) *Bald Meadow Lane*; *Borede Meadow* l.13th; *The Double Gates*; *Dunstall Pitt* (Gough 10 says this is an old marlpit); *The Greene Lane by Newton*; *Lea Lane*; *Old Feild Lane*, *The Olde Feild.*

Great Ness

The parish-name, OE **ness** 'promontory', is discussed in Part **1**.

George Foxall's *TAMap* shows the following divisions: Alderton, Felton Butler, Great Ness, Kinton, Wilcott, and it is convenient to present the place-name material under these. On the Index to Tithe Survey map only Alderton and Felton Butler are shown as discrete townships.

1. ALDERTON (SJ 385174)

Olreton 1271–2 *Ass*, 1309 Ipm, 1339 *SRO 322/136*, 1345 *SBL 3611*
Obreton 1284–5 FA
Alverton 1356 *SBL 10772*, 1385 Cl
Alderton' Hy 8 *RentSur*, *-ton* 1610 PR(L) 20 *et seq*

Unlike its modern namesake in Myddle, *supra*, this appears to be a genuine 'alder settlement', *v.* **alor**, **tūn**. The occurrence of *Alverton* in the 14th cent. may be due to confusion with the place in Myddle: *Alver-* is not a normal development from **alor**.

Field-Names

Forms in (a) are 1847–50 *TA*.

(a) Barn Mdw; The Cockshutt; The Coppice; Dingy Mdw; Dove House Yd (by the single house which is all that is shown at Alderton on 1833 OS and *TAMap*); Fishpool (a large field on S. boundary of parish); Garden Fd; Meadow, Big, Middle, Long, Lown; Middle Lsw; The Rookery, Upper ~; Sheep Cote, Far, Near; Well House, Big, Little.

2. FELTON BUTLER (SJ 394176)

This is a DB manor so was included in Part **1**. The name is a compound of **feld** 'open land' and **tūn**, which occurs three times in Sa. It was suggested in Part **1** 131, 307 that Felton Butler and West Felton, which are 5½ miles apart, are both so named because they are situated on a stretch of raised ground with marsh on either side. This use of **feld** for land on the edge of marsh is much less common than its use for land on the edge of forest or on contours of 400' to 500', but some clear instances are cited in M. Gelling, *Place-Names in the Landscape* 237, and it seems a likely explanation for these two Sa names.

WHITE HALL, *Whitehall Field* and *Leasow* 1847–50 *TA*.

Field-Names

Forms in (a) are 1847–50 *TA*.

(a) Alder Lsw; Banky Fd; Butlers Mdw, Higher, Lower, Little (on the parish boundary, probably short for Felton ~ ~); Close (several); Coppy Lsw; Cow Pasture; The Crofts; Far Clump; Far Mdw; The Farm Lsw (a large field N. of hamlet); Glass House Fd (S.W. of hamlet); Gorsty Lsw; Gravel Hole Fd, ~ ~ Lsw; Greenway; Greenways (not near preceding); Hanmers Bank, Croft; Hawthorn Lsw; Heath Moss Mdw; Kim Cams Croft (FN notes *kim-kam* 'perverse' in SWB); Lady Fern Cottage; Long Lsw; Low Ground; Marsh Lane; Middle Lsw; Moors Flg (by Near Hill Fd, perhaps a small open-field area); Near Hill Fd (Stephen *de le Hull'* is listed under Felton Butler 1327 SR); Old Hew Stick; Patch (2, minute fields); Pool Mdw (by the pool at Folly Fm in Shrawardine); Purcy's Lsw; Sand Hole Fd; School House Yd; Slang (strip by Well House Lane); Swans Well; Walk Moors; Well House Lane (leading to Well House in Alderton); Well Mdw; Wheat Croft; Wheat Fd; Wheat Ridge; White Lsw.

3. KINTON (SJ 370195)

Kinetu', *-ton* 1203–4 *Ass* (p)
Kinton 1271–2 *Ass et passim* with variant spellings *Kyn-* and *-tun'*
Kyngton' 1291–2 *Ass*
Keinton 1659 PR(L) 20

'Royal estate', *v.* **cȳne-**, **tūn**. Neither of the two estates at Ness was in royal ownership in 1086 or TRE, so the reference is obscure.

AEKSEA, *Hexa* 1607, 88 PR(L) 20, *Hecsa* 1688, 91 ib, an obscure name. *TAMap* shows a single, unnamed, small house here.

AEKSEA COPPICE, COTTAGE.

CRANBERRYMOSS, *Cronimosse* 1612, 13, 53 PR(L) 20, *Cronnimosse* 1627, 9, 31, 1725 ib, *Cranymoss* 1635, 9 ib: *v.* **moss**, the first element may be *cranny* as in nook and cranny. The word is recorded from mid-15th cent. *Cranberry* is a rationalisation. The marsh is *Moss* on *TAMap*.

GROVE INN.

KINTON HO, VILLA.

KINTON MOSS, *Moss* 1847–50 *TA*.

SARNCHYRION (Gazetteer), 1619 PR(L) 20, *Sarnehyrion* 1618 ib,

Sarnehyrion 1623 ib. The forms without -*c*- suggest Welsh *sarnauhirion* 'long causeways'.

WOLFSHEAD, (*The*) *Wolf's Head* 1777, 8 PR(L) 20, *Wolf's Head* 1837 OS, *Wolfs Head* 1847–50 *TA*. In PR(L) 20 this is indexed under Inns. In 1384 MGS there is a "Hugo filius Johannis le Wolfs de Nesse": it is not clear what relationship, if any, this surname bears to the house-name.

A residence called *Pentrecoid* (-*koyd*, -*coyd*) is recorded 1591 *et seq* to 1657 in PR(L) 20. 'Farm by a wood', cf. *Pentre-Coed* in Dudleston *supra*. PR(L) 20 also has *The Lodge in the Heath* 1626, *The Lodge in ... Kinton*, *The Heath in Kinton* 1633, *Kinton Heath* 1723.

Field-Names

Forms in (a) are 1847–50 *TA*.

(a) Ash Harbour; Bally Quity; Banky Fd, Lsw; Belland Fd; Birch Tree Croft; Black Wall (probably 'black spring'); The Broaches, Great ~ (Breaches, Big and Little Breaches adjoin in Wilcott township, *v.* **brēc**, **bryce**); Broad Lsw; Cae Reeg; Calves Patch (by Milking Bank); Castle Fd (2 fields at E. end of hamlet); The Common Fd (by Wolfs Head); Corney Howell; Cow Pasture; The Croft, ~ ~ Lands; Day Lsw; Dingle Dongle (FN 18 says "some land by a deep hollow in Great Ness rejoices in the glorious name of Dingle Dongle": the n. is a humorous formation based on *dingle* 'deep hollow'); Far Mdw; Field, Upper, Middle, Banky; The Finger Post (triangle between converging roads); The Fownogs, John Davies's ~ (4 fields by The Moors, Welsh *mawnog* 'peat bog'); Gravel Hole Pce; Green Yd (in Kinton); Hay Moor, Big, Little; Hicksey, ~ Mdw (close, not adjoining); Highley; Hoiduggin, Far, Near (Hoceyduggin adjoins in Wilcott); Hopyard, Lower ~; House Pce (by Aeksea); Hovel (minute enclosure); The Kernel (probably a shape-name, the field is shaped like a hazel-nut); The Lees, Near and Far Lees, Further, Middle and Near Leys; Long Lsw (2); Machine Fd (on outskirts of hamlet); Milking Bank (a very large field, not near a farm); The Moors (there are 8 fields with this n. on N.W. boundary); The Moors, Far and Near Moor, Morgans ~, Parsons ~, Vaughan's ~, Turf ~ (along S.W. boundary); The Moss (several); New Pce; No Man's Lsw; Olives (FN 49 cites two other instances of Olive ns: the reference is obscure); Orchard Fd; Ox Hill Lsw; Paddock (by Aeksea); Pegy Lsw; Pentre Croft, Fd, Mdw (near Pentre in Kinnerley); The Plain, Plain Mdw (*plain* in the sense 'flat meadowland'); Plantation (several); Pool Sheffrey, Far, Near, Middle (by Kinton Moss, Pool Pce also adjoins the Moss); Pun Kiss Pce (tiny enclosure in Kinton, perhaps a corruption of *pincushion*, used of convex land); Raghouse/Righouse/Rughouse Pce, Rughouse Croft (4 adjoining fields: *The Raghouse* 1717, 28 PR(L) 20, 'a building in which rags are stored or prepared for paper-making' NED *s.v. rag* sb[1]); Road Lsw; Rookery Pce; Rowley, Near, Further; Rye Grass Fd; Sandhole Lsw; Seven Acres; The Shipstows (Big and Little Shepstone adjoin in Wilcott township: *Schepstowesrich* 1323 HAC has **rīc** 'small stream' added: *Schepstow* appears to be a compound of **scēap** 'sheep' and **stōw** 'assembly-place'); Shop Croft (on outskirts of hamlet); Six Acres; Slang

Mdw; Sour Mdw (2, close but not adjoining); Suckley West of Turnpike Gate (a sharp projection on N. boundary by the Oswestry road, there is no field called Suckley on *TAMaps* for either of the neighbouring parishes); Sut Lsw (Set Lsw adjoins in G. Ness township); Symore Lsw (Lymore in Wilcott is nearby); Tithe Croft; Turf Pit Lsw; Well Croft, Mdw; Wynnes Croft; Yew Tree Pce.

4. GREAT NESS (SJ 398190)

HOPTON (SJ 388203). The name appears in its modern form from 1271–2 *Ass* onwards. In 1255–6 *Ass* a *Horton'* is mentioned together with Ness and with two places, Milford and Adcot, in Little Ness: this may be a corrupt form for Hopton.

'Settlement in a remote place': this is one of six Hoptons in Sa, *v*. Part **1**. LOWER HOPTON (SJ 380209) is *Little Hopton* on 1837 OS and on *TAMap*, but no specific earlier references have been found for it.

STARTLEWOOD (SJ 388205)
Startcloud 1366 *SRO 103/1/3/68*
Steckloyde 1593 PR(L) 20, *Sterkloyde*, *Sterklloyd* 1604 ib, *Stark Lloyd* 1678–9 *SRO 103/1/3/112*
Starclewood 1601–2 *SBL 1736*, 1622 PR(L) 20, *Starklewood* 1611 PR(L) 20
Startle Lloyd 1678 PR(L) 20
Startle-wood 1678 PR(L) 20, *Startle Wood* 1847–50 *TA*

'Tail-shaped rock', *v*. **steort, clūd**. A narrow ridge called The Cliffe extends from Startlewood to Clifton Ho in Ruyton-XI-Towns.

WILCOTT MARSH, 1793 *SBL 5370*, *Le Marche iuxta Winlecote* 1203–10 HAC (*v.r. Le Merchs*), *WilcotMarsh* 1692 PR (L) 20, *v*. **mersc.**

BROOMHILL, 1847–50 *TA*, *Broomehill* 1612 GT, *Broomhill Field* 1635 GT, 1686 *SBL 1954*, ~ *Fields* 1739 *SBL 6196*. The 1686 reference is to a common field. In the 1635 reference John Broome has an enclosure in this field, but this is probably a coincidence. On *TAMap* there is a group of fields with this name S. of Nesscliff, and the farm building is shown but not named. The building is *Broom Hall* 1833 OS.
CONEY BANK.
THE COTTAGES.
GIBRALTAR, 1833 OS, ~ COPPICE, on parish boundary.
HEATH FM.
HOPTON HILL.

KYNASTON'S CAVE, 1847–50 *TA*. This cave, high on Nesscliff Hill, has "H.K. 1674" carved in the rock pillar which divides it into two compartments. Kelly's Directory for 1934 says it was "formerly the retreat of a celebrated outlaw of that name". Entries in PR(L) 20 show that it was inhabited in the 18th cent. There are references to the burials of "Thomas Griffiths of the Cave, a poor labourer" in 1700, two widows who died there in 1706, an "inhabitant of the Cave at Ness Cliffe" in 1776, and "a soldier and Pensioner who died in the Cave at Ness-Cliffe" in 1783.

LIN CAN COPPICE.

MOUNT PLEASANT, 1833 OS, 1847–50 *TA*.

MOUNT VIEW.

OLIVER'S POINT. There may have been popular association of the adjacent promontory fort with the Civil War.

THE POPLARS.

THE PRILL, 1833 OS: 'spring'. Prill is a metathesised form of Pearl, for which *v*. Part **3** 130.

RUYTON MOSS.

SHRUGG'S COPPICE.

STONE HO.

WELL HO, 1775 PR(L) 20, *Well House Field* 1847–50 *TA*.

On 1833 OS *Forresters* is marked S. of Hopton.

Field-Names

Forms in (a) are 1847–50 *TA* except for those dated 1820, which are *SBL 6217*, and 1824, 41, which are GT. Early forms dated 1322, 3, 8 are HAC, 1612, 85, 1701, 34 are GT, 1675, 1703, 39, 43, 64, 76, 89 are *SBL 6191*, *4134*, *6196*, *4136*, *4137*, *4170*, *4141*, *6200*.

(a) Alderton Gate Fd (on boundary with Alderton); Ash Coppice (this and one of the Oak Coppices are named on 1833 OS); Bank; The Bank; Banky Lsw; Barn Fd (several); Barn Yd (several); Baymos, Upper, Middle, Lower 1820 (*Baymosse Field* 1612, 75, *The Baymosse* 1685, (*The*) *Baymos Dale Meadow* 1703, 64, *Baymos Field* 1703, 40, possibly 'berry marsh', *v*. **beg**, **mos**); Beamhurst, Lower, Middle, Upper, Little, ~ Fd (Beam Ho in Montford lies to the E. of these fields); Big Mdw (1789); Big Pltn; Bradmos(s) Field 1820 (1703, 39, 40, 43, 'broad marsh'); Brake Fd, Pce (*The Brake* 1675, (*The*) *Brake Field* 1703, 40, 64, 89, *v*. **bracu** 'thicket'); Brickhill Fd ('brick kiln'); Brickkiln Fd; Broad Lsw; Broadway Fd; Broadway Lsw (not near preceding); Brook Flg, Far, Near and Middle ~ ~ (a group of furlong-shaped fields W. of Nesscliff Hill); Broom Lsw; Brooms, Lower, Higher, Near; Cabin Croft (*The Cabbin* 1775, 7 PR(L) 20); Calves Croft; Candlins Pce; Catee Hill; Church Croft (by church); Clerks Croft; Closes (cluster on N. boundary); Coopers Yd and Barn;

Coppice Pce; Cotton's Yd 1820 (1743); Cow Pasture; Crabtree Lsw; Criften, Lower, Higher, ~ Croft, The Criftens, Little ~ (a group of normal-sized fields, cf. Criftins in Dudleston *supra*); Croft (*freq*); Crofts (cluster on N. boundary); Crossway Lsw (by crossroads); Double Lsw (2); Ducketts Croft (*Ducketts Fine Butts* 1675, *The Old House late Ducketts* 1703, 64, *Godfrey Ducket's Piece adjoining to Bradmos Field* 1764); Ferny Hough (cf. the same n. in Kenwick Wd township *supra*); Field under Hill (by Nesscliff Hill); Fir Coppice; Fir Pltn (several); Footway Pce (2); Front Pce (by Mount Pleasant); Godfrey's Mdw (*Godfrey's Leasow* 1743, 1820); Gorsty Fd, Lsw (cf. Gosty Bank 1820); Gravestone Flg; Hannah's Mdw; Hawk Castle Hill (*The Aucastle* 1675, by 'Castle Mound' on 1" map: the *TA* form is probably correct, 'hawk castle' being a fanciful term for an earthwork); Hawthorn Tree Hill (*The Hathorns*, *The Hathorne on the Hill* 1675, *Hathorne on the Hill* 1703, Hawthorn ~ ~ ~ 1820: NED gives *hay-*, *haithorne as* 16th-cent. forms of *hawthorn*); Heath Fd, Far, Middle and Near Heath, Lower Heath Lsw; Helks Lsw; Hill, Hill Croft, Field, End, Pce, Ground, Lsw (by Nesscliff Hill, cf. *The Hill House* 1782 PR(L) 20, *The Hill*, 1790 ib); Hoccaloans (the shape suggests a furlong with headland, so -loans is probably -lands in the sense 'open-field strips'); Hopton Hill, Hill Croft; Horse Fd; The Hunch (FN 14 suggests that this is *haunch*, a shape-name referring to a cut of meat); Inclosure; Innis Meadow 1820 (possibly a reference to aniseed, *v.* FN 31); Lawn (by vicarage); The Legs (2 fields which could be considered leg-shaped); Llewyn Came (Welsh *llwyn* 'grove', Came may be a surname); Long Croft (*Longe* ~ 1675); Long Fd; Long Mdw; Marlpit Croft 1841 (1784); Marlpit Close 1824; Marsh, Big, Little and Further ~, ~ Croft, Fd (straddling the boundary with Kinton, cf. *Ness March* 1612, 1776, *The Marsh* 1654, 55, 1791 PR(L) 20, *Marshes Leasow*, *Croft* 1703, 64); Mathews Croft, Far, Near (Matthews Croft 1820); Moat Lsw (by the moated site at Startlewood); Moor Croft, Lower, Upper; Moor Mdw; Moss (several, cf. *The Moss* 1778, 81 PR(L) 20); Moss Mdw; Moss Wall, Higher, Lower and Near ~ ~; Oak Coppice (several); Old Fd (*Old Feild*(*s*) 1608, 12 PR(L) 20); Ox Pasture (cf. *The Ox Leasowe* 1675); Park (3 fields S. of Nesscliff); The Park, ~ Stiles, Little ~ (by Mount Pleasant); Peartree Fd; Pinfold Yd 1820 (1703, 64); Pissing Hill (cf. (*The*) *Pissing Bank Leasow* 1703, 64, Pissing Bank 1820: FN 32 takes this to be a reference to peas); Pit Lsw; Pit Yd; Pool Croft (several); Pool Fd; Pool Hill Lsw ((*The*) *Poole Hill* 1636, 56 PR(L) 20); Pool Pce (2); Puttings Fd ((*The*) *Puttings Field* 1675, 1703, 64, *Puttinsfield* 1739, *Putting Field* 1789); Road Croft; Rough, Lower, Upper, ~ Mdw; Rough Mdw, Far, Near; Round Bank (one curved side); Round Bank (a rectangular field: *Round Bank Leasow* 1739, 43 may relate to one of the 19th-cent. fields); Round Croft (surrounds a smaller enclosure, but has straight sides); Ruddyfern (near Rodefern in Montford *supra*); Rye Lsw (*Ray Leasow* 1703, *Rye Leasow* 1739, 40, 1820, *The Ray Leasow by the Pool* 1764); Set Lsw (2, not near each other); Shop Yd (in Nesscliff); Short Heath; Silken Grove (cf. *Silkehams Greene* 1675); Six Acres; Slang (strip along road); The Snoggs (cf. *Snoggs Croft* 1675, *v.* Snoggs in Colemere *supra*); Square Mdw; Square Pce (oblong); Stackyard Pce; Stocking Mdw, New ~ ~ (*v.* ***stoccing**); Thistly Croft; Towns End (*Townsend* 1789, the *TA* field is a short distance W. of Great Ness village); Turnpike Fd (by Oswestry road); Twelve Acres; Two Butts (1820); Warren Side (adjoins Coton Side in Ruyton-XI-Towns); Weavers Croft 1820; Well Lsw, Mdw; Well Mdw (not near preceding, *The Well Meadowe* 1675 may be one of these); Wet Meadow 1820; White Lsw (several, cf. *The White Leasowe*, *The Wheate* ~ 1675); Windmill Hills (cf. *The Windmill Banke* 1675) Wood

Fd, Pce; Wood Fd, Far and Near ~ ~ (not near preceding: cf. *Wood Field* 1612, 35, 75); Wood Lsw, Pce ((*The*) *Wood Leasow* 1703, 40, 64, 89); Yewtree Lsw.

(b) *Bedows Butt* 1675; *The Bellawne Vaur Fields* 1675 (probably a Welsh n. with *mawr* 'big' added); *Bowker's Lane* 1790, 99 PR(L) 20; *Broad Oak Leasow* 1789; *The Coate Leasow* 1675; *The Gilden Butts* 1675; *The Greate Leasow* 1675; *The Hayes* 1675; *The Heild* 1675 ('slight slope', *v.* **helde**); *Herne* 1327 SAS 2/V (p) (*v.* **hyrne** 'corner'); *Le Hoch* 1322, *Le Hogh* 1323 *Le Hoghz* 1328 (*v.* **hōh**); *Hopton Field* 1703, 39, 64 (a common field); *The Hurst Corner* 1675; *The Lane* 1776, 81, 90, 92 PR(L) 20; *Leat Leasow* 1780; *The Lowe* 1675 (probably **hlāw**); *Nesscliffe Field* 1675; *New Meadow* 1789; *Nursery Piece* 1789; *Place Courte* 1675; *The Poole Leasowe, Lesser ~ ~, Poole Corner* 1675; *Portway Knapp* 1675; *The Port Road* 1739 ("leading from Great to Little Ness"); *St Thomas's Well* 1612; *Sandford* 1675; *Sherewalle* 1323 ('bright spring', *v.* **scīr**, **wælle**); *The Shooting Butts* 1703; *The Vineyard* 1743; *The Well Meadowe* 1675; *Whitewalle* 1323 ('white spring'); *Whirlpool Lane* 1789, 93 PR(L) 20.

5. WILCOTT (SJ 376184)

Winelecote 1203–10, 1258, 1310, 22 HAC, *Wyvelecote* 1284–5 FA
Winlecote 1203–10 HAC
Winelicote 1218–21 HAC
Wyuelcote 1271–2 *Ass*, *Vinelcote* 1275 HAC, *Winelcote* 1320 HAC
Wyle(s)cote 1271–2 *Ass*
Wiflicote 1281 HAC (p)
Weuelcote 1345 *SBL 3611*
Willecote 1448 HAC
Wylcote 1535 VE *et seq* with variant spellings *Wil-* and *-cotte*, *-cot*

Probably 'cottages associated with Wifel'. Spellings with *-n-* have been treated here as mistranscriptions of forms with *-u-*. Two forms suggest a connective **-ing-**.

It is not clear how early a shortened form akin to the modern one was current. *Willecot* occurs in a Haughmond document of 1275 (no. 664), but a variant reading from a mid-14th-cent. copy has *Vinelcote*, so *Willecot* may have been substituted by the 15th-cent. scribe. Another form, *Wilcote*, from document no. 838, dated 1213–15, is not so easily dismissed, however, as other place-names in the charter have not been 'modernised': but it is out of keeping with other evidence. *Wyle(s)cote* 1271–2 *Ass* may be the earliest certain example of this type of form.

The credibility of an OE personal name **Wifel* has been discussed by P. Kitson ('Quantifying Qualifiers in Anglo-Saxon Charter Boundaries', *Folia Linguistica Historica* XIV/1–2, 1994, pp. 75–7) and J. Insley (*Reallexikon der Germanischen Altertumskunde* 17, pp. 426–7).

Kitson demonstrated that in the numerous charter-boundary names where *wifeles-* is compounded with a topographical term this is much more likely to be a collective use of the genitive singular of *wifel* 'beetle' than a personal name. He doubts whether any human being "ever got lumbered with a name the Old English equivalent of 'Cockchafer' or 'Leatherjacket'". Insley accepts this conclusion about charter-boundary names, but argues that in a few place-names with habitative generics there might be an OE personal name **Wīfel*, which would be the equivalent of ON *Vífill*, originally a term for a heathen priest. He feels that this, either as a place-name or as a term for a priest, would be appropriate to the **-ingahām** formation Willingham, which occurs in Ca and twice in Li.

Neither an archaic personal name nor a term for an insect seems obviously appropriate for Wilcott, though an **-ing** formation **wifeling* 'beetle place' might be considered. This is plausibly suggested by Kitson (p. 76) for a Kentish boundary-mark and there may be another instance in a boundary-mark, *wifeling wicon*, in a recently discovered Herts charter. In Sa, however, such formations are, at best, rare, whereas the use of **-ing-** to link a personal name to a habitative term is common.

Details of this Sa name have not been available for use in previous discussions about *wifel-* names. It perhaps offers some support for a personal name **Wifel*, derived from the insect term.

HILLY LANE, leading to Hilly Fm in Shrawardine.

NESSCLIFF, *Nesse Clyff'* Hy 8 *RentSur*, *Nesseclyffe* 1577 Saxton. There are numerous references in PR(L) 20 from 1594 on, with slightly varying spellings. NESSCLIFF HILL is first noted as *Ness Cliffe Hill* 1778 ib.

NESSCLIFF INN.

OLD THREE PIGEONS P.H., *The Pigeon in Ness Cliffe* 1779 PR(L) 20.

WILCOTT HO.

A place called *Lymer*, *Limer* is mentioned 1663 to 1715 in PR(L) 20: this was presumably a dwelling-place. Cf. *Lymore* in f.ns.

Field-Names

Forms in (a) are 1847–50 *TA*.

(a) Bank; Barn Fd; Big Brickkiln Fd (Brickyard and Garden adjoins); Big Fd, Far, Near; Breaches, Big and Little ~ (*v*. Broaches in Kinton *supra*); Brook Flg, Far, Middle and Near ~ ~ (furlong-shaped fields on either side of the Oswestry road N.W. of Nesscliff village: there does not appear to be a brook); Coppice Lsw; Cottage Lsw; Cow Pasture, Lower, Higher; Croft (*freq* in Nesscliff and Wilcott settlements);

Crossleys Croft; Gorsy Fd; Hill Croft (by Nesscliff Hill); Hilly Gate Fd (Hilly Fm is in Shrawardine); Kinton Fd (on boundary with Kinton); Lawn (2 small fields in Wilcott village); Lower Middle Fd (not near Middle Fd); Lymore Fd, Mdw, Big and Little Lymore; Meadow, Near ~; Meadow, Far and Little ~; Middle Fd (this and Oak Fd adjoin Nesscliffe Fd); Moss Moor (by Moss Pool); Nesscliffe Fd, Big ~ ~ (W. of Nesscliff village, not near the Hill); Oak Coppice; Oak Tree Lsw; Pool and Sling (narrow strip); Shepstone, Big, Little (*v.* The Shipstows in Kinton); Slang (one of a set of furlong-shaped fields); Stable Croft; Stack Yd Fd; Staffords Croft; Waltons Mdw; Wet Lsw; Yew Tree Fd.

(b) *Willcott Pool* 1612 GT, Pool Leasow, Piece 1780 *SBL 6192* (a *vivarium* is mentioned in HAC documents).

Little Ness

v. Part **1** for the parish-name and the affixes which distinguish Little Ness from Great Ness.

ADCOTE (SJ 418195)

Addecota c.1240–52 HAC, *-cote* 1265 HAC, 1271–2 *Ass*, *-cot'* 1327 SR (p)
Adecote c.1272 *Ass*, *-kot* 1291–2 *Ass*
Adcot 1655 SAS 1/XLVII, *Adcott* 1656 PR(L) 20, 1807 PR(StA) 3, 1844 *TA*, *Addcott* 1833 OS

'Adda's cottages.'

BENT MILL (lost), *Benetmulne, -mylle* 1268–71 HAC, *Benetmille* 1298 ib, *molendinum de Bent'* 1315–16 ib, *Bentemille* l.15th ib, *Bent Mylle* 1545 SAS 2/XI: 'bent-grass mill', *v*. **beonet**. The name presumably refers to the mill's surroundings. The location is fixed by the occurrence of *Bent Mill Leasow* in the *TA* for Baschurch. This field is on the E. side of the R. Perry, ½ mile upstream from Adcot Mill.

MILFORD (SJ 419210)

Muleford' 1240 Cl *et freq* with variant spellings *-ford*(*e*) to 1291–2 *Ass* (p)
Mulforde 1268 HAC *et freq* with variant spelling *-ford* to 1484–5 *SBL 6147*
Moolford' 1291–2 *Ass*
Mileford' 1291–2 *Ass* (p)
Mulleford 14th *SBL 3583*
Milford 1466–7 *SBL 6147*, *Mylford* 1484–5 ib, *Millford or Millvard* 1777 *SBL 16874*

'Ford by a mill', a recurrent p.n. MILFORD MILL, 1833 OS, is mentioned in 1271 Ipm. The road from Little Ness to Baschurch crosses the R. Perry here. In the 13th–16th centuries there were three mills on a mile-long stretch of the river. Eyton, X 101, conjectures that this one is the mill recorded at Little Ness in DB.

ADCOTE FM.

FLANDERS, on parish boundary.

FOXHOLES, 1844 *TA*.

MARLPIT POOL.

MILFORD HALL.

MILFORD HO: 1833 OS gives the name Milford to this building, not to the settlement by the mill.

NEW HO.

RUYTON LANE.

THE SHRUBS, *Scrubbs Common*, 1844 *TA*.

VALES WOOD, 1833 OS, *Vailswood* 1682 PR(L) 20, *Valeswood Side* 1782 *SBL 4149*.

YEWTREE COTTAGES.

Field-Names

Early forms for which no date or source is given are 1782 *SBL 4142*. Those dated 1685, 93, 98, 1722, 26, 75 are GT.

(a) Antlins Fd; Barley Fd; Barley Pce; The Barns (3 fields); Barn Yd (2); Beamons Hill; Big Mdw; Brickkiln, ~ Mdw; Bridge End (by the bridge at Milford); Brook Lsw; Brooms Ground; Cases; Chapel Mdw, Yd (in village, cf. *Chapel Field* 1722); Cliff Hill Common (by the ridge called The Cliffe in Ruyton); Close(s) (*freq*, there is a cluster in the Vales Wood settlement and there are several in Little Ness); Cock Pit (on outskirts of village); Combdale, Lower ~; Coppice Pce; Corner Mdw (triangular); Cotons Lsw; Cow Pasture; Cowstages; Criftin (*The Criftins* 1782, a normal-sized field); Cross Mdw (between parallel roads, 1685 *et seq* GT); Cross Pools; Far Lsw; Field, Back and Barley Fd (5 fields on N. boundary); Field before the House; Field over the Road; Flax Moors; Flax Yds (on outskirts of village); Flowers Mdw (1685 *et seq* GT); Goose's Foot (not an obvious shape-name, some plants of the chenopodiaceae family have goosefoot ns.); Gorsty Lsw; Gorsty Pce; Great Downs (*The Downes*); Hares Moor, Great ~ ~ (*Yarsmore* 1685 *et seq* GT, *Yardsmoor Field* 1693); Hemp Butt (1782); The Hills; Hills, Lower, Middle, Near (not near preceding); Hill Top; Holly Bank & Lane; Home Mdw (not near a settlement); Leap Hedges (3 sections of what looks like a set of enclosed furlongs S.E. of village); The Lees (*Lees* 1698, 1722); Little Ness Mdw (on N. parish boundary); Long Flg (2, one S.W. and one S.E. of village, one is so named 1685); Marlpit Fd; The Marshes; Mill Mdw, Meadow Bank (by Adcott Mill); New Pce (1722 *et seq* GT, on *TAMap* this is the n. of 3 fields surrounding The Parks); Old Ryegrass; Owens Mdw; Parish of Montford (the n. of a large field near Montford boundary); The Parks (not near any buildings); Patch(es) (5 small enclosures along Little Ness/Hopton road, 2 near Nib Heath); Perry Ground; Perry Lsw, Big, Middle and Upper ~ ~ (Perry ns. are by the river); Piece Above (*sic*); Pinfold Mdw; Potato

Patch (in village); Rushy Mdw; Ruyton Ways (small pentagonal enclosure near road to Ruyton); Salters Mdw; The Sands; The Shaws; Short Broom; Small Wd; Squires Mdw; Stackyard Croft; Stony Bridge, ~ ~ Mdw (by Nib Heath, perhaps a causeway); The Three Lsws; Tinkers Fd; Tongue Hill (1693, 1722, 75, *Tonghill* 1685, 98, *Tongue Field Hill* 1722, the field could be considered tongue-shaped); Townsend, Upper ~ (adjoining Adcott); Upper Clover Pce; Vineyard (by Adcott); Viper Hills; Warthill, Upper Warthills; Weir Croft (*Wear Croft*, by R. Perry); Well Mdw; Welshman's Hill; Wet Reans (drainage channels); Wingfields Land; Withy Reams; (The) Woodside (by Vales Wood, cf. *Valeswood Side supra*); Yewtree Lsw.

(b) *Back Yard*; *The Coles* (*The Coals* 1782 *SBL 4149*, *5369*); *Coiling Headland* 1685, *Collians* ~ 1693, *Colles* ~ 1698, *Collis* ~ 1722, *Collys* ~ 1726, *Colleys* ~ 1775; *Crosspools*; *Dry Bank*; *East Meadow*; *Gelwell Meadow*; *Higher Croft* 1722; *The Homestall*; *Leasow Field* 1698; *Little Furlong*; *Little Leasow*; *Little Patch*; *Long Leasow*; *Perry Meadow*, *Side*; *Pump Yard*; *Waltons Leasow* 1685; *Waltons Stile* 1693; *Wood Leasow*.

Petton

The parish-name, which means 'peak settlement', is discussed in Part **1**.

WACKLEY (SJ 448273), *Wackley Farm* 1752 GT, *Wackley Farm House* 1842 *TA*. Wackley Lodge, in Cockshutt *supra*, is shown on 1833 OS. It is clear from modern and *TAMaps* that there was an area called Wackley which comprised a considerable stretch of land in Cockshutt, Petton and Loppington parishes, which converge N.E. of Petton Park. The 1752 reference is the earliest which has come to light, but it is probable that Wackley is an older name.

CHEVY CHASE COPPICE. The 1900 6" map has this name, but it is not on 1833 OS or *TAMap*. Modern maps do not have it, but it is in Gazetteer. There is an earlier-recorded Chevy Chase in Battlefield, Part **4** 112, and the Petton name may be an imitation of that rather than a direct reference to the ballad.

FISH POND, 1842 *TA*.

THE GRUDGE. The 1900 6" map gives this name to an elongated wood on the E. parish boundary. On *TAMap*, this is *Near Ox Plantation*, adjoining a group of *Ox Leasow* field-names.

PETTON FM, HALL: both 1833 OS, 1842 *TA*.

PETTON GRANGE: there are no buildings here on *TAMap*.

POOL COPPICE.

PUMP HO COPPICE.

RESERVOIR COPPICE.

SERPENTINE WD, by a curved pool in Petton Park.

SEVEN PITS COPPICE.

WEST LO, one of the entrances to Petton Park.

Field-Names

Forms in (a) are 1842 *TA*.

(a) Alder Croft; Brickkiln Fd; Brook Lsw (by Wackley Brook); The Broom (2); Church Bank, Lower ~ ~, ~ ~ Mdw; Clover Fd; Cote Fd (no building); Crabtree Fd; Folly Mdw (on N. boundary, nothing there on 1900 6"); Gravel Hole Fd; Greenfield

(2); Grove Pltn; Hay Shutts; Hock Mdw, ~ ~ Coppice; The Lawn (in Petton Park); Lawns, Broad, Long, Rough, Far, Near, Middle, Near Lawn Pltn (a group of fields between Petton church and S. boundary of parish); Lea, Far, Near; Leas Mdw; Martin Fd; Mill Lsw (adjoins Brook Lsw on Wackley Brook, maps do not show a Mill); The Moor; Near Lsw; Orchard, ~ Rookery; Ox Lsw, Far, Near, South Far, North and South Middle; Park, Great, Little, Pool (fields which were in Petton Park on 1900 6"); Park Lsw, Mdw (on S.E. boundary, Petton Park may have been much larger than it is on *TAMap*); Pleasant Fd; Rough Fd, Big; Rousell (by Rowsel Wd in Baschurch); Thistly Croft; Town End, Great, Little, ~ ~ Fd (adjacent to Petton Fm); Vetches Stubble; Wackley Mdw, Far, Near, Big (*v.* Wackley *supra*); Well Mdw; Weston Gate Fd, Weston Wd (Weston Lullingfield adjoins); Windmill Fd, Lower, Upper; The Yard Side.

Shrawardine

The parish-name is discussed, albeit inconclusively, in Part **1**. It is a compound of **worðign** 'enclosed settlement' with a first element which could be **scræf** 'cave' or **screawa** 'shrew', the latter perhaps used as a personal name or nickname. It was noted in this discussion that the form *Schyreveworthin* 1292 suggested association with *sheriff*, and this is supported by another form, *Schyrreveswordyn* 1339 *SRO 322/137*.

SHRAWARDINE CASTLE (remains of) is *Chastiel Isabell'* 1313 HAC, *Castr' Isabell'* 1320 *SBL 8396*, *Chastel Isabell* 1331 Pat, *Isabell Chastell alias Dame Philip Chastell*, *Castle Philipp* 1397 Pat, *Shrawarden Castle* c.1540 Leland. Isabella de Mortimer held Shrawardine in the late 13th century. No explanation has been noted for the 1397 reference to *Castle Philip*. The references are to the medieval castle, not to the modern farm which has this name. The latter is so called on 1833 OS and on *TAMap*.

AMERICA, 1833 OS, 1844 *TA*. *TA* also has *America Plantation* and fields called *Big* and *Little America*. It appears that an area in the central part of the parish had this name, but it is the plantation which has it on the 1900 6"map and on 1833 OS. Cf. the f.n. America, Part **3** 251, also not an obvious 'distance' n.

BUCKLEY FM, 1641 (1764) *SBL 4170*, 1833 OS, *Buckley* 1844 *TA*.

FOLLY FM, 1833 OS, FOLLY POOL, *Folley*, ~ *Pool* 1844 *TA*, LITTLE FOLLY. *TA* also has fields called *Folley Croft*, *Meadow*, *Field* and *Leasow below The Folley*. There was presumably a building here of the type known as a folly.

HILLY FM, 1833 OS, *Hilley* 1844 *TA*.

SHRAWARDINE LAKE, 1844 *TA*, ~ *Pool* 1833 OS.

Field-Names

Forms in (a) are 1844 *TA*.

(a) Alderley Mdw, Big, Little, Bridge, Alderley Moor (by Hilly Fm, another field called Alderley Moor is ½ mile N.W.); Alderton Lsw (adjoins Alderton in Great

Ness); The Arm Pills (*sic* on Foxall *TAMap*, but in FN 13 he gave it as The Armpits, a shape-name referring to curves in a stream shown on the map); Banky Lsw (2); Barn Yd; Barnyard; Big Fd; Big Lsw; Big Mdw; Bradley; Briar Hill; Brickkiln (2); Broad Mdw; Calves Yd; The Camp, Grassy Camp (one large and two small fields adjoining village on S.E.); Castle Lowes, Meadow at (in N.E. corner of parish); Castle Street, Garden in (by the castle ruins); Close(s) (3 fields by Folly Fm and some small enclosures round Shrawardine); Clover Lsw; Cockshutt (*v.* ***cocc-scīete**); Cow Lsw; Cow Pasture; Cowpasture Mdw (not near preceding); The Crit (a house and enclosure in Shrawardine village: *crit* is a Sa word for a small hut, cf. Crit Pltn in Montford *supra*: Gazetteer cites the Shrawardine n. as extant); Distemper (FN 34 associates this n. with the burial of diseased animals); Dogtree Lsw, Far, Little (FN 48 cites this as a Sa n. for the spindle tree); Duke's Tavern (a field by Folly Pool); Feggy Lsw (coarse grass); Field below House (by Folly Fm); Folley, Big, Little (over a mile W. of Folly Fm); Foxholes, Big, Further and The Long ~ (6 fields in N.E. corner); Foxholes (in N.W. corner); Giglin Croft; Kiteley, Big, Little, ~ Close; The Lawn; Leasow below Stack Yd; Little Lsw; Little Near Lsw; Little Oaks; Little Wd; Long Fd; Long Lsw; Longmore Lake; Marsh, Far, Near, Little; The Marsh, Duke's Marsh (not near preceding); Marsh Lsw (not near other Marsh ns.); Meadow, Lower and Upper ~, Upper Severn ~; Middle Pce; Milking Bank, Old ~ ~ (by Hilly Fm); Moors Prill, Broad ~ ~ ('marsh spring'); Mowing Moors, Little; New Lsw (3); Orchard; The Park (in S.E. corner of parish); Park, Four, Leas, Rushy, Wynn's, Woodley, Big and Little Horse Park (7 fields in S.W. of parish, cf. *Shrawardine Park* 1698 GT); Park Side (on E. boundary); Parson's Mdw; Patch (several); Peggy's Croft; Pentre Lsw (2, Pentre is in Kinnerley); Pigeons Pce; Plane Wd (adjoins Little Wd); Potter's Grave; The Rise; Rough, Big, Little; Rough, Rough near Shraden Lake (strips round three sides of Shrawarden Pool); Rowney (in a bend of the Severn, perhaps 'rough island', *v.* **rūh**, **ēg**); Severn Mdw, Higher, Lower; Sheep Pasture; Shutt, Big, Little, Far, Lower, Broomy (5 fields near S. boundary, the meaning of Shutt is uncertain, *v.* Part **4** 113); Shelwocks Croft, Upper; Sitting Tree Fd (a large field in Shrawardine and a smaller one in Montford, FN 49 cites this as a mysterious tree-n.); Slang; The Snod (*Snodd Field* 1607 GT); Stemports Lsw; Strawberry Bank; Thistly Pce; Three Score Pce; Tinker Lsw, Little; Townsend, Big, Little (at N. end of village); Walk Moors (minute enclosure on N.E. boundary); Wheat Lsw; White Fd; Withies, Big, Little; Wood Green, Pce; The Worthen (possibly from **worðign**, but earlier references would be required before a lost settlement could be presumed: FN 12 lists Worthen(s) ns. in several parishes); Yeld Bank (by Severn, **helde** 'gentle slope'); Yewtree Lsw.

(b) GT, 1607, names *Low Field*, *Middle Field*, *Overfield* as well as *Snodd Field*.

Welshampton

The parish-name is discussed in Part **1**. It means 'high estate' and is one of three Sa examples of this name. The affix *Welsh* was probably added for distinction from Hampton in Worthen: it refers to the proximity of a detached part of Flintshire.

BALMER, BALMER HEATH, 1833 OS. A slip with E. W. Bowcock's writing gives *Baumer Croft* 1664 "Sa deed (private)".

BANK FM.

BREADON HEATH, *Breeden Heath* 1692 *SBL 5275*, *Braden Heath* 1791 *SBL 5278*, *Bradon Heath* 1833 OS, *Bradenheath* 1839 *TA*.

BROOK HO, BROOKHOUSE WD: Adam *del Brok'* appears 1279–80 *RentSur* as a burgage tenant in Ellesmere.

CLAREPOOL MOSS, *Claire Moss* 1664 *SBL 5250*, *Clear Pool Field* 1839 *TA*.

CLAY PITS, *Big* and *Little Claypit* 1839 *TA*.

THE FIELDS, 1833 OS, 1839 *TA*.

HAMPTON GROVE, HO.

HAWTHORN HO.

HILL FM, shown but not named on *TAMap*.

HOLBROOK FM.

THE HOLLIES.

HOLMER PIT, 1833 OS, *Homer Pit* 1839 *TA*.

LOWER FM, shown but not named on *TAMap*.

LYNEAL COPPICE.

THE ROUGH, 1839 *TA*: cf. *The Heltfields Rough*, *The Higher Rye Rough* 1656 *SBL 5243*, *(The) Nant Rough* 1658–9, 1705 *SBL 5246*, *5259*, *Nant Rough*, *Rye Rough* 1726 *SBL 5272*.

STOCKS LANE, Cf. *Stocks Gate* 1839 *TA*.

SUN INN, 1839 *TA*.

TOWERY MOSS, *Moss*, *Towery Croft* and *Meadow* 1839 *TA*.

TAMap shows *Friendly Tavern by* the Methodist chapel in Breadon Heath and *Red Lion P.H.* in the village.

Field-Names

Forms in (a) are 1839 *TA* except where otherwise stated. Early forms dated 1656 are *SBL 5240*, those dated 1664 are from "a private deed" lent to E. W. Bowcock.

Numerous detached portions of Hampton Wood township in Ellesmere (which are shown by linking lines on the Index to Tithe Survey map) have been treated as in Welshampton, and f.ns. in these areas have been taken from Ellesmere *TA*, also 1839. There are some discrepancies between the parish boundaries on *TAMap* and on the 1900 6" OS map. The area treated here is that on the *TAMap*.

(a) Back Side, Low, Top; The Balmer Fd, New ~ ~ (small enclosures called Big, Far, Near Fd adjoin); Bank (2); Banky Fd (3); Barn Fd (2); Battle Hill, Battlehills, Big, Middle and White's Battlehills, Cliffs Battle hill (other 'battle' ns. are noted Part **2** 68, Part **3** 36, 118, 230: it may be worth considering the existence of fixed locations for a formal settling of disputes among people of relatively low social status); Beanhill; Bells Yd; Big Fd (2 large fields); Birch Fd; Birch Mdw; Black Moss, ~ ~ Fd, Mdw; Bond House Fd (in village); Bowldish (a shape-name: NED records this term for a vessel from 1530 to 1725); Brickkiln Croft; Briery Croft; Broad Lsw; Broady Croft (*The Broadway Croft alias The Broadoake Croft* 1656); Bron Fd, Big, Little, Bron Croft (Welsh *bron* 'breast'); Broomy Fd; Broomy Lsw; Brunklet; Bryn Edward, ~ Garrett (adjoining, Welsh *bryn* 'hill'); Cae Baricle, Far and Near (Welsh *cae* 'field', Baricle is unexplained: FN 32 cites this n. and Barnacle Pce in Ashford Carbonel as 'bean' ns., but this seems unlikely); Cae Cooper (*Kay Cooper* 1656); Cae Gwin, Crooked ~ ~ (*Kae Gwyn* c.1619 *SRO Bridgewater Box 458*, 1656, 'white field'); Cae Roughen, Lower ~ ~; Cae Wilkin; Calves Croft (several); Canal Mdw (by Ellesmere Canal); Claypit, Big, Little; Clover Croft; Clover Fd (3); Coffins Fd; Common Fd; Common Pce; Cow Lsw (*The Cowe Leasowe* 1664); Cow Pasture; Cowtail, Big, Little (taking the two fields together this can be seen as a shape-name); Crabtree Fd; Cranemoor, Big and Little ~ Mdw; Croft(s) (*freq*, enclosures called Far, Little, Long Croft etc, are not listed); Crooked Croft (has a protruding corner); Cross Fd (several); Cross Lane Fd (by crossroads); Crowpits; Cuckoo Fd; The Dallacks; Dry Fd; Elts, Big, Little; Far Fd; Far Ground; Far Mdw; Field (*freq*, Far, Near, Long, Lower, Big, Little ~ etc. not listed); Foxyhill, Little ~; Furlong (a large field adjoining High Fd); Gander Fd; Gate Croft; Gilrhos, ~ Croft (a compound with Welsh *rhos* 'heath' does not obviously suit the topography); Glanmoors, Little; Gorse Blathen, Croft, Mdw; Gorsy Bank; Gravelhole Fd, Big and Little ~ ~; Griggy, ~ Fd, ~ Wheat, Little Griggy (*the Gregey Croft* 1656, Welsh *grug* 'heather'); Grooms Mdw; Halt Rough, Middle and Near ~ ~; Hanty Bank; Harder, Thistly ~ (*Hirder*, *The Great*, *The Little*, *The Thistle*, *The Hirder by the Lane* 1656, *Harder*, *Greate*, *Thistley*, *Three Little Harders* 1711, 33–4, 91 *SBL 5263*, *5273*, *5278*, Welsh *hirdir* 'long land'); Hen's Nest (2, one a tiny enclosure between Far and Little Mdw, the other a fairly big field); High Fd; The Hill; The Hole in the Wall 1897 Peake; House Fd; How Mdw, Howe Mdw Fd; Hy Fd; Kill Robin (FN 46 suggests association with the superstition that killing a robin brought bad luck); Kiln Lane, Little Kiln Lsw; Lane Croft, Second and Third ~ ~; Limebricks and Croxens Gate, Limebrick Mdw,

Far, Near; Little Mdw (~ *Meadows* 1656); Long Lsw; Long Pit Fd; Long Wd; Magpie Fd; Marl Croft (*The Marled Croft* 1656); Martins Croft; Meadow, Big, Little, Wood; Meadow, Far, Little; Menlove's Fd; Mere Fd; Mill Mdw; Morris Croft; Moss (several); The Nance (*The Nant* c.1619 *SRO Bridgewater box 458*, *The Naunt* 1656, Welsh *nant* 'valley'); New Fd (2); Newton Ditches (by Newton in Ellesmere); Ney Castle; Oak Fd, Far, Near; Oat Fd; Old Hampton (N. of The Fields, there are no buildings: Peake 1897, p. 50, says that this is a field where "coins and other remains" were dug up); Old House Fd (2); Old House Yd (2); Old Wd, Wood Mdw; Outlet (3, by Hill Fm, Holbrook Fm and a house in Breaden Heath: a term for pasture adjoining winter cattle-sheds); Ox Lsw, Small, Large (*Ox*(*e*) *Leasow* 1726, 47 *SBL 5272*, *5253*); Park, Park Fd, Top and Middle Park (small fields near Balmer); Pit Fd; Plantation Fd; Pulson's Croft; The Rann; Richards Croft; Robin's Mdw; (The) Roe Fd (2); Rogers Lsw (~ *Leasowe* 1656); The Roman Pavement 1897 Peake ("in the road by the Fields Farm", presumably a patch of road metalling); The Rough (2); Round Mdw (one curvilinear side); The Rounds (two curvilinear sides); Rover's Croft; Rye Rough; Salter's Hill; Sandyhill; Sawpit Croft; Slang (narrow strip); Smooth Hazels (*Smeathhassel* 1664, 'smooth hazel (clump)', *v.* **smēðe**); Stack Yd, Stackyard Fd; Stone Hill, Low, High; Thistly Fd; Thistly Angley, Far, Near, Little; Three Cornered Croft (in road fork); Top Fd, Big, Little; Trapps Hill; Turner's Croft; Waggoners Croft; Wallhill; Well Fd, Mdw; Well Fd (2); White's Fd; White Well Croft; Windmill Hill, Low and High ~; Windy Doors, Little ~ ~; The Wood, ~ Fd, Mdw; Worstone ('hoarstone': Peake 1897 says that this is in a field near the railway, but the *TA* n. is in a road fork on the other side of The Fields farm from the railway line).

(b) *The Barne Yard* 1664; *The Big Leasow* 1726 *SBL 5267*; *The Britchin Leasowe* 1656, *Birinton Leasow* 1711 *SBL 5263*, *Birchen* ~ 1726, 47 *SBL 5472*, *5253*, *Birchin* 1733–4 *SBL 5273* ('growing with birch trees'); *The Broadmeadowe Hill* 1656; *The Dallorbe* 1664 (reading uncertain, possibly to be associated with The Dallacks in (a)); *Davys Croft* 1692 *SBL 5275*; *Glade Feild* 1664; *Gough's Wood* 1711, 33–4 *SBL 5623*, *5273*; *Hemp Yard* 1692 *SBL 52 75*; *The Henges* 1656, *The Hengaies* 1705 *SBL 5259*, *The Hengaes* 1726, 47 *SBL 5271*, *5253* (R. Morgan suggests Welsh *Hen Gae*, 'old field', with an English plural added after such a field was divided); *The Highe Broame* 1726 *SBL 5267*; *The Hole Meadow* 1682 *SBL 5262*, *The Whole* ~ 1711, 33–4, 91 *SBL 5263*, *5273*, *5278* (possibly associated with The Hole in the Wall in (a)); *Holmes* 1656; *The Holifield and Rough* 1656; *Kua Castle* c.1619 *SRO Bridgewater/box 458*; *The Long Croft* 1664; *The Lower Leasowe* 1726 *SBL 5267*; *Manwayrings Farme* 1656; *Michells Meadow* 1564 *SBL 5240*, *Michaells Meadowe* 1662 *SBL 1269*; *Morgans Wood* 1656; *The New Meadow and Rough* 1656; *The New Park Leasow* 1726 *SBL 5267*; *The New Peice* 1726 *SBL 5267*; *The Oxe Close* 1656; *Pawlets*, ~ *Croft* 1692 *SBL 5275*; *The Pownd and Meadow* 1664; *Rough Leasow* 1711, 33–4, 91 *SBL 5263*, *5273*, *5278*; *Shutt Hill* 1564, 1603, 62 *SBL 5240*, *5281(A)*, 1269, *Shutt Meadow* 1664 (*v.* Part **4** 113); *Wall Croft* 1664; *Windsors House* 1656.

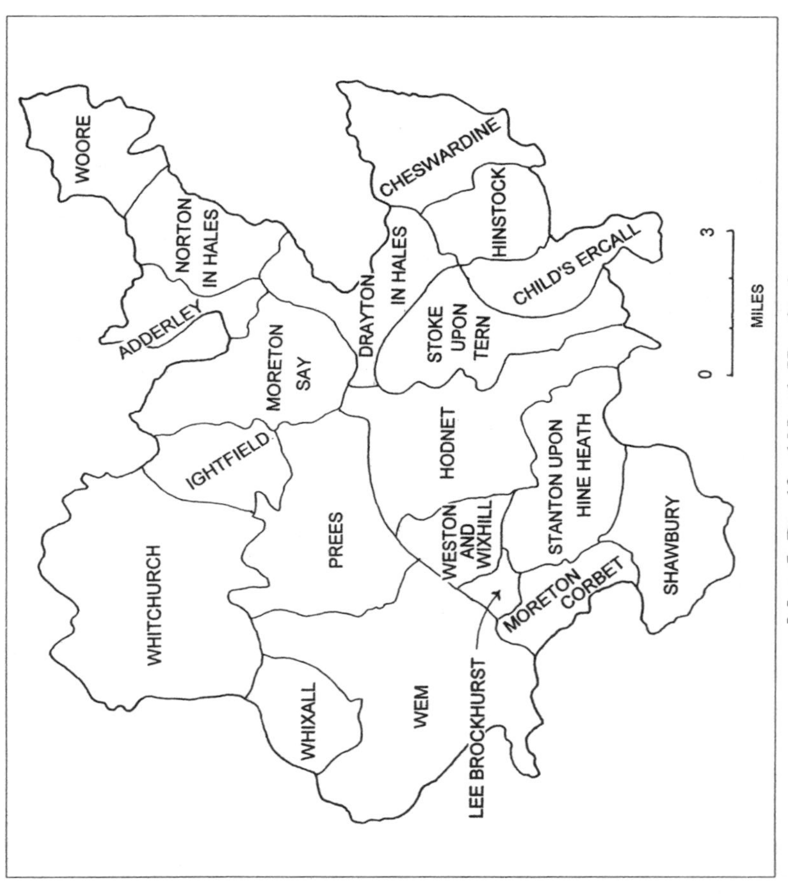

Map 5: Bradford North Hundred.

BRADFORD NORTH HUNDRED

The area treated here is that of the hundred in 1831 as shown on a map by H. D. G. Foxall (*v.* Pimhill Hundred *supra*), except for the inclusion of a small area of Moreton Corbet and Shawbury parishes which Foxall shows as a detached part of Pimhill.

The development of Bradford Hundred is set out in detail in VCH XI, pp. 93–104. It was formed by the amalgamation of the two DB hundreds of Hodnet and Wrockwardine in the mid or late 12th century. This created a very large hundred, comprising a third of the area of the modern county. Records show that from the date of the 1381 poll tax to that of the militia musters of 1539 there were *ad hoc* divisions into two halves, and by 1590 the separation into North and South had become fixed.

Bradford North as treated here consists of the DB hundred of Hodnet with the addition of a substantial south-eastern portion which in 1086 was in Wrockwardine, and the omission of three townships in the north of High Ercall parish which were entered under Hodnet though High Ercall was otherwise in Wrockwardine. It includes Cheswardine, transferred from Staffordshire t.Hy 2, but not Onneley and Tyrley, which, though in Hodnet in 1886, are now in Staffordshire.

The meeting-place of the undivided hundred was at *Bradford* in High Ercall, recorded as the site of a mill in HAC deeds of the mid 12th century. This is in Bradford South, about 1½ miles from the boundary with Bradford North. There is no record of a separate meeting-place for Bradford North.

Adderley

The parish-name was discussed in Part **1**, where it was suggested that **lēah** might be used in its late sense of 'meadow, pasture', rather than in its commoner senses 'wood' or 'clearing'. This suggestion, however, while still seeming relevant to many -ley names in the parts of north Sa round Wem and Ellesmere, seems less relevant in the N.E. angle of the county. Here, and in the adjacent part of St, the -ley names probably indicate ancient woodland, so 'clearing' is the likeliest sense in Adderley. The first element is a feminine personal name in *-þryð*, which could be *Eald-*, *Ælf-* or *Æðelþryð*.

THE LEES (SJ 669386), 1768 PR(L) 4, *villa de Leyes*, *Philippus de Leya* c.1200 SAC, *Leyes* 1320–1 *RentSur*, *Lyes* 1411 SAC, *Lees* 1710 PR(L) 4. A parallel to this is Leese PN Ch **2** 229, which has copious documentation from e.13th cent. on. The forms for both names indicate the plural of **lēah** 'clearing'. There is another instance in Child's Ercall *infra*.

SPOONLEY (SJ 662360). This is a DB manor and was therefore discussed in Part **1**. It is a compound of *spōn* 'chip, shaving' and **lēah** 'wood, clearing', and other instances occur in Gl and K.

TITTENLEY (SJ 648378), shown on modern maps as in Sa, was formerly a township of Audlem Ch, and the name is included in PN Ch **3** 90–1. It means 'Titta's wood or clearing'.

THE WOOD (SJ 650410). This farm is shown on 1833 OS (*Wood House*) and on the 1899 6" map, but neither the building nor the name appears on 1947 and later 1" maps. There is an early reference in the surname of Adam *de la Wode* listed 1327 SR in Adderley. Latin entries in PR(L) 4 in 1721 and 1731 have *Sylva*, *Silva*.

ADDERLEY HALL, 1833 OS.
ADDERLEYLANE FM, this is LANE FM on the 1963 1" map.
ADDERLEY LEES BRIDGE, by The Lees.

ADDERLEY LOCKS.

ADDERLEY LO, 1833 OS.

ADDERLEY PARK, (*in*) *magno parco de Adurdeleye* 1306–7 *Ass*.

ADDERLEY POOL BRIDGE, ~ ~ FM, *Pool House* 1833 OS, *Castle Pool* 1840 *TA*.

ADDERLEY WHARF BRIDGE, 1840 *TA*.

ASYLUM FM, *Adderley Asylum* 1833 OS, *Asylum* 1840 *TA*.

BAWHILL LO, WD, *Baugh Wood* 1833 OS, *Ball Hills* 1840 *TA*.

BLACK COVERT.

CASTLEHILL N.W. of Spoonley, *Castle Hill* 1833 OS, 1840 *TA*.

CASTLE HILL, N. of Adderley: ADDERLEY POOL is *Castle Pool* 1840 *TA*. There is nothing shown on maps which would account for these two names.

COXBANK BROOK, WD, *Cocks Bank* 1731 PR(L) 4. *TA* has *Bank(s)* ns. nearby: *Bank Fd*, *Big*, *Little* and *Near Bank*, *Doolers Bank*, *Carrot Bank Fd*, *Banks*, *Lower Banks*.

DOGKENNEL WD, *Dog Kennel* 1833 OS.

DRY POOL PLTN.

DUCKOW BRIDGE, WD, by R. Duckow.

GAS HOUSE PLTN.

GOLLINGS ROUGH, *Gollings Wood* 1833 OS, *Gollins Rough* 1840 *TA*.

HAWKSMOOR, 1833 OS, 1840 *TA*, ~ BRIDGE, *Hawkesmere* 1770, 3, 7 PR(L) 4, *Hawksmore* 1772 ib, *Hawkesmore* 1779, 86 ib.

LONG POOL.

THE MERE, 1833 OS, *Mere* 1840 *TA*.

MULLINER'S BRIDGE.

NETHERMOST BRIDGE, WD, *Neathers Wd*, *Far* and *Near Neathers* 1840 *TA*.

NEW HO.

NORTH LO.

NORTON LANE, 1833 OS.

PARK FM.

POOL HO, 1833 OS.

RAVEN HO.

SCHOOL PLTN.

SOUTH LO.

SWANBACH BRIDGE, *Swanbach* is in Ch, PN Ch **3** 84.

THE WEMS, 1833 OS, 1840 *TA*, WEMS BRIDGE: a second occurrence of the term which has given the parish-name Wem, *infra*.

YEWTREE PLTN.

Field-Names

Forms in (a) are 1840 *TA* except where otherwise stated. Early forms for which no date or source is given are 1320–1 *RentSur*.

(a) Annette's Stone, Lower, Middle and Near Stone (on S. boundary); Bank, Big, Little; Banks, Big, Further; Banky Fd; Barn Fd; Bates Fd; Billingham Mdw 1824, 41 GT; Birch Fd, Big, Little; Birches; Blackhurst Fd, Further ~ Fds; Blackthorn Lsw; Breach, Little, Oaken Breeches (*v.* **brēc**); Brickkiln Fd (2); Bridge Mdw; Broad Mdw; Brook Fd; Brook Mdw; Broomy Fd; Broughtons Croft; Building Croft; Church Hill, Fd; Clays Yd 1824, 41 GT; Clover Lsw; Cote Lsw, Lower, Upper (no building); Cow Pasture, Big, Little; Dole, Carder, Wilder; Down Wd, Further, Middle, Near; Dudley Park (on border with Audlem Ch, Park and Little Pk adjoin); Field (a cluster of ns. N. of Spoonley includes Scotch, Round, Perry, Marl, Stocking and Five Field(s): there are Flatt and Furlong ns. among these); The Flatts, Hot Flatt (near the Field ns., *flat* probably 'strip in open field'); Frog Lane; Furlong (near the Field ns.); Further Mdw; Gadbridge Moor; Gallantree Fd ('gallows-tree', *v.* **galga**, perhaps in this instance a shape-name, the *TAMap* shows two narrow fields, the shorter one at right-angles at one end of the longer); The Gate Pasture; Gorsy Bank; Gorsy Fd; Grass Common; Grazing Pce; Grimes's Wd; Grinsells Bank; Grinsells Wd (not near preceding); Hall Fd (in the park); Hatch Fd, Lower and Middle ~ ~; The Higher Ground; Hilly Moor; Hop Yd; Horse Hill; Horse Pce; The Intake; Kiln Croft, Further ~ ~; Lady Heys, Further ~ ~; Lane Croft; Lath Moor (*Lathemorhay*, *v.* **mōr**, **(ge)hæg**, first el. uncertain); Lawn, Hall ~ (in the park); Leasow, Higher, Lower; Lies Mdw, Little Ley Fd, Bache's Lees (by The Lees); Little Croft (1698 GT); Little Mdw (2); Llin Fd (the southern part of Adderley Park), Lin Fd, Wd, Pltn (*Lynfeld'*, 'flax field', *v.* **līn**: the Ll- spelling is pseudo-Welsh); Long Fd (several); Long Mdw (several); Lower Ground, ~ ~ Wd (4 fields surrounding The Wood: Neathers, later Nethermost, Wd adjoins); Lower Lsw; Marl Fd (2); Marlpit Fd, Dry Marlpit Lsw; Marl Wd; Middle Fd; Milking Bank Fd (not by a farm); Milking Fd; Mill Mdw; Moat Fd (by The Lees); Moat Wd (adjoins Dogkennel Wd); Moor (2); Moor, Big and Little ~, ~ Mdw, ~ Head (in S.W. corner of parish); Moss, ~ Bank; Muckley Fd; Near Bank; Near Mdw; Near Wd; New Croft; New Lsw, ~ ~ Bank; New Ridges; Oat Fd (adjoins Wheat Croft); Old Pool Mdw; Overis Mdw; Ox Building (also 1833 OS), ~ ~ Fd; Ox Lsw (2); Park Croft; Park Mdw, Middle and Big Park (near S. edge of Adderley Park); Parsons Croft (1682 GT), Upper ~ ~; Pepperhill Mdw, Moor (Pepperhill is in Ch, PN Ch **3** 91: the reference may be to one of the plants which have pepper-names); Piece below House; Pool Croft (2); Pool Fd (by Fishpond); Pool Pce 1849 GT; Pool Mdw, Near, Further; Potter's Croft; Raddle Hill; Red Hill (*Redehul'*, *v.* **rēad**, **hyll**); Ridding ('clearing', on S. boundary); Riddings, Long, Lower and Further Ridding, Grimsalls Near and Further ~ (the fields straddle a footpath near Wems); Ridge Gateway; Rough Fd (2); Row Mdw; Sheep Lsw (2); Sides; Skinners Mdw; Slang; Smithy Croft; Smithy Rough (3 fields on N.E. boundary); Spoonley Mdw, Moor; Spring Pce; Springs; Stable Croft; Strawberry Hill; Sunk Fence Pool (on N. edge of Adderley Park); Swanbach Fd (4 fields in N. tip of parish, Swanbach is in Ch); Swanley (2 very large fields adjoining N. edge of Adderley Park); Tofts Fd, Mdw; Two Moors; Weddish Hill, Further and Near ~ ~; Well Croft; Well Fd; Well Mdw, ~ ~ Bank; Wheat Croft; Wheat Fd; Windmill Fd; Wood, Further, Middle,

Near; Wood, Holly, Cote, Right, Bridges, Three Bridges, Big, Lower, Cottons, Turf, Sadlers, Second, Woods adjoining Road, Further, Two and Five Outwoods (these fields cover a large area E. and S. of Adderley Lo, where no trees are shown on *TAMap* or 6"); Yewtree Fd; Yewtree Mdw.

(b) *Brokherst* (*v.* **brōc**, **hyrst**); *Gradeleye*; *Hallecroft*; *Lichways* 1682, 94, 8, 1705 GT (perhaps a funeral route, *v.* **līc** 'corpse'); *Morhay*, *Netherhay* ('marsh' and 'nether enclosure', *v.* **(ge)hæg**); *Neweparkstokkyng'*, *Le Newestokkyng'* ('clearing', *v.* ***stoccing**); *Nicholas Meadow* 1730 *SBL 1543*); *Normanneshale* ('Norman's nook'); *Wrademersch*.

Cheswardine

The parish contains four townships: Cheswardine and Goldstone, Chipnall, Ellerton and Sambrook, Great Soudley.

The parish-name, which means 'cheese-producing settlement', is discussed in Part **1**.

1. CHESWARDINE AND GOLDSTONE

GOLDSTONE (SJ 706284)

Goldestan c.1200 *ForProc*, 1255–6 *Ass*, *-ston* 1565 *SBL 4712*
Golstan' 1279–80 *RentSur et freq* with variant readings *-ston*(*e*), *-stan* to 1440 Fine
Goldstan 1291–2 *Ass* (p), 1337–8 *ForProc* (p)

v. **gold**, **stān**. This appears to be a clear case of the use of **gold** for an object of golden colour, rather than as a reference to plants.

HAYWOOD FM (SJ 708303), *Haywode* 1327 SR (p), (common wood called) *Haywood* 1635 GT, *Heywood* 1833 OS. On *TAMap* fields with *Haywood* ns. cover an area S. of the farm.

This is a recurring name from **(ge)hæg** 'enclosure' and **wudu**. It is Haywood He, St, Heywood Sr, W, and other Sa occurrences are Heywood in Rushbury (Part **3** 196) and in Aston Botterell.

WESTCOTTMILL FM (SJ 709290), *Westaneskote* 1279–80 *RentSur*, *-cote* 1322 Cl, Ipm, *Westcott Mill* 1833 OS. This name must be considered together with Wistanswick in Stoke upon Tern, 2½ miles west. The two names are 'cottage(s)' and 'dairy farm of Wigstān', and it seems likely that the same man was the owner of both properties.

BLACK WD.
BRICKYARD COVERT.
BRIDLANDS WD.
CHESWARDINE HALL. The present hall and grounds are shown on 1900 6" and later maps. On 1833 OS and 1840 *TAMap* the house is

called *Hill Hall*, and has no grounds. The hall and park shown on later maps are described in Kelly 1934 as "a fine mansion of red brick in the Elizabethan style . . . standing in a park of about 100 acres".

The earlier name, *Hill Hall* is probably *Hull* 1327 SR (p): Thomas *de Hull* is listed in Cheswardine.

CHESWARDINE MARSH, MARSH COTTAGE, the hamlet adjoins Marsh f.ns. *infra*.

CHESWARDINE PARK FM, *Cheswardine Park* 1833 OS, 1840 *TA*. *TAMap* shows the house surrounded by fields which have no names, and there are *Lawn* and *Park* ns. adjoining these. There was perhaps an earlier park here, superseded by the one at the present Cheswardine Hall.

FORESTERS' HALL, in the village.

FOX BRIDGE.

GOLDSTONE BANK FM, *Goldstone Bank* 1833 OS, 1840 *TA*.

GOLDSTONE COMMON, 1833 OS, 1840 *TA*.

GOLDSTONE STUD FM.

HAYWOOD DRUMBLE, this and Lawn Drumble are linear plantations.

HAYWOOD LANE, *Heywood* ~ 1833 OS.

HAYWOOD PLTN.

HILLTOP PLTN.

HOOLES PLTN.

LAWN DRUMBLE (*Plantation* 1840 *TA*), LAWNLANE COTTAGES. These are on the edge of the area here taken to be that of the old park. A large field called *Lawn* is shown on *TAMap* S. of the Drumble.

LITTLE SOUDLEY, 1833 OS, 1840 *TA*: *v*. Great Soudley *infra*.

MANOR HO, in Goldstone.

NEW BRIGHTON, ~ ~ Bridge, by Shropshire Union canal. Perhaps transferred from the 19th-cent. coastal resort in Wirral La.

OLD GORSE PLTN.

OLD HALL, adjoining the church in Cheswardine village.

PINETUM PLTN.

WESTCOT COTTAGE.

WESTCOTT MILL BRIDGE.

WHARF TAVERN.

Field-Names

Forms in (a) are 1840 *TA*. Early forms for which no source is given are GT.

(a) The Alleys, Upper ~ ("a small garden called *le Alees*" 1395 HAC: OFr **alee** 'bordered passage', VEPN gives instances in f.ns. and street-names: this field adjoins the vicarage); Ampool, Upper ~; Barn Fd; Barn Yd (several); Benty Lsw, Far, Lower (growing with bent grass); Big Moor (2); Rig Moor Croft (not near either of preceding); Birch Fd, Far, Near, Birches, Big, Little, Upper, Birch Breach (N. of the Hinstock/Chipnall road), Birches, Big, Little, Far, Near (on the other side of the road) (field-shapes here suggest an enclosed open field: the n. may be **bryce** rather than the tree-name: Birch Field is listed 1635, 85, 93: Green Gore adjoins); Birch, North, South, Blakeley; Black Flat (by a small group of Field ns. on S.W. boundary); Bowling Green; Bradhurst Lsw; Brickkiln Bank; Brickkiln Mdw; Brook Croft; Brook Lsw, Long ~ ~; Broomy Yd; Calves Croft; Castle Croft, Far and Near ~ ~, Castle Pce (these fields are fairly widely spread W. of the castle site: Castle Field is listed 1635, 82, 93, 1701, *Castle Croft with Castle Pitt* 1698); Cordicroft; Copy Bank; Cow Pasture (2); Crany Moor, Near and Far ~ ~ (cf. Cran-y-Moor in Peplow *infra*); Croft(s) (*freq*, there are groups by the habitation sites); Cross Fd, Pce (not adjacent but close, both at right-angles to neighbouring enclosures); Dairy Lsw; Dale Head Land, Dale Headland Bank, Croft (these and Head Lane Pce are near the Birch(es) ns. *supra*, so possibly *headland* in its open-field sense); Doorway, Long and Upper ~ (furlong-shaped strips on E. edge of Birch(es) group); Earp Fd, Far, Near; Elder Stub; Far Fd; Fords, ~ Mdw; Field Pce, Upper, Lower, High Fd (Black Flat and Two Butts adjoin); Five Lane End Pce; Flat Fd (near a group of Field(s), N of Cheswardine); Goldslane, Big, Little; Gorsty Bank; Gravelly Bank; Green Gore, Lower and Upper ~ ~, ~ ~ Mdw (*Greengore Piece* 1693 GT, possibly *gore* in its open-field sense, *v.* Birch Fd *supra*); The Gullet, Little and Great ~ (ME *golet* 'ditch' from OFr *goulet*); Haims Lsw; Hare Pleck, ~ ~ Mdw, Far, Mid, Near; Head Lane Pce; Hay Green, ~ Stile(s) (by Haywood); Heathy Flat, Far, Near (near Birch(es) ns.); Heathy Lsw, Near ~ ~; Hill, Big, Near; Hoar Stone, Lower, Upper (by N.E. boundary); Home Mdw; Horse Pasture; Hough, Far, Near, Old (E. of Haywood, perhaps more likely to be a reflex of **halh** than of **hōh**); Hunger Hill, Near ~ ~, Far ~ ~ Bank; Jones's Lsw; Lawn, Cocks Lawn (both fields adjoin the site of the old park); Leasow, Broomy, Gorsy; Leasow, Holly, Rough, Taskeys; Leasow, Near, Far, Middle, Broomy, Heathy, Gorsty, Broad, Ox, Cote (a group of fields by the canal in S. of township); The Leys; Liget Mdw (by a crossroads, probably 'swing gate', *v.* **hlid-geat**); Little Mdw (several); Long Fd; Long Lsw (2); Long Mdw; Louse Hill; Lower Yd; Madeleys Croft; Manchester, Lower, Upper (on E. boundary: FN 23 classifies this with transferred ns. denoting remoteness); Marl Fd, Marlpit Croft; Marlpit Lane; Marrow Flat; Marsh Fd (1635, 93, 1701); Meadow, Big, Little, Far, Near, Simes, Pool, Cheswardine (group of fields on N. edge of Goldstone Common); The Meadow (several); Meadow, Far, Near, Wilderness (on S. boundary); Meesons Spring Mdw; Minton's Lsw; Moat Bank (the moat is shown on 6" map at the castle site in the village); Moat Bank, Mdw (N.E. of Goldstone); Moor, Big, Little; Moor, Far, Near, Barn (on E. edge of Goldstone Common); The Moors, Winnings Moor; Moss Fd, Mdw, Dry Moss; Moss Pit Fd; Mowing Yd (by Goldstone); Mullinor Lsw; New Pce; Old Lake Fd, Far, Near (adjoining Warlake in Hinstock); The Old Man's Fd; Ox Lsw; Park Lsw, Far and Near ~ ~ (by site of old park); Peggy's Lsw; Pickling, ~ Pce (*pickling* may be related to the *pightel/pingle* terms for small enclosures); The Pingles (ME **pingel** 'small plot', in this instance the n. of a narrow strip running along three sides of Moss Fd, by Goldstone); Plumtree Park; Pool Croft (several); Pool Head, Big, Little, Far, Near (6" map shows Fish Pond here, E. of Haywood: *Vicars Land or Pool Head* is listed 1682, *Vicars Pool Head Close* 1693, 1701); Pool Pce; Reynolds Croft, Far ~ ~; Rough Lsw, Big, Little; Russell's Breach, ~ ~ Coppice, Mdw; Ryegrass Lsw; Sandpits; Silveridge; Slang (several); Snapes, Steadman's, Gorsty, Big, Snape Gate (*Snape Gate Croft* 1693, *enclosure in Marsh Field called Snape Croft* 1701: ***snæp** 'boggy piece of land', the fields are near N.E. boundary); Spoil Bank (by canal); Stile Pce; Stony Pce, Far, Near; Swinnerton's Pce; Strong Pce; Two Butts (adjoins Black Flat); Valley, Far, Near; Water Lands, Great, Little; Well Croft; Well Mdw; Wet Reyns (drainage channels); Wilsons Fd, Mdw, Pce; The Yard, Lower Yd (large fields by Goldstone); Yard, Horse, Stable, House, Well (by Little Soudley).

(b) *Birch Furlong Piece* 1698 (Birch Fd *supra* seems likely to have been an open field); *Hill Cross in Marsh Field* 1693, 1701, *Butt near Hill Cross* 1698 (Marsh Fd *supra*, on E. boundary, seems likely to have been an open field).

2. CHIPNALL (SJ 727314)

Chipnall is a DB manor, and is therefore discussed in Part **1**.

The etymology could be either '*Cippa's knoll' or 'knoll where logs are found'.

COAL BROOK, *Colbrok* 1387 SHC (1910), *Colbrowke* 1554 ib: 'cool brook', *v.* **col**[2], **brōc**. This is a tributary of the R. Tern, partly in St, which forms the N. boundary of Cheswardine near Chipnall Mill.

LIPLEY (SJ 740310). The only early reference found to this name is *Lipley Heath* 1635, 1701 GT. LIPLEY FM and LIPLEYHALL FM are N. and S. of the roadside houses called Lipley on the 1963 1" map. On 1833 OS the name *Lipley* is given to Lipleyhall Fm, and Lipley Heath is shown as an area in Great Soudley. Lipley Fm and *Lipley Heath* are a mile apart. It seems likely that Lipley was an ancient land-unit in spite of there being no available record before 1635. The adjacent settlement called Doley, just in St, is not noted till 1833 OS (*ex inf.* Dr D. Horovitz), but both should probably be considered as ancient names in **lēah**.

CHIPNALL HALL FM.

CHIPNALL LEES, ~ *Lays* 1833 OS, probably **lǣs**, but cf. The Lees in Adderley.

CHIPNALL MILL, 1833 OS, 1840 *TA*, CHIPNALLMILL FM.

CHIPNALL WD.

COALPIT PLTN, near Coal Brook, but probably not incorporating the first element of the stream-name.

GLASS HO, 1833 OS.

GORSEYHILL PLTNS, *Gorse Hill* 1840 *TA*.

JACKSON'S DRUMBLE.

MILL ROUGH, *Wood* 1840 *TA*.

MOSS LANE, along the S. edge of *Moss* fields *infra*.

OLDHOUSE COVERT, a house is shown on *TAMap*.

ROOKERY WD.

RUSHYMOSS WD, *Rushy Moss* 1840 *TA*, one of the Moss ns. by Moss Lane.

SYCAMORE COTTAGE.

TAG LANE (1833 OS), TAGLANE PLTN: perhaps *tag* 'young sheep'.

YEWTREE FM, shown but not named on *TAMap*.

Field-Names

Forms in (a) are 1840 *TA*.

(a) Bank Flg (by Mill Bank); Banky Pce (several); Barlow's Lsw; Barn Fd, Far ~ ~; Barren Fd; Bath Mdw (contains a small pool); Big Fd, Far, Middle, Near; Big Mdw; Bloody Breech (adjoins Clay Breech, perhaps referring to soil colour); Bowling Alley; Broad Water (also 1833 OS, a large pool by Hall Birch, not shown on modern maps); Brook Yd; Browns Lake, Far, Near (probably a drainage channel); Brown's Lsw; Butty Mdw (FN 7 lists *Butty* with open-field terms, but mentions an EDD sense 'a field belonging to two owners but not fenced': for this field, on N.W. boundary of township, there is no obvious open-field context); Caves, Far and Middle ~, ~ Mdw; Clay Breech Mdw, Near ~ ~ (*v.* **brǣc** 'newly-broken-in land'); Common Fd, Far and Near ~ ~, ~ Pce (7 fields on two sides of a block of 7 fields which are called New Inclosure(s): the area is E. of Lipleyhall Fm); Common Pce; Coney Green (*v.* **coninger**); Crabtree Mdw; Croft (*freq*, there is a cluster at N. end of village); Crowed Breech; Cuttock Gate, Big (large field E. of village); Dairy Orchard, Upper Dairy Fd; Davies's Yd; Dove; Dunstall, Little, Upper (small fields N.E. of village, possibly a vanished habitation, *v.* ***tūn-stall**); Earps Black Flat, Earps Well Yd (near but not adjacent, latter a large field W. of village: there is an Earp Fd in Cheswardine); Far Mdw; Far New Lsw; Fatting Pasture; First Fd; Gillion; Grazing Pce; Gravel Hole Fd; Hall Birch, Big, Little (no building); Hall Yd (by Chippenhall Fm); Heath Flat (adjoins Common Fd ns: other Flat ns. are also in S.E. corner of township); Heath Pce, Far and Near ~ ~, ~ Lsw; Hemp Butt; Hilland, Big Hill Croft; Hintwood; Hollywell Breach; House Pce (by Chipnallmill Fm); Hunger Hill; Intake (2); Kinver (possibly transferred from Kinver St); Lancashire Mdw (FN 23 classifies this as a remoteness n., it is on the N. parish boundary); Lane End Pce, Far, Mid; Lawn (by Cheswardine Hall); Lea Mdw, Small, Ley Mdw, Far, Near; Lees Mdw, Pasture (by Chipnall Lees); Lewins Fold, Lower, Upper; Lightmoor, Far, Near (this and Lightwood are recurrent minor ns.); Lightwood, Little ~; Lindop Mdw; Lloyds, ~ Bank, Mdw (*v.* The Lloyd in Market Drayton *infra*); Lodge Bank, Far, Near, ~ Dale; Lord's Lsw; Marwell Breech; Mill Bank, Fd, Hays, Mdw (by Chipnall Mill); Minions Croft, Far, Mid, Near; Moss, Big, Spearman's Big Moss, Rushy Moss, Moss Nook (these fields are on the N. side of Moss Lane); New Inclosure; Norris's Upper Croft; Oat Lsw; Offley Dale, Far, Near, Offley Door; Paddock (2); Ox Lsw; Paradise; Piece, Far, Lower, Road; Pool Mdw, Lower, Upper (by mill pool); Preston

Coalbrook, Far, Near, New, Middle (by Coal Brook *supra*, Preston is unexplained); Rough (several); Rough Ground, Far, Near; Rough Pce; Rushy Mdw, Far ~ ~; Sambrook Pce, Lower ~ ~ (Sambrook, *infra*, is a long way S.); Shoulder of Mutton; Shaw Lsw; Slang; Small Corn Fd; Spearman's Hill (not near Spearman's Big Moss); Stack Fd; Stony Bank, Lower, Upper; Sturps's Gorse; Top Fd; Townsend (at N. end of Chipnall village); Well Lsw; Wheat Croft; Wheat Lsw; Winnings; Yard, Butterton, Brooks, Jackson's, New (on E. side of village); Yewtree Flat, ~ Fd (close but not adjacent).

3. ELLERTON AND SAMBROOK

The Foxall map of this area of Cheswardine has the heading "Ellerton and Sambrook townships", and it is convenient to include here all the names shown on that map, ignoring the complications of its southern part, round Sambrook. Sambrook became an ecclesiastical parish in 1856, and Kelly's 1934 Directory says that this was formed out of the parishes of Chetwynd, Cheswardine Rural and Edgmond. The *TAMaps* for Ellerton and Sambrook and for Chetwynd show detached groups of fields in this area, and the Index to Tithe Survey map has lines connecting the detached portions to Ellerton. Twentieth-century maps show Sambrook as in Chetwynd.

ELLERTON (SJ 716259)

Alartun' 1200 Cur (p), 1203–4 *Ass* (p), *-ton* 1212 P (p)
Ethelarton', *Hethel-* 1255–6 *Ass*, *Ethelarton* 1284–5 FA, *-ton'* 1291–2, 1306–7 *Ass* (p), 1327 SR (p)
Athelarton' 1255–6 *Ass*
Edelharton' 1271–2 *Ass*
Etlarton' 1281 *SBL 4127*
Ellarton 1404–5 MGS, *Ellerton* 1797 PR(L) 13
Allerton 1581–2 *SBL 5304*

'Æðelheard's estate', *v.* **tūn**. Adam *de Alarton*, mentioned 1212 P, is said by Eyton (VIII 93) to derive his surname from this place. If this ascription is correct there must have been an early shortened version of the place-name which had a brief currency.

SAMBROOK (SJ 714246): Sambrook is a DB manor and the name was therefore discussed in Part **1**, where it was taken to be 'sand brook'. This still seems the likeliest etymology. Sambourn PN Wa 221–2 is a partial parallel, but has some *Sand-* forms: these are absent from the available material for Sambrook.

ELLERTON HALL, 1833 OS, 1840 *TA*.
ELLERTON WD, 1833 OS, 1840 *TA*.
SAMBROOK MILL.

Field-Names

Forms in (a) are 1840 *TA*.

(a) Big Links; Britch, Far, Little, ~ Head (*v*. **bryce**); Broad Lsw, Lower; Broomfield; Common Pce; Croft, Far, Middle and Near ~ (by Sambrook); Croft, Barn, Garden (by Stanford Bridge); Cross Green (by a junction of paths); Cross Hills (5 fields by Cross Hills in Hinstock); Custard Mdw (probably a reference to sticky soil); Dains Fd, Far, Near; Danford, Lower, Near, Big, ~ Mdw (by tributary of R. Meese which forms E. parish boundary, probably 'secret ford', *v*. **dierne**); Estray Lsw (on parish boundary, perhaps a reference to stray animals); Five Butts (a tiny enclosure); Flat Tatnall Mdw (other Tatnall ns. adjoin in Chetwynd); Goldstone Mdw (near Goldstone); Gorse Cover; Gravelly Bank; Hay Fd; Hazle Yd; Headlands (probably a feature of a common field in N. of Chetwynd parish); Herschel Lease, Little; Horseholme; Horse Pasture (2); Horse Pipe Mdw (a curious n. which occurs also in Peplow *infra*); The Lawn (by Ellerton Hall); Long Croft; Moor Mdw; New Mdw; New Pool Mdw (by fish ponds E. of Ellerton Hall); Ox Lsws, Big, Little; Ox Pasture, ~ ~ Rough; Pits, ~ Mdw; Pool Croft, Head (by the large mill pond W. of Ellerton, 6" map shows Saw Mill here); Rails; Rogers Yd; Sambrook Mdw; Shooters Flat; The Slang (narrow strip by road); Stanmore Mdw; Tain Tree Fd, Mdw (variant of *tenter* 'cloth-stretching frame'); Talbot Hill (enclosure with house by Stanford Bridge); Taylors Mdw; Town Croft (by Sambrook); Three Crofts, Big, Little (Brook and Dolls Crofts adjoin); Town Fd (N.E. of Ellerton Hall, 5 fields called Field adjoin); Wood, Far, Near, Large, Wood Fd (by Ellerton Wd); Yard, Barn, Lower, Gales, Hall (by Ellerton Hall); Yellow Birch; Yewtree Lsw.

4. SOUDLEY, GREAT (SJ 725290), LITTLE (SJ 716283)
Suthleg', *-lee*, *Suthl'* 1255–6 *Ass*, *alia Suthleye* 1291–2 *Ass*
Sutle 1255–6 *Ass* (p)
Soudleye 1280 SAS 3/VIII (p), *Gt. Soudley or Sowton* 1695 Morden, *Sowdley* 1862 PR(L) 18
Little Soutley 1304 Ipm

'South wood or clearing' (i.e. south of Cheswardine), *v*. **sūð**, **lēah**. The same name, also developed to Soudley, occurs in Eaton under Heywood and in Gl (PN Gl **3** 219).

CROSS GREEN, at a junction of road and footpath.
DOWNAY HO.
DOLEY FM, *Doley* 1840 *TA*. Doley village adjoins, in St.
GREAVES PLTN, *Greaves*, *Big* ~ 1840 *TA*.

HANWOOD FM, *Hanwood* 1833 OS.

HOPSHORT, 1833 OS, 1840 *TA*. A similar name, Dropshort, occurs in O, Bk and twice in Berks, *v*. PN Berks 424, 471. In PN Berks it was tentatively suggested that Dropshort might refer to a position beside a road running at a slightly higher level. Maps suggest that this might suit the houses at Hopshort.

PARK HEATH, 1833 OS, 1840 *TA*, ~ ~ FM, S. of Soudley Park.

ROBIN HOOD INN, the building is shown but not named on *TAMap*.

SHAWBROOM, 1833 OS, 1840 *TA*.

SOUDLEY PARK, 1833 OS, 1840 *TA*. Robert *le Parker de Suthleg'* is mentioned 1255–6 *Ass*. On 19th-cent. maps the name is that of a house, there is no park. SOUDLEY PARK FM, a mile S.E., is shown but not named on *TAMap*.

SOUDLEY VILLA.

THORNEY PITS.

WAGGS BROOK. *Big* and *Little Wag Bank* 1840 *TA* are beside the brook.

WHEAT SHEAF INN.

WHITE HO.

Three canal bridges, Hazeldines, Park Heath and Soudley, are shown on 1900 6".

A house near Park Heath Fm, unnamed on 6", is *Woodside* on *TAMap*.

Field-Names

Forms in (a) are 1840 *TA*.

(a) Adbaston Mdw (Adbaston St is a short distance E.); Barbers Mdw, Yd; Barnyard (several); Black Hole (by Gravel Hole); Blake Breech; Bold Pce; Brick Fd, Big, Little; Brickkiln Fd; Broad Lsw; Brown's Croft; Canal Fd; Carthouse Fd; Castle Ditches (the 1963 1" map marks Castle Mound here and the road from Doley makes a detour round the field); Challinors Fd, Far, New and Lower ~ ~; Chipnall Pce (not near boundary with Chipnall township); Church Fd, Lower, Upper; Cleaver (a shape n.); Cockshut, Far, Middle, Near, ~ Mdw; Common, Big, Little, Common Pces (a large group of rectangular fields in N.E. of township); Common Fd, Little ~ ~ (several fields S. of Park Heath Fd, one is Common Allotment); Conery ('rabbit warren'); Cote Lsw, Far and Near ~ ~ (no building); Cow Lsw; Cow Pasture; Crabtree Pce; The Criftins (larger than surrounding fields, *v*. The Criftins in Dudleston *supra*); Croft (several, with Garden, Peas and Pool ~, round Shawbroom); Croft, Far, Near, Middle, Top (near Doley Fm); Croft(s) (several on outskirts of G. Soudley and by Park Heath Fm); Cross Head, Far and Near ~ ~, ~ Mdw (surrounding a road junction); Dean's Bank; Doorway Fd; Ellerton Fd (near boundary with

Ellerton township); Flat, Hall, Middle, Hob, Near Hob (adjoining fields S. of G. Soudley, near Well Fd ns.); Flatts, Big and Little Flat, Heathy Flat (surrounding Marsh Fd, *flat* in its open-field sense); Foder Heath, Lower and Upper ~ ~; Four Lane End Pce (by crossroads); Foxholes, Little and Middle Foxhole; Gill Lake, Lower and Upper ~ ~ (near Grinsel Lake); Grazing Pce; Griff Fd, Griffs Mdw; Grinsel Lake (*lake* 'drainage channel, ultimately from **lacu**, cf. Lacon Part **1**); Hanwood, Lower, Upper, Middle, ~ Mdw (by Hanwood Fm); Heathy Fd, Middle ~ ~; Hemp Breech; Hilland; Hint Fd, Big, Middle, The Hink Fd; Hoar Stone (by road to Newport, not near a boundary); Holly tree Lsw; Horse Pasture, The ~ ~ Mdw (adjoins Sheep Pasture); House Fd (by Shawbroom); Hunger Hill; Intake; Knighton Croft; Lady Hill; Little Mdw; Lloyds Croft (2); Long Lsw; Lower Lsw; Lower Yd, Big, Little; Low Ground, Middle and Near ~ ~; Lucas's Mdw; The Lunts, Lunts Mdw; Maddocks Breech; Marlpit Close; Marsh Fd, Lower and Upper ~ ~ (probably an open field, Marsh Bank and 3 Marsh Crofts adjoin); Mason's Pce; Masty Pit; Meadow, Little ~; Meadow Bank; Middle Flat (not in an obvious open-field context); Milking Tree Lsw; Mixen Hole ('manure pit'); Moat Bank (near Soudley Park); Moss Fd, Yd; Nan a Bostock; Old Oat Lsw; Ox Pasture; Park Corner (probably marking N. edge of Soudley Park); Pigot's Lsw; Pool Croft (by Park Heath Fm, a large pool on *TAMap* is not there on 1900 6"); Pool Mdw, Pce (there are large pools here, by Shawbroom); Radwell Bank; Robinson's Fd; Rough Lsw (2); Round Croft (one slightly curved side); Rushy Fd; Rye Croft, Far, Near; Sandhole Fd; Sandy Flatt; Sheep Pasture, Little and Middle ~ ~ (5 fields); Slang (narrow strip); Sowdley Fd (adjoins Marsh Fd); Sowdley Hills, Far and Near ~ ~; Staffordshire Mdw (on county boundary); Stile Pce; Thistly Fd; Thistly Pce; Three Cornered Fd (in road junction); Upper Stone; Ward's Pce, Lower, Upper; Well Fd, Big, Little, Lower and Upper ~ ~ (S.E. of Sowdley, perhaps an open field); Wharf Fd (by canal); Wheat Croft (2); Worrall's Mdw; (The) Yard (many in G. Soudley, including Far, Near, Lower, Upper, Hall, Ivy Tree, Corfields, Taylors and Joiners Yd); Yewtree Fd.

Child's Ercall

Ercall was discussed in Part **1**, with the suggestion that the base was an OE **Earcaluw* 'gravelly bare hill', perhaps belonging originally to a settlement at High Ercall, but becoming the name of a district which included Child's Ercall and was bounded on the south by the hill beside the Wrekin called The Ercall. This suggestion, albeit highly tentative, has been accepted by Welsh and English scholars, *v*. H. Wyn Owen, *Nomina* XI 107, and CDEPN.

No evidence has been found bearing directly on the affix Child's. If *child* has the sense 'young nobleman' it might refer to a junior member of the Strange family, which owned the manor. The alternative affix, *Parva* occurs from 1242 to 1705.

The reference 1800 *Map* in this section is to G. Foxall's drawing of a Corbet Estate map *SRO 327/16*. This is with his drawings of *TAMaps* in SRO.

DODECOTE GRANGE (SJ 666244)

Dodecot' 1200 Cur, *-cote* 1201 SAS 2/X (FF), 1253 Ch, c.1291 TN
Dodicot' 1201 Cur, *Doddy Cote* 1800 *Map*, *Dodicote* 1833 OS
Dot(t)ecote 1255 RH
Dotingcote (*Grangia de*) 1301 SAC
Doddecota in feld 1331 Ch
Dodcote 1535 VE

There was probably an **-ing-** in the original name, so 'cottages associated with Dodda'. Combermere Abbey owned the property, hence Grange. The 1331 affix may be an error; there is no other evidence for a district-name *Feld* here.

HUNGRY HATTON (SJ 673268)

Acton' 1257 Cl, *Acton* 1284–5 FA, *Hungery Acton* 1690 *SBL 1960*
Atton 1327 SR
Hungry Hatton 1808 PR(L) 10

This is likely to be *hǣðtūn*, 'heath settlement', rather than *āctūn*, 'oak settlement', with the *Acton* forms due to mistranscription. Eyton, VIII 14, reads *Atton* for the 1284–5 FA form. An area north of the settlement is *Hatton Heath* on 1800 Map, and High Heath in Hinstock adjoins. There are four better-evidenced *hǣðtūn* names in the county, *v*. Part **1**. One of these, Cold Hatton in High Ercall, is 4½ miles S.E., so there would be a need for affixes.

THE LEES (SJ 668263): *La Leye* (p), *Leye* 1279–80 *RentSur*, *Leyes* 1284–5 FA, *Lees* 1800 *Map*, *The Lee* 1833 OS. The same name occurs in Adderley *supra*. It is the plural of **lēah** 'clearing'. OS maps show a moat here.

NAGINGTON (SJ 677254)

Nagitona 1159–60 HAC, *Naggitona* 1160–72 ib
Naggintona 1172 (e.14th) HAC, *Nagynton'* 1271–2 *Ass et freq* with variant spelling *Naginton* to 1359 *SRO 322/175*
Naghinton 1255 RH, *Naghynton'* 1294–9 *Ass*
Nakynton' 1291–2 *Ass* (p), 1327 SR (p)
Nagington' 1339 HAC, *-ton* 1535 VE
Nagvnton alias Naynton' 1540 *SBL 6083*

This is clearly an **-ingtūn** name, and the first element is likely to be a personal name. No such personal name is on record, however, and no such name or element appears to have been noted in other place-names.

ALLFORD GREEN, 1833 OS. On 1800 *Map* there are fields called *Aufords Bank*, *Leasow* and *Meadow* here. Earlier references are *Alford Moore* 1693 *SBL 5317*, *Allford* ~ 1700, 35 *SBL 5319*, *5339*. ALLFORD BROOK is a mile S.W. Possibly 'old ford', the ford was probably a causeway over marshy ground.

BANK HOUSES. 1800 *Map* shows a single house with a field called *Headland Bank* adjoining.

BOG HALL. 1800 *Map* shows the house, in a field called *Croft*, on the N. edge of the area called *Hatton Heath*. The name is ironic.

THE COMMON, on S. edge of *Hatton Heath*. 1800 *Map* shows several fields called *Allotment* here.

CONYBURG WD, 'rabbit warren', from *cony-burrow* (NED). Instances in Abdon and Broseley (Part **3** 91, 110) have the modern form Coneybury.

CROW LANE is *Sayerfields Lane* 1800 *Map*.

ERCALL HEATH, 1794 PR(L) 13, *Ercoll* ~ 1787 ib, *Ercal* ~ 1833 OS. It is "heath between Tibberton and Howle" 1331 Ch.

THE HALL, *Aulam Ercalensem* 1667 PR(L) 20, *Ercall Hall* 1721, 77 ib.

HATTON FM.

HILL LANE COTTAGES. 1800 *Map* shows fields called *Great* and *Little Hill* here.

HOLY WELL, HOLYWELL COTTAGES, FM. 1800 *Map* shows the farm with *Holywell Banks* adjoining. *Holy Well* 1796 PR(L) 13 was presumably a dwelling place.

MALTKILN HO.

MANOR FM. 1800 *Map* has *Capital Messuage* here.

MILE-END COTTAGE, a mile S.E. of Child's Ercall.

NAGGINGTON COTTAGES.

NEW HO, shown but not named on 1800 *Map*.

THE NOOK.

PARK HO, 1800 *Map* shows *Crofts* here, on E. edge of Ercall Heath.

SAYERFIELDS, *Sayer Fields* 1833 OS, *v.* Crow Lane *supra*.

SPRINGFIELD HO, by Park Ho and in same group of *Crofts* on 1800 *Map*.

THE SYTCH (a wood), 1800 *Map* shows *Rough* and *Wet Sytch* here, *v.* **sīc**.

WOOD FM, *Wood* 1800 *Map*.

Field-Names

Forms in (a) are from G. Foxall's drawing of a Corbet Estate map, 1800, except where otherwise stated. Earlier forms dated 1690, 3, 7, 1700, 35 are *SBL 1960*, *5317*, *5318*, *5319*, and 1701, 8, are GT.

(a) Alder Marsh; Allerton Pce (on boundary with Ollerton); Allotment (*freq* round Hatton Heath); Axwells Moor; Balkers Fd, Lower, Upper; Barley Croft (2); Barn Yd; Big Mdw; Bilshams Bank; Birch Fd, Large, Little; Blaze Hill (*blaze*, ultimately from ON **blesi**, refers to a bare spot on a hill-side); Bog or Salts Mdw; Black Flatt; Bolas Fd (on boundary with Bolas); Bradley, Far, Near and Lower ~ (*the two Bradeleys* 1690); Brand Croft; Breaches ('newly-broken-in land'); Bridge Lsw (by a stream-crossing on road to Cherrington); Broad Fd, Big, Little; Broom Fd; Broomy Lsw; Broomy Law, Lower and Upper Broomy Fd; Burley, ~ and Pit; Burrows Lsw; Burying Ground (in village, Parsons Croft adjoins); Calves Croft; China Lsw (listed as a distance n. FN 23); Clay Pits, Far and Near Clay Pit; Clemstead (Clem- ns., probably referring to poor soil, are common in N. Sa, *v.* Prees *infra*); Clerk's Dole 1841 GT (1701, 8); Clover Fd; Colley's Croft; Common Ground (on S. edge of Ercall Heath); Coppy Grove; Cote Lsw Croft; Cottons Lsw; Cow Butts; Cow Lsw; Cow Pasture, Far, Near; Crabtree Fd; Croft, Lower, Middle, Near, Little (normal-sized fields in N. of township); Croft(s) (*freq* round Hatton Heath); Crofts (there is a cluster of Crofts and of fields called House, Garden and Croft, on E. edge of Ercall Heath: the fields and some houses are on 1900 6" map but not on

1963 1"); Crow Croft; Crow Lsw; Dods Moor, Lower and Upper ~ ~ (near Dodicote, *Dodmoore* 1690, *-more* 1693, *Dodmore Lower Feild* 1697, perhaps shortened from **Dodecotemoor*); Eaton Crofts, Fd, ~ Lane Lsw (on boundary with Eaton on Tern); Eight Butts (not in an obvious open-field context); Ercall Lsw; Field, Little, Nether; Fold Pce; Foxhole, Upper, Lower and Middle ~ (6 fields, *Foxall Field* 1690, (*The*) *Foxhole Field* 1693, 7, 1700, 35); Frize Moors (group of fields on N.W. boundary, by Hurst ns., probably a metathesised form of furze); Furlong, Near, Middle, Upper (3 fields on E. boundary); Gorsy Bank; Gorsy Fd, Lower, Upper; Green Fd; Gritty Flatt; Hall Woods, Hall Wood Bank (near Sayerfields); Hatch Lunns (*v.* Lunns *infra*); Hatton Marsh; Heath Lsw (by Hatton Heath); Heath Lsw, Lower or Large, Upper or Small (on N. edge of Ercall Heath); Heath Lsw, Pce (on W. edge of Ercall Heath); Hempbutt; Horseley Butts (near New Fd); Holt Croft, Moor; Hurst Lsw, Little Hurst Croft (several fields on N. boundary); Intake; Inwood Lsw, Upper; Kitchen Lsw; Lady Croft 1841 GT (1701, 8); Lane End; Lea Fd or Lindley; Leasow, Lower, Upper; Leeks Pces; Lees Fd (by Lees); Ley Brook Mdw; Lime Fd (2); Little Mdw; Long Fd (2); Long Flg (1690, not in an obvious open-field context); Long Mdw (2); Long Pce; Lunns, Lower and Near ~, ~ Mdw (from *land* in the sense 'open-field strip', Eaton Fd adjoins); Marl Bank; Marl Fd (2); Marl Pce; Marsh, ~ Bank and Croft, Bald Marsh; Marsh, ~ Mdw, Fd, Freemans Marshes, Elbow Marsh; Meadow, Middle ~, Lower ~ ~; Meadow, New, Long, Town, Horsepasture and Tan House Mdw (group of fields W. of village); Meer Breaches (on E. boundary); Meers, Far and Near ~, ~ Moor, ~ Mdw (group of fields on W. boundary, cf. *The Mear* (a croft) 1693, *The Meare* 1700, 35, *v.* **gemǣre**); Middle Moor; Mill Brooks; Moor (several); Naggington Bank, Lsw; Narrow Lane Croft, Fd; New Fd, Great ~ ~ (5 fields on W. boundary); New Incroachment (on N. edge of Hatton Heath); New Lsw (1693, 7, 1700, 35); Nollock, Birchen, Cote, Ox; Old House Yds; Outcast (on N. edge of Ercall Heath, probably disputed land, cf. Outcast in Cockshutt *supra*); Ox Pasture; Paddock; Pinfold Croft, Far, Near; Pit Lsw; Pool Mdw, Lower, Upper (1900 6" map shows pools here, by Dodicote Grange); Red Slough; Redway Fd; Road at Top; Rough Coppy; Round Mdw (small triangular field, adjacent fields have curved sides); Ryegrass Bank; Sandy Lsw; Shapeless (4 fields S.W. of Lees, probably *The Shepley* 1690, 'sheep pasture', but FN 13 lists it as a shape n.); Shotwell (Well Mdw adjoins); Shut Croft; Shutts (a large field, *v.* the discussion of Shut Part **4** 113: in the Childs Ercall instance 'projecting piece of land' is possible, as the field occupies a corner on the E. boundary); Skarratts Croft; Slang (narrow strip by road); Snake Fd (2 large fields); Square Pce; Sray Hill; Tan House Lsw; Tibberton Lsw, Moor (on boundary with Tibberton); Townsend (at W. end of Childs Ercall); Upper Fd; Way Croft Lsw; Way Fd (2); Wet Reyns, Near and Far ~ ~ (*Whitreanes* 1693, ~ *Croft* 1697, *The* ~ 1700, 35, probably the common n. 'wet reans', i.e. drainage channels); Wharton Pits; Wimble Hill; Wistancewick Brook Mdw, Wistancewick Pce (on boundary with Wistanswick); Woodcock Flat; Yard (3 fields by Hungryhatton); Yard(s) (several round village, including Far, Near, Bolds, Hicks).

(b) *The Bank*, 1697, *The Banke* 1700, 35; *Bank and Heath Leasow* 1693; *Heath Leasow* 1700, 35 (perhaps one of the 3 instances in (a)); *Horse Pasture* 1701, 8; *The Leigh Meadow* 1690; *The Low Field* 1690; *The Marsh* 1690, 3 (cf. 2 groups of Marsh ns. in (a)); *One Heath Leasow* 1697; *The Outwood Bank* 1690 (cf. Inwood Lsw in (a)); *The Pert Greave* 1690; *Town Meadow* 1693, *The Towne* ~1697, 1700, 35; *Weare Croft* 1697.

Hinstock

In the parish-name, discussed in Part **1**, ME *hine* 'domestic servants' has been prefixed to a simplex name from **stoc** 'dependent settlement'. It was suggested in Part **1** that the holders of the Barony of Wem may have used this estate for the upkeep of their household servants. This is conjecture, and any suggestions about the significance of **stoc** in this name and in neighbouring Stoke on Tern must also be conjectural. The names could be taken to indicate that both settlements were once parts of larger estates.

In a Muster Roll of c.1535, published in SAS 3/VIII, a place called *Stoke in the Hamblets* is listed between Cheswardine and Adderley. The editor identifies this with Hinstock, but it is not clear what the significance of such an affix would be, as all the parishes in this area have dispersed settlements which could be called hamlets.

LOCKLEYWOOD, *Boscum de Lockele* 1291–2 *Ass*, *Lokkeleye* 1362, 9 Ipm, *Lokeley Wood*, *Lockeley* c.1566 *SRO 327*, *Lockley Wood* 1698 GT, 1833 OS. 'Wood with an enclosure', *v.* **loca**, **lēah**. Lockwood PN WRY **2** 275 and PN NRY 147 are comparable names.

NUNNELEY (lost, possibly in Hinstock). A *vill* called *Nunnel'* is listed 1255–6 *Ass*, together with Hinstock, Sambrook and Ellerton, and Rog. *de Nunnyleg'* also appears in this roll. 'Nunna's wood or clearing', *v.* **lēah**. Apparently a doublet of Noneley, *supra* 79.

PIXLEY (SJ 682260)

Pichesl' 1255–6 *Ass*, *Pikesl'* 1257 Cl, *Pykesleye* 1291–2 *Ass* (p), *Pickesley* 1599 *PR(Chetwynd)*, *Pick(e)sley* 1690 *SBL 1960*
Piclesleye, *Pykelesle* 1283 InqMisc, *Pykeleslege* 1284–5 FA, 1291–2 *Ass* (p), 1327 SR (p), c.1566 *SRO 327*
Pysleye 1327 SR (p)
Pyckersley 1517 *SRO 327*
Pixley c.1566 *SRO 327*
Pickasly 1664 *PR(Chetwynd)*

'Pīcel's wood or clearing', *v.* **lēah**. Picklescott Part **2** 183 probably contains the same personal name.

SHAKEFORD (SJ 677284)
Sakelford e.13th Lil
Shakelford 1255 RH, *-ford'* 1291–2 *Ass*
Shakerford 1706 *SBL 1547*
Shake Ford 1833 OS

This is an addition to the known corpus of Shackle- names which are discussed in PN Sr 199–200 and in EPN **2** 98–9. The first element is OE **sc(e)acol** 'shackle', the meaning of which in place-names has not been elucidated. There are two other instances of the compound with **ford**, both in Sr. Other generics include **tūn** (Shackleton La), ***tūn-stall** (Shackleton YOW), **well** (Shacklewell MX), **wīc** (*Scacolwic* BCS 834, a swine-pasture belonging to Washington Sx).

A mill here is *Shakelfords Mill* c.1566 *SBL 327*, *Shukaford Mill* 1738 PR(L) 13, *Shakerford Mill* 1837 *TA*.

ASHFIELDS, 1833 OS, *The Ashfield* 1716 *SBL 4897*. The houses called Ashfields are on the W. edge of an area which, on *TAMap*, is divided into fields with Ashfield ns. These include *Big*, *Little*, *Pit*, *Far*, *Middle*, *New*, *Round*, *Five Acres Ashfield* and *Ashfields Dale*. Some of these are furlong-shaped, and this was clearly an open field. The field-pattern survives on 1900 6".

ATCHINGTON, *Ashington* 1833 OS, the house is shown but not named on *TAMap*.

BACK LANE.

BEARCROFT POOL, *Barcroft*, *Barkecroft* c.1566 *SRO 327*, *Barrcroft Field*, *Barecroft* ~ 1682 GT, *The Bar Croft* 1766 *SBL 4897*.

BIG WD, *High Heath Allotment* 1837 *TA*.

BLAKELOW, *The* ~ 1837 *TA*, *Blacklow Field* 1682 GT, *Blake Low Field* 1685 Lees: 'black tumulus', *v.* **hlāw**.

BUTTERMILK HILL, ~ *Bank* 1833 OS. The same n. occurs in Longslow *infra*.

CATLOW (Gazetteer), *Catelow* c.1566 *SRO 327*. *TAMap* shows fields called *Catlow*, *Far*, *Near* and *Round* ~, and *Catlow Hill* near Goldenhill Fm, and *Big Catlow* by Ellerton Mill. Probably 'cat tumulus'. Gazetteer also lists Catley in Sambrook, perhaps the same place.

CHANTICLEER HALL.

CROSS HILLS, ~ *Hill* 1833 OS, 1837 *TA*.

DIAMOND JUBILEE ALMSHOUSES.

ELLERTON HO, near Ellerton in Cheswardine.

FALCON INN.

FERNYDALE, 1833 OS, ~ WD.

FOUR CROSSES INN.

GOLDENHILL FM, LANE, *Golden Hill* 1833 OS, 1837 *TA*.

GOLDSTONE LANE.

THE GORSE.

GRANGE COTTAGE, by Hinstock Grange.

THE HAMSTEAD (Gazetteer). *TAMap* has fields called (*The*) *Hamstead* at S. end of the roadside cluster of houses which form a northern extension of Hinstock village. The name is *Hamstede* c.1566 *SRO 327*, *The Heamsted* 1716 *SBL 4897*.

HIGH FM.

HIGH HEATH, 1837 *TA*: this is part of *Hatton Heath* on 1833 OS.

HINSTOCK GRANGE, 1833 OS, HALL, 1837 *TA*, PARK, VILLA, 1833 OS.

HOMEBROOK HO, *TAMap* has *Homebrook Leasow* here.

HOME FM.

THE HOOKS, 1837 *TA*, HOOKS LANE.

HOWLE LANE.

HUNTERS LO.

JUBILEE PLTN, *Lightwood* ~ 1837 *TA*.

LIGHTWOOD, 1837 *TA*, *Leightwod* 1517 *SRO 327*, *Lyght Wood* 1588–9 *RentSur*, *Lightwood Piece* 1801, 2 *SBL 4887, 8*. 'Light wood', there are two instances in Wo (PN Wo 117, 302) and Lightwood in Ditton Priors, Part **3** 135, is probably another. **lēoht** occurs with several wood and tree terms.

THE LINKS, *Lee Lynkefilde*, *Lynke Leso* c.1566 *SRO 327*, *The Linke Field* 1685 Lees, *The Link* 1833 OS, 1837 *TA*, *v*. **hlinc**, which is generally used in place-names for a terraced road. On *TAMap Links* f.ns. cover a large area to W. and S. of the area with *Ashfield* ns., and many of them are furlong shaped.

LOCKLEY VILLA, 1833 OS, ~ *House* 1837 *TA*.

THE LOCKS (fishponds).

THE LONGPOOLS, 1837 *TA*, *Long Pool* 1833 OS.

LYME COTTAGE.

THE MARSH, MARSH LANE.

MILL GREEN, *Mill Green* 1833 OS. The mill is at Shakeford; *Mill Green* f.ns. on *TAMap* are spread over an area E. of this, interspersed with *Common* ns.

MILL LANE, leading to Saw Mill in Ellerton.

MOUNT PLEASANT, 1833 OS, 1837 *TA*: originally a l.16th-cent hall, *v*. Strain 17.

NAVAL SPINNEY, strip of wood which is shown but not named on *TAMap*.

PIXLEY COTTAGE, shown but not named on *TAMap*.

PRIMROSE DELL.

QUARRY WD.

RED LION INN. Strain (33) says that this was known as The Cat or The Romping Cat, and suggests that Romping is a corruption of Rampant. It ceased to be a public house in 1914, and is now the Gables.

RHODODENDRON WD.

THE ROOKERY.

STAFFORD HO, LO (latter 1833 OS): cf. *Stafford*, *Jellett Stafford*, *Jenetts ~*, *Jellastafford* c.1566 *SRO 327*, *Gill of Stafford* 1702 Strain. Cf. Gill Knobs in f.ns.

SUMMERHILL.

TETTENHALL VILLA.

UPPER GRANGE, 1833 OS.

WARLAKE, 1833 OS, *Whorlakes* c.1566 *SRO 327*, THE HOARLAKE, *Near ~* 1837 *TA*: a canalised small stream forms the N. parish boundary here: *hoar* may have developed a meaning 'boundary'.

WOODLANE.

1833 OS has buildings called *High Fields* and *Malt House*. Highfields is in Gazetteer, *v.* f.ns.

Field-Names

Forms in (a) are 1837 *TA*. Early forms dated 1685, 1706, 1766 are *SBL 3513*, *1547*, *4897*, 1612, 35, 82, 93, 98, 1705, 18, 1824 are GT. Forms for which no date or source is given are c.1566 *SRO 327*.

Most of the land in Hinstock was divided into small fields, and the numbers in the *TA* go up to 1000. A good deal of amalgamation has taken place in the listing of f.ns., and not all compounds with the commonest generics (Allotment, Croft, Meadow, Piece, Yard) have been included. An unusual feature in this parish is that a fair number of fields have two names, as Moor or Cooks Meadow, Smithy Croft and Vetch Croft.

(a) Acres (fields round Mount Pleasant include The Far Acres, The Eight Acres, two instances of The Five and The Twelve Acres, and Ten and Thirteen Acre Pce: these are probably statements of area); The Bank; Banky Fd; Banky Lsw; Barn Yd (several); Bell's Lsw; Belshams Bank; Bickerage, Lower, Upper; The Big Lea; Birchen Croft; The Birches, Far Birches Wd or Old Wd, Near Birches (cf. *Long*

Birches c.1566, *The Lord Birches, Locklaies* ~ 1685); Black Flat (3); Brand Croft; Brick Kiln Fd, Lower Kiln Fd; Briery Fd; Broad Fd; Big, Little; Broad Lsw; Broad Mdw (2) (*Brodmedowe, Brayde Medow* possibly from ***brǣd**, variant of **brād**, *v.* VEPN *s.v.* **brǣdu**); The Brokens, Big and Little ~, The ~ Mdw; Brook Lsw; Broomy or Guttery Fd; Broomy Pce; Butland Head; The Butt (small rectangle among Links ns.); Butter Pce; Calves Croft; Clemsons Park (variant of Clemley Park, *v.* Prees *infra*); Clover Lsw; Clover Mdw; Common Allotment, Pce (groups of fields by High Heath, Lightwood, Lockley Wd, Mill Green); Coney Mdw; Cooks Croft; Cote Lsw, Near, Far (no buildings); Cow Lsw, Far, Middle and Near ~ ~ (*Cowleso*); Croft (clusters of Croft ns. occur in N.W. corner of parish, by Lightwood and Lockley Wd, and by Fernydale); Crooked Lsw (irregularly shaped); Far Bank; Farthing Bank, Big, Little; Flat Lsw, Near ~ ~ (Black Flat adjoins); Foxholes or Hole Mdw; The Furlong (W. of Longpools); Furlong, The Far, The Near (cf. *The Furlonge* c.1566); Gill Knobs (*Jell Knob, Jell Yarde, Gelyarde, The Gill Yard* 1766); Goldstone Britch (*Gostonbriche, Gostanbruche* c.1566 (by Goldstone in Cheswardine, *v.* **bryce**); Gorsy Lsw, Far, Middle, Near; Grange Fd, Lsw, Yd (near Hinstock Grange); Grassy Mdw, Big, Little; Gravelly Pce; Green Fd (2); Green Reans (1682, 93, drainage channels); Hays, Far, Middle, Near; (The) High Fd, Further, Middle and Lower ~ ~ (*Hie Field* 1612, *High* ~ 1635, 82, 1705, N. of village, probably an open field); Hill Wicket Fd; Holly Grove; Holly Tree Fd (Oak Tree Fd adjoins); Hooks Fd (2 fields near The Hooks); Hot Mdw; Howle Lsw (near boundary with Howle); Hutt, Lower, Upper; Ightfields Cross; Intake (several); Lady Hays Mdw, Near Lady Heys (*Lady Heye*, this and other *-hey* ns. in the parish contain ME *hey* 'enclosure'); Lady's Corner; The Lawn, Lawn Fd (by Hinstock Villa); Leasow (*freq* as generic, with a few exceptions the qualifiers have not been listed); Ley, Near, Meeson's; Leys, Far, Middle; Leybrook Mdw (*Laye Brooke Meadowe*); Links Common (a set of rectangular fields W. of Ashfields, *v. The Links supra*); Lockley Wd Fd (a group of furlong-shaped fields adjoining Croft and Common ns. by Lockley Wd Pltn); Long Fd or Lea Fd (*Longher Leafilde, Lee Filde* c.1566, *Lea Field* 1682); Longpools, Far, Near, Middle, Pit (small fields by the house called The Longpools); Lower Fd; The Low Lsw (adjoins Blakelow); Mare Banks; Marl Flat; Marlpit Fd; Marsh Croft, Mdw; Meadow (*freq*); Meadow Bank; Meadow Nook; Meesons Lane (other Meeson's ns. occur in this area); Mill Green Fd (*v. supra*); Mill Mdw (by Hamstead); Mill Mdw, Far Mill Lsw (by Shakeford Mill); Moor or Cooks Mdw; Moor, Middle, Oswald's, Gorsy; Moor, Far, Near; Moor, Grazing, Mowing; Moor Bank or Railly Fd; Naggintons Lsw (*The Nainton Leasow* 1766, by road to Nagginton); Narrow Lane Croft; New Croft; (The) New Lsw (2); New Mdw; New Pce (1705); Old House Lsw; Old Pool and Coppice; Ox Pasture; Palace Yd (ME **palis** 'palisade'); Parvel, Far, Near (Hudson's Paxoil adjoins); Peat Bridge and Heathy Lsw; Pinfold Lane; Pingle (2, **pingel** 'small enclosure'); Pixley Green (funnel-shaped space between roads near Pixley); Pool Fd or Big Fd; Pool Fd, Lsw, Mdw; Potato Fd; Powers Common; Quab Mdw (*The Quabb*, 'marsh'); Ropes, Big, Little, Ropes Bank (*Rope in Link Field* 1682, *Long Rope* 1698, Little Rope 1824, probably referring to rope making); Round Mdw (irregularly shaped but with all sides straight); Rye Grass Lsw Sambrook Lsw (by boundary with Sambrook); Sawpit Bank and Rick Yd; Sheep Lsw; Sheep Pasture; Shoulder of Mutton (small triangle); The Shutts (pointed shape jutting into rectangular fields); The Slang (several); Slang Mdw; Smithy Croft and Vetch Croft; Spender's Barn Yd; Spring Fd, Further, Lower; Stony Bank, Mdw;

Stony Pce, Far Talbots Pce and Tongue Pce; Thirteen Acre Pce or Barn Fd; Three Acre Mdw; (The) Town Fd (several furlong-shaped fields W. of Ashfields); Twining Lsw; Two Gates; Watts Gorsy Fd; (The) Way Fd (2, *The Way Field* 1705); Well Bank; Well Croft, Lsw; Well Mdw, Lower; Well Pce; Well Yd; Weyberry Mdw; Wheathill, Near, Middle, Farther (*Whetehill* c.1S66, *Wheathills* 1705); White Fd; Willow Moor, Big, Little; Wood Fd; Woodfield or Ryegrass Lsw; Wood Lsw; Wynn's Lane, Fd; Yales Croft, Lea; Yard (*freq* by habitation sites); (The) Yelds (cf. *Blanter's Yields* 1693: as with Ashfield and Links ns., Yeld ns. cover an area which could be that of an open field: the n. means 'gentle slope', ultimately from **helde**).

(b) *Barecroft Field* 1682; *Bithome Butt* 1693 (*v.* **bytme** 'valley bottom'); *Blakeley Field* 1612, 35 (perhaps a variant of Blakelow, *v. supra*); *Blak(e)more* ('black marsh'); *Blockley*; *Le Bomer* (said to be in the wood of Pixley); *Briche*, *Le Bruche*, *Bryche* (the c.1566 document has, in addition to these simplex ns., *Hambriche*, *Hethybriche*; *Kaysbriche*, *Lockley Bryche*, *Longebriche*, *Midelbriche*, *Merse*, *More*, *Narrow* and *Oldern Briche*, *Pisbriche* ('peas'), *Pit Breeches*, *Redbriche*, *Roughe Briche*, *v.* **bryce** 'newly-broken-in land'); *Cocks Bacher*; *Colon Furlong* 1698; *Conigree* c.1566, *The Coney Greave* 1766 (*v.* **coninger**); *Elder Tree* 1693; *Fortheyard*; *Gig Hole* 1693, 1705 (referring to flax drying); *The Goldings Furlong* 1766; *Hallcroft*; *Hethe Croft*; *Hewerts Medow*; *Hincks Field* 1612 (possibly an error for *Lincks-*, *v.* The Links *supra*); *Horsepole*; *Houghemorefilde*; *Kechingcroft* (ME **kicchen** 'kitchen'); *The Lay* 1685 (cf. *Lytell Leye*); *Long Fellend*; *Lytill Medowe*; *The Marl Leasow* 1716; *Marsh Field* 1635; *The Moore* 1685; *Moss Furlong*; *The Myers*; *Normanheye*; *Normanstones*; *Oleheye*; *Phipacre*; *Pirriall*, *New*; *Poolebenche* 1685; *Rughecroft* (*v.* **rūh** 'rough'); *Shutmore Poole* 1685; *The Skinners Croft* 1766; *Sparbutter Crofte* 1685; *The Stockins* 1685 (*v.* ***stoccing**); *Stokemorefilde*; *Stonihurst* ('stony wooded hill'); *Vervelt*; *Wawmore*; *Wheat Yield* (*Croft*) 1682, 93 (perhaps part of The Yeld in (a)); *Whorwithy Heath*, *Pool* 1706 (a hoar withy is a whitebeam tree); *Wood Londe Grene*; *Woodleso*.

In a Glebe Terrier of 1685, Lees pp. 66–7, holdings in *High Field*, *Barecroft*, *Blakelow* and *Green Reans* fields are termed *Buts* (*Four*, *Three* ~ etc.), and in *Blakelow* field there is also "one picke".

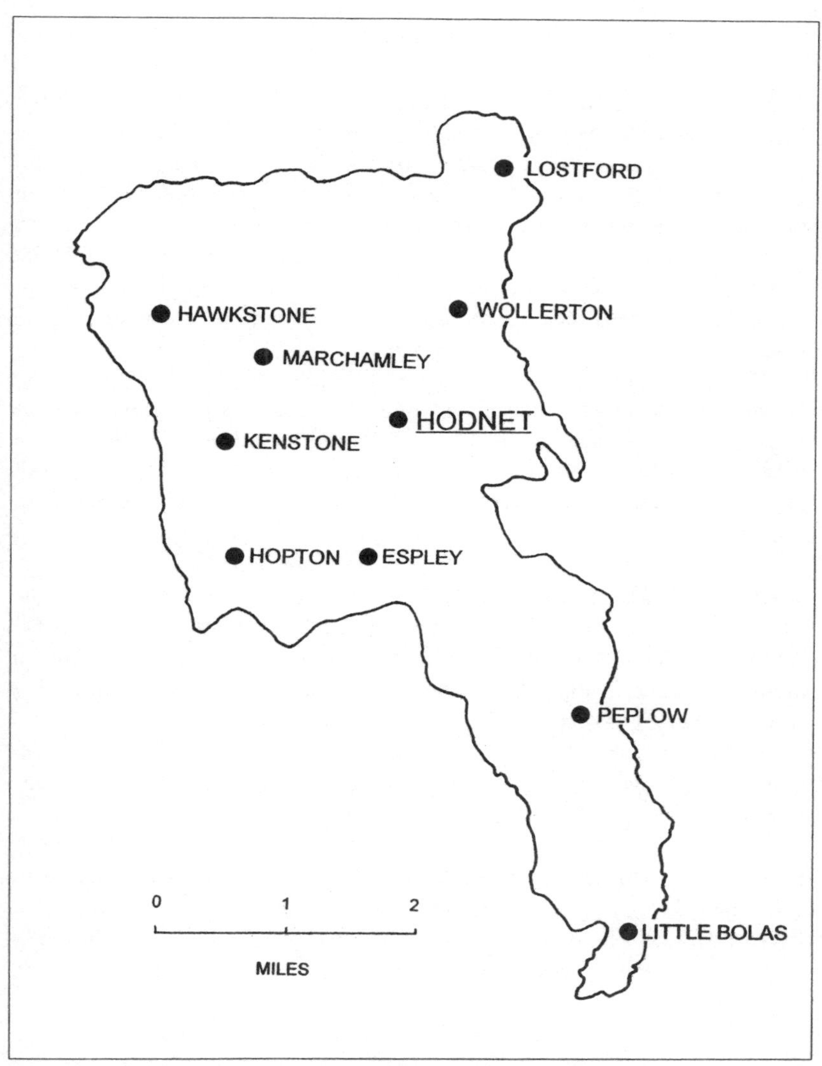

Map 6: Townships in the parish of Hodnet.

Hodnet

The parish-name, discussed in Part **1**, is believed to be identical with the Welsh name Hoddnant. This means 'pleasant valley', and in Hodnet the reference would be to the valley of the R. Tern. There are several examples of Hoddnant in Wales and the Cornish equivalent is found in the forms Hennett, Henon, Huthnance (CornEl 135).

DEPN, where this etymology was suggested, ascribes the loss of the second *-n-* of Welsh *nant* to dissimilation. This parish-name and that of the neighbouring Prees constitute the most striking instances of pre-English linguistic survival in Shropshire.

The Tithe Award recognises nine townships: Little Bolas, Hawkstone, Hodnet, Hopton and Espley, Kenstone, Lostford, Marchamley, Peplow, Weston under Redcastle and Wixhill, Wollerton. Weston with Wixhill was a chapelry as well as a township, and it is shown as a separate unit on the 1967 OS map of Civil Parishes: it has been treated as a parish in this survey.

1. LITTLE BOLAS (SJ 645218)
The name Bolas, which is discussed in Part **1**, is a compound of **wæsse** 'land by a meandering river which floods and drains quickly' and an element **bogel*. In Part **1** it was suggested that **bogel* was a diminutive of **boga** 'bend': this suggestion is noted without comment in VEPN.

Magna or Great Bolas is ½ mile S., on the opposite side of R. Tern, and the parish is in South Bradford Hundred. The affix for Little Bolas is first noted in 1342 Pat (*Parva Boulewas*).

SANDYFORD BRIDGE (Gazetteer), 1833 OS, cf. *Sandfords Breech* 1840 *TA*. The 1833 OS map gives this n. to the road between R. Tern and Potford Brook. The two *TA* fields are by this road, so Breech is probably for Bridge. The ford was probably a causeway.

Field-Names

Forms in (a) are 1840 *TA*.

(a) Adams Pltn; Breech Fd, Lower ('newly-broken-in land'); Broomy Lsw; Buck Breech; Buckle Pits (NED *s.v. buckle* sb. gives *buckle-pit* as the n. of a child's game, with a quotation from 1530, but this is not a likely source for a f.n.); Clay Flatt; Common Pce, Big, Near and Far, Corner, Gorsty; Cows Hay Mdw; Croft, Butchers ~ (in L. Bolas hamlet); Dark Lane Croft; Dawley Mdw; Far and Middle Meadows; Firtree Croft; Forge Lsw; Half Pce (small field); Jacks Mdw; Knowles, Big and Little ~; Landemore(s), Big and Far ~, Landemores Mdw (on N. boundary of township, ultimately from OE *land-gemǣre* 'boundary', a rather rare p.n. el.); Leasow, Higher, Lower; Long Lane Coppice; Long Lsw; Middle Ditch Croft; Middle Pce; New Fd; New Pce; Pinfold Croft; Pit Fd, Marlpit Fd (adjacent); Plantation, Pce adjoining ~; Rock Lsw; Rodens Lsw; Rowley Hill, Big, Long; Rushy Moor; Rye Croft; Walls Mill Pce, Walls Lsw, Walls Pit Fd (not adjacent, the last is by Buckle Pits); Water Furrows, Far ~ ~; Water Pit Fd; Wollastons Lsw.

2. HAWKSTONE (SJ 583300)

Havekestan', Hauekeston' c.1225 SAC (p) *et freq* with variant spellings *-stan, -ston(e)* to 1327 SR, *Hauekistan* 1256 HAC (p)

Haukeston' 1255–6 (p) *et freq* with variant spellings *Hawke-* and *-stan, -ston(e)* to 1728 *SBL 3400*, *Hawkston* 1538 PR(L) 11, 1713 *SBL 14618*, *Hawkstone* 1665 *SBL 8383 et seq*

Hauekston 1276 Ipm

Hakestone 1291–2 Ass (p), *Hakeston* 1308 Ipm, 1570 PR(L) 11

Hackstone 1589 PR(L) 11

'Hawk stone', *v.* **hafoc**, **stān**. The 'stone' is a dramatic sandstone crag.

THE ABBEY, 1833 OS, *Hawstone Abbey* 1804 PR(L) 2, *Lillow Abbey* 1806 ib. The alternative n. is unexplained: a field adjoining the house is *Lillow Hall* 1840 *TA*.

HAWKSTONE PARK. The boundary between Hodnet and Weston under Redcastle runs through the park, the larger portion being in Weston. Names in the park which are shown on the 1900 6" map and Tithe Award maps are mostly in that parish, so are listed *infra*.

MARLPIT SLIP: *slip* is used in this area for narrow strips of woodland.

VALE FM.

WHERLEY ROUGH.

WOOD FM, shown but not named on *TAMap*.

Field-Names

Forms in (a) are 1840 *TA*, and refer to fields in the limited area of the township N. and N.W. of Hawkstone Pk.

(a) The Beechtree Fd; Big Fd; Big Mdw; The Big Moor; Burrow Fd, Top Burrows Fd; Broughtons Lsw; Coppy Fd, Lower ~ ~ (adjoining wood called Coppice); Corsers Mdw; Croft, Far and Middle ~ (small enclosures on N.W. boundary); Croft (cluster by Wood Fm includes Coppice, Near, Pit Crofts); Dole Mdw; Forge Mdw, Big ~ ~; Harvest Stone; Kitchenhurst; Lillow Hall (*v.* The Abbey *supra*); Looms, Big, Little (FN 7 regards this as a form of *land*, like the commoner Loon(s)); Middle Fd; The New Fd; The Old Hey; Orchard Fd; Parsons Mdw; Rough Fd; The Sand Fd.

3. HODNET (SJ 614287)
v. the discussion of the parish-name *supra*.

TUNSTALL (SJ 634264)

Tunstal 1292–5 *Ass* (p) *et freq* with variant spelling *-stall*
Tonstall 1406–7 *SBL 3829*, 1705 PR(L) 11
Tuntshall 1733 *SBL 5277*

v. ***tūn-stall** 'farmstead'. In addition to its use for a number of settlement-sites this compound occurs in f.ns., sometimes as Dunstall, *v.* FN 56 for Sa examples. It may have been used of deserted habitation-sites.

TAMap has *Tunstall Wd* and *Meadow* and fields called *Lower* and *Upper Tunstall*, and the position of these suggests that the name applied to an area not just to the farm.

WEOBLEY (SJ 622263)

Webeleia c.1204–17 HAC
Webbeleye 1333 HAC (p)
Webl(e)y Corner 1728, 9 PR(L) 11

Weobley He (HePN 200) is *Wibelai* in DB and has *Wibe-* and *Webbe-* forms in 12th–13th-cent. sources. It is considered to mean 'Wibba's clearing', though the personal name is not on record.

It seems likely that Weobley in Hodnet is another example of this compound, with the absence of *Wib(b)e-* forms to be accounted for by the scarcity of early references.

The curious modern spelling of both the He and Hodnet names is first noted on the 1833 OS map. CDEPN, discussing the He name, suggests that *Weob-* is due to imitation of Leominster, also in N. Herefordshire. It seems necessary to assume that the spelling of the Hodnet name is due to association with the Herefordshire place, perhaps on the part of Ordnance Survey officers.

ASHCOURT.

BRICKKILN PITS.

COLLEGE HOUSES, 1833 OS.

CRABMILLS, shown but not named on *TAMap*.

GOLDEN GROVE, perhaps a transferred n. from Wales, *v.* NCPNW 113, 228.

GREGGY LEASOWE. *Greggy* is probably an adjective from a variant form of dialect *grig*: 'heather', NED sb[2], ultimately from Welsh *grug*. PN Ch **5.1** 200 ascribes *greg*, *grig* ns. to NED sb[1] 'dwarf', but 'heather' is more likely in p.ns. *Griggy Leasow* 1767 *SBL 8626* appears to be on the S. boundary of the township, so perhaps another instance.

HALL WD, on W. boundary of Hodnet Pk. *TA* calls this *Wood and Water*, there are fish ponds at one end of the strip.

THE HEARNE, *The Horn* 1833 OS, *The Horn Field* 1840 *TA*. If *Horn* is correct the reference might be to the point of land between converging roads S. of the buildings.

HEATH BROOK, ~ WD

HEATH FM.

HODNET HALL, 1682 GT, *Hall* 1840 *TA*.

HODNET HEATH, 1661 PR(L) 11, 1833 OS, 1840 *TA*.

HODNET PK. On *TAMap* the area is divided into rectangular sections called *Broomy*, *Higher*, *Copy Pool*, *Coopers Park*, and *Further Marl Piece*, *Nearer Mall Piece*, *Further* and *Nearer Fall*.

HOME FM.

LAWN COTTAGE, on boundary of Hodnet Park.

LEAR ROUGH, 1833 OS, *Wood in Horn Fm* 1840 *TA*.

OLD SCHOOL, *The Dungeon* 1840 *TA*.

RECTORY, *The* ~ 1833 OS.

THE SLIP, a narrow belt of trees, which is the meaning of *slip* in this area.

SYCAMORE COTTAGE.

TUNSTALL WD, 1840 *TA*, *v. supra*.

THE WORKHOUSE, *Workhouse* 1833 OS. *TAMap* shows *Poor House* with *Workhouse Field* adjoining.

TAMap shows *Bear Inn* and *Unicorn Inn* in village, also *Lock up* and *School House*. *The Bear Inn* is also mentioned 1810 PR(L) 11.

Field-Names

Forms in (a) are 1840 *TA*. Early forms dated 1612, 82, 85, 1701, 5, 19 are GT, 1767 are *SBL 8625*.

(a) Beach, Graftons, Lower, Top (by stream-valley on N. township boundary, *v.* **bæce**); Big Lsw; Big Pce; Birchen Pce; The Blibbs (FN 71 lists this among unexplained Sa f.ns.); Broomy Lsw (several); Calves Croft (2); Common Pce (3 fields on E. edge of Hodnet Heath); Coney Greave ('rabbit warren'); Cotton Gate Fd (on E. boundary of Hodnet Heath); Cote Lsw, Higher, Lower (*Coat Leasow* 1767, large fields with no buildings); Cross Moor, ~ ~ Mdw; Dove Ho Bank (by Hodnet Hall); Field, Big and Little Old Field (7 adjoining fields on S.W. boundary); Field (this and adjoining Crofts, N.W. of village, are furlong shaped); Field (2 fields an N.E. boundary); Fish Mdw (Cottage Pool in Wollerton is nearby); The Flatts (2 furlong-shaped fields adjoining Field on N.E. boundary); The Flatts (adjoins Four Butt Mdw E. of village); Four Butt Mdw; Fox Cover (a small wood); Glebe Pce; Greenway Hedge; Heath Lsw, Lower, Higher; Holloway Mdw, Big ~ ~, Little Holloway (by a road); Hop Yd; Horse Pasture; Hough Mdw; Knights Groves; The Lawn (by Rectory); Lea, Far, Near, Rough, Lea Side, Big and Little ~ ~ (perhaps **lēah** in the sense 'wood', the small wood called Lear Rough is among these fields); Lea, Far, Near (by Oak Coppice on S.E. boundary); The Leasow; Linley Mdw; Little Mdw; Long Fd; Lower Lsw; Marl Fd, Lower, Upper; (The) Moor, Lower ~ (8 fields by R. Tern); (The) Meadow (several); Meadow, Big, Long; Middle Lsw; Oak Coppice; Piece, The Piece, ~ ~ Mdw, End (4 large fields in an area E. of Hodnet which may have been an open field); Pit Fd; Pool Mdw, Long, Lower; The Pools; Reeve Lands (*Revelands Croft* 1701); Round Mdw (3 curved sides); Rown Tree (i.e. mountain ash); Rushy Fd; Sand Fd, Big and New ~ ~ (5 fields E. of village, possibly an open field, *Sandy Field* 1621, 85, 1701, 19, *Sandfield Flatt* 1685, 1705); (The) Tean Tree Croft (*tenter*, referring to cloth stretching); Three Gardens (tiny enclosures); Three Gates, Little, Lower, Near (an adjoining field in Wollerton township is Three Gates, cf. Two Gates in Hinstock); The Three Oaks; Town End Fd (at S. end of village); Unicorn Fd (from Unicorn Inn); Well Croft; Wheat Lawn (by Hodnet Hall); Wheat Lsw; The Wheatly, Far and Middle Wheatly (probably a poor form for Weobley, which adjoins); Withys Hill; Wood and Water (*v.* Hall Wd *supra*); Wood Lsw (2, by Tunstall Wd); Yard, Big, Stack (in village); Yewtree Lsw.

(b) *Hell Lane*, ~ *Wickett* 1767; *Hemp Butt* 1701; *Hopton Corner*, ~ *Hedges* 1767; *Kyneland* (*Croft called*) 1612, *Kineland* 1682, 5 (possibly 'cows'); *Lea Field* 1612, 82, 85, *Lea Croft* 1701, *Leafield Croft* 1705 (cf. Lea ns. in (a); *Meer Fields Gate* (from a boundary description); *Munks Meadow* 1721 *SBL 6521*; *Paddock Well* 1767; *Parsonage Flatt* 1612.

4. HOPTON AND ESPLEY

ESPLEY (SJ 610267)

Espoleye 1172 (e.14th) HAC

Espeleg' c.1230–40 HAC *et freq* with variant spellings *-le*, *-ley*(*e*) to 1395 AD

Esple 1242 Fees (p) *et freq* with variant spellings *-ley*(*e*), *Esply* 1707 PR(L) 11

Aspeleye (p), *Haspeleye* 1291 *Ass*

Eppesley 1398 Cl

'Aspen wood', *v*. VEPN for other instances of this compound. In this heathland area **lēah** is more likely to mean 'wood' than 'clearing'.

HOPTON (SJ 593267)
This is a DB manor, so discussed in Part **1**: the **hop**, 'secluded place', was probably in this instance an enclosure in heathland.

HINEHEATH COPPICE.

HOPE WD, *Hopes Wood* 1833 OS, *Hope Coppice* 1840 *TA*, named from the **hop** of Hopton. Cf. *The Clyffe*, *The Hope alias The Clyffe alias Hope Copie* 1594 *CourtR*, *Le Hope Copie* 1602 *SRO 322 box 2*.

THE LEECH (Gazetteer), 1833 OS, 'boggy stream', ultimately from **læc(c)**.

THE SITCH, 'small stream', ultimately from **sīc**.

Field-Names

Forms in (a) are 1840 *TA*.

(a) Barnyard (perhaps *Banyard* 1600 *CourtR*); Church Butts (in the area of *Parkefelde infra*); Common Pieces (there are two groups, one in the area N. of Hine Heath, the other by Hodnet Heath); Coneys Greaves ('rabbit warrens'); Court Flg (in the area of *Hechefelde infra*); Croft(s) (a row of small enclosures by the road bounding Common Pce ns. near Hine Heath, several (including Gorst Croft) by road to Shrewsbury, 2 by unnamed buildings S. of Hope Wd); Fenny Gates; Heath Mdw; The Hill; Hob Croft; Leasow (Lsw ns. in area N. of Hine Heath include Far, Heath, Middle, New, Rushy, Wet Lsw); Maidens Row (by a small building still there on 1900 6"); The Meadow; New Pce; Park Side, Lower, Upper, Near (adjoining Hodnet Pk); Pudding Flg (in the area of *Parkefelde*, probably a reference to sticky soil); Six Butts (in the area of *Hechefelde*); Tan House Mdw and Jack Horn.

(b) HAC has a document of 1325 leasing land in Hopton. The pieces of land (*acra*) are listed under fields: *le Parkefelde*, *le Hechefelde* and *le Wheystanesfelde*. The first of these open fields will have been in the area adjoining Hodnet Park, where *TA* has Butts and Furlong ns. *Le Hechefeld* (probably from **hæc(c)** 'wicket gate') is said to be in Espley and may correspond to *Espley Feild* 1602 *CourtR*. *Wheystanesfelde* (probably from a pers.n.) contains land near 'Hopley lane', which places it near the W. boundary, where *TA* has a large field called Old Furlong. This may be *Hopton Feild* 1594 *CourtR*. Names from this lease are presented here under the three headings.

(i) In *le Parkefelde*: *Chirchewey* (the road from Hopton to Hodnet, an acre is "ultra" this); *Le Clif* (the steep slope on S. edge of Hope Wd); *Holeweylonde* ('hollow way'); *Schetelonde* ('projecting land', *v*. **scēat**); *Le Stobforlonge* (*v*. ***stobb** 'tree-stump').

(ii) In *le Hechefelde*: *Le Brocforlonge* ('brook furlong', Potford Brook rises N.E. of Espley); *le Hetheyate* ('heath gate' perhaps leading to Hodnet Heath); *Le Slawelonde*; *le Weystreteslonde* ('way street' is a curious n. for a road).

(iii) *Le Barinlonde iuxta Hoppeleyslone*; *Le Duremay Deneswall'* (several of the ns. in this document are corrupt); *Le Elronnegrene*; *Le Hembruche* (*v.* **hemm** 'boundary', **bryce** 'newly-broken-in land'); *Le Hongyngeforlonge* ('hanging', i.e. on a slope); *Johakres*; *Le Lokacr'*; *Le Lydeyate* ('swing gate'); *Le Sondyfurlonge* ('sandy furlong').

Other (b) ns. are: *Eylewardescrofte* c.1230–40 HAC (ME pers.n.); *Hedyate Butthe* 1539–40 *RentSur* (possibly *Hetheyate supra*).

5. KENSTONE (SJ 592283)

Kentenesdene c.1190–4 HAC *et freq* with variant spellings *-den' -den(a)* to 1308 Cl, *Kentenisdene* 1228 BM
Kentesden 1253–63 HAC *et freq* with variant spelling *-dene* to 1600 *SRO 322 box 2*, *Kentesdoun* 1393 Cl
Kentelesdale 1271–2 *Ass*, *Kentenesdale*, *Dennsdale* 1278 Ipm, *Kentalesdale* 1291–2 *Ass*
Kenstanesdon 1271–2 *Ass*
Kendesden 1275 Cl
Ketteneston 1276 Ipm
Ketteston 1276 Ipm
Kemettesden 1317 Cl
Kentelesdene 1327 SR
Kenston(e) 1552 PR(L) 11 *et seq*
Kenteneston(e) 1596 *SRO 322 box 2*, *Kentenstone* 1607 *ib*

Second element **denu**, referring to the sinuous stream-valley which crosses the northern tip of the township and is overlooked by the settlement. There was interchange with ME **dale** in the 13th century.

DEPN says 'perhaps Centwine's valley', and this pers.n. seems the likeliest first element. The *Kenteles-* forms are due to the interchange of *-n-* and *-l-* which is well represented in place-names.

CHIRBURY WD

Cheseburi 1276, 99 Ipm, *Ches(e)bury* 1291–2, 92–5 *Ass*
Chusbor 1308 Ipm

The 1st ed. OS map has *Chirbury Hill* and *TA* calls the wood *Chirbury Hill Plantation*. *TA* also has fields called *Big*, *Cote* and *Pit Chirbury*, *v. Cote* in f.ns.

The second el. of the name is **byrig**, dat. of **burh** 'fort'. Chirbury Wd and the Chirbury f.ns. are on the E. end of the large hill-top which has Bury Walls hill-fort, in Weston under Redcastle on its W. end. The Chirbury ns. are confined to the Kenstone side of the boundary, but there can be little doubt that they preserve the OE name of the fort.

The first el. is likely to be a word meaning 'gravel'. VEPN *s.v.* **cis* discusses names which contain elements **cis*, **ceos*, the latter being a variant suggested by Löfvenberg in PN Do **1** 326 to explain a f.n. *Cheseberghe*. Löfvenberg suggested that **ceos* was due to association with *ceosol* 'gravel', the recorded variant of *cisel*. In the 1308 spelling for the Sa name, *-u-* could be a reflex of *-eo-*.

The contexts of early forms suggest that there was a habitation here in the 13th and 14th centuries, when tenements are said to be "in Chirbury". The houses called Daneswell may be on this site.

Eyton, IX 347–8, gives a form *Chirbere* from a tenure roll of 1285. This is at variance with other spellings and it may be a misreading of **Chisbere*.

HOPLEY (SJ 597280)

Hoppeleia 1155–60 HAC *et freq* with variant spellings *-ley*, *-lega* to 1321 HAC
Hopeley c.1200 HAC, *-lega* 1256 HAC
Hopley 1692 *SBL 5704 et seq*

v. **hop**, **lēah**. It is possible that the area of Hopley, Hopton and Hope Wd was called **hop** in its sense of 'enclosure in waste land', the reference being to cultivated land on the N. edge of extensive heath. **lēah** may mean 'wood' rather than 'clearing' in this instance.

DANES WELL, 1833 OS, DANESWELL. The road to Kenstone runs in a narrow cleft in the S. side of the Hawkstone ridge, and the 6" map marks Danes Well beside this road. The name Daneswell is given to some houses W. of the road. *TA* has *Far* and *Near Dean Well Field* on one side of the road, *Maidens Well* on the other. The latter name is *Greate* and *Litle Maydons Wall* 1615 *SRO 322 box 2*. It is possible that this was shortened to *Dean Well*, the *dean* being taken as the narrow gully, and that there was then association with Danes.

HOPLEY COPPICE, 1833 OS, cf. *Hopley Woodde* 1595 *SRO 322 box 2*.

KENSTONE HILL, 1840 *TA*.

THE LARCHES.

NICCO WD, 1833 OS, 1840 *TA*.

RAKEPARK LO, *Lodge* 1833 OS, *The Lodge* 1840 *TA*. *TA* has two fields called *Rake Park* on the other side of the Weston/Marchamley road, but most of the park is in Weston *infra*.

THE VINEYARD, *Vineyard Plantation* 1840 *TA*.

Field-Names

Forms in (a) are 1840 *TA*. Early forms dated 1596, 1607, 1615 are *SRO 322 box 2*. ME forms for which no source is given are HAC: these relate to Haughmond Abbey's property in Hopley.

(a) Bakehouse Yd (large field by Hopley); Bank, Far, Near; Barn Yd (large field W. of Kenstone near small enclosures called Higher Yd and Stackyard Mdw); Beech Coppice; Big Dale Lsw; Black Britch; Blakeley Fd, Far, Near and Little ~ ~ (among the Lsw ns. W. of the village); Blibbs (this unexplained n. occurs also in Hodnet); Broom Ditch; The Buxtones, Buxton Wd (Big Buxton in Marchamley adjoins: FN 40 notes 3 Sa f.ns., one of which was listed in Part **3** 226 with a 17th-cent. reference: Foxall's suggestion was that these were stones used for beating linen in a farmhouse wash, and in Part **3** it was suggested that the example in All Stretton may have been a shape-n. alluding to such a boulder: for the Kenstone instance a literal sense 'washing stone' seems unlikely, and here again, since The Buxtons is a large field which could be considered boulder-shaped, a shape-name might be suggested: the fields are, however, on the S. edge of the Hawkstone ridge, and actual boulders could have been present: the term is discussed, with examples from a number of counties, in VEPN s.*v.* **bucca**: field-work on all located examples might be enlightening: the 3rd Sa example is in Stoke upon Tern *infra*); Cliffs Fd (cf. *boscus voc. Le Hope alias Le Clyffe* 1596, the *TA* field is by a deep gully); Common Pce (2 fields by a crossroads on S. boundary); Croft, The ~, Ferny and Little ~ (by Kenstone); Croft, Black, Common, Far, Lawn, Middle (along the road S. of Danes Well); Croft, Common, French Wheat (by the crossroads on S. boundary); Dickens Mdw; Dollinger, ~ Bank, Pltn (Gazetteer lists as extant, *vallem voc. Dallinger* 1607); Field before the Door (large field by Hopley); Fields Head, Near and Upper Field Head; Hawkstone Fd (large field by Kenstone Hill, not near Hawkstone); The Hayes, ~ ~ Mdw, Hayes Rough, Hayes Wd ~ Mdw, Lower and Top Hayes, Heys (group of fields on N.E. boundary); Heath Lsw; The Hill, Far and Near Hill Fd, Hill Ground (by Kenstone Hill); Hopley Hill, The Hill (6" map has Hopley Coppice here); Innground, ~ Mdw, Near ~ (probably 'enclosed ground' as opposed to open field); Intake (tiny enclosure on N. edge of Nicco Wd); Leasow (an area of mostly rectangular fields W. of Kenstone includes Docky, Heath, Marl, New, Outmost, Thistly, Wood and Yewtree Lsw); Leasow (8 adjoining fields in S.E. of township are Big, Copy, Ferny, Middle, Pit, Slakey, Lower and Over Wet Lsw); Level Horn, Far, Near; Long Butts (furlong-shaped strip, Ten Butts Mdw adjoins); The Meadow (large field by Hopley); Near Pale Flg (among Lsw ns. W. of village); New Pce, Far, Near; Old Yd (by Croft ns. S. of Danes Well); Rabbit Burrows; Rays Croft; Rodway (by Weston/ Marchamley road); Stone Well; Tanners Mdw; Well Croft, Mdw (*Well Crofte* 1599 *CourtR*); Wildmoor Hill; Yewtree Fd.

(b) *Aldemulnerste* 1203–4 (*Olhmulnehurste* c.1190–1200 is probably a corrupt form, *v.* **eald**, **myln**, **hyrst**, said to be a meadow near *C*(*h*)*ote*); *La Bechemill'* 1256, *Beache Mill* ("now collapsed") 1601 (the account of the mill's position in 1256 places it on the stream overlooked by Kenstone: **bæce** seems a more appropriate term for this narrow valley than the **denu** of Kenstone); *Cote* c.1190–1200, *Chote* 1203–6, *Coate Crofte Furlonge*, *Le Litle Coate Crofte* 1615 (this may be *Cote Chirbury, v. supra*); *Eitaneslache* 1204–17 (*v.* **læc**(**c**), first el. possibly a surname); *Le Merhoke* (probably 'boundary angle'); *Le Portwaye* 1615 (leading from Hopton to Hodnet); *Thestercoumbe* 1256, *Thestrecombe* 1321 ('the eastern coomb', a High Hatton deed of 1607 refers to land "iacens subtus boscum et montem domini vocatur Thestercombe" on Hopley Heath: the **cumb** appears to be the little valley overlooked by Hopley Fm and the "mons" to be the small hill above the farm).

6. LOSTFORD (SJ 627313)

Loscafort 1121 SAC

Luscafort 1138 SAC

Loschesford c.1138 SAC, 1271–2 *Ass*, *Loskesford'* 1212 Fees *et freq* with variant spellings *-ford*(*e*) to 1392 Fine, *Loscusford* 1308 Ipm

Loschefford' 1155 SAC, *Loschefordia* c.1155 SAC, *Loskeford* c.1175 SAC, 1271–2 *Ass*, *-ford'* 1255–6 *Ass*

Lokeswrde 1204 P, *Lokkeswode* 1317 Ipm, Cl

Lochesforde c.1204–24 HAC *et freq* with variant spellings *Lockes-*, *Lokkes-* and *-ford* to 1393 Cl

Luscusford 1271–2 *Ass*, *Luskesford'* 1306–7 *Ass*

Losford 1637, 1706 PR(L) 11, 1672 HTR, 1692 *SBL 5704*, *Lossford* 1738 PR(L) 11

The name is *Losford* on the 1833 OS map and in *TA*. The 1900 6" map is the first instance noted of Lostford.

The commonest early spellings are *Loskesford* and *Lokesford*, with a significant minority of *Loskeford*. It is uncertain whether the original had one or two *s* letters. DEPN suggests OE *lox* 'lynx'. If this were used in the genitive, *loxes* could become *Loskes-* by metathesis or *Lokes-* by dissimilation. BT notes a possible weak form *loxe*, which may be found in a charter-boundary name *loxanwudu*, and this could account for the earliest forms *Loscafort*, *Luscafort*.

The plausibility of this etymology is greatly strengthened by recent research on lynx bones from sites in Yorkshire and Scotland. This indicates that the animal was extant in Britain until the 6th/7th centuries (*The Times* 11.10.05, quoting *Journal of Quarternary Science*).

The ford would be a crossing-place on the R. Tern.

BLEAK HO.

BRADLEY FM, shown but not named on *TAMap*.

LOSTFORD BRIDGE, possibly on the site of the ford of the place-name.

LOSTFORD COPPICE, *Losford* ~1833 OS, *The Coppice* 1840 *TA*.

LOSTFORD HALL and HO. Both buildings are shown without names on *TAMap*.

LOSTFORD LANE, *Losford* ~ 1833 OS.

MANOR FM, shown but not named on *TAMap*.

Field-Names

Forms in (a) are 1840 *TA*.

(a) Barn Yd, Lower, Upper, Far Barn Fd; Big Mdw; Briery Croft; Calves Croft; Clover Croft; Colehurst Mdw; Coppy Lsw; Copy Croft, Mdw (by Lostford Coppice); Cote Flg (2 large fields adjoining Long Fd); Cow Lsw, Far, Near; Dirty Croft; Fifty Acre, Forty Acre (2 tiny enclosures); Green Fd, Far, Middle, Near; Gudgeon Fd (a reference to the fish seems unlikely, but FN 46 lists it as such); Hodnet Fd; Kiln Croft; Long Fd; Long Mdw; Marl Fd; Meadow, Copy, Big, Little, Upper, Middle and Lower Mdw (strips along Bailey Brook); Moat Bank (by Manor Fm); New Fd; Outlet Croft (by Bradley Fm); Ox Lsw, Far, Middle, Near; Park, Far, Near (no apparent reason for n.); Passage, Big, Top, Middle, ~ Mdw (the road from Shrewsbury to Market Drayton crosses the Bailey Brook near these fields, and Drayton *TA* has Passage Mdw by the road on the other side of the stream, so the sense is probably 'river-crossing': this is near the junction with R. Tern, and a causeway may have been needed); Pit Fd; Rough Yd; Sandy Fd (4 fields, another called Barn Yd and Sand Fd adjoins); Shady Mdw; Stoke Fd, Big, Little (not near Stoke upon Tern); Tern Mdw; Tim's Hole Mdw; Weavers Fd; Weir Mdw; White Lsw; Withy Fd, Far, Near and Middle ~ ~; Wood Lsw (by Lostford Coppice).

7. MARCHAMLEY (SJ 597296)

The difficult problems presented by this name were discussed in detail in Part **1**. The etymology suggested in that discussion was 'clearing at the Mercians' (alluding to the boundary of Mercia with the territory of the *Wreocensǣte*). This suggestion is mentioned but deemed not entirely satisfactory in CDEPN. Barthomley Ch and Mortomley WRY have spellings comparable to those for Marchamley, and there is as yet no generally accepted solution to these three names.

FOX COVERT.

HAWKSTONE FM (in Marchamley village).

MARCHAMLEY HILL, 1812 PR(L) 11.

MARCHAMLEY SLIPS, a narrow strip of wood, *v.* Marlpit Slip *supra*.

MARCHAMLEY WD, 1699 *et freq* PR(L) 11, 1833 OS. This is a scattered settlement in the north of the township, with many Croft and Common f.ns. There is no woodland.

MOAT BANK, in village.

RANGER'S LODGE, *Marchamley* ~ 1840 *TA*.

WOOD FM, shown but not named on *TAMap*.

Field-Names

Forms in (a) are 1840 *TA*. Early forms dated c.1320 are AD V, 250.

(a) Ashway, Near, Over; Barn Fd (several); Big Mdw; Blackberry Fd; Bog Easily; Bradeley, Big, Under and Whitfields ~, The Bradeleys (an area N.W. of the village, probably an open field, *Bradeleye Feld* c.1320, 'broad clearing'); Brickyard Fd; Brimstone; Brook Fd, Little Brook Croft; Buxton, Big (*v.* Kenstone f.ns. *supra*); Chapel Yd (in village); Cockshutts (cf. *Le Kokschutelond* c.1320); Common, ~ Pce(s) (a large area by Marchamley Wd has fields with Common ns., including Benbows, Cottons, Duttons Common Pce); Cottons Lower Coppice, ~ Near ~; Croft, Far, Near (in what may have been an open field called Greenway Hedge); The Croft (enclosure with house in N.E. corner); Croft(s) (numerous small enclosures by Marchamley Wd); Croft, Big ~ (by village); Crofts (several by road to Whitchurch); Crooks Britch (*v.* **bryce**); Cross Lsw; Crossway, Little; Dale Lsw, Mdw; Dale Mdw; Dunse Fd; Duttons Ridding, Big ~ ~; The Flat (near Greenway Hedge ns.); Fox Pit Bank; Friday Flg (cf. *Le Frydaieslond* c.1320, probably derogatory); Garden Fd; Goulbournes Britch; Greenway Hedge, Big ~ ~, Atkins' and Harris' ~ ~, ~ ~ Mdw (7 fields E. of the village, possibly an open field); Griftin (probably variant of Criftin, for which *v.* Criftins in Dudleston *supra*); Gwynns Pce; Harpers Fd, The Mdw late Harpers; Haunch Stockings, The Big Haunch, Appletree and Nailors Haunch (the 4 fields joined together could be considered haunch-shaped); Hill Lsw; Hill Pce; Hips Heel; Hodnet Lsw, Near, Far, New (on boundary with Hodnet township); Holmes's Croft; House Mdw; Kitchen Hurst; Lane Croft; Lay Fd; Little Broomy; Little Mdw; Little Ten Acres; Long and Birch Flg; Lower Fd; (The) Meadow (several); Meadow, Little, Long; Meadow Bank; Morris's Croft; Muck Mdw; Moor Mdw, Harris's Moor, Long ~; New Lsw; New Pce; New Pltn; Old Lane; Ox Lsw (2); Paddock(s) (2); Park, North ~ (by Hawkstone Pk); The Piece; Pike Oak, Far and Near ~ ~; Pinch (small field on edge of Croft enclosures by village); Pipers Steel; Pit Lsw, Big, Middle, Near; Rodway (by the road from Weston, cf. *Radeweyforlong* c.1320: 'roadway', several instances noted in PN Ch **5.1** 320 are ascribed to ME **rodeway*); Rough Hays, ~ ~ Mdw (fields called Rough Mdw(s) adjoin); The Stockings, Top ~ (*v. supra* for Haunch ~, 'clearing'); Sweet Appletree Fd; Town Mdw (near village); Townsend Pk (between village and Hawkstone Pk); Turningway (perhaps a variant of Turn Again, Turnabout FN 35, denoting land where a plough could be turned); Upper Coppice, Benbows, Harpers (Big and Little Coppice adjoin); Wheeling Butts (near Greenway Hedge ns.); Whitfields Little Mdw; White Lsw; Witheys Mdw; The Wood, Wood Lsw, Mdw; (The) Wood Fd (2 fields by Marchamley Wd); Wood Lsw, Big, Little, Lower, Top, ~ ~ Mdw (by Marchamley Wd).

(b) The document in AD V lists properties called selions some of which are said to be in *Le Leefeld*, *Gateley Field*, *Radewey forlong* and "the field between Hawkstone and Marchamley". There is also meadow in *Bradeleye Feld*. All the selions have *-lond* ns. Some can be linked to ns. in (a).

Austenesle 1308 Ipm (a doublet of Austonley PN WRY **2** 263, probably from a ME personal n. and ME *lea*, *ley* 'grassland'); *Le Birchlond* c.1320 (in *Le Leefeld*); *Gateleye Field* c.1320 (*sic* in AD, probably 'goat pasture'); *Hawenygge* 1327 SAS 2/I (p) (perhaps a derivative of **haga** 'enclosure'); *Le Hevedlond* c.1320 ('headland', in *Radeweyforlong* which appears to have been an open field); *Le Leefeld* c.1320 (here, as in *Austenesle*, the sense may be 'grassland'); *Lodefordes Marlput* c.1320 (possibly from a surname); *Le Sychelond* c.1320 (*v.* **sīc**, in the field between Hawkstone and Marchamley); *Le Thwelindelond* c.1320 (in *Gateleye Field*, first el. obscure).

8. PEPLOW (SJ 627247)
Peplow is a DB manor, so discussed in Part **1**. The name means 'pebble tumulus'.

RADMOOR (SJ 627246): *Rodmore* 1383 *SRO 322/205*, *Radmore Brooke*, *Radmoore Waye* 1588 *SRO 322 box 2*, *Radmore Meadow* 1839 *TA* (High Hatton), *Radmore Bank*, *Field*, *Leasow* 1840 *TA*. 'Reed marsh' *v.* **hrēod**, **mōr**.

AVENUE FM, by an avenue of trees. Shown but not named on *TAMap*.

THE BIRCHES, 1840 *TA*.

BOWLING GREEN, 1833 OS, *The* ~ ~ 1840 *TA*: a small settlement by the road to Hodnet. There are indications on *TAMap* of an oval enclosure here, *v.* f.ns.

BRICKKILN COPPICE, *TA* has *Brick Field* here.

CRAN-Y-MOOR, *Cranymoor* 1840 *TA*. The same n. occurs in Cheswardine, *supra*. It is probably a variant of the recurrent Cranmere, -more, 'crane pond'; the Hodnet n. has a modern pseudo-Welsh spelling.

DEAKINS WD, *Plantation* 1840 *TA*.

HAWGREEN, ~ COPPICE, *Haw-Green* 1746, 8 PR(L) 11, *Haw Green* 1833 OS, probably 'enclosure', ultimately from **haga**[1].

HIGHWAY COTTAGES, FM.

HOME FM.

ISLE OF WANT, 1840 *TA*. FN 25 lists this with derogatory f.ns., but the 6" map shows it as a small settlement on the boundary with Little Bolas township. There are crofts and a few buildings here on *TAMap*, and the buildings are on 1833 OS.

LONG LANE, 1833 OS, *The* ~ ~ 1790 PR(L) 13.

MILL COPPICE, by Peplow Mill.

OAK COPPICE, 1840 *TA*.

OLD POOL COPPICE, *Plantation* 1840 *TA*, *TAMap* shows a large pool called Peplow Pool.

PEPLOW GRANGE, HALL, MILL: the hall and the mill are 1833 OS, 1840 *TA*.

SHUKER'S COPPICE, LANE, LODGE. If an ancient name, possibly referring to robbers, *v.* **scēacere**. The Lodge building is shown on *TAMap*.

STATION COPSE, by Peplow railway station.

WILLOW COPSE, *Withy Coppice* 1840 *TA*.

Field-Names

Forms in (a) are 1840 *TA*. On *TAMap* the outside boundary of the group of fields called Dinches and Loons forms a curve, part of which is followed by a bend in an E./W. road. The area called The Bowling Green, on the opposite side of a N./S. road, could have been part of an oval enclosure here.

(a) Ashbed, Little Ashway Fd; Badmans Croft; Banky Moor; Banky Pce; Barn Fd (several); Big Cover; Big Pce; The Birches, Far and Near Birches; Black Croft, Far, Near; Boathouse Mdw (Boat House shown on 6" map); Brick Fd; Brickkiln Fd (2); Bridge Mdw (by R. Tern); Buck Britch; Carthouse Fd; Cartwrights Croft; Chatwoods Pce, Far, Near; The Close (among Croft ns. near village) Clover Croft; Clover Lsw; Common Pce (by Hodnet Heath); Cooks Croft; Coppice Pce (by Oak Coppice); Cote Lsw; Cow Lsw, Far, Near; Cow Pasture; Crabtree Dole; Croft(s) (groups by Radmoor and in Isle of Want); Cross Lsw; Dinches, Far and Great ~ (4 fields which, together with the Loons fields, are bounded by a curving outline: if early forms were available the n. might be ascribed to OE **dyncge** 'manured land', but no dialect derivative of this is noted in EDD and the f.n. is probably not ancient); Early Gates, Little ~ ~; Far Pce; Flatt, Ferny, Pinfold; Garden Croft; Garden Mdw (2 large fields between village and R. Tern: there is an enclosure called Gardens in the village); Gorsty Bank, Moor; Gorsty Lsw; Gorsty Pce; Greenfield Moor (near Hawgreen); Halfpenny Hadland; Heath Fd (near Hodnet Heath and Peplow Heath, adjacent fields are The Heathy Lsw, Far, Little, Middle, New, Lower and Upper ~ ~), Hell Hole (derogatory); Horse Pipe Fd (cf. Horse Pipe Mdw in Cheswardine *supra*) Lady Mdw; Loan, Clarks, Pailins (perhaps a form of *land*); Loons, Great Clarkes, Tom ('lands', i.e. 'cultivation strips', Tom may be for Town); Loons, Great, Middle (adjoining Dinches); Lowes Bank, Big Lowes; Marl Pce (2); Marsh, Lower, Over, Marsh Mdw; Meadow, Big, Little; Mill Fd, Big, Little, Mill Mdw; Morgans Yd (within the curved outline round Dinches and Loons); New Cover; Old Mill Mdw (up river from Peplow Mill); Orchard Fd; Orchard Pce; Outlet Fd (by Radmoor); Park (area by Peplow Hall); Pawmoor, Big, Great, Long; Peplow Heath (N. of Cran-y-Moor); Piece over the Road; Piece(s), Far, Near; Pit Croft; Pit Fd, No, Two and Middle ~ ~; Pool Fd (*v.* Old Pool Coppice *supra*); Road Lane; Roundabout (in loop of Tern); Rough Lsw; Rough Mdw (2); Rushy Lsw; Sandy Bridge, Heath; Shade, Hall, Holly; Slade, Little, Lower, Upper (probably fields with wet patches, *v.* FN 18); Space Head, Big, Little; The Stack Fd; Stockings ('clearings'); Ten Acres; Tern Mdw, Great; Townsend, Lower, Upper (at W. end of village); Tunstail Pce, Great (near Tunstall in Stoke upon Tern); Tydesmath Mdw; Wall Thorn (4 fields on S. boundary); Water Flg; Welsh Acres; Wills Croft.

9. WOLLERTON (SJ 620301)

Wollerton is a DB manor, so discussed in Part **1**. The name means 'Wulfrūn's estate'.

CORN MILL, *molendinum de Tyrne apud Wou'ton'* 1291–2 *Ass*. In e.13th SAC there is a reference to *Mulnemedewe* by R. Tern.

COTTAGE POOL, 1840 *TA*.

DRAYTON FIELDS, ~ *Field* 1840 *TA*: by the road to Market Drayton.

THE MOUNT.

NEWHOUSE FM, *The New-House* 1748 PR(L) 11, *The New House* 1762 ib, *New House* 1833 OS.

NORBURY HO (Gazetteer), *Northbury* 1792 PR(L) 2.

WOLLERTON BANK.

WOLLERTON WD, an area with scattered houses in N. of township, no trees shown on 6" or earlier maps.

WOOD END, 1833 OS, in Wollerton Wd.

WOOD FM, by Wollerton Wd, neither farm nor access road shown on *TAMap*.

"The Green, Wollerton" is noted 1750 PR(L) 11.

Field-Names

Forms in (a) are 1840 *TA*. Earlier forms are Hy 8 *RentSur*.

(a) Ban Croft, Big (*Bancrofte*, 'bean croft'); Bank Croft, Further, Middle, Near; Barn Fd; Barn Mdw; Barn Yd (large field by Newhouse Fm); Beach, Flaggy, Little, ~ Croft; Big Mdw; Big New Lsw; The Bradley (13 fields in N.E. corner of township have Bradley ns., with two sets of Near, Far and Lower Bradley, one at N. and one at S. end of the group; also Big and Little Bradley, ~ Mdw); Clover Lsw, Little; Common Pce; Coton Croft, Fd (in S.E. of township); Coton, Big, Hill (4 furlong-shaped fields on S.W. boundary); Cow Lsw, Far and Near (6 fields); Croft (several); The Croil; The Curlong; Eke Hill; Ellands Fd (Ellands Croft, with 3 small buildings, is nearby); Far Bank (between two fields called Moor Bank); Field (a number of fields in N.W. corner of township are called Field(s), among these are Newstree Fd (*infra*) and Barn, Big, Small, Crabtree, Lower, Higher, Rushy Fd); Fingerpost Fd, Mdw; Fish Moor; (The) Flatts, Millens ~ (S. of village); The Golbourn, Golbourns Breach (by a tributary of R. Tern, the n. is in Gazetteer); Goose Croft (normal-sized field adjoining Long ~); Gostneals; Heath Lsw; Hever Fd; The Homsley; Horse Pasture, Lower, Near; Land Fd (2 large enclosures in village, Little Fd adjoins); Little Mdw; Long Croft (large field); Long Fd; Long Shay (variant of *shaw*); Loons, Big, Long (*land*, Long ~ is furlong-shaped); Ludford (by tributary of R. Tern, 6" map marks Spring here: the stream or the spring may have been called *Hlūde* 'loud'); Meadow (several); Meadow, Banky, Englands, Kings, Lower, Mill, Moor, Tan Yd (along R. Tern); Meadow Bank; Mill Mdw (not near R. Tern); Moat Bank (Moat shown on 6" map); The Moor, Far and Near ~, Moor Mdw, The Moor Bank; Newstree Fd (3 fields spread among Field ns. in N.W. of township, Long ~ ~ is furlong-shaped); The Nobridge (possibly 'new breach'); Old Heys (5 fields on edge of Newstree Fd); Over Pit Lsw; Parsons Fm; The Piece (Big and Lower ~, ~ Mdw adjoin); Plantation Fd; Rough (surrounded by Bradley ns.); Ryegrass Fd; Ryegrass Lsw; Shoot Foot Hill; The Slangs; Smiths Mdw; Stackyard Fd (2); Tanpit Fd (Tan Yd Mdw adjoins); (The) Timstow, ~ Mdw (4 fields near Newhouse Fm); Withers Fd; Wood Lsw; The Yard (2 large enclosures in village).

(b) *Le Burche* (*v.* **bryce**); *Myddelmore*; *Wytherslond'*.

Ightfield

The parish-name is discussed in Part **1**. The meaning is 'open land on the R. *Giht*'. This river-name, which occurs also in Islip O, is likely to be pre-English, and it combines with Prees and Hodnet to form a noteworthy cluster of pre-English names in N.E. Shropshire. The stream in question is a tributary of the Tern, which rises S. of the village and is called Bailey Brook lower down its course.

The area treated here is that of the civil parish of Ightfield as shown on the 1963 OS diagram of administrative divisions in Shropshire. This includes Calverhall (also known as Corra) and Willaston which were townships of Prees in 1843 and treated as such in the *TA* for Prees. Field-names for Ightfield, Calverhall and Willaston are listed separately *infra*.

CALVERHALL or CORRA(R) (SJ 602372)
Calverhall is a DB manor, so the name is discussed in Part **1**, where it was suggested that **halh** is used in the sense 'dry ground in a wet area'. Maps show innumerable small pools in the surrounding area. The first element is the nominative, *calfru*, or the genitive plural, *calfra*, of **calf** 'calf'.

PR(L) 18 has the form *Corverhall* in 1699, and this may represent a stage in the development to Corra. The township is *Corrar* in 1843 *TA* and this form is still current locally.

CLOVERLEY (SJ 614373)

Clouerle(gh)' 1291–2 *Ass* (p) *et freq* with variant spellings *Clover-* and *-ley(e)*

Cloreley 1434, 40, 46 Fine, 1479 *SBL 4452*, c.1540 Leland, *Clorley* 1766 PR(L) 8

Cloverley als Cloreley 1686 *SBL 1937*

'Clover clearing' or perhaps 'clover pasture' with **lēah** in its late OE sense.

The ultimate ancestor of ModE *clover* is OE **clāfre**, **clǣfre**, which is a fairly frequent element in place-names. As pointed out in VEPN, *s.v.* **clǣfre**, both OE forms would give ME *Claver-* when the vowels were shortened in compounds, and most 'clover' names have *Claver-* in ME and modern forms: this is the case in Claverley, the other Sa instance with **lēah**. Cloverley is one of a small group of names in which the vowel of **clāfre** was not shortened, and *ā* became *ō*. NED notes "the form clover is very rare before 1600 . . . the usual ME and 16th-c. form was *claver*". MED, however, quotes a single reference "trifoil, wite clouere" from c.1325, so it is likely that this form was in use in the late 13th cent., when Cloverley is first recorded. All the references to Cloverley noted have *-o-*. Bowcock gave a form Claverley from RH (cited in VEPN *s.v.* **clǣfre**), but all the RH references are to Claverley, not to the Ightfield place.

There is no apparent confusion between Cloverley and its near neighbour Calverhall. Men called Will. *de Caluerhale* and Will. *de Clouerle* appear together in 1291–2 *Ass*, and both are mentioned in 1327 SR.

LITTLE CLOVERLEY is *The Little Cloreley* 1654 *SBL 5305, 6*: the same source mentions Great Cloreley Pasture.

The GR given above is for CLOVERLEY HALL.

KEMPLEY, LOWER (THE KEMPLEY on 1999 Explorer map) (SJ 592364)

Kempelegh' 1271–2 *Ass*
Kempeslegth 1271–2 *Ass*
Kempley Parke 1596–7 *SBL 1936*

Probably 'Cempa's pasture', with **lēah** in its late OE sense. A personal name **Cempa*, from **cempa** 'warrior', is probably also found in Kempton, *v.* Part **1**.

Lower Kempley is a single building ¾ mile N.W. of a moated site called UPPER KEMPLEY on 1999 Explorer map. The two sites are *Lower* and *Upper Kempley* 1833 OS, *Lower* and *Higher Kempley* on *TAMaps*. The form from *SBL 1936* probably refers to Upper Kempley.

Higher Kempley with surrounding fields is shown as a small detached portion of Whitchurch on 1841 *TA* and on the 1900 6" map, but it is convenient to include the field-names with those for Ightfield.

WILLASTON (SJ 597357)

Willaueston 1226 SAS 3/VII (FF), *Willaueston'*, *Wylaueston'*, *Wolaweston'* 1255–6 *Ass*
Wyleston', *Wylaston'*, *Wyllaston*, *Willaston* 1255–6 Ass, *Wylaston* 1271–2 *Ass* (p), 1327 SR, *-ton'* 1294–5 *Ass* (p), *-tone* 1327 SR (p)
Willarston 1255–6 *Ass* (p), *Wylareston* 1271–2 *Ass* (p)
Wylardeston' 1271–2 *Ass* (p)

Worlaston 1672 HTR
Wollaston 1655 SAS 1/XLVII, *Woolliston* 1833 OS

'Wiglāf''s estate': the same name occurs twice in Ch with this form, but it has developed to Wollaston in another Sa instance (Part **1**) and in Nth. Cf. also Wollascott Part **4** 174.

WYRLEY (SJ 606357), *Werley* 1271–2 *Ass* (p). A compound of **wīr** 'bog-myrtle' and **lēah**, the latter perhaps in its later senses 'pasture, meadow'; the same name occurs in St.

The identification of the single early form is confirmed by the involvement of the Abbot of Combermere.

THE BELT, a wood.
BIG WD, 1833 OS.
BLACKTHORN PLTN.
CHURCHWALK PLTN.
CLOVERLEY FM, HALL, PARK. On *TAMap* (for Corrar township) most of the park area is occupied by fields called *Big* and *Little Cloverley*.
CLOVERLEY POOL, *The Lake and Island* 1846 *TA*.
CORRA BANK.
CORRA COMMON, ~ ~ FM.
DAIRY HO, 1846 *TA*, *Ightfield* ~ ~ 1833 OS.
FATFARM COVERT. *TAMap* shows a tiny building called *Fat Farm* here, probably ironic.
GRAVELHOLE PLTN.
IGHTFIELD HALL, 1833 OS, 1846 *TA*.
IGHTFIELD HEATH, HEATH FM and ROW. *TAMap* has a large group of Heath ns. in this area, and a row of "allotments" which corresponds to Heath Row on 6" map. The surname *Hethe*, which occurs 1327 SR in Ash Parva, may derive from this.
IGHTFIELD KENNELS.
LAUREL PLTN.
MALTKILN FM.
MANOR FM.
MORETONWOOD FM (by Moreton Say).
OLD JACK P.H.
POOL FM.
SPRING FM.
STOKES COVERT, *Plantation* 1846 *TA*.
UPPER KEMPLEY WD, *v*. Kempley *supra*.

WILLASTON LAWN, *Wollaston* ~ 1731 PR(L) 11, *Woolliston* ~ 1833 OS.

WILLOW PLTN. *Pool* ~ 1846 *TA*, by Cloverley Pool.

TAMap shows *Lamb P.H.* in Ightfield village.

Field-Names

The *TA* names are listed in three sections: (i) Ightfield Parish, (ii) Corrar Township, (iii) Willaston Township. Corrar and Willaston have their own *TAMaps*, as they were townships of Prees. Names from the detached section of Whitchurch round Upper Kempley are listed with (i) but marked (Wh).

(i) Ightfield. Names in (a) are 1846 *TA*, except for those marked (Wh), which are 1841 *TA*, and one n. dated 1828. Some of the *TA* ns. occur also in 1828 GT. Early forms dated 1612, 35 are GT, 1654 are *SBL 5305, 6.*

(a) Acres (2 large fields by Windmill Fd, which may have been an open field); Aldery Fd (Wh); Anne's Fd (Wh); Barn Fd (2); Bowling Green (by Ightfield Hall); Broomy Fd (Wh); Brown Knowl; Burgage (by village); Butchers Pce; Calves Croft (Wh); Calves Croft (1612, 35); Cherry Fd (Wh); Chester's Fd (Wh); Church Fd, Far and Near ~ ~, Church Mdw, Hill (short distance from Ightfield church); Churchwalk (path from Ightfield Hall to village); Clay Fd, Great, Little; Clay End 1828 GT (*Clea End* 1612); Clay Lands; Coalpit Fd (Wh); Coles Rough, Big, Little; Colts Croft; Combermere Fd, Higher, Lower (on boundary with Combermere Ch); Cordnell, Far and Near ~, ~ Mdw; Cow Lsw (2, one 1612, 35); Cow Pasture; Croft (several in village); Crow Bache (a 'stream-valley' in N. of parish); Daisy Pool Mdw; Dove Yd, Far, Near (by village, *Dovehouse Yard* 1612, 35); Dry Pit; Dunsmoor (*Dunkesmore Croft* 1612); Ellen's Bridge Mdw; Furlong (near Heath Fd ns.); Gads Bache, Big, Little (near Crow Bache); Garden Croft; Garden Fd; Gorse Mdw, Far Gorse; Gorsty Bridge, Big, Far, Little ~ ~ Fd; Grove, Near, Middle; Heath End (by Ightfield Heath); Heath Fd, Far, Near, Middle and Little (perhaps an open field, by Ightfield Heath); Hemp Butt; Henshaws; The Hills; Horse Pasture; House Mdw; Jockins Fd (Foukins and Big ~ adjoin); Kempley Fd, Kempley(s) (6 fields by Lower Kempley); Lawn, Higher, Lower, Grove Lawn, Far, Near (near Ightfield Hall); Leasons; Lees (1612, 35); Longhills Bank (Wh); Long Shoot (Wh); Loom, Big, Far, Near (probably *land*, referring to open-field strips, Kempley(s) fields adjoin); Marlpit Fd; Marlpit Fd, Big, Little (Wh); Masseys Fd; Meadow (several); Meadow, Barn, Garden (by Dairy Ho); Meadow, Barn, Garden, Kiln (adjoining Ightfield Hall); Meadow, Big, Little, Waterfall (by Bailey Brook); Middle Fd; Mill Pool Mdw (on N.E. boundary, no mill shown on maps); Moss Fd (2); Mowing Pce (Wh); New Lsw, Far, Near, Big, Little; New Lsws; New Mdw; Oak Moss; Old Orchard (by Ightfield Hall); Paddock (adjoins Park); Park, Further, Higher, Oat, Middle and Londonderry Park (large fields on N. side of Ightfield Hall); Park, Big, Little, Lower, Park Mdw (Wh, by Higher Kempley); Parsonage (large field in village); Pea Mdw; Pinfold Fd; Podmores Pce, Great, Little; Pool (on N. boundary, there are small pools all over the N. of the parish, on the watershed between N. and S. flowing streams); Rindle, Far, Near, Far and Near Rindle Fd (Rindle is ultimately from **rynel** 'small stream', the stream here is a headwater of Bailey Brook); Rose Fd, Big and Far ~ ~, ~ Mdw; Rushy Fd (Wh); St Johns Hill (1612, 35, by the church, which is dedicated to St John Baptist); Sandfords Fd, Mdw (Sandfords Fd and Sandford Mdw occur again in the detached portion of Whitchurch, a mile to the S.: there may have been a causeway here leading to Sandford in Prees); Sandhole Fd, Little ~ ~ (Wh); Shores Ground; Sidney, Far, Near; Slang Mdw; Smiths Croft; Stocking, Higher, Lower, Wiggins ('clearing', Threap Wd adjoins); Stony Fd; Swan Pool Mdw (the same f.n. occurs in Corrar *TA infra*); Threap Wd, Higher, Lower (*Le Trepwode* 1331 Ch, near N.E. corner of parish, 'disputed wood', a recurrent n., cf. Part **4** 122, 136); Townsend Mdw (at S. end of village); Vetch Croft; Wastrell, Big, Little; Well Fd; Whitchurch Bank, ~ Half (not adjacent, both on Whitchurch boundary); White Gate, Big, Little (Wh); Windmill Fd, Far ~ ~ (7 fields by road to Calverhall, probably *Windmill Field* 1612, 35); Windmill Fd (on W. boundary, not near preceding which is on E. boundary); Yard, Kiln, Braughalls, Pembertons (in village); Yard (large field by Heath Fm).

(ii) Corrar Township. Forms in (a) are 1843 *TA*, with one exception. Early forms dated 1654 are *SBL 5305, 6*.

(a) Acre Fd; Banky Fd; The Barlands (*Barrelands* 1652, ME *barre*, usually found in an urban context); Barn Close; Barn Fd (several); Big Barn Fd, Barn Mdw; Big Fd; Big Mdw (2); Black Fd; Black Flatts, Big, Little; Blanthorns Fd, Big ~ ~, ~ Mdw; Brook Fd; Cadman's Wd, Big, Little; Calves Croft, ~ ~ Mdw; Cartwright's Crofts; Chesters Mdw; Clemley, Far, Near (*v.* Prees *infra*); Clough's Fd; Clover Fd; Coits Fd (*Quoyte Feilds* 1654, referring to the sport, cf. Quoitings in Montford *supra*); Common Fd, Field adjoining ~ ~; Copy Croft (2); Cormor Croft; Corrar Orchard; Cow Lsw, Further, Nearer; Croft (enclosures on S.E. boundary include Barn, Far, Upper Croft); Croft (4 small enclosures at a road-junction, also Morris's Further and New Crofts: along the road between these and the village are Little, Middle, Further and Near Trims Croft); (The) Crosses, Near and Little ~ (8 fields S. of village); Dabons Croft; Dickens Fd, Further, Nearer; Dod's Fd, Mdw; Epsley; Ferny Bank (*Fernye Bank* 1654); Field; Five Day Math; Forrest Loons (*The Forrest Loones* 1654, an early instance of the dialect form of *lands*); Further New Lsw; Gorsty Fd, Little ~ ~, Field adjoining ~ ~; Gosling Mdw; Grands Moor Bank; Gravel Flatt, Further, Near (near Black Flatts and Acre Fd); Gravel Hole Fd; Green Fd; Hatch Mdw; Henshaws, Big, Further, Near; Higher Colts Croft; High Oaks, Near and Middle, ~ ~ Croft, Mdw; Hole Croft; Hoodeys, Higher, Lower (*The Howdeyes* 1654); Horse Pasture (2); House Fd; Intake, Stubbs, Whittinghams; The Kempley, Kempley Fd, Long ~ ~, Chesters Kempleys Fd (*v.* Kempley *supra*); Lady Mdw (1654); Little Maddocks Mdw; Long Croft; Long Fd; Long Mdw; Lucerne Croft; Mathews Intake; Milking Bank (not near a farm); Moat Bank, Fd, Moats (approx. GR 618383, no earthworks on maps); Moor Fd; Morris Mdw; Morris's Further and Near Croft; New Lsw, Far, Near; New Street Lane Fd; Orchard Fd (2); Pool Fd; Rents Fd (*Rent Fd* 1654); Rough Fd (2); Rows Croft; Shooting Butts (referring to archery practice); Shoulder of Mutton and Long Mdw; Six Butts (adjoins The Crosses); Slang; Soffings Bank, Mdw; Square Fd, Big, Little; Stable Fd (by Cloverley Hall, Paddock adjoins); Swans Pool Mdw (*Swann Poole Meadowe* 1654, Upper, Middle and Little Pool Fd adjoin: there is another Swan Pool Mdw in Ightfield); Townsend, Further and Middle ~ (at S.E. end of village); Wall Ridding (*The Well Reddinge* 1654, 'spring clearing'); Well Mdw; Wet Fd; Whetstone Flatts; The Wills Fd; Yard(s) (fields round village include Chester's, Goulbourn's, Leathern and Wrights, Schoolhouse Yard).

(iii) Willaston Township. Forms in (a) are 1843 *TA*.

(a) Acorn Croft, Little ~ ~ Fd; Allotments on Moreton Wd (a large area with rectangular fields in S.E. of township, Moreton Say parish adjoins); Barn Fd; Big Fd; Blackwater Fd; Bog; Boosey Pasture (referring to pasture rights, *v.* FN 34); Brickkiln Fd; Cabbage Garden; Calves Croft; Common Fd (among Crofts E. of Willaston); Cow Lsw, Higher, Lower; The Cribben; Croft, Ellis's and Jarvis's Crofts (on S.E. boundary); Croft, Garden, Hempbutt, Lawn (adjacent, normal-sized fields); The Eight Acres; Field, Big, Little, Long, Lower, Middle, Yewtree (adjoining, S.W. of Willaston); Field(s) (a group of fields, some furlong-shaped; E. of Willaston); Field opposite the House; The Furlong (large field E. of Willaston); Green Moor, Lower, Higher; Halfpenny Mdw; Hays; Hitch Cote; The Horse Pasture; Little Croft; Long Croft; Long Fd; Long Mdw (2); March Mdw; Mardrich; Meadow, Dod's, Williams, The Justices, Sheepcote, Meadow Head (a strip of fields running N./S. in middle of township, Halfpenny Mdw is one of these); Moss Pltn; New Enclosures; New Pce, Near, Further; Oaken, The Near, The Ferny, Williams, The Oaken Style (ultimately from dat.pl. of **āc**, Lower and The Big Oaks adjoin); Old House Mdw; Pale Croft; Pool Fd, Mdw (by Claverley Pool); The Rag Fd, Mdw; Roundabout (a road curves round two sides); The Ryley, Justices, Middle, Long and Crabtree Ryley; Skitts Whirley (adjoins Wyrley *supra*, Skitts Croft is also in N.E. part of township); The Slade, Big ~ (along a stream, *slade* in the sense 'small valley' rather than dialect 'wet patch'); The Stocking; Top Fd; White Bread Fd (probably complimentary).

(b) Most of the names in (b) cannot be certainly allocated to any of the three divisions noted above. Forms for which no date or source is given are 1654 *SBL 5305, 6*. Those dated 1612, 35 are GT.

The Bottle Hill; *The Calverhall Haie*, *Haie Wood*; *The Chattles Croft*, *The Chettles Crofte*; *The Chockefeilds*; *The Colte Fleete*; *Grosinor'* 1305–6 *Ass* (Will. de Caluerhale owns a wood *apud Caluerhale* in the place called ~); *The Greene Hill*; *Heath Leasow* 1612, 35; *The Isbell Leas*; *Knoll* 1427 Cl, *The Knowle Feild*, *The Knowles* 1654 (the 1427 reference is to a place by *Callerall*, so this cannot be connected with Brown Knowl in (a), *v.* **cnoll**); *The New Loones* ('new lands'); *The New Pasture*; *Painters Poole*; *The Towne Feild Peice*; *Well Feild alias Manor Leasowe*; *Wood Leasow* 1612, 35.

Lee Brockhurst

The parish-name is discussed in Part **1**. This is one of a group of **lēah** names between the R. Roden and the R. Tern, probably referring to clearings in a patch of ancient woodland. The name was originally simplex. The affix is the name of a wood in Wem, *infra*. This place and Preston in Moreton Corbet were "subtus" Brockhurst in the late 13th century.

Mr Foxall's map for this parish, which he dated 1834–48, combines information from the Tithe Award map with some from an estate map of Sir Roland Hill. The reference *TA* is used for this, but it should be understood as referring in this instance to the map in the Foxall set.

HOLLOWAY LEASOW (Gazetteer), cf. *Holloway Gate* 1828 PR(L) 19, ~ *Croft* 1834–48 *TA*.

KENNELS, *Dogkennel Rough* 1834–48 *TA*.

LEE BRIDGE, 1833 OS. Ogilby's road map, 1675, shows *Hee Bridge* here, an obvious mistake for *Lee*. *TAMap* shows *Lee Bridge Inn*.

LEE ELLS, *Lee Yelds*, ~ ~ *Coppice* 1834–48 *TA*: ultimately from **helde** 'gentle slope'.

LEE FM: cf. Hall Field in f.ns.

LEE HILLS: *TAMap* has *Lee Hill* and two woods called *Lee Hill Plantation*.

A farm called Bradley Gate was probably in this parish: it is named in an Auction Sale Bill of 1796 (slip in E.W. Bowcock's writing), and said to be at Lee Bridge. Earlier references are *Bradley Gate* 1696 PR(L) 9, *Braedly Gate* 1698 PR(L) 19, *Bradeley Gate* 1715 *SBL 5472*.

Field-Names

Forms in (a) are 1834–48 *TA*. Earlier forms for which no date or source is given are 1779 PR(L) 19.

(a) Big Hook, ~ ~ Coppice; (The) Brickkiln Croft; Bridge Fd, Mdw (by Lee Bridge); The Brooms; Clover Fd; Cow Pasture; Cordwell; Crabtree Fd; Croft(s) (the parish has a strip of territory running between Weston under Redcastle and Stanton upon Hine Heath parishes, and in this are small enclosures called Croft(s) and Clover, Devil's, Pig, Near, Far Croft); Crooked Lsw; Ditch Mdw; Donnesley, Far, Near; Drumbel Fd (*v.* The Drumble in Birch *supra*); Farms, New (*The Farmes*, probably NED sb^2 5 'tract of land held on lease'); Flaw (*The Lower Flae*: PN Ch **5.1** 180, 181 notes ns. in *Flay* which are ascribed to a dialect reflex of ON **flaga** 'flagstone' or **flag** 'turf': in Ch there is only the form *flay*, but interchange with *flaw* would be likely: the Sa n. belongs to this group, but the sense is uncertain); Fold (in village); Green Reans (drainage channels); Gwynns Mdw, Far, Near; Hall Fd, Mdw (by Lee Fm, cf. *Lee alias Lee Hall* 1716 (copy) *SBL 5001*); Hill Fd, Little ~ ~ (by Lee Hill); The Intake; Little Meadows; Marsh, Big, Little (The Marsh); Moor Mdw, Big Moor (*The Moor*); Moston Coppice (adjoins Moston); New Lsw; The Oak Lsw; Oat Fd; Old Clover; Old Gate; The Pearl(s), The Little Pearl (*The Pearle*, 'spring', *v.* Part **3** 130); Pigs Flat; Pits and Rough; Ravens Croft; Rookery Fd; Roundabout (roads curve round two sides); Stanherley Mdw; Summer Gates, Big, Little; Team Mdw; The Townsend (on N. edge of village); Turnpike (by one of the roads which converge on Lee Bridge); Underhill Lsw (by Lee Hill); Underhill, Big, Little (not near Lee Hill); The Warren Fd; Weir Fd; Wiggansley Mdw (*Wigginsley*); Yard, Higher, Hemp, Yard at Back (in village); The Yewtree Croft; Yewtree Fd, Lsw.

(b) *The Barn Yard*; *Le Barres* 1336 HAC (furlong called, ME **barre**, there are several ~ Gate ns. in the parish: cf. The Barlands in Ightfield *supra*); *The Gorse Leasow*; *The Green Lane*; *The Hempyard*; *The Hill Door*; *The Lane Croft*; *Lorteleye* 1291–2 *Ass* (*boscus de* ~, 'dirty wood', *v.* **lort(e)**, **lēah**); *Port Meadow*.

Market Drayton

The parish-name is discussed in Part **1**. Drayton is a recurring place-name, interpreted as referring to a settlement where transport involved dragging, either up a steep slope or through marshy land. The second sense is appropriate in this instance. There is an area of wet ground north-east of the town where sledges might have been used rather than wheeled vehicles. The affix Market is first noted c.1540, in Leland. The commonest earlier affix is ~ *in Hales*, others are *Magna*, *Muche*, *Great*. These are set out in Part **1**, and the district-name Hales is discussed *infra*.

LITTLE DRAYTON (now the S.W. part of Market Drayton town) is also documented in Part **1**.

SHIFFORDS BRIDGE: *Shipford* 1166 SHC, *Schipford'* c.1235 SAC, *Schifford'* 1314 *SBL 9894*. 'Sheep ford': other instances occur in O (Shifford), Bd and Berks (Shefford). The ford is on the county boundary at approx. SJ 691349, where the road to Newcastle crosses the R. Tern. Shifford's Grange Fm in St is named from it.

BERRISFORD BRIDGE, cf. *Berresfordeshulles* t.Hen 6 *RentSur*. The bridge crosses the R. Tern a short distance downstream from Shiffords Bridge. If the name is ME the first element may be a surname.

BETTON ROAD BRIDGE.

THE BURGAGE. On the modern street-map a street with this name leads to the site of a large enclosure, which was called *Burgage* on the *TAMap* of the town. Presumably this was a piece of land which was held, perhaps collectively, by burgage tenants in the town.

DRAYTON BRIDGE. Cf. Leland c.1540, "At Drayton a Market Towne . . . is a small bridge."

FIELD HO.

GREENFIELDS.

GREENLANDS.

THE GROVE.

HINSLEY MILL, *Mill* 1840 *TA*.

HOLLY GROVE, 1785 *SBL 4331*: probably *Holygrave* 1738, 75 *SBL*

4247, *52*, from **grǣfe**, variant of **grāf(a)** 'grove'.

HOLLY HO.

KILNBANK NURSERY.

THE LAWN, *Lawn* 1840 *TA*, shown on *TAMap* as one of three large enclosures, without buildings, on N. edge of town.

LITTLE DRAYTON COMMON, 1841 *SBL 4309*.

LORD'S BRIDGE.

MAERS GROUND (Gazetteer), *Mayers* 1840 *TA*. *TA* also has fields called *Big Mere*, *Far*, *Near* and *Middle Mare* and *Mare Lane Field*, so there may have been a pond here, *v.* **mere** and cf. f.ns. The area is Maer Lane Industrial Estate on the modern street-map.

MARKET DRAYTON WHARF, on canal.

MARLEY MOUNT.

THE MOUNT.

NEWCASTLE ROAD BRIDGE.

NEWTOWN, 1738 *SBL 4262*, shown as a district-name on 1900 6", a road on modern street-map.

POLICEMAN'S WD.

RAVEN HOTEL.

RED BANK HO.

ROSEMOUNT.

RUSH LANE CROSSING, SILVERDALE JUNCTION, both on railway.

SPRINGFIELDS.

SPRINGHILL.

SYCH FM. *TA* has *Syche Field*, *Syche Brook Field* here, *v.* **sīc**.

TALBOT HOTEL.

THE TOWERS.

VICTORIA BRIDGE and WHARF, by canal, *Victoria Wharf* 1857 PR(L) 18, *The Wharf* 1862 ib.

VICTORIA MILL, not near preceding.

WALKMILL BRIDGE, RD, *Walkmill* 1738 *SBL 4262*, *The Walk Mill* 1764 *SBL 4335*.

WESTHOLME.

WHITEPIT LANE.

THE WOODLANDS.

The following street-names were listed by H.D.G. Foxall in the mid 1960s:

ALEXANDER RD. BENTLEY'S RD. BUTTS RD. CEMETERY RD. CHESHIRE ST. CHURCH LANE. FROGMORE RD. GREAT HALES ST. HIGH ST. JUG LANE. KILNBANK RD. KING'S AVENUE. LONGSLOW RD. NEWTOWN.

OAKFIELD RD. PHOENIX BANK. PROSPECT RD. QUEEN ST. REDBANK RD. SALISBURY RD. SCHOOL LANE. SHREWSBURY RD. SHROPSHIRE ST. SMITHFIELD RD. STAFFORD ST. STATION RD. WALKMILL RD. WESTLAND RD. There is a large-scale *TAMap* of the town, but the only streets named on this are Cheshire, Shropshire and Stafford Streets, Queen St and High St. Cheshire St is *Chesshere Streete*, *Chessherstrete* 1549 Pat, Shropshire St is *The Shropshire Streett* 1699 *SBL 1511*. These and Stafford St branch off to N.W., S.W. and N.E. from High St.

Salisbury Rd leads towards Salisbury Hill, on the St side of the county boundary, where local tradition says the Yorkist Lord Salisbury camped after the battle of Blore Heath in 1459 (SHC 1945–6, 93).

The key to numbers on the *TAMap* of the town names the following inns: *Cheshire Cheese* (at S. end of Cheshire St), *Corbet's Arms*, *Crown*, *George*, *Lion*, *Phoenix*, *Rock in the Ocean*, *Royal Oak*, *Stag*, *Star*, *Swan*, *Unicorn*.

Other buildings noted in this key are *Cooper's Shop*, *District Bank*, *Hair Factory* (2), *Malt Kiln*, *National School*, *Poor House*, *School*, *Smith's Shop*, *Tan Yard* (2), *Old Tan Yard*. There is also *Bowling Green* which is shown in the same position on the map in *Shropshire Town Centre Maps*, Estate Publications 2001.

In 1518 AD there is a reference to a burgage called *Seynt Marie Hall*. This is *Seyntemarihalle* Hy 6 *RentSur*.

Field-Names

Forms in (a) are 1840 *TA* except where otherwise stated. Early forms dated 14th, 1407–8, 1667, 74, 88, 1722–3, 38, 41, 59, 64, 66, 75, 81, 94, 99 are *SBL 9892*, *9905*, *6531*, *6530*, *5043*, *5044*, *4247*, *5131*, *5047*, *4335*, *4897*, *4252*, *4879*, *5102*, *5052*; those dated Hy 6, Hy 8 are *RentSur*.

On p. 170 of VCH IV (*Agriculture*) there is a map showing the open fields in Market and Little Drayton c.1780. The fields are *Crabtree*, *Gallow Tree*, *Mear* and *Mill Field*. These occupy most of the parish, an unusually large area for north Shropshire.

(a) Allen Croft; Banky Fd; Bowlers Ground; Briary Birch; Broomy Close, Big, Far; Broomy Fd; Cabin Lsw (4 fields), Big ~ ~; Croft, Orchard, Orange (2 enclosures by Burgage *supra*); Croft(s) (some of the strips W. of the town are so called, here also are Frog Lane, Horse Market and Hush Lane Croft); Crofts (5 contiguous strips N. of the town); Cuttings (2 of the strips E. of the town: PN Ch **5.1** lists *cutting* as a ME p.n. el.); Dale Lands (cf. Dale Flatts in Sutton *infra*); Derby Mdw; Dip Dale Fd (possibly *Hibbedale* 1314 *SBL 9894*); Field (strips W. of town include Boots,

Brickkiln, Further, Maltkiln and Pinfold Fd); Field (some of the strips in the area E. of the town have Fd ns: these include Collins, Mare Lane (*v.* Maer's Ground *supra*), Moss, Near, Roberts and Three Cornered Fd); Flatherings (one of the strip fields W. of the town, FN 26 lists this as a marsh n., relating it to EDD *flothers*); Gib Flat (in strip area W. of town); Golden Hadbutt (in Little Drayton, not obviously in an open-field context, but Hadbutt is probably 'headland strip'); Golden Headland (one of the strip fields N. of the town, *The* ~ ~ 1764); Grove Wd (in Park); Hangerhills (perhaps Hunger Hill); The Kitchen Croft (1667, 74, 1730); Long Lands (adjoins Golden Headland); Mare Mdw (on county boundary); Meadow (several); Mill Fd, Big, Little, Mill Mdw (by Hinsley Mill, cf. *Mill Rough* 1794); Park (part of school playing field on modern street-map); Pigeon's Fd; Pigstye Land 1841 GT; Pilsons (4 fields on boundary with Longslow, probably *Pillesdon'* 1271–2 *Ass*, a heath in Longslow part of which was in Drayton, cf. *Puellesdonpulles* Hy 6: apparently a transferred use of Puleston, Part **1** 244, 9 miles S.E., possibly outlying pasture in heathland); Poor Land; Rail Pce; Raven Mdw; Red Bank Fd; Rough Mdw; Round Mdw (one curved side); Shoulder of Mutton (2); Spoonley Fd (on boundary with Spoonley in Adderley); Sych Croft, Farther, Nearer (Syche Fd is nearby, *v.* **sīc**); Talbot Mdw; Triangle (minute enclosure by Hinsley Mill, possibly *Triangle Piece* 1799); Tunstall Fd, Near ~ ~ (on boundary with Tunstall in Norton in Hales).

(b) *The Acres* 1766; *Le Bachous* Hen 6 ('bakehouse'); *The Back* 1766; *Bridgens Crofts* 1766; *Broad Meadow* 1766; *The Bullastree Yard* 1766 ('wild plum-tree', ME *bolas-tre*); *Bushy Croft* 1766; *Butt Field, Butt Land or Moonshine Field* 1799; *Chicken Flatt* 1722; *Churton Medowe* 1518 AD, *Chirton Flat* 1759; *The Cole House* 1667; *Cowsedge* 1741 (said to be a farm, associated with Cliff Grange in Sutton); *The Crofte* 1730; *Cyrle Heyze* 1407–8; *Dallicar* 1706 *SBL 13194*, *Dalacre, Hussey's, Jackson's* 1738; *The Drawell or Well in the Street* 1722–3; *Le Farncros* 14th; *The Gillets Field* 1766; *Gorsty Field, Gorsey Feild* 1667; *Gorsty Hill* 1766; *Gosemere* Hy 6 ('goose pond'); *Grass Croft* 1766; *Grass Leasow* 1766; *The Holts* 1764 ("at the Walk Mill"); *Lease Pasture* 1674; *Lees Meadow* 1766; *The Lesser Flat* 1741; *Leasowes* 1667, 74; *Little Drayton Heath* 1688; *Low Croft* Hy 8; *Marifelde, -filde* 1549 Pat (there was a burgage called *Seynt Marie Hall*); *Marl Field* 1766; *Le Mere, Le Merefulong', Le Nethermere* Hy 6 (cf. Maers Ground *supra*); *The New Lands* 1766; *Ye Nine Lands* 1741; *The Paddock* 1730; *Peartree Croft* 1766; *The Pinfold Pce* 1799; *Pit Croft* 1760; *The Plex* 1741 (pl. of *pleck* 'small piece of ground'); *Sandecote Leasow* 1766; *The Shey Lane* 1766 (variant of *shaw*); *The Sibleys Croft* 1766; *Tern Leasow*, 1738, 75; *The Two Leasows* 1730; *Warwithy* 1781 ('whitebeam'); *White Leasow* 1738, 75; *The Yealds* 1766 (ultimately from **helde** 'slight slope').

Moreton Corbet

The parish-name, 'wet-land settlement', and its affix are discussed in Part **1**. This is one of four Sa examples.

Besford township, included here, was a detached part of Shawbury parish, and is shown as such on the 1900 OS 6" map; but it is territorially in Moreton Corbet and most conveniently treated as a division of this parish. The other townships are Moreton and Preston Brockhurst.

The *TAMap* for Moreton Corbet is blank in much of the Preston area, but there are 1846 maps for Preston and Brockhurst. These were drawn by G. Foxall from a *Map of Lands of Sir Andrew Vincent Corbet, Bt.* Field-names and 1846 forms for map-names in these two townships are taken from that source.

1. BESFORD (SJ 551250)
Besford is a DB manor, so the name, which means 'Betti's ford', is discussed in Part **1**.

Besford is in a sharp bend of a tributary of the R. Roden, and the ford will have been where the road from Shawbury to Wem crosses this stream. The stream was *Fulford Brooke* in 1588 (*v*. Preston Brockhurst f.ns. *infra*), referring to another ford, probably where the Shrewsbury/ Whitchurch road crosses the stream a mile to the west.

BESFORD WD, 1833 OS, 1846 *CorbetMaps 2*: *boscus de Besford'* 1291–2 *Ass*, *Besfordes Woodde* 1588 *CourtR*, *Besford Wode* 1621 PR(L) 19, *Bessford Wood* 1781 ib *et seq*.

CASTLE ROUGH, *Sneeze Coppice* 1846, *v*. f.ns. *infra*.

REDHILL COTTAGE.

Field-Names

Forms in (a) are 1846 *CorbetMaps*. Early forms dated 1588 are *SRO 322 box 2*, those dated 1592, 3, 7, 1601 are *CourtR*.

(a) Barn Yd; Besford Wd Pce, Pltn; Bowling Green (S. of Lee Bridge); The Britches (several f.ns. in the township contain *britch*, from **bryce** 'newly-broken-in land'); The Brooms, Broomy Bank, Yds; Common Pce(s), Lsw, Fd (group of fields covering a large area between Lee Bridge and Besford Wd); Coney Burrow; Coppice (fields by R. Roden on N.E. boundary are Coppice, Lower and Upper Coppice Mdw, Coppice Fd, cf. *Le Copye* 1588); Crabtree Lsw, Far ~ ~; Croft (several in Besford hamlet); Crofts (by Besford Wd); Croft(s) (several between Redhill Cottage and Papermill Bank in Stanton upon Hine Heath); Cross Ash; Forge Croft; Green Fd (by Bowling Green); Idle Bank; Leasow (adjacent fields in N.E. corner are Coppice, Gristy, Hare, Middle, Upper Lsw); Ley Lsw, Near ~ ~ (on boundary with Prestonlea in Preston Brockhurst, *q.v.*); Lincoln Pits; The Low Ground; Marl Pce; The Meadow; Mill Croft (by Lee Bridge, cf. *molendinum de Lye* 1588); Mill Fd, Mdw (by Papermill Bank in Stanton upon Hine Heath); Mill Lane, Mdw (by Harcourt Mill in Stanton upon Hine Heath); Moor Pce, Stile, (The) Moors, The Moors Mdw (adjacent fields in S.E. corner, probably *Besford Moore* 1588); Muck Pce; Near Greaves; New Lsw, Pce (*The Newe Leasowe* 1588); New Pce (2); Phinnis Mdw, Lower Phinnis, The Upper and Middle Finneys (*The Fynnyes* 1588, obscure, cf. The Finish in Sandford); Pool Foot, ~ ~ Mdw, Pool End (pools shown on 1846 map and on 1900 6"); Quickset Croft; The Roadway; Schoolhouse Croft (in hamlet); Sneeze, Upper, The Lower, Near, ~ Mdw (adjacent fields, Sneeze Coppice nearby: an unusual f.n., meaning obscure); Stony Fd; T Pce (part of a large field); Townsend (at N. end of Besford hamlet); Water Pool; Wier Mdw, Weir Lsw; Wheat Lsw; (The) Wood Fd (*Le Woodde Feild* 1588, by Besford Wd); Yard(s), Higher, Lower, The Yard (by buildings S.W. of Lee Bridge, several Crofts here also); The Yard, Little Yd, Tanhouse Yd, The Kiln Yd (in Besford hamlet).

(b) *Besford Feild* 1593; *The Birches* 1588 (in *Moreton Feilde*, "a pasture latelie enclosed", probably *britch*); *The Cryn* 1593; *Edgare Feilde* 1601; *Lytle Moor* 1593; *Margarette Way* 1588 (the perambulation places this "Footeway" in S.E. of township; *The Meare Greaves*, *The Meare Oake* 1588 (in perambulation, on E. boundary, the oak stands in *The Hooke Hedge*, probably 'oak hedge'); *Myll Oxe Leasow* 1593; *Neither Yard* 1597; *Organs Fold* 1592; *Le Smyethe* 1588, *The Smythe*, *The Smeeth* 1592, *Smeeth* 1600 (a wood: the forms suggest a substantive use of *smēðe* 'smooth', but this is not an obviously appropriate term for a wood).

2. MORETON CORBET (SJ 559232)

CRIFTIN COPPICE, 1840 *TA*, *Le Criftinge Copy* 1607 *SRO 322 box 2*. Cf. *Le Cruftinges* 1340 *SRO 322/142*, *The Criftyng*, *Le Criftinges*, *Criftinge Poole als Shawbury Poole* 1588 *SRO 322 box 2*. *v*. Criftins in Dudleston *supra*.

ASH COPPICE, 1833 OS. This is *Brickkiln Coppice* 1840 *TA*.

BOLAS WASTE, 1588 *CourtR*, 1840 *TA*. *TAMap* shows the house called THE WASTE, and fields called (*The*) *Waste*, *Bolas Waste*, ~ ~ *Coppice* N. and S. of the house. *Moreton Waste* is also mentioned 1588 *CourtR*.

Field-Names

Forms in (a) are 1840 *TA*. Early forms dated 1342 are *SRO 322/146*, 1588, 90, 92 are *CourtR*, 1602, 7, 15 are *SRO 322 box 2*, 1612, 35 are GT, 1712 are *SBL 1662*.

(a) Besford Croft, Lsw; Big Mdw; Birches Mdw, Big Birches (*Birches* 1588, *Birch Field* 1612); Brickkiln, ~ Pce, Little ~ (*Brickhill Leasowe* 1588, 1612, 35); Bushy Lsw; Carradine Croft, New ~ ~, ~ Mdw (Carradine is in the adjacent part of Shawbury); Castle Court, Yd, Mdw (surrounding castle ruins); Clun Lsw; Crabtree Lsw; Croft, Far, Middle; Cross Lsw; Deepmoor, ~ Bank (*Depmore* 1588); Far Croft, Mdw (on N.E. boundary); Forge Mdw (cf. *Morton Forge* 1702 *SBL 5533*); Gravel Pit Lsw; Green Lsw, Far, Near; Hatton Lsw; Hawbirch; Lawyers Lsw; Long Croft; Long Lsw; Middle Lsw (1612, 35); Moor(s), Moors Mdw (5 fields, cf. *Moreton More* 1588, ~ *Moors*, *Moore Meadow* 1712); New Pce; Parks (on S. boundary); Pinfold, Big and Little ~ (*Le Pynfold Leasow* 1607); Preston Lsw; Rickyard Pce; Rook Wd (*Roodwood* 1696 PR(L) 1 is probably an erroneous form); Sandy Lsw; Slang Coppice (narrow strip); Square Lsw; Swines Wd (*Swynes Woodde* 1588); Warren, Far, Little, Middle (cf. *Coneygrave* 1712); Waxford Mdw (*Waxford More* 1592); Yewtree Lsw, Mdw.

(b) *Bandheath alias Byneheath* 1588; *Banisters Meadow* 1712; *Blakeland More* 1590; *Clynke* 1588 (perhaps OE *clinc*, dialect *clink* 'rough ground', *v.* VEPN *s.v.* ***clenc**); *Croamers* 1712; *Le Greate Meadowe* 1615; *The Greene* 1588; *Grenhullesmille* 1342; *Hambor Brooke* 1602; *Le Ham Meadow* 1607; *Hempe Butt* 1588; *Kyngusfort* 1342; *Lea Field* 1612; *Lowe Sytche* 1590; *Masons Meadow* 1712; *Meare Greaves* 1592; *Moreton Feild* 1588; *Moreton Lea*, *The Lea* 1588 (cf. Prestonlea *infra* and *La Lea Woodde* 1607); *Morton Pool* 1786, 98 RTH; *Neither Woodde alias Moore* 1588; *Rushey Peice* 1712; *Rye Lsw* 1588; *Sandy Feild* 1588, ~ *Field* 1612; *Scotts Meadow in Wall Feild* 1602; *Le Walnut Tree Yarde* 1607.

3. PRESTON BROCKHURST (SJ 537247)

This is a DB manor, so discussed in Part **1**. It is one of five Sa instances of the recurring name which means 'estate of the priests'. Brockhurst, which is also used as an affix in Lee Brockhurst *supra*, is discussed under Wem *infra*.

BRIDLEWAY GATE (SJ 543262). A perambulation of Besford, 1588 *SRO 322 box 2*, has "the ferme of Bradeley" at this point on the boundary between Preston Brockhurst and Besford, and *Bradeley Gate* is mentioned in the same source. PR(L) 1 has *Bradeley Yate* 1682, ~ *Gat*(*e*) 1686, 1763, *Breadley-Gate* 1781, *Bradley Gate* 1808. In 1635 GT there is a reference to "Preston Brockhurst and Bradeley Gate". The 1846 map of Preston Brockhurst names the house *Bridleway Gate* and shows fields called *Bridleway* and *Big*, *Little*, *Lower Bridleway* on either side of one of the two roads which cross the township boundary here. This is the road to Whitchurch for which bridleway is not an appropriate term, and the modern name may be considered a rationalisation of the earlier name *Brad(e)ley*, probably 'broad clearing' from **brād** and **lēah**. The currency of the two names overlapped, *Bradley Gate* 1808 in the parish register being balanced by *Bridleway Gate* 1786, 1803 RTH. These fields and the farm are on the western edge of Besford Wood.

BLAZE COPPICE, 1831 OS. Cf. *Blasbanke* 1599 *CourtR*, *Blaze Bank* 1777 *CorbetMaps*. Probably 'bare spot on a hillside', ultimately from ON **blesi**.

DREPEWOOD GORSE. It is clear from this and from 19th-cent. field-names that the wood which gave name to Drepewood in Clive (Part **4** 122) extended into Moreton Corbet. A slightly earlier form than those quoted in Part **4** is *Dreepe Woodd* 1588 *SRO 322 box 2*.

PRESTON HALL, 1833 OS.

PRESTONLEA COPPICE, *Prestoneslee* ("une place de bois") 1340 *SRO 322/140*, *The Lea Woodd* 1588 *SRO 322 box 2*, *Lea Coppice* 1846 *Map*. This is near Actonlea Coppice, Part **4** 98. There was probably a wood with a simplex name from **lēah**.

PRESTON SPRINGS, 1833 OS, ~ ~ *Coppice* 1846 *Map*: *spring* has the meaning 'copse' in a number of place-names.

ROCK HALL, 1846 *Map*.

Corbet Arms P.H. and *Elephant and Castle P.H.* are shown on 1846 *Map* in village.

Field-Names

Forms in (a) are from the 1846 *Map* described *supra*. Early forms for which no date or source is given are 1588 *SRO 322 box 2*. Those dated 1340 are *SRO 322/140*, 1599, 1607 are *SRO 322 box 2*.

(a) Bakehouse Lsw; Barley Mdw; Barn Yd (2); Big Fd; Big Turnpike Rough, Rough Pce (by road to Wem); Birchen Coppice; Brockhurst Lsw; Brook Lsw; Broomy Banks, Big ~ ~; Broomy Hayes; Calves Croft; Catherines Hayes, Further, Middle and Upper ~ ~ (5 fields on W. boundary, *Katherynes Hay*, ~ *Hey* 1588); Church Stile; Clay Flg (by Rake ns.); Clemley (*v*. Clemley in Prees *infra*); Clive Wd Lsw (on boundary with Clive, *The Clyve Woodde* 1588); Cote Mdw (no building); Cow Lsw; Cow Pasture, Far and Near ~ ~; Croft (enclosures with buildings in village); Croft(s) (enclosures with buildings by Bridleway Gate and Besfordwood); Cross Mdw (by a road fork); Cuckoo Britch; Dark Lane Fm; Drepewood, Dreepwood Mdw (by Drepewood *supra*, some fields have erroneous Deepwood spellings); The Far Ground; Ferny Bank; Fold Lsw; Foot-tree Lsw; Garden Lsw; Gorsty Britch;

Gough's Wd, Lower, Upper and Near ~ ~ (*Goughes Woodd*, adjoining Sherwood in Clive, Part **4** 122); Grassy Lsw; Greenway Croft, Side; Grinshill Fd (on boundary with Grinshill); Hammer Way; Hazle Gates, The Near ~ ~ (adjoins Bridleway ns. discussed *supra*); Hill, Middle, Top; Hollytree Lsw; House Mdw, Lower; The Lady Flg, Top Lady Flg (3 fields E. of village); Lady Mdw; Lawyer's Lsw (the same f.n. occurs in Moreton township); Lea, Lower, Upper, Middle, The Lea Croft, Lsw; Big Lea Croft, The Lea Horn (Lea Horn, which has a point, is *The Lea Hornes* 1588); Lee Mdw; Long Mdw; The Lower Orchard; Marl Pce; Meadow; Meadow, Little, New; Mill Hill, Far, Near, Old (probably a windmill); Moathouse Coppice (in N. tip of parish); Muddy Croft; New Breech (*Newebruche* 1340, *v.* **bryce**); New Farm (no building); New Lsw (3); Norton, The Little Norton; The Oatlands (cf. *Owtelandes Gate*, *Lane*); Paddock; Pinfold Croft; The Pingle (variant of **pightel** 'small piece of land'); Pits; Plain Pce; Preston Brook Mdw, Brook Lsw (by *Fulforde Brooke infra*); Preston Lsw; Preston Pce, Far, Near; Price's Pce; Rabbit Bank, Close; Rake Fd, Far, Near, Rake Mdw, Rake Sitch, Big ~ ~, Rake Hill, Far ~ ~ (*Rake Lane* 1602, *Le Rake Brooke* 1604, dialect *rake* 'narrow path': the fields are on either side of a footpath leading N.W. from Preston: possibly an open field, Clay Flg adjoins: Sitch is ultimately from **sīc** 'small stream); Reeves Pce (cf. *Reeves Meadow*(*e*) 1588, 1712); The Riddings, Riddings Mdw (*Le Riddyng Meadow* 1607, 'clearing'); Rock Pce (near Rock Hall); Rough Pce; Shop Mdw; Shut Lsw (2); Sockets Croft, Far, Near; Spring Lane; The Stocking, Big, Little and Simmonds Stockings (*The Stocking* 1588, 'clearing'); Stony Pits; Thistles; Townsend (2, at N. and S. ends of village); Wadlands, Little, Long (The Big Woodlands adjoins, probably 'woad land'); Well Croft; Well Lsw; Well Mdw; Wood, Little, Tanners, Far, Near, Horse (N. of Drepewood); Yard, Barn, Clover, Banky (by Bridleway Gate); (The) Yard, Hall, Kite and Maypole Yd (in village); Yewtree Lsw.

(b) *Besford Brytches*; *Birchhull* 1340; *Brounesbruche* 1340 (several f.ns. in this township contain reflexes of **bryce** 'newly-broken-in land'); *Fooford* ("a little brooke", the same source has *Fulford Brooke* and *Meadow* in Besford, this is the tributary of R. Roden which runs through Preston Brockhurst and curves round Besford hamlet: the 'foul ford' was probably where the Whitchurch road crosses this brook); *Haynes Crofte*; *Heynesfordesmedewe* 1340; *Nicholesbuttes* 1340; *Powes Lane*; *Le Querchey* 1340; *Redwey Gate*, *Redwaye* ~; *The Shrugges* ('brushwood', ME **scrogge**); *Wilcastell Yate* 1599, *Wilkaston* ~ 1607; *Wodewardesmedewe* 1340.

Moreton Say

The parish-name is discussed in Part **1**. It is one of four Sa examples of a common name which means either 'marsh settlement' or 'moorland settlement'. In Sa all the instances refer to marsh, and Moreton Say contains a large area of wet ground called Smythemoor. The affix, a family-name, distinguishes this place from Moreton Corbet *supra*.

The parish contains the townships of Bletchley, Longford, Longslow, Moreton Say, Shavington, and Styche and Woodlands. The Foxall *TAMap* does not show township boundaries but these can be recovered from the Index to Tithe map. Shavington has its own *TA* as a detached portion of Adderley; it was transferred to Moreton Say in 1883. Longslow, which was transferred to Moreton Say in 1914, is included in Market Drayton *TA*.

1. BLETCHLEY (SJ 622336)

Ble(c)hell 1199 (1265) Ch, *Blecheleya* e.13th Lil *et passim* with variant spellings *Blecche-* and *-leg(a)*, *-legh'*, *-le(e)*, *-leye* to 1543 PR(L) 11, *Blechcheleye* 1309 Ipm

Bleggeleg c.1220–30 Lil, *-leg'* p.1236 Lil, *Bledgley* 1618 PR(L) 11

Blechesley c.1222 HAC, *Blechesl'* 1255–6 *Ass*, *Bletchesley*, *Blecchesley* 1389 Cl

Blechlegh' 1271–2 *Ass* (p), *Bleçhley* 1536 PR(L) 11

Blaccheleye 1306–7 *Ass* (p)

Bletcheley 1322 Pat, *-leye* 1334 SR, *Bletchley* 1596 PR(L) 11

Bleashley 1696 *SBL 4992*

Second element **lēah**, probably in its late sense 'pasture, meadow'. First element a personal name, probably **Blecca*. The personal name *Blæcca* is recorded, and is sometimes given as the first element of place-names such as Bletchley Bk, Bletchingley Sr, which have early forms with *-a-* as well as with *-e-*, *v*. PN Bk 17, PN Sr 308. There is a single *-a-* form for the present name, but this is outweighed by the mass of *-e-* spellings, and *Blecca* is the likeliest form of the personal name in this case. CDEPN and DEPN note the occasional forms with *-s-* and postulate a strong form **Blecci* as an alternative, but a full collection of forms gives strong support to *Blecca*.

BAILEY BROOK. This stream, which forms the S.W. boundary of Moreton Say, joins the R. Tern near Tern Hill. It is convenient to discuss the name here, as the *TA* has fields called *Far* and *Near Bailey* and *Bailey Meadow* beside the stream in this township. Bailey may be an interpretation of the first part of an earlier name of the stream, *Bulebrok* 1331 Ch, which occurs in the bounds of Tern Hill discussed *infra*: this may mean 'bull brook'. This tributary of the Tern had the pre-English name *Giht*, preserved in Ightfield *supra*.

OVER (lost), *Oure* 1199 (1265) Ch, *nemus quod vocature Overe* c.1243 Lil, *Over* 1253–5 Lil, *villa de Overe* 1265 Lil. The bounds of the wood called *Over*, as set out in a grant of c.1243, begin at Bletchley mill, for which *v.* f.ns. *infra*; and it is clear that the wood lay by Bailey Brook. The name probably refers to a low, flat-topped ridge of the sort regularly referred to by the term **ofer*, for which *v.* LPN 199–203 and CDEPN xlvii.

Field-Names

Forms in (a) are 1838 *TA*.

(a) The Ashes; Aychley Mdw, The Aychley (Aychley is in Prees *infra*); Backside, Long and Middle ~ (by the village); Barn Fd; Blake Flatt; Bletchley (2 fields on the edge of Smythemoor); Brickkiln Croft; Calves Croft; Castle Hill (in village); Cow Pasture, Lower, Near; Crofts (*freq*); Cross Fd; Dunnible Pce, Far, Near, Middle; Far Mdw; Fishpond; Furbers Croft; Gadbury Bank; Green Loon and Ox Lsw (Loon is probably *land*); Hoolbridge Lsw (a road crosses a tiny tributary of Bailey Brook here); The Hungerhill; Ipsons Corner; Jennings Mdw; Lane Flatt; The Leas, Long Lees, Lower Lees Croft; The Lidget ('swing-gate'); Little Wood Croft; Longley, Big ~, ~ ~ Mdw; The Meadow; Mill Hill, Outer Hill, Long and Mill Mdws (by Bailey Brook, cf. *molendinum de Blecheleya* e.13th Lil: in a deed of c.1220–30 Lil a grant of the mill has the whole of *Lemunlnehul'* (*sic*) attached); Little Oaks; Paddock; Pea Fd; Sheep Hill, Near, Further, Middle; Town Fd, Higher and Little ~ ~ (possibly a small open field, Blake and Lane Flatts adjoin); Town Mdw and Wall Moor; Vantages, Far, Near (cf. Vantage in Moreton *infra*); Withinbridge, ~ Mdw (between a road and Bailey Brook, 'willow bridge').

(b) *Ar(i)mitdeleford* c.1213 Lil, *Armitelgeford* 1253–5 Lil (in the first reference this is one of the bounds of *Over* wood, in the second it is near a road from Bletchley past Bletchley mill, so the ford is a crossing over Bailey Brook: if the first form is correct this is 'hermit-hollow ford', *v.* **ermite, dæl**); *Bromleia* c.1220–30 Lil (2 acres of assart *versus Bromleiam* are near *Lemunlnehul'*, i.e. Mill Hill *supra*: 'broom clearing', *v.* **brōm, lēah**); *Longefordegate* c.1243 Lil (one of the bounds of *Over* wood, probably on the boundary with Longford township).

2. LONGFORD (SJ 646340)

Langeford' 1232 Cur

Longeford 1271–2 *Ass* (p), 1520 AD, *-forde* 1638 PR(L) 11, 1690 PR(L) 8

Longford 1535 VE *et seq*

Longforthe 1538 PR(L) 11

Lonkeford 1553 PR(L) 11

Lomnford alias Longford 1728 *SBL 4336*, *Lomford* 1745 PR(L) 8, *Lomford otherwise Longford* 1777 *SBL 4338*, *Lumford* 1783 PR(L) 11

Langford 1702 PR(L) 8

'Long ford' with **ford** probably in the sense 'causeway across wet ground'. This is a common place-name, widespread in England with modern forms Longford and Langford.

The settlement in Moreton Say is just over a mile from the Roman road called The Longford, which forms the S.W. boundary of the township and parish. This road is "the causeway of *Longeford* between the towns of *Bleccheleye* and *Neweport*" 1319 Pat, in a grant of pontage for a bridge across the R. Tern (repeated 1322 Pat), and *Le Longford* 1331 Ch in the bounds of Tern Hill for which *v. infra*.

The name was discussed in Part **1** together with the other Sa example, which is the name of a parish near Newport. It was suggested there that the parish-name, rather than referring as the Moreton Say name does to the road, may refer to a causeway over marshy land by Strine Brook. The parish of Church Aston lies between Longford near Newport and the Roman road, and this makes it less likely that the Roman road is the referent.

A recent paper by K. E. Jermy and A. Breeze, SAS LXXV 109–10, repeats a suggestion in DEPN that -ford in the Sa names is Welsh *ffordd* rather than OE **ford**, but the postulated use of *ffordd* in English place-names after it was borrowed from OE and had developed the new meaning 'road' seems improbable, especially in the Jermy and Breeze scenario which envisages this for a considerable number of -ford names elsewhere in England. Neither this paper nor the DEPN entry makes allowance for the probable use of OE **ford** for causeways over wet ground as well as (much more commonly) for river-crossings. The St/Sa road is explicitly a causeway in the 1319 reference, and place-names along its route give ample evidence of marsh. Jermy and Breeze note that there is a place called Longford by part of Watling Street S. of Cannock St (GR 967093): this also is a stretch of Roman road where a causeway over wet ground may have been needed. There is a fourth example of the n. in the f.ns. of High Hatton *infra*.

The possible correlation between 'long ford' names and causeways would be a suitable subject for investigation, but this would require examination of all the Longford/Langford names in the country, which is outside the scope of a county survey. For the present it may be noted that the suggestion that these names are indicators of Roman roads and that -ford in many English names may be the Welsh word which was borrowed from English, does not appear convincing to the present writer.

CASTLEHILL WD, *The Castle Hill, Castle Hill Meadow* 1707, 65 *SBL 5355, 4264*, 1838 *TA*. There is nothing on maps to account for the name here or in Bletchley village, where *TA* has another *Castle Hill*.

FORD HALL, *Foord* 1690–1 *SBL 5091*, *Fourdhouse* 1563 PR(L) 11, *The* ~ 1600 ib, *Fordhall* 1707 *SBL 5335*, *Fourd Hall* 1708 PR(L) 8, *Ford Hall* 1711 *et seq* ib. FORDHALL COTTAGES, VILLA: the Villa is *Fordlake* 1838 *TA*. This group of buildings lies between Longford village and the R. Tern, but there is no road leading to the river, so the name is not likely to refer to a ford over it. The nature of the referent is unclear.

LONG COVERT, a strip of woodland.

LONGFORD COTTAGE, HO, VILLA.

SMYTHEMOOR, *Smithmoor Common* 1635 GT, *Smith Moor* 1718 GT, *the common of Smethmoor* 1728 *SBL 4336*, *Smythymoor* 1803 *SBL 4375*, *Smithsmoor* 1867 *SBL 4351*, *Smithy Moor Meadows or Smith Moor Meadows* 1826 *SBL 4357*, *Smithymoor* 1838 *TA*. On 1833 OS *Smith Moor* occurs twice, applied to groups of houses nearly a mile apart at the N. and S. ends of a long, narrow marsh on the boundary of Bletchley and Longford townships. On *TAMap* this strip is divided into rectangular enclosures, many called *Smithymoor*, some called *Inclosures*, *Allotments* and *Crofts*. The name may be identical with Smedmore PN Do **1** 86 and Smithy Moor in Cockshut *supra*, which are considered to be 'smooth marsh', from **smēðe**. However, *TAMap* has a field called *Lower Yard and Smithy* at the N. end of the marsh, and a *Smithy Green* nearby, so in this instance the meaning may be 'marsh near a smithy'.

WATERLOO COTTAGE, by the parish boundary.

TAMap shows *Red Lion Inn* and *Castle Inn*, both on The Longford.

Field-Names

Forms in (a) are 1838 *TA*, except for those dated 1803, 04, 07, 16, 33, 34, 40, which are *SBL 4342, 47, 53, 58, 75, 5652, 3*. Earlier forms dated 1707, 12, 25, 65, 94, 98 are *SBL 5535, 4261, 64, 4339, 40, 53*.

(a) Acres Mdw; Asps; Bank, Far, Near, Big, Little, Clarke's (*Far*, *Near*, *Clarkes Banks* 1712); Barn Fd (2, one 1725); Big Fd; Birkin Hill; Black Flat (by Shaw Dale); Bluegate Fd; Broad Fd; Broad Mdw; Brook Mdw; Brown's Lsw; Butcher's Fd; Butty Mdw, (Quillets in, by R. Duckow); Butty Pce (a tiny strip is Quillet in ~ ~, by Shad Dale); Calves Croft (*Bigger* and *Lesser* 1707, 25); Carrion Fd (perhaps a reference to burial of diseased animals, this is an addition to the instances noted Part **4** 113); The Church Stiles 1803, Lower, Upper ~ ~ *TA*; Clover Fd; Colts Cote Fd; Common Pce 1807, *TA* (*~ ~ otherwise Suker's Piece* 1712); Crabtree Lsw; Crib Head 1833, *TA* (the crib may be a manger); Croft(s) (a large number along E. edge of Smythemoor, a few in village); Crossways (*Further Cross Ways*, *The Near Cross Ways otherwise Mill Croft* 1712, Further ~ ~, Near ~ ~ otherwise called Mile Croft 1807, the *TA* field is by a road-fork); The Curiner otherwise The Curinery Dole 1816 (perhaps **coninger** 'rabbit-warren'); Drayton Fd (near boundary with Market Drayton); Flash, Far, Near ~ ('shallow pool'); Fordhall Lsw; Galley Pit, Higher 1803, Galleymore, Galley Pot 1834, Galleymore, Galley Pit *TA*, Little Gallipot or Lower Galley Pit Fd, Big Gallipot Fd or Higher Galley Pit Fd 1840 (possibly a shape-n. from some feature resembling an earthen vessel, but if the correct form is Pit then Galley may be a derivative of *gall* 'spongy ground'); Garden Croft; Gig or Sparrow Croft; Gravel Fd, Long and Little ~ ~ (a line of small rectangular fields with others called N. and S. Fd at either end, on E. edge of Smythemoor); Green Lane, Far ~ ~; Headford, ~ Croft, Fd, Mdw (the Longslow road crosses R. Duckow here, the n. is The Eddsford 1803, Edford 1816); Hempbutt or Town Corner 1816, Hempsbutt 1834; Herdmans Pce, Far, Near; Hill, Low, Round, The Low Hills 1804, Round Hill 1833, Round, Middle, Clarkes Lower Hill, Prees Hills, Lower ~ ~ *TA* (*Low Hills*, *Low Round Hill* 1798); Lane Enclosure; Lane End 1803, *TA*; Lane Fd 1834; Leasow, Lower ~, Lower and Upper New Lsw; Lees, Lower, Big Leas; Little Bridge; Little Mdw (1725, 65); Long Butts or Lane Fd; Longford Turnings (in a road-fork); Long Mdw; Meadow (several); Meadow, New, Old; Meadow, Worrall's, Paynes, Swinchats; The Member Flatt 1816, Member Flat *TA* (adjoins Town Fd); Middle Shaw (not near Shade/Shaw ns.); Mill Dam (on R. Duckow); Millings Cop otherwise Millions Cop 1816, Milling Cop 1833, Milling, Big, Little, Milling Croft *TA* (Mill Gate adjoins); Moor or Quag Ends; The Moorland Broad Mdw; Moss, Far, Near, Middle, Top Moss, Rough Moss, Far and Near Moss Croft; The Moss, Little ~, Moss Croft(s); New Mdw, Pce; New Pltn; Oak Lsw; Oak Pce; Patch (tiny enclosure, *The Patch* 1712); The Piece 1804; Pool Croft; Pool Yd; Pye Nest ('magpie nest'); Rock Hill (*Rock Hill otherwise Roaches* 1712, *roach* is from ME **roche**[1] 'rock'); Roger Wall; Rough Pce (2); Round and Cunnery Mdw (one curved side, Cunnery is 'rabbit-warren'); Rut Bag; Ryegrass Fd; Shade Dale, Big, Far, Lower, Upper, Big Shaw, Little Shaw Dale (*Bigger* and *Lesser Shaw*, *Shaw Meadow* 1725, probably an open field, Butty Pce and Black Flat adjoin, *v.* Shay *infra*); Shay, Far, Near, Middle, Big (on opposite side of Shrewsbury road from preceding, *shay* is a variant of *shaw*, ultimately from **sceaga** 'small wood'); Smithy Green, Lower Yd and Smithy (*v.* Smythemoor *supra*); Sparrow

Croft, Fd; Stackyard Fd; Swinchatts Smithymoor; Sytchbridge Mdw 1816, Sitch Bank, Bridge, Pool Sitch Mdw 1834, Sych Bridge, ~ ~ Mdw, Sych Bank, Pool Sych Mdw *TA* ('small stream', ultimately from **sīc**); Ten Brooks (by R. Duckow); Terne Mdw, Far, Near, Far Terne Lsw (*Far Tern Leasow* 1712); Tern Mdw, Lower, Upper (down river from preceding); Thistly Fd, Lower, Upper; Top Yd; Tough Horn, Far and Near ~ (probably Rough Horns 1833: in a road-fork); The Town Fd (otherwise The Intacke) 1803, (The) Town Field 1816, *TA* (S.E. of village); Town Mdw and Stocking; Two Butts; Two Trees Fd; Wall Flat; Well Mdw (2); Wheat Croft; Yard, New, Lower and Pool Yd (in village).

(b) *Bigg Meadow* 1725, *Big* ~ 1765; *Gollins Field, Meadow* 1707, 65, *Higher Meadow alias Gollins* ~ 1725; *(The) Gorsty Field* 1707, 25, 65; *Kiln Yard* 1707; *Moor, Further, Nearer* 1725, 65; *Orchard, Old* 1707, *Old and New* ~1765; *The Sands* 1765.

3. LONGSLOW (SJ 655354)

The township name, which means 'Wlanc's tumulus', is discussed in Part **1**, and the possible significance of such names is also discussed there under Beslow.

THE BATH. On the 1900 6" map this is the name of a strip of wood, part of which is shown as *Plantation* on *TAMap*.

Field-Names

Forms in (a) are 1840 *TA* (Market Drayton).

(a) Bank Fd; Banky Fd; Black Pits; Bottoms; Brick Kiln; Buttermilk Hill; Clay Pits (2); Cockpit Croft (near village); Croft, Far and Horse ~ (in village); Cut End; Daniel, Big, Little; Dickens Six, Eight and Nine Acres, Big Dickens Fd; Dugnalls, ~ Mdw; Gorsy Fd; Greasy Fd; Green (tiny triangle by village); Green Fd Brick Kiln; Greys Yd (in village); Guady Bit (probably *recte* Gaudy, a reference to dyer's greenweed, FN 31); Halfway House Croft (no building); Herons Pit; Hildick Fd, Near; Horse Pasture; Lees; Little Fd; Little Mdw (2); New Longford Fd (on boundary with Longford); Long Friday, New (possibly a derogatory name: Friday in f.ns. presents problems which are discussed in J. Field, *English Field-Names* 107); Low Hill, Far and Near ~ ~; Marlpit Fd; Masseys Fd; Meadow, Nobridge, Near, Townsend, House, White Gate, Far, Moor(s) (along W. boundary by R. Duckow); Mill Fd (probably a windmill); Moors, Far and Grazing ~, Moor Head, Far and Near ~ ~; Near Mdw; New Lsw, Far, Near, Big, Little; New Pce; Nobridge Fd, Lane (*v.* Nobridge *infra*); Paddock; Pear Tree Croft (large field), Lsw; Perkins Nook; Pooles End; Pool Fd; Sawpit Bank; Shut Flat (by Spoonley Fd); Spoonley Fd, Far and Little ~ ~, ~ Mdw (on boundary with Spoonley in Adderley); Styche Bank and Long Croft (*v.* Styche *infra*); Well Moor; Yard Fd (by village).

4. MORETON SAY (SJ 630345)

AUDLEY BROW (SJ 634353)

Aldeleg 1274 Ipm, 1395 *SRO 322/217*, *-leye* 1284–5 FA
Audeley 1323 Cl

This settlement may be *Lai* 1086 DB: *Lai* follows Moreton Say, and both manors are held from Roger de Lacy by a tenant named William. If this identification be correct the name may have been originally simplex, but alternatively the DB form could be an erroneous rendering of the compound of **ald** 'old' and **lēah** which is represented by the later forms.

Audley is one of a cluster of **lēah** names which lie between the headwaters of the Duckow and Tern, on a narrow watershed between north- and south-flowing rivers. The group includes Bletchley in this parish. This is wet land where **lēah** is perhaps more likely to have its late OE meaning 'meadow, pasture' than to refer to woods or woodland clearings.

The significance of **ald** is uncertain. Many compounds with this qualifier recur, but this instance with **lēah** is rare, possibly unique.

The modern house-name, Audley Brow, occurs 1833 OS, 1838 *TA*.

OLDFIELDS (SJ 628364)

Oldefeld 1284–5 FA, 1436 Fine
Ye Oldfields 1720 PR(L) 8, *Old Field* 1833 OS, ~ *Fields* 1838 *TA*

On *TAMap* the house called *Old Fields* is surrounded by a large group of fields with ~ *Field* names, three of them called *Old Field*. The others are listed in f.ns. *infra*. It seems likely that **feld** here means 'open field', with 'old' indicating that the area had been used for communal cultivation for a long time.

CHEADLE ORCHARD.

HIGGINSWOOD, *Higgins Wood* 1833 OS, 1838 *TA*.

HILL FM (Gazetteer, in Moretonwood): *William de Hulle iuxta Morton' Say* is mentioned 1314 *SBL 6595*, and other members of the family appear in later 14th-cent. records.

LOCKETT'S GORSE.

MORETON HALL, 1833 OS, 1838 *TA*.

MORETON MILL, 1833 OS, 1838 *TA*.

MORETONWOOD. In 1199 SAS 2/X(FF) there is a reference to "a third part of the wood of Moreton". Later references include *Mortoneswod*

1317 AD, *Moreton Wood* 1709 *et seq* PR(L) 8. On 1833 OS the name occurs three times denoting scattered groups of houses.

PEDSMORE PLTN.

STYCHE FM, 1833 OS, 1838 *TA*, *v*. Styche *infra*.

Field-Names

Forms in (a) are 1838 *TA*.

(a) Allotment(s) (with Common ns. on W. boundary); Bakehouse Croft; Banky and Hoddy's Fd; Barley Fd; Barn Fd (several); Big Mdw (2); Big Wood Fd; Brickkiln Fd (2); Broad Mdw; Broad Orchard, Big and Far ~ ~; Broomy Fd; Calves Croft (2); Church Mdw; Clemley (2, *v*. Prees *infra*); Common Fd, Big, Higher, Lower, Little, Common Allotment, Pce (with Croft and Allotments ns. on W. boundary); Copnalls Mdw; Cops Ditch; Cote Lsw (no building); Cow Lsw (Ox Lsw adjoins); Croft(s) (several groups by W. boundary, also a large area designated Crofts and Inclosures); Croft(s) (group by Higginswood); Cross Fd, Bottom, Top; Cross Fd, Far and Near ~ ~, Lower Cross Mdw (not near preceding); Daughtys Fd, Ground; Daisy Bank; Dockfield Fd; Dovehouse Bank (by Moreton Hall); Field (a large group of fields surrounding Oldfields has ~ Field names: these include Barn, Big, Broad, Clench, Common, Cote, Far, Green (2), Hill (3), High, Hopper, Long, Middle, Mill (4), Pit, Rushy, Thistly, Three Pit, Wash Fd); Fisher's Croft; Fislow; Fox Cover, ~ ~ Mdw; Garden Fd; Glovers Bank; Goosberry Mdw; Gorsty Bank (2); Gravelly Wheeley, Far ~ ~; Hare Ground, Big, Little, Far, Near; Haywood, Far, Near, Big; Henshaw Bank; High Wd; Hill Head; Hoar Croft; Hole Ground (3 fields on N.E. boundary, Hale Croft adjoins); Holly Bank, Little Holly Bush; Hopes Croft; Horse Croft, Far, Near; House Fd; House Mdw (3); Kitchens Croft; Little Mdw; Long Fd (2); Long Mdw, Meadow Head; Loons, Near ~ ('lands', in the group of Fd ns. listed *supra*); Manlove Mdw; Milking Bank (by a building on W. boundary); Moor, Moor Pce; Moor (3 fields on W. edge of Smythemoor); Moores Croft; New Croft; New Lsw, Far, Near, Little; Old Lane; Ox Lsw (2); Parker's Croft; Peartree Croft, Little ~ ~; Pigtrough Mdw; Plungeon Yd; Pool Dam or Horse Pasture; Pool Side and End (by Mill Pool); Riders Mdw; Rough Fds; Rushy Mdw; Ryegrass, Big, Little; Sand Fd, Far and Near ~ ~; Single Fd; (The) Slang (2); Slang Mdw; Stannerley's Croft, Fd; Teece's Croft; Three Crofts (this and Two Crofts are tiny enclosures by houses); Vantage, ~ Mdw (perhaps a complimentary n., cf. Vantages in Bletchley); Well Fd, Far, Near; The Wood (by Higginswood).

5. SHAVINGTON (SJ 636388)

The township name, which means 'estate associated with Scēaf(a)', is discussed in Part **1**.

MORREY, LOWER, MIDDLE, HIGHER. This name is *Morrey* in Adderley parish register (PR(L) 4) from 1693 to 1795. This is a possible development of **morgen-gifu** 'morning gift', well evidenced in place-names for land given by husband to wife the day after marriage; but earlier forms would be required for confirmation of this possibility. Morrey in St, one mile W. of Yoxall, is first recorded with that form in 1499 (*ex inf.* D. Horovitz).

The 1833 OS map gives *Old Morrey House* for Higher Morrey, and *Morrey*, twice, for both houses called Middle Morrey on 6" map. Lower Morrey is not shown in 1833. There is a moated site near the houses.

HOME FM, 1840 *TA*, 1833 OS.
SHAVINGTON HALL, PARK, 1848 *TA*.
SHAVINGTON WD, 1709, 80 PR(L) 4.
SNAKES PLTN, *Wood* 1840 *TA*. The plantation has the shape of a snake seen from above.
THE SPINNEYS, *Plantations* 1840 *TA*.
WALL PLTN.
YEWTREE HO.

Field-Names

Forms in (a) are 1840 *TA*. Shavington has a separate *TA* as a detached township of Adderley.

(a) Ash Croft; Ash Tree Fd; Banky Fd, Little ~ ~; Barn Fd; Black Croft; Boggy Moor; Brick Kiln Fd; By Hand Mdw; Calves Croft; Cheshire Fd Mdw; Clover Fd; Cockshutt Fd; Griffiths Fd; Heifer Mdw; Horse Wd, Lower; House Fd (by Shavington Wd); Hughs Wd; Kiln Fd, Mdw; Little Fd; Little Wd (2); Long Croft; Long Mdw; Lower Croft; Marl Fd, Lower ~ ~; Middle Pce; Moor Mdw; Morrey Lane Fd, Morrey Mdw (*v. supra*); New Lsw, Lower, Upper, New Pce; Old Garden; Old Yd; Ox Pasture and Mdw; Pan Croft; Parson's Fd; Penthouse Croft, Lower; Pinfold Croft; Pit Fd, Lower, Higher; Platt Fd (*v.* **plat**[1] 'footbridge', a path crosses a stream here); Richardson's Pce; Rush Fd; Rye Grass Fd; Sandhole Fd; Slang, Lower; Smiths Wd, Lower; Spring Fd; Way Mdw; Well Fd; Wilkesley Ley (by boundary with Wilkesley Ch).

6. STYCHE AND WOODLANDS (Styche Hall is SJ 645357)

Stuche 1203–4 *Ass* (p) *et freq* to 1430 Fine, *Stuyche* 1548–9 *SBL 2002*

The Stich 1645 PR(L) 12, *Stich* 1655 SAS 1/XLVII, *Stych* 1760, 71 PR(L) 8, *Styche* 1833 OS, *The Styche* 1838 *TA*

OE **stycce** 'a piece' has been noted in minor names and field-names in some counties: EPN gives examples from C, Ess, Hu, Nt, and six instances are noted in Ch (PN Ch **5.1** 357–8). It is a rare element, and the material available does not provide evidence for a precise meaning. The

Sa instance may be the only one which can be classified as a settlement-name.

WOODLANDS. This survives as part of the township-name, but no settlement called Woodlands appears on *TA* or later maps. It is *Woodlands* 1655 SAS 1/XLVII, 1693 GT, *Woodsland* (township) 1701 PR(L) 8, *Woodland* 1706 ib, *hamlet of Woodlands* 1742 GT. *TAMap* shows six adjoining fields called *Green*, *Middle*, *Higher*, *Lower Wood* in the W. of the township; if the hamlet was in this area this would balance Styche, which is near the E. boundary.

BIG POOL, 1833 OS, *The New Pool* 1838 *TA*. A small *Old Pool* is shown upstream on *TAMap*.

BIG WD, 1833 OS, *Shavington* ~ ~ 1838 *TA*.

CLOVERLEY DOLE, 1833 OS, *Clawleydole or Cloverley Dale* 1838 *TA*. Cloverley adjoins, in Ightfield *supra*. Dole is probably shared meadow land.

CLOVERLEY WALL PLTN.

MOAT FM, PLTN (latter 1838 *TA*), by the moat at Newstreet Lane.

MOAT PLANTING, by a moat called *Warren's Moat* 1838 *TA*. There is relevant information in a note by Michael Fradley in *Shropshire Archaeology and History Newsletter* no. 61, Spring 2006: "Recent research has located the site of *Warandashale*, a house held by Richard de *Puleston* which was granted a License to Crenellate in 1296. ... The location of *Warrenhall* is a levelled moated site (SJ 6429 3747) ... The moat is depicted on early OS editions as enclosing an island of about 45m × 60m, but is now only visible as a cropmark on aerial photographs. The site was pinpointed by seventeenth and early eighteenth century documents in the Powis Estate Records of the Styche Estate in the Shropshire Record Office which use the name *Warrenshall* alongside that of Rhiews, which is a seventeenth century farmhouse to the west of the moated site and which probably replaced the earlier settlement site."

NEW STREET LANE, probably *Newsted Lane* 1730, 51 PR(L) 8.

NOBRIDGE, 1831 OS, *Noebridge* 1608 PR(L) 20, *Noe-Bridge* 1676, 83 ib, *No Bridge* 1676 ib. Possibly 'new bridge', cf. Nobold Part **4** 149. A road crosses R. Duckow near the farm.

PARK GORSE.

RHIEWS, ~ FM, *Rhews* 1833 OS, *The Rhewes* 1838 *TA*, Welsh *rhiw* 'hill' with an English plural, probably a fairly recent coinage. *v.* Welchman's Piece in f.ns. *infra*.

THE ROOKERY.

SHAVINGTON GRANGE.

SPRINGS PLTN, *Springs* 1838 *TA*, probably *spring* in the sense 'coppice'.

STYCHE FM, 1838 *TA*, *Stych Farm* 1833 OS.

STYCHE WD.

Field-Names

Forms in (a) are 1838 *TA*.

(a) The Bank; Barley Fd; Barn Fd; Barn Mdw; Barn Yd; Big Mdw; Brickkiln Fd; Calf Cote Close, Little Calf Croft; Calves Croft (2); Carthouse Croft; Clem Ley (*v.* Prees *infra*); Clover, Far, Near; Coney Green, Big, Little (**conygre** 'rabbit warren'); Corner Croft; Croft(s) (with Inclosures along the road by New Street Lane); Croft(s) (by Rhiews); Dairy House Fd (Dairy Ho adjoins, by Styche Hall); Daisy Fd; Dods Croft; Far Fd; Fenny Bank; Flashes; Forest Loons, Long ~ ~ ('lands'); Gosling Mdw; Grassley, Big, Little; Great Mdw; Green Lane; Hall Fd (by Rhiews); Hare Fd; Hawthorn Fd; Heath Fd, Styche Heath; Horse Mdw; Horse Wash Croft; House Mdw (by New Street Lane); Hussey's Fd; Lamb Mdw and Inclosure; Little Wd; Marl Fd (2); Meadow (a line of Mdw ns. along R. Duckow includes Captain's, Moat, Middle (2), New, Nobridge, Rushy and 3 Water Mdws); Milking Bank (by Nobridge); Mud Fd; Near Fd (2); New Lsw, Further; New Mdw; New Pce; New Street Lane Ground (a short distance from the hamlet); The Park, Park Fd (by Styche Hall); Pit Fd; Rhew Fd; Rose, Further, Near Lower, Near Top (probably Welsh *rhos* 'moor, heath': these 3 fields and Welchman's Pce are near Rhiews, which probably had a Welsh-speaking owner at some time); Rough Croft, Far, Near; Round Mdw (one curved side); Ryegrass Fd (2); The Slang (atypically, a large triangular field); Stone Croft; Strawberry Fd; Tenlow's Fd; Way Fd; Welchman's Pce, Far, Near (a Welsh-speaking occupant of Rhiews may have been responsible for that n. and for Rose *supra*); Well Fd, Mdw; Well Fd (not near preceding); Wood, Big, Little, Rough, Styche; Wide Fd and Inclosure.

Norton in Hales

The parish-name, discussed in Part **1**, is one of seven examples of this name in Sa. 'North' in this instance may refer to the position of the settlement in the district called Hales, which stretched at least as far south as Hales in Tyrley St, three miles away. The modern affix is first noted 1271–2 *Ass*. In the 13th and early 14th centuries the affix *sub Liman*, *under Lyme* was also used, referring to the position at the southern extremity of the district called Lyme on the western edge of the Pennines. Details of these affixes are given in Part **1**.

The modern civil parish includes the township of Betton, which was transferred from Market Drayton in 1914.

1. BETTON IN HALES (SJ 692370)
This is a DB manor, so discussed in Part **1**. The name may be identical with Betton in Berrington, Part **2** 93, 95, also discussed in Part **1**, but the etymology of both names is uncertain. 'Beech-tree settlement' is accepted in VEPN (*s.v.* **bēce**) but some early spellings for both names are difficult to equate with this.

RIDGWARDINE (SJ 680381)
Rugwordin c.1182 SAC *et passim* with variant spellings *-wrthin*, *-ward'*, *-worthin*, *-warthin*, *-wardyn*, *-worthyn* to late 14th SAC, *Rugwardyn in Halys* 1349 Pat
Wrugwrthin a.1240, c.1242 (p) SAC
Ruggewardyn 1411 SAC, *-worthyn* Hy 6 *RentSur*
Rygerton 1540 *SBL 6083*, *Rigerdine* 1723 PR(L) 20
Ryghtwarden c.1550 SAS l/VI
Rudgardin 1637 PR(L) 9
Ridgewarden 1698 Morden, *-wardine* 1704 PR(L) 4, *Ridgwardine* 1693, 1849 PR(L) 18
Richwardine 1833 OS

'Enclosed settlement on a ridge', *v.* **hrycg**, **worðign**. The low ridge is shown clearly on the 1833 hachured map.

TUNSTALL HALL (SJ 690355)

Tunstal c.1135 SAC (p) *et passim* with variant spellings *-stal'*, *-stall*
Tonstale c.1235 SAC
Tunestal l.14th SAC

v. ***tūn-stall**, which may sometimes be used in place-names for a deserted settlement-site.

BENNET'S COVERT.

BETTON COPPICE FM, *Betton Coppice* 1833 OS.

BETTON COPPICE TURNOVER BRIDGE, on Shropshire Union canal.

BETTONHALL, BETTONHALL FM.

BETTON HO, LODGE.

BETTON MOSS, 1833 OS, 1840 *TA*, ~ ~ FM, MOSS COTTAGE, MOSSLANE COTTAGES, FM: *Le Mos* 1411 SAC, *v.* **mos**.

BETTONWOOD FM, *Nemus de Beitona* 1175–c.1190 SAC, *Boscus de Becton'* (? *recte Betton'*) 1256 SAC, *Boscus de Betton'* 1306–7 *Ass*, *Bettonwode* 1411 SAC, *Betton Wood* 1602 *et freq* PR(L) 18: cf. *Betton' Woodhouse* Hy 8 *RentSur*.

BRICKKILN WD (by brick works).

BROWNHILLS, ~ FM, WD, *Browne Hill* Hy 8 *RentSur*, *Brown Hill* 1833 OS.

CINDERHOLE WD.

DOVEPOOL WD, *Dove Pool* 1840 *TA*.

GARDEN COVERT.

GLADE WD.

THE GORSE.

GREENHILL FM, WD, *Green Hill* 1840 *TA*.

HEATH WD: *TA* has a cluster of *Heath* ns. here, *v.* f.ns. *infra*.

LOCKETT'S FM, *Locketts Piece* 1840 *TA*.

HILL COTTAGES, by Mill Ho in Oakley St, *TA* has (*Oakley*) *Mill Field* here, *v.* f.ns.

NORTON LANE.

NUTDRUMBLE WD, *v.* The Drumble in Baschurch *supra*.

OLDPOOL LANE.

OXLEASOW WD, *Ox Leasow* 1840 *TA*.

THE PARK, *Park* 1840 *TA*, by Tunstall Hall.

QUARRY WD, *Big* and *Little Quarry* 1840 *TA*, cf. *Quarrellforlong* 1411 SAC.

ROOKERY WD.

ROOMS FM.

THE ROUGH.
SANDHOLE WD.
TWIN COVERT.
WAGTAIL WD.
WALKER'S WD.
YEWTREE WD.

Field-Names

Forms in (a) are 1840 *TA* (Market Drayton). Early forms dated 1411 are SAC, Hy 8 are *RentSur*.

(a) Acton Rough; Armes Lsw, Far, Near; Banks; Barn Fd, Little ~ ~; Barn Yd Fd; Betton Lsw, Big, Little; Big Bottom Fd; Big Hall Fd; Blake Flats; Boozy Pasture (2, the n. refers to pasture rights); Bowers Lsw; Brick Kiln Fd; Broadhurst, Near, Far Broadhurst Heath; Cabin Lsw (the same n. occurs a short distance away in Market Drayton); Chapel (large field in village); Cherry Tree Fd; Clock Hill (perhaps land used for maintenance of the church clock, but a reference to dandelions is also possible); Coal Barn Fd, Cole Barn Mdw; Clover Fd; Coopers Fd (cf. *Cowperesbruche* 1411); Cote Fd, Big, Little (no building); Crab Tree Fd; Cross Fd, Big, Little (by a road-junction, *Le Croffeld'* 1411 may be a mistranscription for *Cros-*); Custard Croft (tiny triangle in road junction by some roadside buildings, *custard* is sometimes from **cot-stōw**); Dove Ho Croft (by Betton Hall); Drayton Fd; Ellis Fd; Far New Dams; Fern Fd; Fern Hill, Far, Middle, Near (*Fernhull* 1411); Fuel Ho Fd (by Tunstall Hall); Furlong, Far ~ (not in an obvious open-field context, cf. *Le Furlong'* Hy 8); Gallimore Fd (probably dialect *gall* 'wet spot in a field'); Gorsy Croft, Big Gorsy Lsw; Great Wd; Grove Fd; Gully Tree, Far, Great, Little, Three Cornered (FN 48 lists this as a mysterious tree-name); Hall Yd (large field by Betton Hall, cf. *Le Hallefeld'* 1411); Harpers Mdw; Hazle Moor; Heath, Broad, Flat, Wardley, Heathway Fd (near Heath Wd); Hedge Croft, Edge Croft (adjacent, cf. Will *de Egge* 1411, probably 'edge'); Hill Lane Fd; Hole Birch; Horse Hayes, Far, Near, Horse Pasture; House Croft (no building, Milking Bank adjoins); House Croft (by Mill Cottages); House Fd (by Brownhills Fm); House Mdw (by Bettonmoss Fm); Kiln Fd; Leg, Big, Little (a shape n.); Little Fd; Long Fd; Lower Lsw; Lower Mdw; Marl Fd (2); Meadow (several); Micklin, Near, Over, Top (5 adjoining fields, Micklin Tops is nearby); Middle Fd (*Le Middelfeld'*, *Le Middelfeldes-heystowe* 1411, the precise meaning of *hegestow* has not been established, there are several instances in Ch, PN Ch **5.1** 220); Mill Fd; Oakley ~ ~, Billon ~ ~ (6 fields, some furlong-shaped, on opposite bank of R. Tern from Mill Ho in Oakley St, Mill Cottages adjoin); Mill Fd, Lower and Upper Mill Mdw (downstream from preceding, *TAMap* shows Mill, 1900 6" map shows Weir and Pump House: Mill Fd is very large, and this and preceding could both have been open fields, cf. *Le Mullefeld'* 1411); Moss Croft, Mdw (several by Betton Moss, cf. *Mosse Croft* Hy 8); Monmouth Mdw, Big and Little Monmouth (FN 23 lists this as a transferred n.); Moor Mdw; Mud Fd; Naggintons Fd (cf. *Nagyntonescroft* 1411, Will. *de Nagynton'* mentioned); New Croft; Norton Fd, Big, Little (on boundary with Norton); Ox Lsw; Partridge Flat; Peaks and Woodleys Croft; Podmore Mdw, Six Acre Podmore, Four ~ ~ (cf.

Podmoresforlong 1411, perhaps a surname from Podmore St, 5 miles E.); Porters Head; Randles, Field up to, Field behind; Rick Yd Mdw; Ridding Brook (*Le Rudyngbrok'* 1411, *v.* ***ryding**); Rookery Fd; Rushy Croft; Rushy Fd, Lower, Top; Rye Grass Fd; Seven Acres; Shade Fd; Shaw, Big, Little; Shay Dowler Mdw (Alder Birch adjoins, the n. may contain *oller* 'alder', cf. *Straggedoldremedewe* 1411); Sheep Fd; Slang (3 fields in line, tapering to a point); Spoonley Fd; Stentons Croft, Near, Middle; Steventons Fd; Stones Fd; Strangers Fd, Far ~ ~ (*Strangersfeld'* Hy 8); Tripple Croft; Twelve Score (average-sized field, FN 12 notes a Twelve Score Mdw in Neenton and lists it with size names); Underwood; Walkers, ~ Ground; Wardleys New Croft; Wardleys Paddock, Little ~ ~; Wheat Birch; Wheat Still; Whittle, Far, Near and Middle ~; Withy Fd.

(b) *Alesgrenefeld'* 1411; *Bowkeresflat* 1411 (Thomas *Bowker* mentioned); *Brewesacre* 1411; *Brokelonescroftes* 1411 ('brook lane's croft'); *Byrche, Lyttle Clerk' and Tunstall'* Hy 8 (*Byrche*, like some Birch ns. in (a), may be from **bryce** 'broken-in land', or it may be a surname, John *Byrche* is mentioned); *Clerkesbruche* (*v.* **bryce**); *Cock' Furlong'* Hy 8; *Colyaresfeld'*, *Colyaresmedewe* 1411; *Cowlesowe* Hy 8; *Ethdredesh', nemus de* 1175–c.1190 SAC; *Gorstyfeld'* Hy 8; *Grene* 1291–2, 92–5 *Ass* (p); *La Helde* c.1242 SAC ('gentle slope', *v.* **helde**); *Le Hemmedewe* 1411 ('border meadow', *v.* **hem**); *Hethilee* c.1240 SAC, *Hethileye* c.1240 ib (said to be *quondam legam*, so probably a ME n. 'heathy grassland'); *Kylcroft* Hy 8; *Londemeressiche* c.1240 SAC ('boundary rivulet', *v.* **landgemǣre**, **sīc**); *Low Croft* Hy 8; *Mokysdon* Hy 8; *Le Moreforlong* 1411 ('marsh furlong'); *Mowumore* 1411; *Muculhullwey* 1411 ('big hill way'); *Le Newdom* 1411; *Palmerescroft* 1411; *Le Portewey* 1411; *Stordylane* 1411; *Whyterondes* 1411, *Le Whyte Roundes* Hy 8, *The White Rownd* c.1550 SAS l/VI (apparently 'white circles'); *Wodebruches* 1411; *Wyndybruche* 1411 (*windy* is a rare p.n. el.).

2. NORTON IN HALES (SJ 703387)

BELLAPORT HALL FM, LO, *v.* ~ Old Hall in Woore *infra*.

BRAND FM, HALL: *Brand* 1599–1600 *SBL 2201*, 1689 *et freq* PR(L) 18, *Brands* 1625 *SBL 4604*, *The Bran* 1630 *SBL 2202*, *Brond* 1695 Morden, *Ye Brand* 1747 PR(L) 18, *Brand Hall* 1825 ib. 'Place which has been burnt.' VEPN *s.v.* **brend** notes the predominantly south-west-midland distribution of forms with *-a-*, but it seems likely that this more northerly name is also an example. The use of this past participle as a simplex name is quite common.

PR(L) 18 has *The Brand-Common*, *Brand Common* 1807, 15.

BETTON WD, not near Bettonwood Fm, *supra*.
BRADLING STONE.
COBSCOT, 1852, 73 PR(L) 18.
NORTON FM.
NORTON FORGE, 1694 *et seq* PR(L) 18, *The Forge* 1795 ib.

NORTON WD, 1600 *et freq* PR(L) 18. This farm and nearby NORTONWOOD FM are both *Norton Wood* on 1822 *FoxallMap*.

Field-Names

There are two tithe awards and maps for Norton: one is dated 1822, and resulted from an act for inclosure of commonable lands and tithe commutation, the other is 1864, when rent charges were reviewed. The 1864 award repeated the field-names of the 1822 one. George Foxall's map was based on that of 1864, but he dated it 1822 as the field-names were identical, and the earlier date has been adopted for the present list. It seems better, however, to use *FoxallMap* rather than *TA* as the reference. A more detailed account of the two maps can be obtained from SRO.

Early forms are GT.

(a) Allotment (several fields by Brand Hall); Anne's Moor, ~ ~ Mdw; Banky Fd; Barn Coppice, Far and Near Coppice, Coppice Mdw (by Norton Wd); Bearstone Fd (1635, 1701, Bearstone in Woore adjoins); Benty Moor, Big, Little (Big and Little Belty Moor adjoin, Benty is probably correct, referring to bent grass); Beswicks Croft; Betton Croft, Fd, Lsw (on border with Betton); Big Mdw (2); Black Moor; Blackpit Coppice (adjoins Coppice fields *infra*); Blake Flat (adjoins Crabtree Flat); Bradeley, Far, Middle, Near, ~ Mdw (*Bradley Field* 1612, *Bradeley Meadow* 1701); Brand Common Croft; Brand Croft, Fd, Mdw (by Brand Hall); Broomy Croft (2); Broomy Lsw; Broomy Pce; Browns Moor; Butty Mdw (*butty* has several meanings, *v.* FN 7–8, PN Ch **5.1** 124); Chasemoor Hill; Churn Moors, Churn Moor Mdw; Clough, Higher and Middle ~, ~ Mdw (6 fields near Norton Wd); Coppice, Big, Far and Little ~ (7 fields on N.W. boundary); Corder Bank, Croft; Corsy Close; Crabtree Flat, Big, Further and Middle ~ ~; Crevor, ~ Mdw; Croft (small enclosures in village include Farther, Near, Churchyard, Poppy Croft); Crofts (large field near village); Crooked Birch, Little, Near, Middle (perhaps *britch* 'cleared land'); Cross Lsw (extends between two roads); Cross Lsw, Mdw (by a road junction); Curkstool Croft (*sic*, but Cuckstool in FN 56, by R. Tern, near village: 'ducking stool'); Darleys; Drake Pit; Fords, Middle ~, Fords Mdw (either side of Norton/Adderley road, perhaps a causeway); Foxholes, Bigger, Farther and Long ~ (6 fields which, with Long and Further New Lsw and Further Sandpit Moor, form a group of furlong-shaped strips on N.E. boundary); Furlong (one of a small group of furlong-shaped fields on N. boundary); Furnace, ~ Bank, Mdw (by R. Tern, some distance upstream from Norton Forge); Furness Mdw (not near preceding); Gorsy Croft; Gorsy Fd; Grove, ~ Fd; Hall Ground, Mdw (by Brand Hall); Hammer Croft, Near ~ ~, ~ ~ Mdw (downstream from Furnace Bank, *Hammer Croft* 1701); The Hayes; Higher Pce; Hill Fd, High ~ ~, Far Hill, Hill Mdw, Little ~ ~; Homestone Croft; Hop Yd; House Coppice (by Norton Wd); House Mdw (by Norton Fm); House Yd (by Nortonwood Fm); Jack Acres, Big and Middle ~ ~, ~ ~ Mdw; Jacksons Coppice, Far, Near; Knowles Fd; Lady Mdw; Landgate (adjoins Park End); Lea Fd, ~ ~ Mdw; Lees; Lindley, Farther, Middle, Little and Long ~; Long Croft; Long Lawn (by Brand Fm);

Long Leys; Long Mdw; Mail Croft; Meadow; Meadow, Far, Near, Middle; Merry Croft; Moat Mdw (by Brand Hall); Monks Mdw (1682, 1701, *Muncksmeadow* 1635); New Pce, Far ~ ~, ~ ~ Mdw; New Croft; New Croft Mdw; New Lsw; New Lsw, Further, New, Big, Long (furlong-shaped strips by Foxholes); New Mdw; Oven Mdw; Ox Lsw, ~ ~ Mdw, Big, Little, Far, Near, Middle, Further and Pit Ox Lsw, Ox Mdw (13 fields in N.W. corner of township); Paddock; Park End, Little, Near and Far ~ ~, Lower Park, Park Croft (Bellaport Lo adjoins, the park was perhaps attached to Bellaport Old Hall in Woore *infra*); Peas Fd; Pigstye Mdw; Pingle (ME **pingel** 'small enclosure'); Pit Fd, Black, High; Pixley, Pixley's Yd (not adjacent); Pump Mdw; Radway Lane (a series of fields along a ½ mile stretch of the Norton/Audlem road includes Big, Near, Far, Further ~ ~, ~ ~ Croft, Mdw: the n. could be 'riding way' or 'red way', *v.* LPN 95); Reed Mdw; Ridding, Clarke, Long; Ridding, Cromers, Lower, Upper ('cleared land'); Round Mdw (sub-circular); Sand Bank; Sandbank Fd, Sandhole Fd (adjoining); Sandpit Moor, Little, Farther, Near, Middle; Schoolhouse Fd, Mdw; Shootingbutt Croft (on edge of village); Shores Coppice; Sidling (2; not near each other, both on parish boundary, nothing distinctive in shapes); Stonery Croft; Storking Hill; Tern Croft, Fd (1635, by R. Tern); Tillers Ridding; Timberway, Big ~, ~ Lane; Tinkers Croft (cf. *Tinkers Lane* 1635); Townsend, Far, Near (at N. end of Norton village); Turners Lsw; Watering Pit (tiny enclosure); Well Lsw; Winningtons Croft; Yd (*freq* in village, including Far, Near, Handsons, Pixleys, Higher); Yewtree Mdw.

(b) *Backside* 1701; *Intake* 1682; *Mill Field* 1612; *Parsonage Croft* 1635; *Town Field towards Bearstone* 1612.

Prees

The parish-name is discussed in Part **1**. It is a pre-English name from PrW ***pres** 'brushwood', which became Modern Welsh *prys* 'copse, thicket'. The discussion in Part **1** requires emendation as regards the date of lengthening of the vowel in the PrW word. This was said (following LHEB) to be 7th-century, but subsequent studies, for which *v.* EPNS *Journal* 25, p. 55, show it to have happened in the 6th century.

As treated in the tithe award the parish contains seven townships: Darliston, Fauls, Mickley, Millenheath, Prees, Sandford, Steel and Whixall. Whixall has been treated *infra* as a separate unit, as it is a civil parish. The townships are uneven in size, ranging from Millenheath, with only 64 numbered fields, to Prees with 1,737.

1. DARLISTON (SJ 582334)

Derloueston 1199 SAS 2/X (FF)

Derelaweston' 1255–6 *Ass*, *Derlawston* 1291–2 *Ass*, *-ton* 1308 Ipm, 1327 SR

Darlaston 1577 Saxton, 1655 SAS 1/XLVII, 1695 Morden, *Darleston(e)* 1721, 61 PR(L) 11

'Deorlāf's estate', *v.* **tūn**. There are two instances of this name in St.

THE FORD, 1833 OS. A road crosses a tributary of Bailey Brook here, *TA* has *Ford Meadow*.

GREENLANE.

HEATHGATES, *Heath Gates* 1833 OS.

LOWER COLLEGE, *The College* 1833 OS.

PREES LOWER HEATH, 1833 OS, *v.* 201.

ROSE COTTAGE.

UPPER COLLEGE: 1833 OS has *Hills Arms* here.

Field-Names

Forms in (a) are 1840 *TA*.

(a) Astley's Fd; Bank Fd; Barley Fd; Barn Yd (2); Bentley's Banks; Big Yd; Black Acre; Black Bank; Cage, Far, Near, The Little, The Cage Mdw (VEPN *s.v.* **cage** gives 'enclosures and lockable buildings', also several more specific usages, none of which seems appropriate here); Church Fd; Clemley (6 small rectangular enclosures at N. end of Prees Lower Heath are Second, Third, Fourth, Top, Long and Far Clemley: *v.* Prees *infra*); Clover Fd; Common Fd (2); Common Pce, Near and Top ~ ~; The Corner Croft; Cover (several plantations on edge of Prees Lower Heath, including Causeway, Big and Little Slang); Croft (*freq* in Prees Lower Heath settlement, including Bottom, Top, Calves, Flash, Marl, Old, Pigsty, Well); Croft (*freq* in village, including Pinfold, Rye, Sir Rowland's); Croft (clusters on N. boundary include Darlaston, Far, Near, Long, Marl, Road); Cross Hays (by road-junction); Dodd's Fd; Field, Barn, Broad, Long; Field, Barn, Far, Garden, Rough; Field, Ferny, Long, Middle; Fingerpost Fd (by crossroads); Four Lane End Fd (other side of crossroads from preceding); Gale Bank, Mdw (bog myrtle); Grassy Mdw, Yd; Griggy Fd, Pces (heather); Haynes's Fd; Heath Fd, Bottom and Top ~ ~ (on boundary with Millenheath); Heath Fleck; Hoofords Mdw (Hoofoot Croft in Darliston adjoins); Long Fd; Lower Fd; Marsh Mdw; Massey's Fd; Meadow, Far, Near, Prestons, below the House, Old, Moss; Meadow, Brook, The Hop, Long, Rye Croft, Sandfords, Well, below House; Meadow, Big, Orchard, Rough Wd; Meadow, ~ Bank; Middle Croft; Mill Fd Mdw (by Old Mill in Sandford); Moor, The First, Near, Stubble; Moor, Big, Little, Far, Near (N. of Sidleymoor Brook); The Moss (2 small fields in N.E. corner); Mowing Mdw; Parkins Hay; Pea Fd; Pennsylvania (small enclosure by a group of Moor ns.); Piece, The Far, The New; Plantation Fd; Platt Bank, Far, Near (**plat**[1] 'footbridge', road crosses brook here); Pool Fd, Lsw (by Sandford mill pool); Poverty Patch (one of a cluster of small enclosures at N. end of Prees Lower Heath); Sandhole Fd (2); School Fd (school shown on *TAMap* and on 1900 6"); Shinglers Fd, ~ Top (not adjacent); Shooting Butts (near village); Stable Croft; Three Corner Pce (tiny triangle); Tidley, Bottom, Middle (*v.* Fauls f.ns. *infra*); Townsend, Big and Little ~, ~ Mdw (at N. end of village); Watsfords Fd; Well Lw, Mdw; Weston's Fd, Far; Wheat Bank; Yard (*freq* in Prees Lower Heath settlement); Yard (*freq* in village, including Back Lane, Great, Old, the last is a large field); Yard, Jones, Big, Little, Old (on N. boundary with Croft ns.); Yem Croft, Mdw.

2. FAULS (SJ 590327)

Le Faall 1301 BM

Le Falles 1363 Ipm, *Falles* 1383 SBL 265, *Fawles* 1672 HTR

OE *(**ge**)**fall**, which is considered to mean 'clearing'. The term is well represented in Ch, PN Ch **5.1** 173, sometimes, in Wirral, referring to turf mosses. 'Woodland clearing' seems appropriate in the present instance, as blocks of fields called *Stocking* and *Ridding* in *TA* adjoin the settlement.

The GR given above is for the settlement called *Fauls Green* on 1833 OS, Faulsgreen on later OS maps. The 1900 6" map has Fauls Fm to the S. of this. FAULSGREEN is *Farsgreen* 1695 Morden, *Fauls Green* 1782 *SBL 6253*, *Faux Green* 1806 PR(L) 11; and *Green Field* and *Meadow* adjoin on *TAMap*. This settlement is at a road junction and may represent a short migration from an earlier site.

NORTHWOOD: *Northwude* 1199 SAS 2/X (FF), *Northwode* 1308 Ipm, *Northwood* 1699 PR(L) 13, probably named in relation to the vanished Marchamley Wd *supra*.

The 1900 6" and 1833 OS maps give the name Northwood to two farms ½ mile apart. The 1961 1" map calls the northern farm Northwood Grange and the southern one Northwood Fm.

MOAT HO: the moat is shown on 6" map.

Field-Names

Forms in (a) are 1843 *TA*.

(a) The Acre, Black Acre (in N.E. of township, near Leen ns.); America Fd (on N. boundary); Barn Fd (2); Black Acre, Far and Near ~ ~ (adjoining Tidley); Black Birch (adjoins Black Acre in N.E. of township: this and nearby Vaughan's Birch may contain a metathesised form of Britch 'newly-broken-in land'); Blank Lake; Brickkiln Fd; The Butcher's Fd, Butchers Mdw; Cockshutt, Near, Far, ~ Bank; Common, Far, Near, Long (on S. parish boundary); Common Fd, Lower, Middle, Top (on boundary with Darliston); Copy, Far, Near; Cote Fd (no building); Crabtree Bank; (The) Crim Cram (FN 11 lists Crim Cram as a term for a small piece of ground, but these two fields are of average size: perhaps a variant of *kim-kam* 'perverse' FN 25); Croft (*freq* in Faulsgreen, including Calves, Common, Long, Top); Croft, Far, Near (on W. boundary); Dulsons (*Dullsons Yard* 1762 *SBL 5483*, *Dulson's Crofts* 1763 *SBL 5498*); Eccleston's Croft; Field, Barn, Bottom, Middle, Top; Flat, Lower, Upper; Flax Butt; Further Moor; Garden Croft, Mdw; Goose Croft, Big, Little; Gorsty Bank; Green Fd, Mdw (by Faulsgreen); Hay Knowl, Little and Middle ~ ~, The Hay Knowles; Hays; Hill Park (not near The Park, no apparent reason for either n.); House Croft; House Fd, Mdw; Hurst, Big, Little, ~ Mdw; (The) Inclosure, The Enclosure (adjoining Common ns. on S. boundary); Intake (2, both enclosed from road edges); Lane Pce; The Lawn Mdw; The Leen, Round Leen, The Big and Little Leen, Long and Old Leen Hill, Leens, Leens Bank, Mdw (11 fields E. of Faulsgreen, this may have been an open field: the n. may be from ME *layne*, *lain*, an unexplained field- and minor n. element discussed *supra* under Lionlane in Ellesmere); Leg of Mutton (shape-n.); Little Croft; Little Fd; Little Mdw; Long Acre (adjoins Tidley); Long Lsw (2); Massey's Croft; Meadow (fields along brook on S. boundary are Dawson's, Doghole, Forge, Middle, Park, Rushy, Long Mdw); Meadow, Big, Little; Middle Fd; Middle Lsw; Muck Fd; North, Big, Little, Big and Little Northwood Fd, Northwood Croft (W. of Northwood Fm); Old Yards; Orchard Fd; Ox Lsw; (The) Ox Mdw; Painter's Croft; The Park (Park Mdw adjoins); Pinfold Croft, Mdw; Pit Holes; Plain, Big, Little; Property (field in Faulsgreen); Rail Mdw; Randles Fd; The Ridding, Big, Little and Near Ridding (by Faulsgreen); Rough Moor; Rushy Pce; Rye Bank; Rye Lsw; Sawpit Fd; Seven Acres; Shutt Fd (Short Fd adjoins); Shutt (not near preceding); Sitch Fd ('drainage channel'); The Slang; Stackyard Fd; Stocking(s), Big, Little, Top, Upper, (The) Stocking (adjoining Ridding ns. N. of Faulsgreen, both are clearing terms); Stocking (not near preceding); Tall Tree Bank; Tidley (fields near boundary with Darliston are Tidley, The Tidley, ~ ~ Fd, Big, Lower, Higher, Long, Middle and Rough Tidley, with Bottom and Middle Tidley adjoining in Darliston: this may have been an open field); Well Fd; Wheat Croft; Whitley Ford, ~ ~ Mdw (6" map shows a footpath crossing a stream on N. boundary); Withy Fd, Little ~ ~; The Wood Fd, Northwood Fd; Wood Lsw; Yard (several in Faulsgreen including Gregory's, Top).

3. MICKLEY (SJ 615326)

Mitteleg' 1241–9 Lil, *Mitteleye* 1327 SR (p)
Mittonley 1308 Ipm, *Mittomleye* Ed 3 *SBL 5924* (p)
Mutteleye 1327 SR (p)
Mittley 1655 SAS 1/XLVII, 1672 HTR, *Mitley* 1765 *SBL 4264*
Mickley 1833 OS, 1843 *TA*

An etymology 'wood or clearing at a junction of streams', from **(ge)mȳðe** and **lēah**, would be sustainable on topographical grounds. Two forms suggest that the first element was dative plural. Mickley is between Bailey Brook and another tributary of the R. Tern, and there is a junction of these and several other streams with the Tern about 1½ miles downstream. Mickley could have been on the N. edge of a wood through which these streams flowed.

It is, however, difficult, perhaps impossible, to find parallels for development of *ð-l* to *tt-l*, and the forms are more compatible with a first element **mytt*, which would be totally obscure.

The 1900 6" map shows two farms, Mickley Fm and Upper Mickley, ⅓ mile apart.

HOARSTONE 1833 OS: the farm is not on a boundary, but *TA* has fields called *Big*, *Lower* and *Upper Hoarstone* W. of the farm, and these are on the boundary with Fauls township.

Field-Names

Forms in (a) are 1843 *TA*.

(a) Barn Fd (2); Barn Pce; Big Fd; Big Mdw (2); Brickkiln Fd, Little ~ ~; Calves Croft; Carthouse Lsw; Chamber End (2 fields by Hoarstone, near Mickley Wd: VEPN *s.v.* **chambre** gives 'hunting lodge' as one of the meanings); Clover Fd, Big, Little; Clover Lsw, Large, Little, Middle; Common Fd, Big, Little, Lower (by Mickley Fm); Cow Lsw; Daisy Bank; Ferny Bank; The Holmes (possibly a reflex of **hamm** but the field is a strip on the outside of a stream-bend, so not typical); House

Mdw, Little ~ ~ (by Mickley Fm); Kiln Croft; Long Croft; Marl Fd, Big, Near; Meadows, The Mdw; Mickley Fd, Mdw; Mickley Wd, The Long Wd, The New Wd, Second, Lower and Hopkins New Wd, Great and Little Wd Mdw (a group of fields occupying the centre of the township); Old House Fd, Bottom, Top (no building); Pool Mdw; Purgatory Mdw, Long; Rough; The Rough Yds; Ryegrass Fd; Sand Fd (2); The Shutt Fd; The Slade (a strip by Bailey Brook); Slang; Smith's Mdw; The Thistle Fd; Tobacco Fd (FN 32 lists this as one of two Sa f.ns. reflecting "attempts to grow tobacco"); Wall Fd (adjoins Well Fd); Well Fd (3); Withings Bridge Mdw ('willows').

4. MILLENHEATH (SJ 578354)

Milneheth 1282 InqMisc, 1283 Pat
Mulnethe, *Mulnehethe* 1283 InqMisc
Mill-heath 1672 HTR
Millenheath 1796 RTH, *Millen Heath* 1833 OS

'(Wind)mill heath', *v.* **myln**, **hǣð**.

BRICKFIELD PLTN.
LARCH PLTN.
MILLENHEATH BRIDGE, COTTAGES (*TA* has *Old House* here), PLTN.

Field-Names

Forms in (a) are 1843 *TA*.

(a) Black Butts (probably referring to open-field strips); Broom, Higher, Lower, ~ Mdw; Brown Hill; Far Middle Fd; Flatt, Far, Near, Middle (this and Middle Fd, Black Butts, Stony Loom and Gorsty Flat suggest a tiny open field area); Great Mdw; Griggy Pce ('heathery'); Hatch Pce; Hazle Croft; Heath Pce; Henberry Mdw; Higgins Pce; Innage, with Rough; Kempley; Lime Pce; Long Croft; Long Fd; Marlpit Croft; Moors, Big ~, Great and Round Moor (a road curves round Round Moor); New Pce; Park, ~ Mdw (no apparent reason for n.); Patch (tiny enclosure); Pentre Cloud (Welsh *pentre(f)* 'hamlet', but there are no buildings in these two fields: Cloud might represent Welsh *clwt* 'patch of land'); Piece of Common (by Prees Higher Heath); Pingle (tiny enclosure, *pingle* is a form of **pightel**); Quab Mdw ('marsh', ultimately from ***cwabba**); Sandy Croft; Sow Fd Horn (pointed field in stream-junction); Stony Loom (a 'land' n., near Flatt); Town Mdw; Triangle Fd; Weary Oak (FN 48–9 lists this with "mysterious tree-names"); Wet Gate, Great, Little, Near (by road to Calverhall); Yard, Old Yd (by Millenheath hamlet).

5. PREES (SJ 557335)

CLEMLEY (field-name). A reappraisal of the field-name Clemley and its variants (of which the most frequent is Clemley Park) is appropriate in the context of Prees township as the Tithe Award has seven instances, and these fields are in a clearly defined topographical setting. Details of the seven are given below. *Clem-*, *Clemley* ~ names were discussed briefly in Part **2** 8, Part **3** 70 and Part **4** 123, with references to previous discussions in PN Db 759, and PN Ch **3** 47. The most recent treatment is in VEPN *s.v.* **clām**.

Two suggestions have been made for the first element *Clem-*, sometimes *Clam-*. The earliest was by Cameron, PN Db 759, listing Clam Park as an infertility name, associating it with the verb *clem* 'to starve'. This is the interpretation of Sa instances followed in FN 25, but more credence has generally been given to the later suggestion by Dodgson, in PN Ch **3** 47, of derivation from an OE **clǣme* 'muddy place' from **clām**, modern dialect *cloam*. This second suggestion led to the field-name term being discussed under **clām** in VEPN, but with the acknowledgment of the Cameron alternative. 'Muddy place' was adopted without qualification by John Field in *A History of English Field-Names* 39, with Clemley Park Db 142 cited as one of the examples.

Work in progress on the Shropshire survey is revealing that this group of names is exceptionally well represented in north Shropshire, where several townships have two instances and Prees has seven. The context of the Prees examples gives strong support to the 'hunger' interpretation. Five of them are in the north of the township in the area called Prees Higher Heath. On the *TAMap* this area is partly occupied by 'plantations' and 'allotments'. These are surrounded by a dense fringe of tiny enclosures, each with its own name; and among these are four Clemleys, also a Hunger Hill and a Labour in Vain, the latter adjoining one of the Clemley fields. Gorsty, Grig and Griggy are frequent qualifiers. Adjoining the southern edge of this belt of tiny enclosures are four larger fields called The Clemley and Little, Lower and Top Clemley: these are at approx. GR 567346, between The Fields and Manor Ho. In the south of the township, in Prees Lower Heath, there is another cluster of tiny fields, of which two adjacent ones are called The Clemley and two elsewhere in the group are Big and Little Clemley: here also Gorsty ~ and Griggy ~ names are prominent.

There can be little doubt about the nature of the land on these two heaths, and infertility is much more likely to be referred to than mud. Another piece of evidence (acknowledged to be significant in the VEPN article) is the field-name Clem Guts in Wem *infra*, and there is also the delightful Clem Gander, cited in FN 25. *Clem-gut* is noted in EDD as a Sa term for poor food. Clemson in Sutton upon Tern adjoins Famish Croft.

The second element in Clemley might be -ly used as an adjectival suffix and assimilated to the common place-name ending -ley. Against this, but not necessarily fatal to it, is that the usual adjectival suffix is -y, as in Gorsty, Griggy, and that Clemley could be used as a simplex name, sometimes with the definite article. The frequent addition of Park can be explained as ironic if the reference is to exceptionally poor land.

Clemley (Park) is one of several field-name terms which were in use in the 19th century and must have been understood by farmers in groups of counties, but which did not find their way into written sources and thence into dictionaries, and presumably did not survive late enough to get into EDD. Another such is Puppies Parlour, discussed in EPNS *Journal* 22; this was known in Berkshire, Hertfordshire, Oxfordshire, Warwickshire and Worcestershire.

As regards the date of the Clemley names, valuable evidence has recently come to light in the discovery of forms *Clemley* and *Clemley Park* in a document of 1615 in *SRO 322 box 2* for a f.n. which survived as Chelmley Park in the *TA* for Acton Reynald (Part **4** 99, *v*. Addenda *supra*). This is considerably earlier than the 1756 reference noted on p. 91. As NED says, however, "the simplex verb [i.e. *clem*] hardly appears before 1600", so the names are not likely to be of ME or OE origin.

PN Ch **2** 52 notes a minor name Clamhunger Wood and field-names Clemonga, Clamhanger, Clemhunger, which Dodgson (followed by VEPN and LPN) explained as from a compound of **clām** or **clǣme* with **hangra** 'sloping wood'. Dodgson says "the form has been influenced by ModEdial. *clam*, *clem* 'to starve' and **hungor**". In the light of the Sa evidence for Clem-, Clam- names it seems likely that this also is a 19th-century infertility name rather than an older name meaning 'muddy hanging wood'. The forms given in PN Ch are 19th-cent.

LEETON (lost). Entries for 1352 and 1356 in Pat refer to "Le(e)ton within the manor of Prees". This is a third instance of the name discussed (under Leaton) in Part **3** 82 and Part **4** 143. It appears to be a compound of **lēah** with **tūn**. This example, like Leaton N. of Shrewsbury, is in a heathland setting where woodland would be notable and valuable, so perhaps **lēah** has the sense 'wood' rather than 'clearing'.

LINFORD (SJ 562303): *Lymford'* 1291–2 *Ass*, *Linfoord* 1666 PR(L) 11, *Lindford* 1807 ib. 'Flax ford', *v*. **līn**, identical with Linford Bk, Lynford Nf. The Shrewsbury road crosses a small stream here.

PREES HIGHER and LOWER HEATH. Prees Higher Heath occupies a large area in the northern tip of the parish, and a settlement here may be the one designated *Hethe* 1199 SAS 2/X (FF), *La Hethe* 1255–6 *Ass*, 1352 Pat, and later *Heathe* 1655 SAS 1/XLVII, *Prees Heath* 1794 *et seq* to 1802 RTH. Prees Lower Heath, S.E. of Prees village, is so called 1792 PR(L) 10, 1798 PR(L) 2. This may be *Prees Town Heath* 1800 ib. RTH distinguishes between Prees Heath 1794 *et seq* and *Prees Lower Heath* 1783 *et seq* to 1803.

ALDERSEY, 1797 RTH, 1833 OS.

THE BRADES.

BRICK BARN.

BROADHAY, 1795 RTH, *Broad Hay* 1833 OS.

CORN MILL, *Prees Mill* 1833 OS.

CROOKMOOR, 1833 OS, ~ LANE, *Cruckmoor*, ~ *Bank* and *Meadow* 1843 *TA*.

CUMBERBATCH WD, perhaps transferred from Comberbach Ch.

DICKEN'S WD.

DOGMOOR, *Dogmorgate* 1779 PR(L) 10, *Dog Moor* 1833 OS, 1843 *TA*. T. Rowley, *The Shropshire Landscape* 165–8, gives an account of the enclosure of this 'typical marsh-common' in the 16th cent.

FERNYLEES, *Ferney Lees* 1787 RTH, *Ferny Leys* 1833 OS, *Ferny Ley* 1843 *TA*.

THE FIELDS.

GREEN'S GORSE.

THE GROVE.

HILL COTTAGE: the hill is the escarpment round the S. side of the block of raised ground on which the village stands. *TA* has fields called *Little*, *Long*, *Sandford's* and *Tylers Hill* curving round the cottage.

HOUGH, 1833 OS, 1843 *TA*, *The Hough* 1804 PR(L) 2. If an ancient name, probably **halh** in the sense 'water meadow'. PN Ch **5.1** 211 cites a number of instances of Hough from **halh**. The house is by Sidleymoor Brook.

JOHNSON'S COVERT.

LIGHTEACH, 1833 OS, ~ *Coppice* 1843 *TA*, *Leighteache* 1596–7 *SBL 1936*, *The Lighteach* 1658 PR(L) 9, *The Lightech* 1659 ib. Probably an ancient name 'light-coloured oak', from **lēoht** and **ǣc** dative of **āc**: **lēoht** is frequently combined with tree-species names.

LILYFIELDS, LILY HALL, *Lilly Hill* 1833 OS. *TA* has *New*, *Lower* and *Further Hall Field* here.

LOWER HEATH COPPICE.

MANOR HO, LANE: these are in the fringe of tiny fields on S. side of Prees Higher Heath.

THE MANSE.

MANSFIELD COTTAGE.

MILL HO, 1833 OS: on Prees Higher Heath, so a windmill.

THE NOOK, 1833 OS, NOOK COPPICE, LANE: *Nook* 1798 RTH.

PLAT, *Platt* 1833 OS: 'footbridge'.

PREESGREEN, *Prees Green* 1784 *et seq* RTH.

PREES HALL, 1843 *TA*.

PREES WD, 1801 RTH, 1833 OS, PREESWOOD FM.

RAG LANE FM, *Rag Lane* 1833 OS.

ROUND COVERT.

SANDYLANE, *Sandy Lane* 1833 OS, 1843 *TA*.

SIDLEYMOOR BROOK, *Big, Near, Far Sidley Moor, ~ ~ Field, Meadow* 1843 *TA*.

TWEMLOWS BIG WD: Twemlows is in Whitchurch *infra*.

TAMap shows *Lion P.H.* at the crossroads in the village. Ogilby's road map, 1675, shows a large house called *hare lane* a short distance N. of Prees Heath.

Field-Names

Forms in (a) are 1843 *TA*. This Award contains 1,737 named fields. In several areas of the township the land is divided into very small enclosures, and the names of these have not been listed. There is a fringe of such enclosures round Prees Higher Heath and a large cluster round Prees Green. Smaller clusters are at Prees Wood and Prees Lower Heath. Many of these tiny enclosures have ~ Croft or ~ Yard names. Most of the names of larger fields have been listed, but some ~ Croft and ~ Field names with obvious surnames have been omitted.

(a) Aldersay Croft (a short distance from Aldersey); Ash Croft (2); Bakehouse Croft; Bank, Big, Little (near but not adjacent); Banks, Far, Near, Middle, Cote Bank, The Broomy Bank; The Banks (2); Barn Croft, Fd (by Fernylee); Barn Fd (several); Barn Yd (several); Batty Crofts; Bears Mdw; Bentley's Bank, The Bank; Big Fd (several); (The) Big Hill, Big and Little Lower Hill; Big Mdw; Bishop's Mdw, Far and Middle ~ ~; The Bit (very tiny); Bleak Ends, Far ~ ~ (two fields called Blake Ends are ⅔ mile N.); The Boilet (*recte* Bylet, this is a short distance from Prees Mill and refers to a small island between brook and mill-stream, *v*. FN 41); The Booten, Broad, Big, Long, Top or Footway and Tyler's Booten (Booten Lane runs through the fields, The Broughtons, The Vicar's ~ adjoin); The Bran Pce; Brickkiln Fd (several); Bridge Mdw; Britains Rough, Big, Little; Broad Hay; Broad Lane;

Brockley, Big; Bromley Croft, Further, Great; Broomy Bank; Calves Croft; Calves Yd; Cardigan's Hayes; Carthouse Mdw; Castle Hays (near Crookmoor); Chidlow's Bank, Chidley's Crofts; Clemley (7, this recurrent f.n. has been accorded a separate article *supra*); Coalpit Lsw; (The) Common Fd (*freq*); Common Moor; Coppy Croft (by Lighteach Coppice); Corner Croft; Cotton Lane, Mdw (Cotton is in Wem); Countess Pltn; Cover (some woods in the two heaths have ~ Cover ns.); Cow Lsw; Cow Pasture, Far, Near; Crabtree Cover, Lsw; Crabtree Mdw (2); Croft(s) (*freq*, applied to tiny enclosures round habitations); Crow Birch (perhaps Britch); Dainty's Mdw; Daisy Croft; Dogkennel Fd; The Double Fd; Far Fd; Fence, Little; Flat Mdw (a division of Dogmoor); Footroad Mdw; Frog Pits; Four Square Fd (ironic, the field is irregularly shaped); Gansey Croft; (The) Gawmoor, Big ~ (*gall* 'barren place', ultimately OE **galla**); Gorsty Fd; Green Fd, Big, Little; Halfpenny Fd; Hall Mdw (by Prees Hall); Heath Fd; Heath Mdw; Helyards; Hemp Fd; Heys Mdw, The Big Heys, The Vicar's ~; The Hollins, Far, Near and Middle ~, Hollins or Crabtree Fd ('holly'); Hollins Bank; The Hollins, ~ ~ Bank (divisions of Dogmoor); Holly Birch Mdw (as elsewhere in this township Birch may be for Britch 'newly-broken-in land'); Hopwood, Big, Little; Hopwood Croft (not near preceding); Horse Pasture (2); Horse Pool, Far, Near; Intack (alongside road); Intake; Junkins Bank; Kiln Fd; Lacon Mdw, Top, Bottom, Further; Lady Mdw (2); Lime Pce; Little Intake; Little Patch; Long Fd (several); Long Lane; Lower Heath Cover (part of a large area of trees in Prees Lower Heath); Malthouse Croft, Maltkiln ~; Mare Pce; Marestalls (near Prees Mill, 'stagnant pond', OE *mere-steall*, noted 7 times in Ch, PN Ch **5.1** 281, and 5 in Sa, FN 22: the OE occurrence is noted in BTSuppl); Marl Croft; Marl Lsw, Further and Old ~ ~; (The) Meadow (several); Meadow (small fields surrounding Aldersey are Betton's, Chidlows, Foresters, Hands, Jones, Lady, Smith's, Wythens, Long, Broad, Lower Mdw); The Meadow, Broad, Dovehouse, Long and Pool Head Mdw; Meadow, Little, Long, Far, Middle, Hopyard; The Meagres; Middle Fd (several); Middle Pce; Milking Bank (by Brades); Mill Fd, Big, Mill Pool, The Pool Mdw (by Brades, downstream from Prees Mill); Moor, First, Second, Third, Small, Large, Long, Broad, Moor Cover; Moor (the portions of Dogmoor, which was enclosed in 16th cent., include Aldery, Far and Near Best, Bridge, Leaton and Shed Moor); Moor, Far, Middle, Near; Moors, Far Moor; The Moss; Moss Pit Fd; The Mound; Mud Fd; The Nagleys, Lower Nagneigh, Nagneigh Croft; New Mdw (a division of Dogmoor); Nook Mdw; Old Weir Hole; Ox Lsw (several); The Park, Park Mdw (no apparent reason for n.); Penny Knowles Bank, Mdw; Pingo, The Pinger, Pingel (small enclosures in Prees Lower Heath, *v.* **pingel**); Pit Hole Mdw; Pit Lsw (2); (The) Platt Gate Fd (by Plat); Pool Mdw, Pool Head Mdw (by Prees Mill pool); Prees Fd; Prees Mdw; Raddle Gates, Big, Little; Rail Pce, Lower and Top Railed Fd; The Red Hills, Red Hill Fd, Mdw (at W. end of semi-circle of hill-names for which *v.* Hill Cottage *supra*); Road Fd; The Rose Fd; Rough Lsw; Rough Pce; Round Mdw (2, both with a road curving round one side); Round Thorn; Rushy Fd; Rushy Pce, Big, Little; Ryegrass Fd; Sandford's Mdw, Further, Middle, Near; Sandhole Fd; Sandlands Mdw, Far Sandlands; Sergeant's Croft; Sheffield Walls; Sheep Fd; Sullins; Shepherd's Acre, Higher, Lower; Shutfield, Far (Near Shit Fd adjoins); Six Looms (i.e. six open-field strips, adjoins Way Butts); The Slang (between road and stream); Smithy Fd; Smithy Pce; Stack Bank; Tanpit Croft, Mdw, Tan Yd (by mill); The Tea Fd, Lower ~ ~ (not T-shaped); Temple Fd; Thistle Fd; Thorntree Fd; Three Cornered, Three Corner Fd (both triangular); The Townsend (at N. end of village);

Turnpike Fd, Far, Near (by Whitchurch road); Wall Lsw (2); Way Butts (adjacent to furlong-shaped fields S. of village); Weir Mdw; Well Fd, ~ Slade; Well Yd; White Birch (probably Britch); Windmill Fd, Big and Little ~ ~ (*Wynnemelfeld* 1413 Pat); Wood Fd (several); Wood Pce; Woodfint Mdw; Woolly Mdw, Little; Workhouse Fd; Yard, Brook, Lower (by Aldersey); Yewtree Fd.

6. SANDFORD (SJ 583340)
The township-name, which means 'sandy ford', is discussed in Part **1**, as Sandford is a DB manor.

AYCHLEY FM (SJ 608343), COTTAGES
Amcheleg 1241–9 Lil
Acheleg c.1243 Lil, *Acheley* 1655 SAS 1/XLVII
Achesleye 1327 SR (p)
Aytchley 1766 PR(L) 8
Ocheley (*Common*) 1843 *TA*

lēah may be 'wood' rather than 'clearing'. The first element might be an adjective *ǣcen* 'growing with oaks', as suggested in DEPN for Eachwick Nth but since 'oak wood' is so frequently Oakley, from **āc**, such a variant seems unlikely. A personal name **Ǣca* would suit. The 1241–9 form can be considered erroneous.

ASHFORD COVERT, GRANGE, ASHFORD GRANGE COTTAGES: *Ashford Pool* 1833 OS, *Assford's Pool*, *Plantation* etc. 1843 *TA*.
THE HALL, *Hall* 1833 OS.
HIGHTREES, the house is shown but not named on *TAMap*.
THE LAWN, *Sandford Lawn* 1833 OS.
OLD MILL.
SANDFORD POOL.

1833 OS shows *Wathens Rough*, *Whitacre Barn*, *Sandford Wood*. The last is probably *boscus de Saunford'* 1255–6 *Ass*. *Whitacre Barn* is near *Whittowell* f.ns. *infra*.

Field-Names

Forms in (a) are 1843 *TA*.

(a) Ash Flg; Barn Croft, Fd, Yd; Black Croft; Brandhurst, Big, Higher, Lower (if an old n. 'burnt wood', *v.* **brand**, **hyrst**); Broomy Bank; Broomy Lsw; Burys Ground; Cage Wd, Further, Near, Middle (perhaps referring to a lockable enclosure); Calves Croft; Clay Piddings (*sic* on *TAMap* but given as Clay Puddings FN 26, and listed with 'boggy' ns.); Clover Croft; Cockshade; Copnalls, Copnall Pce; Cow Lsw, Near ~ ~; Cows Mdw; Crabtree Fd; Crabtree Pce; Croft, Further, Near, Hands, Higher, Long (adjacent normal-sized fields); Deborah Loon, Higher (adjoins Ash Flg, Loon may be 'open-field strip'); The Dunsters (possibly Dunstall from ***tūn-stall** 'farm-site'); Ferny Fd; The Finish; The Foisiege; Further Wd; Frith Mygig; Gilt Hays; Goodridge Bank; Heath with Rough; Higher Fd and Barn; Hill, Further, Middle, Little Whittowell; Hill Lsw; Holding Croft, Near, Third, Fifth; Horse Pasture; Jackson's Pce; Large Wd; Leasow, Garnsey, Great, Long, Great Wd (adjoining, in N.W. corner); Lees, ~ Mdw; Lime Lsw; Long Croft; Marl Fd; Marl Lsw; Marsh Meadow (strips along Bailey Brook are Sandford, Mill, Bank, Little Orchard, Long (2), Mossy, Brook, New, Further Little and Cottage Mdw); Middle Fd; Mill Bank, Sandford Mill Pool (by Old Mill in Sandford hamlet); Moor (2); New Hay; Newlands; Old Yd; Pigtrough Mdw; The Platt (probably 'footbridge', adjoins Bailey Brook); Ollery Croft (alders); Pool Mdw, Long ~ ~; Rail Pce; The Reap and Moor; Rushy Fd; Rushy Pce; Ryley, The Ryley (2 fields a short distance apart); Salt Work(s) Rough (2 fields in centre of township); Sandford Heath; Sandy Croft; Sandy Pce, Further, Near; Sandy Pce, Bottom, Far, Long; Sir John's Pce; Slade (field with a wet patch, FN 18); The Square Pce; Thistly Fd; Top Mdw; Weston Fd; Wheat Lsw; Whittowell, Great, Little, ~ Barn and Fold (possibly connected with Whitacre Barn, which 1833 OS shows in this area); Wood Fd, Mdw; Yard, Barn, Brickkiln, Little (by hamlet).

7. STEEL (SJ 549365)

Steel is a DB manor, so forms are set out in Part **1**. The name is OE **stigel**, modern *stile*, probably referring to a passage through a fence or hedge. There is nothing remarkable in the topography, so a transferred sense such as 'steep ascent' is unlikely.

MOSS COVERT.

PADDOCK, 1843 *TA*.

PITHOLES PLTN, SLIPS PLTN: both *Plantation* 1843 *TA*.

STEEL GRANGE FM: the 2004 Landranger map has two farms called Steel Fm and Steel Grange Fm.

STEEL HEATH, 1806 PR(L) 10, 1833 OS, 1843 *TA*.

Field-Names

Forms in (a) are 1843 *TA*.

(a) The Acres; Bare Croft, Big, Little; Barn Butts; Barn Fd; Boar Croft; Brick Kiln Fd; Briery Fd; Broad Irons; Broomy Fd (2); Bull Yd; Calves Croft; Childs Croft, ~ ~ Mdw; Colts Croft; Croft(s) (small enclosures round Steel Heath include Croft before Door, up to House, at the end of the Barn, and Big, Little Croft); Croft, Lower and Middle (by Paddock); Flock Fd, Far, Near, ~ ~ Mdw; Foxholes, Big, Little; Grindley's Lsw, ~ New Lsw, ~ Big Fd, ~ Little Mdw, ~ Yds; Hawmoor Mdw, Haw Moor Lane; Heath Fd, Big, Little; High Fd, Far, Near (Low Fd adjoins); Leys

Fd; Littleworth, Near; Long Mdw; Madeley Fd, ~ ~ Corner; Marl Croft; (The) Meadow (other Mdw ns. along a stream which rises near Steel Heath and the stream which it joins on E. boundary are Big, Curn, Middle, Bottom Mdw, Mdw by the Stocks, Hawmoor, Lysters and Prees Mdw); Oak, Big, Little; Ox Fd, Big, Little; Patch, Big, Little (tiny enclosures at Steel Heath); Rough Fd, First, Second, Third, Fourth; Stockings, Big, Rough; Stocks Bank, Lower ~ ~; Whips Croft; Yard, Clover, Top (by Steel Heath); Yeoman's Fd.

Shawbury

The parish-name, 'manor-house by a small wood', is discussed in Part **1**.

There is a *TAMap* with the title *Lands in Shawbury Parish*. This shows fields in Acton Reynald, Shawbury, Edgebolton and Wytheford, but not in Charlton Grange or Muckleton. There is a map of Charlton Grange, 1846, in *CorbetMaps 2* (referred to as *Map* in this section), but nothing is available for Muckleton. Charlton Grange and Muckleton are the only areas designated as townships on the Index to Tithe Survey map, but as Edgebolton and Wytheford have clearly discernible areas on the *TAMap* it has seemed best to treat them also as discrete units.

Acton Reynald was included in Part **4** as a township of the Liberties of Shrewsbury, so is not treated here.

1. CHARLTON GRANGE (lost)

The township occupied the northern tip of Shawbury parish. It was a DB manor, so the name is discussed in Part **1**. It is one of two Sa instances of this common name, these being the furthest west examples in the Midlands.

The name means 'peasants' settlement', and the precise significance of the compound has been much discussed. The latest discussion is in VEPN *s.v.* **ceorl**, and this draws attention to suggestions other than the one put forward by H. P. R. Finberg in 1964, which was cited in Part **1**. The name survived into the mid-19th century as that of a township, but there appears to be no knowledge of the exact site of the settlement. It was a grange of Lilleshall Abbey.

CRIFTIN COPPICE, 1833 OS, 1846 *Map*: *v.* **cryfting**, literally 'small croft', common in N. Sa.

DAWSON'S ROUGH, ~ ~ *Coppice* 1833 OS, *Deacon's Rough* 1846 *Map*.

FORGE COPPICE, *Birchen Coppice* 1833 OS, *Birchy* ~ 1846 *Map*. On the 1846 map *The Forge Coppice* is a nearby field on R. Roden.

MORETONMILL. The mill is shown 1846 *Map*. It presumably belonged to Moreton Corbet, from which it is separated by this township.

Field-Names

Forms in (a) are from the 1846 *Corbet Map*, for which *v. supra*. Early forms are 1610 *SRO 322 box 2*, except where otherwise stated.

(a) Aldrey Rough (probably alders); Bannister Mdw; Cote Lsw (*Le Cote Leasow*); C(r)oomer Mdw, Croomers Coppice, The Big and The Little Coomer (6 fields, 1833 OS has Cromer Coppice here: cf. *Cromes Pytte* 1610, a surname *Cro(o)me* appears in this source); Deepmoor Mdw; The Far Fd (The Middle Fd adjoins); Griggy Fd (6 adjacent fields in centre of township, *grig* is a borrowing from Welsh *grug* 'heather'); Jebb's Croft; The Long Lsw; (The) Marl Fd; Moss Holes (*Moshale* 1248–9 *SBL 5408*, *Le Mossalles*, *v.* **mos**, **halh**); The New Pce; Paradise Mdw; Park(s) (4 adjacent fields on W. boundary are Big Parks and Middle Park, a nearby field is Binnals Park); Park Croft (not near other Park ns.); The Pool Mdw, Little ~ ~ (by the mill pond for Moreton Mill); Stanton Banks (on boundary with Stanton upon Hine Heath); The Stocking Mdw, Little ~ ~; Triangle Pce; Wood Pce.

(b) *Alyeteslege* 1334 *SBL 5413*, *Alietesleghe* 1340 *SRO 322/142* ('Ælfgeat's wood or clearing'); *Birchen Leasow*; *Bromfeld* 1494 Ipm, *Bromefeild Meadowe* ('broom field'); *The two Bromye Feilds*; *Calder Crofte*; *Charleton Heath al. Le Oxe Heath*; *Eykens Meadowe*; *Farthing Meadow*; *Le Grasse Leasowe*; *Hole Meadowe*; *Le Horsse Heath*; *Peplowes Meadow*; *Symcocke Meadowe*; *Welmedowe* 1336 HAC ("at Cherleton": there is some editorial confusion in HAC with another 'spring meadow' in Sleap in Crudgington).

2. EDGEBOLTON (SJ 572220)

The township name is a doublet of Edgebold, S. W. of Shrewsbury, and was discussed in Part **1** together with that name: *v.* also Part **4** 148. In spite of the modern forms both names are clearly shown by early spellings to be compounds of **hām** with a personal name *Ecgbeald(a)*.

WYTHEFORD WD: *Wythyford Wood* 1833 OS, *Rumours Coppice or Witheford Wood* 1839 *TA*. *Rumours* may be 'rough marsh' from **rūh** and **mōr**; there is another instance in Pontesbury, Part **2** 39. *Rommore Lake* 1725 *SBL 6526*, in neighbouring Muckleton, probably contains the name, with *lake* 'small stream'.

Field-Names

Forms in (a) are 1839 *TA*. Early forms for which a date but no source is given are from *SRO 322 box 2*. Those without date or source are 1588 *ib*. Some of the 1588 ns. are from a perambulation but these have been presented in alphabetical order.

(a) The Acres; Almshouse Lsw; Backsides (the gardens of the hamlet back onto this field); Barn Yd, Near, Far, Middle; Breech, Big, Smalls, Far, Lower, Near; Brick

Croft, Lower; Brook Lsw; Broom, Big, Little, Near, Middle; Cow Lsw; Davies's New Pce; Gouge Pce; Hollybush Lane; Hough Mdw (by a stream, probably **halh**); Little Park (no apparent reason for the n.); Hare Lsw; Morgan's Croft; New Lsw (a group of fields on N. edge of Wythemore Wd includes Lower, Upper, Middle, Far, Near and Little New Lsw); Turnpike Pce (by road to Market Drayton, *Toll Gate* shown on *TAMap*).

(b) *Brade Meadow* 1615; *Coltresich* l.14th HAC, *Culsuche*, *Cultersich Pool* 1588, *Cultesiche* 1594 (*v.* **sīc** 'small stream drainage channel', first el. ME *culter*, ModE *coulter* 'knife on the blade of a plough', perhaps in a transferred topographical sense: the word has not hitherto been noted as a p.n. el.); *Edgbaldon Heath*, *Moss*; *Le Harde Wey* l.14th HAC; *Hernesall* 1600; *Le Hilles* 1594; *The High Heades* ("a small bancke or rysinge" in Hine Heath); *Hyne Gate*, *Heath*, Lane; *The Incheharne*, *Walles Incharne*; *Lapech*, *Lapeche Gate*; *Mucheshurste* l.14th HAC, *Mychelhurst* (the 1588 perambulation goes "betwixt Muckleton Mychelhurst and Edgbaldon Mychelhurst", which indicates a 'large wooded hill' straddling the township boundary, *v.* **mycel**, **hyrst**); *Nomans Pleck* 1601 *CourtR*; *Olyvers Dych*; *Oswastreuswei* 1338 *SRO 322/131*, *Oswestree Lane* (Oswestry is about 20 miles N.W. so it is curious that this should be seen as a route leading there: in the 1588 perambulation it is "an olde lane called ~"); *The Oxe Waste*; *Le Quabbe Pitt* 1595 (*quab* 'marsh', from ***cwabbe**); *Le Salemos* l.14th HAC ('willow bog', *v.* **salh**, **mos**); *Le Slades* 1594 (probably an early instance of *slade* 'wet patch in field'); *Staunton Mosse*; *Woodde Dole* (shared meadow by a wood); *Woodwalles Waste* (ME *wodewal*, dialect *woodwall*, a bird-name).

3. MUCKLETON (SJ 594210)

Muchelitune c.1200 *SBL 5392* (p)

Moclyton 1255–63 HAC, *Mokelyton'* 1291–2 *Ass*, *Mocliton* c.1307 *SBL 407*, *-ton'* 1320 *SBL 5410* (p)

Muclinton' 1255–6 *Ass*, *Muklinton'* 1271–2 *Ass*

Moklinton' 1271–2 *Ass*, *Mokelinton* 1284–5 FA, *Moclinton'* 1291–2 *Ass*, *Moclynton* 1336 *SRO 322/133*

Muglynton' 1291–2 *Ass*, *Moglynton* 1387 *SRO 322/208*

Mokelton 1327 SR (p), 1397 InqMisc, 1398 Pat, *Mokylton* 1401 Pat, *Mocleton* 1564 *SBL 10775*

Mokleston 1345 Pat, *Mukleston* 1701 PR(L) 11

Muckleton 1577 Saxton *et seq*, *Muccleton* 1589 *SBL 6512*

Moculton 1590 *SBL 6511A*, 1626 *SBL 6511*

'Estate associated with Mucel', an -**ingtūn** compound.

BROOMS COPPICE and HOARHEATH COPPICE: this is an elongated wood, the northern part is *Brooms Coppice* 1833 OS, the southern part is *Greens Coppice* ib.

THE GORSE.

MUCKLETON BANK, 1806 PR(L) 20.

MUCKLETON MOSS, 1833 OS, *Muckleton Heath or Moss* 1588 *CourtR*.

OLD POOL (a wood), *Hazles Coppice* 1833 OS.

POOL HO, *The* ~ ~ 1833 OS.

Field-Names

No 19th-cent. f.ns. are available for Muckleton. Earlier names dated 1701 are *SBL 6524*, 1725 are *SBL 6526*.

(b) *Annes' Leasow* 1725; *Backside, The Further* 1701; *The Birchen Leasow* 1725; *Brattings Meadow* 1725; *Broad Lakes* 1725 (*lakes* probably in the sense 'drainage channels'); *The Brooms* 1701; *Butchers Croft* 1701; *Butt Croft* 1725; *Calves Croft* 1701; *The Causy Pitt Leasow* 1701 (probably 'causeway'); *Cooks Meadow* 1725; *The Cow Leasow* 1725; *The Cross Pavement* 1725; *Duff House Yard* 1725; *Embry's Croft* 1725; *The Flax Butt* 1725; *The Furlong or Wheate Leasow* 1701; *Golden Meadows* 1725; *Gossages Leasow* 1701; *Hengorst* 1725; *The Hill Field, Leasow* 1701; *Hodgkiss Field* 1617–18 *SBL 2993*; *Hopyard* 1701; *Lawley's Yard* 1725; *The Leayes* 1701; *The Lowes* 1617–18 *SBL 2993*, *The Lows* 1701; *Marlefield* 1701; *The March* 1701; *Masons Wast* 1669 *SBL 1662*; *Mill Croft* 1701; *The Monney Crofts* 1701; *The New Piece* 1725; *The Olde Feild* 1725; *The Peas Crofts* 1725; *Ye Port Way Feild* 1617–18 *SBL 2993*; *Portway* ~ 1701 (there is no obvious portway here); *Ribbitchyard* 1701; *Rommore Lake* 1725 (*v.* Wytheford Wd *supra*); *Sapling Britch* 1701; *The Six Butts* 1725 (i.e. six open-field strips); *Steynesbruche* 1255–63 HAC (*v.* **bryce**); *Town Meadow* 1701; *The Twelve Score* 1725 (Twelve and Ten Score f.ns. are noted FN 12, *v.* also Part **4** 118); *Wallsich* 1701, *Little Woolsich* 1725 (*v.* **sīc**); *Watt Croft* 1701; *White Britch* 1701; *White Leasow* 1701; *Whittmore Fields* 1701, *Whitmore Feild* 1725.

4. SHAWBURY (SJ 558214)

CARRADINE (lost, approx SJ 551217)

Kaderwardynes Gorstes 1348 *SRO 322/155*

Carwardyne 1588 *SRO 322 box 2 et freq* with variant spelling *-dine*, *Old Carwardine* 1760, 82, 4 PR(L) 1

Carradine 1660 PR(L) 1, 1833 OS, 1900 OS 6"

Second element **worðign**. The single ME spelling suggests that the first element could be PrW ***cadeir** 'chair', Modern Welsh *cadar*, which has been postulated in a number of names, including Catterlen PN Cu 182, Chadderton and Chatterton PN La 50, 64, Chatterley St (DEPN), Catterton PN WRY **4** 236–7, Caterham PN Sr 311–12. However, Richard Coates, in CV, regards the suggestion of such a derivation for these names questionable, and he says in the glossary (p. 348) "*cadeir* 'chair' has not been safely disentangled from other early elements; the representation of these in English names needs further careful study".

In addition to the caution induced by this statement it should be noted that the transferred use of ***cadeir** as a hill-name, found, e.g., in Cader Idris in Wales, would not be appropriate for Carradine. For the present the Shawbury name can only be added to the list of names in C(h)ader-, C(h)ater-. The superficially similar names, Carwardine HePN 140 and Carden PN Ch **4** 53–4 are both **worðign** compounds with different spellings for the first elements.

On the 1900 6" map Carradine is the name of a single house by a road from Shawbury to Grinshill. The area is now part of an airfield.

BROOKS PLTN.

THE DOG.

FOX & HOUNDS P.H.

THE GROVE, 1833 OS.

MATTHEWS COPPICE, 1833 OS, 1839 *TA*.

NEW MOSS.

THE ONE HO, *v.* Wain Ho in Wem *infra*.

SHAWBURY BRIDGE.

SHAWBURY GROVE.

SHAWBURY HEATH, 1588 *SRO 322 box 2*, 1666 *SBL 5894*, 1833 OS, *Shabrie Heathe* 1511 *SBL 5853*. In 1588 this is "magnum vastum sive bruera".

SHAWBURY PARK, 1807 PR(L) 20, 1833 OS, *Le parke de Schauburi* 1338 *SRO 322/131*. SHAWBURY PARK WD, *Park Coppice* 1839 *TA*.

THE SLIPS.

SPRINGFIELD COTTAGE.

STONE HO.

WHITEGATE.

Field-Names

Forms in (a) are 1839 *TA*. Earlier forms for which no source is given are *SRO 322 box 2*. Those for which neither date nor source is given are 1588 *ib*.

(a) Appletree Croft; Bargymoor, Lower and Upper ~, ~ Mdw (8 fields S. of church, *Bargamore* 1679 GT); Barn Lsw; Barn Yd (large field adjoining Shawbury Park); Bolas Waste (1679 GT, c.1760 *CorbetMap*, possibly a detached property of Bolas, 6 miles east: most of the area, in N. tip of township, with this n. is blank on *TAMap*); Brakes, Big, Near; Brickley's Pce; Brook Mdw, Big and Little Brookes;

Broomy Lsw; Chantry Lsw (1679 GT, a church maintenance n.); Clemley, Far, Near (*v.* Clemley in Prees *supra*, these fields are *Gorsty Pces* on *CorbetMap* of c.1760: they are between Great Gosty Lsw and Marl Waste); Common Pces (on N. edge of Shawbury Heath); Coney Burrow; Coppice Mdw (by Park Coppice); Cote Lsw, Far, Near; Cureton's Croft; Ditchers Pce; Ferny Lsw; Fridays, Big, Little and Cowleys (3 fields called Saturdays adjoin); Gorsty Lsw, Great; Head(s), Lower; Heath Ground (on N. edge of Shawbury Heath); Heath Lsw; Henshaw Lsw (not near following); Hornshaw Mdw (*The Hornesow Meadow* 1720 *SBL 6532*); Horse Course; Knaves Castle, ~ ~ Mdw (1900 6" map shows a small building here); Lawns, Sandy ~ (near Shawbury Park); Lime Lsw; Long Lsw (2); Lower Ground; Marl Waste, Lower, Upper (cf. *Marl Piece* 1679 GT); Middle Heath, Far, Near, Middle, Lower (*Le Middleheth* 1269–82 HAC, *Middleheath* 1597 *CourtR*); Middle Waste (adjoins Marl Waste); Moors, Moor Coppice, ~ ~ Bank, Mdw (cf. *The Moore*); Moss Lakes; Mount, Broad, Green, Horseleap, Marlpit (4 fields S. of Park Coppice); Nessage, Long, Near; New Mdw; New Pce; Oaktree Lsw; Outlands Pits; Ox Lsw, ~ ~ Coppice; Paddock, Paddocks Pce (by Shawbury Park); Park Lsw, Far, Near, Park Mdw, Big ~ ~ (perhaps marking limits of a park round the house called Shawbury Park, *Park Meadow* 1679 GT); Rail Pce; Rushy Pce, Far, Near; Sandy Hole; Sheep Lsw; Sow & Pigs (another in Alveley, *v.* FN 44); Steadman's Folly (near Shawbury Park); Stony Flg; Sythe Ground; Tanner's Pce; Thompson's Pce; Townsend, Far, Near (near N.W. corner of village, cf. *Townsend Leasow* 1679 GT); Twelve Score, Far and Near ~ ~ (*v.* Muckleton f.ns. *supra*); Wheat Croft; Wood Pce; Yard, Far, Long.

(b) *Le Barbican* 1338 *SRO 322/131*, *Barbican* (OFr **barbecane** 'outer fortification of a city or castle, fortified gate or bridge' (VEPN) occurs in a number of town-names, but it is unexpected in the present context: in the 1338 reference it is associated with Shawbury Park, and in 1588 it is a *clausum terre*); *Le Bekenesbrugge* 1249 *SBL 5402* (apparently 'bridge of the beacon'); *Berringtons Yarde*; *The Blacke Lakes* 1589 (probably drainage channels); *Broadyard Ends* 1593, *Le Broad Yard* 1599; *Le Bruche* 1249 *SBL 5409*, *Le Britche* 1593 (*v.* **bryce**); *Le Chirchemedewe* 1279 Lil, *Church Meadowe* 1589; *Cressewalbroke* 1269–82 HAC, *Crassewallebroke* 1279 Lil, *Creswall Brooke*, *steppinge stones called Creswall Stones* 1589 ('cress spring'); *Crokesforlonge* 1269–82 HAC; *Cronckhill* 1588, *Cronkhills* c.1760 *CorbetMap* ('crane hill', *v.* **cranoc**); *Le Crosmeduwe* 1388 *SRO 322/131*; *Crukson's More* 1596 *CourtR*; *The Double Harrowes*; *Le Dynnemor* 1334 *SBL 5414* ('Dynna's marsh'); *Graungehull* (Charlton was a grange of Haughmond); *Halycros Gate*; *Hemmesleg* c.1240–60 HAC, *-le* 1242 SAS 4/VI (a wood, first el. possibly pers.n. *Hemmi*); *Le Heymore*, *-mer* c.1240–60 HAC, *Le Haymor* 1338 *SRO 322/131*, *Hay More* 1588 *CourtR* ('hay marsh' *v.* **hēg**, **mōr**); *Home Barne*, *The Home Barne Gate*; *Huyt Crofte*; *Ingriythemedewe* 1269–82 HAC ('Ingrith's meadow', from ME fem. pers.n.); *Knysich* 1596 *CourtR*; *Leas Yarde*; *Lorteleye* 1291–2 *Ass* ('dirt wood', *v.* **lort(e)**, **lēah**, the same compound occurs in Loatleys PN ERY 207); *Molkebur* 1269–82 HAC; *Moreton Waste*, *The Waste Gate*; *Neither Yard Hedge* 1593; *Owse Britches*; *Prestley Wood* 1592 *CourtR*; *Sacheburywey* 1244–67 HAC, *Schaubureseye* 1279 Lil, *Schawebureye* 1285 Ch, *Eye Meadowe* 1588, *The Eye Meadowe alias Shawbury Haye* 1589 (*v.* **ēg**, here probably in the sense 'well-watered land'); *Shawbury Poole alias Criftinge Poole* (cf. Criftin Coppice in Charlton Grange *supra*); *Le Sicheforlonge* 1269–82 HAC (*v.* **sīc**); Stodefolde 1269–83 HAC ('stud-ford'); *Tunstall Feild* 1593, *Dunstall Feild* 1599 (*v.* ***tūn-stall**); *Le Waste*; *Wemmewode* 1291–2 *Ass* (cf. The Wems in Adderley *supra*, this may be a third instance of the term which gives the parish-name Wem); *Whetenebruche* 1334 *SBL 5414* ('newly cultivated land with wheat', *v.* **hwǣten**, **bryce**); *The Whyte Syche*, *Le Whitesiche* (in Shawbury Heath, 'white drainage ditch'); *Wolfusbruche* 1338 *SRO 322/131* (*v.* **bryce**, first el. probably a pers.n.); *Wymehurst Gate*; *Le Yarde Meadowe*.

5. WYTHEFORD (SJ 572192)

The township-name, which means 'willow ford', is discussed in Part **1**. There are two small settlements (Great and Little) on either side of R. Roden, both of which are DB manors.

WYTHEFORD BRIDGE.
WYTHEFORD FORGE, 1833 OS.
WYTHEFORD HEATH, 1833 OS, *Wythiford* ~ 1588 *SBL 322 box 2*.

Field-Names

Names in (a) are 1839 *TA*. Forms dated 1588, 9 are *SRO 322 box 2*.

(a) Aldrey Lsw (probably alders); Birchtree Lsw (cf. *Birchen Leasowe* 1589, 1593 *CourtR*); Brooms Hill; Calves Croft; Common Pce (on N. edge of Wytheford Heath); Cote Lsw; Fox Mdw; Gorsty Fd; Hell Mdw; Hill, Big, Little; Horse Croft; Inn Mdw; Long Lsw; Marlpit Lsw; Muck Lsw; Noghouse Mdw (*nog* is coarse hemp, *v.* FN 31); Park Lsw (Ercall Park adjoins); The Three Crofts; Troy Mdw (probably referring to a turf maze, *v.* PN O 235: the field is at approx. SJ 576184); Walton Wd (by road to Walton in High Ercall); Wass Moor (probably from ***wæsse** 'alluvial land which floods and drains quickly', *v.* Part **1** under Bolas and Buildwas: the field overlooks a meandering stretch of R. Roden, with two Water Fields adjoining, one on opposite bank); Water Fd (2); Wood, Big, Little.

(b) *Fole Bridge* 1588; *Le Knoll* 1589; *Organs Folde* 1589; *Pemleye, boscus de* 1588.

Stanton upon Hine Heath

The parish-name, which means 'settlement on stony land', and the affix, 'heath of the servants', are discussed in Part **1**. There are five Stantons in Shropshire, and in this county the name refers to stony soil rather than to the proximity of megaliths. The significance of the Heath name is problematical. OE **hīwan**, gen. pl. **hīgna** usually refers to a monastic household in pre-Conquest names, but in those of later origin, as Hine Heath probably is, the ME reflex **hine** is considered to refer to the servants of a lay household. Cf. Hinstock *supra*.

There are *TAMaps* for four townships, Harcourt, High Hatton, Moston and Stanton. A fifth township, Booley, is shown as a separate entity on the Index to Tithe Survey map, but the Foxall set does not contain a map for it.

1. BOOLEY (SJ 574256)

Boleleiam 1121 SAC, *Bolelegam* 1155 SAC
Bole c.1175 SAC, *Boleye* 1302 Ipm, 1327 SR (p), 1348 *SRO 322/152*, *Boley* 1421 *ib/236*
Bolle 1235 Cl, *Bolleg'* c.1245 SAC, *Bollege* 1306–7 *Ass*
Boeleye 1291–2 *Ass* (p)
Buleye 1327 SR (p)
Bowley 1494 Ipm, 1552 Pat, 1588 *SRO 322 box 2*
Booley 1588 *SRO 322 box 2*, 1672 HTR *et seq*

'Tree-trunk clearing', *v.* **bol** (VEPN), **lēah**.

BLAKELEYHILL, *Blakelow Hill* 1588 *CourtR*, *SRO 322 box 2*, *Blakeley Hill* 1833 OS. 'Black tumulus', *v.* **hlāw**; a number of ns. in this area suggest the presence of burial mounds, but none have been located on the ground.

BOOLEY BANK, *Booley Bank* 1833 OS.
BOOLEY HO.
MORGAN'S COPPICE.
NEW LODGE, LODGE BANK, both 1833 OS.
QUARRY COPPICE.

Field-Names

No 19th-cent. ns. are available for Booley as the Foxall set of *TAMaps* does not include one for this township. Early forms for which no date or source is given are 1588 *SRO 322 box 2*; some of the ns. in this source occur in a perambulation of the township.

(b) *The Banke* 1588 *CourtR*; *Blakelow Brytch alias Gorsty Leasow* (v. **bryce**); (*an apple tree called*) *Booley Crosse*; *Burtons Poole* (this appears also in the perambulation of High Hatton *ib*); (a pasture called) *The Clyffe*, *The Clyffe Gate* (there is a steep escarpment along W. boundary); *Dearne Poole* (v. **derne** 'hidden'); *Farefeild* 1588 *CourtR*; *Jenkyns Closse*; *Maglyns Poole*; *The Meare Oake* ('boundary oak'); *The Mosse Lake*; *The Oldefeild* 1588 *CourtR*, *Peplowes Oldfeilds*; *The Poole Lane*; *Staunton Feild*; *Stertelond* 1302 Ipm (v. **steort**); *The Strynde* (ME **strind** 'stream', a rare p.n. el: EPN cites one instance, in Db, PN Ch **5.1** 357 cites 3: the boundary-mark appears also in the High Hatton perambulation *ib*).

2. HARCOURT (SJ 570250)
The township-name, which means 'cottage(s) of the harpers', is discussed in Part **1**. The manor house became known as Har(e)court, rather than *Har*(*e*)*cot*, in the early 19th century.

THE CAVE: this building is shown but not named on *TAMap*.

HARCOURT MILL, 1833 OS, *Harecote Mill* 1495 Ipm, *Harpcott Myll* 1588 *SRO 322 box 2*.

HARCOURT PARK, 1833 OS, *Harecote Park* 1495 Ipm, *Harpcott Park* 1588 *CourtR*, *Harcott Park* 1810 PR(L) 2.

Field-Names

Forms in (a) are 1839 *TA*.

(a) Barn Yd; Big Mdw; Bog Coppice, Mdw; Brickkiln Fd; Burnt Tree Fd; Cow Pasture; Croft, Lower, Middle, Upper; Crofts (by buildings on N.W. boundary); Geary Mdw; Holly Well, Hollywell Fd (*Hallywell Meadow* 1588 *SRO 322 box 2*, 'holy spring'); Horse Pasture; Long Acre (a building on N. boundary); Long Mdw; Marl Fd; Middle Fd; Mill Croft Fd (by Harcourt Mill); Moat Mdw (nothing shown on 6" map); Moston Door (on boundary with Moston); Near Fd, Mdw; Ox Lsw; Plantation Fd; River Fd; Rock Bank; Round Mdw (shape does not suit n.); Sunny Side.

3. HIGH HATTON (SJ 611248)
The township-name, which means 'heath settlement', and the affix are discussed in Part **1**. It was suggested there that 'high' means 'more

important', as the actual height is not significantly different from that of Cold Hatton, 2½ miles S.E.

DRAKE LEY HEATH (SJ 617244), *Drakelowe* 1376 *SBL 5433*, *Drakeley Heath* 1588 *CourtR*, ~ *Feild* 1605 *ib*, 1833 OS, 1839 *TA*. 'Dragon tumulus', *v.* **draca**, **hlāw**. This recurrent compound, which is found also in Bd, Db, La, Wo, refers to the belief, recorded in OE poetry, that treasure in burial mounds was guarded by dragons. Several names in this area contain **hlāw**. Peplow, 'pebble tumulus', is a mile to the east, cf. also Blakeleyhill in Booley township.

EXPRESS (lost). The 1833 OS map gives the name *Express Wood* to the farm at SJ 633234 which later maps call Wood Fm. *Express* is earlier *Espris* 1333 HAC, *Espres* 1588 *SRO 322 box 2*, *Esprees* 1594 *ib*, *Espree* 1692 *SBL 5704*. This is a wood, *magnus boscus* in 1588, *boscus domini* in 1594. The name appears to be unique, and is unsolved. The document of 1333 is in French, and it is possible that a French etymology should be sought.

AVENUE COTTAGES.

DOGKENNEL COTTAGE: *TAMap* shows *Crofts* with small buildings here.

GREENFIELDS, GREEN LANE: *Le Greenfeild*, ~ ~ *Lane* 1588 *SRO 322 box 2*, *Le Heath Feild al. Le Greenfeild* 1600 *ib*, *Green Fields* 1767 *SBL 8625*, 1833 OS, *Greenfields Farm* 1839 *TA*.

GREENHURST, shown but not named on *TAMap*, ~ LANE: *Grenehurst* 1600 *SRO 322 box 2*.

HALL COPPICE.

HEATH HO, 1692 *SBL 5704*, 1833 OS, *The Heth Howse* 1495 Ipm, *Le Hethehowse* 1539–40 *RentSur*, *Heath House Farm* 1588 *CourtR*, *The Heath Farm* 1839 *TA*.

HIGH HATTON HALL, 1833 OS.

NEW COPPICE.

PLATT BROOK, **plat**[1] 'footbridge'.

SIDE SADDLE LAKE. In the 1588 perambulations of Booley and Hatton townships this n. occurs as *Sett Saddell Lake* (Booley), *Syde Sadlelake* (Hatton). *Lake* is presumably a ME reflex of OE **lacu** 'small stream', referring to the tributary of Platt Brook by which the farm stands, but the use of *side-saddle* as a p.n. qualifier is unexplained.

THE SUMMER HO, *Summer House Cottage* and *Field* 1839 *TA*.

WOOD FM, *v. Express supra*: WOODMILL FM, 1839 *TA*.

1833 OS names a small wood W. of Wood Fm *Bates Rough*.

Field-Names

Forms in (a) are 1839 *TA*. Early forms dated 1343, 4, 6 are *SRO 322/147, /150, /152*. Forms dated 1588[1], 1594[1], 1595, 6, 7, 1599[1], 1600, 1602[1], 1603, 1605[1], 1607, 15 are *SRO 322 box 2*. Forms dated 1588[2], 1590, 2, 3, 1594[2], 1599[2], 1602[2], 1605[2] are *CourtR*. Some of the 1588[1] names are items in a perambulation of the township.

(a) Bank, Cross, Round; Bank, Gorsty, Meadow, Rye; Barn Yd (*Le Banyard* 1600 may be a corrupt form); Bates's Fd; Bath Lsw (there is a small pool in one corner); Big Hoo Sitch; Big Lsw; Black Breech (*Blake Britch alias Longe* ~ 1588[1], ~ ~ *alias Rough Britch* 1590, *v.* **bryce** 'newly-broken-in land', a common f.n. term in heathland); Breech, Cross and Sandy Breech (*Crosse Britche* 1590); Breech Moor; Bridle Road; Broad Moor; Broom Hill; Brown's Moor; Cartwright's Croft; Challenor's Fd, ~ Far Fd; Clover Lsw; Common Pce(s) (fields marked as such occupy a large area of N.W. of township); Corrow Fd; Crane's Horn (2 fields with Breech between them, *Cranes Horne* 1599[1], *Cranes Horne in Michell Feild* 1600); Croft, Lower, Upper (normal-sized fields); Croft(s) (there are clusters by habitation sites and a large group on N. boundary); Crook Headges (*Le Cruck Hedge* 1595, *Crooke Hedge also Crucke* 1605); Deptill (*Depdale* 1588, *Depdale or Swynes Woode* 1590, *Dep-Dale-Yate* 1605, *v.* **dēop**, **dæl**); Devil's Nest (a small field); Dod's Fd, Moor; dwebreech (*sic*); Ferny Flg (*Feyrn(e)y Furlonge* 1588, 90); Fishes Mdw; Flemmings Fd; Gate Lsw; Giggy Lsw (probably *griggy* 'heathery'); The Gorse Cover; Hackhurst (*Ackhurst* 1588, 'oak wood': *hurst* is not common in Sa but occurs 4 times in this township); Hadley Yd (1595, ~ *House* 1600); The Hall Coppice; The Hassocks (i.e. clumps of coarse grass); Heathy Lsw, Big, Little; Hoar Stone (not on a boundary); Hob Fd (probably, like Hassocks, a reference to grass tussocks); Hodge Mdw (cf. *Hodge Lane* 1605, first el. 'hog': Hodge ns. are common in Ch, PN Ch **5.1** 229); Hunger Hill; Kiln Croft (*Kyllcrofte* 1588, *Killcroft*, *Kylnecroft* 1595[2]); Lane End Lsw; The Lawn (2 large fields by Hall); Little Mdw; Long Flg (*Longe Forlonge* 1594[2]); Long Mdw (2, cf. *Longe Meadowe* 1590); Lower Middle Fd; Meadow, Broad, Glover's, Lower, New (adjoining fields); Meadow, Big, Little; Moor, Far, Near, Stockett, Moor Bank; New Pce, Bates's and Teece's ~ ~; Old Fd; Orchard Fd (~ *Feild* 1588); Out Breech; Ox Lsw (*Le Oxe Leasowe*, 1588); Pritchard's Banks, Moor; Rough Beech Mdw (*sic*, *Rough Briche Meadowe* 1599, *Rough Britch Meadow* 1600, a **bryce** n. with corruption to Beech, cf. Black Breech *supra*); Shoulder of Mutton (not the usual shape for this f.n.); Stable Croft (by Greenfields); Stony Fd; Thistly Croft; Vineyard (by Greenhurst); Walker's Croft (large field); Washway Lsw; White Hill; The Wren (large field); Yard, Calves, Dock, Hallens (in hamlet).

(b) *Astmor* 1344 ('east marsh'); *Bircheford Heath* 1605[1]; *Blakeland Moore* 1588[1]; *Brodmeadowe or Brodde Meadow* 1590 ('broad meadow'); *The Broomes* 1590; *Burtons Poole* 1588[1] (also in the perambulation of Booley *supra*); *Byrchen Meadowe* 1590; *Caldwell Feild* 1593, *Caldwall* ~ 1605[1] ('cold spring'); *Le Chappell Yarde* 1588[1]; *Cressedge Brytch* 1588[1]; *Crucksons Moore* 1595; *Darneford Lane* 1588[1] ('hidden ford', a recurrent compound); *Daw Crofte End* 1605[2]; *Drakeley Dore* 1595 (*v*. Drakeley *supra*, 'door' used for an opening of some kind ("ruptura" in this deed) is fairly common in this area); *Espley Meare* 1588[1] (a boundary mark, *v*. **(ge)mǣre**, Espley is in Hodnet); *Espley Feild* 1602[1]; *Ferringtons Shutt* 1605[1]; *Flax Butt alias Hempe Butt* 1590; *Fooleacre Furlonge alias Oxe Leasow* 1588[2]; *Gorsty Crofte*, *Pitt* 1596; *Hadley Yarde* 1595, ~ *House* 1600; *Hancockes Britche* 1588[1]; *Hatton Moore* 1588[1]; *Heathy Pleck* 1590; *Hedgewood* (*boscus voc.*) 1602[1]; *Hell Wickett* 1588[1]; *Le Hetheforlong* 1343; *Hill Furlong* 1605[1]; *The Hilles* 1593; *Hopton Feild Corner* 1588[1] (a boundary mark); *Hydebritche* 1588[1], *Hidebritche*, *Le Highbritches* 1600 (probably 'newly-broken-in hide of land'); *Jenkyns Closse* 1588[2]; *Jow Briches*, *Jowbriche*, *Jowbridge* 1605[2]; *Knolle Meadowe* 1605[1]; *Le Lakeforlong* 1343 (*v*. **lacu**); *Lylly Well*, *Lyllie* ~ 1588[1] (Gazetteer lists a number of Lilly- ns., cf. Lillyfields in Prees *supra*); *Longebritche* 1615 ("una parcella vasti nuper inclusa de mora de Hatton", a good example of **bryce**); *The Longe Foorde* 1588[1] (*v*. the discussion of this n. in Part **1** and under Longford in Moreton Say *supra*: this 1588 form, which is a boundary-mark probably on the W. boundary of Hatton, is a 4th example in an area of E. Sa and W. St); *Longe Forlonge* 1594[2]; *The Longe Hurste* ("a ferny banke whereupon divers oakes did grow") 1588[1], *Long Hurste* 1590; *The Long Moore* 1588[1]; *The Lowe Sytche* 1588[1]; *Le Lowe Yarde* 1605[1]; *The Lowes Waie* ("a greene way called") 1588[1] (said to "come between the two lowes", *v*. **hlāw** and cf. Blakeleyhill in Booley *supra*); *Lycoras Well*, *Licoras* ~ 1594[1] (J. Field, *English Field-Names* 100, cites ns. which refer to the cultivation of liquorice, but in a spring-n. the reference may be to some characteristic of the water); *Le Marshe Meadowe* 1599[1]; *Le Middulforlong* 1343; *Le Moore Peece* 1599[1]; *Mychell Feilde* 1588[1], *Michell Feild* 1600 ('great field', *v*. **mycel**); *Newe Bryche* 1590; *New Leasowe* 1602[2], *The Newe Leasow alias Aylewarde Croft* 1615; *Le Newelond* 1346; *Owsiche Bank* 1588[2], *Owsiche* 1594[2], ~ *Croft* 1599 (*v*. **sīc** 'drainage channel', as *freq* in this township); *Owtewoodd* 1602[1]; *Parke Well* 1588[1]; *Le Pike* 1605[1]; *Le Poole Gate* 1602[1] (*porta vocat'*); *Le Greate Portfurlonge* 1615; *Prese Furlong* 1594[1]; *Le Puddinge Yarde* 1605[1]; *Rowndhurste* 1599[2], *Roundhurst in mora de Hatton* 1600; *Ryecroft Siche* 1595; *Seates* 1597 (a virgate); (*Le*) *Slades Hill* 1588[1], 1592; *The Slades* 1594[2], *Sladehill* 1607 (*v*. **slæd**); *Le Snapes* 1588[1] (***snæp** 'boggy piece of land'); *Springles* 1605[1] (a virgate in *Esprees* wood); *Stancastle Feild*, *Hill* 1594[1] (the field occurs also 1605[1]: 'stone heap', *v*. discussion in VEPN *s.v.* **ceastel**: the compound is well evidenced in charter boundaries, rare in later sources); *Stodleyfurlong* 1344, *Stodley* 1588[1] ('stud clearing or pasture', a recurrent compound); *Stannton Field*, ~ *Heath or Moss* 1588[2]); *The Strynde* (*v*. Booley f.ns. *supra*); *Takes Feild* 1602[1]; *Thistly Britche* 1588[2]; *Tom Brytche* (*Tom* in f.ns. is frequently for *town*, *v*. FN 7); *The Wallebrooke* 1603; *Le Walleforlong*; 1343, *Walfurlong*(*e*) 1588[1] (probably 'spring furlong'); *Well Crofte* 1600; *Whitley Britche* 1595; *The Whorre Crosse alias Hatton Crosse* 1588[1] (in a perambulation, probably *hoar* in the late sense 'boundary'); *Withaw*(*e*)*feild* 1594[2]; *Workhurste Feilde*, *Haye* 1588[1], *Wockhurste* ~, ~ 1590 (first el. possibly **weorc** 'building, structure'); *Woodd Meadow* 1594[2]; *Worrall Feild* 1603; *Yarde*, *The Greate*, *Le Jacke*, *Le Neither*, *Le Upper* 1615; *Yarde End* 1605[2].

4. MOSTON (SJ 561265)

The township-name, 'bog settlement', is discussed in Part **1** as Moston is a DB manor. The spelling on 1833 OS is *Mostyn*, with the Welsh substitution of *-tyn* for *-ton*.

BOOLEY FM (by Booley).

MOSTON COPPICE, 1839 *TA*, *Mostyn Rough* 1833 OS.

MOSTON HO.

MOSTON POOL (Gazetteer), 1809 PR(L) 19, *Moston Pole Wicket* 1630 ib: the pool has been drained. The "pond of Moston" is mentioned 1308 Ipm.

OLD BOAT HO, 1833 OS, "the boat house at Moston Boat" 1812 PR(L) 19, presumably a ferry for crossing the Pool. *TAMap* shows *Wheelwright's Shop* here.

PAPERMILL BANK, BRIDGE, *Paper Mills* 1833 OS, *Papermill Meadow* 1839 *TA*, by R. Roden.

Field-Names

Forms in (a) are 1839 *TA*.

(a) Acres, Big, Little; Barley Fd; Big Fd; Big Flg; Blot Fd; Booley Coppice, Big and Little Coppice Fd (on boundary with Booley); Bowling Green (by Booley Fm); Breech, Big, Black, Little, Gwynn's; Broomy Lsw, Big, Little; The Brooms (2); Brown Heath, The Big, The Little; The Clemley, Clemley Croft (*v*. Clemley in Prees); Clover Fd (2); Common Pce, Far, Near (among Croft and Field ns. on E. boundary); Coppy Fd; Cote Lsw; The Cow Pasture; Cranberry Moss; (The) Croft, Clover and Pit Croft (in Moston hamlet); Croft (small enclosures on E. boundary include Middle, Lower, Top, Square, Stackyard and Booley Croft); Drumble Lsw (*v*. The Drumble in Baschurch *supra*); Fallow Fd; Field, Long, Middle Gorsty, Moston (among Croft ns. on E. boundary); Field before the House; Fridays, Big, Little; Garden Fd (by Booley Fm); Gorsty Lsw (2); The Grigg Fd ('heather', ultimately from Welsh *grug*); Grooms Fd; Hamin Fd; The Haymaker; Heath Lsw (2); Hempbutt; Highway Lsw, Big, Little; The Hill; Horse Pasture, Big, Little; Little Coppice; Lloyd Hill, Big, Little (FN 21 suggests that Lloyd is a development of **hlūd** 'loud' used as a stream-name: the hill overlooks a small tributary of R. Roden); Long Fd, Bottom, Top; The Looms ('lands', i.e. open-field strips); Marl Lsw; Meadow, The Big, The Little; Meadow, Lower, Top; Middle Fd; Moors (by R. Roden); Mosses Croft; New Croft; The New Lsw; New Road; Old Shops, Yd and Garden (by Old Boat House); Park Fd (near Harcourt Pk); The Ploughed Flg; Pool Mdw; Rushy Fd; The Slangs (long strip by stream); Solid Horn (*horn* occurs several times in this part of Sa in ns. of fields which are not horn-shaped: this field is sub-rectangular); The Three Birches; Top Fd; Triangle Fd; Wettings Dale, Dale Mdw.

5. STANTON (SJ 568240)

SOWBATH/SOWBATCH (SJ 576229)

Suthbeche 1291–2 *Ass*, *Southbece*, *-bache* 1339 HAC, *Southbeche*, *-bache* 1339 *SRO 322/137*

Sowbech 1366 *SRO 322/189*, *Sow(e)bache* 1389 *TA*, *Sowbach'* 1539–40 *RentSur*, *-bach* 1654, 92 *SBL 1661*, *5704*, *-batch* 1695 Morden
Sobath 1661 *SBL 6516*, *Sowbath* 1698, 1720 *SBL 6518*, *6517*, 1773 PR(L) 20, 1833 OS
Sowbich 1729 PR(L) 20

'South stream-valley', *v.* **sūð**, **bæce**. There is a small gully a short distance north of the farm, and the 1833 OS map shows a tiny stream running down this to R. Roden. The stream does not appear on later maps. *TAMap* has fields called *Far*, *Middle* and *Near Beech*, *Beech Croft* and *Meadow* where the stream shown on 1833 OS enters the Roden, and these probably preserve the second element of the name. For Beach or Beech as a reflex of **bæce** *v.* Part **2** 25–6, 161.

There is a longer gully through which a stream runs through Stanton village to the Roden, and the Sowbatch feature is 'south' in relation to that.

The late substitution of -bath may be due partly to the insignificance of the little stream-valley, and partly to the comparative rarity of **bæce** ns. in the north of the county. This is the present form of the name, though Gazetteer gives Sowbatch.

WAXFORD (?lost, SJ 549247): *Waxford* 1366, 76 *SRO 322/189*, *SBL 5433*, *Waxforde More* 1592 *CourtR*, *Far* and *Near Waxford*, ~ *Meadow* 1839 *TA*. This is strictly a field-name, but it deserves a separate entry as **w(e)ax** is a rare p.n. element, and its occurrence in *TA* makes it possible to locate it with some precision at the above GR. A road crosses R. Roden S. of Harcourt Mill here.

It is generally assumed that **w(e)ax** in p.ns. refers to places where beeswax is produced.

BUTLERS BANK, *Butler's Piece* 1839 *TA*.

COOLMOOR, possibly *Collesmoore* 1578 *SBL 5982*.

HAZLE GORSE, 1833 OS.

THE HAZLES, 1833 OS, *Hassells* 1682 GT. The wood called HAZLE GRIGG S. of the farm covers an area with fields called *Griggy Leasow* and *Hazles Bank* 1839 *TA*. *Griggy* is an adj. from *grig* 'heather'.

LONGLEY.

MANNINGS COPPICE, *Hayles Coppice* 1839 *TA*.

NEW FM.

POTFORD BROOK.

STANTON HEATH.

STANTON MILL, 1730 GT, 1839 *TA*.

STONEHOUSE FM and THE WOODLANDS are both shown but not named on *TAMap*.

WOOD VILLA.

1833 OS shows *Browns Rough* near Sowbath, and *TA* has *Brown's Rough* and *Brownes Yates* here.

Field-Names

Forms in (a) are 1839 *TA*. Early forms dated 1612, 79, 82, 98, 1718, 30 are GT: those dated 1661 are *SBL 6516*.

(a) Adder Bank; Bakehouse Mdw (in village); Barley Croft; Barn Yard (several); Bean Bank; Beech, Near, Far, Middle, ~ Croft, Mdw (near Sowbath *q.v.*); Besford's Lsw; Bet Yds; Big Fd; Big Hill Lsw; Big Mdw (2); Bitter Sweet Fd (FN 49 says "probably Woody Nightshade"); Black Britch; Booley Fd, Near, Upper (Booley adjoins); Breech, Black, Long, Howbreech; Brickkiln Fd (2); Broad Graves (adjoins Nangraves); Brown Bank; Calves Croft (several); Cliff, Little, Long, Ox (steep slope by The Woodlands); Clover Fd; Colley's Marl Fd; Common Fd, Far, Near, Middle, Top (10 fields by a line of Crofts); Coppice, Near, Timber, Great and Little Coppice Fd, ~ Croft; Coppice Mdw; Copy Fd; The Corder Warder (FN 71 lists as unexplained); Cote Lsw (2); Cow Lsw (2); Cowley's Fd; Crib, Big, Little (probably 'manger'); Croft (a line of small enclosures along a road S.E. of the village includes several Crofts, also Hanmers, Lower, Middle, House Croft); Croft (the eastern tip of the parish, containing Coolmoor, Stonehouse Fm and Longley, is divided into small enclosures many of which have Croft ns.: those near Stonehouse Fm include Crabtree, Old Man's, Clover and Well Croft); Crossway Fd (by a crossroads); Dial Bank (small enclosure by village, *dial* in f.ns. is thought to refer to sundials); Dingle Fd, Lsw, Mdw (fields with Dingle ns. occur by both the stream gullies noted under Sowbath *supra*); Dovehouse Bank; Dovehouse Yd (large field by Sowbath, cf. *Dovehouse Croft* 1682); Elder Bottom; Far Fd; Ferny Bank, Large, Small; Flanders, Near, Middle, Far (perhaps a distance n. but not near township boundary); Flash Lsw; Frog Coppy Fd; Gardener's Fd, Far, Near; Gorsty Breech; Gravel Hole Fd; Grazing Pasture; Grindleys Fd; Gutter Fd (by Dingle Fd); Hassocks (*Hassock Furlong* 1612, 1718, *hassocks* are clumps of coarse grass); Hazle Mdw, Hazles Lsw (not near Hazles Fm); Heath Fd, Far, Near; Heath House Fd, Mdw (Heath Ho is in Hatton township); Heath Pce; The Hett, Far and Near ~ (*Heytt Bank* 1612, *Hett* ~ 1698, *Height* ~ 1718, 3 large fields by village, perhaps *height* in the sense 'high place'); The Hill; Hill Lsw; Horse Pasture; House Lsw; The Isle of Want (by a line of Croft and Common ns.); The Lawn, Lower ~ (across a road from The Hazles); Leas, Big and Little ~ (*Leas* 1679, *Lees* 1682); Ley Pce; Little Fd; Long Fd; Long Lsw (2); Long Mdw (2); Marl Fd (2); Marlpit Bank, Far, Near; Marlpit Lsw; Marsh, Far, Near, Middle; Marsh, ~ Mdw, Willow Pltn in the Marsh; Middle Lsw; Middle Pce; Millers Croft; Mill Mdw (by Stanton Mill); Moor Bank, ~ ~ Mdw; Moss, Near, Far,

Further; Nail Shop (in cluster of tiny enclosures E. of Stonehouse Fm); Nangraves, Far, Near, Middle; New Lsw, Lower, Upper (2); New Pce, Far, Near, Small (by Isle of Want); Oaktree Lsw; Oat Lsw; Old Woman's Garden (near Stonehouse Fm); Ombrey's Pce; Ox Lsw (2); Park Croft, Fd, Mdw (7 fields N. of Stanton village, cf. *The Park* 1679, *Park Croft* 1698); Paxall's Lsw; Peg's Fd; Permy Breech; Perry Yates; Petticoat Park, Far, Near (by a small building on S.E. boundary, among Croft and Yd ns.); Pit Fd; Pit Lsw, Little, Great, Lower; Pool Mdw; Poverty Bank (by the cluster of Crofts near Coolmoor); Rabbit Burrow Fd; Raddledan; Rough Moor; Rough Mdw; Rue Flg; Rushy Pce; Shone's Croft, Fd; Square Fd; Stanton Bank(s) (2); Stanton Croft, Lower, Upper; Strawberry Breech, Big, Near; Tett's Fd; Third Fd; Three Butts; Three Cornered Croft; Triangle Fd (this and preceding are in road junctions); Upper Fd; Waltons Fd, Far, Near (*Walton Fields* 1612); Wet Moor, Big and Little ~ ~; Wet Reans (drainage channels); Wheat Lsw; Wicketty Fd (perhaps for *wicket tree* 'mountain ash'); Wicket Pce, Near, Far; (The) Yard (several round village, also Pit, Stack Yd); Yard (several among Crofts in E. tip of township); Yard (ns. near Stonehouse Fm include Appletree, Granny's, Old Mary's, Far and Long Yd); Yewtree Fd.

(b) *Bank* 1698; *Bullfords* 1661; *Corbettesbruche* ("un assart") 1340 *SRO 322/143*; *Corfield* 1661; *Halstons Croft* 1612, *Hulstone Croft* 1718; *Holbache, Vicars* 1612, *Howbach* 1679, *Howbaches* 1682, 98, *Vicars Holbaches* 1718 ('hollow stream-valley'); *Hood Mill* 1730; *Leenes* 1698; *Leighs* (2 closes) 1718; *The Pitts* 1661; *Le Portwey* 1341 *SRO 322/144*; *Over Leasow* 1612, 1718; *Rea Fields* 1661; *Redhopesty* 1376 *SBL 5433* (final el. probably **stīg** 'climbing path'); *The Riddings* 1661 ('clearings'); *Le Sladewey* 1341 *SRO 322/144*, *The Slade* 1661 (*v.* **slæd**); *Stanton Heath and Moss* 1698; *Twenty Penny Grounds* 1661; *Upper Field* 1698; *Viccaridge Lands* 1661; *Waddens Field* 1698; *La Were* 1376 *SBL 5433* ('weir').

Stoke upon Tern

The parish-name is discussed in Part **1**, and details are given there of the affixes *North ~*, *~ Say* and ~ upon Tern.

The Foxall *TAMap* does not give township boundaries, but the 19th-cent. Index to Tithe Award map shows Eaton upon Tern, Ollerton, Stoke upon Tern and Wistanswick as discrete areas. The material has been arranged in accordance with this.

1. EATON UPON TERN (SJ 654230)

Eton' 1255–6 *Ass et passim* with variant spelling *-ton* to 1361 Cl, *Eton upon Tyerne* 1389 Cl, *~ upon Tierne* 1394 Cl

Heton 1255 RH (p)

Eaton alias Yeaton upon Tern 1684 (1796) *SBL 14677*, *Eaton* 1702 PR(L) 18, 1713 *SBL 14618*, *Yeaton otherwise Eaton* 1787 *SBL 14669*

'River settlement', *v.* **ēa**, **tūn**, a recurrent name which occurs six times in Sa: *v.* the discussion in Part **1**.

BRICK-KILN COTTAGE: *TA* has fields called *Clay Hole*, *Clayhole Meadow* here, cf. *Clayhole* 1684 (1796) *SBL 14677*.

THE CHESTNUTS: the house is shown but not named on *TAMap*.

CRAMER COTTAGES, *Cramoor* 1684 (1796), *Cramer Hill* 1780, 7 *SBL 14677*, *56*, *69*, *Craymoor Hill*, *Cranmoor Hill*, *Cranmoor* 1840 *TA*: 'crane marsh', *v.* **mōr**, the *TA* ns. cover an area extending to R. Tern.

DODMORE LANE (Gazetteer): *Big*, *Higher*, *Lower Dodmore*, *~ Meadow* 1840 *TA*.

EATON COPPICE.

EATON GRANGE.

EATON MILL, *Mill* 1833 OS, 1840 *TA*.

EATON VILLA: the house is shown but not named on *TAMap*.

TURNPIKE GATEHOUSE: *TAMap* shows *Smithy* here.

Field-Names

Forms in (a) are 1840 *TA*. Early forms dated 1684 (1796), 1718, 22, 80, 87 are *SBL 14618*, *22*, *56*, *69*, *71*.

(a) Big House; Blakeley Bank; Blakely, Blakelow Mdw; Bran Hill, Brant Hill, Brantail Mdw; Broadway, Breadway, ~ Mdw, Badiway; Brook Lsw (*The Ford otherwise The Brooke Leasow* 1787); Bull Heads; Cow Lsw (1684 (1796)), Far ~ ~, ~ ~ Moor; Cranberry Moor; Crancow Mdw, Big and Little Croncow, Cronkwell, Cranmore (6 adjacent fields on S. boundary, ½ mile from Cramer Cottages *supra*, *Crankow* 1684 (1796), *The Rod Meadow otherwise The Rood*, *otherwise Cankow* 1787); Ditches (*The* ~ 1780); Duns Bridge; Eaton Mdw (on township boundary); Ercall Fd (Child's Ercall adjoins); Forge Land, Mdw (*Eaton Forge* 1750, 82 PR(L) 13); Frill Hill; Gravel Hole Yd; Hay Flg, Far, Near, Heys Mdw ((*The*) *Hay Furlong*(*s*) 1684 (1756), 1780, 7); Hazle Buts; Hook Moor (a shape n.); Horne (an oblong field, nearby Dodmore Horne is irregularly shaped: cf. *The Two Hornes* 1684 (1796)); Horse Croft, Far, Near, Middle (*Horse Croft* 1684 (1796), 1780); Hot Hill (3 fields); Howle Mdw; Landiniver Mdw (on boundary with Hodnet, FN 22 suggests 'boundary', ultimately from **land-gemǣre**); Lunds, Far, Near (one of many forms of *lands*, 'open-field strips'); Marsh, ~ Croft, Mdw (*The Marsh* 1722); Mastalls; New Pce; Oak Lsw; Oatfield; Odd Acres; Ollerton Croft (on boundary with Ollerton); Ouverlane, Big, Little; Padford Bank; Parrs Moor; Peas Lsw; Piece, Far, Near; Flatley Mdw (*Plattly Meadow* 1684 (1796), *Plattley* ~ 1780); Prestoos Britch; Seven Acres (Eight Acres, of similar size, adjoins); Shop Lsw (Smithy in corner); Skeldons Mdw; Soonds ('sands'); Speatley (*Sperteghe* e.14th *Wom*, *Speertley* 1780, *The Partley otherwise Spertley* 1787: the e.14th form suggests a compound of **ēg** 'raised ground in marsh' with the rare p.n. el. ***spyrt**, ***spert**, for which various suggested meanings are given in EPN: PN Ch **5.1** 348 notes a few Ch examples and gives 'a spurt, a jet of liquid' as meaning: the *Wom* ref. says "mora . . . super ripam de Tyrne", but the 2 small fields in *TA* are a short distance from the river, next to Marsh ns.); Whitley Pit; Yard (large field by hamlet, with smaller Barn, Old and Taylor's Yd adjoining); Yard, Upper, Lower.

(b) *The Field Meadow* 1787; *Froghole Meadow* 1722; *The Furlong towards Ollderton* 1718, 87; *The Ling Meadow*, *Long Bank*, *Lsw* 1722; (*The*) *Marsh Watthill* 1780, 87; *The New Leasow* 1718, 87; *The Pitt Meadow*(*s*) 1780, 7; *Wear Mdw* 1722.

2. OLLERTON (SJ 650253)

Alvereton 1284–5 FA
Alverton 1317 Cl *et freq* to 1371 Cl
Alworton 1360 Ipm
Ollerton 1535 PR(L) 11, 1672 HTR *et seq*
Allerton 1577 Saxton, *Alerton* 1696 *SBL 4992*

Probably 'Ælfwaru's estate', from a feminine personal name. Alverton Co, which is ascribed to this origin in DEPN, has comparable spellings without the late development to Oller-.

BACON HALL: this is *Sydney End* 1833 OS, and fields on either side of the house are *Sidney End* 1840 *TA*. If this is an ancient name it may be 'wide island', *v.* **sīd**, **ēg**. The site is enclosed by streams.

BLAKELEY (BLAKEWAY on 1963 1" map): *Blackley Meadow* 1684 (1796) *SBL 14677*, *Blakeley* (a field with no house) 1840 *TA*. There are fields called *Blakeley*, *Blakelow* in Eaton township, ½ mile distant.

OLLERTON FM.

OLLERTON LANE, 1833 OS.

OLLERTON PARK: the area of the park shown on 1900 6" is divided into fields on *TAMap*.

Field-Names

Forms in (a) are 1840 *TA*.

(a) Allen's Bank; Badgers Lsw; Big Lsw (2); Big Mdw; Bitham (perhaps a derivative of **byðme** used for a hollow, there is no valley); Bradley Moor; Britch; Brook Lsw; Butt (a tiny strip between fields); Carthouse Gate; Dods Wall; Eaton Stales; Five Butts (in S. part of township where field-shapes suggest enclosure of open field); Fords (2 fields by R. Tern); Gighole Croft (Hemp Butt adjoins); Gravelly Flat (in same area as Five Butts); Hagram Flat, Hagrane Flats (in same area as Five Butts); Head Moor (5 fields S. of Ollerton); Hemp Butt (2 in hamlet); Higher Fds; Hoddy Well Mdw (perhaps a reference to flax, cf. FN 31); Hot Croft (not near Hot Hill in Eaton); Holes; Intake; Jones Croft; Leasow, Middle, Long, Near New, Far; Long Lsw (4 fields, 3 of them strip-shaped); Marl Lsw; Marsh; Meir (on parish boundary, *v.* **(ge)mǣre**); Morny Marl Pits; New Pce; Ollerton Lsw; Pantry (FN 48 suggests 'pine tree', but it seems more likely to be the word *pantry* used in some transferred sense: the field is a narrow L-shaped enclosure between fields called Head Moor); Pit Croft; Pit Lsw; Rushtomley; Sandy Flat; Sheep Hay & Mdw; Shuts; Sidney End (*v.* Bacon Hall *supra*); Slang; Tan House Yd (in hamlet); Taylor Mdw; Touchay Croft; Town Mdw (7 fields bordering R. Tern); Towns End (at S. end of hamlet); Trindle Lsw, Mdw (the Mdw and one of the Lsw fields share a curved side); Well Croft, Mdw; Woodside (adjoins Wd ns. in Stoke township); Yard (Ollerton hamlet is surrounded by fields called Yard).

3. STOKE UPON TERN

THE BENDLES (SJ 652261), 1833 OS, 1840 *TA*, *The Benulle* 1371 Cl, *The Oxe Bendle* 1688 *SBL 4968*: 'bean hill', *v.* **bēan**, **hyll**, and f.ns. *infra*.

BURNHILL (lost)
Burhullam 1155 SAC
Burne 1271–2 *Ass*
Borwhull c.1291 TN

Burnhull 1331 Ch
Burnell 1696 *SBL 4992*

v. **hyll**. The forms are insufficient for a firm etymology of the first element, but **byrgen** 'burial place' is possible. This was suggested for Burnhill PN Bk 165 on the grounds that there is a burial mound on that hill.

The context of the early references is discussed in Part **1** 77, together with those for *Chesthill*. The suggestion in Part **1** that *Bran*(*t*) *Hill*, a *TA* f.n. in Eaton township, might preserve the name now seems ill-advised. *Burnell* 1696 is likely to be the latest reference found.

CHESTHILL (lost). This was a DB manor, and the name is discussed fully in Part **1**. The first element is probably **ceast** 'strife, contention', occasionally used in names of places on boundaries. *Chesthill* appears to have been a land-unit which was divided between Moreton Say and Stoke upon Tern. The latest occurrence of the name is *Chatsall Grange otherwise Stoke Grange* 1813 *SRO 327/1*.

COTTON (SJ 631278), 'cottages'. This is one of six Sa instances of Cot(t)on. Eyton's identification of the Stoke upon Tern place with DB *Ludecote* has been generally accepted, and the name was therefore discussed in Part **1**, where it was suggested that the DB affix, probably the personal name *Luda*, was a temporary addition to an originally simplex name.

HELSHAW GRANGE (SJ 639296)
Heselschawe 1253 HAC (p) *et freq* with variant spelling *-shawe* to 1327 SR (p), *Heseleschawe* 1271–2 *Ass* (p), *Hesilshawe* 1389 Cl
Haselschawe 1255–6 *Ass* (p), 1317 Cl (p), *Hazelschawe* 1320 *SBL 4531* (p), *Haselsewe* 1331 Ch, *-shawe* 1332 Ipm (p), 1344 Cl (p), *Hasilshawe* 1394 Cl
Helshawe Hy 8 *RentSur*, *Helshaw* 1696 *SBL 4992*

'Hazel wood', *v.* **hæsel, sceaga**. 1833 OS has *Helshaw Grove* and *Wood* N. of the house.

PETSEY (SJ 637277)
Pechesey(*e*) 1255–6, 1253–63 *Ass* (p), *Pechchiseye* 1256 HAC (p), *Peccheseye* 1271–2 *Ass* (p)
Pethesey 1284–5 FA

Picheseye 1291–2 *Ass* (p)
Pettsey 1778 PR(L) 20, *Petsey* 1833 OS

Second element **ēg** 'island'. Petsey is beside the R. Tern, a short distance S.W. of Stoke upon Tern village. The river has side-channels in this stretch, and a water-enclosed or a slightly raised site here would deserve the term **ēg**.

The first element is problematic. *Pethesey* 1284–5 is likely to be a mistranscription, and most of the spellings indicate an original *Peces-*. Pitsea PN Ess 167 has analogous spellings but with regular *Pic*(*h*)-, occasional *Pe*(*t*)*ch-*, indicating an original *Pices-*. The Essex name is usually ascribed to a recorded OE personal name *Pīc*. For Petsey the only available suggestion is an unrecorded personal name **Pĕ̄c*.

The occurrence of two similar (?related) personal names with **ēg** can reasonably be ascribed to coincidence: monothematic personal names are the most frequent qualifiers in *-ēg* compounds.

In the Essex name the change to *-t-* is recorded from 1488. In the Shropshire name there is a gap in available forms after 1327, so the change was probably earlier than its appearance in 1778. This is a development found in other names, e.g. Bletsoe Bd, which is *Blechesho*(*u*) in DB.

WOODHOUSE FM (SJ 643266): *Wudehuse* 1221–2 *Ass*, *Wodehus* 1271–2, 91–2 (p) *Ass*, 1284–5 FA, *Wood House* 1833 OS. This is a recurring name, particularly common in Sa, *v.* Part **1** where details are given for this and another seven examples. It was suggested there that this might be a term for buildings housing people who had specialised woodland functions. *TA* field-names, *infra*, suggest the former presence of woodland in this part of the parish.

THE FENNERS, 1833 OS, *Finners* 1840 *TA*. On *TAMap* the names *Finners*, *Near* ~, *Finners Meadow* cover twelve fields, eight of which have the rectangular shapes characteristic of reclaimed wetland.

GALLANTRY HILL, HO: *The Gallowtree Hill More* 1696 *SBL 4970*: cf. *Gallantry Bank* Part **2** 9.

GRANGE WD, 1833 OS, *Wood* 1840 *TA*.

HEATHCOTE, 1732 PR(L) 9.

HURST FM, *The Hurst* 1833 OS, *Hurst* 1840 *TA*.

MANOR HO, 1833 OS.

MILL ROUGH, by New Mill in Lostford.

THE MOUNT, 1833 OS.

POOR HO, 1833 OS.

SALTERSHILL, *Salters Hill Field* 1682 GT, *Salters Hill* 1840 *TA*.

STOKE BRIDGE: *TA* has *Bridge Field* here.

STOKE GRANGE, 1833 OS, STOKEGRANGE COTTAGES: probably the property owned by Shrewsbury Abbey, *v.* SAC 38 and cf. *Chesthill supra*.

STOKEHALL FM: the building is shown but not named on *TAMap*.

STOKE HEATH, 1612 GT, 1833 OS: cf. *Stoke upon Tyrne and La Hethe* 1317 Ipm.

STOKEPARK FM: *Stoke Park* 1765, 98 *SBL 4264*, *4304*, *Park House* 1840 *TA*. The *TAMap* shows three houses called *Park House*, and 1833 OS calls two of these *Stoke Park*. The area called Stoke Park on 1900 6" map is divided into fields on *TAMap*.

THE SYTCHPITS, *Sitch Field* 1840 *TA*, 'small stream', *v.* **sīc**.

WHITE HALL, 1833 OS, *Whitehall* c.1566 *SRO 327 uncat*.

YEWTREE HO.

Field-Names

Forms in (a) are 1840 *TA*. Early forms dated 1689, 96, 1743, 71 are *SBL 4969*, *70*, *80*, *5748*, those dated 1612, 82 are GT. Forms dated 1331 are Ch, and are from the bounds of *Chesthill* and (Tern) Hill.

(a) Ash Fd, Far, Near; Bailey Brush (small enclosure in Stoke Heath with a building which is still there on 1900 6"); Bakehouse Bank (by Petsey); Bank; Bank Hay; Barn Fd (several); Bay Fd(s), Big, Little, Great, Middle (these fields extend N. from a tributary of R. Tern, and are separated by a row of Moor fields from Weir Fd: *Bay* may be "*bay* ME dam, weir" as listed in VEPN); Bean Fd (adjoins The Bendles *supra*); Bendles, Crabtree, House, Robin (surrounding the house called The Bendles, *Further* and *Neither Benders Lownes* 1696 is probably 'Bendles lands'); Big Coppice; Big Mastiff Fd, Pit; Big Mdw; Birch (*The Byrtch* 1696, *The Birch* 1743, probably *britch*, the *TA* field is by Heath Lsw); Brick Bank, Lower, Upper, Lym; Brickfield, ~ Mdw; Brickkiln Fd (several); Brickyard and Orchard; Bridge Fd (by Stoke Mill); Bridge Fd, Little, Big, ~ Mdw (by R. Tern but not at a crossing-place); Broad Fd; Broad Mdw; Brook Fd (2); Brook Flg (1612, *Brooke Furlongs* 1696, 2 fields by Helshaw/Shaw ns.); Broomy Bank; (several, one 1696); Broomy Fd; Bucklin Fd (adjoins Buxton); Burnage Fd, Far, Near, Marl; Buxton, Great, Little (*v.* Buxton in Kenstone township *supra*); Calves Croft; Carthouse Mdw; Church Mdw (1696, adjoins Stoke church); Cloggers Croft; Clover Fd; Cockshot; Colts Croft; Common (adjoins Heath Lsw); Common (among Crofts on Stoke Heath); Common Pces (adjoining Croft fields by Heathcote); Cote Lsw (no building); Cowhouse Lsw; Cow Lsw (1696), Mdw; Cow Lsw Bank; Cow Pasture; Crabtree Fd (2); Croft(s) (clusters in Stoke Heath, by Yewtree Ho, by Heathcote and by Rosehill in Stoke upon Tern); Cross Croft, Croft Fd; Cross Fd, Far, Near; Cuch House Fd; Dilly Bank (daffodils); Dovehouse Bank; Dyers Yd; Eight Butts (near Helshaw Fd); Ellams

Common; Fearny Fd; Field, Big, Little, Middle; Five Butts (1682, by Shaw Fd); Flat Croft, Big (between Shaw Fd and Stoke Fd); Francis Pce; French Wheat Pce (*The ~ ~ Peice* 1743); Gambrell (FN 14 lists under shape-names and quotes SWB for a meaning 'crooked piece of wood used by butchers to hang carcases', but this is a large kite-shaped field: the other main meaning of *cambrel/gambrel* in NED, 'horse's hock', is also not appropriate); Garden Fd, Mdw; Gorsy Bank; Gorsy Croft, Long, Little ~ Fd; Great Yd Fd; Green Fd; Green Pce; Grosvenors Mdw, Yd; Grove (Wood Fd adjoins but no trees are shown on *TAMap*); Hall Bank; Heath Allotment, Croft, Pltn; Heath Fd or Nine Acres; Heath Lsw (several); Heath Pce; Helshaw Corner (1682); Helshaw Fd, Far and Near ~ ~ (5 Shaw Fds adjoin: 1612 GT refers to 'lands' in *Shawe Field*, and *TA* has Butts, Flat and Flg ns. in this area: *Helshaw Field* occurs 1743); Hill (large field S. of village, cf. *The Hill* 1743, 71); Hill Fd; Hog Yd (*The Hoggyard* 1696); Holly Bank (2); Honey Spot; Hooters Hill, Far, Near; Horse Moor; Horse Pasture (2); Horsewash Mdw; Hurst Mdw (by Hurst Fm); Kiln Garden; King's Mdw (2); Land (a group of rectangular enclosures by Yewtree Ho); Lane Croft; Lawn (near Stokepark Fm); Lawn, Dry, Wet, Long, Middle, Near (on W. edge of Stoke Pk); Lees Mdw; Ley Croft, Little Ley; Little Mdw; Lodge Mdw, Near ~ Lsw (small building shown on *TAMap*); Long Fd; Long Mdw; Meadow, Big, Little, New, Lower; Meadow, Long, Mill, Weir; Middle Fd; Middle Well Croft; Mill Fd (near Walkmill, 1612 GT mentions 'lands' in *Mill Flatt* and on *Mill Pool Head Flatt* in *Mill Field*); Mill Mdw (by Stoke Mill, 6" map has Corn Mill (disused) here); Moat Lsw (by Hurst Fm); Moor, Big, Little, ~ Bank; Moor, ~ Mdw, Bank; Moor, Near, Rushy and Horse ~; Moores Pool, ~ ~ Banks; New Pce; Nursery; Nut Bank, Big, Little; Old Gardens & Orchard; Ox Lsw; Paddock, ~ Moor (by Stokepark Fm); Park, Little, Great, New, Heath, Park End, Lsw, Mdw (in or near Stoke Pk); Parks (N. of Ollerton Pk); Patch and Plank Mdw; Piece, Brickkiln, Coppice, Garden, Pond, Workhouse; Pingle (*The* ~ 1743 'small enclosure'); Pit Lsw; Plantation (a large area in the N. of the township is divided into rectangles with this n.); Plat End (adjoins Bridge Fd by Stoke Bridge, *plat* is probably 'footbridge' here); Pool, Pool Head, Croft (*Pool Head Flatt* 1612); Pool Sitch Bank; Pudding Croft; Puking (large field by Manor Ho); Quag(s) Mdw (a rare 'bog' term, PN Ch **5.1** 315 lists one instance); Ravens Nest; Ravens Oak; Rough Lsw (2); Rushy Flat; Rushy Pce; Scald Britch; Seven Pits (large field near Heathcote); Shaw Fd (*The Shafield Leasow* and *Pingle* 1696, *The Shawfield or Shayfield* 1743, *v.* Helshaw Fd *supra*); Sheep Walk (several); Shop Croft (6" map shows Smithy here); Shoulder of Mutton (shape-n.); Shut Mdw; Skelands; Slade; Sniggle (cf. Sniggle Bogs in Baschurch *supra*); Stable Croft (by Cotton); Stable Fd; Stew Fd (probably fish-pond); Stocking Mdw (*meadow called Stockings* 1612, *v.* ***stoccing**); Stoke Fd (2 fields among Helshaw and Shaw Fds); Stoke Mdw; Strote Mdw; Stubble; Sty Lsw, Big; Sullen Fd, Moor (FN 12 lists some Sullins, Sullen(s) ns. and suggests a connection with OE **sulh** 'ploughland', but a 19th-cent. derogatory n. seems more likely); Tern Mdw (2, cf. *Tern Meadow or Big Meadow* 1743); Thirty Acres (1612 GT mentions 'lands' in *Thirty Acre Field*); Thistly Fd; Thorny Pits; Town Fd (4 fields E. of Shaw and Stoke Fds, *The* ~ ~ 1743); Town Mdw; Two Dale; Two Four Loaves; Upper Mdw; Walker's Croft (by Heathcote, encircled by a narrow strip called Walk, possibly referring to a rope-walk); Walk Mill Croft, Mdw, Mill Fd (*Walkmill Croft* 1682, a fulling mill); Warrenter's Pce; Weir Fd (2); Weir Mdw, Moor; Whalley's Lsw, Far, Near, Wolley's Lsw, Mdw; Wheat Croft; Whitening Yd (for bleaching linen, FN 40);

Wirland (adjoins Weir Mdw); Withy Eye ('willow island', between streams); Wood, ~ Mdw, Pce (by Grange Wd); Wood, ~ Pce, Woodside Pce (5 fields, no trees shown on *TAMap*); Wood, Big, Little (as with preceding, no trees on map); Wood Fd (several); Workhouse Pce.

(b) *Aldeleye* 1332 Ipm (a wood, *v.* **ald**, **lēah**); *Le Bromhock* 1331 (*v.* **brōm**, **hōc**); *The Coate Croft* 1696; *Cockhill Ridgbutts in Shawe Field* 1612; *The Dingle* 1771; *Ethelasmedwe* 1351 SRO 322/160, *Hethhallesmedewe* 1378 *ib/197* (a meadow in Cotton, first el. uncertain); *The Fouldeyarde* 1610–11 *SBL 1483* ("adioyning to the mote of the manor house of Stoke uppon Tearne"); *Grymbaldesweye* 1331 ('Grimbald's way'); *La Haie* 1199 SAS 2/X (a wood, probably ME *hay* 'fenced-in enclosure'); *Helshaw Cornhill* 1696; *The Long Flats* 1696; *The Lower Houses* 1689; *Monekes Halstede* 1314 InqMisc (a plot of ground containing 12 acres and a rood, leased out by the Abbot of Combermere and said to be in *Chesthill*, which is associated with Stoke Grange: presumably the monks of Shrewsbury Abbey, who owned nearby Wollerton, or those of Combermere, had an establishment here: p.ns. derived ultimately from an OE **heall-stede*, literally 'hall-place', are listed and discussed by Dr K. I. Sandred, *English Place-Names in -stead* 101–2, with the suggestion that the meaning is "something like 'farm-stead'"); *The Parsons Heyes* 1689, ~ ~ *Hays* 1743, 71; (*The*) *Pickin* 1696, 1743, 71; *Platley Mdw* 1696, *Platly* ~ 1743; *Redehull* 1331 ('red hill'); *Shawe Platt* 1612 (a headland in ~ ~, *v.* Helshaw/ Shaw Fd *supra*, *platt* is a side-form of *plot*); *Stratford* 1331 (probably on the Roman road called The Longford, *v.* **strǣt**); *The Wheat Flatt* 1771.

4. WISTANSWICK (SJ 667290)

Wistaneswic 1209 For (p) *et passim* with variant spellings *Wystanes-* and *-wyk'*, *-wyk*(*e*) to Hy 6 *RentSur*
Westaneswvk 1326 Pat
Wystonswyke c.1566 *SRO 327 uncat*
Wistanswicke 1672 HTR

'Wīgstan's farm, *v.* **wīc**.

BROOK HO: 1833 OS shows a house called *The Grove* here.
RED LION INN.

Field-Names

Forms in (a) are 1840 *TA*.

(a) Banky Pce; Black Flat(s), Big Black Flat; Bow Butts; Broomy Fd, Lower, Upper; Bullock Fd; Calves Croft; Coppice Bank, Moor or Coppy Mdw; Crabtree Fd; Croft (several round village, including Crooks, Chapel, Kiln, Lane); Croft Horn (irregularly shaped with sharp points); Dross Dole; Fenny Grig (2) ('marshy heather'); Folly (by Suttonheath Cottages, on parish boundary); Green (2); Green Pce (3 small fields a short distance along road from Wistanswick Green); Jenkins, Big, Little; Lea; Lewers; Little Fd; London Lsw (by The Longford); Long Croft; Marsh

Mdw (2); Meadow, Big, Little; Middle Fd, Lower and Upper ~ ~; Moor (an area in N.W. of township is divided into numerous small fields with Moor ns: North Moor (*infra*) is the commonest: there are also Moor, Upper ~, Mare ~, Moor Bank: Mare Moor is on township boundary); Moor (8 fields S.W. of village are Moor, Big ~, Freeze Moor and Mdw); Moss Mdw; Mount Corner, Mdw (by The Mount in Stoke township); Nellock, ~ Fd; New Pce; North Moor (*North Moorfield or North Moor Piece* 1712 (copy) *SBL 4985*); Nub Bank Mdw; Oaks (2); Orchard Bank; Paddock; Pell Butts (FN 35 relates this to *pelled* SWB, 'eaten by sheep or cattle'); Penny Knowl, Pennet ~; Pikes (the field has two points); Porter's Lsw, Middle, Near; Purcell's Britch, Big and Little ~ ~; Richardson's Croft; Seven Sands (perhaps an error for *~ Lands); Shaddock (there is a large group of fields in S.E. corner of township with Shaddock ns., those with prefixes are Far, Near, Middle, Broomy, Gorsy, Oak, Big, Little, Road ~, also Shaddock Mdw: perhaps 'boundary oak', *v.* **scēad**, **āc**); Slaney; Two Butts (narrow strip in a small group of furlong-shaped fields); Well Fd; Wet Reins (drainage channels); White Flg; Wistanswick Green (narrow strip by road); Yard (several round village, including Kiln (by Malt Kiln), Long, Round and Seed Yd: Seed ~ may be *The Side Yard* 1712 (copy) *SBL 4985*).

Sutton Upon Tern

The parish-name is discussed in Part **1**. It is one of seven 'south settlements' in the county, and is so called in relationship to Market Drayton. It was earlier *Sutton by* (or *in*) *Drayton*.

The civil parish was formed out of Market Drayton in 1914, and the whole area is included in the Drayton Tithe Award. The 19th-cent. Index to Tithe Survey map shows Woodseaves as a separate township.

1. SUTTON UPON TERN (SJ 667317)

BUNTINGSDALE HALL (SJ 654325)

Bontanesdale 1291–2 *Ass* (p)
Buntanesd' 14th *SBL 9892* (p)
Buttanysdole 1416 Fine
Buntyngsdale 1517 *SRO 327*, *Buntingsdale* 1680 *SBL 4243 et seq*, ~ *Hall* 1833 OS
Buntinsdale 1776 *SBL 4259*

Perhaps a ME name, from *dale* 'valley' and a surname. *Bontan-*, *Buntan-* does not look like the reflex of an OE word or personal name. The surname *Bunting*, believed to be from the bird-name and recorded from the 12th century (VEPN), has modern variants such as *Bunton*, *Buntain*, but without evidence it would be rash to postulate such forms as ME alternatives to *Bunting*.

The Hall overlooks the valley of the R. Tern. *Buntingsdale Mill* is mentioned 1758 *SBL 4248* and *Buntinsdale Mills* 1776 *SBL 4259*.

COLEHURST MANOR (SJ 661313). This name is discussed in Part **1**. Identification of Colehurst with DB *Corselle* and 13th-cent. forms such as *Coleshasel* supersedes an earlier one with Cross Hills in Hinstock. The name means 'Col's hazel clump'.

TERN HILL (SJ 636323) is *Terynhyll* 1520 AD, *Tirnhull* 1535 VE, *Ternehill* c.1540 Leland, 1716 PR(L) 4, *Ternhill* 1711 *et freq* PR(L) 8. The modern crossroads settlement is on the boundary between Sutton upon Tern and Moreton Say parishes. Land here was earlier called *Hulle* 1231, 2 Ch, *Hull'* 1271–2 *Ass*, *Hull* 1284–5 FA. This was attached to *Chesthill supra*, in the vicinity or Stoke Grange. *Hulle* and *Chesthulle* were granted to Combermere Abbey in 1232, and the 1331 reference is to the bounds of the "manor of *Chesthulle* and all the land called *Hulle*".

It was suggested in Part **1**, *s.v. Chesthill*, that **hyll** in these and two other names in the 1331 bounds was used for slight eminences in an area adjoining the valleys of the R. Tern and its tributary, Bailey Brook.

BRICKKILN COVERT.

BROWNHILL COTTAGE, WD, *The Brown Hill* 1706 *SBL 13194*, *Brown Hill* 1833 OS.

CHESTNUT FM.

CLIFF GRANGE, 1833 OS, *Clift* ~ 1741 *SBL 5131*.

COLEHURST BUILDING, COTTAGES, WD: the wood is shown on *TAMap*.

DRY POOL, *Wood and Pleasure Ground* 1840 *TA*, by Buntingsdale Hall.

FLASH WD.

FOX INN.

THE GRANGE.

GRIGGY WD, *Plantation* 1840 *TA*. *Griggy* is an adjective from *grig* 'heather'.

HOLLYGROVE, *Holley Grove Flatt* 1706 *SBL 13194*, *Holly Grove* 1833 OS, 1840 *TA*.

LOSTFORD HALL, COPPICE, LANE, *v.* Lostford in Moreton Say.

MILL COTTAGES, *Mill* 1840 *TA*.

NEW MILL.

ROCK HO, *TA* has *Rock Leasow* here.

THE ROOKERY.

SALISBURYHILL COTTAGES, shown but not named on *TAMap*, *v.* Market Drayton street-ns. *supra*.

STONE COTTAGES, by Old Quarry, *TA* has *Quarry Field* here.

TERNHILL BRIDGE, *TA* has *Bridge Meadow* here.

THE VILLA.

WARRAN FM, shown but not named on *TAMap*.

Field-Names

Forms in (a) are 1840 *TA*, except for those dated 1823, 37, 51 which are *SBL 4297*, *4300*, *4311*: the first two documents are associated with Cliff

Grange. Early forms for which no date or source is given are 1706 *SBL 13194*. Those dated 1368 are *SBL 5454*, 1790 are *SBL 4256*.

(a) Axons Pce; Backside Croft (2, by houses); Banky Fd; Barn Fd; Barn Fd, Lsw (2 large fields); Bayley, Near (Bayleys Yard); The Bent (*The Fur Bent*, *Big* and *Middle Bent*, *The Bent Head*, *Long Bent Meadow*, 'bent grass', PN Ch **5.1** 102 lists several simplex ns. from this source); Big Barn Hill Pce; Birch, Big, Little (probably *britch*); Bogs, Bog Top, Plantation Bogs 1837; Boots Yd; Bowbridge Bank, Mdw (*Bowbridge Meadowe* 1688 *SBL 5043*, by a crossing of R. Tern on N. boundary); Brick Mdw; Brittaines Croft; Broad Pool; Brook Fd; Brook Lsw (*The* ~ ~); Bushy Grove Flat (*Bush Grove Flat*); Chuton Cop; Clemson (adjoins Famish Croft, *v.* discussion of Clem- ns. in Prees *supra*); Close Fd; Common, ~ Pces (large group of fields between Colehurst and The Longford); Common Pce (2); Coopers Lsw (1706); Cote Lsw (2, *Two Coate Leasows*, *The Little Coat Leasow*); Croft (several, small enclosures round habitations); Dale Flats (*Two Dale Flatts*); Dove Fd; Dovehouse Fd, Far, Near; The Eight Acres (adjoining Ten Acres is slightly larger); Eight Lands (1706, adjoins Dale Flats); Famish Croft (*Fammish* ~, Clemson adjoins); Field back of the House); Five Acres and Long Fd Top; The Flat (2 large fields near Dale Flats); Flat, Far, Near, Middle; Flat Fd; Four Loaves and Eight Acres 1837 (Loaves may be *recte* Loans 'lands'); The Giol Wicket 1823, Gaol of Wicket 1837; Gorsy Fd (2); Green Fd; Grinsell Pce; Hall Fd (2, one near Buntingsdale Hall); Handkerchief (a curiously shaped field which could be considered to resemble a neckerchief); Hatchetts Pce (~ *Croft*, *The Hatchett Peece*, possibly cf. *Hatch Gate Croft ib*); Heath Fd (adjoins Common); Hill Fd; Hoar Croft; Holly Tree Mdw; House Mdw; Island Mdw, Lower, Upper (by R. Tern); Lawn (by Buntingsdale Hall); London Fd (by The Longford, London Lsw in Wistanswick is 1½ miles S. on same road); Long Sutton Fd; Lousey Mdw; Mare Fd (on county boundary); Marl Pit Fd (Marley Pit Croft); Meadow, Lower, Near, Barn, Hall, Dovehouse (by Colehurst); Meadow, Lower, Middle, Upper, ~ Bank (along Tern); Mill Mdw (1706, by Mill Cottages); Moles Lsw, Upper, Moles Mdw, Lower, Upper; Moor, Long, Lower, Upper, ~ Bank (*The Moors*); New Inclosure; New Pce (~ *Peece*); Oak Hill, Lower, Upper; Oat Stubble (1706); Ox and Harpers Lsw; Ozier Bed 1823; Paddock; Passage Mdw; Pool Fd; Quarry Bank; Rickyard Fd; Rock Lsw; Rough Pce; Rushy Fd; Sandy Croft; Short Sutton Fd; Sitch Fd, Mdw (*The Sitch*); Slang; Smooth Wd, Near Swerving ~ ~; The Sniggle Bogs 1823 (the same n. occurs in Boreatton township in Baschurch *supra*: a similar term, *sniddle-bog*, occurs in Ch dialect, PN Ch **3** 225); Stoky Fd, Far, Near, Little (*Stokey Field*); Stone Wall; Styche, Big, Little (various meanings are suggested for *stitch* in f.ns., *v.* discussions PN Berks 907, PN Ch **5.1** 353, 357–8); Sutton Mdw; Taylors Mdw; Teylant Lsw, Mdw (possibly *Teal Lane Leasow*); Town End Lsw (at N. end of Sutton, *Townsend Piece*); Turnips; War Fd, Mdw (*Wear Meadow* 1790, 'weir', by a stream); Weavers Fd 1837; Well Mdw; White Gate Fd; White Lsw (1706); Wood Lsw; Yard, Bullock, Low, Over and Far Yd (by Sutton); Yester (*The* ~, *Great* and *Little* ~, 'sheepfold', *v.* **eowestre**).

(b) *Allcock Hill*; *The Annatts*; *Brightly Well* 1790; *Butts*, *The Three*, *The Two*; *Church Hill Cop*; *Coat Croft*; *The Horne*; *Leasow*, *Colledge*, *Coopers*, *Farther*, *French Wheat*, *Gorsty*, *Grass*, *Hawthorn*, *Higher*, *Little*, *Marle*, *New*, *Oake*, *Old*, *Ox*, *Pease*, *Rough*, *Tern*, *Thisteley*, *Triangle*, *Webbs*; *The Line Peece*; *Long Lands*; *The Long Meadow*; *Marl Furlongs* 1368; *The Moats*; *Newett Corner*; *The Plecks* (ME

plek 'small plot'); *Rye Croft*; *Shop Latches Leasow* (there is a street in Shrewsbury called Shoplatch, Part **4** 31–2); *Steventons Meadow*; *The Wall Croft*; *The Whittning Yard* (cf. Stoke upon Tern f.ns.); *Winter and Lent Fields* 1368; *Wythnale Furlong*, 1368 (probably 'willow nook', *v.* **wīðign**, **halh**); *Yard*, *Barn*, *Bigg*, *Bullock*, *Carthouse*, *Clover*, *French Wheat*, *Hall*, *Higher*, *Farther*, *Middle*, *Nar*, *Spires*.

2. WOODSEAVES (SJ 687310): *Woodseivs* 1517 *SRO 327* (reading of second el. uncertain), *Wodseves* 1548 *SBL 4545*, *Woodseves* 1550–1 *SBL 5193*, *Woddeseves* 1569 *SBL 5458*, *Woodseaves* 1776 *SBL 4874*. 'Wood's edge', *v.* **efes**.

THE SYDNALL (SJ 684305), LOWER SYDNALL

Sydenhale e.14th *SBL 4543*, *Sidenhale* 1315 *SBL 5449*, *Syddenhall* 1529 *SBL 5441 et freq* with variant spellings *Sidden-*, *-halle* to 1627 *SBL 5698*, *Sydenhall* 1548 *SBL 4544*

Sydnall' 1547–8 *SBL 5094 et seq* with variant spelling *-al(l)*

v. **sīd** 'wide, spacious' and **halh**: this is a recurrent p.n. compound. It is not obvious which of the numerous senses of **halh** is the relevant one in this case. The reference could be to a shallow bowl of land, as in Shifnal (Part **1**).

Many of the later shortened forms have *als Syd(d)enhall/or Sydenhall* added: the name is *Sydnall or Sydenhall Farm* 1825 *SBL 5647*.

BERRINGTON, 1833 OS.

BROAD VIEW.

CHESWARDINE ROAD BRIDGE, HIGH BRIDGE (canal bridges).

THE COMMON, 1840 *TA*.

CRICKMERY BANK, *Crickmerry Bank* 1833 OS, *Crickmary* 1840 *TA*.

CROW WD. *Wood* 1840 *TA*.

DAIRY HO, shown but not named on *TAMap*.

THE DINGLE, *Wood* 1840 *TA*.

THE GROVE, 1833 OS.

LIGHT WD, LIGHTWOOD FM. The 6" map shows these names in Woodseaves and also gives Lightwood for a small roadside settlement ⅓ mile E. in Hinstock. The name is discussed under Hinstock, *supra*.

ROSEHILL, *Rose Hill* 1833 OS. ROSEHILL MILL, *Mill* 1833 OS, 1840 *TA*.

SUTTON HEATH, 1776 *SBL 4874*, 1833 OS.

Field-Names

Forms in (a) are 1840 *TA* except where otherwise stated: those dated 1801, 2, 24, 37, 51, 70 are *SBL 4886*, *4888*, *4889*, *4301*, *4311*, *4379*. Earlier forms dated c.1566, 1667, 74, 1729, 30, 82 are *SRO 327 uncat*, *SBL 6531*, *6530*, *6529*, *4883*, *4884*.

(a) Acres, ~ Nook; Adder Fd; Bache (ultimately from **bæce**); Bailey Birch; Bank Lsw; Banky Fd (2); Barley Fd; Barn Yd; Big Fd (2); Big Mdw (several); Birch(es) 1801 (the 1801 list has Great Arcon and Elkins Birch(e), earlier sources have *Elkins ~*, *Lockley ~*, *Poolebirch* 1667, 74, *Nether Lowe Birch* 1674: the 1824 list has "The Great Elkin or Arkin Birches in two parts divided": *Birch* is a form of *britch* 'newly-broken-in land'); Birch, Near, Pool (Clay Birch is nearby, probably *britch*); Black Flat; Bogs, Bog Top 1837; Bone Mdw 1801; Bowler Croft; Brick Fd, Little, Big Brick Lsw; Brick Kiln Fd (several); Broad Lsw; Broad Mdw; Brockley; Broom Croft 1801; Broomy Croft; Canal and Spoil Banks; Chalton or Chorlton Fds; Chambling Bank, Far, Near; Cherringtons Lsw 1801 (1729, 30); Charringtons Lsw; Clover Fd; Clover Lsw; Cockpit Fd, Lower, Over (on N. edge of the straggling Woodseaves settlement); Coat Lsw (1729, 30), The Coat Grounds (1730), The Coat Mdw 1801 (*TA* has Cote Lsw); Common (several, large cluster of Common ns. on boundary with Hinstock and Stoke upon Tern); The Cow Lsw 1801 (1732, *Cowes Lessowe* 1667); Cow Moor 1801; Crabmill Croft 1802; Crabtree Fd ("a butt in") 1841 GT (1722–3); Croft (cluster by Woodseaves includes Big, Heath, House, Pit and Turnpike Croft, cluster by Rose Hill includes House, Lane, Long and Maw Croft, cluster on Wistanswick boundary includes Barnt, Graftons and Well Croft); Cunniga ('rabbit warren', *v.* **coninger**); Door House Mdw; Daily Lsw; Eight Acres; Far Mdw; Far Moors; Field, Little, New, Stable; Flax Butts, Far, Near; Ford Rough (narrow strip, EDD *foredraught* 'lane or path for the purpose of draught between two farms'); Fordyhough (Forty Trough 1870, probably garbled versions of preceding, this field is also a narrow strip); The Further Ground 1801; Gate Fd, Lower; Gill Fd, Far, Near, Lower, ~ Lane; Gravel Pit Fd, Little Pit Fd; Greasley, Common ~, Smooth ~, Far Smoothey ~, Big and Little Rough ~ (group of fields on E. boundary); Grove; Hawthorn; Honey Spot 1870; Horse Hays; Horse Moor; Housefield Mdw, House Fd and Mdw, House Mdw; Intake (several); Jacks Lsw; Kings Lsw; Lambs Cote Lsw; Land Lsw 1801; Lane; Lane Croft, Far, Near; Lawrences Lsw 1801 (1729, 30); Lee Lsw, The Two Lea Lsws 1801 (*Lea Leasow* 1729); Lions Yd (among Croft ns. on Wistanswick boundary); Little Croft 1801; Little Heath 1801; Lodge, Front Lodge, Two ~ ~, Three ~ ~ (no buildings in these 4 fields); Long Fd; Long Mdw; Longston, Far, Long, Lower; Mare Fd; Marl Fd (*The Little ~ ~* 1788); Meadow (several); Merry Tree Fd (wild cherry); Moor, The Lower, Nearer, Little, Moor Bank 1801 (*Near* and *Lower Moor* 1782); New Fd; New Mdw 1801; Near Moors (short distance from Far ~); Oat Lsw & Mdw; Oat Moor 1801; Over Fd (Over Mdw and Over Common Fd are nearby); Ox Lsw (several); The Paddock 1801 (1782); Pea Croft, Fd; Pool, Pool Bank, Fd, Mdw, Lightwood ~; Pool Fd, Mdw (this and preceding are by pools on a tributary of R. Tern); Poor Lsw, Near; Potato Fd, Lower; Rail Pce, Big, Little; Road Pce; Rough Fd (2); Rough Lsw; Rough Pits & Wash (cf. *Wesshing Pittfilde* c.1566); Round Orchard 1801, 24 (1730); Rubbing Post Fd; Sand Lsw 1801; Sheet Croft;

Shukers Fd; Shutts; Sixteen Acres (4 fields); Slang, ~ Mdw; Sniggle Bogs (another in Sutton township *supra*); Soldiers Fd, Holes; Spout Pit Bank; Stantons Lsw, Far ~ ~; Stanyards Bank 1801; Stony Bank; The Stony Hurst 1801 (*Stainehurst Pasture* 1667, *The Stonyhurst* 1730, *v.* **stānig**, **hyrst**); Tattenhall; Tunstall, Far, Little, Long, Near, ~ Mdw (5 fields between Woodseaves and St border, perhaps indicating that Woodseaves is a shrunken settlement: cf. Tunstall in Betton township *supra*); Vetches Fd; Way Fd; Well Fd (2); White Lsw; With Pce; Wood, Over, Near, Lower, Wood Mdw; Wood Fd, Far, Near; Wood Mdw (c.1566); Wycherleys, Far; Yelves, New ~.

(b) *Blakemedow* 1439, 47 AD, *Blackemedowe* c.1566; *Chalkingfilde*, *Chockfilde*, *Chokin Briche* c.1566; *Daffolde ib*; *Dewks Hill ib*; *Pitcrofte ib*; *Strabury Bryche ib*; *Woodcrofte ib.*

Map 7: Townships in the parish of Wem.

Wem

The parish-name, which is considered to mean 'marshy ground', is discussed in Part **1**.

The parish contains 12 townships, Aston, Edstaston and Coton, Horton, Lacon, Lowe and Ditches, Newtown, Northwood, Sleap, Soulton, Tilley and Trench, Wem and Wolverley. These have separate Tithe Awards, varying in date from 1840 to 1846. A high proportion of these, all except Lowe and Ditches, Newtown, and Tilley and Trench, are DB manors.

1. ASTON (SJ 530287)
One of 10 Sa instances of the common name which means 'east settlement', east of Wem in this instance. As a DB manor this Aston is documented in Part **1**.

BROCKHURST (SJ 540287): *Brokhurst*, *Brochurste* 1290 Ipm, *Brochurst* 1342 HAC, *Brokhurst* 1369 Ipm, *Brockhurst* 1588 *SRO 322 box 2*.

A compound of **brocc** 'badger' and **hyrst** 'wooded hill', which occurs also in minor ns. in Ch, Db, Wa. The above references are to a wood in Wem. The settlement is *Wem Brocaist* 1748, *Brockhorst* 1750, *Brockhurst* 1758, all PR(L) 10. This settlement and a house called The Hill stand on an oval hill of 300', a classic **hyrst** site.

ASTON BRIDGE, HALL (1732 PR(L) 9, 1833 OS), HO, PARK, RD.

ALDERLEY LANE, *The Owlery Lane* 1768 PR(L) 10, *The Alderly Lane* 1802 ib, *Alderey Lane* 1833 OS, *Big* and *Far Howler* 1842 *TA*. Garbet, 1818, has *Sowford Lane now Oller Lane*. Ultimately from **alor** 'alder'. PN Ch **5.1** 92 gives Aldery, Howlery, Owlery among f.ns. from this source.

BARKERS GREEN, 1833 OS, 1842 *TA*, *Barker's Green* 1658 *et seq* PR(L) 9.

BROCKHURST COVERT.

BROOK HO, 1833 OS, *The Brooke* 1722 *et seq* PR(L) 9.

HILCOP BANK, *Hill Cop Bank* 1842 *TA*. Garbet, 1818, has "The Hill Lane or Hill-cop-bank, corruptly called Held-cop-bank", which may indicate that the first element is from **helde** 'gentle slope'. This is the E. side of the Brockhurst Hill.

THE HILL, 1818 Garbet, 1833 OS, *v.* Brockhurst *supra*.

MOAT HO, 1789 RTH, 1818 Garbet, 1833 OS, *The Mothouse* 1659 PR(L) 9, *Mott House* 1660 ib, *Mote House* 1719 ib. The moat is shown on modern OS maps.

THISTLEFORD BRIDGE, *Lower Thistleford Meadow* 1842 *TA*.

THE WEIR, 1833 OS, *Weare* 1599 PR(L) 9, *The Ware* 1769 ib 10, *The Were* 1789 ib 7.

Field-Names

Forms in (a) are 1842 *TA*.

This township contains a large number of small fields. Most of the names have been listed, but divisions such as Big, Little, Far, Near have not been noted.

(a) (The) Bank (2); Barn Fd (2); Barnyard (2); Big Fd; Big Mdw; Black Ford (by Alderley Lane, probably a causeway); Boot Heath, Fd (3 fields, possibly a shape n.); Brickkiln Fd (several); Brick Yd; Brook Croft, Pce; Brook Mdw (several); (The) Brooms (several); Broomy Lsw; Brown Robin; Bull Croft; Burdens Moor, Far, Little; Calves Yd (by Cow Lsw); Church Gates (by road, N. of village); Clover Fd; Clemley Park (*v.* Clemley in Prees *supra*); Coal Mdw; Coppice Fd; Cote Mdw (no building); Crabtree Fd; Creamore Stones; Croft (*freq*, clusters round habitations); Crow Croft; Cuckoo's Corner (2, both small, irregularly shaped fields); Cutters Pce; Dovehouse Fd (by village); The Exchange (cf. Exchange Mdw in Wellington and The Change in Rushbury, Part **3** 70, 189, which are cited in VEPN under OFr *change* with the comment "In f.ns the term probably denotes exchange transactions"); Far Wall (Well Mdw adjoins); Field under Wood; Firtree Croft; Flams (dialect *fleam* 'artificial water channel' is sometimes Flam in Ch, PN Ch **5.1** 181–2: *TAMap* shows a straight channel by R. Roden, not shown on later maps); Foxes Marsh; The Furlong (probably in Winsorton Fd); Garden Fd (2); Gorsy Lsw; Hadley; Halloway Mdw; Hay Butts, Haybutt Mdw; Heart's Head; Hill (group of fields in S.W. corner of township); Hill Fd, Lower Hill; Hollybush Fd; Horse Moor (2 groups of fields on N. boundary); House Fd; House Road Bank (by Brockhurst); Irelands Mdw; Lady Mdw (*The* ~ ~ 1651 Garbet); The Lawn (by Aston Park); Lessage; Long Square (narrow oblong); Marl Fd; Marl Lsw (2); The Moors, Moors Fd; Moors, Far, Old; Mill Fd; Milking Bank (by The Hill); Modus Pce (NED 4, 'money payment in lieu of tithe'); Muddy Mdw; Nailor's Mdw; New Lsw (several); New Mdw (2); New Pce; Oaks, Mealing ~; Orchard Fd; Owen's Britch; Patch, Little; The Robins (not near Brown Robin); Rough Lsw; Rushy Fd; Frye Croft (2); Ryegrass Fd; Sawpit Fd; Sharp's Mdw; Sheep Lsw (Cow Lsw adjoins); Shop Fd (by Smithy Croft); Shutt Lsw; The Slade (strip beside R. Roden); Slang (several); Smithy Croft (near village); Soulton Fd (Garbet places a common field called Barley Fd in this area); Stackyard Mdw; Steward's Mdw, Pce; Stockholms Croft, Hill, Pce; Stockings ('clearings', 4 fields by village); Sycamore Mdw; Thistly Lsw; Thistly Mdw; Three Cornered Pce; Three

Gates (on E. boundary, by Wem road); Townsend (by a house which may have been considered the easternmost in Wem, Town Fd adjoins); Water Mdw; Weir Croft (not by river); Weir Mdw (by R. Roden on E. boundary); Well Fd (2); Well Lsw; Well Mdw (several); Well War Moor (Far and Long Wall Moor adjoin); Wem Mdw; Wheat Fd (several); Widow's Lsw (Lord's Lsw adjoins); Wing Marsh, The Wings (adjoining Marsh ns.); Winserton Fd, Little Winserton (Garbet gives Winsorton Fd as one of Aston's 3 open fields, "name preserved in Winsorton Bank"); Wycherley Fd; Yewtree Fd.

2. EDSTASTON AND COTON

This large township can conveniently be treated in two parts, with the boundary between Edstaston and Coton taken to be the tributary of Soulton Brook from which the hamlet of Quina Brook is named. This stream joins Soulton Brook at SJ 540326.

(i) COTON (SJ 536350)

Coton is a DB manor so the name is discussed in Part **1**. It is one of six Sa instances of Cot(t)on, 'cottages'.

BANK HO, 1792 RTH, *The Bank* 1842 *TA*.

BULL AND DOG P.H., *Dog and Bull* 1799 RTH.

COCK'S BRITCHES (a small wood which is *Cox Birch Pltn* on *TAMap*), *Cocks Britches* 1699 *SBL 3411*, *the two Cocks Britches* 1700 *SBL 3414*, *Cockes Britches* 1711 *SBL 3419*, 'newly-broken-in land', *v.* **bryce**.

COTON FM.

COTON GROVE.

COTON HALL: Garbet says the hall was there t. Ed 6.

COTON HO.

COTON PARK FM.

COTON WD, 1833 OS, *Cotton Wood* 1695 PR(L) 9. The settlement is Cotonwood on the 1899 6" map and a small wood nearby is *Coton Wood*. Cotton Wood appears twice on 1833 OS, applied to N. and S. parts of the sprawling settlement.

GANDERSBANK: the house is shown but not named on *TAMap*.

HEATHS COVERT, *Big*, *Far*, *Near Heath*, *The Heaths* 1842 *TA*, perhaps *Wem Heathes* 1702 PR(L) 9.

HOME FM.

MILL HO, 1833 OS, *The Millhouse* 1761 PR(L) 10, *Old Windmill Field*, *The Old Mill Field*, *Old Mill Meadow* 1842 *TA*: "Old Windmill" is marked on 1899 6".

ROOKERY 1833 OS.

WOODEND HALL, 1833 OS, *Wood End Hall* 1785 RTH.

WOODSIDE FM, 1833 OS.

Field-Names

Forms in (a) are 1842 *TA*.

(a) Adrey Fd; Ashley's Fd; Back Fd, Far, Near, Bottom; Backside Fd, Backhouse Fd; Bakehouse Croft; Bakehouse Fd; Bansage Fd, Mdw; The Barley Bank; Barn Fd (several); Barn Mdw; Barnyard Fd; Big Fd; Big Mdw (several); Birch, Creamore, Rean (near Cock's Birch *supra*); Brickkiln; Brickkiln Fd; Briery Bank; Broad Mdw; Brook Lsw; Broomy Lsw; Chidlow's Croft; Chimney Lsw (not an obvious shape n.); Clemley Park (among Croft ns. on S. outskirts of Cotonwood: the n. recurs in this parish, as it does in Prees); Clover Fd; Common Fd, Pce (large group of enclosures in Cotonwood); Cote Fd, Big, Little, ~ Mdw (no building); Cotton's Fd; Cow Lsw; Cow Pasture, Higher, Lower; Crew Hall Yd (Garbet mentions Crew Hall and Lane); Croft (*passim* in Cotonwood); The Crofts (large field); Dovehouse Mdw (by Coton Hall); Field, Big, Far, Footroad, Shop, Well (cluster of small fields S. of Coton Ho); Field (enclosures in Cotonwood include Back, Banky, Barnyard, Big, Clover, Corner, Cottage, House, Pit, Tilers, Westons ~); Footroad Fd (Footway Fd adjoins); The Furlong, The Furlongs (among Croft ns. S. of Cotonwood); Grooms Pce; Higginson's Yd; Hill Fd, Upper ~ ~ (Garbet says this was a common field, W. of Cotonwood); Hills Fd; Hinton's Pce; Hoar Stone (large field by Woodend Hall); Horse Moor, Far and Little ~ ~; Horse Pasture; The Knowles, Far, Near and Middle ~, Knowl Bank; Kyngston's Fd; The Lawn (tiny field by Cotongrove); Ley, Far, Near; Long Fd (several); Long Mdw (2); Maddox Moor, Big, Little; Marl Fd; Marl Lsw, Far, Near; Meadow, Big, Little, Baugh's; Meadow, Big, Brook, Dole, Wet (5 parallel strips, still there on 1900 6"); Middle Pce; Milking Bank (near Bank Ho); Milking Bank Fd (large field, not near a house); The Miller's Fd; Millington's Fd, Mdw, Big, Little Millingtons; Moor, Far, Horse; Moor, Little, Long; Newlands Fd, Mdw; New Lsw; New Mdw; Old Wd Pce; The Old Yd; Ox Hay; Oxons Fd; Pale Stiles; Peas Croft; Phibs Croft; Pingo (variant of **pingel** 'small enclosure'); Pit Fd, Black, Top; Plantation; Pool Mdw, Big, Little; The Pools (near preceding); Rails Pce; Ratcliff's Mdw; Raven Fd; The Rough; Rough Croft; (The) Roundabout (3 fields S. of Cotonwood); Rowley's Fd; Rushy Croft; Rushy Moor, Big, Little; Rye Flg, ~ ~ Mdw (by Coton Hall); Sandlands Mdw, Little ~ Fd; The Six Butts (tiny enclosure in Cotonwood); Slang (several); Stable Croft; Stone & Cross Fd, Pltn (RTH, 1787, gives *Stone & Cross, Coton* as a place where he delivered a baby); Tall Tree Bank; Tench Pit Fd; Three Cornered Croft (2); Thistly Fd; Tollgate Fd (by Whitchurch road); Top Fd; The Two Butts (tiny enclosures near Gandersbank); Wall Lsw, Big, Little; Warmoor Lane, Far, Near (Moor Lane now called Warmoor Lane, Garbet); Water Lane Fd; The Way Croft; Way Lsw; Well Fd; Whitfields Mdw; Wood Fd; Woodgate Fd (in Cotonwood); Wood Pce, Far, Near; Yard (enclosures in Cotonwood include Barnett's, Bottom, Evans, Middle, Stackyard).

(ii) EDSTASTON (SJ 519319).
The name, which means 'Ēadstān's estate', is discussed in Part **1**.

CREAMORE (SJ 517303): *Cramer* 1610 *et seq* PR(L) 9, *Cramar* 1655, 8 ib, *Cramore* 1701, 20 ib, *Creamer* 1778 *SBL 3337*. CREAMORE BANK is

Chramor Bank 1753 PR(L) 10, *Chramer* ~ 1756 ib, *Cramor*(*e*) 1758, 68 ib.

Possibly 'crow pond' or 'marsh', *v.* **crāwe**, **mere**, **mōr**. Available forms do not support Garbet's "Creamore, rightly Cranmore".

PADDOL GREEN (SJ 505323), 1833 OS. Forms from PR(L) 9 and 10 are: *Para Green* 1687, 9, *Pady Green* 1737, (*The*) *Padergreen* 1762–72, *Paddoe Green* 1786, *Paddock Green* 1794, 1803. Probably 'paddock', ultimately from OE **pearroc**.

PEPPER STREET (SJ 533326), 1758 PR(L) 10, 1793 RTH, 1833 OS: *Peper Street* 1683, 8 PR(L) 9. There is an excellent discussion of this name in PN Ch **5.1** 17–18. Dodgson gives a number of urban examples from Ch and other counties which can be explained as trade names; but he notes that "it is not clear what the name Pepper Street means as a road-name in the countryside or in small villages", and he lists a number of examples in that category to which the Wem instance can be added. He also notes some examples in the Netherlands and Flanders.

No entirely convincing explanation is available. Dodgson notes the possibility of an allusion to dust on these roads, also that *pepper* is a dialect term for an itinerant pedlar or horse-dealer. Pepper Hill, one instance of which occurs in the enclave of Ch near Adderley, 8 miles N.E. of the Edstaston Pepper Street, may be a related name.

QUINA BROOK (SJ 525330), *Kinabrook* 1762 PR(L) 10, *Quinabrook* 1777, 1808 ib, *Quino Brook* 1810 ib, 1818 Garbet. The settlement is a short distance S. of the tributary of Soulton Brook which is here treated as the boundary between Coton and Edstaston. The name resembles that of Quinny Brook in Wistanstow, mentioned in ERN with the spellings *Quen*(*n*)*y* 1577, *Queneie* 1586. Other forms for Quinny Brook are *Quenn*(*i*)*y* (*Lands*) 1687 PR(H) 17 and probably *Winewesbrok* 1301 SAC. The duplication suggests a stream-name, albeit of obscure origin. There is no likelihood of a compound with **ēa**, as that term is applied to major rivers.

ASHFIELD HO: probably *The Ash House* 1656 PR(L) 9, 1818 Garbet.
BANK HO.
BIRCHTREE FM, shown but not named on *TAMap*.
COTON PARK FM (a mile from Coton).
CREAMORE MILL, VILLA: *v. supra*.
EDSTASTON BRIDGE, over canal.

EDSTASTON GORSE.

EDSTASTON HALL, 1687 PR(L) 9, 1833 OS: Garbet says "leased 1591".

EDSTASTON PARK, t.Eliz *RentSur*, 1833 OS, EDSTASTON HIGHER PARK. Garbet says that the "new park" was a wood in 1561 "now divided into pastures and meadows", and that Park House is "a convenient dwelling belonging to the larger of the two farms". Cf. (wood called) *Le Newepark* 1299 Ipm.

FOXHOLES 1833 OS, applied to two sites: *The* ~ 1644 *et seq* PR(L) 9.

HIGHFIELDS, 1687 *et seq* PR(L) 9, *High Fields* 1833 OS.

MOORHEAD.

MUNT COTTAGE.

OAKLANDS.

PARKGATE: *Edstaston Park Gate* is mentioned 1794 RTH as a place where a baby was delivered.

POOLHEAD, 1786 *et seq* RTH, 1833 OS, *Pool Head* 1688 Garbet. Garbet 270 says "Messuage called the Pool Head, at head of Castor's pool, formerly 1 mile in compass, mainly in Whixall. Long drained."

RYEBANK, *The Riebank* 1654 PR(L) 9, *Rye Bank* 1696 ib, 1783 *et seq* RTH, *The Rye Bank* 1807 PR(L) 10. RYEBANK HO, 1833 OS, is a "good house at Rye Bank" 1818 Garbet.

SYDNEY BRIDGE, over canal.

YEWTREE HO, *Yew Tree House* 1833 OS.

The moated site N.E. of Creamore is *Drigadrake* 1833 OS. FN 67 says "the field named *Drake Hill* or *Drigadrake* (Wem) was said to be the haunt of a dragon". The name is not in *TA*.

Field-Names

Forms in (a) are 1842 *TA*.

(a) Alder Fd, Higher, Lower; Alderley, Far, Near; Ashes Fd, Mdw; Aston Fd (not near Aston); Baggley's Mdw; Bakehouse Mdw, Yd; Barn Fd (several); Barn Mdw; Barn Yd (several); Beggarman's Bank; Besford's Backside; Big Fd (several); Big Mdw (2); Birch Mdw; The Birches (2, probably *britch* 'newly-broken-in land'); The Black Mdw; Bostock's Fd; Bottom Fd (2); Bottom Mdw; Brankelow, Far and Near ~, ~ Mdw; Briary Croft; Brickkiln, Big, Little; Brickckiln Mdw; Brickyard, Big, Little; Brook Mdw (several); Brooms (several); Broomy Lsw; Caster/Castor Pool (4 fields near Poolhead *q.v.*); Chapel Fd, Mdw (Garbet says this was an open field); The Clemley, Clemley Park (⅓ mile apart, *v.* Clemley in Prees); Clover Fd (2); Clover Lsw; The Coppice; Croft (small enclosures by Ryebank include Far, Near, Middle, Pinfold and Yewtree Croft: small fields near Coton Park Fm include Ann's,

Croxon's, Jenkins, Rowleys, Briery, Fingerpost and Gorsy Croft); Cross Fd, Lower, Top (by road junction, Garbet says this was one of 3 common fields); Dunn's Britch, Lower, Upper, Near; Far Fd (on E. boundary); Far Moor; Fazely Oak; Feggy Fd, Further ~ ~ (coarse grass); Field (small enclosures in Quina Brook include Clover, Crabtree, Middle, Read's and Well Fd); Field, Big, Bottom, Little; Field, Barn, Brook, Long, Near, Thistly, Top; The Five Butts (large field by Whitchurch road, Garbet places an open field in this area); Furlong (adjoining fields N.E. of Quina Brook are Chicken ~ and Hares ~); Garden Fd (several); George's Bank; Gorsy Britch, Gorsy Lsw; Gravel Hall Fd (probably Gravel Hole); Green Fd; Green Lane; Grimes, Far, Near; The Grove; Hall Mdw (by Edstaston Hall); Harper, Big; Hinds Pce; Hopyard; Horse Moor; Horse Pasture (several); Inklings Croft; Intake (tiny enclosure by road); Jebb's Moor, Big, Little, Near, Jebbs Mdw, Far, Near; John Hays, Far, Near, ~ ~ Mdw; Kiln Mdw (Malt Kiln adjoins); Lane Mdw, Big, Out; (The) Lawn (3, by Edstaston Ho and Park and Ryebank Ho); Leasow, Allen's, Hill, Little; Leg and Foot (shape n.); Limestone, Far, Near, Limestones, Lower and Middle ~ (round Ryebank Ho); Long Croft; Long Fd; Long Hayes; Long Lsw; Long Moor; Machine House & Meadow (by canal wharf); Marl Fd (2); Marl Lsw; Matty's Croft; The Meadow (several); Meadow, Big, Broad, Dole, Hoo; Meadow, Hinton's, Tinman's, Welves; Meadow Bank, Big, Little; Middle Fd; Milestone Fd (by Whitchurch road); Milking Bank (2, by Birchtree Fm and New Ho); Moat Bank, Fd (by Highfields, moat shown on 6" map); Moat Fd (by Poolhead, 6" map shows Old Clay Pit); Mosspit Fd, Croft (tiny enclosure called Pits adjoins); Mossy Pool, Pce; Near Fd, Bottom, Top; New Mdw, Pce; Nick Brich, Far, Near; Norton Fd, Lower, Upper; Nuttree Fd; Oak, Big, Little; Oakley Mdw, Benders Oakley (on Wem boundary, Garbet mentions "the little and Great Okenel now called Okeleys"); Offal, Higher, Lower; Old Man's Bank; Orchard Mdw; Ox Hay; Ox Lsw (Cow Lsw adjoins); Park Fd, Mdw (by Coton Pk Fm); Pea Lsw; Pen Bank; Penny Rent; Piece, Barkers's, Jennings, Further, Near; Piece, Middle, Far, New, Top, Canal, Braynes, Hinton's, Powell's, Wrights; Piece, Wells, Wycherleys; Piper's Moor; Pit Fd; Pool Pce; Potato Croft (several); Prescott's Pce; Rails Pce, Far, Near; Richmond Hill (probably transferred from London); Rough Hayes; Rough Mdw; Round Mdw (one curved side); The Rushy Fd; The Ryegrass; Sambrook Mdw; Sawpit Fd; Shop Croft, Far and Near Shop Fd; Sidney, Far, Near, ~ Mdw (either side of canal); Silver Pit, Big, Little; Slang; The Sneds (on W. boundary, 'cut-off land', ultimately from **snǣd**); Stable Mdw (by Highfields); Stiff Fd; Stockalls Croft; Stockings (2, 'clearings'); Swanacks; Thistly Fd; Throats, Long, Rushy (strips by stream); Town Fd (minute enclosure by Ryebank); Trench Pit Fd; Turnpike Croft (by Wem/Whitchurch road); Warehouse Croft, Wharf (by canal); Well Lsw; Whitchurch Road, Lower, Top; Windsor Fd; Wollary Husk (Wollery refers to alders, Husk is possibly *hassock* 'coarse grass'); Wood, Big, Far, Middle; Near Wood Fd, Mosspit Wd; Wren's Nest (enclosure with house by canal); Yewtree Fd (2).

(b) Garbet, 1818, gives two early ns: *Chetal Wood* 1561 and *Whorrow Field* n.d. He says that the wood, "still preserved, oak, a mile in circuit", was sometimes written *Chetwal*, *Chittal*, *Chitto*, and that Whorrow was the n. of an open field between Creamore farm and the first house on the Whitchurch road. The n. of the open field was "still retained by one or more closes".

3. HORTON (SJ 490298)

This is a DB manor, so the name is discussed in Part **1**: it means 'dirt settlement' and is one of three Sa instances of this recurrent name.

CHALK HILL: another *Chalk Hill* occurs in *TA*.

FIELDS, FIELDS FM: neither building is shown on *TAMap*.

HORTON GATE: *TAMap* shows *Turnpike House* on Wem/Wolverley road.

HORTON HALL.

PRIMROSE BANK.

LONG WOLVERLEY, plantation on border with Wolverley, *Big* and *Little Wolverley*, ~ *Pltn* 1845 *TA*.

Field-Names

Forms in (a) are 1845 *TA*, except for those dated 1818, which are Garbet.

(a) Alders, Bottom, Top, Little; Barn Yd; Black Croft Mdw; Bradley Moor; Brickkiln Fd; Calves Croft; Chalk Hill (not near Chalk Hill at Horton Gate, *TAMap* shows a depression marked Sand Hole in the field); Cinder Fd, Cinders Croft *v. infra*); Coppy Fd; Common Mdw; Croft (cluster on N.E. boundary includes Big, Second, Far, Near Croft); Croft (cluster by Horton Gate includes Chicken, Pingo, Well Croft); The Dole Mdw; Field (cluster S. of Horton includes Blakeway's, Briery, House, Pigstye, Thistly, Yewtree Field); Flax Mdw; Gravel Hole Fd; The Green Lane 1818; Green's Grave; Hannah Mdw; Horse Pasture (2); Horton Fd; Horton Mdw; The Lawn (by Horton Hall); Leasow, Brook, Hill, New; Long Croft; Lord's Mdw (1653 *SBL 2503*); Lynors; Marlpit Fd; Meadow, Flax, Rough, Tags; Mile Ash (by Wem road, about a mile from edge of town); Moody's Fd; Moor Lane 1818; Nicoll's Breech 1818; Old Land, Far, Near; Orchard Croft; The Pinfold; Pit Fd (2); Pool, First, Second, Pool Lane Mdw, Pltn; The Rough, Little ~, Rough Fd, Mdw; Rough Bank; Roundhill, Far, Near, ~ Pltn; Rushy Mdw; Ryley Lane 1818 (*v. infra*); Sparks Britch, Near, Middle, ~ ~ Mdw; Spentfords Fd (by Spenford Bridge in Loppington *supra*); Spruce Pltn; Swattock Mdw; Tags Mdw; Tile House Pce; Tupnals, Big, Little Tupneys Pltn; Turnpike Fd (by Wolverley/Wem road); Way Lsw, Higher, Lower, Middle (by road to Loppington, possibly *The Wey Field* 1799 PR(L) 10); Wollaston's Mdw.

(b) Garbet, 1818, says that there were 4 common fields in 1561: *Homon*, *Homore*, *Holmor* or *Holman Field*, near Old Pool of Wem; *Gronow*, *Grannow* or *Granno Field*, between the town and Northwood Hall; *Sindons*, *Sinders* or *Sinder Field* (Cinder Fd in (a)); *Ryley Field*, also called *The Little Field* (Ryley Lane in (a)).

4. LACON (SJ 539326)

Lacon is a DB manor, so the name is discussed in Part **1**. It is the dative plural of **lacu** 'water-channel', probably here referring to drainage channels in marshy land.

There are three settlements, Lacon, and Lower and Upper Lacon. 1833 OS gives the name without qualification to all three.

LACON GORSE, *Fox Cover* 1846 *TA*.
LACON HALL, 1577 Saxton, 1685 PR(L) 9, 1846 *TA*.

Field-Names

Forms in (a) are 1846 *TA*.

(a) Baggy Moor, Baggy Fd Moor (apparently the same n. as Baggy Moor *supra*, about 8 miles S.W., for which there are ME forms: the meaning of ***bagga** in these ns. and in Bagley is uncertain); The Bank, Far ~; Barn Fd (2); Barn Mdw; Barn Yd; Big Fd; Big Mdw; Birch Coppice; The Bottom Fd; Brand Mdw; Brickkiln, Far, Middle; The Broad Mdw; Brooms, Far, Middle, Near; Calves Croft; Coach Bank; Colts Moor, Far and Middle ~ ~; Cote Lsw (no building); Cow Lsw (several); Creamore Stones (by Creamore); Cunnery, Big, Little ('rabbit warren', 2 large fields making an egg-shape); Damn Mdw, Lane (by stream); The Duke's Garden (plantation with pools on 6"); Feggy Fd ('coarse grass'); Garden Croft; Garden Fd; Gorsy Bank; Gorsy Croft; Green Bank; Gully Bank; Hollings Bank (probably 'holly', ultimately from **holegn**); Lacon Lsw, Far, Near; Little Moor; Long Fd; Middle Fd; Moor, Banky, Drain, Far; Moss, The Mosses; Near Marsh; New Lsw; The Old Fd; Ox Lsw; Palace Croft, Fd ('palisade', *v.* **palis**); The Patch (minute enclosure); Peartree Croft; Pool Fd; The Pools; Spans Bank; Rushy Mdw; The Sandy Bank, Fd, Sandy Pit Fd (Pit Fd adjoins); Spittle Fd, Far, Near (perhaps a charitable endowment for a hospital); Springs, Further, Middle, Near; Square Croft; Stackyard Fd; Well Fd; Well Lsw, Big, Little; Well Mdw, Big, Little; Wem Bank and Mdw; Wheat Lsw, Far, Near; Withy Pit Croft; Wood Fd, Far, Near; Yewtree Bank, Moor.

5. LOWE AND DITCHES

DITCHES (SJ 496294): *La Diche* 1255–6 *Ass*, *Dyche* 1290 Ipm, 1586–7 *RentSur*, *Dyches* 1291 *Ass* (p), 1294–9 *Ass*, 1327 SR (p), *The Dyches* 1621 PR(L) 9, *Diches* 1657, 8 ib, *Ditches* 1672 HTR.

v. **dīc**. The evidence is slightly in favour of the original name being singular. The reference is probably to an earthwork, but no archaeological remains are shown on maps.

The house is *The Diches Hall* 1674 PR(L) 9, *The Ditches Hall* 1818 Garbet.

LOWE (SJ 501306)
La Lawe 1255–6 *Ass*
Lowe 1290 Ipm *et seq*, *La Lowe* 1291–2 *Ass*, *The Low(e) freq* from 1654 PR(L) 9

La Louwe 1306–7 *Ass*
The Lo(o)e freq from 1596 to 1700 PR(L) 9

'Tumulus', one of three Sa instances of simplex names from **hlāw**. No trace has been found of the eponymous burial mound.

Lai, a DB manor in Hodnet Hundred, has sometimes been considered to be Lowe, but Audley in Moreton Say, *supra*, is a more likely identification.

F. and C. Thorn, in the Phillimore edition of DB (note 4.14.4) note *Dichelowe* from a l.13th cent. survey of Bradford Hundred.

CROSSBANK, 1732 PR(L) 9, 1833 OS, 1844 *TA*, *Crosbank* 1728, 30 PR(L) 9: by a road-junction, a common meaning of *cross* in Sa.

LOWE COTTAGE, FM.

LOWE HALL, 1833 OS, 1844 *TA*.

LOWE HILL, 1833 OS, 1844 *TA*, *The Low Hill* 1660 PR(L) 9.

NEW HO, *Newhouse Field* 1844 *TA*.

POOLS FM, 1833 OS, *The Pools*, *Pool Meadow* 1844 *TA*.

PYMS COTTAGE, HO, latter 1833 OS. Garbet says that a man called *Pym* was killed at Pyms Fm in the Civil War.

Field-Names

Forms in (a) are 1844 *TA*, except for those dated 1818, which are Garbet.

(a) Balcroft 1818; Bank Croft; Banks Pce; Barn Croft (2); Barn Fd (2); Barn Yd; Big Fd; Big Mdw; Black Mdw; Brickkiln Fd (2); Broomhill Fd; Broomy Croft Mdw; Broomy Fd, Big, Little; Calves Croft (2); Catherine's Pce; Chapel Fd 1818 ("formerly belonging to St. John's Chapel in Wem"); Common Lake, Big and Little ~ ~ (by a stream); Coppice Fd, Big, Little; Cow Lsw, Big, Near; Crabtree Croft; Days Pit Fd; Dial Yd (by Ditches, *dial* in f.ns. is considered to refer to sundials); Dogkennel Croft, Far, Middle, Near, Long (by Pyms Cottage, RTH has Dogkennel House 1796 *et seq* to 1803); Drake Fd, Lane 1818, Drak(e)y Fd, Drake Hill Fd, Drakey Lane Fd (7 fields along road on W. boundary: cf. *Drigadrake* in Edstaston *supra*: Garbet mentions Drake Lane in Horton); Far Fd (2); Far Pce; The Ferny Fd; Fingerpost Mdw (by road-junction); Flat Fd; Forgham, Higher, Lower; Gorsy Fd; Goulburn, Big, Little; Green Fd (several); Hall Mdw (by Ditches); Hill Broomhill (not near Broomhill *supra*); Hollow Fd; Home Fd (by Ditches); Hopyard Mdw; Horton Fd (on boundary with Horton); Liners, Lower, Long, Middle (the n. occurs also in Newtown); Long Fd (2); Lord's Land, Near, Middle, Far, Lord's Mdw, Big, Little (7 fields in N. tip of township, near Lowe Hall); Marigold Fd; Marlpit Fd; Meadow, Big, Little, New; The Meadow, Mdw Bank; The Meadow (several); Middle Fd; Orchard Mdw; Outlet (by Lowe Hill); Ox Lsw, Little ~ ~; Pit Fd (2); Rough Fd, Lower ~ ~; Rough Pce; Round Mdw (irregularly shaped, some curves); Rye Croft;

Ryegrass Croft; Sandhole Fd; Sandy Bank; Shop Fd; Shoulder of Mutton; Square Fd; Stackyard Fd; The Ten Acres; Thistly Fd; Washpit Fd; Well Fd, Big, Little; Windmill Fd (Garbet gives Windmill Croft as one of 6 closes in this township).

6. NEWTOWN (SJ 484314): *Neuton by Wemme* 1373 Cl, *Newton vill* 1586–7 *RentSur*, *Newtowne* 1588–9 *ib et freq* to 1695 PR(L) 9, *Newtown* 1652 ib *et seq*, *Newton* 1673, 1726 ib.

'New settlement', a common name in Sa as elsewhere. Cf. Newton in Ellesmere *supra*.

CHURCH FM.
ELM COTTAGE, shown but not named on *TAMap*.
MOAT FM, moat shown on 1900 6" Map.
NEWTOWN COTTAGE, 1845 *TA*, NEWTOWN FM, ~ *Villa* 1833 OS.
NORTHWOOD HALL, 1845 *TA*.

Field-Names

Forms in (a) are 1845 *TA*, except for those dated 1841, which are GT.

(a) The Acre; Alders, Far, Middle; Allmands Croft; Bakehouse Croft; Barn Fd (several); Big Ditch Fd; Big Fd; Black Fd; Brand Mdw; Breech Pce; Burrow Mdw; Calves Croft (several); Calves Yd Fd; Cartrick, Bottom, Top, Middle, ~ Mdw; Chapel Fd (by Newtown Chapel); Cow Pasture; Croft (series along road by Newtown includes Far, Near, Middle, Stony Croft); Croft(s) (cluster in N.E. corner); Dip Yd, Further, Near, Little; Glassy Hedge; Gorsy Croft; Hall Mdw (by Northwood Hall); Hareshorn (probably Hares Head 1841, *v*. Stag's Horn *infra*); Hollow Croft; Horton Mdw (on boundary with Horton); House Fd (by Elm Cottage); Husbands Croft 1841; Kenrick, Big, Little (the n. occurs again in Northwood, about ½ mile away); Lady Pce 1841; Liners (cf. same n. in Lowe and Ditches); Long Croft; Long Fd; Lord's Land; Marl Mixen; The Meadow (several); Meadow before House; Milking Bank (2); Milking Birches; Mud Fd; New Mdw (2); Newtown Mdw (2, on E. and W. boundaries); Orchard; The Old Fallow; Peas Croft, Lsw; Peats Mdw, Big, Little; Pinfold Mdw; Pit Fd; Potato Garden; Rock Fd, Big, Little; Rough; Rough Fd; Round Banky Pce (rectangular); Round Fd, Further (irregularly shaped with some curves); Round Hill (rectangular field); Sawpit Fd; Slangs; Stag's Horn (the field has a sharp point: Hareshorn, also with a point, is nearby); Stockings, Big, Little ('clearings'); Swan's Nest (2); Three Cornered Croft; Turma's Yd; Walk Fd; Well Mdw; Wood Mdw (2); Wood Pce 1841.

(b) *Espinfeild* 1641 *SBL 1493* (probably 'spinney').

7. NORTHWOOD (SJ 466333): *Northwode* 1290, 1368 Ipm, *Northwood* 1586–7 *RentSur et seq* with variant reading *-woode*. The township forms the N.W. tip of the parish. The Ipm references are to woodland. Ellesmere, *supra*, also has a Northwood township.

1833 OS gives the name to two houses in the township, as well as to the village. RTH, 1793, mentions *Northwood Gate* as a place where a baby was delivered.

BLACKHURSTFORD BRIDGE (on parish boundary, by Blackhurst Fm in Bettisfield, Fli): *Blackhurst Ford* 1561 Garbet, 1795, 7 RTH, 1833 OS. Garbet also gives *Blackford Brook* from his 1561 source, and says that *Black Waterford* is on the W. boundary of Wem; and *Blakeford Forde* is given in PR(L) 9 as the residence of a woman buried at Wem in 1598. It is not clear whether these other names refer to Blackhurst Ford, or whether there was another crossing of R. Roden nearby.

FIELDS.
GRANGE.
GREENBANK.
GREENFIELD, *Greenfields* 1788 RTH.
HAZEL HO.
HORNSPIKE, 1808 PR(L) 10, *The Horne Spick* 1680 PR(L) 9. An earlier reference is to "a mosse or seathe called Hornspike" t.Eliz *RentSur*. The building, near Wem Moss, is at the base of a sharply pointed projection of the parish boundary, on slightly raised ground which intrudes into the southern edge of a large area of moss in Fli. The name appears to be a compound of *horn*, used in Sa for pointed fields, and *spike* 'pointed object'. The latter term, which NED notes from the late 14th cent., is rare, perhaps hitherto unnoted, in place-names. The Elizabethan reference may be to a marshy hollow (NED *seath*), since the area is not a moss.
HORSE AND JOCKEY P.H.
THE LAWN.
PINFOLD, 1833 OS, *The* ~ 1792 PR(L) 10.
RED FALLOWS MEADOW, field-name 1840 *TA*. The *TA* fields are on either side of a tributary of R. Roden which Garbet, 1818, calls *Redfellis Brook*. It is possible that *Redfellis* is a stream-name.
THE ROOKERY.
WEM MOSS, 1833 OS. This area is *Wem Heath* 1840 *TA*, and there are two *Heath Fields* and two *Moss Fields* adjoining.

1833 OS shows *Northwood Green* by the village; this is *Northwodegrene* 1745 PR(L) 10.

Field-Names

Forms in (a) are 1840 *TA*, except for those dated 1818, which are Garbet.

(a) Acres (a number of fields in S.E. projection of township have Acre ns., Two, Three, Six, Seven, Eight Acres, Four Acre and Half); Banky Fd; Barklums Bank; Barn Fd; Battle Fd (Battle ns. are discussed in the f.n. section of Welshampton *supra*); Betchfield Morass 1818 (Betchfield is Bettisfield Fli, with development of *-tes-* similar to that sometimes seen in *-des-*, cf., e.g., Frodesley Part **1**, Edgeley *infra*); Birch Mdw; Birches Yd; Black Pce; Brickkiln Fd (2); Bridge Pce; Butler's Mdw; Bythorn, Big, Little; Calves Croft (several); Clays Fd; Clemley Fd, Mdw (large fields by hamlet), Clemley Mdw, Big, Little (near Pinfold, *v.* discussion of Clemley in Prees *supra*); Clover Fd; Coltsfoot Croft; Cooper's Yd; Coppice, Lower, Higher, Far, Upper (fields called Springs and one called Little Copy adjoin); Coppy, Big, Little; Cow Pasture; Crabmill Fd; Crabtree Bank; Crabtree Fd (2); Croft, Back, Povey's, Wotters (by Foxholes in Edstaston); Croft, Barn, Calves, Carthouse (by Hornspike); Croft (cluster round Northwood village includes Brook, Green, Hassells, Pigstye Croft); Croft (small enclosures by The Rookery include Alder, Far, Lane, Little, Long, Top Croft); Croft(s) (clusters by Poolhead in Edstaston and on county boundary by Wem Moss); Crooked Pce; Cross Hedges; Edstaston Mdw (on boundary with Edstaston); Egerton's Croft; Ferny Bank; Field (*freq*, with Big, Bottom, Far, Near, Long etc.); Field (small enclosures by The Rookery include Clover, Corner, Orchard, Potato, Six Corner, Square Fd); Field, Egerton's, Lowery's; First Pce; Garden Fd; Gravel Hole Fd (Sandhole Fd adjoins); Grazing Fd; The Great Wd 1818; Green Fd (not near Greenfield); Hassall Fd, Near; Hemp Fd; Hemp Lsw (2); Higginson's Pce, Far, Near; The Hollins, Near ~; Homer, Great (large field S. of Wem Moss, small pool shown: perhaps **holh**, **mere**); Horse Pasture (2); House Fd (by Greenbank); House Mdw (near The Rookery); Intake (small enclosures on county boundary, by Wem Moss); Kenrick (cf. the same n. in Newtown *supra*); Kilvert's Pce, Little, Large; Lady's Pce; The Leans, Big and Little ~ (probably ME *leyne* of uncertain meaning); Leasow, Far, Rough, Rushy; Leg and Foot (shape n.); Long Slang (several); Lord's Pce; Lurf y land (*sic*); Maidens Lsw; Marl Bank; Meadow (*freq*, with Big, Far, Long etc.); Milking Bank (2, by Greenbank and The Rookery); Moor, Top, The Third; Newfoundland (by village); New Pce; Newtown Mdw (near boundary with Newtown); Oak Fd; Oak Lsw; Oat Headish ('oat enclosure'; **edisc**, common in Ch, is found occasionally in N. Sa, as in Edgeley *infra*); The Old Fd; The Old Folds 1818; The Old Grazing Pce; The Outlet (2, by Hornspike and Northwood village); Ox Lsw, Big; Piece, Big, Black, Far, Long, Higginsons; Piece, Far, Middle, Near; Piece, Mannings, Wright's; The Pingle (tiny enclosure); Pit Fd; Pits, Dry, Far; The Pond; Pond Fd, Mdw; Potato Croft; Powell's Fd; Road Fd (2); Rough Fd; Rough Moor; Round Mdw (one curved side); Rye Grass; Sand Bank; Sandford's Fd, Mdw; Sheep Fd; Slades; Springs, Big, Little, Old (adjoining Coppice); Stag's Horn (the field has a small pointed projection); Strawberry Fd; Swithin, Further, Second, Third, Blackswithin (possibly 'burnt ground': if so, the ultimate source would be ON ***sviðinn** 'land cleared by burning', which is found in minor names and field-names in Yorkshire (PN WRY **7** 254): appearance in Sa would suggest a dialect derivative outside areas of Norse influence: another instance may be Swithin's Door in Pontesbury, Part **2** 46, though that n. has been ascribed to a church dedication: EDD gives *swither* 'to burn', in Nt, Wa, Wo, Gl as well as in northern counties); Thieves' Bridge Fd (by Ellesmere/Whitchurch road, no stream, Thieves Bridge Lane 1818); Townsend (by village); Two Days Math; Vetch Croft; Wally Mdw (perhaps 'wallet' referring to a hollow, *v.* FN 18); Washing Pit; Watering Mdw; Well Yd; Wem Mdw; Wheat Fd; Woods Pce; The Yard (large field by Top Ho).

8. SLEAP (SJ 486267)

Sleap is a DB manor, so the name, which means 'slippery place', is discussed in Part **1**. OE **slǣp** is used in place-names for specific topographical features rather than being a term for a marsh. The identification of such a feature would be difficult in this case because of the presence of an airfield. It might have been where the road crosses the brook which separates Sleap hamlet from Sleap Hall in Myddle (*supra*). The township is a very small area between Sleap Brook and a tributary.

SLEAP BRIDGE (over Sleap Brook), HO.

Field-Names

Forms in (a) are 1840 *TA*.

(a) Allen's Mdw; Barnyard (large field by hamlet); Big Fd; Black Heath; Broad Mdw; Brook Mdw; Broom Fd, Brooms, Far, Near, Second; Calloways, First, Far, Middle; Croft, Lloyds, Marl, Near, Sleap, Stackyard (along Noneley road); Dee Bank (there is an unnamed house here on *TAMap* and 1900 6"); Gighole Croft; Hawthorn Mdw; Heath, Far, Near, Long, Middle, ~ Mdw; Hollins, The Left Hand, The Right Hand (either side of road to Myddle); Hollins Fd ('holly', ultimately from **holegn**); Honey Croft (this and Ferny Croft are large fields on the other side of road from Croft ns. *supra*); House Pce (not near a building); Husk, Far, Near, Usk Mdw (possibly a contraction of *hassocks*, *hussocks* 'tufts of coarse grass'); Lloyd's Mdw; Mathews Yd; Moor, Lower, Top, Rough, Gayley, Moor Mdw, Bank; New Pce; Noneley Mdw (on boundary with Noneley); Ox Lsw; Pit Mdw; Richards Mdw; Round Mdw (3 curved sides); Slang (strip by road); Stock Bank, Mdw, Pce; Well Fd, Mdw (Wall Fd adjoins); Withy Bed; The Yard, Big and Little Yd; Yewtree Fd.

9. SOULTON (SJ 544303)

Soulton is a DB manor, so the name is discussed in Part **1**. The first element is **sulh** 'plough', probably used in place-names in the sense 'gully'. Soulton Brook runs in a gully immediately E. of Soulton Hall.

BALL'S BRIDGE: the *TA* for Prees township has *Ball's Moor*, a division of the enclosed Dogmoor, near this crossing of Sidleymoor Brook; cf. *Ball's Brook* 1799 RTH.

BROOK HO, 1833 OS.

DAIRY HO, 1833 OS, *Soulton* ~ ~ 1795 PR(L) 11.

MASSEY'S ROUGH, 1833 OS, 1842 *TA*: *TA* also has *Massey's Piece, Field, Barn Field.*

SOULTON BRIDGE.

SOULTON HALL, 1833 OS, 1842 *TA*.

SOULTON WD, 1842 *TA*, ~ *Coppice* 1833 OS.

Field-Names

Forms in (a) are 1842 *TA*.

(a) Bank Pce (by R. Roden); Barn Fd (2); Big Paddock, Big Parks (by Soulton Hall); Brickkiln Lsw, Far, Near; Brooms, Far, Near; Burley Hurst, Big, Little; Calves Croft; Carrion Pits Lane (probably a burial place for diseased cattle); Challinors Fd; Clay Fd (not near Clays); Clays, Big, Far, Middle, Near, Clays Bank (5 fields along boundary with Lacon); Dogmoor Bank, Mdw (most of Dogmore is in Prees, *supra*); The Dole, Big Dole (communally held meadow); Dove House Garden (by Soulton Hall); Gors(t)y Croft; Hall Mdw; Hawk Fd, Big, Little; Heath Lsw, Big and Little ~ ~; Black Heath; Horse Close, Hayes; Lady Mdw; Long Fd; Long Mdw; Mill Croft, Fd (perhaps a windmill); Mill Mdw, Pool (by R. Roden); Moss Pit Croft; Nursery; Parks, Big, Further (near Soulton Hall); The Pieces; Pool Mdw, Pool Weir or Parks Mdw; Rabbit Yd; Rail Mdw; Robinsons Mdw, Pce; Rough Lsw (2); Rough Mdw (by Massey's Rough); Round Lsw (curved sides); Rushy Mdw; Slang; Smiths Pce, Far Smiths Fd; Spring Mdw; Weir Fd, Pce (by Soulton Brook); Wood, Far, Middle, ~ Mdw; Yewtree Mdw.

(b) *Hawode* 1255–6 *Ass*.

10. TILLEY AND TRENCH

The area of this township is bisected by the Shrewsbury/Wem road. Tilley, except for Tilleygreen, is on the W., and Trench on the E. of the road. As it is a fairly large township it is convenient to treat each part separately.

(i) TILLEY (SJ 508278)

Tyleweleg' 1221 SAC, 1255–6 *Ass*, *Tilewel* 1283 Cl, *Tylewele* 1291–2 *Ass* (p), *Ty'leweleye* 1337 SR

Tululeye 1271–2 *Ass* (p)

Tilvelegh 1290 Ipm

Tylley 1586–7 *RentSur et freq* from 1600 in PR(L) 9, 10 with variant spellings *Till(e)y*

Tyllele alias Tylley 1625 *SBL 278*

Second element **lēah**, probably in the sense 'clearing', cf. Lee Brockhurst *supra*.

The first element is uncertain. The *Tylewe-*, *Tilewe-* forms probably rule out **tigel** 'tile', which is found in Tyley Do, Gl and Tilehurst Berks. None of those names has forms which indicate metathesis of *-g-* and *-l-*. OE *tili(g)a* 'husbandman' would suit formally, but that appears to be a literary term, not hitherto noted in place-names.

Smith, EPN, listed Tilley under **telga**, ***telg**, 'shoot, twig, sucker', surviving in dialect *tiller*, *tillow* 'sapling', noted in a few names in K and Sx; but spellings for the Sa name indicate something like **tilga*, not *telga*.

TILLEY BRIDGE, COTTAGE.

TILLEYGREEN, *Tylly Green* 1695 PR(L) 7, *Tilley Greene* 1700 PR(L) 9, ~ *Green* 1791, 8 RTH.

TILLEY PARK, 1783 RTH, ~ *Parke* t.Eliz *RentSur*. Garbet says this was The Old Park, as distinct from The New Park in Edstaston. It is *Le Holdepark* 1290 Ipm, where both parks are referred to as woods, *v.* f.ns.

TILLEY VILLA.

PR(L) 10 mentions *Tilley Brook* and *Tilley Gate* under 1811.

Field-Names

Forms in (a) are 1845 *TA*. Some fields in the N. tip of the township as shown on *TAMap* are in Wem Urban on the 1900 6" map. These have been included in the Tilley and Trench lists.

(a) Bannox, Far ~; Barn Fd (2); Barnyard; Billow Mdw (on S. boundary, Garbet gives Billow Brook as boundary with Liberties of Shrewbury); Black Abbey, Far ~ ~; Brickkiln, ~ Lsw; The Britch ('newly-broken-in land'); Brockley, Big, Little, ~ Mdw (Garbet gives Brockley as one of 3 open fields); Brookfield; Brook Mdw (2); Calves Croft; Clover Lsw; Coe Mdw; Cooper, Big; Cow Lsw (2); (The) Croft(s) (cluster round hamlet, which also includes Marl and Yewtree Croft); Downes Pce; Fold Pce; Gorsy Lsw; Grass Lsw, Big, Little; Green Bank (2); Green Fd; Gregory Pce; Hempyard Pce; The Hollins; Holy Husk (Holly Husk in Noneley *supra* adjoins); Horse Hayes; Johnson's Mdw; King's Pce; Meadow (several); New Lsw; Newnes Bank; Noneley, Big ~ (not on boundary with Noneley); Ox Lsw; Park (there are fields called Park Croft, Fd, Mdw, Orchard, Big Park Fd and Near, Middle, Far, Lower Tilley Park in the area between the house and the Shrewsbury road: another Park Croft and Old Park Fd are a short distance W. of the house: no park outline is discernible on *TAMap*); Pit Fd; Randley Mdw, Pool; Ridley Mdw; Rough Lsw, Little Rough; Rough Mdw; Sawpit Fd; Slang; Tilley Fd, Far, Near, Middle, Tilley Mdw (among Tilley Park fds); Tilley Fd, ~ ~ Mdw, Tilley Lsw, Pce (on N. boundary);

Turnpike Fd; Weir Croft (by Tilley Bridge); Whitfields Mdw; Windmill Fd; Wycherley Mdw (2, not adjacent); Yard (large field near hamlet).

(ii) TRENCH (SJ 514269): *Le Trench* 1290 Ipm, *La Trench* 1291–2 *Ass*, *Trenche*, *Trench Farm* Eliz *RentSur*, (*The*) *Trench*(*e*) *Farm*(*e*) *freq* from 1600 to 1745 PR(L) 9, 10. The specialised sense of OFr, ME **trenche** for roads through woodland is noted *supra* under Trench in Ellesmere.

There are two settlement-sites. The GR above is for Trench Hall, which is *Trench Fm* on 1833 OS. On the 1900 6" map Trench Hall and Trench Fm adjoin. UPPER TRENCH, ½ mile S., is also called *Trench Fm* on 1833 OS. The 1833 map gives the name *Trench Lane* to a road leading from Tilleygreen to Tilley Park, and this appears in PR(L) 9 under 1700, PR(L) 10 under 1770, and in Garbet.

WAIN HO (SJ 529269). This is a rationalisation of One House, forms for which are *The One House* 1676 *et seq* to 1744 PR(L) 9, 1768 ib 1. There are two houses on either side of the Wem/Moreton Corbet boundary. 1833 OS calls the eastern one, in Moreton Corbet, *One House*. The western one is not named on 1833 OS or on *TAMap*, but Garbet's *One House* is likely to refer to it.

For other instances of this and analogous names *v.* VEPN *s.v.* **ān**. Onehouse Sf appears in an 11th-cent. will, and Onehouse Ch has 12th and 13th-cent. forms, so the Sa name may also be ancient. Dodgson (PN Ch **1** 140) suggests an OE appellative comparable to *ānseld* and *ānsetl* with **ān** perhaps meaning 'isolated'.

WOOD HO (SJ 517277), 1833 OS, *Woodhowsen'* Eliz *RentSur*: PR(L) 9 has *The Wodehouse* 1601, (*The*) *Woodhouse freq* from 1687 to 1741, (*The*) *Woodhousses* 1615, 39, 40, *The Woodhousen* 1616, 18, 21. Garbet has *The Wood-houses*, echoing the dialect plural of earlier forms.

This Wood Ho was listed in Part **1**, *q.v.*, as one of eight instances in Sa, but this is the only one which has plural forms.

BATH COPPICE, *Plantation* 1845 *TA*, pool shown on 6" map.

BLACK WD, *Plantation* 1845 *TA*.

CASTLE STEAD (Gazetteer), (close called) *The Castle Stead* 1561 Garbet. The 6" map shows a rectangular enclosure, marked "camp", by Trench Hall. The field is *The Banks* 1845 *TA*.

HOUGH LANE, 1818 Garbet.

MILL HO, 1818 Garbet, 1845 *TA*, near Wem Mill.

NEW INN, *New House* 1833 OS, *Newhouse* 1783 *et seq* to 1789 RTH.

OAKLANDS, 1833 OS.

PALMS HILL, 1833 OS. In PR(L) 9 *Palms Hill* and *Pams Hill* alternate from 1695 to 1741, with *Pams Hill* predominating, and a single *Parms Hill* in 1738. PR(L) 10 has *Pames Hill* 1746.

PANKEYMOOR COTTAGES, VILLA.

SUMMER HO.

TEAKINS. PR(L) 10 *The Teakins* 1761, *The Teakings* 1766, *The Takins* 1801.

WOODHOUSE COPPICE.

Field-Names

Forms in (a) are 1845 *TA*, except for those dated 1818 which are Garbet.

(a) Alderley Mdw; Ash Fd; Bakehouse Mdw (this and Carthouse Mdw are by Upper Trench); Barn Croft; Barn Fd; Big Hill, Big and Little Hill Mdw, Hill Valley, Little Hill Top; Big Mdw; Brantlet; Brickkiln Fd (2); Bridge Fd, Mdw (by Sutmore, perhaps a causeway); Blackthorn Mdw; Burley, Big (2 large fields on N. boundary, Garbet gives Burley Fd as one of 3 open fields); Calves Croft; Carriers Croft; Celery, Big, Little; Clee Butts; The Common (tiny triangle near Palms Hill); Common Pce (in Tilleygreen); Cote Fd (no building); Cow Lsw; Cow Mdw Rean; Croft, Far, Near, Middle, Road (by New Inn); Croft (cluster round Tilleygreen includes Far, Middle, Pit, Top Croft); Cross Croft, Mdw, Near Cross (by road junction); Downes Rough, Far, Near; Far Fd; Field, Far, Near, Lane (row of 5 fields on N. boundary); Garden Fd; Gravel Hole Fd; The Grazing Fd; Green Fd; Greenland; Grooms Croft, Mdw; Hempbutt Lsw; Hill Fd, Far, Middle and Top ~ ~ (by Palms Hill); Horse Fd; Horse Pasture; Hough Croft, Mdw (by Hough Lane); House Pce (by Pankeymoor cottages); Jenkins, Big, Little, Lower, Jenkins Mdw; Johnny Cock; Lane Croft; Ley, Big, Little, Orchard; Long Fd; Long Lsw; Marl Lsw; Marlpit Bank; Mathews Britch; (The) Meadow (*freq*, some with Big, Little, or with surnames); Meadow Bank; Milliners Moor; Millington's Mdw; The Moor, Coppy Moor; The Muck Lsw; Orchard Croft; Ox Lsw (2); The Paddock (by Teakins); Palms Hill Mdw; Pan Pudding Rough (*panpudding* NED 'pudding cooked in a pan': Panpudding Hill in Oldbury is a motte, but the 6" map shows nothing in this field by Teakins); Pickel Ends, Far ~ ~ (*v.* **pightel**); Pigstye Fd; Pingo (tiny enclosure, *v.* **pingel**); The Pools 1818 ("formerly a wood called the Little and Great Pollys, between Trench Farm and the Clive wood"); Potato Croft; Pugh's Fd; The Ridgels; Pough Lsw (2); Rushy Pce; Ryegrass Fd; The Seven Acres; Slacks Pce; The Slang; Spindles Pce; Stable Fd (by Teakins); The Stockings, Far ~ ('clearings'); Stoneybutts, Stannibutts (N. of Tilleygreen, where field-shapes suggest a small open field: Garbet places *Tilleley* Fd here); Sutmoor, Big, Little; Tilley Fd (between Tilleygreen and Woodhouse: Garbet gives *Tilleley* Field "beyond the Woodhouse" as one of 3 open fields in this township); The Virgins; Well Lsw; Well Mdw; Wood, Big, Little.

Garbet gives Goo Lane and Stones Lane in this township: these could be in (i) or (ii).

11. WEM (the parish church is SJ 515290)

(i) WEM URBAN

The area including the town which is shown on the 1900 6" map as Wem U.D. contains the following:

ASTON VILLA.

CLAY'S BUILDINGS.

THE FIRS.

FORNCET: a house here is *The Lane* 1833 OS, probably the place of that n. mentioned 1805 PR(L) 10. *TAMap* has *Lane Field* adjoining.

FOXLEY: the house is just inside the Wem Urban boundary. In the area of Wem Rural between the house and the E. boundary of the township *TA* has fields called *Foxley*, *Big*, *Little*, *Further*, *Near*, *Far* and *Lower Foxley*, *Foxley Meadow*, and there is a common field called *Foxley* c.1680, 1696 GT. The *TA* fields are dispersed, suggesting an open field larger than most in this part of Sa.

THE GROVE.

MILL HO.

RODEN LODGE, VILLA.

THE SHRUBBERY.

In addition to these 6" map names, Gazetteer has THE ALLEYS. *TAMap* has an area called *The Alleys & buildings* on the S. edge of the town, by Roden Lodge. Gazetteer gives several Sa instances, including the one in Cheswardine f.ns. *supra*: *v.* VEPN *s.v.* **alee**.

Street-Names

Street-names on the 1900 6" map are:

BANKHOUSE LANE, *v.* Uggerley Lane *infra*.

DRAWWELL WALK: cf. *Drawwell* 1649 PR(L) 9, ~ *House* 1657 *et seq* ib, *The Drawell* 1775 ib 10.

ELLESMERE ST.

HIGH ST.

MILL ST, leading to Wem Mill: Garbet, 1818, says that two water mills and a windmill were leased in 1553.

WEMBROOK RD: *TA* has *Wem Brooks Meadow* along the road.

Streets shown without names on 1900 6" map which are named in the County Red Book are:

ASTON ST.

BARNARD ST.

CROWN ST, *Crown Street otherwise Maiden Lane* 1761, 1828 'private deeds' (E. W. Bowcock's slips): Garbet, 1818, says "Maiden-lane, only three houses, name little known".

LEEK ST: cf. *Licklane* 1588–9 *RentSur*, "Leek-lane commonly called old Chapel-street" 1818 Garbet.

MARKET ST, "formerly Cripple Street" Gazetteer: the earlier n. occurs 1669 *SBL 3411*, cf. *Cripple Gate* 1711 *SBL 3419*: Garbet, 1818, also has *New Cripple Street*: *v.* Part **4** 24–5 for a discussion of this name.

NEW ST, *Newestrete* 1588–9 *RentSur*.

NOBLE ST, *The Noble Street* 1722 'private deed' (E. W. B.'s slip): Garbet, 1818, says "Noble-street vulgarly called the Back-street" and RTH has *Back Street* 1802.

SOULTON RD.

Other street-names are:

DARK LANE, Gazetteer says "now Leek St" but Garbet 1818, gives *The Dark Lane* and *Leek-lane* as two of the four lanes in Wem: Garbet says "hollow situation, covered by trees, the sink of the town, very dirty in winter".

UGGERLEY LANE (Gazetteer): *TA* has *Far*, *Near*, *Little Uggeley*, *Uggerley Meadow*, *The Huggerley/Huggaley*, *Far Huggerley*, fields S.W. of the town approached by the modern Bankhouse Lane: earlier forms are *Big*, *Little Uggaly* 1717 *SBL 36*, *Little Hugerley* 1809 Sale Bill (E. W. B.'s slip).

Garbet has *The Horse Fair* "lately called Ireland". *The Pig Markett* occurs 1751 'private deed' (E. W. B.'s slip).

Public houses are *Buck's Head Inn* and *Castle Inn TA*, *The Black Lion* 1812 PR(L) 10, *Bull's Head* 1790 RTH, *Crown Inn* 1802 RTH (*The Crown in Wem* 1723 SAS 2/IV), *Packhorse* 1787, 1801 RTH, *The 7 Stars* 1808 PR(L) 10, *White Horse* 1796 RTH.

1833 OS shows *Kensington House* on N. outskirts of town. *Lacons Hall* in Cripple Street is mentioned 1699, 1700 *SBL 3411*, *14*.

Field-Names

Forms in (a) are 1845 *TA* except where otherwise stated. Some fields in the S. of the Wem Urban area appear in the *TA* for Tilley, and these have been listed under Tilley.

(a) Barn Fd; Barnetts Bank; Brad Mdw 1818 Garbet; Coblers Pce; Cooks Mdw; Cordwell, ~ Mdw, Big Cordwell Hill (the ns. apply to several fields, not all contiguous, S.E. of the town: Garbet has Cordway Hill and Cordwall); Crabtree Croft; (The) Croft (several); Crosses, Big, Little, Far, Near, Middle (by Prees road: Garbet says this was a common field "named from a cross erected on that road"); Dog Kennel Fd; Field adjoining House; Field behind House; First Fd; Gravelhole Fd; Harris's Croft; Higginson's Pce; Horton Fd, Upper ~ ~ (by road to Horton: Garbet names a common field called Chapel Fd "towards Horton", and *Chapel Fields* appears as a common field c.1680, 96, 1832 GT); Humpreyson Pce; Jacks Fd; John's Orchard; The Lawn (small field on N. edge of town); The Lawn (by Rectory); Lawn (by The Grove); Long Mdw; Lowe Hill Croft; Lower Way Fd; Madman's Pce; Marl Croft; Marlpit Fd, Smith's Marlpit; The Meadow (2); Middle Fd (named as a common field c.1680, 96, 1832 GT, and by Garbet); New Pool Mdw; Parsons Croft; Pipers Pool or Lawn (contains a fishpond, next to a building called Hall); Rushy Mdw; The Slang; Townsend (there are 2 groups of Townsend ns., N. and E. of the town: cf. *Townsend Leasow, Meadow, Further Townsend* 1727 *SBL 8608*); Town Fd (near Townsend ns. at E. edge of town); Waterfall (tiny enclosure near Wem Mill); Water Mdw; Woodhouse Croft.

(ii) WEM RURAL

BELLEVUE, 1833 OS: Gazetteer lists 15 instances in the county.

GREEN HILL: houses are shown but not named on *TAMap*.

POOLS FM, *The Pools* 1842 *TA*. *TA* has *Pool* names extending E. along R. Roden, including *Duck*, *Rushy* and *Swanwicks Pool*. Garbet 1818 says "the pool lands, about two miles in compass, all pasture ground, in the winter much exposed to floods". Cf. *Wem Pooles*, *Poole Meadow*, *Two Pool Peeces* 1699 *SBL 3411*: a note by E. W. Bowcock on the slip for these says "The Pools is a district about a mile from Wem, now drained, but formerly under water to a great extent. Even now is like a lake in wet times."

Field-Names

Forms in (a) are 1842 *TA*.

(a) Bank Fd, Gorsy Bank; Barkers Pce; Barnes Croft; Barn Fd; Bazeley, Little, Middle, Near; Big Fd; Black Croft; Brickkiln Fd (2); Broomy Lsw; Broughalls Pit; Clemley Park (2, fairly large field by Bellevue and small field on E. boundary, *v.* Clemley in Prees *supra*); Cooks Mdw; Creamore Pce, Upper ~ ~, ~ Corner (by Creamore in Edstaston: *Creamore Field* is one of the open fields of Wem c.1680, 96 GT); Drain Mdw; Far Fd; Field leading to Broomfield; Footroad Fd, Far Road Fd; Footway Fd; Foxley (*v.* Wem Urban *supra*); The Fridays, Upper ~, ~ Mdw (4 fields N.W. of town, a derogatory n.); Further Fd, Far, Near; Gospel Butt (on boundary with Wem Urban); Gravel Hole Fd; Guttery Mdw; Half Mile Ash (on Ellesmere road); Harris's Croft; Honey Bridge Croft, Bridge Mdw (by crossing of R. Roden);

The Hopyard, Big and Little ~; Horse Moor; Horse Pasture; Hughes Pce; Kings Hill, Hither, Further, Lower, Lower Hill Fd (*The Kings Hill* 1739 *SBL 14636*); Lane Fd; Long Fd; Meadow, Bottom, Top; Meadow, Cooks, Higher, Rushy, Tays (on E. edge of Pool ns.); Patch, Big, Far, Middle; Paul Pugh, Far, Near; Pidgeons Fd (Garbet mentions Pigeons Barn on the line of Civil War rampart); Pool Fd; Poor Man's Fd; Primrose Fd; Race Pce; Rags Pce; The Rector's Fd; Road Tree Fd; Round Dale, ~ ~ Mdw (slightly curved sides); Round Hill, Big, Little; Round Mdw (curved sides, adjoins Square Fd); Sambrook Mdw, Little; Sisters, Far, Near; Snape, Little ('boggy place', ultimately OE ***snæp**); Square Fd; Stall Mdw; Tarver, Further, Near, Higher, Lowermost (2 groups of fields ½ mile apart); Top Fd (2); Washpit Fd; Wem Brooks Mdw, Big, Little and Top ~ ~ ~; Wheat Fd, Far, Near, Middle; Wheatley Mdw; Windmill Fd (4).

12. WOLVERLEY (SJ 469312)

Wolverley is a DB manor, so the name, which means 'Wulfward's clearing', is discussed in Part **1**.

BLACK PLTN.

HOLLY FM, shown but not named on *TAMap*.

THE LEES.

MOUNT COTTAGE.

NEW HO, 1833 OS.

PARK FM.

ROOKERY PLTN.

SLANG PLTN: a narrow strip.

WOLVERLEY BRIDGE, 1801 RTH.

WOLVERLEY HALL: Garbet gives a date of 1404.

WOLVERLEY LODGE: the 1900 6" map shows two lodges, both in the grounds of Loppington Ho. One of these is shown on 1833 OS.

WOODLANDS, 1840 *TA*.

RTH names *Wolverley Gate* as a place where a baby was delivered in 1802.

Field-Names

Names in (a) are 1840 *TA*: those marked * belong to fields in a small detached area situated in Northwood township.

(a) Barnyard (2); Big Fd; Birchen Coppy/Coppice; Birchen Lsw; Broomy Plat; Bull Gate(s); Butty Mdw (FN 7–8 gives several dialect uses for *butty*); Chaise Mdw (FN 8 notes Chaise Dole in Longford parish, which also suggests a connection with meadow); Clark's Croft; Coalbrook; *Crabmill Fd; Crimplin, Big, Little and Upper ~ (5 fields S. of Woodlands: possible a derivative of the word discussed under

Crimps Fm in Ellesmere *supra*, but a meaning such as 'small piece' is not appropriate as the fields cover a substantial portion of the township); *(The) Croft; Croft, Bridge, Duns, Pit, Peas (surrounding hamlet); Deakins Fd; Dungeon Mdw (cf. Whixall f.ns. *infra*); Field before House (by New Ho); Fingerpost Fd (by road junction); Fold; Four Butts (strip adjoining Crimplin); Gailey Moor; Garden Fd; Gorsy Bank; Gravel Flg, Big (by Crimplin); Hill Fd; Hill Lsw, Far, Near; Liners, Long, Square; Marl Lsw, Further, Long, Little and Lower ~ ~ (8 fields near E. boundary); Meadow, Big, Far, Middle, Near, Meadow Bank; Meadow, Big, Little, Far, Lousy, Shay (FN 44 ascribes Lousy to **hlōse** 'pigstye', but it is more likely to be derogatory); Milliner, Big, Little (cf. Milliner's Moor in Tilley *supra*); Mist Ground (by The Moor); Oak Lsw; Peat Moor (adjoins Moor ns.); The Piece (large field, New Pce adjoins); Pit Fd (2); Pool Mdw; Quabs ('bog', adjoins Moor ns.); *Quale Fd, Mdw (perhaps *quail* used for the corncrake); Quile Mdw (cf. *Quale Mdw one mile N.); Rabbit Burrow; *Rough Mdw; Round Mdw (some curved sides); *Sawpit Fd; Stone Mdw; Toll Mdw (by R. Roden, not near a road); Weir Corner, Great, Little (by R. Roden); Wem Fd; Wolverley Fd (2 fields in S.W. corner, also small field on N. boundary); Wolverley Lawn (large field by Loppington Ho); Wolverley Pool; Yard, Kiln, Stack, Well, Wolverley (round hamlet); Yewtree Fd, Little.

The following ns. are in Wem parish but have not been assigned to townships: *Bennette Lands* 1586–7 *RentSur*; *Crosbrethe ib*; *Dewkehill* 1588–9 *ib*; *The Folegate* 1767 PR(L) 10; *The Godsheyes* 1739 *SBL 14636*; *Rodweie* 1221 SAC (between the field of Tilley and that of Sleap); *Shutt Leasowe* 1641 *SBL 1493* (in Horton or Newtown); *Shuttles* 1369 Ipm (manor of Wem called ~); *Sow Leasows, The Two* ~ ~ 1739 *SBL 14636*; *Thorneyfeilde* 1586–7 *RentSur*.

Weston-under-Redcastle

The parish-name, one of 10 instances in the county, is discussed in Part **1**. Together with Wixhill this formed the western part of the ancient parish of Hodnet. In the Tithe Survey it is treated as a township of Hodnet, described as "chapelry of Weston under Redcastle and Wixhill", but it has been treated separately here as a civil parish.

The castle, a 13th-cent. ruin in Hawkstone Park, is first noted as *Rubeum Castrum* 1255 RH; a full set of forms is set out in Part **1**.

WIXHILL (SJ 560287)

Wynekeshull 1252 Ch *et freq* with variant spellings *Winekes-* and *-hul* to 1378 Pat

Wynkeshull' 1291–2 *Ass*

Wenekeshull' 1291–2 *Ass*

Wykeshull' 1291–2 *Ass* (p) *et freq* with variant spellings *Wickes-* and *-hull* to 1472 *SRO 322/273*

Wekineshull c.1285–1315 HAC (p)

Wyxhull 1325 Pat (p), *Wikshull* 1472 *SRO 322/273*, *Wixhill* 1589 PR(L) 11

Wyxel 1580 PR(L) 19, *Wixsele* 1590 PR(L) 11, *Wixsell* 1592, 1675 ib, *Wixill* 1623, 93 ib, *Whicsell* 1635 ib

'Winuc's hill.' This personal name is recorded once, on a coin.

DEPN cites *Witekeshill* 1203 Eyton, but this form belongs to Whixall *infra*. In his account of Wixhill (IX 346) Eyton notes the difficulty of distinguishing between Wixhill and Whixall, 4½ miles apart. They are linked in records because "by an extraordinary accident the Lords of both places were identical". A full range of spellings for both, however, makes it possible to assign early spellings to the correct names.

HAWKSTONE PARK, 1833 OS. The main part of this is in Weston. In the early 18th century Sir Richard Hill built the house at Hawkstone and laid out a park which was transformed into a sort of Gothic playground at the end of the century by Sir Rowland Hill.

The earlier park here is *Radeclif Park* 1228 BM, *Redcastel Park(e)* 1542 *SBL 4462*, 1588 *SRO 322 box 2*, *Red Castle Broad Park*, *Castle Park* 1665 *SBL 8383*. Henry *de Aldithele* is given a licence in 1227 Pat to build a castle at *Radeclif*, 'red cliff', evidently the name of the sandstone massif on which the castle stands.

A park called *Ludeparck* is mentioned 1308 Ipm together with Redcastle, Weston and Wixhill. The first element may be ***hlȳde** 'loud stream'.

The 1900 6" map shows the following names in Hawkstone Park:

BIRCHES PIT: *Birches Park* 1841 *TA*. A large field between Birches Park and Weston village is *Inn Close*, *The Headlands*, *Bullers Trees & Birches*.

THE CITADEL, 1841 *TA*, *Citadel* 1833 OS.

DUNGEON, in Castle ruins.

ELYSIAN HILL, *The* ~ ~ 1841 *TA*.

FOX COVERT.

GIANT'S WELL.

GROTTO HILL, 1841 *TA*.

HAWK LAKE, *Hawk River* 1840 *TA*: this was made in 1790.

IVY LODGE.

MENAGERIE POOL, 1841 *TA*, *The Menagerie* 1792 PR(L) 11, *Menagerie* 1833 OS.

NEPTUNE'S WHIM, 1833 OS, *The Whim*, *The Whim Pool*, *Neptune's Bank* 1841 *TA*. Cf. *Neptune's Cottage* 1792 PR(L) 11.

NORTH PARK, LODGE, 1840 *TA*.

RAKE PARK 1841 *TA*, *Rake Parke*, *Little* ~ ~ 1665 *SBL 8383*.

RANGER'S LODGE.

VINEYARD.

WHITE TOWER.

1841 *TA* also has *Inn Park*, by Hawkstone Inn, and *Vale Park*, possibly connected with Vale Fm in Hawkstone.

HOLLOWAY (SJ 557284), 1665 *et seq* PR(L) 11, *Holewey* 1291–2 *Ass*, *Halloway* 1675 Ogilby: *v*. **hol(h)**, **weg**, a common term for a sunken road. The name applies to a few houses in a road fork on the Shrewsbury/ Prees road.

ABBEY SLIP, *Plantation at the Abbey* 1841 *TA*.

BURY WALLS, 1833 OS. This is a prehistoric hill-fort, the OE name of which is preserved in Chirbury Wd in Kenstone, *q.v.* Associated with the fort are BURY FM, 1833 OS, *The Burys* 1841 *TA*; BURY PARK; BURY ROUGH, 1833 OS, *Burries Coppice* 1841 *TA*; BURYTUMP, 1833 OS, a small wood by Bury Fm, called *Under the Fir Trees* 1841 *TA*; BURY WD, *The Burry Walls Coppice* 1841 *TA*.

CANNON BANK.

THE COTTAGE.

CRABHALL (Gazetteer), 1619 PR(L) 11.

HAWKSTONE HOTEL, *Hawkstone Inn*, ~ ~ *Farm House* 1792 PR(L) 11, *Hawkstone Inn* 1841 *TA*. *v.* SAS 77 p. 124 for an account of the Swedenborgian group which met here from 1806 to 1823.

THE HERMITAGE, 1681 *et seq* PR(L) 11, ~ *Farm House* 1792 ib: *TAMap* shows *The Malthouse* here.

LINFORD BRICK WORKS, ½ mile from Linford in Prees.

MOAT BANK, 1833 OS, by Bury Walls hill-fort.

THE MOUNT, *Mount Meadow* 1841 *TA*: 6" map shows a small earthwork.

NEW HO, shown but not named on *TAMap*.

OLD COPPICE, 1833 OS, *The* ~ ~ 1841 *TA*.

POOLDAM.

POOL ROUGH, 1833 OS, 1841 *TA*.

SLADE, 1833 OS. If an ancient name this is 'small valley', *v.* **slæd**.

SPINNEL WD, *Spring Coppice* 1833 OS, *Spinhill Coppice*, ~ *Wood Leasow* 1841 *TA*.

THE TERRACE.

TOP MOSS, 1833 OS, *The Moss* 1841 *TA*. Moston adjoins.

WESTON HEATH, 1787, 8, 1802 RTH, 1833 OS, 1841 *TA*.

WINDMILL, *Ye Mill* 1798, 1800 PR(L) 11, *The Wind Mill* 1805 ib.

WIXHILL HILL: *TA* has *Hill* names in this area.

Field-Names

Forms in (a) are 1841 *TA*. Early forms dated 1665 are *SBL 8383*, 1383 are *SBL 265*.

(a) Aldery Lsw; Ansterley, Clover and Rough ~; Astley's Fd; Back Lsw (2); Banks; Banky Lsw; Barn Fd (several); (The) Big Fd (2); Big Mdw; Big Moor; Briery Pce; Brook Fd; Calves Croft; Church Fd; Cockshutt; Cold Chair Lsw (FN 25 suggests 'cold cheer'); Cote Lsw (2, no buildings); Cow Pasture; Crabba Mdw, Croft (possibly connected with Crabhall *supra*, the fields are near Holloway); The Crin (a semicircular enclosure on S.W. boundary, close to the road from which Holloway is named, is called "Inclosure at The Crin": Gazetteer lists this and another instance in Clive: *crin* is noted in EDD only from Sa with the meaning 'a small ravine in a hill' and a single quotation); Croft (enclosures near Holloway include Marlpit and Well Croft); Croft(s) (small enclosures on N. edge of Hine Heath); Croft(s) (many small fields on N. edge of Weston Heath); Crow Sytch (*v.* **sīc**); Cuttings; Dogpool (a strip along a stream on N. boundary is Linford or Dogpool, cf. Dogpole in Shrewsbury, Part **4** 12–13); Double Pce; Dunse Fd; Far Common (by Weston Heath); Fingerpost Mdw (at a crossroads); Galey Bank, Mdw; Garden Pce; Gateley Mdw; Glidewell; Hawkstile & Peplow's Yd; Heath Lsw (by Weston Heath); Hempbutt; High Park (small field near Holloway); Holloway, Big, Near, ~ Fd, Mdw (7 fields round Holloway hamlet, The Five Butts and Wood Flg occur in this area so possibly an open field); Horse Pce, Pool; Kenstone Lsw (on boundary with Kenstone); Leighs, ~ Mdw; Linford, Big, Little, ~ Mdw (adjoining Linford in Prees *supra*); Long Croft; Long Lsw; Long Mdw; Marl Fd, Big, Little (Marl Pit shown on *TAMap* and on 6"); Moor, Astleys, Jebbs, Near, Moor Bank, Mdw; New Pce (several); Noman's (not on a boundary); Nook Mdw, Bentley's Nook (adjoining The Nook in Prees); Oakhouse Mdw; Oaks, Big ~; Oat Croft & Clay Pits; Oil Mill, ~ ~ Pool (1833 OS calls the pool *Bath* and 6" map shows Bath House here); Parlour Mdw; Pike Flg & Five Butts (not in an obvious open-field context); Pool or Watering Place; Pool Bank, Mdw; Pool Rough; Priest Mdw; Purshills; Rail Pce; Rock Yd; Rough Fd; Rowley Hill; Rye Croft; Sandfords Lsw, Mdw; Settings, Far, Near, Little, Rough; Sheep Birch; Sim Fd; Slang; Stocking, Lower, Upper, ~ Mdw; Stocking, Far, Near ('clearing', *v.* ***stoccing**); Sytch, Marsh, Near; Triangle; Turnpike Croft (by Toll Ho on Whitchurch road); Waggon Ho Fd; Well Lsw; Watkins Moor; Weir Mdw (2); Weston Fd; Wet Mdw; Winstone Bank; Wixhill Fd, Shores ~ ~; Wixhill Pltn (no trees on *TAMap*, but this is a wood on 1900 6"); Wood Flg; Yard (enclosures in Wixhill include The Yard and Cote, Hemp, Rick, Robinsons Yd); Yewtree Fd.

(b) *Abbotts Yarde alias The Tythe Barne Yard* 1615 *SRO 322 box 2*; *Bechemulne* 1299 Ipm (*v.* **myln**, first el. could be 'beech' or **bæce**, 'stream valley'); *Hill Top* 1665; Little Ease 1665 (an early instance of a derogatory n.); *Peete Mdw* (family called *Peete*) 1665; *Petybruche* 1383 (*v.* **bryce**); *Smallmoors* 1665; *Stokesbruche* 1383; *Three Leasowes* 1665; *Trillmill* 1665 (apparently another instance of the n. discussed in Part **4** 82–3); *Westbrokemulne* 1299 Ipm ('west brook mill').

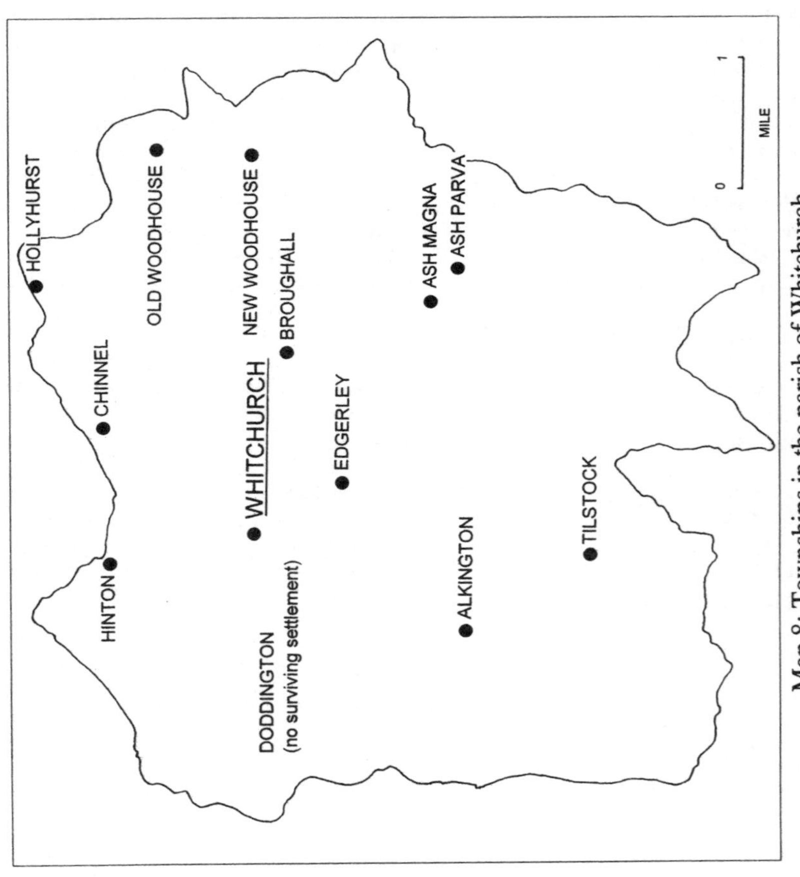

Map 8: Townships in the parish of Whitchurch.

Whitchurch

The parish-name, 'white church', is discussed in Part **1**. The English form is first noted in 1271–2, preceded by Latin *Album Monasterium* (1199) and French *Blancmustier* (c.1200). In DB the estate was *Westune*, one of 10 Sa examples of that name.

A Romano-British settlement called MEDIOLANUM was situated at Whitchurch. This Celtic name, which is the origin of Milan, is widespread on the Continent, 42 instances having been noted (Rivet and Smith, *The Place-Names of Roman Britain*, 415–16). The meaning could be 'central plain' or 'place in the middle of the plain'. There has not been a systematic topographical study of the whole corpus of *Mediolanum* settlements. It may be relevant to the meaning that Whitchurch is on a watershed between drainage to the north-west, to the Dee, and that to the Severn.

The Tithe Survey recognises 12 townships — Alkington, Ash Magna, Ash Parva, Broughall, Dodington, Edgeley, Hinton, Hollyhurst and Chinnel, Tilstock, Whitchurch, New Woodhouse, Old Woodhouse — and the place-name material has been arranged within the framework of these units. They vary in size from Hollyhurst and Chinnel, with 72 numbered fields in the *TA*, to Tilstock, with 712.

Alkington, Dodington, Edgeley and Whitchurch have entries in DB. The other townships are first recorded in the 13th century, except for the Chinnel component of Hollyhurst.

1. ALKINGTON (SJ 531392)

Alkington is a DB manor, so the name was discussed in Part **1**, where the etymology 'estate connected with Ealha' was proposed. This still seems the best option, but the treatment of the name in DEPN, which was not mentioned there, requires discussion.

Ekwall put the Sa name together with Alkington Gl (PN Gl **2** 207) and derived both from the personal name *Ealhmund*. This is likely for the Gl Alkington, but that name is not as well-documented as Ekwall thought; he mistakenly ascribed to it charter-forms such as *Alhmundingtune* which actually belong to Elmstone PN Gl **2** 81. Without the charter-forms, however, the Gl Alkington has forms with *-m-* (*Almintune* 1086, *Alkminton'* 1194) which support derivation from

Ealhmund. The Sa Alkington has no *-m-* spellings and a monothematic **Ealh*(*a*) is therefore likely.

It is probably coincidence that Whitchurch parish church is dedicated to St Alkmund.

ALKINGTON FM.

ALKINGTON GRANGE: the house is shown but not named on *TAMap*.

ALKINGTON HALL, 1841 *TA*.

CHAIN HO: buildings are shown here but not named on *TAMap*.

DEARNFORD HALL, 1833 OS, 1841 *TA*. This is probably an ancient n. despite absence of records. 'Hidden ford', *v*. **dierne**. There is no river, but the reference could be to a causeway through marsh.

SPRINGHILL, the house is shown but not named on *TAMap*, with fields called *Further* and *Near Spring Hill*, *~ ~ Field* and *Meadow*: *spring* probably in the sense 'coppice'.

Field-Names

Forms in (a) are 1841 *TA*.

(a) Alkington Fd (on boundary with Tilstock); Bache Fd (by a small stream, *v*. **bæce**); Bake House Croft (by Alkington Grange); Barn Croft (Bran Croft adjoins); Barn Fd (several); Barn Mdw; Big Fd (2); Big Mdw (several); Black Lane (leading to Dearnford Hall); Boosey Pasture, Higher, Lower (a reference to pasture rights, FN 34); Bradeley Fd (3 fields, Furlong Fd adjoins); Bromley Fd, Big; Bromley Fd (not near preceding); Brook Fd; Broomy Fd, New ~ ~; Colts Croft; Corner Croft; Croft(s) (small clusters by habitation sites); Cuckoo Fd (large and irregularly shaped); Dodington Fd (on boundary with Dodington); Dogkennel Croft (by Alkington Hall); Far Croft or Calves Croft; Fernyhill; Field (3 fields E. of Whitchurch road, near Chain Ho, are called Field: Barn, Green, Owens and Wicksteads Fds adjoin: Huntitout is among these); Finches Mdw; Fourteen Acres; Furlong Fd; Further Fd; Glanthorn, Lower (Higher Glanton adjoins); Glass Mdw; Gorsy, Gorsy Croft; Gorsy Fd; Green Fd; Halfpenny Croft; Higher Fd, Further, Near; High Fd; Hob Lane Croft; Holly Pce; Horse Moor; House Fd; Huntitout (cited in John Field's *English Field-Names: A Dictionary* as "fanciful name for a small secluded field", but it is neither small nor secluded: FN 11 notes that 1841 *TA* gives its area as 5 acres, and suggests that the reference is to difficulty of access, but it lies beside the Whitchurch road); Kennersley Croft, Higher, Lower, Middle; Late Murhall; Little Ley Fd; Little Mdw; Long Croft (2); Long Fd; Lords Mdw; Lythes Mdw; Marl Fd; Meadow (several); Meadow, Further or Big, Middle or Rough; Milking Bank Fd, Lower ~ ~ ~ (near Alkington Hall); Mowing Mdw; Near Ridding; New Hey; Oat Fd; Ollery Fd, Big, Little, ~ Mdw (alder trees); Orchard Fd; Ox Hey; Ox Lsw; Paddock; Parlour & Yd; Pea Fd; Peartree Fd; Peas Croft; Pinfold Fd; Poolstead; Ridding Moor; Rough Fd; Rye Hill; Shammerridding, Big, Little (Near and Far Shammer Ridding adjoin in Dodington); Stackyard Mdw; Stone Fd; Taylors Pce, Far, Near; Ten Shillings Fd,

Mdw; Thistly Croft; Thistly Fd; Three Nooked Croft (triangle in road junction); Tom Sullen, Big, Little; Wash Mdw; Way Fd; Welch's Fd, Little; Well Croft; Well Fd (2); Well Mdw (2); Wheat Fd; White Moor (2); White Ridding; Wood Pce.

2. ASH MAGNA (SJ 574396)

Esche 1255–6 *Ass*

Ash 1712 *et seq* PR(L) 4, *The Ash* 1770, 9, 87 ib, *Ashe* 1786 ib, *Ash Magna* 1831 OS, 1841 *TA*.

OE **æsc** 'ash tree' occurs fairly frequently as a simplex settlement-name, this and Nash (Part **1**) being the two Sa examples.

The two settlements, which are ¼ mile apart, are *Asshe Magna* and *Assh Parva* 1401–2 Talbot, *Essh Major*, *Essh Parva* 1419–20 ib.

ASH GRANGE, GROVE, HALL.

BANK HO and CHURCH FM are both shown, but not named, on *TAMap*.

Field-Names

Forms in (a) are 1841 *TA*.

(a) Barn Fd (several); Beddow Croft; Big Fd; Blackwater, Lower ~ (on E. edge of Brown Moss in Edgeley); Brickyard & Pltn; Brooms; Croft (clusters by habitations); Cross Fd (by a road-fork); Dayloom (*-loom* may be for *land*, i.e. open-field strip, 5 fields called Field adjoin); Falls (adjoins Stanner Ridding, both ns. refer to tree clearance, *v.* ***(ge)fall**); Flakes (FN 30 takes this to be flax); Fledgenett; Further Fd; Green Mdw; Hintons Ground; Horsley (7 fields near N. boundary are Big and Little Horsley, Horsley Ground and Mdw, and adjacent fields are Field(s) and Big and Little Field: Horsley may have been an open field); House Mdw; Intake (tiny enclosure by road); Jacksons Croft; Lawn (by Ash Hall); Long Fd; Langford, Gosy, Top, Well (by a road which skirts the edge of Brown Moss, so the 'long ford' is probably a causeway); Long Yd; Long Mdw; Loughnill (8 fields on E. boundary, by Ash Magna church); Madeley Ground; Marsh; Mawkins Croft; Middle Fd; Mill Fd, Mdw (probably a windmill); Moss Fd; Oak Flat (adjoins Field ns. by Dayloom *supra*); Peat Moss, Little; Pinge (*sic*, probably *pingo* 'small enclosure'); Pit Fd; Rough Mdw; Shoulder of Mutton (triangle in road-fork); Socknell, ~ Thorneycroft (3 fields adjoining Loughnill); Stanner Ridding (possibly 'stony clearing' from **stǣner**: Shammeridding in Dodington *infra* may be a corrupt version of the same n.); Town Mdw, Big; Wall End, Long ~ ~, ~ ~ Mdw (Wall may be from WMidl form of **welle**); Watergate Fd (by Edgeley Hall, significance not apparent); Well Mdw.

3. ASH PARVA (SJ 576395)

v. Ash Magna for the township name. There is little difference in size between the settlements, but Ash Parva is the larger of the two townships.

ASHACRES, *Ash Acres* 1833 OS, 1841 *TA*: *acres* perhaps in the sense 'open-field strips'. *Further* and *Near Ash Field* adjoin on *TAMap*.

ASH CORNER, COTTAGE, COVERT.

ASH FIELDS, *The Fields* 1833 OS, possibly a farm built on earlier open-field land.

ASHWOOD, 1654 PR(L) 9, 1841 *TA*, *Asshewoodes* 1483–5 Harl 433. In the 15th-cent. reference this is one of a group of woods in Whitchurch lordship. 1833 OS gives the n. Ash Wood to two farms.

ASHWOOD COTTAGE: the house is shown but not named on *TAMap*.

LEA HALL, 1833 OS, 1841 *TA*. This is a moated site, so the n. is probably ancient: 'clearing', *v.* **lēah**.

MELVERLEY: the house is shown but not named on *TAMap*.

THE SPRINGS, 1833 OS, SPRINGS WD, *Wood* 1841 *TA*: 'coppice'.

TWEMLOWS HALL, 1833 OS, 1841 *TA*, *Twembloes* c.1750 Garbet. Possibly from a surname derived from Twemlow Ch ('place at the two tumuli'), cf. Tilstock f.ns. *infra*. The establishment called TWEMLOWS on 1900 6" and later maps is *Dairy House* 1841 *TA*.

TWEMLOWS OLD WD, *Cover* 1841 *TA*.

Field-Names

Forms in (a) are 1841 *TA*.

(a) Acre; Arable; Ash Lane Fd; Ash Mdw, Big, Near (on county boundary); Ash Mdw (by Lea Hall); Bache ('stream-valley', adjoins Waterfall Lsw); Bank, Barn, Glade; Barley Fd, Lower ~ ~; Barn Croft; Barnett's Pce; Barn Fd (*freq*); Barn Yd (large field); Beech Fd, Garden; Bentley's Mdw; Bessy's Fd, Mdw, Bessy's Second Mdw; Big Fd (2); Big Mdw (2); Big Spring ('coppice', Little Coppice adjoins); Bookley Hill (Bootley Hill adjoins); Brewhouse Fd (by village); Brickkiln Fd (2); Broad Fd (2); Brook Mdw, Little; Brooms; Broomy Lsw; Burgess Pce; Calf Colt Fd; Carthouse Mdw (by Lea Hall); Catherine Pce; Cat Pit Fd; Chidlow's Ground (5 fields); Clayley, Little ~; Clemley (adjoins Heath Fd, about a mile S. of Clemley Park); Clemley Park (among Crofts on boundary with Ash Magna, *v.* Clemley in Prees, *supra*); Clover Fd (2); Comans Butt, Little ~ ~; Comans Knowl (not near preceding); Combs Hill, Higher, Lower; Cote Lsw, Little, Rough, Far; Cow Lsw (2); Crabtree Fd; Daisy Fd; Doe Butts; Dry Pce; Ewe Fd; Field, Little, Further, Middle; Field Pce, Higgins, Further, Near; Flat Fd; Flax Croft; Fowler's Fd, Great; Fox Hill, Big, Little; Further Fd; Gold Mdw; Gollins Mdw; Gorsy Bank; Gorsy Fd (2); Gouge Fd; Green, Far, Near; Green Fd; Griggy Pce (dialect *grig* 'heather'); Grindley's Moor; Hall & Clover Fds; Harrison's Pce; Heath Croft (2); Heath Fd, Big, Little; Hempbutt; Horse Pasture; Ightfield Mdw, Pce (near boundary with Ightfield); Improved; Intake (tiny field on township boundary); Jackson's Croft; Jenkins Heys, Mdw; Jenkins Moor; Kempley, Little, Great (the fields are nearly 2 miles from Higher Kempley *supra*, which was a detached part of Whitchurch); Lea Hall Fd; Lea Wd, Little, Ley Wd, Great (½ mile from Lea Hall); Ley, Big, Soldiers, Leys Mdw,

Moor; Little Fd, Little Mdw; Little Worth (small strip, a derogatory n.); Londonderry Park (strip along brook by Ash Woods, Derry Fd adjoins); Long Croft (2); Long Fd (several); Lower Fd; Lower Pce; Maddocks Mdw; Madeley's Moor; Malkins Mdw; Marl Moor; Meadow, Big and Little ~; Merryshire Wd; Mill Fd (probably a windmill); Moat Mdw (by Lea Hall); Moor; Moss Mdw (2); New Lsw; New Pce; Norcopps Yd; Old Fd; Ox Pasture, Great, Little; Peartree Fds, Further ~ Fd; Piece, Far Middle, Near Great; Pingo, Little Pingot ('small enclosure'); Pit Fd; Poor Fd; Queen Fd (King Fd adjoins); Rough Mdw; Round Hill; Round Oak; The Rue (Rue Bridge Fd is a short distance away: probably a reference to cultivation of the herb); Rushy Mdw; Sampson, Great, Little; Sawpit Fd; Six Day Math; Steels Fd; Thistly Fd; Thorny Croft, Mdw; Three Quarters; Three Thorns; Town Fd, Lower ~ ~ (4 fields W. of village); Trenched Fd; Turning Croft; Vetch Fd; Wall Crofts, Mdw, Wall Stone; Ward Fd, Mdw; Waterfall Lsw (by brook on S.E. boundary); Whitchurch Heath; Whittingham's Croft; Wood, Big, Low and Brook Wd, Wood Pce (near Ashwood); Wood Pce.

4. BROUGHALL (SJ 566414)

Burnthale, *Burnhale* 1255–6 *Ass*, *Bungale*, *Bughale* 1271–2 *Ass*
Worch'al' 1327 SR
Borhalle 1402 Talbot
Burgall 1419–20 Talbot, *Burghalle* 1483–5 Harl 433
Broughall 1712, 18 PR (L) 4

The Assize Roll forms are inconsistent and probably unreliable as regards the first element, and the 1327 form has been transcribed, probably incorrectly, with *W*-. The name is probably a compound of **burh** and **halh**, but as both these elements have various meanings in OE and ME usage it seems impossible to assign a precise meaning. There is no ancient fortification which could explain **burh**, and the ME sense 'borough' is not obviously suitable for the adjacent Whitchurch. Two of the established senses of **halh** might suit. The settlement is in a slight hollow, the most frequent sense, but this is an area where 'raised ground in marsh' is also possible.

ABBEY FM, *The Abbey* 1831 OS.

BROUGHALL COTTAGE, FM, HO: these are all shown but not named on *TAMap*.

BROUGHALLFIELDS: the farm is shown on *TAMap* surrounded by ~ *Field* ns.

CATTERALSLANE, *Ceteralls Field* 1841 *TA*.

FIELD FM: *TAMap* shows a group of furlong-shaped fields by a building and *Croft*.

OAKLANDS: there are no buildings here on *TAMap*.

Field-Names

Forms in (a) are 1841 *TA*.

(a) Aldertree Fd, Mdw; Almarks Fd; Ash Fd (on boundary with Ash Magna); Bank; Barn Fd; Barn Mdw; Barn Pce; Becketts Mdw; Big Ash Fd; Big Fall (probably 'clearing', *v.* ***(ge)fall**); Brandish Bank; Brickkiln Fd, Far ~ ~; Brickyard Fd; Broad Fd; Broughall Cross, Big, Little (by Cross Fd: there is a road-junction, but the fields are spread fairly widely); Chesters Fd; Clequirley, Higher ~, Cliquirley; Clover Fd; Coopers Fd, Lower, Higher; Crofts (4 equal-sized enclosures by Nantwich road); Croft (clusters at W. end of village and on N.E. boundary); Dainty Fd (2); Daisy Bank; Dawson's Moss Mdw; Fallow Fd; Far Fd; Field (many fields in the S.E. half of the township are called Field: there are also a few on N.W. boundary); Fingerpost Fd (in road-fork); Fishpond Mdw (by Broughall Ho, Fish Pond marked on 6" map); Five Acres; Gorsy Fd (2); Hail Bank, Big, Little; Hales Fd; Hatch Fd; High Stile Mdw; Hollins Knowle Fd; Horse Fd, Middle; Little Mdw (several); Long Mdw; Lovells Pce; Meadow (*freq*); Mere Bank (on boundary); Padmores Fd; Pale Croft (large field); Palmers Fd; Pea Stubble; Peat Fd; Peat Mdw; Peat Moss; Pingo (tiny strip by road); Pool Hill, Big Pool Pce; Pool Mdw; Ridding ('clearing'); Robinsons Fd; Rough Fd (2); Ryme Mdw (on E. boundary, perhaps **rima**); Shones Fd; Slang; Stack Fd; Suttons Fd, Little ~ ~; Top Fd; Vaughans Fd; Wall Stone (2, one S. of village, the other at the road-junction by Catteralslane); Well Fd (2); Well Lsw; Welch Harrow (possibly a mistake for Welsh Harp, which would suit one of the 2 fields); Wet Mdw; Wood Fd; Wood Mdw; Wood Pce.

(b) *Burghallewo*(*o*)*d* 1419–20 Talbot.

5. DODDINGTON (only surviving as a street-name on S. edge of Whitchurch town)

This is a DB manor, so the forms are presented in Part **1** and the etymology is discussed there under Detton (earlier *Dodington*). Sa has five names which are derived from OE **Dodingtūn* or **Dudingtūn*, and there are at least another 15 in the whole country. It has been suggested that these names mean 'estate at *Doding*', from an **-ing** place-name based on an unrecorded OE **dod** 'hill'; but the absence of such a word in other Sa names and the absence or extreme rarity of **-ing** names in this county tells against this. The alternative is 'estate associated with Doda', from a personal name and **-ingtūn**. This necessitates the assumption that the personal name, which (like the variants *Dodda*, *Dud*(*d*)*a*) is well recorded, was in frequent use at a time when **-ingtūn** formations were being coined.

HADLEY (SJ 519414), *Hadleye* 1327 SR (p). Clearly an ancient name in spite of poor documentation. 'Heath clearing', *v.* **hǣð**, **lēah**.

RED BROOK, *Le Redebrok* 1317 Pat ("stream called ~ ~ which is the division between co. Salop and the Welshery"). There is a small settlement called Redbrook across the county boundary in Iscoyd Fli.

BATHFIELDS, *Bath Field* 1841 *TA*.

BELTON (SJ 528408), *The Farm* 1833 OS, 1841 *TA*. This is a possible site for the settlement from which the township is named. The n. Belton has not been noted earlier than the 1898 OS 6" map.

BLACKOE, 1841 *TA*, *Blacko* 1796 *SBL 5374*, 1833 OS. BLACKOE BRIDGE, COTTAGES.

CHEMISTRY, 1833 OS, by the Ellesmere road, W. of the town. Two instances of Chemistry Lane in Ch, PN Ch **4** 125, **5.1** 75, are references to chemical works.

THE FIELDS, FIELDS COTTAGES, both shown but not named on *TAMap*. Probably a farm built on enclosed open-field land.

JUBILEE PARK.

MOSSFIELD; the house is shown but not named on *TAMap*.

PAN CASTLE, 1833 OS, *Panntonescastelhey* 1418–20 Talbot, *v.* **(ge)hæg** 'enclosure': this is an unusual instance of ME **castel** used for a motte and bailey. *Pannton* is a surname.

PAUL'S MOSS, 1841 *TA*.

RISING SUN COTTAGES, WD.

SMALLBROOK FM.

TILSTOCKROAD FM, shown but not named on *TAMap*.

VINEYARD, *The Cottage* 1833 OS.

Field-Names

Forms in (a) are 1841 *TA*.

(a) Alkington Lane Croft, Fd (by road to Alkington); Bake House Croft; Banky Fd; Barley Fd; Barlows Fd; Barnett's Fd; Barn Fd (*freq*); Bath Fd (nearly a mile S.E. of Bathfields *supra*); Benyons Fd; Big Fd; Big Mdw; Birtchinley Croft; Black Lake, Little ~ ~ (by canal, Lake is probably the dialect reflex of **lacu** 'small stream'); Bottoms (along a stream); Brickkiln Mdw; Britains Fd; Broad Congley; Brook Fd; Brook Mdw; Broom Fd; Brow Rough; Burtons Ground; Butchers Fd; Carther Ridding, ~ ~ Mdw; Clover Bank; Clover Fd; Cold Croft, Great; Cornhill Mdw, Pit Corn Hill; Corn Mill & Croft, ~ ~ Fd, Mill Pool, Near Mill Fd (these and Walk Mill Fd are by the stream on N. boundary); Croft (small fields round a building S.W. of Hadley include Bottom, Ferny, Long Hill, Moss, Penny and Spencers Croft); Croft(s) (clusters by habitations); Cuckoo Well Mdw, Cuckoo's Walls; Daisy Bank; Dodington Fd (on E. boundary); Downs Fd; Far Mdw; Fat Beast Fd; Ferny Croft; Field (many fields in the N.E. third of the township are called Field(s): some of these are furlong-shaped); Field, High, Middle, Lower; Fingerpost Mdw (by road-junction); Footway Fd (2); Fishers Fd, Mdw; Foxholes, Little, Madeley's; Glass Fd; Gorsty; Gorsy Fd; Great Fd; Great Mdw; Great Mdw and Petty France; Green Fd (several); Grindley's Ground; Gritty, Near Grit; Gritty Sawpit; Hadley Fd (½ mile E. of Hadley); Higher Wood Pce; High Fd; Hill Fd (2); Hollins & Brickkiln Croft; House Fd; Intake; The Island; Jervis's Fd; Kiln Fd; Kinleys Croft; Little Fd (2); Little Mdw (2); Little Worth; Long Croft (several); Long Fd (2); Long Mdw (several); Lower Fd; Lower Heath; Mallions Mdw; Mangill Fd, Nangill Mdw; Marl Croft; Marl Fd (2); Meadow; Mercers Fd, Flats; Middle Croft; Middle Fd; Millingtons Croft, Fd; Moss Fd; Mullocks Mdw; Near Mdw; Nursery; Orchard Hill; Outlet (near Blackoe); Ox Pce, (2); Pan Castle Mdw, Yd (*v. supra*); Penny Croft; Pit Fd (*freq*); Plat Fd; Pool Pce; Quakers Croft; Ravens Oak, Reins Oaks (adjacent); Roberts Ground; Rough Fd; Round Fd (one curved side); Round Mdw; Rushy Mdw; Sand Fd; Sandpit Fd; Savage Fd; Sedgeford Fd Mdw; Shammer Ridding, Near, Further (Ridding adjoins and Carther ~ is nearby, *v.* ***ryding** 'clearing': Shammer is possibly a corrupt spelling for Stanner 'stony', *v.* Ash Magna f.ns. *supra*); Sheep Fd (2); Shingle Bank, Near ~ ~ (by canal); Shoulder of Mutton; Shuters Hill (possibly a transferred n. from Shooters Hill, London); Six Butts (2 strips on edge of the group of Field(s) which adjoins The Fields farm); Slade (field with a wet patch, *v.* FN 18); Snow House Fd (1833 OS has Snow Hill here); Spring Bottom (by Red Brook); Spring Pce; Swamp; Swanwick's Mdw; Tilstock Fd (by Tilstockroad Fm); Timber Stile Fd, Mdw; Top Fd; Trims Pce, ~ Great ~; Two Ashes; Vetch Croft; Walk Mill Fd; Well Croft (2); Well Fd (several); Well Mdw (several); Wheat Fd (2); Whitchurch Croft; Windmill Fd; Wood Pce, Little ~ ~; Wycherley's Fd; Yards.

6. EDGELEY (SJ 557402)

Edgeley is a DB manor, so the name was discussed in Part **1**. The likeliest etymology was said there to be 'clearing at an enclosed park' from **edisc** and **lēah**, which would make the name identical with Edgeley in Cheadle Ch (PN Ch **1** 248). This conclusion still appears valid, but the discussion requires some modification.

The abundant spellings for the Ch name include many with *Ediss(e)-*, *Edis-* and some with *Edis(s)he-*, *Edyssh-* which certainly point to **edisc**, whereas the DB form for the Sa name and the few available 13th-cent. forms have only *Ed(d)es-*, which could indicate 'Ēad's clearing'. The suggestion in Part **1** that the development to Edgeley tells in favour of **edisc** is invalid. In names with *-desl-* development to *-dgl-* can sometimes be clearly demonstrated. This is seen in Frodesley, also discussed in Part **1**, which was *Frodgley* 1584 *et seq*, and in Mudgley So, which was *Mudesle* 1157, and this is a possible explanation of the development to Edge- in the present name.

The evidence for Edgeley Sa is compatible with an alternative etymology, 'Ēad's clearing', but telling against this is the occurrence of a second Edgeley in Ch, PN Ch **3** 309, with forms which, like those for the Sa name, are compatible with either etymology, and of a field-name *Eddesley*, c.1275, in Middleton Priors Sa, Part **2** 137. While several examples of a name meaning 'Ēad's clearing' are not beyond the bounds of coincidence, the four names probably belong together, and derivation from **edisc**, certain in one Ch example, is probably the best bet for the other three.

BROWN MOSS, 1833 OS, 1841 *TA*.
EDGELEY HALL.
FIELD'S FM.

Field-Names

Forms in (a) are 1841 *TA*.

(a) Ash Croft; Aphrons Fd; Barn Fd (several); Barn Yd; Bensons Fd; Big Fd (several); Big Mdw (2); Brickkiln Croft; Broad Hill, Hill Fd; Buckleys Fd; Chetwoods Fd; Comberbatch Fd; Crabtree Fd; Croft (several near Heathlane in Tilstock); Dykes Fd; Far Fd; Far Pce; Green Fd; Green Fd, Big, Little, Higher; Heath Lane Fd (Heathlane is in Tilstock *infra*); Hollin Croft, Big, Little; Hop Yd; Jones's Mdw; Keays Fd; Land Fd; Laywood Fd, Mdw; Little Fd (2); Long Fd; Lower Fd (2); Mill Fd (on outskirts of Whitchurch, probably a windmill); Moss Fd, Mdw; Moss Croft, Far Moss Fd (by Brown Moss); New Garden; The Riddings; Riddings, Far, Little; Sheep Fd; Short Croft; Slang (between road and stream); Stew Croft (by Edgeley Hall, 'fish pond', *v.* **stewe**); Taylor's Fd; Top Fd; Top Pce; Well Yd; Wheat Fd; Whitehalls Mdw.

7. HINTON (SJ 541434)
Hyneton' (p), *Hineton'* 1255–6 *Ass*
Hayneton 1255–6 *Ass*
Hynton' 1291–2, 1327 SR (p), *-ton* 1302 Ipm, 1381 Cl, 1577 Saxton

'Estate of the religious household' or 'estate of the domestic servants', *v.* **hīwan, hīgna**. Other Sa instances are Hinton in Pontesbury, Part **2** 38, and Hinnington (*Hineton'* 1255–6 *Ass*) in Shifnal. Hinstock and Hine Heath have the same first element.

BRICKKILN PLTN.
THE FIELDS, 1833 OS, 1841 *TA*.
GRINDLEYBROOK FM.
HINTON HALL.
HINTON OLD HALL, *Hinton Hall* 1675 Ogilby, 1833 OS, 1841 *TA*. There is no village, and GR above is for the Old Hall.

Field-Names

Forms in (a) are 1841 *TA*. Earlier forms are 1690 *SBL 1960*.

(a) Barn Fd (2); Big Mdw; Brickkiln Fd; Bridge Fd (6" map shows footpath crossing stream on S. boundary); Brocha Hill, Big, Little and Short ~ ~; Bythom, Lower, Middle, Large, Cheshire (along the Whitchurch/Tarporley road, the n. is from **bytme**, variant of **botm**: the feature is not obvious from maps but may be identifiable on the ground); Clapgate Fd; Close, Big, Little (2 large fields); Clover Fd; Cotmore Hill, Big, Little, Hill Fd; Cunnery, Lower ~ ('rabbit-warren'); Duck Mdw; Ferny Fd; Fishpond Fd; Five Acre Mdw (Six Acre Mdw adjoins); Flat Fd (2); Footway Fd; Fox Cover; Green Fd; Horse Pasture; Horse Pasture Mdw; House Fd (2, by Grindleybrook Fm and The Fields); Hussey's Fd; Innage (*v*. **inheche**, a ME term for land cultivated after being fallow); Marlpit Fd; Middle Fd; Moss Mdw; Old Mdw; Oxford Mdw; Ox Lsw; Paddock (by Hinton Old Hall); Pool Mdw (cf. *Hyntonespole* 1419–20 Talbot); Rough Croft, Fd; Round Croft (curved sides); Rye Bank; Town Fd; Wall Fd (*The Wall Fields*), Well Fields (Wall from WMidl form of **welle** 'spring'); Well Fd; Well Mdw; Wells Croft.

(b) *Broomy Fields*; *The Great* and *Little Intack*; *Oate Fields*; *The Readings* ('clearings').

8. HOLLYHURST AND CHINNEL

HOLLYHURST (SJ 574445)
Halehurst 1268 AD
Hollehirst 1401–2 Talbot
Holehurst 1419–20 Talbot
Holhurst Cheynell 1532–40 SAS 3/VIII
Hollyhurst 1672 HTR, 1833 OS

Hollyhurst Lodge and Wood are in Sa, but the tiny settlement is in Marbury Ch, which was a parochial chapelry of Whitchurch. The name is listed in PN Ch **3** 105, where it is ascribed to **holegn** 'holly'. The 1268 form, however, which occurs in a context associating the place with Marbury, suggests derivation from **halh** and **hyrst**, 'wooded hill by a valley or hollow'. It is clear that the association with holly is late.

CHINNEL FM (SJ 557435)
Chenhull 1401–2 Talbot, *Chene Hull* 1419–20 ib
Cheynell 1532–40 SAS 3/VIII.

v. **hyll**: the forms are insufficient for identification of the first element.

BROOK FM, *Brook House* 1833 OS.

HOLLYHURST LO, YD.

LARDER LO, WD, on W. edge of Combermere Pk.

Field-Names

Forms in (a) are 1841 *TA*.

(a) Aldery Croft; Barn Fd (2); Barrack, Lower (probably a temporary shelter, PN Ch **5.1** 98 lists a few instances); Big Oak Fd; Brickkiln Fd; Brickkiln Yd; Brickley Bank; Broomy Bank; Calves Croft; Chinnel Fd; Clover Fd; Cote Croft (2 fields, no buildings); Drumble Croft (*v*. The Drumble in Baschurch *supra*); Fairy Fd; Field, Far, Middle; Further Pce; Gorsty Bank (2); Green Fd; Handley Sion, Great, Little (possibly a chapel); Horse Pasture (2); Long Mdw; Mossy Bank, Little; Meadow, Big, Little; Meadow, Great and Little ~; Moss (Branklow Moss Ch adjoins); Paddock (adjoins Horse Pasture); Park (by Combermere Pk); Ryegrass Fd (2); Sandy Croft; Slovens Fd; Sour Croft; Thistly Croft; Triangle Fd.

9. TILSTOCK (SJ 543379)

Tildestok 1211 Cur (p) *et freq* with variant spellings *Tylde-* and *-stok'*, *-stoke* to 1327 SR

Tilstoke 1401–2 Talbot, *-stok* 1512–13 *SBL 1934*, 1577 Saxton, *Tylstoke* c.1535 SAS 3/VIII, *Tilstocke* 1599, 1674 PR(L) 9, *-stock* 1704 ib

Tillestoke 1419–20 Talbot

Tystoke 1483–5 Harl 433

'Tīdhild's dependent settlement', *v*. **stoc**. The pers.n. is feminine.

BRICKWALLS, by Brick Works next to canal: *TAMap* shows *Limekilns & Wharf* here.

GLEBE COTTAGE.

HEATH COTTAGE.

HEATHLANE, *Heath Lane* 1833 OS, cf. *two Heath Lane fields* 1690 *SBL 1960*.

HEATH VILLA: this is the name given on 6" map to one of the small buildings in a patch of enclosures on Whitchurch Heath: these are called *Croft*(*s*) in *TA*.

HOLLINS FM, HO, LANE.

INGLESIDE, IVY HO.

MALTKILN COTTAGES, *Malt Kiln & Plantation* 1841 *TA*.

OAK FM: *TAMap* shows buildings and crofts here.

ORGAN HO, 1833 OS, *v*. FN 59. This was the official residence of the organist of the parish church, and adjoining small fields in *TA* are *Bass's Croft*, *Tenor Croft* and *Treble*.

TILSTOCK PK, LOWER and UPPER ~ ~: 1833 OS gives the name to all three sites.

WARREN HO, 1833 OS, 1841 *TA*.

WHITCHURCH HEATH.

WITNEYS FM.

WOODLANE FM.

Field-Names

Forms in (a) are 1841 *TA*.

(a) The Acre; Apprentices Mdw; Bache, Further, Near ('small stream-valley', *v.* **bæce**); Bakehouse Croft (2, by Brickwalls and Lower Tilstock Pk); Bakehouse Fd, Far, Near (by Heathlane); Bank Pce, Big, Little; Barefoot Flat, Big, Little (probably derogatory); Barley Bank; Barley Croft, Big and Little ~ ~; Batho's Croft, Fd; Bean Fd; Bayleys Bank, Big, Little; Big Fd (*freq*); Big Hills (Little Hills Mdw adjoins); Big Mdw (*freq*); Big Pit Fd; Birch, Big Pool, Park (probably *britch* 'newly-broken-in land'); Black Cuttings; Black Mdw; Black Pit Fd (2); Black Waste; Boosey Pasture (probably referring to a type of tenure, *v.* FN 34); Boot Leg (shaped like a boot); Brassy Mdw; Brickkiln Croft; Brickkiln Fd (2); Briery Croft; Broad Lsw; Broad Mdw; Brookes Bank; Broom Fd; Broomfields & Joshua's Yd; Broomy Croft; Broomy Fd (2); Bucks Pasture; Butty Fd (*v.* FN 7–8 for various meanings); Calves Croft; Calves Fd; Carthouse Croft; Catley, Further and Near ~, ~ Mdw; Chapel Fd; Chidlow's Fd; Church Hill; Clover Bank; Clover Fd (several); Clover Yd; Colts Croft; Common Fd, Higher, Lower (by Hollinwood Common); Coppice Fd (2); Cornist, Big Cornisk; Cote Pce (no building); Crabmill Mdw; Crabtree Pce; Cranberry Mdw; Crofts (small fields by Organ Ho are Barley, Barn, Rushy Croft, also Bass's and Tenor Croft, and Treble, for which *v. supra*); Darling Pce; Darlingtons Yd; Diglake Croft, Mdw (by a small stream, probably canalised, *v.* Ellesmere f.ns. *supra*); Duggins Moor; Egg Hill (FN 50 suggests a plant-n.); Ellis's Green Fd, Ellis's Mdw; Far Fd; The Farm (tiny field by Steel Heath); Flat; Flax Fd; Footway Fd; Further Ground (2); Gig Hole (2, pits for drying flax); Gill Mdw; Gorsy Croft; Grass Fd; Grazing Mdw (Mowing Mdw adjoins); Green Fd; Gumbersage; Hamnett Croft; Hannah Pits; Heath Fd (several); Hempyard Mdw; Henshaws Croft, Mdw; Higgins Fd (2); Higgins Oak; The Higginsons; High Fd, Mdw; High Shoot; Higher Wd; Hills Croft; Holly Pce; Hopkins Pce, Big, Little; Horse Moor (several); Hose End; Jack Birch (probably *britch*); Kempsters Fd; Kens Tail; Kettles Big Fd; Kinnersley's Lane; Kins Croft; Lane Fd; Lawyers Croft; Light Birches; Lodge Pce (by Heath Cottages); Lodgets Fd; Long Croft (several); Long Fd; Long Hills; Lower Fd; Lower Yd; Malt Kiln & Pltn; Marl Croft; Marl Pce; Meadow, Higher, Lower; Meadow behind Barn; Mellors Croft; Middle Fd; Midleys Yd; Milking Bank (2); Minshulls Mdw; Montford's Croft; Moody's Croft; Moor; Moor, Further and Near ~, Jonah's ~, Lady ~; Moor, Middle, Round; Moss Fd (on edge of Brown Moss); Moss Mdw; Moss Moor; Mowing Croft; Mowing Pce; Musgrave Mdw; Nell Fd;

New Fd (several); New Intake; New Lsw (2); New Pce; New Yd; Nungrave, ~ Mdw; Oakley Marsh, Big and Little ~ ~; Old Barn; Old Marl Fd; Ollery Fd (alders); Ollery Mdw; Outlet Fd; Paddock (by Lower Tilstock Pk); Park Fd (2, by Lower and Upper Tilstock Pk); Parry's Croft; Pea Moss; Phillips Fd; Piece, Long, Middle, Near, Nearer; Pindle Rindle Fd, Mdw (listed as obscure FN 71 but also mentioned ib 14 as a possible shape-n., Rindle being perhaps associated with *rondel* 'circle': the latter suggestion does not suit the fields); Pinfold Fd; Pingo; Pingot (as preceding, form of **pingel** 'small enclosure'); Pointon, Big, Little; Pool Mdw; Poplar, ~ Fd, Little Poplar (6 fields S.E. of village, these and adjacent Rowley Fd include some furlong-shaped strips); Potato Butt; Quillet Hills, Big and Little ~ ~ (Quillet has various sense in f.ns., *v.* FN 8 and J. Field, *A History of English Field-Names* 129); Ravens Bank; Ridding, Lower, Pipe ('clearing', *pipe* perhaps referring to a canalised stream); Rough Fd (2); Rough Wd; Round Bank (2 slightly curved sides); Rowley Fd, ~ ~ Moor, Lower ~ ~, Higher Rowley; Ryegrass Fd; Rye Lsw (2); Sam's Pce; Sandford Mdw; Sandhole Fd; Sawpit Fd; Spring ('plantation'); Stannary Hill, Big, Little, Stanner Hill Fd ('stony hill', *v.* **stǣner**); Stocking, Big, Little; Stoddy Fd, Big and Lower ~ ~; Sunny Croft; The Suttons; Swanwicks Fd, Mdw; Taggs Fd; Three Crofts; Tilstock Mdw; Tonge Sharp (another field, by Whitchurch Heath, is Tongue Sharp: both are small, elongated enclosures, but not obviously like tongues); Top Fd (several); Twelve Swath (i.e. breadth of scythe cuts); Twemlows, ~ Fd, Mdw (7 fields, perhaps the property of someone from Twemlow Ch, *v.* Twemlows Hall in Ash Parva *supra*); Wall Fd; Wall Mdw Bank, Fd; Washing Pit Fd, Higher, Lower; Washpit Fd; Waste Mdw; Way Fd; Weir Mdw; Welch's Croft, Fd; Well Mdw; Wheat Fd; Whetstone Fd, Big, Little; Whitneys, Whitney Pits; White Ridding; Whixall Croft; Wilbraham Head; Wild Swan Leys; Wood, Higher, Lower; Wood Lane Croft; Wood Pce; Yespleys Crank.

Between Whitchurch Heath (*Prees Heath* in *TA*) and the stream which forms the boundary with Prees, the *TAMap* shows a belt of mostly very small fields, the pattern of which is still discernible on the 1900 6" map. These were presumably enclosed from the western edge of the heath. The names can be summarised under the generics Croft, Field, Meadow, Moor and Piece.

Croft(*s*): a large number of the fields are labelled Croft(s), there are also Crabtree, House, and Big and Little Moss Croft.

Field: ns. with this generic are Broomy, Crabmill, Crabtree, Heath (2) and Minshulls Field.

Meadow: Brook, Crabmill, Further, Jenkins, Parsons, Titley, Weir, Well, Whittakers.

Moor: Bratts, Heath, Middle, Rushy, Well.

Piece: New and Summer, both large fields.

There are also two relatively large fields called Six Acres and Tongue Sharp (*supra*).

10. WHITCHURCH

The 1899 6" OS map shows Whitchurch Urban and Rural as discrete areas, but there is no division on the Index to Tithe Survey map and the Foxall *TAMap* is for the whole area.

BLAKE MERE (SJ 560425)

Blackmere 1334 Strange, *Blakmere* 1377 Fine, *Black Mere* 1796 *SBL 5374*, 1808 Baugh

Blakemere 1360 Pat *et freq* to 1577 Saxton, *Blake Mere* 1833 OS

'Dark lake', *v.* **blæc**, **mere**. The earlier references are to the medieval residence of the Talbot family, which was on the S. side of the lake, and the GR given above is for this site. There is an account of the house in the Introduction to Talbot. It ceased to be habitable between 1538 and 1561, and there is now only a mound.

BLACK PK, 1833 OS, (*Le*) *Blakeparke* 1401–2 Talbot, *Blakepark* 1419–20 ib, *Black Parke* 1672 HTR: probably short for **Blakemereparke*. The Talbot house was within the park.

BUBNEY (SJ 519428), *Bubney* 1483–5 Harl 433. 'Bubba's island', with **ēg** in the sense 'raised ground in a wet area'. The nature of the site is shown clearly on the hachured 1833 OS map.

YOKINGSGATE: *Ȝokkynsȝatte*, *Yokkinsyatte* 1401–2 Talbot, *Yockynesyate*, *Yockenesyate* 1411–12 ib, *Ȝockenȝate* 1417–18 ib, *Yokings Gate* 1833 OS, 1841 *TA*. This was a grange of Blake Mere.

v. **geat** 'gate'. The first element may be a surname.

BATHOS WD.

BLACKPARK COTTAGE, FM.

BLACK WD: *TAMap* has strips called *Plantation* here.

BLAKEMERE COTTAGE.

BRICKKILN LANE, 1841 *TA*, BRICKKILN LANE FM.

BROOK LANDS.

CLAP GATE, *Clapgate Field* 1841 *TA*.

THE COTTAGE, 1841 *TA*.

CRANBERRY MOSS COVERT, *Cranberry Moss* 1841 *TA*.

DANSON'S BRIDGE, COTTAGE, *Danson's Farm* 1833 OS.

THE FOUNDRY.

GORSE COVERT, 1833 OS.

GRINDLEYBROOK: the brook forms the county boundary and the name is documented in PN Ch **4** 47. Grindley was *Grenleg'* 1230, 'green wood or clearing'. GRINDLEYBROOK FM is in Hinton township.

THE GROVES: the house is shown but not named on *TAMap*.

HORSE AND JOCKEY P.H. (in Grindleybrook).

LILY WD.

THE LODGE, 1833 OS, 1841 *TA*: in Black Pk.

MILE BANK, ~ ~ CREAMERY.

MOSS COVERT.

MOSS FM, *The Moss* 1833 OS.

THE MOUNT, *Mount House* 1841 *TA*. MOUNT FM is shown but not named on *TAMap*.

NEW HO, 1833 OS.

OSS MERE, 1833 OS, 1841 *TA*, OSSMERE COTTAGES, WD.

TERRICK HALL, 1833 OS, *Terrick House* 1841 *TA*. The houses called TERRICK which adjoin in Hinton township are represented on Hinton *TAMap* by a building and a *Croft*.

WAYMILLS, *Waymill Feild* 1735 *SBL 5327*, ~ *Field* 1841 *TA*.

Street-Names

Street-names on the 1899 OS 6" map are:

BARGATE.

BRIDGEWATER ST.

BROWNLOW ST.

DODINGTON.

EGERTON ST.

GREEN END, 1841 *TA*, *The ~ ~* 1735 *SBL 5327*.

HIGH ST, 1841 *TA*.

NEWTOWN.

STATION RD.

TALBOT ST.

WATERGATE.

WEST END.

The map in *Shropshire Town Centre Maps* (Estate Publications 8th ed.) shows CLAYPIT STREET (not named on 6" but so called on *TAMap*) and SHERRYMILL HILL, which is near *Sharrow Mill Field* on *TAMap*. There are references to the mill in Talbot: *Shreffmylne* 1401–2, *Shrifmull* 1420. Probably 'sheriff mill', *v.* **scīr-(ge)refa**.

A set of accounts for 1419–20 in Talbot (p. 138) mentions a 'manor' called *Hethhous* and a place in Whitchurch called *Le Pendas*. This last, also mentioned 1401–2 (p. 53), is a 'penthouse', *v.* NED *s.v. penthouse*, *pentice*.

Field-Names

Forms in (a) are 1841 *TA*, except for those dated 1806, which are *SBL 12169*. Earlier forms dated 1401–2, 1417–18, 1419–20 are Talbot. Those dated 1735 are *SBL 5327*.

(a) Abbey Moor; Allens Fd; Aston Shut, Far, Great, Little; Back House Croft (by Brickkiln Lane Fm); Bank; Bank, Beggary, Eton's, King Tree, Sandy; Bank, Clover, Near; Bank, High, Low, Great; Bank Croft; Banky Fd (several); Barn Bank; Barn Croft; Barn Fd (*freq*); Barn Mdw; Barn Yd (large field by Rectory); Barrow Pce; Bench Fd; Bentley Mdw; Big Fd (several); Big Lancashire; Blake Mere Fd (½ mile W. of Blake Mere); Boat Fd, Boathouse Fd (both by canal); Bolands Fd; Brickkiln Fd (several); Brickley Croft; Bridge Fd; Brook Fd; Broom Fd (2); Broomy Fd; Calves Croft; Calves Grass, Far, Near; Causeway Mdw; Clem Park (by Mount Fm); Clemley Park (adjoins Heath Inclosure: *v.* Clemley in Prees *supra*); Coppice, Far, Near; Cote Pce (no building); Cotton's Fd, Mdw, Pce; Cow Pasture; Croft(s) (a large number of fields in the centre of the township, N. of the town, are called Croft(s)); Davies Fd, Mdw; Daxon's Fd, Mdw; Deer Leaps (by Yokingsgate); Deermoss Croft, Mdw; Dickens Mdw; Edgeley Fd (on boundary with Edgeley); Far Fd (several); Festick Fd, Far, Near; Field (in an area W. of the town, between the Malpas road and Bubney, many fields are labelled Field); Field back of House (by Blackpark Cottage); Field, Higher, Near; Fingerpost Fd (in road-fork); Fishpond Mdw; Fleets House Croft; Flewellyns Fd, Far, Near, Middle (cf. *Lewellins Croft* 1735); Footroad Fd; Footway Fd (2); Fowler's Pce, High and Low ~ ~; Fox Cover Fd; Fox Fd; Fox Oaks, Far, Great, Little; Garden Fd; Glade Fd (cf. *Gladesdale* 1401–2); Gollins Mdw, Little; Gorsty Fd; Great Fd; Great Mdw; Green Fd (2); Heath, ~ Fd (6 fields); Hall Mdw (by Terrick Hall); Harpers Fd, Far, Near; Hill Fd (2); Horse Pasture (2); Horton's Bank, Mdw (cf. *Horton's Croft* 1735); House Fd (by Mount Fm); Improved, Great, Little; The Island 1806; Kerrystone Fd; Keys Fd; Knowle; Lane Croft; Lane Fd (2); Leaf Grass (near Calves Grass); Little Croft; Little Fd; Little Mdw (2); Little Worth (tiny enclosure); Lodge Moor, Great, Little (by The Lodge); Long Croft (2); Long Fd (several); Long Lands, Lower; Long Shoot (2 elongated fields); Lower Fd; Malpas Croft; Manor Mdw, Moor (by Blake Mere); Marbury Fd (Marbury is in Ch); Marl Fd (2); Meadow (*freq*); Meadow, Big, Great, Far, Near, Lease; Meadow, Far and Near Great, Far and Near Little, Andersons Great); Mere Fd (by Blake Mere); Middle Fd (several); Milestone Fd (by Malpas road); Minced Pie (FN 28 suggests a reference to soil consistency, associating this n. with Pastrycrust); Moor Croft; Moss; Moss Croft; Moss Fd (2); Moss Fd, Great ~ ~, Little Windsor Moss; Mossy Mdw; Mount, Big, Little, Lower Mount Fd (by Terrick Hall, not near The Mount or Mount Fm); Murray, Far, Cow and Horse ~ (FN 62 suggests **morgen-gifu** for this and Black Morray in Bolas Magna, but earlier documentation would be desirable); Near Fd (2); Nells Park (adjoins Clemley Park); New Mdw; New Mill Fd; New Pce; Old House Fd; Ownes Fd, Further, ~ Hill, Near; Park Fd, Big, Little (no obvious reason for n.); Pea Fd; Phillips Great Mdw, Moor; Pigstye Fd; Pinfold Fd; Pit Fd (several); Pool Fd (several); Potato Garden; Public House Fd (P.H. shown); Quillet (minute strip by church); Ridge; Ridgeway Bank; Road Fd; Roes Fd; Rough Bottom; Rough Croft; Rough Pce; Roy's Croft; School Mdw; Shooting Butts, Lower, Higher (on N. edge of town); Slang (several); The Smallbrookes or Brook or

Footway Fd 1806; Spa Well Fd (at approx. GR 533422); Square Fd; Stack Yard Fd; Steppingstones Fd, Big, Little, Hippingstone Fd; Stubble Close; Sweet Fd; Syllabub Close (FN 26 suggests a reference to rich pasture, alluding to the cream used in making syllabub: there is a Cae Cylabab in Llanyblodwell); Thistle Close; Thistly Fd; Tinkers Bank; Tollgate Fd, Pce (by Tollgate Ho on Malpas road); Tollgate Fd (by Tollgate Ho on Market Drayton road); Tree Bank; Triangle Fd; Two Pit Fd; Walnut Close, Little; Wash Pit Fd; Water Fd, Far, ~ Mdw (by Blake Mere); Watson's Mdw; Way Fd (several); Welch Croft; Well Fd (several); Well Mdw; Wet Marl Pit (possibly *Marleput* 1327 SR (p)); Wheat Fd, Far, Near; Whitley Lane Fd; Whittinghams Croft, Pce (not near each other); Wibberley, Big, Great, Little, Lower and Middle ~ (6 fields on S.E. boundary: *Wyburley* (a meadow) 1401–2); Wicksteads Fd, Mdw; Wilkinsons Fd; Wilsons Great Fd; Windmill Fd; Wood, Far, Near, ~ Mdw; Wood Pce (several); Worrall's Fd.

(b) *Bans(s)hawe* 1419–20 (*v.* **sceaga**); *Blakemerehulle* 1417–18; *Braceysheth* 1419–20; *Brasymedowe* 1401–2 (possibly the same surname as in preceding); *Bromefurlong* 1419–20 (*v.* **brōm**); *Chapell Meadowe* 1401–2; *Ebbefurlong* 1419–20; *Ellesmore* 1401–2 ('Elli's wet ground', *v.* **mōr**); *Espley* 1401–2, *Esperley* 1419–20; *Fissherndyng* 1419–20; *Furthermill Fd* 1735; *Glesmore* 1401–2; *Halghyate* 1419–20 (*v.* **halh**, **geat**); *Hethmore* 1401–2 (*v.* **hǣð**, **mōr**); *Heyrndyn* 1419–20; *Launceturfeld*, *Launceterfeld* 1419–20; *Longley* 1419–20; *Monkesmore* 1419–20; *Mundesmede* 1419–20; *Murymede* 1419–20 ('pleasant mead', *v.* **myrig**); *Neuelecroft* 1419–20; *Neupole* 1419–20 ('new pool'); *Parkmill Field* 1735; *Polested* 1401–2 ('pool place'); *Reodymore* 1417–18 ('reedy wet ground'); *Rostwode* 1327 SR (p) (perhaps 'wood where roof-beams are obtained', from **hrōst** and **lēah**, cf. Rossley PN Gl **1** 169); *Roule* 1419–20; *Sawpitt Croft* 1735; *Schellefelde* 1417–18; *Somereshull* 1419–20; *Walmore* 1401–2 (*v.* **mōr**, first el. probably **wælle** 'spring'); *Le Withianesleghe* 1337 Pat (perhaps 'clearing of the willow holt', *v.* **wīðign**, **lēah**); *Wolfencrofte* 1419–20.

11. NEW WOODHOUSE (SJ 591420)

v. Old Woodhouse *infra*. This settlement is *Newewodhous* 1401–2 Talbot, *Newodehous* 1419–20 ib, *New Woodhouses* 1782 *SBL 4318*.

ANCIENT BRITON P.H.

ASHWOOD COURT: Ashwood is in Ash Parva *supra*.

BANK FM, shown but not named on *TAMap*.

BROADOAK FM, shown but not named on *TAMap*.

BROADOAK COPPICE.

CRAB MILL: cf. *Crab Mill Field otherwise Gamons Pool Field*, *Crab Mill Meadow formerly Meadow of Dukes* 1834 *SBL 8622, 3*.

FIRTREE HO, 1833 OS.

GRUB GREEN: *TAMap* shows one building and a cluster of *Croft(s)* here.

IVY FM, shown but not named on *TAMap*.

LONG WD, *Rough* 1841 *TA*.

NEW FM, shown but not named on *TAMap*.

OAK COTTAGES.

Field-Names

Forms in (a) are 1841 *TA*.

(a) The Acre; The Acres; Adderley Mdw; Bache (in a small stream-valley); Bache, Far and Near ~ (at the head of a small stream-valley: lower down the valley is Blue Bache Fm PN Ch **3** 103); Bank Mdw; Barn Fd (*freq*); Barn Pce; Benyons Fd; Big Fd; Big Mdw; Birches Wd; Brickkiln Fd; Broad Oak (not near Broadoak Fm); Calves Croft (Cow Lsw adjoins); Cater House Croft; Cateralls Fd (not near Cateralls Fd in Broughall); Chapel Fd; Clover Fd; Cookes Mdw; Cooks Fd; Coppice Mdw; Corner Croft; Corner Fd; Cutters Fd, Higher Cappers, Far Scapers (adjoining); English Fd; Far Fd; Fowlers Mdw; Gorsty Fd; Grazing Mdw; Great Fd; Great Twopenny Cut (tiny enclosure); Green Fd; Hill Fd (several); Hoare Stone Fd, Mdw (on boundary); Horse Pasture (2); House Fd; Juney Hill; Lady Moor Mdw; Lawn (by Oak Cottage); Little Lsw; Little Mdw (2); Little Pasture; Long Mdw (2); Meadow (several); Merricks Fd; Middle Fd (2); Montgomery; New Fd; Outlet (by Bank Fm); Ox Lsw; Parlour Croft (one of the Crofts S. of Grub Green); Peartree Mdw; Pinfold Fd; Pingo (tiny enclosure, *v.* **pingel**); Pit Fd; Pool Fd, Big, Little; Pool Head, Little ~ ~; Rabbit Mdw; Riddings ('clearings'); Rough Fd; Rye Croft, Far; Sand Fd; Sandy Croft; Scubo, Further, Middle, ~ Mdw; Shentons Fd, Far, Near; Sillabub Croft (cf. Whitchurch f.ns. *supra*); Stocks Fd; Tom Ridding, Far and Near ~ ~ (probably 'town clearing', *v.* FN 7); Trick Fd; Walnut Croft; Way Fd (2); Well Fd (several); Wet Fd; Wheat Eddish (**edisc** is usually rendered 'enclosed park', but in f.ns. it is frequently qualified by crop terms, *v.* PN Ch **5.1** 166); Whitfield Fd.

12. OLD WOODHOUSE (SJ 592429)

Wodehous 1271–2 *Ass*, 1327 SR, *Blakemere Wodehous* 1388 Pat
Wodhous 1401–2 Talbot, *Oldewodhous* ib

This is a recurring name in Sa, *v.* the discussion under Woodhouse in Stoke upon Tern *supra*.

BRIDGE PLTN, *Plantation* 1841 *TA*.
COMBERMERE COTTAGE, shown but not named on *TAMap*.
MARTIN'S ASH, 1833 OS.
SHROPSHIRE GATE FM, shown but not named on *TAMap*.
SHROPSHIRE LANE FM.
STEEL'S ROUGH PLTN.
WELLINGTON LO, 1833 OS, *Wellington Cottage* 1841 *TA*.
WHITCHURCH LO.
WOODHOUSE FM.

Field-Names

Names in (a) are 1841 *TA*.

(a) Barn Fd; Big House Fd (by Shropshire Gate Fm); Big Mdw; Brook Croft; Calves Croft; Cow Hay; Croft (cluster by Martin's Ash); Field (many fields are called Field, there is a row of these along W. boundary); Field across the Road; Gorsty Croft; Green Fd; Inclosure Fd; Little Mdw (2); Manus/Menos Fd (4 fields on S. boundary); Meadow (several); Meadow Fd; Moss Mdw; Oak Fd; Paddock; Park (on edge of Combermere Pk); Pars Fd, Old Pars Mdw; Peartree Fd, Big; Pingo (*v.* **pingel**); Rough, Great, Little; Rough Fd; Sand Fd; Sandhole Fd; Whitehouse Fd; Wood Pce.

Whixall

The parish-name, 'Hwittuc's **halh**', is discussed in Part **1**. This is a clear instance of **halh** in the sense 'dry ground in marsh'.

ABBEYGREEN, *The Green* 1847 *TA*.

ALDERS, 1833 OS, ALDERS LANE.

BANK HO.

BARLEYBIRCH, *Barley Birch* 1833 OS, 1847 *TA*: *Birch* is probably the metathesised form of *Britch*, ultimately from **bryce** 'newly-broken-in land', which is common in N. Sa.

BOSTOCK HALL, 1798, 9 RTH, *Bostocks Hall* 1833 OS. A list of Sa gentry in 1663, SAS 2/IV, includes *Bostock* of Whixall: the house is 16th-cent.

BRIDGE FM, by Dobson's Bridge *infra*.

BROOK HO, 1833 OS.

BROWNSBROOK: the *TAMap* shows *Crofts* here.

CHAPEL LANE.

CUMBERLAND FM, LANE (1849 GT), *Cumberland* 1833 OS.

THE FARM, 1833 OS.

GARNER'S LANE, 1798 RTH.

GILBERT'S LANE.

GOBLIN'S LANE, 1796 RTH, 1833 OS, 1847 *TA*.

GREEN LANE.

HIGHER HO.

HOLLINWOOD, 1795, 6 RTH, *v*. **holegn**.

HOLLY HO.

LADYWELL 1803 RTH, 1847 *TA*.

LORD HILL, *Lord Hill Inn* 1847 *TA*.

LOWER HOUSES.

MANOR HO: a small building on N. boundary, shown but not named on *TAMap*.

MARL ALLOTMENT, *Marl Piece* 1847 *TA*.

MILL HO.

MOAT, *Moat House* 1833 OS.

MOSLEYWELL, 1789 RTH, 1833 OS, *v*. f.ns.

MOSS COTTAGES, by Whixall Moss.

MOSS FM.

MOSS LANE.

OAK COTTAGE.

OAKFIELDS, *The Oak* 1833 OS.

OSSAGE BRIDGE, LANE, 1833 OS, *Hossage Field* 1847 *TA*, *Hostage Lane Croft* 1849 GT. There is a Horsage Fm in Wichenford Wo (PN Wo 181) which is *Ossage* 1884.

PHEASANT P.H.

PINFOLD HO.

PLATTLANE, *Platt Lane* 1801 RTH, 1833 OS: **plat**[1] 'footbridge'.

POOLBANK: *The Pools*, *Castor Pools* adjoin 1847 *TA*.

POST OFFICE LANE.

RACK LANE: an adjoining field is *Rock Field* 1847 *TA*.

RODEN VILLA.

ROUNDTHORN BRIDGE, 1833 OS, *Round Thorn* 1847 *TA*.

ROVING BRIDGE, 1833 OS.

RYE FIELDS.

RYE HILL, *Rye Hill* 1847 *TA*.

SANDYBANK, *Sandy Bank* 1792 RTH.

SHIRLEY COTTAGE.

STANLEY GREEN, *Standlane Green* 1833 OS.

WATERLOO, ~ BRIDGE, *Waterloo Lime Kilns* 1833 OS, 1847 *TA*.

WELSHEND, *Welsh End* 1798 RTH, *Whixall Welsh End* 1833 OS.

WHIXALL HALL, 1847 *TA*.

WHIXALL MOSS, 1803 RTH, 1833 OS: part of a large moss straddling Sa/Fli border.

WHIXALL WINDMILL, *Whixall Mill* 1833 OS, *Windmill & Croft* 1847 *TA*.

WORLDSEND, 1833 OS.

Bridges over the Shropshire Union Canal include, in addition to some listed above, ALLMANS, BOODLES, DOBSON'S, MORRIS'S, STARKS. Some buildings listed above are shown without names on *TAMap*: these include Bank Ho, Lower Houses, Poolbank, Roden Villa, Shirley Cottage.

The 1833 OS map shows *Newfoundland* and *Windy Arbour* in Whixall Moss.

Field-Names

Forms in (a) are 1847 *TA* except where otherwise stated. Early forms dated 1683, 1715, 17, 32, 56, 62, 66, 70, 75, 76 are *SBL 5470*, *5471*, *2*, *8474*, *5484*, *5485*, *5483*, *5501*, *1681*, *5493*, *5502*.

(a) The Acres (adjoins Grimes/Groins); Alder Fd; Aldery Mdw; Allotments (a large area on the edge of Whixall Moss has rectangular fields so labelled); Ash Croft; Backhouse Fd; Bank, Daisy ~; Bank Lsw; Barn Fd (*freq*); Barn Mdw; Barn Yd (several); Barrows Fd; The Beach (*v.* **bæce**); Bean Fd; Bentley's Mdw; Big Fd (several, one 1762); Big Leash Mdw; Big Mdw (2); Birch Orchard; Black Croft (several); Blake Fd; Bold Darner; Brickkiln; Brickkiln Croft; Brickkiln Fd (2); Brickkiln Pce (by "brickworks, maltkilns etc." adjoining canal); Brickyard Fd; Broad Mdw (2); Brockhurst, Hill; Broomy Lsw; Burnthouse Fd; Burrows Fd; Callcots Fd; Calves Croft (2); Calves Yd; Castor Birch, Pools (near Poolbank *supra*, Casters Britch, Pools, The Pools 1810 *SBL 5459*); Chap Fd; Chapel Mdw (cf. *Chappell Croft* 1683, 1766, *Chapel Field* 1762); Clay Hill, Mdw; Clothes Hedge Fd; Clover Bank; Clover Croft; Clover Fd (2); Coal Croft; Colley's Croft; Common Mdw; Common Pce(s) (scattered fields on the edge of Allotments and Crofts are so labelled); Common Pce (near Abbeygreen); Cook's Pce; Cow Lsw (2); Cow Pasture; Crabtree Fd; Croft(s) (clusters round habitations); Croft(s) (some smaller rectangles fringing the Allotments fields are so labelled); Croft Pit Fd; Dace Pit Fd; Dock'd Pce; Double Pit Fd; Dovehouse Bank, Mdw (by Bostock Hall); Dovehouse Mdw, Big ~ ~; Dudleston's Yd (*Dudlestons Yords* 1683, *Dulstands Yard* 1776); Dungeon (by Ladywell: the usual explanation, 'deep hollow' (FN 18, PN Ch **3** 250), does not seem appropriate here); Field, Big, Further, Lower, Whixall (group of small fields on W. boundary); Forty Shillings Fd (adjoins Four Pound Fd); Furlong Mdw, Hatch Flg (near Mossley); Garden Fd; Garden Pasture; Gighole Fd (a reference to flax drying); Glass Birch (*birch* for *britch* as *freq*); Goblins Lane Fd, Goblins Fd, Pce (by Goblins Lane); Gorse Cote Fd; Green Fd (1776); Green Lsw; Groins, Lower, Middle, Little, Higher (Near and Far Grimes adjoin, and two fields in Edstaston called Grimes are a short distance S., cf. Higher, Middle, Lower, Little Grimes 1810 *SBL 5459*: this may have been a small open field); Hall Mdw (by Bostock Hall); Hall's Croft; Haunch (a shape-n.); Hawthorn Hills; Hemp Butt; Hemp Yd; Higher Yd (2); Hobson's Croft; Horse Pasture (2, cf. *Near(er)*, *Farther Horse Pasture* 1732, *Higher*, *Further* ~ ~ 1762); House Croft; (The) Intake (tiny strips by road); Jailor's Croft; Jebb's Rye Hill; Keay's Fd; Kiln Fd; Kiln Pit Fd; Lane Pce; Lilly Flg (adjoins Furlong Mdw); Little Worth; Long Common, Common Pce (on S. boundary); Long Croft (2); Long Fd (2); Long Mdw; Marl Croft; Marl Fd (1763); Marlpit Croft; Marlpit Fd, Higher, Near; Mat's Croft; (The) Meadow (several); Meadow, ~ Bank; Meadow, Big, Little, ~ Bank; Middle Fd; Middle Lsw; Moat Fd (not near Moat *supra*: cf. *The Moate Bank* 1732, *Moat Bank* 1762, 3, 6, 75, 6, 8); Moors; Mossage Fd (near Hossage Fd, *v.* Ossage Bridge *supra*); Mossley, Big, Little, ~ Mdw, Mossley Well Fd (*butts* and *furlong* ns. in same area suggest an open field); Moss Mdw (1762); Mud Fd; Mullock Mdw, Orchard; New Lsw; New Mdw (2); Old House Croft; Old Mdw; Old Yd; Orchard Pce; The Orchards; Ox Mdw; Paddock; Paradise; Park (by the vicarage); Parson's Pce; Part Birch; Peas Croft; Peas Fd; Piece, Bottom, Far, Near, Common (with Croft and Field ns. on W. boundary); Piece, Little, Rough;

Pigstye Croft; Plant Yd; Pond Fd; Pool Mdw; Prescott's Fd (*Prescots Piece* 1683, *The Prescott Field* 1732, 63); Pump House Fd; Rake Lane Croft (fairly near Rack Lane *supra*); Raven's Nest; Red Marl Fd; Rickyard; Road Pce; The Roughs, Rough Acres, Mdw (*The Two Roughs* 1683, *Higher* and *Lower Rough* 1762, *The Two Ruffs* 1776); Roundabout (enclosed by roads); Rushy Fd; Rushy Mdw; Sandyhole/ Sandhole Fd (Sandy Hole 1810 *SBL 5459*); Sandland Croft; School House Fd; Scotch Orchards; Sharemore Mdw (Big and Little Sharmon adjoin, *Shearmoore* 1683, *The Sharemoor* 1762, *The Shermoor Meadow* 1766, *Shermon Meadow* 1775: perhaps 'shared marsh', *v.* **scearu**, **mōr**); Shut Fd, Large, Little; Shut Fd, Big, Little, Large, ~ ~ Mdw (this or preceding may be *Shutfeild* 1683, *The Shutt Field* 1732, 66, *Shut Field* 1772: Shut Fd is a common f.n. in N. Sa, but the meaning has not been ascertained); Sidbrook; Slade ('field with a wet patch' FN 18); Slang Mdw; Stack Yd Mdw (2); Thistly Croft; Thistly Fd (2, *Thistley Field* 1776); Tinkers Croft; Top Mdw; Tree Croft, Lower, Middle, Higher; Trefoil Fd; Two Acre Fd (larger than adjoining Ten ~ ~); Two Butts (tiny strip between fields near Mossley); Waringshorn (not an obvious shape-n.); Washpit Fd; Watery Mdw; Way Fd; Well Fd; Wild's Yd; Windmill, Big, Little; Windmill, Thornley's, Whitfield's; Worsted Hills; Wright's Mdw; Yewtree Fd (several); Yoahall Green.

(b) *The Espen Croft* 1683; *Hadlands*, *Higher* 1683; *The Har alias Higher Field* 1756, 66; *Hodges Croft* 1715; *Hollins Lane* 1798 RTH; *Kinastons Croft* 1683, *Kynastons* ~ 1715; *The Marled Feild* 1732, 66; *Monks Feild*, *Old*, *New* 1683; *New Marled Peice* 1717; *The Owller Croft* 1732, *The Oller* ~ 1766, *Owllery Croft* 1776 ('alder croft'); *The Snape Moor Meadow* 1715 (John *Snape* mentioned, *The Slipe Moor Meadow* 1732 may be the same field); *Wheat Stuble Field* 1762.

Woore

The parish-name, which is a substantive use of the adj. **wæfre** 'wavering', is discussed in Part **1**. EPN outlines various possible uses of this element. In Part **1** it is suggested that in Woore it may refer to the appearance of trees on the ridge which runs through the parish.

Woore became a civil parish in 1841, having previously been part of Mucklestone. The rest of Mucklestone was transferred to St in 1866. There are *TAMaps* for the townships of Bearstone, Dorrington, Gravenhunger and Woore. These are filed under Mucklestone at SRO.

1. BEARSTONE (SJ 724397)
Bearstone is a DB manor, so the name, 'Bæghard's estate', is discussed in Part **1**. It appears to have developed from a shortened form *Byarston'* (1291–2 *Ass*) by association with the word *bear*. There is another shortened form *Berson*, c.1535 SAS 3/VIII, which was not noted in Part **1**.

BELLAPORT OLD HALL (SJ 709405): *Beleporte* c.1540 Leland, *Bellaporte* Hy 8, 1596 AD, *Belaport* 1577 Saxton, *Bellaport* 1608 PR(L) 18. This is a name coined for a manor house on the common French or Italian model, as seen, e.g., in Belmont, Bellevue. The use of *port* in such a formation appears to be unique to this name.

BEARSTONE BRIDGE, MILL (*Mill* 1838 *TA*).
BELLAPORT WD: *TA* calls this *Bearstone Wood*.
LADIES WD, 1833 OS, *Lady's Wood* 1838 *TA*.
ROOKERY WD, *Bellaport Wood* 1833 OS, *Norton Wood* 1838 *TA*.
WET BUTTS PLTN, 1833 OS, *Wet Butt* 1838 *TA*.

Field-Names

Forms in (a) are 1838 *TA*.

(a) Aston Shutt, Big, Little; Barley Croft; Barn Fd; Bentall's Mdw; Brickkiln Fd; Broad Lsw, Far, Near; Broad Mdw; Broomy Fd (2); Butty Lsw (*v*. FN 8 for possible senses of *butty*); Close Yd; Connery, Little ~ ('rabbit warren'); Court Croft (near Bellaport Old Hall); Dry Marlpit; Edward Fd; Filly Ford; Forge Pce (by R. Tern);

Forrest Mdw (by Bearstone hamlet, Forest ns. in Dorrington are fairly close); Garland Mdw; George Ash; Gorsty Lsw; Gravel Hole Pce or Wood End; Great Mdw; Hall Mdw (large field by Bellaport Old Hall); Harbour Hill, Far, Little (on W. boundary, possibly referring to a temporary shelter); Harrison's Pce; Heath Croft; Hicks Fd; Hill's Pce; Holly Ford, Near ~ ~, Far Ford (by R. Tern); Horse Close, Far, Near; Horse Pasture, Near; Horsley Pools; Joan Snores; Long Fd; Lower Croft; Man Fd, Lower, Upper, Long, Far, Middle, Near, Near and Far Upper, Manfield Mdw (11 fields on N.E. boundary, possibly 'common', *v.* **(ge)mǣne**); Means, Great, Little (possibly ME *main* 'demesne land'); Middle Fd; Mid Fd, Near, Great; Mill Croft, Fd, Mdw (by Bearstone Mill); New Pce; Nott Fleck; Old Brook, Far, Near; Ox Lsw; Paddock; Peas Croft; Peas Lsw; Pinfold (in hamlet); Plants Mdw; Pool Mdw; Puncheon Croft (a *puncheon* is a pointed tool, so possibly a shape-n., the field has a sharp point); Rickardine Hall; The Ridding ('clearing'); Ridding, Brown, Little; Rough Lsw; Rough Mdw (several); Round Lsw (curved sides); Shaw's Mdw; Sherrod's Yd (2 large fields); Shooting Butts; Skirmy Fd (FN 35 suggests dialect *skirm* 'to mow or dig lightly'); Spinney Close; Stanley's Middle Fd; Stone Quarry (6" map shows Old Quarry); Sytch Mdw (*v.* **sīc**); Thorp's Mdw; Townsend, Big, Little (on edge of Bearstone hamlet); Wheat Fd; Whitly Mdw; Windmill Bank; Wood End Mdw; Wood Fd, Far, Near, Meredith's (by Ladies Wd); Wood Fd, Mdw (by Bellaport Wd).

2. DORRINGTON (SJ 732409)

Dorrington is a DB manor, so the name is discussed in Part **1**. For the purposes of this place-name survey it is taken to be 'estate associated with Dēora', a formation of the personal-name + **-ingtūn** type which is common in this county. There is another instance with *Dēora* in Sa, Derrington in Ditton Priors (Part **3** 134); and Dorrington Li, Durrington Sx, W have the same etymology. The problems presented by groups of **-ingtūn** names which are formed from the same personal name are discussed in Part **1** under Detton.

It should be noted that Dorrington in Condover (Part **3** 134) was earlier *Dodington*.

BIRTLES (?lost), 1838 *TA*: *The Birtles* 1638–9 *SBL 1980*, *Birckles* 1639–40 *SBL 2228*, *The Bertles* 1692 *SBL 2348*, *The Two Birtles* 1705 *SBL 2041*.

Gazetteer lists Birtles Fm, Woore, but there are no buildings shown on maps in the area where *Birtles* f.ns. occur. *TAMap* shows fields with this name covering an area about ½ mile wide between Dorrington village and the N. township boundary.

Birtles is probably the plural of a name derived from OE ***bircel** 'little birch trees', discussed in Part **3** 150 s.n. Birtley. This element was previously noted in Db, La, Ch and St with modern forms Birchill(s), Birtles. It is tentatively noted in VEPN *s.v.* **birce**.

CARTER'S ROUGH, 1833 OS, probably *Cardas Rough* 1728 *SBL 2026*.

COLLEGE FIELDS, 1786 *SBL 5037*, *Colledge Feildes* 1594 PR(L) 18. The 1963 1" OS map gives this name to an area straddling the Ch/Sa border. On the 1899 6" map the name is given to three farms, one in Dorrington, the others in Ch. Land here may have belonged to a religious house or to an Oxford or Cambridge college.

DORRINGTON BOGS, *Plantation Bogs* 1838 *TA*.

DORRINGTON FM, DORRINGTON HALL FM.

DORRINGTON OLD HALL, 1833 OS.

THE FIELDS: the farm is shown but not named on *TAMap*.

FOX COVERT.

IRELAND'S CROSS 1681 *et seq* PR(L) 18, 1833 OS. This is a hamlet at a crossroads, Ireland may be a surname.

PIPE GATE, 1833 OS, *The Pipe Gate* 1724 *SBL 2056*, *Pipe Gate Field*, *Piped* and *Pipped Leasow* 1838 *TA*: *v. Cudelsford* in Gravenhunger, *infra*.

ROOKERY WD.

SQUARE PLTN.

WILLOWBRIDGE FM (Gazetteer), *Willowbridge* 1872 PR(L) 18.

Field-Names

The head forms in (a) are 1838 *TA*. Earlier forms are from E. W. Bowcock's notes on *SBL* documents which he examined in the early years of the English Place-Name Society's activities, when he was acting as "County Organiser for Shropshire" (Allen Mawer, 'Shropshire and a Survey of English Place Names', in E. W. Bowcock, *Shropshire Place Names*, 1923). The numbers of the documents for each date given are listed below:

1348–9, *2158*: 1354–5, *1973*: 1416–17, *2288*: 1419–20, *2169*: 1421–2, *2178*: 1426–7, *2370*: 1450 and 1474–5, *2172*: 1483–4, *1976*: 1523–4 *2374*: 1539–40, *2177*: 1554, *2232*: 1558, *2192*: 1616, *2248*: 1630, *2202*: 1636–7, *2350*: 1639, *2344*: 1639–40, *2228*: 1641, *2211* and *2213*: 1645, *2270*: 1652, *2271*: 1656, *2205*: 1660, *2023*: 1665, *2329*: 1672, *2156*: 1674, *5725*: 1677, *2223*: 1677–8, *2223*: 1679, *2204*: 1680, *2138*: 1686, *2347*: 1686–7, *2040*: 1691–2, *2352*: 1692, *2348*: 1705, *2041*: 1718, *2326* and *2070*: 1719, *2071*: 1720, *2025*: 1721, *2026* and *2072*, *3*: 1722, *2076*: 1723, *2326*: 1724, *2027* and *2057*: 1726, *2029* and *2054*: 1727, *2058*: 1728, *2030* and *2060*: 1730, *2080*: 1731 *2063*: 1736, *2075*: 1740, *2064*: 1744, *2034*: 1753, *2045*: 1760, *2082*: 1783, *2105*: 1786, *2036* and *2037*.

(a) Barley Moor, Big, Far and Little ~ ~ (*Barleymow* 1483–4 (*sic* transcribed, assumed to be *-mor*)); Barn Fd (2); Big Mdw; Big New Pce; Birchin Croft (*Two Birchen Crofts* 1692); Broad Moor, ~ ~ Mdw (*Brodemore* 1419–20, *Broadmoor Meadow* 1786); Broomy Fd; Broomy Lsw; Brothers Low Pce (*Stephen Shaw's Brothers Low Piece and Meadow* 1740); Browns Pit; Butty Fd (on *TAMap* a dotted line divides this from part of Butty Fd which may support the sense 'field belonging to two owners but not fenced', FN 7); Butty Pce; Calves Croft (1718); Clark's Ridding, Higher, Lower and Little ~ ~ (*Clarke Ridding* 1641, Marjory *Clark* mentioned 1665); The Cliffe, Cliff, Cliffe Iron (*Le Clyf* 1421–2, *The Clyffe*, *Clyf Iron* 1641, *Cliffe Meadow* 1652, 92, *Cliffe Iron* 1677, *Clift Iron* 1731: maps show two areas of ground over 500', the Cliff fields are beside the northern one, which extends into Woore township: this presumably has a fairly steep edge (**clif**) and an angle (**hyrne**)); Common, ~ Fd, ~ Allotment; Croft (cluster by Ireland's Cross includes Cokers, Crabtree (*The Crabtree Croft* 1686), House, Middle, Top Croft); Croft (several along road W. of village); Croft (cluster by Common ns. in S.E. projection of parish includes Little, Higher, Road Croft); Cross Fd (1641, on outskirts of Ireland's Cross); Custard Croft (tiny enclosure in village, perhaps **cot-stōw**); Damask Hey (*The Big* and *Little Damasheys* 1718, *The Damas Heays* 1727, *Dammas Heys* 1731: J. Field, *English Field-Names: A Dictionary*, suggests that ridge-and-furrow ploughing sometimes produced a damask pattern); Duns Croft, Fd; Fishpond Fd; Five Butts; Five Oaks, Big, Little (*The Five Oakes* 1718, 60); Flatt, Higher, Lower (*The Flatt* 1630, 1728); Forest, Higher, Lower, ~ Mdw (the significance of *Forest* in this n. is not clear, the fields adjoin those with Common and Heath ns. in S.E. projection of parish); Garratts Pce (*Garrard Peece* 1691–2, *Jarrards Piece*, *Great Gerards Piece* 1724, cf. *Gerrard's Cross* 1726); Gorse Cover; Gorsty Fd, Near, Further (*Le Gorstyfyld* 1558, *The Two Gorsty Fields* 1718, *Gorstey Field* 1727); Hammerway (*Homer Way* 1679, *Hammerway Croft* 1719, *The Hammerway* 1726); Hampton Croft (2, one has Hampton Court nearby); Heath Close, Fd, Mdw, Great Heath Lane (adjoining Common ns: *The Heath Fields* 1652, *Dorrington Heath* 1660, 1722, *Leasowes or Heath Ground* 1724); Hewitt's Mdw (1718); Hill Fd, Mdw; Jack Mdw; Lane Croft; Leyfoot (Leaford in Gravenhunger adjoins, *Leaford* 1639, *Loford Flatt* 1656, *The Layford* 1686, *Lefort* 1721: the road crosses a stream by Ireland's Cross); Long Fd; Long Fridays (*Long Frydaies* 1554, 1652, *The Bank Peice or Long Fryday* 1736, probably a derogatory n., *v.* PN Ch **4** 115); Mago Mdw (*Maghole Meadowe* 1636–7, *Madgehoale* 1639, *Maghole* 1656, *Madgehole Meadow* 1656, 79: PN Ch **5.1** lists a number of f.ns. under ModEdial *madge* 'magpie'); Man Fd, Little; Masters, New, Long and Little ~ (possibly *The Musteys or Mustyns* 1705 and (*The*) *Mastives* 1720, 21, 30); Middle Fd; Mud Mdw (*Mudd Meadow* 1728); Near Mdw; New Lands (*Newelond* 1450, *Heathground als Newlunts* 1554, *Neweland* 1523–4, *The New Loonts* 1726, *The New Lunts* 1728); New Pce (several); Nixon's Well, Mdw, Barn Fd (Well Fd, Mdw adjoin, cf. *Nixon's Tenement* 1786, Joseph *Nixon* of College Fields is mentioned 1763); North Croft; Old Barn Fd, Mdw, Barn Croft; Ox Lsw (2, *Ox Leasow*(*e*) 1636–7, 1718); Piece, Far, Middle; Pinfold Croft (by village); Pingle, Lower ~, ~ Mdw (*Pingow Meadow* 1554, *Pingle* 1740, *v.* **pingel**); Piped Lsw, Little ~ ~, Pipped Lsw (by Pipe Gate); Pit Croft; Pool Croft; Pool Fd (1798, *Poole Fieldes* 1652, *The Poole Feild* 1692); Range Moor, Big, Little (*Rangemoor* 1727, *Range Moore* 1731: these are 2 large fields, the meaning of *range* is uncertain); Hough Mdw (2); Sapling Bank (1692, 1718); Senches, Far, Witmore (*The Whitmore's*

Senches 1718, probably *Schench(e)hurst* 1416–17, 1419–20, *Sanchehurst* 1426–7, *v.* **hyrst**, first el. obscure); Shoulder of Mutton (appropriately shaped); Slang(s) (there are fields called "Slang in Butty Fd" and "Slangs and Butts in Sytch Mdw"); Smithy Fd (cf. *The Smithy Leasow* 1718); Stean Fd, Lower and Upper ~ ~, ~ Mdw; Stony Lake, Far, Near (*Stoney Lake* 1692, *Near Stony Lake* 1718); Sytch Mdw Croft (*Sitch Meadowe* 1554, "a Butty meadow called the Sitch Meadowe" 1679, "one butt and one dole in the Sich Meadow" 1686–7, "the dole in ~ ~" 1721, *v.* **sīc** 'small stream, drainage channel'); Tag Fd, Big, Little (possibly *teg* 'young sheep', cf. *Tagge Flatt* 1636–7, 1686); Tenement (row of small fields on E. boundary); Top Lsw; Townsend (on edge of villlage, possibly *The Townes End* 1674); Watering Hole Pce (*Wateringe Place Flatt* 1636–7, *Watteringe Place* 1639–40); Weir Fd, Mdw (by R. Tern); Well Fd, Mdw (by Nixon's Well, *Well Meadow* 1720); Wood, ~ Mdw; Wood, Big, Little; Wreakin Top, Far, Near (*The Two Rekin Tops* 1692, ~ ~ *Reakin* ~ 1718, perhaps a jocular allusion to the Wrekin, the fields are a short distance E. of a patch of high ground marked by the 500' contour); Yard, Near, Over, Yard End, Mdw (by village, cf. *The Two Yoards* 1705, *Yords Ends* 1728, *Yerds Ends* 1736).

(b) (*The*) *Bache Meadow* 1630, 1719 (*v.* **bæce**); *Battell Flat* 1639–40 (the same n. is noted PN Db 583 (*Batayleflat* 1351), and other compounds with **bataille** are listed in VEPN: *v.* discussion of Sa instances in Welshampton f.ns. *supra*); *Beremedoe* 1474–5 (possibly **bær** 'bare'); *Bogg Flatt* 1686–7; *Boozey Pasture* 1745; *The Bottom Mill* 1786; *Bradebroke* 1419–20, *Bradbroke* 1450 ('broad brook'); *Breremor* 1523–4 (*v.* **brēr** 'briar', **mōr**); *Broad Meadow* 1692; *Bruche* (*v.* **bryce**); *Bulley Piece* 1718; *Le Byrchynfyld* 1539–40, *Burchenfeildes* 1616 (*v.* ***bircen**); *The Bytaks* 1726 (FN 34 suggests another term for an intake); *The Clayes Peece* 1554; *Clayflatt* 1639–40, *Clayes Flatt* 1645; *Clover Grasse* 1691–2; *Cokkeslowe Forlong* 1419–20; *Cookes Croft* 1724; *Crooke Lane* 1639–40; *Crooked Lane* 1645; *Cross Croft* 1724; *Eight Butt Peeice* 1660; *The Eight Buts* 1786; *Le Forefeld* 1483–4 (*v.* **fore**); *Gorsty Hill* 1483–4; *Gorstie Leasowe* 1616; *Gubbotrudyng* 1419–20 (*v.* ***ryding**); *Halle Rogh* 1474–5, *The Hall Roughe* 1630, *Hall Rough* 1719, 28; *Haselhurst* 1419–20; (*The*) *Homestall* 1727, 31; *Horse Riddings* 1724; *Hough Moores* 1639–40, *The Five Hough Moores* 1686, *Hough Moor* 1786 (probably **halh**); *Hullebache* 1419–20 (*v.* **hyll**, **bæc**); *Knife Meadow* 1692; *The Lenche Meadow*, *The Greate Lenches*, *The Hill* ~1630 (*v.* **hlinc** 'terrace'); *Levitt's Higher Ground* 1721 (Robert *Levitt* mentioned 1665); *The Lowe Piece* 1718; *The Little Masslins* 1718; *Monhey* 1419–20; *Murreys New Peece* 1724 (Leonard *Morrey* mentioned 1665); *Newe Leasowes* 1645, 1718; *New Marled Croft* 1636–7; *The Paddocke* 1705; *The Penlington Folley* 1718 (Benjamin and Thomas *Pendlington* mentioned 1723); *Preston's Farm* 1679; *Ravensmore* 1641, *Ravensmoor* 1677–8, *Ravenmoors* 1718; *Rowheye* 1348–9, *La Rowehaye* 1354–5 ('rough enclosure', *v.* **rūh**, **(ge)hæg**); *Rowley* 1523–4, *Proleies or Rowleies* 1672, *Owleies or Rowleies* 1680 (probably *Rolowe* 1450, correct form uncertain); *Shertebache* 1348–9, 1354–5 ('short stream-valley'); *Southehurst* 1421–2; *Kocstockyng* 1348–9, *Lecokstockynge* 1354–5 (other ***stoccing** ns. in these deeds are *Chrystian Stokkynge* 1474–5, *Gibbestockynges* 1348–9, *Hykocstokyng* 1416–17: the first els. are probably surnames); *Tenter Yard* 1736, ~ *Croft* 1744; *Tybbemedowe* 1416–17; *Tythe Barn Flatt* 1554, 1679, *Tyth Barn(e) Flatt* 1728; *Weet Reans* 1656, *Weete Reans* 1783 ('wet drainage channels', referring to the furrows between strips, FN 3); *Withietree Croft* 1660, *The Withy Tree Croft* 1724; *The Yoakins Hey* 1630, *The Yokins Hey* 1652.

3. GRAVENHUNGER (SJ 743426)

Gravenhunger is a DB manor, so the name is discussed in Part **1**. It is there taken to mean 'hanging wood with a coppice'. There is a steep bank opposite Gravenhunger Hall and the house called Banktop, and this would be a suitable site for the **hongra**.

CUDELESFORD (lost). A deed of a.1210 in Lil provides for a mill and a fishpond to be established on a watercourse between Gravenhunger and Dorrington, and the *mora de Cudelesford* is donated for this purpose. A rental of c.1250 ib lists the mill, and a dispute about multure is recorded in a deed of 1275–84. The name is spelt *Cudelesford* and *Cudeslesford* in the a.1210 deed, *Cudelesford* in the rental and in 1275–84. It is *Cudeleford*, *Cudelesford* and *Chudelesford* in rubrics. An *SBL* deed, *2172*, dated 1450 mentions *Cutlesfordruddyng*.

The first element may be ***cuttel** 'artificial water-channel', which has been noted with **myln** in several counties. It must be noted, however, that interchange of *-t-* and *-d-* has not been recorded elsewhere in this element, and it is rare in other names with *-tel-*. Titlington Nb is *Tedlintona* 1123–8, *Titlingtona* 1154–81 (DEPN). Bridlington ERY 100–2 is a clear instance, in which the interchange makes it difficult to decide between original *-d-* and *-t-*. Another possibility is a diminutive, **Cudel*, of the personal name *Cuda*.

The position on the Gravenhunger/Dorrington township boundary places the ford near Pool Hall, in an area where there are a number of canalised water-courses.

BANK FM, BANKTOP, both shown but not named 1838 *TAMap*.

BLAKE HALL, 1833 OS.

CROW HO.

GRAVENHUNGER HALL, 1833 OS, 1838 *TA*.

GRAVENHUNGER MOSS, *Butter Hill Moss* 1833 OS (*v.* f.ns.), *Gravenhunger Bottom* and *Top Moss* 1838 *TA*: probably *Le Mos* 1323 AD.

GREAVES, 1833 OS, *Lower* ~ shown ½ mile N.: *v.* **grǣfe** 'coppice', variant of **grāfa** which is first el. of township-name.

HOLLY COTTAGE.

HOLLYHURST FM, 1833 OS, *Holliehurst* 1593–4 *SBL 2265*.

LANCERBARN, *Lancer Barn* 1833 OS, *The Lancer Meadow* 1838 *TA*: *TA* has a field called *The Lankers* a short distance away.

MOSS FM, by Gravenhunger Moss.

ONNELEY HALL, 1838 *TA*, *Onnely* ~ 1727 *SBL 5510*, *Onnily* ~ 1742

SBL 5513, Onneley St adjoins.

PHYNSONHAYS, *Finson Hays* 1833 OS, *Phinsons Hay Meadow* 1838 *TA*.

POOL HALL, 1833 OS.

SHENTONHILL, *Shenton Hill* 1838 *TA*.

Field-Names

Forms in (a) are 1838 *TA*.

(a) Banky Fd, Little; Barn Fd (several); Bear Mdw (cf. *Beremedoe* in Dorrington, *supra*); Bebeton's Mdw, Orchard; Big Fd, Far, Near; Big Fd (Little Fd adjoins); Birches; Bird Ridding, Big and Little ~ ~; Black Croft, Far, Near, Little; Boss Mdw; Boundary Croft (on St boundary); Boylas Fd; Brickkiln Fd (several); Briery Fd, Pasture; Broad Lsws; Broomy Fd; Bulloes Tree Bank (*bullace*, wild plum); Butterhill, Big and Little ~, ~ Pltn (adjoining Hungary Hill); Calf Croft (several); Carthouse Croft; Castle Fd (*Le Castell* 1327 SR (p), large field by Gravenhunger Moss); Catch, The Great ~ (on county boundary: FN 21 explains *catch* as a boundary term for land not in a parish where the tithe went to the first parson to claim it); Clover Fd (2); Cow Pasture Mdw; Croft (Croft ns. round hamlet include Barn, Crabtree, Hassall's, Lower, Madam's, Pinfold, Well); Crofts (by Onneley road); Cross Heath; Crown Bank; Custard Fd (probably a reference to sticky soil); Cutlake Croft, Big Cutlock Fd, Little Cutlack Fd (perhaps a drain, *lake* ultimately from **lacu**); Down Moor, Near and Far ~ ~, ~ ~ Mdw); Drumble (2, both wooded strips along streams, *v*. The Drumble in Baschurch *supra*); Eight Shillings Worth, Higher, Lower; Fallow; Far Fd; Field, Brown's, House, Lower, Middle; Field, Sargeants and Matthews ~ (an area divided into strips by dotted lines on *TAMap*); Field above House; The Flatts; Grandfather's Croft; Gravenhunger Fd, Far; Greaves Fd, Little (a short distance from Greaves); Growecocks Croft; Hares Fd; Hemp Fd, Big, Little; Hilly Moor, Big, Little; Horse Lsw; Horse Pasture (several); House Fd (2); Hungary Hill, Big, Little ('hungry'); Intake (small strip by road); Isobel's Croft; Langet, Far, Near (narrow strips, a rather rare f.n., PN Ch **5.1** 264 notes 2 instances); Leaford, ~ Mdw (adjoins Leyfoot in Dorrington *supra*, *q.v.*: Big and Little Langford, adjoining, may have another version of the n.); Leather Fd (possibly referring to hard soil); Lincolns End or Ems Mdw; Little Fd; Little Mdw (several); The Long Croft; Longfield; Long Mdw; Lower or Gravenhunger Mdw; Lower Ground; Lower Moor; Marl Fd (2); Maypole Ridding; Meadow, Big, Lower, Rough; Meadow, Big, Little; Meadow, Lower, Upper; Meghill; Moor(s) Ends; Mill Fd (by Onneley Ho, probably a windmill); New Lsw; New Mdw; Nicklin's Croft; Oak Fd; Ox Lsw, Mdw; Park Fd (not near a building); Pen Fd; Pentong (*v*. Pentingtons in Woore, *infra*); Phillips Croft; Pillington Hole; The Pit Fd; Poor's Land; Raddymoor Bank, Raddymoors (another instance in Woore, *infra*); Ragshaw; Rough Fd; Rough Mdws; Rusky Mdw; Rye Croft; Ryegrass Fd; Sandy Croft; Sandy Fd, Farther, Little; Senas, Far, Near, Senats Mdw; Shad Fd; Sheep Fd; Ship Fd; Shoulder of Mutton (several); Sisley Mdw (~ Fd is nearby); Snows Mdw; Spout Croft (2); Sprink (possibly *spring* 'coppice'); Stew Croft (by Onneley Hall); Stockings, Big, Little; Stonyford; Three Cornered Fd; Three Shire Fds (at Ch/St/Sa boundary point); Tom Fleck, Far, Near ('town plot');

Townfield, Near, Middle, Farther (Gravenhunger Fd adjoins, possibly a small open field); Turnpike Fd (by Newcastle road); Wall Fd, Far, Near; Wards Croft, Garden; Water Mdw; Well Fd; Wheat Croft; Wheat Fd; Wood, Little Wd Fd; The Wood, Wood Fd; Wood, Big, Little (the Wood f.ns. are on N. and N.E. boundaries; Woorstong (perhaps ME *stank* 'pond', the field is by Phynsonshays and 6" map shows pools by the house: ON **stǫng** 'pole' is unlikely as it has not been noted in Ch).

(b) *Bridisruding* n.d. AD (*v.* ***ryding**); *Derintoneplek'* 1340 AD ('Dorrington plot'); *Grene* 1327 (p); *Haywode* 1327 (p) ('enclosed wood', the surname may be from an instance elsewhere); *Mosihald* n.d. AD; *Scotch Backside* 1691–2 *SBL 2352*; *Sonde* 1327 SR (p) ('sand').

6. WOORE (SJ 730423)

ASH MOUNT.

BUCKLEY HALL, 1838 *TA*.

CANRIDDEN WD, *Carriden Wood* 1833 OS, *Canridden*, ~ *Meadow*, *Camedan* (*sic*) *Wood* 1838 *TA*.

CHERRYTREE FM, ~ *Field* 1838 *TA*: there is no building on *TAMap*.

CRAB WD.

ELMHURST.

FIELD FM.

FLASH FM, 1833 OS, ME **flasshe**, used in Sa for a shallow pool formed by flood water.

THE GORSE.

GORSY BANK.

THE HOLLIES.

THE HOLLOWS: *TAMap* has *Hollow Meadow* and *Hollyway Meadow* nearby on either side of the road.

IVY COTTAGE.

MANOR HO, shown but not named on *TAMap*.

MILLHAY WD, *Mill Haywood* 1838 *TA*, *Mill Hey*, ~ ~ *Meadow* adjoin: probably a windmill.

MOAT.

OAK COTTAGE.

OAKHOUSE FM.

PARK FM.

SANDYFORD, 1833 OS, *Sandifords Meadow* and *Pasture* 1674 *SBL 5725*: the Audlem road crosses a stream here.

SPRING COTTAGE.

SUNNYBANK.

SYLLENHURST FM, *Syllenhurst* 1594–5 *SBL 2406 et freq*, *Sillinghurst* 1641 *SBL 2211 et freq*, *The Sillinhurst* 1802 PR(L) 18, *Sillenhurst* 1833

OS. This is probably an ancient name, there is a moat at the farm. The first element might be an inflected form of **sele**[2] 'willow copse'.

THREE BROOKS, at the confluence of three streams.

WOORE HALL, 1833 OS.

1833 OS has *Woore Green* W. of village, cf. *Sibilla de la Grene de Wou'ere* 1291–2 *Ass*. *TAMap* shows *Falcon Inn* and *Swan Inn* in village.

Field-Names

Forms in (a) are 1838 *TA*.

(a) Bank, Far, Near; Barn Fd; Barn Mdw (2); Birchney Fd, Great ~ ~; Black House Croft or Barratt's Croft; Blaze Fd (cf. Blaze Bank in Baschurch *supra*); Brickkiln Fd; Briery Copy (Long Coppy adjoins); Broad Runlet; Brookhouse Fd, Big ~ ~ (by the building called The Hollows on 1899 6" map); Brook Mdw; Butcher's Croft; Calf Croft Mdw; Calf Hey Mdw; Carter's Rough Fd; Cockset Fd (probably *cockshoot*); Common (by Audlem road); Corcus Mdw; Cow Pasture, Lower; Cow Pasture Mdw; Croft(s) (around village); Cross Fd, Far, Near (by road to Ireland's Cross); Daddle Pool Mdw; Depmoors (The Moor, Little Moor adjoin); Down Moor Mdw, Further ~ ~; Duffet Croft; Endless, First, Second, Third, Pit (between village and S. township boundary: First, Second, Third form a long, narrow strip); Fucis, Lower, Middle, Upper (probably *Higher*, *Lower*, *Fooseys* 1674 *SBL 5725*); Glass House Mdw; Gorsty Fd; Grass Flat, Big; Green Fd; Greenlock, Big, Little and Lower ~, ~ Mdw; Hall's May, Hall Mays, Hollowsmee (adjacent fields by Hall Croft, a short distance from Woore Hall); Hanging Hill (2); Harkey, Higher, Middle, Harkey Bank, Mdw (Lower Harker Lsw is fairly close); Hollow Mdw; Honey Bank, Far, Middle, Little; Horse Pasture (*freq*); House Fd (large field by Buckley Hall); Hussey's Mdw; Jacks Croft; Key Fd; Kiln Croft; Little Croft; Marl Fd, Marlpit Fd; Meadow, Near, Top, Rough, Jack; Moat Mdw (by Woore Hall); Mobhay, Big and Little ~, ~ Mdw; Moss; Moss Mdw; Old Wd; Paddock & Spring Croft; Pentingtons Lower Ground, Higher Pce (near Pentong in Gravenhunger, which may be a version of the same n.); Pool Fd; Prince's Croft; Quice Tree Hill (perhaps dialect *quice* 'wood pigeon', *v.* FN 27); Raddymoor, Big, Little, Far (not near Raddymoors in Gravenhunger); Raven's Croft; Ridding Mdw, Hill ~; Roberts Fd; Sandy Croft; Silverters Lane; Spring Brightstall; Town Fd (2); Wallstone Fd, Higher and Lower ~ Mdw; White Leys; Windmill Fd; The Wood Mdw, Wood Fd (by Mill Haywood); Yewtree Bank.

The following names from *SBL 5725*, dated 1674, are in Woore parish but cannot be assigned to townships:

The Two Brockhursts; *Bromhill Peice*; *Chappell Flatt*; *Culey Top*; *Highfield*; *Hoorestone Leasow*; *Leas Flatt*; *Long Acre*; *The Moore*; *Two Ollery Crofts* (alder trees); *Lower Ragbrook*; *Ragshawe Feild*; *Rough Leasowe*; *Shellow Ridding*; *Shingletree Hill*; *The Townefeild Ground*.

INDEX